Poetry
for Students

Poetry for Students

**Presenting Analysis, Context, and Criticism on
Commonly Studied Poetry**

Volume 9

Ira Mark Milne, Editor

Foreword by David Kelly, College of Lake County

GALE GROUP

Detroit
New York
San Francisco
London
Boston
Woodbridge, CT

Poetry for Students

Staff

Series Editors: Mary Ruby and Ira Mark Milne.

Contributing Editors: Elizabeth Bellalouna, Elizabeth Bodenmiller, Angela Y. Jones, Michael L. LaBlanc, Polly Rapp.

Managing Editor: Dwayne D. Hayes.

Research: Victoria B. Cariappa, *Research Team Manager.* Cheryl Warnock, *Research Specialist.* Corrine A. Boland, Tamara Nott, Tracie A. Richardson, *Research Associates.* Timothy Lehnerer, Patricia Love, *Research Assistants.*

Permissions: Maria Franklin, *Permissions Manager.* Margaret A. Chamberlain, Edna Hedblad, *Permissions Specialists.* Erin Bealmear, *Permissions Associate.* Sandra K. Gore, *Permissions Assistant.*

Production: Mary Beth Trimper, *Production Director.* Evi Seoud, *Assistant Production Manager.* Stacy Melson, *Production Assistant.*

Imaging and Multimedia Content Team: Randy Bassett, *Image Database Supervisor.* Robert Duncan, *Imaging Specialist.* Michael Logusz, *Graphic Artist.* Pamela A. Reed, *Imaging Coordinator.* Dean Dauphinais, Robyn V. Young, *Senior Image Editors.* Kelly A. Quin, *Image Editor*

Product Design Team: Cynthia Baldwin, *Product Design Manager.* Pamela A. E. Galbreath, *Senior Art Director.* Gary Leach, *Graphic Artist.*

Copyright Notice

Since this page cannot legibly accommodate all copyright notices, the acknowledgments constitute an extension of the copyright notice.

ISBN 0-7876-3570-7
ISSN 1094-7019
Printed in the United States of America.

10 9 8 7 6 5 4 3 2

National Advisory Board

Table of Contents

Just a Few Lines on a Page

I have often thought that poets have the easiest job in the world. A poem, after all, is just a few lines on a page, usually not even extending margin to margin—how long would that take to write, about five minutes? Maybe ten at the most, if you wanted it to rhyme or have a repeating meter. Why, I could start in the morning and produce a book of poetry by dinnertime. But we all know that it isn't that easy. Anyone can come up with enough words, but the poet's job is about writing the *right* ones. The right words will change lives, making people see the world somewhat differently than they saw it just a few minutes earlier. The right words can make a reader who relies on the dictionary for meanings take a greater responsibility for his or her own personal understanding. A poem that is put on the page correctly can bear any amount of analysis, probing, defining, explaining, and interrogating, and something about it will still feel new the next time you read it.

It would be fine with me if I could talk about poetry without using the word "magical," because that word is overused these days to imply "a really good time," often with a certain sweetness about it, and a lot of poetry is neither of these. But if you stop and think about magic—whether it brings to mind sorcery, witchcraft, or bunnies pulled from top hats—it always seems to involve stretching reality to produce a result greater than the sum of its parts and pulling unexpected results out of thin air. This book provides ample cases where a few simple words conjure up whole worlds. We do not actually travel to different times and different cultures, but the poems get into our minds, they find what little we know about the places they are talking about, and then they make that little bit blossom into a bouquet of someone else's life. Poets make us think we are following simple, specific events, but then they leave ideas in our heads that cannot be found on the printed page. Abracadabra.

Sometimes when you finish a poem it doesn't feel as if it has left any supernatural effect on you, like it did not have any more to say beyond the actual words that it used. This happens to everybody, but most often to inexperienced readers: regardless of what is often said about young people's infinite capacity to be amazed, you have to understand what usually does happen, and what could have happened instead, if you are going to be moved by what someone has accomplished. In those cases in which you finish a poem with a "So what?" attitude, the information provided in *Poetry for Students* comes in handy. Readers can feel assured that the poems included here actually are potent magic, not just because a few (or a hundred or ten thousand) professors of literature say they are: they're significant because they can withstand close inspection and still amaze the very same people who have just finished taking them apart and seeing how they work. Turn them inside out, and they will still be able to come alive, again and again. *Poetry for Students* gives readers of any age good practice in feeling the ways poems relate to both the reality of the time and place the poet lived in and the reality of our emotions. Practice is just another word for being a student. The information given here helps you understand the way to read poetry; what to look for, what to expect.

With all of this in mind, I really don't think I would actually like to have a poet's job at all. There are too many skills involved, including precision, honesty, taste, courage, linguistics, passion, compassion, and the ability to keep all sorts of people entertained at once. And that is just what they do with one hand, while the other hand pulls some sort of trick that most of us will never fully understand. I can't even pack all that I need for a weekend into one suitcase, so what would be my chances of stuffing so much life into a few lines? With all that *Poetry for Students* tells us about each poem, I am impressed that any poet can finish three or four poems a year. Read the inside stories of these poems, and you won't be able to approach any poem in the same way you did before.

David J. Kelly
College of Lake County

Introduction

Purpose of the Book

The purpose of *Poetry for Students* (*PfS*) is to provide readers with a guide to understanding, enjoying, and studying poems by giving them easy access to information about the work. Part of Gale's "For Students" Literature line, *PfS* is specifically designed to meet the curricular needs of high school and undergraduate college students and their teachers, as well as the interests of general readers and researchers considering specific poems. While each volume contains entries on "classic" poems frequently studied in classrooms, there are also entries containing hard-to-find information on contemporary poems, including works by multicultural, international, and women poets.

The information covered in each entry includes an introduction to the poem and the poem's author; the actual poem text; a poem summary, to help readers unravel and understand the meaning of the poem; analysis of important themes in the poem; and an explanation of important literary techniques and movements as they are demonstrated in the poem.

In addition to this material, which helps the readers analyze the poem itself, students are also provided with important information on the literary and historical background informing each work. This includes a historical context essay, a box comparing the time or place the poem was written to modern Western culture, a critical overview essay, and excerpts from critical essays on the poem, when available. A unique feature of *PfS* is a specially commissioned overview essay on each poem by an academic expert, targeted toward the student reader.

To further aid the student in studying and enjoying each poem, information on media adaptations is provided when available, as well as reading suggestions for works of fiction and nonfiction on similar themes and topics. Classroom aids include ideas for research papers and lists of critical sources that provide additional material on the poem.

Selection Criteria

The titles for each volume of *PfS* were selected by surveying numerous sources on teaching literature and analyzing course curricula for various school districts. Some of the sources surveyed included: literature anthologies; *Reading Lists for College-Bound Students: The Books Most Recommended by America's Top Colleges;* textbooks on teaching the poem; a College Board survey of poems commonly studied in high schools; and a National Council of Teachers of English (NCTE) survey of poems commonly studied in high schools.

Input was also solicited from our expert advisory board, as well as educators from various areas. From these discussions, it was determined that each volume should have a mix of "classic" poems (those works commonly taught in literature classes) and contemporary poems for which information is often hard to find. Because of the interest in expanding the canon of literature, an emphasis was also placed on including works by international, multicultural, and women authors. Our advisory board members—current high school and college teachers—helped pare down the list for each volume. If a work was not selected for the present volume, it was often noted as a possibility for a future volume. As always, the editor welcomes suggestions for titles to be included in future volumes.

How Each Entry Is Organized

Each entry, or chapter, in *PfS* focuses on one poem. Each entry heading lists the full name of the poem, the author's name, and the date of the poem's publication. The following elements are contained in each entry:

- **Introduction:** a brief overview of the poem which provides information about its first appearance, its literary standing, any controversies surrounding the work, and major conflicts or themes within the work.

- **Author Biography:** this section includes basic facts about the poet's life, and focuses on events and times in the author's life that inspired the poem in question.

- **Poem Text:** when permission has been granted, the poem is reprinted, allowing for quick reference when reading the explication of the following section.

- **Poem Summary:** a description of the major events in the poem, with interpretation of how these events help articulate the poem's themes. Summaries are broken down with subheads that indicate the lines being discussed.

- **Themes:** a thorough overview of how the major topics, themes, and issues are addressed within the poem. Each theme discussed appears in a separate subhead and is easily accessed through the boldface entries in the Subject/ Theme Index.

- **Style:** this section addresses important style elements of the poem, such as form, meter, and rhyme scheme; important literary devices used, such as imagery, foreshadowing, and symbolism; and, if applicable, genres to which the work might have belonged, such as Gothicism or Romanticism. Literary terms are explained within the entry, but can also be found in the Glossary.

- **Historical and Cultural Context:** This section outlines the social, political, and cultural climate *in which the author lived and the poem was created*. This section may include descriptions of related historical events, pertinent aspects of daily life in the culture, and the artistic and literary sensibilities of the time in which the work was written. If the poem is a historical work, information regarding the time in which the poem is set is also included. Each section is broken down with helpful subheads. (Works written after the late 1970s may not have this section.)

- **Critical Overview:** this section provides background on the critical reputation of the poem, including bannings or any other public controversies surrounding the work. For older works, this section includes a history of how poem was first received and how perceptions of it may have changed over the years; for more recent poems, direct quotes from early reviews may also be included.

- **Sources:** an alphabetical list of critical material quoted in the entry, with full bibliographical information.

- **For Further Study:** an alphabetical list of other critical sources which may prove useful for the student. Includes full bibliographical information and a brief annotation.

- **Criticism:** at least one essay commissioned by *PfS* which specifically deals with the poem and is written specifically for the student audience, as well as excerpts from previously published criticism on the work, when available.

In addition, most entries contain the following highlighted sections, set separately from the main text:

- **Media Adaptations:** a list of audio recordings as well as any film or television adaptations of the poem, including source information.

- **Compare and Contrast Box:** an "at-a-glance" comparison of the cultural and historical differences between the author's time and culture and late twentieth-century Western culture. This box includes pertinent parallels between the major scientific, political, and cultural movements of the time or place the poem was written, the time or place the poem was set (if a historical work), and modern Western culture. Works written after the mid-1970s may not have this box.

- **What Do I Read Next?:** a list of works that might complement the featured poem or serve as a contrast to it. This includes works by the same author and others, works of fiction and nonfiction, and works from various genres, cultures, and eras.

- **Study Questions:** a list of potential study questions or research topics dealing with the poem. This section includes questions related to other disciplines the student may be studying, such as American history, world history, science, math, government, business, geography, economics, psychology, etc.

Other Features

PfS includes a foreword by David J. Kelly, an instructor and cofounder of the creative writing periodical of Oakton Community College. This essay provides a straightforward, unpretentious explanation of why poetry should be marveled at and how *Poetry for Students* can help teachers show students how to enrich their own reading experiences.

A Cumulative Author/Title Index lists the authors and titles covered in each volume of the *PfS* series.

A Cumulative Nationality/Ethnicity Index breaks down the authors and titles covered in each volume of the *PfS* series by nationality and ethnicity.

A Subject/Theme Index, specific to each volume, provides easy reference for users who may be studying a particular subject or theme rather than a single work. Significant subjects from events to broad themes are included, and the entries pointing to the specific theme discussions in each entry are indicated in **boldface.**

Illustrations are included with entries when available, including photos of the author and other graphics related to the poem.

Citing Poetry for Students

When writing papers, students who quote directly from any volume of *Poetry for Students* may use the following general forms. These examples are based on MLA style; teachers may request that students adhere to a different style, so the following examples may be adapted as needed.

When citing text from *PfS* that is not attributed to a particular author (i.e., the Themes, Style,

Historical Context sections, etc.), the following format should be used in the bibliography section:

"Angle of Geese." *Poetry for Students.* Eds. Marie Napierkowski and Mary Ruby. Vol. 1. Detroit: Gale, 1997. 8–9.

When quoting the specially commissioned essay from *PfS* (usually the first piece under the "Criticism" subhead), the following format should be used:

Velie, Alan. Essay on "Angle of Geese."*Poetry for Students.* Eds. Marie Napierkowski and Mary Ruby. Vol. 1. Detroit: Gale, 1997. 8–9.

When quoting a journal or newspaper essay that is reprinted in a volume of *PfS,* the following form may be used:

Luscher, Robert M. "An Emersonian Context of Dickinson's 'The Soul Selects Her Own Society.'" *ESQ: A Journal of American Renaissance* 30, No. 2 (Second Quarterl, 1984), 111–16; excerpted and reprinted in *Poetry for Students,* Vol. 2, eds. Marie Napierkowski and Mary Ruby (Detroit: Gale, 1997), pp. 120–34.

When quoting material reprinted from a book that appears in a volume of *PfS,* the following form may be used:

Mootry, Maria K. "'Tell It Slant': Disguise and Discovery as Revisionist Poetic Discourse in 'The Bean Eaters,'" in *A Life Distilled: Gwendolyn Brroks, Her Poetry and Fiction,* edited by Maria K. Mootry and Gary Smith (University of Illinois Press, 1987, 177–80; excerpted and reprinted in *Poetry for Students,* Vol. 1, Eds. Marie Napierkowski and Mary Ruby (Detroit: Gale, 1997), pp. 59–61.

We Welcome Your Suggestions

The editors of *Poetry for Students* welcome your comments and ideas. Readers who wish to suggest poems to appear in future volumes, or who have other suggestions, are cordially invited to contact the editor. You may write to the editor at:

Editor, *Poetry for Students*
Gale Group
27500 Drake Rd.
Farmington Hills, MI 48331–3535

Literary Chronology

circa 700: *Beowulf* is composed at about this time.

1300–1699: Humanism as a philosophical view of the world is prevalent in this period.

1300–1699: The Renaissance begins in the fourteenth century and continues for the next 300 years.

1558–1603: The Elizabethan Age begins with the coronation in 1558 of Elizabeth I as Queen of England and continues until her death in 1603. Elizabethan literature is recognized as some of the finest in the English language.

1564: William Shakespeare (whose exact birthdate is unknown) is baptized on April 26, 1564, in Stratford-upon-Avon, the eldest son of John Shakespeare, a glove maker and wool merchant, and his wife, Mary Arden, the daughter of a prominent landowner.

1575–1799: The literary style known as Baroque arises in the late-sixteenth century and remains influential until the early eighteenth century.

1600–1799: The Enlightenment period in European social and cultural history begins in the seventeenth century and continues into the eighteenth century.

1600–1650: Metaphysical poetry becomes a prominent style of verse in the first half of the seventeenth century.

1603–1625: The Jacobean Age begins with the coronation in 1603 of James I of England and continues until his death in 1625.

1609: Sonnet 19 is published as one of a collection of 154 sonnets by Shakespeare. Probably written in the early to mid-1590s, when the sonnet was a fashionable literary form, these poems are generally regarded as the finest sonnet sequence in the English language.

1611: Psalm 8 is published as part of the new version of the English Bible, commissioned by King James I of England.

1616: William Shakespeare dies in Stratford on April 23, and is buried within the chancel of the Holy Trinity Church.

1625–1649: The Cavalier Poets, a group of writers that includes Robert Herrick, Richard Lovelace, and John Suckling, are active during the reign of Charles I of England (1625–1649).

1660–1688: The Restoration Period begins when Charles II regains the throne of England, and it continues through the reign of his successor, James II (1685–1688). Restoration literature includes the first well-developed English-language works in several forms of writing that would become widespread in the modern world, including the novel, biography, and travel literature.

1675–1799: Neoclassicism as the prevailing approach to literature begins late in the seventeenth century and continues through much of the eighteenth century.

1700–1799: The English Augustan Age (the name is borrowed from a brilliant period of literary creativity in ancient Rome) flourishes throughout much of the eighteenth century.

1700–1725: The Scottish Enlightenment, a period of great literary and philosophical activity, occurs in the early part of the eighteenth century.

1716: Thomas Gray is born in the Cornhill district of London to Dorothy Antrobus Gray, a milliner, and Philip Gray, a scrivener.

1740–1775: Pre-Romanticism, a transitional literary movement between Neoclassicism and Romanticism, takes place in the middle part of the eighteenth century.

1740–1750: The Graveyard School, referring to poetry that focuses on death and grieving, emerges as a significant genre in the middle of the eighteenth century.

1750–1899: The Welsh Literary Renaissance, an effort to revive interest in Welsh language and literature, begins in the middle of the eighteenth century and continues into the following century.

1751: Thomas Gray's "Elegy Written in a Country Churchyard" is first published, although it was probably begun in 1742, shortly after the death of Gray's close friend Richard West.

1771: Thomas Gray dies, having held the position of Regius Professor of Modern History at Cambridge from 1768.

1775–1850: Romanticism as a literary movement arises in the latter part of the eighteenth century and continues until the middle of the nineteenth century.

1795: John Keats is born, the son of a stablekeeper.

1800–1899: The Gaelic Revival, a renewal of interest in Irish literature and language, takes place throughout much of the nineteenth century.

1809: Edgar Allen Poe is born in Boston, the son of Elizabeth Arnold Poe and David Poe, both minor professional actors.

1809: Oliver Wendell Holmes is born on August 29 in Cambridge, Massachusetts.

1809–1865: The Knickerbocker School, a group of American writers determined to establish New York as a literary center, flourishes between 1809 and 1865.

1819: John Keats's "Bright Star! Would I Were Steadfast As Thou Art" is composed.

1821: John Keats dies of tuberculosis in Rome at the age of 26.

1830–1860: The flowering of American literature known as the American Renaissance begins in the 1830s and continues through the Civil War period.

1830–1855: Transcendentalism, an American philosophical and literary movement, is at its height during this period.

1836: Oliver Wendell Holmes's "Old Ironsides" is published in his *Poems*, which is Holmes's first collection and earns for him a reputation as a humorist.

1837–1901: The Victorian Age begins with the coronation of Victoria as Queen of England, and continues until her death in 1901. Victorian literature is recognized for its magnificent achievements in a variety of genres.

1848–1858: The Pre-Raphaelites, an influential group of English painters, forms in 1848 and remains together for about ten years, during which time it has a significant impact on literature as well as the visual arts.

1849: Edgar Allen Poe dies on October 7 in Baltimore.

1849: Edgar Allen Poe's "Annabel Lee" is published, just two days after Poe's death on October 7. It appears in two newspapers, the *Richmond Examiner* and the *New York Tribune*, and then in the 1850 edition of *The Works of the Late Edgar Allan Poe*. The poem has since become one of Poe's most popular works.

1850: The poets of the so-called Spasmodic School are active in the 1850s.

1871: Stephen Crane is born on November 1 in Newark, New Jersey, as the last of fourteen children to Mary Helen Peck Crane and the Reverend Dr. Jonathan Townley Crane, who is an elder in the District of the Methodist Episcopal Church of Newark and later becomes the Methodist pastor in Port Jervis, New York.

1875–1899: Aestheticism becomes a significant artistic and literary philosophy in the latter part of the nineteenth century.

1875–1899: Decadence becomes an important poetic force late in the nineteenth century.

1875–1925: Expressionism is a significant artistic and literary influence through the late nineteenth century and the early twentieth century.

1875–1925: The Irish Literary Renaissance begins late in the nineteenth century and continues for the next several decades.

1875–1925: The Symbolist Movement flourishes in the closing decades of the nineteenth century and the opening years of the twentieth century.

1875–1950: Realism as an approach to literature gains importance in the nineteenth century and remains influential well into the twentieth century.

1890–1899: The decade of the 1890s, noted for the mood of weariness and pessimism in its art and literature, is known as the Fin de Siècle ("end of the century") period.

1894: Oliver Wendell Holmes dies at his Boston home on October 7.

1899: Stephen Crane's "War is Kind" is published as the first poem of his second collection, *War is Kind and Other Lines*, which appears in print less than a year before Crane dies.

1900: Stephen Crane suffers a tubercular hemorrhage and dies at 29 years of age.

1900–1999: The philosophy of Existentialism and the literature it inspires are highly influential throughout much of the twentieth century.

1900–1950: Modernism remains a dominant literary force from the early part to the middle years of the twentieth century.

1905: Phyllis McGinley is born on March 21 in Ontario, Oregon.

1907–1930: The Bloomsbury Group, a circle of English writers and artists, gathers regularly in the period from 1907 to around 1930.

1910–1920: Georgian poetry becomes a popular style of lyric verse during the reign of King George V of England.

1910–1930: New Humanism, a philosophy of literature, is influential for several decades, beginning around 1910.

1912–1925: The Chicago Literary Renaissance, a time of great literary activity, takes place from about 1912 to 1925.

1912–1922: Imagism as a philosophy of poetry is defined in 1912 and remains influential for the next decade.

1916: Peter Viereck is born in New York City.

1919–1960: The Scottish Renaissance in literature begins around 1919 and continues for about forty years.

1920: The Harlem Renaissance, a flowering of African American literary activity, takes place.

1920–1930: The label Lost Generation is applied to a generation of American writers working in the decades following World War I.

1920–1930: The Montreal Group, a circle of Canadian poets interested in dealing with complex metaphysical issues, begins in the late 1920s and flourishes for the next decade.

1920–1970: New Criticism as a philosophy of literature arises in the 1920s and continues to be a significant approach to writing for over fifty years.

1920–1960: Surrealism, an artistic and literary technique, arises in the 1920s and remains influential for the next half century.

1924: Lisel Mueller is born in Hamburg, Germany.

1927: Galway Kinnell is born on February 1 in Providence, Rhode Island, as the fourth child of James and Elizabeth Mills Kinnell, immigrants from Scotland and Ireland.

1929: Thompson William Gunn is born in Gravesend, Kent, England, on August 29.

1930: Gary Snyder is born in San Francisco.

1930–1965: Negritude emerges as a literary movement in the 1930s and continues until the early 1960s.

1930–1970: The New York Intellectuals, a group of literary critics, are active from the 1930s to the 1970s.

1934: Mark Strand is born in Summerside, Prince Edward Island, Canada.

1934: Amiri Baraka is born (birthname Everett LeRoi Jones) in Newark, New Jersey.

1935–1943: The Works Progress Administration (WPA) Federal Writers' Project provides federally funded jobs for unemployed writers during the Great Depression.

1936: Marge Piercy is born to working-class parents Robert Douglas and Bert Bedoyna (Bunnin) Piercy in Detroit, Michigan.

1940: The New Apocalypse Movement, founded by J. F. Hendry and Henry Treece, takes place in England in the 1940s.

1940: Postmodernism, referring to the various philosophies and practices of literature that challenge the dominance of Modernism, begins in the 1940s.

1947: Jane Kenyon is born on May 23.

1948: Peter Viereck's "For an Assyrian Frieze" is published in his first book, *Terror and Decorum*.

1948: Leslie Marmon Silko is born in Albuquerque, New Mexico, to a family of mixed white and native blood.

1949: Peter Viereck's first book, *Terror and Decorum*, which contains "For an Assyrian Frieze," wins the Pulitzer Prize for poetry.

1950: The so-called Beat Movement writers begin publishing their work in the 1950s.

1950: The Black Mountain Poets, emphasizing the creative process, become an influential force in American literature in the 1950s.

1950–1975: Structuralism emerges as an important movement in literary criticism in the middle of the twentieth century.

1951: Phyllis McGinley's "Reactionary Essay on Applied Science" is published in the *New Yorker* and in *A Short Walk from the Station*.

1960–1970: The Black Aesthetic Movement, also known as the Black Arts Movement, takes place from the 1960s into the 1970s.

1960:–1999: Poststructuralism arises as a theory of literary criticism in the 1960s.

1961: Amiri Baraka's "In Memory of Radio" is published in his first collection of poetry, *Preface to a Twenty Volume Suicide Note*. Baraka is still known as LeRoi Jones.

1961: Phyllis McGinley's "Reactionary Essay on Applied Science" is published in *Times Three*, which spans three decades of McGinley's work, and which also wins the Pulitzer Prize.

1968: Mark Strand's "Eating Poetry" is published in his collection *Reasons for Moving*. This is Strand's second collection and earns him national recognition as a poet.

1970–1999: New Historicism, a school of literary analysis, originates in the 1970s.

1973: Marge Piercy's "Barbie Doll" appears in her 1973 collection *To Be of Use*.

1974: Gary Snyder's "Anasazi" is published as the first poem in his collection *Turtle Island*.

1975: Leslie Marmon Silko's "Four Mountain Wolves" is published in the anthology *Voices of the Rainbow: Contemporary Native American Poetry*.

1978: Phyllis McGinley dies in New York City.

1980: Galway Kinnell's "Saint Francis and the Sow" is published in his *Mortal Acts, Mortal Words*.

1986: Lisel Mueller's "The Exhibit" is published in her collection *Second Language*.

1986: Jane Kenyon's "Trouble with Math in a One-Room Country School" is published in her second volume of poems, *The Boat of Quiet Hours*. It is published again in her collection of new and selected poems, *Otherwise* (1996).

1992: Thom Gunn's "The Missing" is published in his collection, *The Man with Night Sweats*, a title that refers to a symptom that is frequently experienced by sufferers of AIDS.

1995: Jane Kenyon dies from leukemia on April 23, one month before her 48th birthday, having lived nearly twenty years in rural Wilmot, New Hampshire, with her husband, poet Donald Hall.

1998: Mark Strand's *Blizzard of One* wins the Pulitzer Prize.

Acknowledgments

The editors wish to thank the copyright holders of the excerpted criticism included in this volume and the permissions managers of many book and magazine publishing companies for assisting us in securing reproduction rights. We are also grateful to the staffs of the Detroit Public Library, the Library of Congress, the University of Detroit Mercy Library, Wayne State University Purdy/Kresge Library Complex, and the University of Michigan Libraries for making their resources available to us. Following is a list of the copyright holders who have granted us permission to reproduce material in this volume of *Poetry for Students (PFS)*. Every effort has been made to trace copyright, but if omissions have been made, please let us know.

COPYRIGHTED EXCERPTS IN *PFS*, VOLUME 9, WERE REPRODUCED FROM THE FOLLOWING BOOKS:

Concerning Poetry, v. 10, Spring, 1977. Copyright © 1977, Western Washington University. Reproduced by permission.—*North Dakota Quarterly*, v. 60, Fall, 1992. Copyright 1992 by The University of North Dakota. Reproduced by permission.— *Philological Quarterly*, v. 69, Summer, 1990 for "Gray's Political Elegy: Poetry as the Burial of History" Richard C. Sha. Copyright © 1990 by The University of Iowa. Reproduced by permission of the author.—*Poe Studies/Dark Romanticism*, v. 6, June, 1973 for "A Note on Annabel Lee'" by Julienne H. Empric; v. 17, June, 1984 for "Mrs. Osgood's The Life Voyage' and

Annabel Lee'" by John E. Reilly. Both reproduced by permission of the publisher and the respective authors.— *Saturday Review of Literature*, 1949. © 1949 Saturday Review Magazine, © 1979 General Media International, Inc. Reproduced by permission.

COPYRIGHTED MATERIAL IN *PFS*, VOLUME 9, WERE REPRODUCED FROM THE FOLLOWING BOOKS:

Baraka, Imamu Amiri. From *Preface to a Twenty Volume Suicide Note*. Totem Press, 1961. Reproduced by permission of Sterling Lord Literistic, Inc.—Ellis, R. J. From "Plodding Plowmen: Issues of Labour and Literacy in Gray's Elegy'" in *The Independent Spirit: John Clare and the Self-Taught Tradition*. Edited by John Goodridge. John Clare Society, 1994. © the individual contributors, 1994. Reproduced by permission.—Gunn, Thom. From *Collected Poems*. Farrar, Straus & Giroux, 1994. Copyright © 1994 by Thom Gunn. Reproduced by permission of Faber & Faber Limited. In North America by Farrar, Straus & Giroux, LLC.—Jones, Buford and Kent Ljungquist. From "Poe, Mrs. Osgood, and Annabel Lee'" in *Studies in the American Renaissance*. Edited by Joel Myerson. University Press of Virginia, 1983. Copyright © 1983 by Joel Myerson. All rights reserved. Reproduced by permission of the editor.—Kenyon, Jane. From *The Boat of Quiet Hours*. Graywolf Press, 1986. Reproduced by permission.—Kinnell, Galway. From *Mortal Acts, Mortal Words*. Houghton Mifflin, 1980. Reproduced by permission of

Houghton Mifflin Company.—McGinley, Phyllis. From *Times Three: Selected Verse from Three Decades with 70 New Poems*. Viking Press, 1960. Reproduced by permission of Viking Press, a division of Penguin Putnam Inc.—Mueller, Lisel. From *Alive Together: New and Selected Poems*. Louisiana State University Press, 1996. Copyright © 1996 by Lisel Mueller. Reproduced by permission.—Piercy, Marge. From "Barbie Doll" in *To Be of Use*. Doubleday, 1973. Reproduced by permission of the Wallace Literary Agency, Inc.—Roe, Nicholas. From "'Brightest Star, Sweet Unrest': Image and Consolation in Wordsworth, Shelley, and Keats" in *History & Myth: Essays in English Romantic Literature*. Edited by Stephen C. Behrendt. Wayne State University Press, 1990. Copyright © 1990 by Wayne State University Press. All rights reserved. Reproduced by permission of the publisher and the author.—Silko, Leslie Marmon. From "Four Mountain Wolves," in *Voices of the Rainbow*. Edited by Kenneth Rosen. Viking Press, 1973. Reproduced by permission of The Wylie Agency.—Snyder, Gary. From *Turtle Island*. Shambhala Publications, Inc., 1993. © 1974 by Gary Snyder. Reproduced by permission of New Directions Publishing Corporation.—Strand, Mark. From "Eating Poetry" in *Reasons for Moving*. Atheneum, 1968. Copyright © 1968 by Mark Strand. Reproduced by permission of the author.

PHOTOGRAPHS AND ILLUSTRATIONS APPEARING IN *PFS*, VOLUME 9, WERE RECEIVED FROM THE FOLLOWING SOURCES:

Baraka, Amiri, standing in a doorway, photograph. AP/Wide World Photos. Reproduced by permission.—Gunn, Thom (standing by window, in tie-dyed tank shirt), photograph. Hulton-Deutsch Collection/Corbis. Reproduced by permission.—McGinley, Phyllis, Connecticut, 1964, photograph. AP/Wide World Photos. Reproduced by permission.—Mueller, Lisel, Illinois, 1997, photograph. AP/Wide World Photos. Reproduced by permission.—Piercy, Marge, photograph by Jerry Bauer. Reproduced by permission.—Poe, Edgar Allen (facing forward, blank expression), photograph. AP/Wide World Photos. Reproduced by permission.—Silko, Leslie Marmon (wearing black shirt, parrot pin), photograph by Robyn McDaniels. © Robyn McDaniels. Reproduced by permission.—Snyder, Gary, photograph. AP/Wide World Photos. Reproduced by permission.—Viereck, Peter, Photo by Clemens Kalischer. Mount Holyoke College. Reproduced by permission.—Kinnell, Galway, photograph by John Reeves. Reproduced by permission.

Contributors

Emily Archer: Emily Archer holds a Ph.D. in English from Georgia State University, has taught literature and poetry at several colleges, and has published essays, reviews, interviews, and poetry in numerous literary journals. Entries on *St. Francis and the Sow* and *Trouble with Math in a One-Room Country School*. Original essay on *Psalm 8*.

Bryan Aubrey: Bryan Aubrey holds a Ph.D. in English Literature from the University of Durham, England. He has worked as an editor for Lynn C. Franklin Associates and as a freelance writer and editor. Entry on *Sonnet 19*.

Greg Barnhisel: Greg Barnhisel holds a Ph.D. in American Literature from the University of Texas at Austin. He has taught English as Assistant Professor at Southwestern University in Georgetown, Texas. He has published articles on Ezra Pound, and has worked as a freelance writer and editor. Entries on *For an Assyrian Frieze* and *Four Mountain Wolves*. Original essays on *For an Assyrian Frieze* and *Four Mountain Wolves*.

Jonathan N. Barron: Jonathan N. Barron is associate professor of English at the University of Southern Mississippi. He has co-edited *Jewish American Poetry* (forthcoming from University Press of New England), *Robert Frost at the Millennium* (forthcoming from University of Missouri Press), as well as a forthcoming collection of essays on the poetic movement, New Formalism. Beginning in 2001, he will be the editor-in-chief of

The Robert Frost Review. Original essays on *Eating Poetry* and *St. Francis and the Sow*.

Robert Bee: Robert Bee is in the doctoral program in English Literature at Rutgers University, where he teaches English. Bee is a freelance editor and writer, who has published over 20 short stories and a number of book reviews. Original essay on *The Missing*.

Adrian Blevins: Adrian Blevins, a poet and essayist who has taught at Hollins University, Sweet Briar College, and in the Virginia Community College System, is the author of *The Man Who Went Out for Cigarettes*, a chapbook of poems, and has published poems, stories, and essays in many magazines, journals, and anthologies. Original essay on *The Exhibit*.

Jeannine Johnson: Jeannine Johnson received her Ph.D. from Yale University and is currently visiting assistant professor of English at Wake Forest University. Original essays on *Annabel Lee* and *Bright Star! Would I Were Steadfast As Thou Art*.

David Kelly: David Kelly is an instructor of creative writing at several community colleges in Illinois, as well as a fiction writer and playwright. Entries on *Annabel Lee, Bright Star! Would I Were Steadfast As Thou Art, Elegy Written in a Country Churchyard, Old Ironsides*, and *Psalm 8*. Original essays on *Annabel Lee, Bright Star! Would I Were Steadfast As Thou Art, Elegy Written in a Country Churchyard, Old Ironsides*, and *Psalm 8*.

Aviya Kushner: Aviya Kushner is the Contributing Editor in Poetry at *BarnesandNoble.com* and the Poetry Editor of *Neworld Magazine*. She is a graduate of the acclaimed creative writing program in poetry at Boston University, where she received the Fitzgerald Award in Translation. Her writing on poetry has appeared in *Harvard Review* and *The Boston Phoenix*, and she has served as Poetry Coordinator for *AGNI Magazine*. She has given readings of her own work throughout the United States, and she teaches at Massachusetts Communications College in Boston. Original essays on *Bright Star! Would I Were Steadfast As Thou Art*, *Eating Poetry*, *Elegy Written in a Country Churchyard*, and *Trouble with Math in a One-Room Country School*.

Mary Mahony: Mary Mahony earned an M.A. in English from the University of Detroit and a M.L.S. from Wayne State University. She is an instructor of English at Wayne County Community College in Detroit, Michigan. Entry on *Reactionary Essay on Applied Science*.

Tyrus Miller: Tyrus Miller is an assistant professor of comparative literature and English at Yale University, where he teaches twentieth-century literature and visual culture. His book *Late Modernism: Politics, Fiction, and the Arts Between the World Wars* is forthcoming. Original essay on *In Memory of Radio*.

Marisa Anne Pagnattaro: Marisa Anne Pagnattaro, J.D., Ph.D. in English, is a freelance writer and a Robert E. West Teaching Fellow in the English Department at the University of Georgia. Original essay on *The Missing*.

Dean Rader: Dean Rader is Assistant Professor of English at Texas Lutheran Univerity in Seguin, Texas. Original essay on *Four Mountain Wolves*.

Cliff Saunders: Cliff Saunders teaches writing and literature in the Myrtle Beach, South Carolina, area and has published six chapbooks of verse. Entry on *The Missing*.

Chris Semansky: Chris Semansky holds a Ph.D. in English from Stony Brook University and teaches writing and literature at Portland Community College in Portland, Oregon. His collection of poems *Death, But at a Good Price* received the Nicholas Roerich Poetry Prize for 1991 and was published by Story Line Press and the Nicholas Roerich Museum. Semansky's most recent collection, *Blindsided*, has been published by 26 Books of Portland, Oregon. Entries on *Barbie Doll*, *In Memory of Radio*, and *War Is Kind*. Original essays on *Barbie Doll*, *In Memory of Radio*, *Reactionary Essay on Applied Science*, *Sonnet 19*, and *War Is Kind*.

Pamela Steed Hill: Pamela Steed Hill, the author of a collection of poetry titled *In Praise of Motels*, has had poems published in more than 90 journals and magazines and has twice been nominated for a Pushcart Prize. She has an M.A. in English from Marshall University and is an associate editor for university communications at Ohio State University. Entries on *Anasazi*, *Eating Poetry*, and *The Exhibit*. Original essays on *Anasazi* and *The Exhibit*.

Alice Van Wart: Alice Van Wart is a writer and teaches literature and writing in the Department of Continuing Education at the University of Toronto. She has published two books of poetry and has written articles on modern and contemporary literature. Original essays on *Barbie Doll* and *Trouble with Math in a One-Room Country School*.

Anasazi

Gary Snyder
1974

Gary Snyder placed "Anasazi" as the first poem in his 1974 collection *Turtle Island*. Its placement is significant because the first poem often sets the tone for the rest of the book, and this is the case here. *Anasazi* is a Navajo word most often translated as "ancient ones," and it designates a group of Native Americans thought to be the predecessors of the modern Pueblo Indians. From about 200 to 1300 A.D., the Anasazi inhabited the Four Corners region of the United States, encompassing southern Utah, southwestern Colorado, northwestern New Mexico, and northern Arizona. As Snyder's poem indicates, the Anasazi people were very adept at horticulture, pottery making, basket weaving and architecture, and were remembered especially for their villages built into the sides of steep cliffs. Although opinions vary on what eventually scattered these Native Americans throughout the southwestern United States and Mexico, there is widespread agreement that they were a very sophisticated, highly developed people who left behind a wealth of remarkable wares and intriguing structures.

"Anasazi" is a celebration poem, much like a chant or a song of praise. Its creator is both poet and anthropologist, and he combines the two callings to produce works of vivid imagery and in reverence for a humankind that lives simply and in harmony with nature. While the poem may be sparse in language, it is full of meaning, evidenced by strong, descriptive words and effective cadence. It engages both history and myth, presented with striking metaphors and alliteration. And, too, it re-

Gary Snyder

flects Gary Snyder's fervor for depicting the strength and beauty of Native American culture and his ability to express great praise in a minimal amount of words. For these reasons, the poem provides a fit beginning for *Turtle Island* whose own title refers to the original name of North America handed down through Indian mythology.

Author Biography

Gary Snyder was born in San Francisco in 1930. His parents separated when he was very young, and he spent most of his early years living with his mother and sister on small farms in Washington and Oregon. Even as a youngster and teenager, Snyder was an avid outdoorsman and developed a strong reverence for all things natural—mammals, insects, trees, mountains, rivers, and anything else that was a part of the earth. He also held ancient North American and Far Eastern cultures in high regard and would eventually make their study and practice a part of his everyday life.

In 1951, he received degrees in both literature and anthropology from Reed College in Portland, Oregon. There, he became a part of the intellectual crowd that was often also the "party" crowd, and

he and his friends experimented not only with a variety of hallucinogenic drugs and alcohol, but also with eastern philosophy, Indian mythology, and communal living. He spent most of his college years in one of the "Reed houses," which were typically old houses close to campus that students rented, sharing in the household duties and monthly utility bills. Snyder had a preference for a home life that was village-like, similar to most Native American cultures in which all members were part of an extended family, and group effort and shared responsibilities—as opposed to individual achievement—were major tenets.

Snyder's interest in Zen Buddhism was heightened by three years of graduate study in Asian languages at the University of California-Berkeley during the early 1950s. In 1956, he moved to Japan where he remained for 12 years studying, researching, and practicing Zen philosophy and also traveling throughout Asia. Returning to the United States in 1969, he and his wife (along with a dozen or so friends) erected a Japanese-style house in the foothills of the northern Sierras of California where the poet/anthropologist still lives today.

To date, Gary Snyder has published 16 books of poetry and prose. *Turtle Island,* containing "Anasazi," won a Pulitzer Prize in 1975. The work he has produced over the decades has continued to transcend mere words on paper. Perhaps more than any other writer—and certainly more than most—Snyder lives the life that he advocates in his poems. He has supported the causes of environmentalism, Native American rights, communal living, and spiritual and sexual freedom from the political venue to the streets to his own home. The poignancy of work and community so prevalent in the Anasazi culture has always been a primary component of the poet's own life, and what he writes is essentially what he lives. In his essay, "'Thirty Miles of Dust: There Is No Other Life,'" Snyder's longtime friend Scott McLean tells us that "one cannot read Gary's poetry without being constantly made aware of how much it is an expression of community life. His work argues that if one wants to touch the deepest levels of our humanity, one must learn within the relationships of responsibility that bind family, community, and place."

Poem Text

Anasazi,
Anasazi,

tucked up in clefts in the cliffs
growing strict fields of corn and beans
sinking deeper and deeper in earth   5
up to your hips in Gods
    your head all turned to eagle-down
    & lightning for knees and elbows
your eyes full of pollen

    the smell of bats.   10
    the flavor of sandstone
    grit on the tongue.

    women
    birthing
at the foot of ladders in the dark.   15

trickling streams in hidden canyons
under the cold rolling desert

corn-basket   wide-eyed
    red baby
    rock lip home,   20

Anasazi

Poem Summary

Lines 1-2:

A discussion of the *meaning* of "Anasazi" must include mention of its style, as the form of the poem—its rhythms, its sounds, even its look—is intrinsic to what it tells us. The first two lines appear to be only a repetition of the title. In fact, they are. And, yet, these two one-word lines also set the tone for the poem's celebratory effect. Read aloud, they should be read slowly, allowing each syllable equal voice in the incantation: ah-nah-sah-zee, ah-nah-sah-zee. On an obvious level, they simply describe the subject of the poem, but they also imply the author's feelings about that subject. In essence, he prepares us for the "song of praise" that follows.

Lines 3-4:

Line 3 of the poem refers to the cliff dwellings that the Anasazi people constructed on the steep sides of the mountains, particularly in the Mesa Verde, Colorado, region. They eventually built hundred-room villages in the cliffs and caves of this area, and many of these remarkable structures still stand today. The cliff houses were blocks of rectangular living and storage spaces, tucked into rocky walls, providing shelter from inclement weather as well as aggressive enemies. As the people themselves moved into the cliffs, so did their livelihoods, and they used their excellent stone masonry skills to construct cliffside granaries. As line

4 indicates, the Anasazi also planted their crops on the mountains and were able to grow "strict fields of corn and beans" even on such unlikely terrain. The word "strict" here is not used as in "austere" or "harsh," but in the "absolute" or "accurate" sense. Maize horticulture had been the driving force behind turning the ancestors of the Anasazi from a hunting-gathering culture into the more settled crop-growers, and it became a mainstay of their economy. The addition of beans and squash provided a nutritious supplement to their diet, and remaining evidence indicates that they were very precise and skilled farmers.

Line 5:

Line 5 of the poem may be interpreted both literally and figuratively, for the Anasazi sank "deeper and deeper in earth" in more ways than one. In the actual sense, the Anasazi people of 200 to 500 A.D. stored their goods (as well as their dead) in deep pits in the ground. Over the centuries, the Anasazi increased the size of partly underground spaces until they became their actual living quarters, now known as pithouses, consisting of several rooms. When the people began to move up into the cliffs, the earth dwellings did not disappear, but, rather, took on a new significance in the culture. By 900 A.D., the pithouses were completely subterranean, and they were used in the ceremonial role of the village "kiva." Kivas are prominent throughout the history of all Pueblo tribes and are typically underground chambers used especially by men to hold council and to perform religious ceremonies. In this literal sense, then, the Anasazi did sink "deeper and deeper in earth." Line 5 may also be seen as a metaphor for the deep ties these Native American people had with nature. They grew their food in the earth, lived in the earth, and worshipped in the earth, requiring an obvious respect and love for the land.

Lines 6-9:

Lines 6-8 carry the metaphor a bit further by highlighting the rituals often performed in the kiva and addressing in particular the intertwining of natural elements in a celebration of life for all. The "Gods" are of the earth, and eagle feathers become headdresses; the dancing of "knees and elbows" appears like lightning, and the eyes are "full of pollen" because pollen represents fertility and growth. All these natural entities—eagle-down, lightning, knees, elbows, eyes, pollen—blend into the poem to help create its praise of nature and of the people who themselves had such a strong al-

Media Adaptations

- Snyder recorded a collection of his prize-winning essays called *Practice of the Wild.* The two audiocassettes (1991 edition) pertain to the relationship between humans and the land that Snyder believes must occur, for both our sake and the earth's.

- In 1992, Snyder recorded a series of Zen master Dogen's "lessons" regarding self-liberation on two cassettes entitled *The Teachings of Zen: Master Dogen.* One review called the writings "practical and down-to-earth, paradoxical and mystical."

- *Art of the Wild* is a VHS tape based on interviews with 14 writers of prose and poetry discussing their love of the natural world and what motivated them to "give back to the earth." Writers include Gary Snyder, Garrett Hongo, Sandra McPherson, and Pattiann Rogers, among others.

---

liance with the natural world. In his essay, "Gary Snyder: The Lessons of *Turtle Island,*" critic Michael Castro describes the poet's response to the common overuse and misuse of natural resources in the industrialized world: "Snyder pointed to Indian societies as models of human organization that do not self-destruct by exploiting and exhausting their resources. Their relationship to the land is characterized by protection rather than production." And although pollen may indeed represent reproduction and growth, it is not used here to indicate an explosive and overriding increase, but one that lives in harmony with the earth and its creatures.

Lines 10-12:

These lines (as well as all the remaining ones) may be viewed as chunks of imagery that depict the Anasazi lifestyle and its interdependence on and with natural surroundings. "The smell of bats" reminds us that these people lived in caves and on steep cliffs and shared their dwellings with other mammals who made their homes in the rocks. "The

flavor of sandstone/ grit on the tongue" refers not only to the cliff houses, but to the pottery created by the Anasazi for both utilitarian and decorative purposes. These Native Americans were very adept at masonry and working in clay, and stone was so prevalent that it must have gotten into their mouths, as well as their eyes and noses.

Lines 13-15:

While these lines may seem to imply a terrible hardship in the lives of Anasazi women—giving birth to their children in the night at the bottom of steep ladders which they had to climb to their houses—it is not written in a bemoaning style or with a harsh tone. Instead, there is a *softness* in its simple statement, made more evident by the two-syllable, one-word lines: wo-men/ birth-ing. Line 15 again reiterates the remarkable dwellings the Anasazi constructed and tells us how they had to enter and exit their homes.

Lines 16-17:

Lines 16 and 17 give us a panoramic view of the natural setting in which the Indians lived. The imagery pulls us away from the people themselves and takes us to the "trickling streams," the "hidden canyons," and the "cold rolling desert." Although brief, these phrases paint a vivid picture of the natural beauty that surrounded the Anasazi. Since the desert is "cold," we must assume it's nighttime, and, therefore, the lines provide an idyllic connection between the childbirth "in the dark" addressed in the previous lines and the beginning of a new life with the cliff dwellers cited in the next.

Lines 18-20:

The Anasazi were not only skilled potters, but fine basket weavers as well. They found many uses for their baskets, including hauling corn and carrying babies. If lines 18-19 were turned into a complete sentence, it may read something like, "The red and wide-eyed newborn was carried to his home in the cliffs in a corn basket." The effect, of course, would be greatly diminished.

Line 21:

Snyder ends his poem the way he began it. Not only does the repetition of the word *Anasazi* bring a sense of "roundness" or of coming full circle to the work, but it reemphasizes the "sound" of it. Speaking the name of the people one more time, slowly—ah-nah-sah-zee—completes the song of praise on a peaceful and very resonant note.

Themes

Humans and the Environment

Gary Snyder the poet is inseparable from Gary Snyder the anthropologist. He has a distinct interest in studying human life not in isolation, but as an integral part of everything that is natural. The need to recognize the earth itself as a living being—along with all its trees, rocks, plants, and animals, including humans—is a major theme in much of Snyder's work, and such is the case for "Anasazi." Throughout the poem, there is interplay of humans, animals, plants, even sandstone and rock canyons. While many of us may not visualize living in the crags of a mountain as a very comfortable existence, here the lifestyle is portrayed as almost cozy. The Anasazi are "tucked up" in the cliffs, a phrase usually reserved for a softer, warmer form of protection or comfort. Along the same lines, "sinking deeper and deeper in earth" may not evoke a pleasant image, and yet in this poem, it is a wonderful experience, one that moves people closer to a spiritual (as well as a physical) oneness with the land. They are up to their "hips in Gods" because the supreme beings live in the earth that surrounds them. During their religious dance rituals, there is again a mixture of natural beings. Humans, eagles, and pollen seem to celebrate together.

In the essays contained at the end of *Turtle Island,* Snyder points out that many Native Americans, the Sioux in particular, consider things other than human beings as "people" too, such as insects, trees, birds, and fish. Snyder, too, believes that all of nature should be given a voice on our planet and tells us that "what we must find a way to do is incorporate the other people—the creeping people, and the standing people, and the flying people, and the swimming people—into the council of government." In "Anasazi," this incorporation is evidenced in the humans sharing the cliffs with bats, as opposed to killing them or driving them out, and in the "flavor" of sandstone, implying such a closeness to their surroundings that they can taste it. Even one of a woman's most intimate moments is intertwined with her environment. There is no complaint about giving birth at the foot of a ladder on a cold, dark night. Rather, this kind of childbirth is merely a part of the natural course, just as the "trickling streams" and "rolling desert" nearby. There is no resentment toward the natural surroundings here. The mother simply places her new baby in the basket she has brought with her and totes him home. We must understand that the child is only one of the living organisms in her presence,

Topics for Further Study

- Consider all the environmental issues that have come to the forefront along with technological advances—from the invention of the gasoline-powered engine to space modules landing on Mars. Select one issue in particular and write an essay on its pros and cons for both human beings and for the environment.

- Choose one Native American tribe and research its beginnings in North America through to its sudden end or to its gradual dispersion into other tribes. Write an essay that concentrates on what happened to the tribe when the Europeans arrived and how the members' lives changed.

- Write a poem about the natural environment that surrounds your home. Try to pattern your poem after "Anasazi," using strong descriptive words and brief phrases.

- Gary Snyder's introductory note in *Turtle Island* states "The 'U.S.A.' and its states and counties are arbitrary and inaccurate impositions on what is really here." Write about what you think he means by this statement and why you agree or disagree with it.

- Many architects today are designing homes that "respect" the natural environment. If you were going to build an unconventional home on any type of land, describe what it would be like and how/why you would make your choices.

for she is also among streams, canyons, trees, rocks—all a part of the living earth.

Understanding Place

A theme related to humans and our relationship with the environment that Snyder touches upon in "Anasazi" is that of the need for human beings to have a thorough understanding of the place we inhabit on earth. By "place," he does not mean our own country, our own state, nor even our own city, but, instead, our own *land.* Whether that encompasses a backyard, a field on a farm, or thousands of acres surrounding a close-knit village, without a knowledge of the animals, insects, wild berries, soil types, and prospering crops that share our small piece of the planet, we really do not know the place where we live. In his 1977 collection of essays called *The Old Ways,* Snyder claims that we will one day "reinhabit this land with people who know they belong to it" and we will "learn to see, region by region, how we live specifically—in each place." Living *specifically* in a place means knowing your surroundings *completely.* It means understanding the plants and animals indigenous to a region, the crops that will grow best, the wild foods that are edible and the ones that are poison, and the best means of preserving the natural resources available. It means truly knowing how to live off the land and how to do so without destroying it.

In "Anasazi," the people live "specifically." They are able to grow "strict fields of corn and beans" because they know just how to tend the crops in order to gain the best yield from the desert land. They know "the smell of bats" because they live with them, and they know "the flavor of sandstone" because they work the rock into utensils, into pottery, and into walls for their homes. They know, too, the sound of streams in the canyons, even though the water may be only "trickling" and even though the canyons may be "hidden." In truth, nothing in the environment is hidden from the Anasazi, for they genuinely *know* the land they inhabit.

Religion

A discussion of Snyder's general themes in this poem (and in many others) would be incomplete without mention of his belief in and practice of Zen Buddhism. Whether we view Buddhism as a religion or as a philosophy, or both, its tenets are very similar to that of most Native American beliefs. Buddhism maintains that every being in the universe is interrelated, and that nothing can exist separately from other beings. The world is essentially a network of all creatures and all natural objects, and each lives in relation to another. Examples from "Anasazi" that demonstrate this theme would simply be the same as those addressed above, illuminating the philosophy of environment in Indian culture, as well as that within the poet himself.

Style

Style in "Anasazi" is intrinsic to the poem's presentation and meaning. A song of praise or celebration needs rhythm and a discernible cadence to bring its full bearing to life. Snyder uses two predominant mechanisms to convey the adulatory intent of this work—alliteration (similar vowel sounds and similar consonant sounds) and line length.

While the first two "lines" are merely exact repetitions of the title, they set an alliterative tone for the rest of the poem. Not only do the first three syllables of the word "ah-nah-sah-zee" rhyme, but they also carry a soft, pleasant rhythm that warrants the repetition. The alliteration continues in the very next lines with the short *u* sound in "tucked up" and the *cl* sound in "clefts" and "cliffs," followed by the hard *c* in "corn." Lines 5, 7, and 8 all end with the short *e* sound in "earth," "eagle-down," and "elbows," and toward the end of the poem, we have "canyons," "cold," and "corn-basket" blended with "rolling," "red," and "rock." The last line rounds out the work by simply bringing us back to its rhythmic beginning.

Line length plays a major roll in the presentation of this poem by the gradual flow of nearly complete sentences into briefer phrases and finally into one- or two-word lines that wind us down as though a dance or song is coming to an end. In his *Ideogram, History of a Poetic Method,* critic Laszlo Gefin tells us that in *Turtle Island* "the form is coextensive with the material. As Snyder comments, 'Each poem grows from an energy-mind-field-dance, and has its own inner grain.' —.[In other words], energy invades the mind, expands out into a field from which the poem, the dance of words, comes into being." In "Anasazi," Snyder moves from the longer cadences of lines such as "your head all turned to eagle-down/ & lightning for knees and elbows" to the briefer "—smell of bats/ the flavor of sandstone/ grit on the tongue" to the drum-like beat of the last few lines. Read these phrases slowly and notice how the accents fall at the beginning of each to give them a TA-dum, TA-dum rhythm: Corn-basket. Wide-eyed. Red baby. Rock lip. Clearly, Snyder's form here relates directly to the subjects of the poem as well as the feelings he has for them. While the work may be "officially" free verse, there is much evidence of careful crafting by the poet to create a specific sound, a specific rhythm, and a specific movement. In doing so, he has composed a piece whose form can be heard and felt, as well as seen.

Historical Context

Gary Snyder wrote most of the poems in *Turtle Island* in the late 1960s and early 1970s when he re-

Compare &*Contrast*

- **1970:** The first "Earth Day" observation was held throughout the world. More than 20 million people took part, making it the largest organized demonstration in history.

- **1970:** The Environmental Protection Agency (EPA) was created by Congress to control water and air pollution.

- **1973:** Members of the American Indian Movement seized the village of Wounded Knee, South Dakota, the site where Sioux Indians had been massacred by the U.S. Cavalry in 1890. Two Indians were killed by police in the 70-day occupation, and the village of Wounded Knee was destroyed by fire.

- **1973:** A global energy crisis emerged, and President Richard Nixon encouraged Americans to conserve. He pointed out that the United States had 6% of the population but consumed nearly 35% of the world's energy.

- **1989:** Brazil, South America's wealthiest country, began to regulate previously uncontrolled land clearances in the Amazon basin after profiting for years on the destruction of the land.

- **1992:** Seven prominent Native Americans filed a lawsuit against the NFL's Washington Redskins, citing the nickname and mascot as offensive to American Indians. In 1999, the Trademark Trial and Appeal Board canceled federal protection of the trademark name, but it was still in use during the 1999-2000 season.

- **1995:** The construction of a man-made mountain of 10,000 trees was begun in Finland, as organized by environmental artist Agnes Denes. Called "Tree Mountain-A Living Time Capsule-10,000 Trees-10,000 People-400 Years," the project invites people from around the world to plant a tree which will bear their name and those of their heirs for the next 400 years.

- **1999:** Bangladesh Water Resources Minister Abdur Razzak announced that dwindling water supplies and poor water quality will soon threaten the lives of hundreds of millions of people in South Asia. Razzak noted that 80% of illnesses and 30% of unnatural deaths in the developing countries were caused by drinking polluted water.

turned to the United States from his 12-year hiatus in Japan. The influence of Far Eastern culture and Zen Buddhism on his work is clear in many poems, including "Anasazi," but considering the similarity of Native American philosophy to Zen, we cannot always tell where references to one end and the other begin. Fundamentally, it makes little difference, for these poems were written in a time of large-scale revolution in American thought, politics, and behavior, much of it leaning toward—if not completely enveloping—the same sentiments and ideas that Snyder had been promoting for decades. A sampling of only the *titles* of the journals in which many of *Turtle Island*'s poems first appeared is indicative of the world the poet lived in and the values he held: *Rising Generation, Not Man Apart, Unmuzzled Ox, Peace & Pieces,* and *Marijuana Review.* And while it may be easy to place Snyder in the "hippie" category of 1960s

America, his personal beliefs and lifestyle existed long before and go well beyond any cultural fads or pseudo-political movements that came about.

The time setting of "Anasazi" and that of the poet when he wrote it are hundreds of years apart. Even so, Gary Snyder was living in the same general region of the country as these ancient Indians, performing many of the same daily routines and taking on the same daily responsibilities. He and his family built their own home (not in "clefts in the cliffs," but with their own hands and a "village" of friends), grew their own food, used water from mountain streams for bathing and cooking, and prepared most meals over an open fire set in a pit in the middle of the living room. While the Anasazi people had no other methods from which to choose, Snyder opted for an environmentally conscious life that did not depend on technology, and he was happy to welcome neighbors and strangers alike to his home rather than put up fences and walls to keep them out.

The poetry that Snyder wrote during the 1960s and early 1970s was often didactic, or "preachy," in nature. His essays also addressed political and social issues, reflecting the American shift in attitude toward the government, the environment, war, drug use, and other controversial topics. It was a turbulent time, and there was much fuel for anyone looking to light a fire under social reform. The war in Vietnam dragged on, and the streets in America filled up with more and more protesters. Various factions of the population who had historically had little say in government and in society began to organize movements, from Black Power to women's rights to the American Indian Movement. Also during these years, many people became concerned about pollution and the misuse of natural resources. A "greens" movement developed, and its followers advocated an earthy spirituality, believing in "Gaia," or in the earth as a living organism. Many environmentalists turned against hunting wild animals for sport, and a large vegetarian crusade developed. Amidst all these movements, the use of recreational drugs increased dramatically, especially within the younger generation, but hippies and peaceniks by no means invented "getting high." Hallucinogenic herbs and powders have been used for centuries all over the world for both relaxation and in cultural and religious rites, and Native Americans often included peyote in their rituals. Gary Snyder, too, has been noted for his experimentation with a variety of drugs and for the common use of them during meditative group gatherings at his home in the mountains.

"Anasazi" is a poem that Snyder could have written at any point in his career, considering his lifelong interest in Indian culture and in living in harmony with the environment. The inclusion of it, however, in *Turtle Island,* as well as the publication of that book in 1974, allowed its message to be even more pertinent. The world was *ready* for it, so to speak. There was widespread acknowledgement that minority populations deserved an equal voice, and there was general appreciation of the lessons the majority could learn—from artistic style to soil conservation—from diverse cultures. There was a growing outcry to protect the natural resources that industrialized nations had been treating as "endless," and part of that protection meant treating the earth more gently and with greater respect. The Anasazi had already done that. And though these people faced the hardships of enemy tribes, inclement weather, and disease, they never struggled with nor pillaged their natural environment. Instead, they took care of it and, in turn, prospered from its resources.

Critical Overview

Gary Snyder's first few books of poetry were reviewed by only a handful of critics, but all of them wrote very favorably of the poet's work. Most comments centered on Snyder's easy lyrical style and precise portrayal of the natural world, some noting that he was simply writing the life he was living. After this positive beginning, Snyder moved to Japan and little was heard from him back in the States. When he returned and began construction on his home in the Sierra Nevadas, he wrote the poems for *Turtle Island.*

This book was not received favorably by many critics at first. It was considered too limited in scope, most of the poems drawing on the poet's own regional environment and on his own friends and experiences. In his "'Thirty Miles of Dust: There Is No Other Life,'" Scott McLean states that, "scholars lamented his departure—from the purely imagistic lyric for forms that were too overtly political or were too centered on one locality." Later, however, critics came to regard the book as one of Snyder's best, and it was awarded a Pulitzer Prize in 1975. McLean attributes this change in critical attitude to readers developing a better understanding of the importance that social issues and community involvement held for the poet. McLean points out that "these poems represented for Gary a series of notes in an open scale, a range of poetry that community life and involvement demanded. For when the developers are right there at a neighbor's property line it is important to have a poem that ends, 'And here we must draw/ Our line.'" (This line appears in the poem "Front Lines.")

Criticism

Pamela Steed Hill

Pamela Steed Hill has had poems published in close to a hundred journals and is the author of In Praise of Motels, *a collection of poems published by Blair Mountain Press. She is an associate edi-*

tor for University Communications *at The Ohio State University.*

To understand and appreciate fully Gary Snyder's "Anasazi" we need to know something about the Native American people who are the subject of the poem. The Anasazi are thought to be ancestors of the modern Pueblo Indians, and they inhabited Utah, Colorado, New Mexico, and Arizona from about 200 to 1300 A.D. They are remembered for their skills at horticulture, pottery making, basket weaving, and architecture, especially their "cliff houses." These dwellings—literally two- and three-story structures carved into the sides of steep cliffs and requiring ladders for entry and exit—replaced the partially underground homes where the Anasazi had lived for centuries. As they began to move to the cliffs and to expand their skills at masonry and architecture, the underground rooms were reserved as "kivas," or places to hold council or perform religious rituals. The most important aspect of Anasazi life, as well as of all Native American cultures, was their respect for the land they lived on and their ability to care for it and prosper from it without destroying it.

Gary Snyder himself was greatly influenced by Indian customs and lifestyle, and he patterned his own life and surroundings after them. With an interest in anthropology as well as poetry, he often combines the two areas in his work, frequently sending messages of pro-environmentalism through essays, lectures, and poems. In a 1977 collection of essays entitled *The Old Ways,* Snyder addresses the issues of technology and industrialization gone out of control. He defends a need for "modern" human beings to take a hard look at what we have done to the earth—to the trees, the soil, the mountains, the animals, the air—and to begin to reverse the damage by seeing our planet as a living organism. One way that each person can help turn things around, according to Snyder, is to "reinhabit this land with people who know they belong to it." By doing so, we will come to understand how we "live specifically in each place."

The poem "Anasazi" exemplifies a people who lived specifically in their place. They took time to get to know their region of the world, including the plants that grew there, the animals that lived there, the fish that filled the streams and rivers, and the best types of crops for the soil they had. These were people who truly could live off the land and did so without exploiting its resources. The Anasazi not only took care of the environment, but also celebrated it. Snyder's poem reveals and imitates this

> *What makes Snyder's poem a bit different is that his subject is not just about respecting the earth or convincing people that nature is beautiful and worth protecting. Rather, this poet writes from a perspective of an absolute necessity for human beings to pay critical attention to their relationship with the natural world. The Anasazi people not only recognized that their existence depended upon nature, but they knew that nature depended on them as well.*"

celebration through its soft, rhythmic cadence and its strong imagery. Each line reads as though it was written in reverence for the thing or person being described, and the mixture of human life, animal life, and nature is reflective of the poet's opinion on how all life should be lived.

Not only is the line "tucked up in clefts in the cliffs" a wonderful use of alliteration, but it also indicates how the Anasazi felt about their rock homes. Contrary to how people in contemporary society may view a seemingly harsh, rough existence, Snyder describes the Native Americans as "tucked up," a pleasant phrase connoting gentleness and comfort. The Anasazi were so in tune with the earth that they chose to live, literally, among its natural stone and craggy mountainsides. Their knowledge of the surrounding soil is evident in the fact that they were able to grow "strict fields of corn and beans" on terrain that would likely prove impossible for less skilled, less caring farmers. Snyder merges nature with spirituality in the lines "sinking deeper and deeper in earth / up to your

What Do I Read Next?

- *The Back Country* (1971) is one of Gary Snyder's most Eastern-influenced collections of poetry. What makes it especially interesting is his blending of East Asian thought and western United States culture.

- Probably the most prolific collection of poems dealing with Buddhist thought is the 358-page *Beneath a Single Moon: Buddhism in Contemporary American Poetry,* published in 1991. Edited by Kent Johnson and Craig Paulenich, and with an introduction by Gary Snyder, this massive volume contains dozens of poems by writers from around the world, including Stephen Berg, Diane Di Prima, Allen Ginsberg, and Anthony Piccione.

- Most people know author Jack Kerouac for his Beat-movement "bible" *On the Road.* But he is also the author of *Dharma Bums,* an autobiographical work, published in 1958, relating his experiences with Buddhism while living in California in the mid-1950s. The character "Japhy Ryder"—a poet, woodsman, and Buddhist—is actually Kerouac's real-life friend and mentor, Gary Snyder.

- *American Indian Studies: An Interdisciplinary Approach to Contemporary Issues* provides a new and provocative way of looking at many facets of Native American life. Edited by Dane Morrison and published in 1997, this book is a collection of essays by writers drawing upon their expertise in diverse disciplines—economics, education, film, history, linguistics, literature, museum studies, popular culture, and religion—to highlight a particular aspect of the American Indian experience.

- Gerald Hausman's *Tunkashila: From the Birth of Turtle Island to the Blood of Wounded Knee* reads more like a complex novel than a collection of fables, folktales, and myths concerning Native Americans. Published in 1994, this book tells the stories of the continent's beginning through 88 myths and 100 illustrations and brings Indian legends to life in the contemporary world.

- Robin Attfield's *The Ethics of a Global Environment* is a very accessible, reader-friendly book that discusses the ethical principles of humans to nature, natural resources, and the planet. Attfield offers some startling, future scenarios, including a limited water supply, changing climates, overpopulation, and the destruction of ecosystems.

---

hips in Gods," implying a religious connection between the people, the land, and a divine presence. He carries the union further by pairing human physical attributes to animals and natural phenomena: head and eagle-down; knees, elbows, and lightning; and eyes and pollen. The lines containing these elements describe a ritual taking place, probably in a kiva, since we know the underground rooms were converted for such after the Anasazi moved into the cliffs.

The concept of living specifically in a place and of being keenly aware of the nature that shares the space is nowhere more evident than in the middle three lines of the poem. "[T]he smell of bats. / the flavor of sandstone / grit on the tongue" present images that touch directly upon the senses and indicate how close the Anasazi people were to their environment. Most of us do not know what bats smell like because we don't live where bats live. Nor do we know what sandstone tastes like or how it feels on the tongue because we don't have reason to come into such close contact with it. While we may be able to imagine these sensations and to carry them even further into the senses of sight and sound—we can "see" bats in our minds and we can "hear" sandstone grinding in one's teeth—but the Anasazi knew them firsthand. Instead of "overtaking the land with" man-made comforts and bombarding the natural setting with unnatural inventions, these Native Americans got to know their environment as though it were a "neighbor" and came to live at peace with it.

For most people in industrialized, technology-centered nations today—and especially for the women—the idea of giving birth to a child without taking every measurement of comfort into consideration is unthinkable. From special beds to numbing drugs, we want to make childbirth as easy and painless as possible. Therefore, reading about "women / birthing / at the foot of ladders in the dark" can send chills down the spine of anyone who has been through, or can imagine going through, the process of having a baby. But this section of "Anasazi" is not there to horrify and dismay. Nor is it there to imply any complaints from the Indians about how and where the women gave birth. Instead, the image leads directly to a description of the surrounding natural beauty: "trickling streams," "hidden canyons," and "the cold rolling desert." Again the connection is made between human phenomena and natural phenomena, with a bit of ambiguity thrown in to make any separation even harder to distinguish. If our first notion is to see the "trickling streams in hidden canyons" line as a shift to a description of the natural setting, we may also consider it a continuation of the depiction of real childbirth. With the presence of both water and blood during birth, the use of "trickling streams" works as well as a metaphor as it does a simple description of a nearby creek or river. The point here is that there is an undeniable interconnectedness and interdependence between people and nature.

It is fitting that the poem ends with a new beginning, so to speak. The baby described in the last few lines signifies not only a new life among the Anasazi people, but also a new creation out of the union with nature. Here, the images are extremely brief and the syllabic pattern makes a very pronounced cadence, all in tune with the celebratory effect of the poem. The four distinct images—"corn basket," "wide-eyed," "red baby," and "rock lip home"—may be seen as separate entities, but more likely there is an intentional pairing of the object with the human. That is, corn basket pairs with wide-eyed and red baby pairs with rock lip home. This match-up would be in keeping with the blending of people and environment that we find throughout the poem. On the literal level, this string of images tells us that the wide-eyed newborn will be carried to its home in the cliffs in a corn basket. The Anasazi, we recall, were excellent basket weavers, and their wares served a variety of purposes, from toting crop yields to infants. And on the metaphorical level, these words illuminate the necessary alliance between humankind—from infancy on—and the world around us.

Even with an understanding of the history of the Anasazi culture, some readers may find Gary Snyder's poem difficult because it seems disjointed or incomplete. But the style and the presentation lend themselves well to what the poet is trying to convey. His ability to select just the right words and brief phrases to portray an entire philosophy and lifestyle is actually more effective than belaboring the points with long, explanatory sentences and a didactic, or "preachy," defense. With such exact imagery and unadorned detail, the poet simply shows us a picture of true environmentalism and of how one group of people accomplished living in harmony with nature.

The theme of "Anasazi" is not unique in the world of poetry. Countless poets over the centuries have penned verses of praise for the natural world, including many in more recent times who have used the venue to make social statements in favor of environmentalism. What makes Snyder's poem a bit different is that his subject is not just about respecting the earth or convincing people that nature is beautiful and worth protecting. Rather, this poet writes from a perspective of an absolute necessity for human beings to pay critical attention to their relationship with the natural world. The Anasazi people not only recognized that their existence depended upon nature, but they knew that nature depended on them as well. In the poem, this is demonstrated by the continuous blending of people, animals, earth, rocks, and so forth. With such an interweaving tie between all living things, Snyder makes a very strong case for taking our current notion of environmentalism to a much higher level.

Sources

"Anasazi," http://www.crystalinks.com/anasazi.html, accessed February 9, 2000.

Castro, Michael, "Gary Snyder: The Lessons of *Turtle Island*," *Critical Essays on Gary Snyder*, edited by Patrick D. Murphy, Boston: G.K. Hall & Co., 1991, pp. 131-144.

Gefin, Laszlo, *Ideogram, History of a Poetic Method*, Austin: University of Texas Press, 1982.

"The History Channel," http://www.historychannel.com/, accessed December 3, 1999.

McClean, Scott, "'Thirty Miles of Dust: There Is No Other Life,'" *Gary Snyder: Dimensions of a Life*, edited by Jon Halper, San Francisco: Sierra Club Books, 1991, pp. 127-138.

"Native Americans and the American Indian Movement," http://www.letsfindout.com/subjects/america/aim.html, accessed December 8, 1999.

Snyder, Gary, *The Old Ways: Six Essays,* San Francisco: City Lights Books, 1977.

————, *Turtle Island,* New York: New Directions, 1974.

For Further Study

Brody, J. J., *The Anasazi: Ancient Indian People of the American Southwest,* New York: Rizzoli, 1990.
    This is an oversized book containing 222 illustrations and text written for the non-specialist. It highlights the land the Anasazi inhabited, their social and cultural rise, their architecture, and their ultimate dispersion throughout the Southwest.

Mails, Thomas E., *The Pueblo Children of the Earth Mother,* Garden City, New York: Doubleday, 1983.
    This book provides insight into the ancient Indians even before the Anasazi group settled in America. It tells the story of both the Anasazi and Pueblo Indians, from their roots in Peru in 2000 B.C. to the first Anasazi basket makers in the American Southwest, highlighting their centuries of living at peace with the environment.

Snyder, Gary, *Earth House Hold,* New York: New Directions, 1969.
    This is Gary Snyder's first collection of prose, containing both essays and journal entries. Most pieces concentrate on his life and studies in Japan and address issues of wilderness life, community, and the philosophy of Zen Buddhism.

Annabel Lee

Edgar Allan Poe
1849

Written in 1849, "Annabel Lee" was published the same year, just two days after Poe's death on October 7. It appeared in two newspapers, the *Richmond Examiner* and the *New York Tribune*, and then in the 1850 edition of *The Works of the Late Edgar Allan Poe*. The poem has since become one of Poe's most popular works. Using a melodious narrative form, the speaker laments the death, many years ago, of his beloved young bride Annabel Lee. His loss moves him to state that envious angels caused the girl's death to "dissever" (separate) the young married couple. He tells briefly of her funeral and entombment "in her sepulchre ... by the sea." The narrator then reveals that he has been unable to accept their separation. Since her death, he has spent night after night at her tomb, an astonishing and perverse example of the immortality of young love.

Author Biography

Poe was born in Boston in 1809, the son of Elizabeth Arnold Poe and David Poe, both minor professional actors. Both his parents died before he was three years old, and he was subsequently raised in the home of Frances Keeling Valentine Allan and her husband John Allan, a prosperous exporter from Richmond, Virginia. As a youth, Poe attended the finest academies in Richmond, his stepfather overseeing his education, and he entered the Uni-

Edgar Allan Poe

versity of Virginia at Charlottesville in 1825. He distinguished himself academically at the university but was forced to leave due to inadequate financial support from his stepfather. Poe returned to Richmond in 1827 but soon left for Boston. There he enlisted in the army and published his first collection of poetry, *Tamerlane, and Other Poems.* Poe was discharged from the army in 1829, the same year he published a second volume of verse. Neither of his first two collections attracted much attention. After briefly attending West Point, Poe went to New York City and soon after to Baltimore. He married his cousin Virginia Clemm in 1836 after receiving an editorship at *The Southern Literary Messenger* in Richmond. Poe thereafter received a degree of recognition, not only for his poetry and fiction, but as an exceptional literary critic. He also occasionally achieved popular success, especially following the publication of his poem "The Raven."

Poe's wife Virginia died from tuberculosis in 1847. After a period in which he was involved in various romantic affairs, Poe planned to remarry, but in late September, 1849 he arrived in Baltimore for reasons unknown. In early October he was discovered nearly unconscious; he died on October 7, never regaining sufficient consciousness to relate the details of the final days of his life. Since his

death Poe's work has been variously assessed, with critics disagreeing on its value. Today, however, Poe is acknowledged as a major literary figure, a master of Gothic atmosphere and interior monologue. His poems and stories have influenced the literary schools of Symbolism and Surrealism as well as the popular genres of detective and horror fiction.

Poem Text

It was many and many a year ago,
    In a kingdom by the sea,
That a maiden there lived whom you may know
    By the name of Annabel Lee;
And this maiden she lived with no other thought   5
    Than to love and be loved by me.

She was a child and *I* was a child,
    In this kingdom by the sea,
But we loved with a love that was more than
        love—
    I and my Annabel Lee—   10
With a love that the wingéd seraphs of Heaven
    Coveted her and me.

And this was the reason that, long ago,
    In this kingdom by the sea,
A wind blew out of a cloud by night   15
    Chilling my Annabel Lee;
So that her highborn kinsmen came
    And bore her away from me,
To shut her up in a sepulchre
    In this kingdom by the sea.   20

The angels, not half so happy in Heaven,
    Went envying her and me:
Yes! that was the reason (as all men know,
    In this kingdom by the sea)
That the wind came out of the cloud, chilling   25
    And killing my Annabel Lee.

But our love it was stronger by far than the love
    Of those who were older than we—
Of many far wiser than we—
    And neither the angels in Heaven above   30
Nor the demons down under the sea,
    Can ever dissever my soul from the soul
Of the beautiful Annabel Lee:

    For the moon never beams without bringing me
        dreams
Of the beautiful Annabel Lee;   35
    And the stars never rise but I see the bright
        eyes
Of the beautiful Annabel Lee;
    And so, all the night-tide, I lie down by the side
Of my darling, my darling, my life and my bride,
    In her sepulchre there by the sea—   40
In her tomb by the side of the sea.

Poem Summary

Lines 1-2:

Poe introduces the setting of "Annabel Lee" in these lines. Though vague, his use of "many and many a year ago" shows with its repetition that the poem will tell about an event that occurred in the far past. The physical location "a kingdom by the sea" and the use of the abstract time frame produce a romantic, legendary quality for the narrative setting. These lines also establish the rhythmical use of anapests and iambs. Here, however, the first two syllables may be read as a spondee, a combination of two stressed syllables in a row. If one emphasizes both words, "It was," and keeps stress also on the first syllable of "many," the poem begins with the strong effect of three stressed syllables in a row.

Lines 3-4:

These lines introduce the character of Annabel Lee. Her description as someone "whom you may know" adds to the legendary quality of the poem, and the use of the personal pronoun "you" creates a feeling of intimacy between the speaker and the reader.

Lines 5-6:

The speaker's relationship to Annabel Lee is introduced in these lines. Her devotion to the speaker, whom we later learn (in line 39) was her husband, appears in the fact that her only thought was to "love and be loved" by the speaker. The repetition of "love"/"loved" emphasizes the relationship between the two.

Lines 7-8:

The repetition of the word "child" in line 7 establishes the youth of both characters at the time of Annabel Lee's death. It implies that their love was an innocent love, removed from the corruption that may be associated with the adult world. The repetition in line 8 of line 2 from the first stanza presents the phrase as a refrain, creating a harmonious, linking effect every time it is used in the poem.

Lines 9-12:

These lines associate the relationship between the speaker and his bride with heavenly qualities. Through repetition of the words "love" and "loved" the magnitude of their feelings develops. The suggestion that angels—"the wingéd seraphs"—envy or covet the lovers' feelings for one another elevates this relationship above any other on earth or in heaven.

Lines 13-16:

In line 13, The pronoun "this" refers to the jealousy of the angels introduced in lines 11-12, while line 14 repeats the refrain from the first two stanzas. In line 15 the speaker names the cause of Annabel Lee's death. A chilling wind emerges from the sky, and so her death is tied to heaven and the jealousy of the angels. He places the action in the "night," an appropriate time for an insidious deed to be executed by the covetous angels.

Lines 17-20:

The speaker describes Annabel Lee's funeral in these lines. Also she is further characterized; with the reference to her "highborn kinsmen" the reader discovers that she belonged to an upper-class family. The use of the formal word, "sepulchre," rather than a more common word such as "tomb," adds to this impression of the girl's birthright. The word "sepulchre" also has a more formal tone to it, suggesting the finality of the couple's relationship. This finality—the speaker's total isolation from his love—is also developed by using the words, "shut her up" and "away from me" rather than using a phrase such as "placed her there." Note that this stanza concludes with the refrain, which also lends a note of completion to the lovers' relationship. However, in the final two stanzas of the poem, the reader will learn that in spite of Annabel Lee's death, the speaker has not stopped loving her.

Lines 21-26:

This stanza repeats the speaker's belief that the envious angels caused Annabel Lee's death by blowing a chilling wind from the cloudy sky. All this repetition serves to emphasize the conflict in the poem, the loss of the speaker's love. Line 21 uses alliteration in its repetition of *h*, a sound that suggests the airy blowing of wind. The word "Yes," followed by an exclamation mark, creates the first hint of a frantic tone that will develop in the last two stanzas. The phrase "as all men know" in line 23 adds to that legendary quality of the poem. The refrain appears again in line 24. And a rhyme link occurs in "chilling" and "killing" (lines 25 and 26) which emphasizes the horror of Annabel Lee's death and sets the mood for the desperate method of mourning that the speaker unveils in the last stanza.

Lines 27-29:

These lines continue to elevate the relationship between the speaker and his bride by repeating the word, "love," and by stating that they love more than even older and wiser people.

Media Adaptations

- Dover Press Audio Thrift Classics has produced *Listen and Read Edgar Allan Poe's "The Raven" and other Favorite Poems* (1998) as a book and audiocassette.

- Marianne Faithful renders "Annabel Lee" on the audio compact disk *Closed On Account of Rabies: Poems and Tales of Edgar Allan Poe* (1997) by UNI/Polygram.

- Arts and Entertainment Network has produced the videocassette *Biography: Edgar Allan Poe* (1996).

- Educational Insights, Inc., has produced the book and audiocassette *The Best of Poe* (1999).

- Caedmon (publisher) presents *Poems and Tales of Edgar Allan Poe* (1955) on audiocassette with Basil Rathbone.

- Michael Cain renders "Annabel Lee" on the audiocassette *The Silver Lining: The World's Most Distinguished Actors Read Their Favorite Poems* (1995) for BMP, Ltd.

- Guidance Associates presents the videocassette, filmstrip and teacher's guide *Edgar Allan Poe and the Literature of Melancholy* (1980).

- Monterey Home Video has produced the videocassette *Edgar Allan Poe: Architect of Dreams* (1995).

- A&E Home Video has produced the videocassette *The Mystery of Edgar Allan Poe* (1999).

- GRJ Productions has produced the 16mm film *Poe: A Visit With the Author* (1968).

Lines 30-33:

In these lines the speaker asserts his faithfulness to Annabel Lee, a loyalty that transcends death. The "angels" have already been referred to as those jealous of the extraordinary love between the speaker and his bride. The phrase, "demons down under the sea," brings to mind the Greek myth of Andromeda, who is about to be devoured by a sea monster when she is rescued by the hero Perseus. Note the alliteration of the letter "d" in the words "demon," "down," "under," and "dissever" to create a heavy sound; the internal rhyme of "ever dissever" to create a melodious effect; and the repetition of "soul" to emphasize the extent of the lovers' union. These lines have been connected to St. Paul's *Epistle to the Romans* by Richard Wilbur. St. Paul's eighth chapter reads "I am persuaded that neither death, nor life, nor angels, nor principalities, nor powers, nor things present, nor things to come, nor height, nor depth, nor any other creature, shall be able to separate us from the love of God."

Lines 34-37:

The speaker offers proof that his love for Annabel Lee is eternal. He explains that the "moon" and the "stars" are celestial messengers which bring her love to him in the form of "dreams" and in visions of her "eyes." Association of Annabel Lee with these heavenly bodies immortalizes her and her love. Alliteration of the consonant *b* occurs in the words "beams," "bringing," "beautiful," "but," and "bright." Internal rhyme exists in "beams" and "dreams" and in "rise" and "eyes."

Lines 38-41:

In these lines the speaker finally reveals the shocking fact that he visits Annabel Lee's tomb nightly, reposing there next to her. It is also in line 39 that the speaker reveals the fact that Annabel Lee was his "bride." The love he feels for her finds expression in repetition of the words, "my darling," and in the statement that she is his "life." The rhymes "tide," "side," and "bride" create an auditory link between lines 38 and 39. The final two lines, in their parallel construction, both beginning with "in her" and ending with "the sea" create a strong sense of finality. For some readers, the double naming of the location to identify Annabel Lee's burial chamber ("sepulchre" and "tomb") as the setting of this eternal exchange has the eerie effect of allowing the theme of death to overshadow the theme of love in this poem.

Themes

Memory and Reminiscing

Readers are urged by the tone and setting of this poem to question how well the speaker actually remembers his relationship with his dead lover. From the very first line, the speaker admits that he is talking about things that happened "many and many years ago." Repeating the word "many" emphasizes the amount of time that has passed since Annabel Lee's death. This encourages readers' suspicions, since memories, especially extremely pleasant memories, are often idealized versions of reality. In the third stanza, the poem makes a point of mentioning once more that there is a considerable distance of time between the events being described and the speaker as he is recalling them. It becomes even more difficult to believe that his brief, youthful love affair could have been as pure and beautiful as he describes it. If his claim was that a recent love had died because of angels' jealousy, or that he thought every day about a lover who died the year before, then his obsession could be attributed to strong but normal grief. With the distance of time indicated here, though, there has to be a strong possibility that he is not actually responding to the love affair that he lived, but instead to a false, inflated memory of Annabel Lee.

The sea is used here as a poetic device to represent memory. It is linked to the life the speaker had with Annabel Lee because they lived together in a kingdom next to it. It is linked to her death, as he makes a point of mentioning twice in the last two lines that her body is put to rest beside the sea. As a vast, mysterious force, a traditional place of enigma and danger, the sea is a fitting symbol to represent the past, which is as attractive to the speaker as the sea is to those who sail it. In line 31 he speculates that the demons who might come to disrupt his memory of Annabel Lee—who might "dissever" his soul from hers—lurk under the sea.

Death

Like many of Edgar Allan Poe's short stories and poems, "Annabel Lee" concerns itself with the human problem of having to carry on and make sense of the world after the permanent disruption that death causes. In this particular case, the speaker of the poem is so distraught over his loss that he bends reality to find a cause for her death that his mind can accept. Readers are not given a physical, medical explanation for her death, other than that a "chill" came down upon her, because in his mind mere physics would be too simple to destroy a grand love like the one he remembers. The explanation that is offered instead is that the angels envied the young couple's happiness and, most uncharacteristically for angels, killed her out of jealousy. For the narrator, this explanation makes sense of the randomness of disease and death by providing a culprit; he needs this in order to accept

Topics for Further Study

- In this poem, Poe places an ideal love in "a kingdom by the sea." Write a poem in which you give a location to be the site of a perfect love— would it be rural, urban, mountainous, coastal? Write about what you think it would be like to have a loved one buried at that place that you associate with living, vibrant love.

- At the time this poem was written, 1849, America was still an expanding country, with conflicting opinions between the North and South over whether newly formed states should allow slavery. By contrast, "Annabel Lee" takes place in a well-established social structure, a kingdom. Explain what you think nostalgia might have been like for Americans at that time, both for those who were part of the established order and those who were expanding the frontier.

- Like much of Poe's poetry, "Annabel Lee" has an easily recognizable rhythm. Set this poem to music, using either original instrumentation or melodies sampled from other songs.

- Research the seven stages of death as described by psychologist Elisabeth Kubler-Ross. Explain which of these stages the narrator of the poem is undergoing at each point in the poem.

the idea that his love might not have been great enough to stop death. In fact, he cannot accept death as a separation from the girl he loved, but believes that they are still linked, which may be true for him in a psychological sense, although there is no way of knowing if the deceased, wherever she may be, might also feel this way. The situation related in this poem is real more in a psychological sense than in any other sense, and this makes death (which is an absolute, unchangeable limit in the real world) serve as an appropriate tool for Poe's type of writing.

Class Conflict

The speaker of this poem presents himself as an underdog, struggling throughout his entire love affair against those who attempt to use their superior social positions against him. At first, the speaker implies that the world looked down on his relationship with Annabel Lee because they were both children, making a point of emphasizing *she* and *I* to show their common bond against the opposition, presumably from adults. If, as most critics agree, this poem is based upon Poe's relationship with his cousin Virginia Clemm, then he has altered the facts here to fit this theory of opposition: even if Virginia was only thirteen when they married, Poe himself was twenty-seven. By presenting himself as a child, he puts himself and Annabel Lee on one side and the adult world on the other. Later in the poem, there is opposition from the angels, who are jealous because the young couple has more happiness than they themselves have in heaven. The angels, obviously from a higher and more privileged class than a couple of children on Earth, have killed Annabel Lee, the narrator says. After Annabel Lee's death, her body was taken away by "her high-born kinsmen." Although it is not directly stated, the implication here is that the speaker is prohibited from visiting his deceased love or from participating in her funeral because of class distinctions. The love affair in this poem is opposed by forces more powerful—adults, angels, and the upper social class. The endurance of the youngsters' love against all of these is a testament to its strength.

Style

"Annabel Lee" consists of six stanzas that range from six to eight lines each. The poem uses repetition and rhyme to create the qualities of unity and euphony, or a pleasing musicality. The repeated use of the end rhymes "sea," "Lee," "we," and "me" offer a link from stanza to stanza throughout the poem. The name "Annabel Lee" appears at least once in every stanza, and the phrase "kingdom by the sea" also appears frequently, adding to the unified structure. Repetition of key words within lines gives the poem its pleasing sound while at the same time emphasizing main ideas. For example, in line 1, "many and many" establishes the fact that a long period of time has elapsed since the speaker began mourning, an important fact to recognize if the reader is to understand the extent of the speaker's grief.

The poem's rhyme scheme begins simply with an *ababcb* pattern but gets more complicated as the poem progresses, repeating rhymes within a line (known as internal rhyme) and ending with the pattern *abcbddbb* in the last stanza. The lines increase in length and in number in this last stanza. These devices—the increasingly complex rhyme scheme and lengthening of lines—allow the poem to intensify in dramatic pitch.

The predominant rhythm that the poem uses is the anapest. An anapest is a type of meter consisting of three syllables, with one stressed syllable occurring after two unstressed syllables. For example in the first line, the first syllable of "many" and the word "year" receive stress after two unaccented syllables, as shown below:

> Itwasma / nyandma / nyayear / a go.

The anapest rhythm is an exciting, climactic one that builds in momentum just as the overall structure of the poem does. To vary the rhythm, the poem also uses iambic feet, or pairs of unstressed and stressed syllables, as in "ago" in the line shown above.

Historical Context

In 1849 America was still expanding westward, and the addition of each new state stirred anew the debate between supporters of slavery and the reformers (referred to as "Abolitionists") who wanted to abolish slavery. The slave trade had developed as the country was developing during the sixteenth and seventeenth centuries. Many of the settlers of the original thirteen colonies brought "indentured servants" from Europe. These were usually citizens of the lower classes who were willing to sell their freedom for a time, usually seven years, in exchange for the price of passage to the new continent. From that practice, the practice of permanently keeping people with different physical characteristics seemed a natural progression. Some colonies, most notably Virginia, dabbled in keeping American Indians for slave labor, but, possibly because of the bloody confrontations that had served to take the country from the Indians, the European property owners never felt comfortable keeping them around. The Dutch built a profitable trade selling captured Africans in the colonies and in the Caribbean. Slavery was first legally recognized in the colonies in 1650. By 1676, Dutch traders were selling 15,000 Africans in the Americas each year. There were several reasons why slavery became a Southern institution. The slaves

Compare & Contrast

- **1849:** Two months after "Annabel Lee" was published, Edgar Allan Poe was found in a tavern in Baltimore, muttering incoherently. He was admitted to the hospital, where he died four days later.

  Today: Despite the claims of earlier biographers who wrote that Poe had been on a self-destructive drinking binge, modern historians guess that his condition probably had a physiological cause, such as a stroke.

- **1849:** The discovery of gold in California the year before sparked a "Gold Rush" to that territory. Seventy-seven thousand people, dubbed "'49ers," rushed to California that year, travelling across unpopulated plains and the Rocky Mountains. California mines yielded $450,000,000 in gold.

  Today: California is the most populous state in the union, with over ten million more people than the next most populous, New York.

- **1849:** The safety pin was invented by Walter Hunt, also known for inventing the sewing machine and the paper disposable shirt collar. To pay off some debts, he sold the rights to the safety pin for $400.

  1942: A Swiss manufacturer invented Velcro, a device used to fasten two strips of cloth together without the use of pins.

  Today: Safety pins are still available, but are seldom used anymore.

- **1849:** Harriet Tubman escaped from slavery and began her career with the Underground Railroad, the secret organization that helped slaves escape to freedom in Canada. She went on to make nearly twenty trips between the North and South, freeing 300 slaves.

  Today: Harriet Tubman is recognized as an American hero.

- **1849:** The first talk of secession came from the Southern states, in response to President Zachary Taylor's decision to let Californians vote for whether they wanted slavery in their state when it was admitted into the union. Hardcore supporters of slavery thought this was a betrayal of the Missouri Compromise, which decreed that slavery should be allowed anywhere below thirty-six degrees latitude.

  1860: The South did secede from the United States, provoking the Civil War.

  Today: The United States is a prosperous and fairly harmonious country, with no powerful separatist movements.

- **1849:** The Women's Rights movement was on the rise in America: the first Women's Rights Convention was held in Seneca, New York, in 1848, with the first national convention held in 1850.

  Today: After strong advances in the 1960s and 1970s, the Women's Rights movement has suffered a great drop in popular support. Some of its detractors say that it favors women at the expense of equality. Others feel that the movement has become irrelevant.

---

were from agricultural societies, and, as the colonies developed, the South, which was warmer and more fertile, became agricultural, while the northern states tended toward manufacturing economies that would have more required for training the slaves than would have been practical.

Around the time of the Revolutionary War, the issue of slavery was hotly debated. In 1768 the Mason-Dixon Line established the boundary between Pennsylvania and Maryland, providing a line of demarcation between the slave-holding south and the free north. The first American society for abolishing slavery was founded in Pennsylvania in 1775. A number of states, including southern states, passed laws outlawing the barbaric slave trade (it was eventually outlawed on a national level in

1808). The laws were empty gestures, though, because there were already more than enough slaves in the country with little need to import more. In Virginia, for example, there were as many slaves as there were whites, while South Carolina had twice as many slaves a free whites. Slavery was firmly established as part of Southern society, but Southern politicians could feel the pressure from Abolitionists to end the practice. To support their way of life, southerners felt that they had to assure that slavery was accepted in as many new states as possible.

The first half of the 1800s was marked by expansion, and as each new state joined the Union there were bitter debates in Congress about whether slavery would be allowed there. For the most part, the South remained slave territory and the North remained free, but there were bitter fights for states near the border or those west of the Mississippi river. The Missouri Compromise, in 1820, was one notable case of Congressional decision-making: there were 11 slave states and 11 free states when Missouri, a slave territory, applied to enter the Union, so Northern politicians insisted that the territory had to give up slavery if it wanted statehood. As a compromise, Maine, a free territory, was admitted, and Missouri was allowed to keep its slaves, and a new dividing line for states that came from the land bought in the Louisiana Purchase was established. The next major occasion for setting boundaries came in the 1840s, when President Polk, unsuccessful in his attempt to buy land from Mexico, sent troops to the Southwest to start a war against Mexico. With the American victory, Mexico gave up everything north of the Rio Grande, losing 35% of its land and opening up the opportunity for new states. The struggle between Abolitionists and the supporters of slavery who felt threatened reached new levels as the government prepared to decide which new states, if any, would have slaves.

As the struggle continued between those who fought for the moral cause of freedom and those who fought to hold onto their traditions, the debate over what to do with slaves who escaped to free lands became more intense. Freed slaves became more prominent. Frederick Douglass, an escaped slave, published his autobiography and started an Abolitionist newspaper, *The North Star,* which he supplemented with money raised from speaking fees in Europe. In 1838 a secret organization called the Underground Railroad established a path of safe hiding places that escaping slaves could follow north to Canada. In an effort to calm the growing rift between the North and the South, Congress enacted a new, harsh Fugitive Slave Law in 1850, toughening the penalties against escaping slaves and the people who assisted them. Free blacks in free territories could be arrested and taken south into slavery if anyone so much as accused them of being escaped slaves, while people accused of helping escaped slaves faced time in jail. The law was found unconstitutional in 1854 and then upheld by the Supreme Court in 1857. When "Annabel Lee" was published, eleven years before the outbreak of the Civil War, the question of slavery and its legal and moral ramifications was part of everyday American life.

Critical Overview

One of the first critics to comment on a connection between Poe and the speaker in "Annabel Lee" is John Cowper Powys, in his 1915 work *Visions and Revisions: A Book of Literary Devotions.* He writes that in poems such as this Poe expresses "a certain dark, wilful melancholy," a cold mood that Poe "must surely himself have known." Powys's suggestion may spring from Poe's experience with loss, and in particular the death of his child bride, Virginia Clemm. Virginia's death occurred in 1847, two years prior to the writing of this poem, and her loss could have created for Poe the atmosphere or mood that he reproduces in his poetry. Even before her death, however, Poe had experienced the death of his actress mother when he was a small child, and then the death from brain cancer of Jane Stanard, a friend's beautiful mother whom the fourteen-year-old Poe had idolized; and he had already stated in his "Philosophy of Composition" that the most appropriate subject for poetry is the death of a beautiful woman because it carries with it the most emotional power.

Despite the coldness and "artificiality" he observes in Poe's poems, Powys remarks that "to say they are artificial does not derogate from their genius." Early assessments of Poe's verse dismissed it as overly musical and vulgar, but later critics have found more to praise in it. Noting that Poe wrote several kinds and degrees of poetry, George Saintsbury wrote in a 1927 essay, later included in *Prefaces and Essays,* that "I know nothing that can beat, if I know anything that can equal, 'Annabel Lee.'" He explains: "It begins quite quietly but with a motion of gathering speed and a sort of flicker of light and glow of heat: and these things quicken and brighten and grow till they finish in the last stanza, that incomparable explosion of rapturous regret that towers to the stars and sinks to the sea."

Rather than focus on the subject of the poem, Floyd Stovall in his book *Edgar Poe the Poet* recognizes the "hypnotic effect of the repetition of harmonized sound and sense through the poem, building up to a climax in the last stanza." He commends this effect as the poem's most "pleasing" quality and contends that "the value of the poem subsists more in its form than its meaning." Not all critics would agree with Stovall, however. The well-known modern poet Richard Wilbur admires the deeper meaning in Poe's poetry. In a 1981 talk delivered to the Poe Studies Association and later published in *The University of Mississippi Studies in English*, Wilbur connects "Annabel Lee" to the divine love of God. Using references to St. Paul's *Epistle to the Romans*, Wilbur suggests that Poe has been inspired by it to create in the character of Annabel Lee the symbol of a "kind of blessed communion," one in which the speaker experiences a love that is "more than love." Wilbur supplies the excerpt from St. Paul which states that "neither death, nor life, nor angels … shall be able to separate us from the love of God." From this allusion, Wilbur concludes that "Poe asserts that the soul of Annabel's lover shall never be severed from hers, or from the divine love and beauty which her soul communicates."

Criticism

Jeannine Johnson

Jeannine Johnson received her Ph.D. from Yale University and is currently visiting assistant professor of English at Wake Forest University. In the following essay, Johnson argues that what inspired Poe to compose "Annabel Lee" was not his affection for any one person but his interest in contemplating the general nature of beauty and love.

"Annabel Lee" was the last of Edgar Allan Poe's poems to be published, appearing October 9, 1849, in the *New York Tribune,* two days after the author's death. Since the poem first appeared in print—and continuing to the present day—there have been competing claims as to the source of Poe's inspiration for this work. His wife Virginia had died in 1847 after suffering a prolonged illness, and many readers have believed that the poem was

> *In other words, the poet has boasted of the strength and significance of his spiritual bond with Annabel Lee. Yet, in his need to be near the body of his beloved, he seems to contradict his own assertions and indicate that a physical connection is just as important as a non-physical one."*

written in her memory. Frances ("Fanny") Osgood, a poet and a friend of both Poe and his wife, stated unequivocally that the poem was written to celebrate his love for Virginia (A. H. Quinn, *Edgar Allan Poe: A Critical Biography*). Fanny, with whom Poe carried on a long and intimate (though largely literary) correspondence is herself thought by some to be a candidate for the muse of "Annabel Lee." In addition, there are two other women who might have inspired Poe in the writing of this poem: Nancy ("Annie") Richmond and the poet Sarah Helen Whitman, both of whom Poe met and fostered relationships with in 1848. According to the literary critic J. Gerald Kennedy, Poe "seems to have regarded [Annie Richmond] as a virtual reincarnation of the dead Virginia Poe" (*Poe, Death, and the Life of Writing*), and Kennedy has no doubt that it is with Richmond in mind that Poe writes. Other readers have imagined that a more likely muse was Sarah Whitman, to whom Poe was briefly engaged in late 1848.

Of all the possibilities, the case for Virginia seems strongest, if only because the narrator of "Annabel Lee" emphasizes that "*She* was a child and *I* was a child." When Poe married Virginia, she was indeed a child: his wife was just 13 years old at the time of their wedding, while Poe was a less youthful 27. Of course, in composing the poem Poe chooses his words in large part for their figurative value. The quality of their youth—especially the

What Do I Read Next?

- The poems by Poe that are most often associated with this one are "Lenore" and "To Helen," which are also about the deaths of young women. All of his works can be found in the Library of America's superior collection *Edgar Allan Poe: Poetry and Tales,* published in 1984.

- Poe is considered the first serious literary critic in America. His ideas about art are evident in his nonfiction prose, collected in a different Library of America volume entitled *Edgar Allan Poe, Essays and Reviews: Theory of Poetry, Reviews of British and Continental Authors, Reviews of American Authors and American Literature.*

- Tundra Books has a hardcover book-length edition of this poem, released in 1987. *Annabel Lee* has text by Edgar Allan Poe and watercolors by award-winning children's book artist Gilles Tibo. It is usually cataloged with children's books.

- One of the best biographies of Poe available is Kenneth Silverman's *Edgar Allan Poe: Mournful and Never-Ending Remembrance,* published in 1992 by Harper Perennial. This book is not only richly detailed, but it tells an engrossing tale of the poet's life.

- John Evangelist Walsh concentrates on the four days leading up to Poe's death (which was two days before "Annabel Lee" was published) in his brief 1998 book *Midnight Dreary: The Mysterious Death of Edgar Allan Poe.* Poe's whereabouts for those days and the exact circumstances of his death have always been matters of controversy, and Walsh is meticulous in gathering evidence about what might have really happened.

- Daniel Hoffman's 1998 analysis of the poet, entitled *Poe Poe Poe Poe Poe Poe Poe,* has been received with some controversy: readers generally respect his intellectual approach but find fault with the conclusions he draws about Poe's work.

- Poe is considered to be a primary influence on the French Symbolist school, that came a generation after him. Charles Baudelaire, in particular, did much to save Poe from obscurity with his translations and reviews. The most notable collection of French Symbolist poetry is Baudelaire's *Les Fleurs Du Mal (Flowers of Evil),* which is available with commentary from Cambridge University Press series Landmarks in World Literature.

---

speaker's—seems more metaphorical than literal: Poe uses the word "child" to emphasize the innocence and purity of their bond. Because of his beloved's youth and their untainted love for each other, he is a child in spirit, if not in chronological age.

Given the importance of figurative meaning, we cannot depend solely upon literal interpretations of poetry, nor read them as simple statements of autobiographical fact. Thus perhaps we need not choose from among the several candidates for a specific source of inspiration for "Annabel Lee," or even enter this debate at all. Poe indirectly offers some insight into his purpose for the poem in the essay "The Philosophy of Composition" (1846).

In it, Poe dissects his earlier work "The Raven" (1845), reconstructing the deliberate process by which he chose the style, form, tone, and subject of his most famous poem. It is not clear whether Poe intends for us to take seriously every detail of his sometimes outrageous "philosophy." Nevertheless, he is sincere on at least one point: that "the death … of a beautiful woman is, unquestionably, the most poetic topic in the world—and equally is it beyond doubt that the lips best suited for such topic are those of a bereaved lover" (*Edgar Allan Poe: Poetry, Tales, and Selected Essays*).

Poe developed this theory of the "most poetic topic in the world" several years before he composed "Annabel Lee," which suggests that the general theme was a greater influence on its composition than was a particular person. He used the death of a beautiful woman as his topic not only in "Annabel Lee" and "The Raven" but in many of his other poems, most notably "Lenore" (1831) and "Ulalume" (1847). Poe also visited this grim subject several times in his fiction, and the narrator mourns the loss of his fair beloved in the tales "Ligeia" (1838) and "Eleonora" (1841).

Not only is the theme of "Annabel Lee" one that is common to multiple works by Poe, but several of its phrases echo earlier compositions. For instance, many critics have noted the similarities between "Annabel Lee" and Poe's first published poem, "Tamerlane" (1827). In "Tamerlane" the love of which the poet speaks "was such as angel minds above might envy," while in "Annabel Lee" "The angels, not half so happy in Heaven, / Went envying her and me." "Thus," comments Poe's biographer, Arthur Hobson Quinn, "in his first and in his last poem he thought in terms of a spiritual passion that transcended human limits" (*Edgar Allan Poe: A Critical Biography*). This is an idealized view of love which Poe held throughout his life, from the time before he met Virginia to the time after her death. And it is largely his interest in examining a "spiritual passion that transcended human limits" which inspired Poe to write this poem.

Though Poe argues in "The Philosophy of Composition" that the death of a beautiful woman is the most poetic topic, he makes a slightly different claim in the article "The Poetic Principle." The essay is based on the text of a lecture frequently presented by Poe during 1848 and 1849, and it overlaps with "Annabel Lee" both in the time period in which it was written and in subject matter. In "The Poetic Principle," Poe declares that though beauty is the goal of poetry, its proper topic is love: "Love … love—the true, the divine Eros—the Uranian, as distinguished from the Dionaean Venus—is unquestionably the purest and truest of all poetic themes" (*Edgar Allan Poe: Poetry, Tales, and Selected Essays*). "Uranian Venus" refers to love that is spiritual, pure, and eternal. It is a rare love that transcends the physical world, as opposed to a "Dionaean," or earthly, common, and finite, type of love.

In "Annabel Lee," the poet celebrates this true Uranian love: "we loved with a love that was more than love." Poe repeats the word "love" three times, as if to demonstrate the inadequacy of that human word for a condition that is divine. Even though

Annabel and her lover were young, the speaker contends that their feelings surpassed those of all others: "our love it was stronger by far than the love / Of those who were older than we— / Of many far wiser than we…." The poet argues that wisdom and age do not determine one's power to love deeply and honestly, and he then goes on to proclaim that "neither the angels in Heaven above / Nor the demons down under the sea / Can ever dissever my soul from the soul / Of the beautiful Annabel Lee."

Even though the speaker claims to possess an everlasting love that transcends all physical boundaries, he feels compelled to visit Annabel's grave again and again. The poet tells us that not only does he visit the gravesite, but he enters her tomb in order to lie down next to her corpse. What is more, it is clear from the present verb tense that this is a repeated action: "all the night-tide, I lie down by the side / Of my darling, my darling, my life and my bride / In her sepulchre there by the sea— / In her tomb by the side of the sea." The poem ends by emphasizing the material location of their union: the final two lines are nearly identical as they point us to the "sepulchre" or "tomb" in which the lovers lie. Given these circumstances, J. Gerald Kennedy asks, "why does he try to achieve physical proximity to the corpse if his love is indeed spiritual and lasting? His action seems an unconscious betrayal of anxiety, a reflexive acknowledgment of the very separation which the poem itself seeks to deny" (*Poe, Death, and the Life of Writing*). In other words, the poet has boasted of the strength and significance of his spiritual bond with Annabel Lee. Yet, in his need to be near the body of his beloved, he seems to contradict his own assertions and indicate that a physical connection is just as important as a non-physical one.

We may better understand this apparent contradiction if we recall that the poet's tale is poignant because he loses not only love but beauty. Poe revised the poem a few times, making some minor alterations which nevertheless affect the overall meaning of the poem. In an earlier version of the poem, Poe writes in the third stanza, "A wind blew out of a cloud, chilling / My beautiful Annabel Lee." In the final version of the poem, Poe changes the lines to read: "A wind blew out of a cloud by night / Chilling my Annabel Lee." With the revision, Poe infuses the event with the mysterious and potentially sinister characteristics of night-time. Furthermore, the addition of two syllables ("by night") to the third line requires Poe to shift "Chilling" to the fourth line, and it allows him to delay using the word "beautiful" to describe Annabel. He does not include this word until the fifth stanza, at which point we know that she has died. This is significant because one of Poe's main projects in this poem is to explore the link between beauty and death.

Through the first two-and-a-half stanzas, the speaker never explicitly reveals that his beloved has died. In the first four lines of the third stanza, he refers to a time at which Annabel was still alive: when she experienced a fatal chill. The action of death is so abrupt that the poet appears not to have the time to name it: "A wind blew out of a cloud by night / Chilling my Annabel Lee; / So that her high-born kinsmen came / And bore her away from me, / To shut her up in a sepulchre / In this kingdom by the sea." One moment Annabel Lee is hypothermic, and the next moment she is being buried by her relatives. Only a semi-colon signals the change from life to death, and the sentence recreates the swift and sorrowful transformation that occurs in the lovers' history.

In the fourth stanza, the poet is able to slow his recollections somewhat, and there he speaks directly of that moment which is so painful to him: "the wind came out of the cloud, chilling / And killing my Annabel Lee." The poet has explicitly acknowledged her death, and in the final stanzas he can now refer to her beauty. Between the fifth and sixth stanzas, the speaker repeats the phrase "Of the beautiful Annabel Lee" three times. The poem is full of repetition—this is a favorite technique of Poe's—but this triple refrain is unique because it occurs in such rapid succession, and the poet thus calls attention to this line.

Why does the poet want to underscore at this point in the piece that Annabel Lee was beautiful? Surely we are led to believe that she was attractive in life, but there is a particular kind of beauty that comes with her death. In the fifth and sixth stanzas the poem shifts from narrative to memorial. That is to say, in the first part of the poem, the speaker has told the story of his relationship with his beloved and of her death. In the latter part, he tells us what his life is like now and the way that he tries to honor her memory. As the poem turns from story to commemoration, the vocabulary also changes. There is in the sixth stanza a notable emphasis on visual imagery that is not present in the rest of the poem. For instance, the poet mentions the moon and the stars in which he observes "the bright eyes" of his dear Annabel. His love becomes not just something to feel or imagine but to touch and to see. In fact, the beauty that he conjures

comes to replace the "love" about which the poet has spoken earlier in the poem: he uses "love" eight times in the first five stanzas, but this word disappears in the sixth. The theoretical idea of "love" gives way to a more concrete notion of loveliness, and the absence of the former term in this last stanza suggests that, though we may want to value the ethereal qualities of true love, its tangible elements are what we ultimately cherish most.

Source: Jeannine Johnson, in an essay for *Poetry for Students,* Gale, 2000.

David Kelly

David Kelly is an instructor of literature and writing at several community colleges in Illinois, as well as a fiction writer and playwright. In this essay, Kelly examines whether the verbal excesses of "Annabel Lee" are justified, or if the poem is just an exercise in cleverness for its own sake.

A sure sign of weak poetry—and if Edgar Allan Poe had any weakness as a writer, it was his poetry—is that it is padded with extra words that serve no purpose but to fill out its metrical scheme. The word "extra" is key here. We all think that we can recognize which words can be considered useless to a poem, but that concept is open and is constantly interpreted in different ways. The interpretation of what is necessary and what can be dismissed as filler seems to be at the root of the controversy about whether Poe was a good poet or a bad one. A poem like "Annabel Lee" provides the author with a good forum for clever word trickery. Some people praise such cleverness, while others immediately become suspicions of a poet who might be more enamoured with the sounds of words than with what ideas they represent—in other words, there is a good chance, if his poems are *too* musical, that Poe may be willing to settle for weakness in his poem's thoughts if he feels audiences are kept amused enough with the excellence of his music.

Poe's supporters, who have grown in number through the generations, encourage readers to be skeptical, but to keep open, unprejudiced minds about the fact that such suspicious could turn out to be unfounded. Serious content is possible even when the style is as conspicuous as it is in "Annabel Lee." Just because it is is possible, though, is no evidence of whether he has achieved it or not, just as the music of the poem is no true sign that it is only light verse, popular but lacking content.

Some of the brightest lights in the English-speaking literary establishment, including Henry

James and T. S. Eliot, dismissed Edgar Allan Poe's poetry as juvenile, as the kind of stuff that could only appeal to underdeveloped tastes. It is certainly easier for a person in their teens to appreciate Poe than to even follow what is said by James or Eliot, but we have to be careful to not identify universality as a weakness, or obtuseness as a strength. The charge against Poe has to be examined, though, if only because there have been many weak poets who write like Poe. Our first piece of evidence would be the strong, unavoidable rhythm of his poems, evident in "Annabel Lee": it is exactly the sort of thing that a poetaster with nothing to say would use to simulate profundity.

It does not help Poe's case to note that the speaker of the poem actually *is* juvenile in his attitude. This is not to say that it is immature to grieve, but there has to be a question, when one holds onto grief for "many and many a year," of whether the emotion really is not fading or whether the person finds that he likes striking the pose of a griever. Grief is not forgotten, but there is more to it than latching onto the first flush of emotion and staying frozen in that state for years. An immature point of view only knows the initial feeling, having, of course, never matured beyond it. It is small wonder that young people are able to relate so well to this poem, given that its speaker looks at life from a young person's perspective.

To counter the charge of juvenility, one only needs to focus on the fact that emotions are the business of poetry, and that if learning to get past them were the standard for maturity then all poems would just have to be juvenile. That the speaker of "Annabel Lee" cannot grow out of his grief, which some people might consider an embarrassing personality weakness, can actually be a source of pride in the experience-obsessed world of a Poe poem. To him, "maturity" in the sense of being able to put a lost love out of one's mind would be a wasteful, soul-deadening thing. The "highbrow kinsmen," the angels and demons, and those who are older and wiser all expressed their objections to the young lovers' affair, and the maturity that they represented proved useless in stopping passion. Readers get the sense that it is their opposition that, at least in part, has given the speaker the tenacity to hold on to his memories. Youth rises to its best when it has to oppose the challenge to grow up, act mature, and to keep its unruly emotions in check. One gets the feeling that Poe would accept the accusation that his mournful poetry was juvenile, that his only objection would be in calling this label an accusation.

> *The style with which Poe presents his ideas really ought to be juvenile, in order to give the idea of unstoppable love and inconsolable grief their right presentation."*

There is long and ongoing aesthetic argument to be made about whether an artist can be considered successful simply because she or he is able to provoke the response they intended. This question frequently is raised in modern art, with artists who use offensive materials or abuse cherished symbols to create works that are meant to shock: if audiences are in fact shocked, does that necessarily make the work art? What if a work is agreeable, and that is all that it aspired to be: are we to consider Liberace an artist in the medium of schmaltz?

It seems that, at least in certain cases, the objection to juvenile writing should be lifted from works that intend to be accessible to a wide age range. Accepting Poe's juvenile subject matter as artistry because he intended it to be juvenile would mean that some of his detractors would have to, however grudgingly, keep their objections to themselves, providing he had a good reason for intending to write that way. One good case to be made in favor of juvenilia is that it is so familiar to everyone, being a part of the human experience. Not everyone lost someone close to them in youth, but almost everyone who has gone through adolescence knows what it is like to suffer and feel that the world does not understand suffering of such depth. Even the most mature reader—even James or Eliot—must be able to find within themselves some echo of this poem's emotional overkill.

The style with which Poe presents his ideas really ought to be juvenile, in order to give the idea of unstoppable love and inconsolable grief their right presentation. This is the time to consider whether or not the extra words, which seem added for purely cosmetic reasons, might actually prove their worth. Throughout the poem, there are plenty of cases where Poe uses more words than should be needed if he were only trying to make his point cerebrally. The most glaring example of verbal excess seems to be the constant reiteration that all of this happened in "a kingdom by the sea." Mentioned once or even twice, and this phrase gives the poem a fairy-tale aura. When the sea is repeated seven times, though, and always at the ends of lines, readers cannot help feeling that the author was dragging around a handy little chock of a phrase that he could rhyme with "Annabel Lee" whenever he felt the need. The same suspicion of padding holds for the second "many" in line one, all of line ten, and the inclusion of both "chilling" and "killing"—they could be left out without any loss to the meaning of the poem, and exist only to serve a rather gaudy form.

But poetry isn't only about meaning—the aspect of sounds is involved as well. If it didn't care about the work's musicality, a poem might as well be a work of prose. The objection that is raised to "Annabel Lee," as well as to Poe's other poems, is that sound has not only been acknowledged but has been given the main role. Most students of literature agree that the intellectual aspect should dominate, that the sound does its work well when it supplements the meaning, not when it rules it.

In poetry that aims to stand up straight and look squarely at life's mysteries, Poe's method of melodiousness at the expense of quiet thoughtfulness would be inexcusable. This poem is told through the speaker's eyes, though, and it is therefore not free to address reality straight-on: it is filtered through his mind and his vocabulary. It is the character of the young man who lost his lover that is talking to us in this sing-song way, and is adding phrases to make the song come out right. This rhythm and repetition may not describe grief at its rawest, but they do describe grief as this character sees it. In the end, it turns out to be unfair to accuse Poe of weakness if his verse sounds like the work of someone who is immaturely obsessed. The voice seems right to the mind of the character, and, juvenile or not, the character deserves to be examined. Whether Poe wrote this way because of his own limitations is a debate for biographers, but it is not the issue here. However he came up with it, "Annabel Lee" provides an excellent, whole psychological snapshot of a particular personality.

Source: David Kelly, in an essay for *Poetry for Students,* Gale, 2000.

John E. Reilly

In this essay, Reilly disputes the contention of Buford Jones and Kent Ljungquist that Frances Sargent Osgood's poem "The Life-Voyage. A Ballad" served as the model for Poe's "Annabel Lee."

Professors Buford Jones and Kent Ljungquist exercise more ingenuity than care in arguing that there are enough "internal parallels alone" to make Frances Sargent Osgood's "The Life-Voyage. A Ballad" a "probable model" for "Annabel Lee" [see "Poe, Mrs. Osgood, and 'Annabel Lee,'" *Studies in the American Renaissance* (1983)]. Noting that Poe must have been familiar with "The Life-Voyage" when he wrote "Annabel Lee," Jones and Ljungquist cite what they believe are five "parallels" between the two poems: 1) both contain the phrase "sounding sea"; 2) both "are ballads"; 3) both "begin in fairy tale fashion beside the sea"; 4) both present a fair maiden "who is envied by the angels in heaven"; and 5) both share the "theme of angelic-demonic ambivalence." But Jones and Ljungquist fail to make their case: two of these alleged "parallels" do not exist, and though the remaining three are genuine, none can be adduced as convincing evidence that Mrs. Osgood's poem served as a "probable model."

Of the three genuine parallels, the phrase "sounding sea" does occur in the first and second stanzas of Mrs. Osgood's poem and in the closing stanza of the earliest version of "Annabel Lee." But why should Mrs. Osgood's use of the phrase be considered a "probable" source for Poe when, as Jones and Ljungquist admit in a footnote, Poe must for years have been familiar with Milton's use of "sounding sea" in "Lycidas"? The fact that the phrase occurs in Blake's *The Four Zoas* and in Tennyson's "The Lover's Tale" (works not published before Poe's death which cannot, of course, have influenced "Annabel Lee") suggests that it was not sufficiently uncommon to identify any single work as its "probable" source in Poe's poem. Moreover, according to the *Oxford English Dictionary,* the word "sounding" appears as an adjective "frequently in 18th century poetry." One such appearance especially noteworthy here, though not cited by the *Dictionary,* occurs in the story of Lysander and Aspasia at the close of "Night V" of Edward Young's *Night Thoughts,* a work with which Poe was familiar. As in "Annabel Lee" the love of Lysander and Aspasia was "envied" by "all who knew" and their sorrowful tale related in *Night Thoughts* is played out upon "the sounding beach."

The second genuine parallel cited by Jones and Ljungquist is that both "Annabel Lee" and "The Life-Voyage" are ballads. But the fact that the two poems can be considered ballads is meaningless because the ballad as a genre is an omnium-gatherum of such generous proportions that it includes works having little in common. Poe's poem is a personal story of lost love which achieves its unique effects largely through its narrative voice and its haunting repetitions. It is not written in stanzas of traditional ballad quatrains. Osgood's poem is a didactic tale addressed to a young child, a moral allegory tracing the journey of personified "Innocence" as she bears the "divine gem" of "Truth" across the perilous seas of life to her "home" in "yonder skies." Though Mrs. Osgood's poem is written in ballad quatrains, the kind of repetition we associate with the traditional ballad plays almost no role in her poem. Jones and Ljungquist's third point—that both "Annabel Lee" and "The Life-Voyage" begin in fairy tale fashion beside the sea—is also valid. In Poe's poem, however, "a kingdom by the sea" is the locus of all the action, whereas in Mrs. Osgood's, "beside the sounding sea" is only a point of departure: by line twenty her heroine has "bravely put to sea" on a voyage which occupies the remaining one hundred and eight lines, a voyage which is the subject of the poem.

The fourth parallel alleged by Jones and Ljungquist—that the heroine of each poem "is envied by the angels in heaven"—does not, in fact, exist. Nowhere does Mrs. Osgood's poem suggest that the "fair maiden" (that is, "Innocence") is envied by anyone, least of all by the angels in heaven. Quite the contrary, the "angels" are instrumental and faithful in assisting "Innocence" in her effort to reach the safety of heaven. Even the "evil spirits" who beset her are not motivated by envy: they simply play their role in a conventional contest in which "Innocence" traditionally finds herself the prize. The last parallel, what Jones and Ljungquist call the "theme of angelic-demonic ambivalence," is also non-existent. This theme, which alleges that angels are transformed into devils and vice versa, is one of the longstanding interpretations of that controversial passage in Poe's ballad where Annabel Lee appears to have been the victim of both angels and demons or of angels as demons. Jones and Ljungquist hold that the angels in "The Life-Voyage" are similarly transformed into "demons" and back into angels as they alternately assault and assist the maiden on her voyage. But Mrs. Osgood's scenario is quite otherwise. "The Life-Voyage" is an old-fashioned Christian allegory laced with a distinct element of Manichaeism, furnished here by a cast made up of good characters who assist the maiden and of evil characters who tempt and threaten her. The good characters,

> *But nowhere in her allegory does Mrs. Osgood burden her reader (identified as 'my pure and simple child') with those disturbing ambiguities of devilish angels that people the paranoid world of 'Annabel Lee.' "*

the angels, put in their first appearance in lines 23–24, where they "whisper'd her from Heaven, / To loose … or to reef" the sail of her "shallop"; thus, they function as a kind of mission control advising the maiden on the trim of her craft as it makes its "way" to its "home" in "yonder skies," a "way" or course illuminated by the pearl of "Truth." But the maiden is beset by two distinct bands of hostile beings. The first, the "false, evil spirits" of lines 37–72, represent a moral threat to the maiden by tempting her first with "costly lure" and then with "rank," "power," and "pleasures free" in their effort to bribe her into surrendering her "white pearl" of "Truth." But they fail. The second hostile band is the "dark-wind demons" … representing a physical threat to the maiden by trying her courage through a violent storm. But she prevails again…. In the midst of this "blinding storm," an "angel" finally leaves heaven to join the maiden on her frail vessel … (note that the angels of lines 23–24 had only whispered advice from heaven). Guided through the dark storm by the light of the pearl on the maiden's shallop, this angel "Flew down the fairy helm to take, / And steer the boat aright," piloting the vessel to its "designated port." Here … the maiden passes from storm and temptation to heavenly peace with her "Innocence" intact. But nowhere in her allegory does Mrs. Osgood burden her reader (identified as "my pure and simple child") with those disturbing ambiguities of devilish angels that people the paranoid world of "Annabel Lee." As Jones and Ljungquist point out, there can be no doubt of Poe's "exposure" to Mrs. Osgood's "The Life-Voyage," but this fact, even when coupled with the parallel occurrence of the phrase "sounding sea," does not justify swelling still further the ranks of "probable" sources of Poe's poem.

Source: John E. Reilly, "Mrs. Osgood's 'The Life Voyage' and 'Annabel Lee,'" in *Poe Studies*, Vol. 17, No. 1, June, 1984, p. 23.

Buford Jones and Kent Ljungquist, "Poe, Mrs. Osgood, and 'Annabel Lee,'"

In this essay, Jones and Ljungquist argue that Frances Sergent Osgood's "The Life-Voyage" served as the model for Poe's "Annabel Lee."

In Poe's contacts with literary ladies of his time, no relationship stimulated more controversy than that with the poet, Frances Sargent Osgood. For the literary biographer, suspicions of adultery and charges of moral impropriety had to be balanced against Virginia Poe's apparent fondness for Mrs. Osgood. Citing the many innocuous but fashionable literary flirtations of the era, Arthur Hobson Quinn delicately dubbed the relationship "a literary courtship" in which Poe found a convenient outlet for his amatory poems. Expressing doubt that Poe was ever seriously infatuated, Sidney P. Moss has claimed that Mrs. Osgood clearly took the initiative in the flirtation. Adopting a more speculative stance, John Evangelist Walsh has put forth the theory that Poe was the father of Mrs. Osgood's child, Fanny Fay. It is more likely that Poe's relationship to Mrs. Osgood was an injudicious but innocent involvement, but as Edward Wagenkneckt has noted, the Poe-Osgood relationship does not lend itself to clear distinctions between fact and fiction: "Nowhere in Poe's story is it more difficult to disentangle truth from falsehood than there." In spite of Thomas Ollive Mabbott's careful annotations of Poe's poems dedicated to Mrs. Osgood, biographical speculation has exceeded the study of literary indebtedness that may have existed. Of particular interest are Mrs. Osgood's comments on "Annabel Lee," in which she stridently claimed that Virginia Poe, "the only woman Poe ever loved," was the sole possible subject of the poem. Mabbott, calling her comments "ingenious and poetic," added: "her motives were certainly complicated. She wanted to minimize the importance of all the women in Poe's life save Virginia Poe and herself." Mrs. Osgood clearly showed special knowledge of "Annabel Lee." She explained the problematical reference to "high-born kinsmen" as "*kindred angels*" of God who took away the speaker's lost love. Her gloss has generally been accepted by early and

later commentators on Poe. Mrs. Osgood's insights transcended self-concern as well as defensiveness about Virginia's reputation. Her remarks were further complicated by her authorship of a poem, entitled "The Life-Voyage," which probably served as a model for "Annabel Lee."

The sources of "Annabel Lee" have received fairly rigorous attention. Perhaps more in the realm of legend than fact is a newspaper obituary mentioning an infant named Annabel Lee. A possible literary source, "The Mourner," displays many similarities to "Annabel Lee," but the date of its appearance in the Charleston, South Carolina, *Courier* (1807) makes Poe's knowledge of it doubtful. Another literary lady, Sarah Helen Whitman, provided a possible model with her "Stanzas for Music," printed in the *American Metropolitan Magazine* of February 1849. Poe claimed to have written "Annabel Lee" in May 1849; thus the publication date of "Stanzas for Music" and Poe's relationship to Mrs. Whitman make likely his exposure to her poem. Other literary ladies vied for favor in the "Annabel Lee" contest. Elmira Shelton and Annie Richmond have both been mentioned as candidates, but a more notable claimant was Stella Lewis. Mrs. Lewis' claim, reported at third or fourth hand, triggered Mrs. Osgood's outburst, which should be quoted at length:

> I believe that she [Virginia] was the only woman he ever loved; and this is evidenced by the exquisite pathos of the little poem, lately written, called Annabel Lee, of which she was the subject, and which is by far the most natural, simple, tender and touchingly beautiful of all his songs. I have heard that it was intended to illustrate a late love affair of the author; but they who believe this, have in their dullness, evidently misunderstood or missed the beautiful meaning latent in the most lovely of all its verses—where he says,
>
> A wind blew out of a cloud, chilling
> My beautiful Annabel Lee,
> So that her *high-born kinsmen* came,
> And bore her away from me.
>
> There seems a strange and almost profane disregard of the sacred purity and spiritual tenderness of this delicious ballad, in thus overlooking the allusion to the *kindred angels* of the Heavenly *Father* of the lost and loved and unforgotton wife.

In large measure because of Mrs. Osgood's comments, Virginia's role as a source of inspiration for "Annabel Lee" has received more serious attention than other rival claims.

But Mrs. Osgood's involvement with "Annabel Lee" goes further than her explicit comments indicate. Poe reviewed at length her *Poems*

(1846), which contains the following ballad, from which we quote the first two stanzas:

"The Life-Voyage"

Once in the olden time there dwelt
Beside the sounding sea,
A little maid—her garb was coarse,
Her spirit pure and free.
Her parents were an humble twain,
And poor as poor could be;
Yet gaily sang the guileless child,
Beside the sounding sea.

The most outstanding phrase that this poem shares with "Annabel Lee" is in the second stanza. There Osgood uses the alliterative "sounding sea," an epithet that appeared in the first version of "Annabel Lee." It has generally been agreed that Poe's final phrasing ("In her tomb by the side of the sea") was a mistake to achieve metrical regularity. This change from "In her tomb by the sounding sea," according to one authority, was unfortunate, "since it marred the concluding line, widely regarded as one of the great lines of English verse." In any case, "The Life-Voyage" is the probable source for Poe's phrase "sounding sea."

Other parallels exist between the two poems. Both "The Life-Voyage" and "Annabel Lee" are ballads that begin in fairytale fashion beside the sea. Osgood's "Once in the olden time" is far more conventional than Poe's roughly anapestic "many and many a year ago." Both poems present a fair maiden of "bright eyes" who is envied by the angels in heaven. In "The Life-Voyage," the angels come down from heaven to win her prized pearl. Roughly conforming to Osgood's published remarks on "Annabel Lee," these angels eventually usher her safely to heaven; they act almost as kinsmen of God or the Heavenly Father. In "Annabel Lee," "the angels, not half so happy in Heaven, / Went envying her and me." It is noteworthy, that, in both poems, these angels are later transformed into demons that threaten the figure of female beauty. The transformation from angels to demons is occasioned by the announcement of death. In Osgood's poem, "A stillness of death" is attended by "dark wind-demons," which attack the pearl maiden. In "Annabel Lee," after wind brings death to his beloved, the speaker is locked in a never-ending conflict between "the angels in Heaven above" and "the demons down under the sea." This theme of angelic-demonic ambivalence appealed to Poe, not only in "Annabel Lee," but also in "The Raven" where the student initially believes that the raven is sent by the angels of the lost Lenore. While Poe is infinitely more successful in approximating

> " *The most outstanding phrase that this poem shares with 'Annabel Lee' is in the second stanza. There Osgood uses the alliterative 'sounding sea,' an epithet that appeared in the first version of 'Annabel Lee.'* "

the sound of the ocean's ebb and flow, both poets attempt onomatopoetic effects associated with oceanic rhythms. While the theme of adolescent love is absent from "The Life-Voyage," it contains a theme that appealed to Poe as well as other American Romantics. This is the "Voyage of Life" theme, which attempted to "telescope" the human cycle from infancy to death in a single work of literature. The Hudson River painter Thomas Cole employed this theme in his pictorial series "The Voyage of Life." And Poe, in "The Domain of Arnheim," projected the theme of life-voyage in his narrator's trip down a winding stream. Thus, because of Poe's predilection for this theme, Osgood's treatment in her poem would have been congenial to him.

Poe's review of Osgood's 1846 volume makes his exposure to "The Life-Voyage" clear. Subsequent reviews and printings of the poem suggest that his memory may have been refreshed at a time close to his claimed date of composition for "Annabel Lee." Furthermore, the possiblity of mutual or reciprocal influence between "Annabel Lee" and "The Life-Voyage" should not be discounted. Mrs. Osgood's comments on "Annabel Lee" reflect a knowledge of the poem that exceeded any of her contemporaries. Rather uncharacteristically of Poe, he circulated a manuscript of "Annabel Lee" more widely than any of his other poems, sending a copy to Rufus Griswold, Mrs. Osgood's literary executor, in June 1849. By the same token, Poe may have seen a draft of "The Life-Voyage" independently of its publication. Such interchange is not unlikely in view of the Poe-esque titles among Osgood's poems: "Ermengarde's Awakening," "Lenore," and "Leonor." Another poem on a theme similar to that of "The Life-Voyage" is "The Spirit's Voyage," an elegy on the death of a child which echoes Poe's most famous refrain:

No more!—ah! never, never more!
Her precious feet will tead,
Like light, our dwelling's coral floor,
By young affection led.

As if in reciprocation for these poetic efforts that bring to mind his characters, themes, and vocabulary, Poe wrote a series of poems to Mrs. Osgood. He also lauded her poetry in his reviews, showing particular fondness for a dramatic poem *Elfrida* in which the hero is a king named Edgar. The literary relationship reached its conclusion with her elegiac tribute to Poe, "The Hand That Swept the Sounding Lyre." In all this give-and-take, the connection between "The Life-Voyage" and "Annabel Lee" may have had the most fruitful and significant literary consequences.

In any case, examination of internal parallels alone would seem to make "The Life-Voyage" a probable model for Poe's final poem. In view of Mrs. Osgood's personal and literary relationship extending from 1845 to 1849, "The Life-Voyage" merits inclusion in any survey of the provenance of "Annabel Lee."

Source: Buford Jones and Kent Ljungquist, "Poe, Mrs. Osgood, and 'Annabel Lee,'" in *Studies in the American Renaissance,* edited by Joel Myerson, University Press of Virginia, 1983, pp. 275–80.

Julienne H. Empric

In this brief essay, Empric delves into the psychological factors driving the poem's narrator.

The child's vision of reality is, in relation to the larger proportions and understanding of the adult mind, a vision of the grotesque. Time, for example, exists for the child as a present in which, somehow, past and future are simply amalgamated rather than sequential, separate entities. The narrator in "Annabel Lee" says he was a child when he knew and loved his child-bride. From the subsequent workings of his mind, the narrator's perspective seems to have changed little since that time. He has remained a child, because of inability or unwillingness to change, and this frozen perspective is lent a peculiar strength by the characteristic and simple cadences of the ballad form. The narrator tells his story until stanza three, when, in an attempt to account for the disproportion of his feelings of loss, he creates a child's explanation for

these feelings: the vision of the angel-murderers. As simple as it appears among the lulling rhythms of the poem, the vision is grotesque. To justify the loss, to find some cause proportionate to the effect he has experienced, the narrator must temper his idea of the seraphic with the demonic. He confirms his rationalization of angel-murder by re-asserting it and lending it the weight of common knowledge in stanza four. The final stanzas represent the conflation of time into the ever-present faithfulness and the nightly ceremonial act whereby the narrator tries to overcome the fact of separation he has earlier tried to explain. And the conventionally macabre "sepulchre" and "tomb," given rhythmic emphasis in stanza six, transform, in context, into the blessed place of union for the lovers, among the soothing, familiar elements of nature. It is toward this unconscious wholeness in nature, in sleep, in death, that the distraught consciousness of the child mind strives through the simple narrative poem.

Source: Julienne H. Empric, "A Note on 'Annabel Lee,'" in *Poe Studies,* Vol. 6, No. 1, June, 1973, p. 26.

Sources

Hammond, J. R., *An Edgar Allan Poe Companion,* Totowa, NJ: Barnes and Noble Books, 1981.

Kennedy, J. Gerald, *Poe, Death, and the Life of Writing,* Yale University Press, 1987.

Poe, Edgar Allan, *Edgar Allan Poe: Poetry, Tales, and Selected Essays,* edited by Patrick F. Quinn and G. R. Thompson, Library of America College Editions, 1996.

Powys, John Cowper, "Edgar Allan Poe," in *Visions and Revisions: A Book of Literary Devotions,* G. Arnold Shaw, 1915, pp. 263-277.

Quinn, Arthur Hobson, *Edgar Allan Poe: A Critical Biography,* Johns Hopkins University Press, 1988.

Rice, C. Duncan, *The Rise and Fall of Black Slavery,* Evanston, IL: Harper and Rowe, Publishers, 1975.

Saintsbury, George, "Edgar Allan Poe," in *Prefaces and Essays,* edited by Oliver Elton, Macmillan & Co., 1933, pp. 314-23.

Stovall, Floyd, *Edgar Poe the Poet: Essays New and Old on the Man and His Work,* University Press of Virginia, 1969, 273 p.

Wilbur, Richard, "Poe and the Art of Suggestion," in *The University of Mississippi Studies in English,* Vol. III, 1982, pp. 1-13, reprinted in *Critical Essays on Edgar Allan Poe,* edited by Eric W. Carlson, G. K. Hall and Company, 1987, pp. 160-171.

For Further Study

Buranelli, Vincent, *Edgar Allan Poe,* 2nd ed., Boston: Twayne Publishers, 1977.

Buranelli's concise book briefly discusses each of the author's works of poetry, prose and criticism, providing a good general sense of context but not much depth.

Carlson, Eric W., ed., *The Recognition of Edgar Allan Poe: Selected Criticism Since 1829,* Ann Arbor: The University of Michigan Press, 1969.

This book contains essays of critics ranging from Poe's early publications through to the 1960s. Some of the most important literary figures of the last two hundred years are represented here: Baudelaire, Swinburne, Henry James, Dostoevski, T. S. Eliot, W. H. Auden, Richard Wilbur, and many more. Of particular interest is the obituary published by the Reverend Rufus Griswold using the pseudonym "Ludwig": the slanderous lies told in this article haunted Poe's literary reputation for years.

Dayan, Joan, "Amorous Bondage: Poe, Ladies and Slaves," in *The American Face of Edgar Allan Poe,* edited by Shawn Rosenheim and Stephen Rachman, Baltimore: The Johns Hopkins University Press, 1995, pp. 179-209.

This scholarly essay draws the connection between the institution of slavery in the South, where Poe lived, and his treatment of female characters in his love poetry.

Fletcher, Richard M, *The Stylistic Development of Edgar Allan Poe,* The Hague: Mouton & Co. Publishers, 1973.

This book attempts to understand Poe's stories and his poems together: in particular, it pairs "Annabel Lee" with the short story "Hop-Frog."

Murray, David, "'A Strange Sound, as of a Harp-string Broken': The Poetry of Edgar Allan Poe," in *Edgar Allan Poe: The Design of Order,* edited by A. Robert Lee, Totowa, NJ: Barnes and Noble Books, 1987.

This essay questions Poe's reputation as a late figure in the Romantic movement and a forerunner of the Symbolist movement.

Porte, Joel, *The Romance in America: Studies in Cooper, Poe, Hawthorne, Melville and James,* Middletown, CT: Wesleyan University Press, 1969.

One of the clearest and most understandable works to put Poe into proper context among other figures who are not always thought of as his peers.

Stampp, Kenneth M., *America in 1857,* New York: Oxford University Press, 1990.

This book gives a good overview of the social situation in America two years before this poem was published, in the year that Poe's wife, who is presumed to be the model for Annabel Lee, died.

Thomas, Dwight, and David K. Jackson, *The Poe Log: A Documentary Life of Edgar Allan Poe, 1809-1849,* New York: G. K. Hall & Co., 1987.

With an almost day-by-day breakdown of events in and related to Poe's life from birth to death, this is an indispensable guide for anyone interested in doing research on the poet.

Barbie Doll

Marge Piercy

1973

"Barbie Doll" appears in Piercy's 1973 collection, *To Be of Use.* By using the iconic image of the Barbie doll as a kind of straw "man," Piercy implicitly criticizes the ways in which women are socialized into stereotypical feminine behavior. Written as a fairy-tale of sorts, "Barbie Doll" suggests that the enormous social pressures on women to conform to particular ways of looking and behaving are ultimately destructive. Her ironic tone barely conceals a simmering rage at prescribed gender roles that eat away at women's self-confidence and wreak havoc on their self-image. Piercy suggests that corporate America, embodied by Barbie's maker, Mattel Toys, participates in our patriarchal system by perpetuating gender stereotypes. The Barbie doll, one of the best-selling "toys" of all time, has become an icon of U.S. culture for the way it idealizes the female body. For more than 40 years parents have been buying the doll, along with Barbie's companion, Ken, for their daughters, who attempt to emulate Barbie's appearance and the values that that appearance embodies. Indeed, in some segments of society, the term "Barbie Doll" itself has become a term of derision, signifying an attractive, but vapid, blonde who will do what she is told. Piercy skewers this image, implying that it is inherently destructive. Piercy's poem has been reprinted a number of times. Its accessibility and clearly defined—yet not simplistic—stance toward its subject make it one of her more popular pieces.

Author Biography

A feminist activist as well as a poet, novelist, essayist, and playwright, Piercy melds the personal and the political in her writing. She writes frequently about women's issues, particularly the ways in which women have been made to feel inferior, both about their minds and their bodies. Born to working-class parents Robert Douglas and Bert Bedoyna (Bunnin) Piercy in Detroit, Michigan in 1936, Piercy began writing—both poetry and fiction—when she was fifteen. Her early literary influences include Emily Dickinson, Walt Whitman, and the Romantic poets Byron, Shelley, Keats, Wordsworth, and Coleridge, but Piercy learned about storytelling through listening to the women in her family, especially her mother, her Aunt Ruth, and her maternal grandmother, Hannah, who gave Piercy her Hebrew name, Marah. Piercy received a full fellowship to the University of Michigan, where she co-edited the literary magazine her senior year and also won a prestigious Hopwood Award for her poetry. After receiving her bachelor's degree, she entered Northwestern University, from which she graduated with an M.A. in 1962.

Piercy's grandfather was a union organizer who was murdered while organizing bakery workers. Piercy too has fashioned an overtly political life for herself. An active member of Students for a Democratic Society in the 1960s, she helped organize protests against U.S. involvement in Vietnam and for civil rights for all Americans. Her involvement in the women's movement, however, has come to define her writing. By infusing her poetry, fiction, and essays with autobiographical elements, Piercy gives her writing an urgency and edge frequently lacking in so much contemporary poetry. Her description of the girlchild in "Barbie Doll" is a not-so-thinly-veiled reference to herself. Piercy, however, did not sacrifice herself to patriarchy's image of what an "ideal" woman should be; rather, she made herself into a crusader for women's rights. The majority of her novels, most of which contain autobiographical material, address some aspect of recuperating women's identity from the snares of a society that does not have women's interests at heart. The author of numerous novels, poetry collections, essays, and plays, Piercy writes full time and occasionally teaches workshops. Her writing has appeared in more than 150 anthologies and has been translated into more than a dozen languages. She lives with her third husband, writer and publisher Ira Wood, and five cats in Wellfleet on Cape Cod in Massachusetts.

Marge Piercy

Poem Text

This girlchild was: born as usual
and presented dolls that did pee-pee
and miniature GE stoves and irons
and wee lipsticks the color of cherry candy.
Then in the magic of puberty, a classmate said: 5
You have a great big nose and fat legs.

She was healthy, tested intelligent,
possessed strong arms and back,
abundant sexual drive and manual dexterity.
She went to and fro apologizing.   10
Everyone saw a fat nose on thick legs.

She was advised to play coy,
exhorted to come on hearty?
exercise, diet, smile and wheedle.
Her good nature wore out   15
like a fan belt.
So she cut off her nose and her legs
and offered them up.

In the casket displayed on satin she lay
with the undertaker's cosmetics painted on,   20
a turned-up putty nose,
dressed in a pink and white nightie.
Doesn't she look pretty? everyone said.
Consummation at last.
To every woman a happy ending.   25

Media Adaptations

- Marge Piercy has her own website: http://www.capecod.net/~tmpiercy/index.html

- A compilation of essays about the Barbie doll's cultural significance can be found at this website: http://www.dolliedish.com/barbie/onbarbie.html

- For another point of view on how Barbie has been marketed, examine Mattel's own website for Barbie: http://www.barbie.com/

- In 1976 Watershed Tapes released a cassette of Piercy reading her poems, *At the Core.*

Poem Summary

Lines 1-4:

The title of this poem refers to Mattel's Barbie Doll, a popular toy for young girls. The original Barbie—tall, shapely, with blonde hair and blue eyes—debuted in 1959 at the American Toy Fair in New York City. Mattel has manufactured a variety of "Barbies" since then—everything from Action Adventure Barbie, to "Mod" Barbie, to Francie, an African-American "Barbie." The poem begins in a fairy-tale vein, the archaic term "girlchild" being used to underscore the mythic quality of the story. The dolls, stove, iron and lipstick are all traditional playthings for young girls, but they are also markers of an identity in the making, the things that young girls grow to idenitfy with their own social roles. The doll presents an idealized image of the body, and stove and irons tell them what kind of work is expected of them as adults. Lipstick, perhaps the most sexualized cosmetic for women, signals to young girls that they will be valued for their physical appearance.

Lines 5-9:

The "magic of puberty" introduces the theme of growth. It is a magical time because the body changes rapidly. Girls begin to menstruate and their bodies change. Piercy uses the term ironically here,

as she is also referring to the pain that comes with puberty. Adolescents become more aware of one another as sexual and social beings and are frequently cruel towards one another. The "girlchild" is told she has "a great big nose and fat legs" even though she is smart, healthy and strong. The latter descriptors, however, are seen as being positive only for males, not females. Being good with one's hands (manual dexterity) is a conventional male trait. Similarly, while having an "abundant sexual drive" for boys might be seen as "sowing oats" or being a "real" man, for girls it is often considered aggressive or the mark of a "whore."

Lines 10-14:

The girl was made to feel guilty for who she was, for her intelligence and abilities, and also for not being slim and "beautiful." She apologized to everyone for not being the person they wanted her to be, but all they could see was her body and how it did not match their idea of what a woman should look like. They tried to help her be more of an idealized woman by suggesting how to compensate for her unfeminine qualities. It is important to understand that for Piercy the "girlchild" is "everygirl," not some poetic character with no relation to the real world. Children are socialized through family, culture, and education from the day they are born. Piercy is symbolically examining the process of how children come to inhabit their gendered identities and the destructive consequences of those processes for women.

Lines 15-18:

Fan belts wear out because of overuse. Fan belts are also commodities—things—like Barbie dolls themselves and, Piercy suggests, like women. This simile is interesting because it uses an image we associate with cars, and cars are a symbol of masculinity in American culture. Her "good nature," that part of her that sought to accommodate others, has been so exploited that she can no longer continue. She "offers up" (a gesture of sacrifice) her nose and legs, the symbols of her oppression, but to whom we do not know: presumably patriarchal power itself.

Lines 19-25:

These lines are laden with irony. The very person that the girlchild could never be is the person "appearing" in her casket, after a makeover by the undertaker. "A turned-up putty nose" and "a pink and white nightie" are features of Barbie-doll-like beauty and femininity. It is ironic that the very people ("everyone") who could not appreciate the girl-child for who she was in life, now admire the person she is *made* to be in death. In Piercy's fable, it is society (not the girl) that achieves consummation, for it has made the girlchild into what it wanted. "Consummation" is a term used to describe completion or fulfillment. The last line of the poem echoes the happy ending of fairy-tales. In this case, of course, Piercy is saying that because of women's subservient position in society, it is often difficult for their lives to have happy endings.

Themes

Obedience

"Barbie Doll" symbolically describes the inherently destructive nature of patriarchy. A system of social organization in which male prerogative is the ruling principle, patriarchy demands women's obedience to men. Historically, this obedience has been externally manifest through law; for example, until the twentieth century women had been denied voting privileges in the United States. But patriarchy also exhibits its power through the shaping of mind and self-image. A "good" woman is one who conforms to patriarchal expectations: she is feminine, domestic, pretty, and accommodating. When you are not these things, as the girlchild in Piercy's poem is not, you will be punished. Society will shun you, you will be judged a freak, and your own strengths (e.g., the girlchild's physical strength and intelligence) will appear to you as shortcomings because you will not be recognized for them. Piercy's poem presents a girl of many talents who is worn down by an image of herself created by others which she could not, literally, live up to. In an act of "self" sacrifice, she cut off her nose and legs, those parts of her which did not conform to how a "beautiful" woman should look. This act of mutilation echoes the mutilation other women endure in tyrannically patriarchal societies. In parts of lower equatorial Africa, for example, young girls are forced to have "clitorectomies," procedures which medically remove the clitoris. This deprives the woman of sexual pleasure, and is a constant reminder that her only value is as a child-bearing machine for the man who will own her. In the West, eating disorders such as bulimia and anorexia are consequences women suffer in attempting to conform to the ideal of the Barbie body. In "Barbie Doll" the girlchild fulfills the patriarchal prescription for obedience by destroying herself. She perpetuates patriarchal power in death by being transformed into someone she could not be in life.

Sex Roles

"Barbie Doll" speaks to the destructive influences of rigid sex roles in modern society, and how women, especially, have been socialized into making their bodies and behavior conform to those roles. We see this socialization at work when the "girlchild" is "presented dolls that did pee-pee / and miniature GE stoves and irons / and wee lipsticks the color of cherry candy." Taught from early childhood that a woman should be pretty, intellectually passive, and domestic, the girlchild is apologetic for being none of these. Society, however, offers her compensatory strategies: she is urged to "play coy, / exhorted to come on hearty, / exercise, diet, smile, and wheedle." This was too much for the girlchild and, as a result of her inability to please those who want her to be someone else, she grows

Topics for Further Study

- What was Barbie's first date with Ken like? Write a short story about this from a 1960s Barbie's point of view, then do the same for a 1970s Barbie and a 1990s Barbie. What do your stories tell you about how you think of these decades?

- Make a list of all the toys you can remember playing with as a child. Write an essay on how these toys contribute to a child's sense of him- or herself as a boy or a girl.

- Interview an equal number of men and women, asking them what they consider to be their own most appealing attributes, and what they consider to be the most appealing attributes in a mate. Write an essay describing what similarities and differences you find and what this tells you about how we see ourselves in terms of our gender identity and how others see us.

- Write a poem called "G.I. Joe" about a "boy-child's" socialization.

to loathe herself and finally destroys herself in an act of sacrifice, "cut[ting] off her nose and her legs / and offer[ing] them up." The irony of the last lines of the poem, when the undertaker constructs a woman the girlchild could never be, suggests that societal expectations for sex roles transcend death itself and that, fight as they may against such repressive stereotyping, women will always lose. The moral of Piercy's parable is in the reader's response. The lesson is contained in the audience's outrage at the ways in which women have been (and continue to be) forced to conform to an ideal of femininity—often in ways antithetical to who they are as human beings. Piercy would have her readers take their rage at the poem's last line as a spur to action.

Style

A narrative poem written in free verse [verse having irregular meter, or rhythm that is not metrical], "Barbie Doll" can be read as a parable of what often happens to women in a patriarchal society. Parables are short narratives with a moral. Well-known parables are found in religious texts such as the Bible. The moral of Piercy's poem also functions as a warning: it urges readers to be aware of the ways in which society shapes our (gendered) identities and urges women not to compare themselves to idealized notions of feminine beauty or behavior.

Piercy's diction is occasionally archaic. That is, she uses words and grammatical constructions which we would not use today, for example "girlchild," "that did pee-pee", etc. By weaving these archaisms into a story told in contemporary language, the speaker achieves an effect of timelessness, suggesting that the instance of modern women modeling themselves after Barbie dolls is only the latest in the history of women's oppression.

Piercy employs irony to drive her point home. Irony, which comes from the Greek word "eiron," refers to the way in which a speaker "hides" or in some way understates what she really means. The end of Piercy's poem is ironic because the only thing that is consummated is the "girlchild's" death. When the speaker wishes "every woman a happy ending," she is actually expressing disgust at what has happened to the girlchild and what regularly happens to women who have been socialized to make men's desires their own.

Historical Context

In her essay, "Through the Cracks: Growing Up in the Fifties," originally published in *Partisan Review* and later reprinted in *Part-Colored Blocks for a Quilt*, Marge Piercy describes the social pressures exerted on women to conform in mid-twentieth century America, claiming that those who did not were labeled "sick." Piercy writes, "If you wanted something you couldn't have easily or that other people did not want or wouldn't admit to wanting, if you were angry, if you were different, strange, psychic, emotional, intellectual, political, double-jointed: you were sick, sick, sick." Commenting on the demands to physically conform, she notes that women's clothes were meant to accentuate breasts and hips while simultaneously "squashing" any parts of the body, such as the stomach, which might stick out. Piercy's mother bought her a girdle when she was twelve years old, telling her that she "was now a woman." Images of restraint are common in Piercy's writing about her childhood and adolescence, as is her anger at the pain such restraint caused. "Women must accustom themselves to a constant state of minor pain, binding themselves in a parody of the real body to be constantly 'attractive' …. We didn't have bodies then, we had shapes. We were the poor stuff from which this equipment carved the feminine." Piercy's anger at the ways in which ideas of beauty destroyed women's self-confidence and enslaved them to male desire is evident in the cynical and bitter irony of "Barbie Doll," which symbolically tells the story of a woman who could not resist, or accommodate, society's demands. Of late 1950s America, Piercy says that "Even the notion of acceptable beauty was exceedingly limited and marred a whole generation of women who grew up knowing it (training in self-hatred) and a whole generation of men who felt they were entitled to it, and any actual woman not resembling the few idols was very second best: or Everyman has the right to the exclusive possession of Marilyn Monroe."

In 1959 when Piercy was twenty-three years old, Mattel created and sold the first Barbie doll. Named after Barbara, the daughter of the founders of Mattel Toys (Ruth and Elliot Handler), Barbie was the first doll with an adult body to appear in America. She was a doll of idealized proportions but with no genitals or nipples. This allowed the doll to be feminine and sexual but non-offensive at the same time. The Handlers claimed they got the idea while watching their growing daughter begin to imitate adult conversation and behavior. They wanted to give their daughter (and potential con-

Compare & Contrast

- **1959:** Mattel Toys introduces the first Barbie Doll.

- **1966:** Francie, Barbie's "mod" cousin, is introduced in a polka-dotted top and gingham bikini bottom.

- **1967:** African-American Francie "Barbie" is introduced.

- **1976:** Barbie is given a place in "America's Time Capsule" at the nation's bicentennial celebration.

- **1971:** Discarding any submissive undertones, Barbie's eyes, once adverted in a side-glance, now look straight ahead.

- **1975:** During the Winter Olympics, Barbie is marketed abroad as the athlete of the year, appearing as a swimmer, skier, and skater, with a gold medal draped around her neck.

- **1982:** "Punk" Barbie is released.

- **1985:** "Day to Night" Barbie, Mattel's version of the yuppie lifestyle, is released. She has everything from modern office equipment (a tiny calculator) to an evening gown designed for the night out on the town.

- **1986:** "Astronaut" Barbie is released.

- **1988:** "Dr. Barbie" is released.

- **1990:** Mattel sponsors the "Barbie Summit" in New York City. Thirty-nine children from around the world meet and discuss world hunger, environmental degradation, and war and peace.

- **1995:** "Karaoke" Barbie is released.

- **1993:** Barbie sales reach $1 billion in 1993. She and related products account for 34 percent of Mattel's overall sales.

- **1997:** Mattel announces plans to give Barbie a more realistic figure and tone down the makeup. The new Barbie will reportedly have a wider waist, slimmer hips and a smaller bustline, and will be phased in gradually.

---

sumers) a doll that would represent the teenager she and other children would become. Special attention was given to Barbie's outfits, which were designed to appeal simultaneously to a young girl's idea of teenage independence and fun and a parent's idea of wholesomeness. The original Barbie had a tennis dress, a bathing suit, a ballerina outfit, a wedding dress, and a football game outfit, encompassing all of the (gendered) roles of a conventional suburban, middle-class American life. By playing with Barbie, young girls learned what was expected of them. They were given the illusion of freedom, of inventing themselves through the many Barbie costumes. As the country changed in the 1960s, however, so did Barbie. Her facial features were softened, along with her skin tone, and she was given a new hairstyle—a bubblecut—to reflect the changing times. In the 1970s Barbie changed yet again. Now Barbie's bright blue eyes looked directly ahead, signaling an assertive, confident woman who makes her own decisions. The sexual revolution and women's liberation helped to create a new image of what girls could be. Barbie has continued to "evolve" along with society. Mattel has put out a number of different Barbies to reflect those changes. Their stable of dolls has included Betsy Ross Barbie (to commemorate the bicentennial) Twist and Turn Barbie, Color Magic Barbie, Action Adventure Barbie, Francie (an African-American Barbie), and a host of other Barbies meant to reflect the changing values of American society and the opportunities available to women.

Critical Overview

Perhaps the real mark of "Barbie Doll's" reception has been the numerous times it has been reprinted and anthologized. Appearing in 1973, at the crest of feminism's second wave, "Barbie Doll" embodied the rage many women felt at being sexually objectified and treated as second-class citizens. The poem remains popular in large part because it continues to represent women's experience.

Most of the criticism and reviews of Piercy's poetry have underscored its politically committed nature. Leapfrog Press has built a website (http://www.capecod.net/~tmpiercy/over.htm) excerpting reviews of Piercy's poetry. Erica Jong calls Piercy "one of the most important writers of our time who has redefined the meaning of the female consciousness in literature and in so doing has begun to redefine the meaning of literature." Writing in the *Washington Post* on Piercy's *Selected Poems*, poet and critic Carolyn Kizer says "Marge Piercy is my idea of the very model of a modern major feminist. There is a deal of sheer, toe-curling pleasure to be gained from reading this robust, protean and hilarious woman's selected poems … her earthiness, her wonderful physicalness." "Barbie Doll" has also been reprinted in a number of classroom anthologies, and teacher Robert Perrin has written an essay on using the poem to acquaint his students with gender issues.

Criticism

Chris Semansky

Chris Semansky's most recent collection of poems, Blindsided, *has been published by 26 Books of Portland, Oregon and nominated for an Oregon Book Award. In the following essay, Semansky examines Marge Piercy's "Barbie Doll" as a symbolic story about women's socialization in a patriarchal world.*

Marge Piercy's poem, "Barbie Doll," is a mythic rendering of the destructive ways in which women have been socialized into thinking of their bodies and behavior in relation to a patriarchal ideal. This ideal, represented by Mattel's popular Barbie doll, is a thin yet curvy body, with symmetrical, perfect facial features. The girlchild in Piercy's "Barbie Doll" sacrifices her own gifts to fulfill the social dictates of patriarchy, a system of social organization based on male privilege. The doll is symbolic of the ways that women themselves have been "plasticized," turned into creatures who have been riven of their humanity.

After the Barbie doll came out in 1959 many women literally attempted to emulate her look. This was virtually impossible, since Barbie's body measures the human equivalent of 39-18-33. However, one woman, Cindy Jackson, founder of the Cosmetic Surgery Network, has dedicated her life to trying to achieve a "Barbie look," putting herself through more than twenty operations. It is not only Barbie's body that young girls aspire to but Barbie's life as well. The original Barbie came with a tennis outfit and bathing suit, as well as a wedding dress. She embodied the ideals and values of a middle-class suburban housewife who spent her days at the country club and her afternoons cooking dinner for her husband. To become a Barbie doll is for many girls and young women a dream. For Marge Piercy it is a nightmare. Her poem is a frontal assault on the socialization (for Piercy, "Barbie-ization") of young girls.

The process of constructing an identity based on gender and the consequences of this construction for women are popular subjects in the sociology of gender. The *Dictionary of Sociology* lists four primary features: 1) women are ascribed specific feminine personalities and a "gender identity" through socialization; 2) women are often secluded from public activities in industrial societies by their relegation to the private domain of the home; 3) women are allocated to inferior and typically degrading productive activities; 4) women are subjected to stereotypical ideologies which define women as weak and emotionally dependent on men.

Socialization is the process through which human beings learn how to be in the world. They internalize rules—some spoken, some unspoken—and these rules come to form a part of the image we develop about ourselves. "Barbie Doll" addresses the various stages of socialization: childhood, adolescence, and adulthood. The girlchild is presented with toys—presumably by her family—which help to set expectations for what her interests and behavior should be. Dolls, stoves, irons, and lipstick are all conventional things that little girls, especially in the West, are given to clue them in to societal expectations. This is not an intentional or necessarily coercive process but one which adults themselves have gone through and have come to believe is "natural." That is, they believe that little girls will enjoy pretending to be a homemaker or a Barbie doll because these are desires with which little girls are born.

The domestic realm has long been a space relegated to women. It is expected that they cook, clean, bear children, and take care of their men, who work and provide for the family. The public realm, the realm of politics, business, war, and large-scale decision-making, belongs to men. Academia, until recently, has also been a male province, as women were not valued for their intelligence. If women taught at all, it was elementary school where teaching was considered closer to baby-sitting, something in which women were considered well-versed. That the girlchild, when she reached adolescence, "tested intelligent" suggests that she was doomed, for such a quality is not valued by a society which considers "smarts" to be the mark of a strong male. Intelligent women present a threat to male power. Similarly, a woman who is good with her hands ("manual dexterity") or who has "abundant sexual drive" is considered to be unfeminine, as these qualities are also normally associated with maleness and masculinity.

Because she did not conform to social expectations, Piercy's girlchild did not "consummate" the process of socialization. Because she could not "play coy, / … come on hearty, / exercise, diet, smile and wheedle," the girlchild suffered intense emotional conflict, which eventually resulted in her taking her own life. The poem is not clear as to the girlchild's emotional state when she "cut off her nose and legs." We can read the statement that "Her good nature wore out / like a fan belt" to mean that she became angry and killed herself in disgust, or we can read the lines to mean that she was exhausted with constantly trying to be something that she was not. She did not, however, make it to adulthood, which means she failed to pass on the expectations that she herself could not meet. The only way that society could ensure that future generations would grow into the gender roles that the girlchild did not would be if the girlchild were not around to be a negative role model. When she did "offer" herself up, the undertaker, symbolically representing the destructive power of patriarchal desire, was ready to transform her, to have her conform to the gendered role she could not inhabit during her life.

Piercy's poem symbolizes what happens to young women in real life. In her essay "klaus barbie, and other dolls i'd like to see" from the anthology *Adios, Barbie: Young Women Write about Body Image and Identity,* Susan Jane Gilman writes that "We urban, Jewish, Black, Asian and Latina girls … realize that if you didn't look like Barbie, you didn't fit in. You were less beautiful, less valuable, less worthy. If you didn't look like Barbie, companies would discontinue you. You simply couldn't compete." Piercy herself, an urban Jewish woman and a burgeoning intellectual, did not fit in. Before she became politically active in the 1960s Piercy was a part of the Barbie-ized culture of

> " *Because she did not conform to social expectations, Piercy's girlchild did not 'consummate' the process of socialization. Because she could not 'play coy, / … come on hearty, / exercise, diet, smile and wheedle,' the girlchild suffered intense emotional conflict, which eventually resulted in her taking her own life.* "

1950s America. It was not just men who controlled women, though. Male desire permeated society. Piercy writes that "Women policed each other in the fifties with a special frenzy, being totally convinced nothing but death and madness lay outside the nuclear family and the baby-doll-mommy roles. How could we have believed that when we saw the toll of death and madness inside the roles?" These roles began to expand in the 1960s as more opportunities developed for women. Rising female employment offered women economic possibilities, and the sexual revolution gave them "permission" to seek sexual satisfaction outside the bounds of marriage. Helen Gurley Brown's 1962 blockbuster book, *Sex and the Single Girl,* described the "new woman" as a sexy, financially independent, upwardly mobile professional who made her own decisions, and Betty Friedan's 1963 *The Feminine Mystique* argued strongly for equal rights for women. In 1964 Congress passed Title VII, which banned gender discrimination in employment and helped create the Equal Employment Opportunity Commission, a federal agency which addresses issues of gender equality and discrimination in the workplace. Piercy herself embodied America's cultural changes, as she divorced her first husband partly because he did not take her writing seriously and held conventional notions of how a wife should behave.

*What
Do I Read
Next?*

- *Barbie Unbound: A Parody of the Barbie Obsession,* by Sarah Strohmeyer and Geoff Hansen (photographer), treats the Barbie doll as a contemporary American woman and spoofs her. She assumes roles including Safe-Sex Barbie, Barbie Antoinette, Anita Hill Barbie, Marie Curie Barbie, and in honor of her upcoming 40th anniversary, Hot Flash Barbie, who comes complete with tiny estrogen supplements.

- Published in 1997 by Orchises Press, Denise Duhamel's collection of poems, *Kinky,* treats Barbie as a "real" character, asking and answering questions such as: What if Barbie were in therapy? What if she were a religious fanatic? Do you know why Barbie and Ken don't dress in underwear?

- Richard Peabody and Lucinda Ebersole's *Mondo Barbie* collects poems and stories about this American icon, many of which are from Barbie's own point of view.

- *Early Grrrl: The Early Poems of Marge Piercy,* was published in 1999 by Leapfrog Press and contains many of the poems that helped launch Piercy's career as both feminist-activist and writer.

- *Adios, Barbie,* edited by Ophira Edut, collects first-person accounts of young women reflecting on the relationship between body image and race, ethnicity, and sexuality.

As a result of the changes in American society, gender roles for women have expanded greatly since the 1950s. These changes have been tracked by the Barbie doll, which literally has had scores of incarnations, including Francie the African-American Barbie, and "Punk" Barbie, a 1980s doll. More recently Mattel has announced plans to give Barbie a makeover. She will have a "less graduated profile," in response to children's interest in more realism in their toys.

Source: Chris Semansky, in an essay for *Poetry for Students,* Gale, 2000.

Alice Van Wart

Alice Van Wart is a writer and teaches literature and writing in the Department of Continuing Education at the University of Toronto. She has published two books of poetry and has written articles on modern and contemporary literature.

In her essay "Rethinking the Seventies: Women Writers and Violence," Elaine Showalter says women writers in the 1970s were experiencing the beginning of an exciting new phase where they "seemed at last able to express anger and passion, to confront their own raging emotions...." Marge Piercy's "Barbie Doll" is a highly polished and ironic poem that perfectly demonstrates Showalter's thesis. In "Barbie Doll," Piercy scathingly condemns contemporary expectations placed on women concerning their appearance. The view she expresses in the poem is a feminist one, consistent with the political views she expresses in her numerous poetry collections, novels, and essays, particularly those views that condemn society's attitudes towards women.

"Barbie Doll" tells the story of a girl who grows up to find out she does not look quite as she should. Because she wants the approval of others she attempts to compensate for her imperfections in other areas. She soon grows tired of her efforts and in desperation chops off the offending parts of her body, taking her life as she does. In the hands of the undertaker, however, she finally achieves what she could not in life: perfection and hence approval.

The apt title given to the poem points to the central and controlling device of irony and the symbolic associations between the doll and the women in the poem. The Barbie Doll, more than being a favorite with adolescent girls, is a cultural icon of femininity that carries with it complex associations of ideal beauty and desirability. Piercy wishes to expose the destructiveness behind such ideals by showing the extent to which many women will go to achieve them.

Told through the third person point of view in four stanzas of free verse, the poem delineates the far-reaching consequences of a women's concern with her appearance as measured by an external ideal. The use of the third person point of view reinforces the increasing sense of alienation and self-loathing the woman in the poem experiences towards herself because she does not conform to this ideal. In the first stanza, Piercy shows the early indoctrination of young girls into feminine stereotypes. The second stanza conveys society's concern with women's appearance, in general, while the third stanza shows the extent to which women will go to conform to an ideal. The fourth stanza provides a concluding ironic twist showing how the woman in the poem achieves in death what she could not in life.

In the first line of the first stanza the poet introduces the subject of her poem as the "girlchild." Distinguishing her only by gender serves to objectify her, and the fact that she is "born as usual" suggests there is nothing out of the ordinary about the birth of this girl. The enjambment between lines one and two, however, clarifies that "as usual" also means she is greeted into the world as girls usually are with presents of "dolls that did pee-pee / and miniature GE stove and irons / and wee lipsticks the color of cherry candy". The images of "dolls," "stoves," "irons," serve to show the early indoctrination of girls into the woman's world of motherhood and domesticity, while the image of "wee lipsticks the color of cherry candy" begins her introduction into the guileful art of femininity.

In the fourth line the poem's focus shifts from childhood to "the magic of puberty." The use of the word "magic" to describe this period of the girl's life suggests the powerful and extraordinary nature of the emotional and hormonal changes that transform her from a girl into a young woman capable of bearing children. However, the magic of puberty is destroyed for her when a classmate tells her she has "a great big nose and fat legs."

In the second stanza the young woman has become so preoccupied with her imperfections that she is unable to see her positive qualities. Although she is "healthy, tested intelligent / possessed strong arms and a back" and even possesses "abundant sexual drive and manual dexterity," she is so conditioned to be over-concerned with her appearance that these positive qualities fail to have any value. Because she only sees her imperfections and believes she has no value because of them, she goes "to and fro apologizing." So obsessed is she with her imperfections that she begins to believe that what "everyone saw" when they looked at her was "a fat nose on thick legs."

By collapsing the images of "a great big nose and fat legs" into the comic image of "a fat nose on thick legs," Piercy uses synecdoche [a figure of speech in which the part stands for the whole, or the whole stands for the part], to draw attention

> *As an artifice of desire that measures itself against an impossible ideal, the female body requires endless maintenance to shape it for public acceptance and idealization, and this woman fails to shape herself into the image of what is desirable. Eventually she tires of her efforts and breaks down."*

both to her use of irony and to the sad fact that the young woman can only see herself in the terms of some artificial ideal.

In the third stanza the woman is "advised to play coy / exhorted to come on hearty / exercise, diet, smile and wheedle." She is pressured into trying to mold herself into what she is not and to compensate for her shortcomings. The verbs "advised" and "exhorted" suggest the insistence placed on the woman to please others, particularly men, while the advice to "play coy" and to "come on hearty" point to the artificial means women are encouraged to use to make themselves desirable.

As an artifice of desire that measures itself against an impossible ideal, the female body requires endless maintenance to shape it for public acceptance and idealization, and this woman fails to shape herself into the image of what is desirable. Eventually she tires of her efforts and breaks down. As the poet puts it, her "'good nature' wore out / like a fan belt."

The poet's use of simile [a figure of speech comparing two unlike things, often introduced by "like" or "as"] shows the extent to which the woman has accepted society's objectification of her body. Like the fan belt in a car that wears out and is discarded, the woman wears herself out in her attempts to perfect herself. Her body becomes an alien thing.

Because of its imperfections it has no value, "so she cut off her nose and her legs / and offered them up." Since she is the sum of her imperfect parts, "a fat nose on thick legs," by offering them up she is in fact sacrificing her life. The image of the woman cutting off parts of her body points to a growing popularity among women of using cosmetic surgery to perfect their appearances. More generally, it also suggests the history of abuse that women have inflicted on themselves in the name of beauty.

In the final stanza the woman lies in a casket made up for public display. Her face has been "painted on" by the undertaker's "cosmetics" and her "putty" nose has been "turned up." She lies on "satin" dressed "in a pink and white nightie." Everyone who comes to see her says, "Doesn't she look pretty?" Ironically, she achieves "consummation at last." "Consummation" in this context means literally to complete through perfection. The woman achieves in life what she could not in death.

The last two lines of the poem move beyond ironic expression and are rich in implication and scathing in intent. Piercy satirizes the traditional ending to many conventional fairy tales that conclude with the female protagonist living happily ever after with the consummation of marriage. Piercy subverts the traditional implication of sexual consummation to consummation in death. By sacrificing herself the woman finally receives the approval she had always wanted from others. The last line moves from the specific woman to women in general as Piercy concludes her poem: "to every woman a happy ending." The irony is clear. The woman lying in her casket is made up to look just like a Barbie doll; even her nose has been turned up. The woman, however, no longer bears any resemblance to the person she was. She is made-up and false, and, just like a Barbie doll, lifeless and perfect.

In "Barbie Doll," Piercy has found the perfect vehicle to express her anger and to criticize both women and the society they live in. By equating the woman in the poem with the image of the Barbie Doll and by using irony as a controlling device within the poem, the poet shows both the insidious way in which women are objectified as well as their own cooperative part in the process.

Source: Alice Van Wart, in an essay for *Poetry for Students,* Gale, 2000.

Sources

Abercrombie, Nicholas, Stephen Hill and Bryan S. Turner, eds., *Dictionary of Sociology,* London: Penguin, 1984.

Doherty, Patricia, *Marge Piercy: An Annotated Bibliography,* Westport, CT: Greenwood Press, 1997.

Duhamel, Denise, *Kinky,* Alexandria, VA: Orchises Press, 1997.

Edut, Ophira, ed., *Adios, Barbie,* Seattle: Seal Press, 1998.

Peabody, Richard and Lucinda Ebersole, eds., *Mondo Barbie,* New York: St. Martins Press, 1993.

Perrin, Robert, "'Barbie Doll' and 'G.I. Joe': Exploring Issues of Gender," *English Journal,* Vol. 88, January, 1999, pp. 83-86.

Piercy, Marge, *The Twelve-Spoked Wheel Flashing,* New York: Knopf, 1978.

Shands, Kerstin W., *The Repair of the World: The Novels of Marge Piercy,* Wesport, CT: Greenwood Publishing Group, 1994.

Showalter, Elaine, "The Femininst Critical Revolution," in *Feminist Criticism: Essays on Women, Literature, and Theory,* New York: Pantheon Books, 1985.

Strohmeyer, Sarah, *Barbie Unbound: A Parody of the Barbie Obsession,* Norwich, VT: New Victoria Publishers, 1997.

Walker, Sue, ed., *Critical Essays on Marge Piercy,* Westport, CT: Greenwood Publishers, 2000.

For Further Study

Lord, M.G., *Forever Barbie,* William Morrow and Co.: New York, 1994.
   Lord's examination of Barbie's historical impact on U.S. culture and consumer society is the most complete published thus far. Lord provides a detailed examination of Barbie's "roots" and traces her changes through the latter half of the twentieth century.

McDonough, Yona Zeldis, ed., *The Barbie Chronicles,* New York: Touchstone Books, 1999.
   This anthology collects essays and poems about the plastic icon at the 40th anniversary of her creation. The best essays in this collection discuss Barbie as seen through the lenses of sexuality, gender, and race.

Piercy, Marge, *Parti-Colored Blocks for a Quilt,* Ann Arbor: University of Michigan Press, 1982.
   This collection of interviews, essays, and reviews provides a first-hand account of Piercy's involvement with the women's movement and her views on her own, as well as others', poetry.

Varaste, Christopher, *Face of the American Dream: Barbie Doll 1959-1971,* Grantsville, MD: Hobby House Press, 1999.
   This book is a fresh look at the early Barbie dolls as "time capsules of the past" that mirror popular culture. The fashion trends, make-up and hairstyles of the 60s are embodied in photographs of vintage Barbie dolls. Actual advertisements for beauty products are shown to document the fashionable trends of the period. The author points out the revolutionizing influences on the fashions and selects dolls that perfectly embody the various styles, giving us a first hand look at the changing American Dream.

Bright Star! Would I Were Steadfast as Thou Art

John Keats

1819

In the summer of 1819 Keats and his friend James Rice left for an extended stay on the Isle of Wight off the southern coast of England. Keats had spent time alone on the Isle in the spring of 1817, reading Shakespeare and receiving the inspiration that led to the long poem "Endymion" as well as some of his most famous insights about the nature of art. He hoped the 1819 journey would prove equally invigorating, but he was distracted by his troubled love for Fanny Brawne. Keats had met her in December, 1818, but he was having trouble fully committing to their relationship. He wrote several letters to Fanny during his stay on the Isle, and one in particular seems to give insight into "Bright Star! Would I Were Steadfast as Thou Art." In the letter, he writes, "I have two luxuries to brood over in my walks, your loveliness and the hour of my death. O that I could have possession of them both in the same minute." Keats's biographer Aileen Ward writes that while composing the letter, Keats witnessed the planet Venus rising outside his window. At that moment, Ward says, "doubt and distraction left him; it was only beauty, Fanny's and the star's, that mattered."

"Bright Star!" considers a similar moment, and the sonnet is considered one of Keats's loveliest and most paradoxical. The speaker of the poem wishes he were as eternal as a star that keeps watch like a sleepless, solitary, and religious hermit over the "moving waters" and the "soft-fallen mask / Of snow." But while he longs for this unchanging state, he does not wish to exist by himself, in "lone splendor." Rather, he longs to be "Awake for ever" and "Pillowed upon my fair love's ripening breast." Unfortunately, these two desires—to experience love and to be eternal—do not go together. To love, he must be human, and therefore not an unchanging thing like the star. The speaker seems to reveal an awareness of this in the final line of the poem. He wishes to "live ever" in love, but to be in love means to be human, which means that the speaker and the love he feels for the woman will change and eventually die. The only other possibility he can imagine is to "swoon to death." This can be interpreted to mean that he wishes to die at a moment when he is experiencing the ecstasy of love. Despite the awareness that the speaker seems to express about the paradox of having love and immortality, the poem as a whole can also be seen as the speaker's plea to have both of these qualities, however impossible that may be.

Author Biography

Born in 1795, Keats, the son of a stablekeeper, was raised in Moorfields, London, and attended the Clarke School in Enfield. The death of his mother in 1810 left Keats and his three younger siblings in the care of a guardian, Richard Abbey. Although Keats was apprenticed to an apothecary, he soon realized that writing was his true talent, and he decided to become a poet. Forced to hide his ambition from Abbey, who would not have sanctioned it, Keats instead entered Guy's and St. Thomas's Hospitals in London, becoming an apothecary in 1816 and continuing his studies to become a surgeon. When he reached the age of twenty-one, Keats was free of Abbey's jurisdiction. Supported by his small inheritance, he devoted himself to writing. Keats also began associating with artists and writers, among them Leigh Hunt, who published Keats's first poems in his journal, the *Examiner*. But within a few years the poet experienced the first symptoms of tuberculosis, the disease that had killed his mother and brother. He continued writing and reading the great works of literature. He also fell in love with Fanny Brawne, a neighbor's daughter, though his poor health and financial difficulties made marriage impossible. He published a final work, *Lamia, Isabella, The Eve of St. Agnes, and Other Poems*, which included his famous odes and the unfinished narrative, *Hyperion: A Fragment*. Keats travelled to Italy in 1820 in an effort to improve his health but died in Rome the following year at the age of 26.

John Keats

Poem Text

Bright star! would I were steadfast as thou art—
Not in lone splendor hung aloft the night,
And watching, with eternal lids apart,
Like Nature's patient, sleepless Eremite,
The moving waters at their priestlike task   5
Of pure ablution round earth's human shores,
Or gazing on the new soft-fallen mask
Of snow upon the mountains and the moors—

No—yet still steadfast, still unchangeable,
Pillowed upon my fair love's ripening breast,   10
To feel for ever its soft fall and swell,
Awake for ever in a sweet unrest,
Still, still to hear her tender-taken breath,
    And so live ever—or else swoon to death.

Poem Summary

Lines 1-4:

In the opening lines, the poet establishes the image of the star that is the central focus of the poem. The star is said to be eternal ("patient"), unchanging ("sleepless"), and beyond the speaker's immediate grasp ("aloft"). Furthermore, the star is described as watching over earth, rather than being watched by someone. As a result, the star nearly pushes the speaker's presence out of the octave—

Media Adaptations

- Spoken Arts, Inc., has produced an audiocassette entitled *Treasury of John Keats* (1989).

- Anthony Thorlby can be heard on two audiocassettes entitled *Keats and Romanticism* (1973) for Everett/Edwards.

- Blackstone Audio Books presents *John Keats* (1993) on two audiocassettes.

- Archive of Recorded Poetry and Literature, Library of Congress, has produced *Cheryl Crawford and Greg Morton Reading Poems and Letters of John Keats, May 1952* (1952) on audiotape reel.

- The King's Collage has produced an audiocassette entitled *John Keats' Pursuit of Essence* (1972) with Kathryn Ludwig.

- Harvard Vocarium Records has produced a 78 r.p.m. record album entitled *Poems of John Keats* (1941) with Robert Speaight.

- Annenberg/Corporation for Public Broadcasting Project has produced an audiocassette entitled *John Keats and the Romantic Agony* (1987) from the "Introduction to Modern English and American Literature" series.

- Listening Library has produced an audiocassette entitled *The Essential Keats* (1989), selected and with an introduction by Philip Levine.

- Monterey Home Video has produced a videocassette entitled *The Glorious Romantics: A Poetic Return to the Regency* (1993).

- Encyclopedia Britannica Corporation has produced a videocassette entitled *John Keats: His Life and Death* (1991), written by Archibald MacLeish and narrated by James Mason.

- Films for the Humanities and Sciences has produced a videocassette entitled *The Last Journey of John Keats* (1998).

- Landmark Media has produced a videocassette entitled *John Keats, Poet: 1795-1821* (1994).

- Center for Cassette Studies has produced an audiocassette with graphics entitled *The Quintessential Keats: Dr. John Theobald Lectures on the Life of the Immortal Romantic Poet* (1970).

---

the poem's first eight lines: the word "I" is mentioned only in the first line. This is indicative of a change that occurred in Keats's work as his career progressed. His earlier poems are more concerned with self-consciousness and personal matters but his later work, such as "Bright Star! Would I Were Steadfast as Thou Art," include a more harmonious acceptance of nature for what it is, beyond the self's interpretation of it.

Lines 5-8:

The second part of the octave describes what the star watches. Here, two symbols emerge, both suggesting the idea of pureness. The first is the "moving waters" the star watches over. The waters here take on a spiritual significance, their "ablution" suggesting religious purification, "a priestlike task" that is performed on the "human shores." The second symbol is contained in the image of snow: "the new soft-fallen mask" that covers "the mountains and the moors." By introducing these images, the speaker seems to identify with those things that can, in some sense, make humans pure or spiritual. Perhaps he feels this to be a way to transcend the limitations of human life—the changes and eventual decay that result in death.

Lines 9-14:

In the sestet, the speaker turns from the star's existence to his own. Keats uses related imagery to emphasize this process. In lines 5 and 6 he spoke of the moving waters washing the shore, an image that suggests the rising and falling of ocean waves. In line 11, the reference is made to the "soft fall and swell" of the woman's breast, which also suggests water and waves.

In comparing himself to the star, however, the speaker wishes for something the star does not have: steadfastness without solitude. Though he wishes to be "still unchangeable" like the star, he wishes his eternity to be in the context of human love: to be "Pillowed" upon his love's breast. The breast, itself a symbol of fertility, is described as "ripening." But while fertility is the organic basis of life, the star's steadfastness is "aloft," or far above such this process. Thus, a paradox is created. While the star is merely "watching" the "moving waters," the speaker wishes to actually "feel" his love's living body. His desire is not to exist in "lone splendor" but rather to be in "unchangeable" proximity with his love—to be, in other words, eternally human.

This, of course, is impossible. The qualities that make the star eternal are non-human ones. While the star fails to sense the procession of time—it is "patient"—the speaker envisions an eternity of "sweet unrest." Thus, in the final two lines there are two mutually exclusive possibilities. On the one hand, the speaker can live in the sensual experience of love, which, because it is characterized by the slipping away of apparent time, seems to be "for ever." Failing that, the speaker hopes he might "swoon to death" at the moment of purest happiness.

Themes

Art and Experience

The qualities that Keats attributes to the star in this poem are the qualities of the artist—it is said to be "watching, with eternal lids apart," while remaining uninvolved in the events that it is witness to. In this particular case, the observations are made of nature, which is described as being holy, "priest-like" acts, while the star that observes them is also described with the religious term "Eremite." There is a difference in their religious qualities, though, as the observer keeps aloof, removed from the situation. It all adds up to the reverent stance that Keats took toward his artistry and the things that he wrote about, particularly when the subject matter was nature, which he held in the kind of esteem that many people reserve for God. To Keats, it was the artist's goal to be able to observe and fully understand her/his subject without interfering with it, so that it could be recorded as it existed, with no bias or interference. The reference in line 7 to "grazing" the "mask" of snow might be meant to

imply that, as the poet saw it, the star could undo that mask to know the reality beneath, or it could mean that observing the contours of the mask closely enough could lead one to understanding what the mask hides. Keats's view of the relationship between the artist and experience is somewhat unique and unexpected from a poet who led an active life: in countless novels and memoirs, artists are seen trying to immerse themselves in experience in order to give themselves true understanding of their subjects. In this poem Keats draws a line between observation and experience, presenting the two as mutually exclusive, so that a person cannot, try as he might, have both at the same time.

Change and Transformation

The problem facing the speaker in this poem is that he would like to stop all change, to freeze things at one particularly wonderful moment, but he realizes that doing so would be the opposite of living life, that life *is* change, even when that change is something as small as the motion of his lover's breathing. In the first part of the poem, the octet, he focuses on images of nature that either do not change or else show changes that are part of a larger pattern that does not change. The oceans do move constantly, from our earthly perspective, but from a star's perspective they would look as constant as a star would from Earth. Similarly, snowflakes fall but the snow that blankets or "masks" hills and fields of a countryside changes the color but retains the land's original shape. From a great distance, no transformation is discernable. Keats, aware of his impending death from tuberculosis, would naturally have a reason to fear change, and he would have wished to stop the clock before his life ran out of minutes, but, as he admits here, doing so would mean missing out on life's pleasures. In the end he notes that the ideal would be for time to stop at a moment when he is wrapped up in one of those pleasures, such as when lying with his lover. He could live within such a moment for the rest of eternity. In the last four lines he punctuates this idea with the phrases "To feel for ever," "Awake for ever," and "And so live for ever." The poem's sad tone comes from the fact that the speaker knows that it could never be, that as a living being he could never, like the star, stay the same from one moment to the next.

Death

The sudden appearance of death in the last line of this poem might take readers by surprise, especially since the preceding lines of the sestet had

Topics for Further Study

- In this poem, the speaker says that the star has qualities—steadfastness, watchfulness, fidelity—that he would like to have himself. Write a poem about an object of your choosing, in which you give that object qualities you admire.

- Do you think a star is a powerful way for an author to imagine his relationship with his lover? Point out the strengths and weaknesses of this image.

- Keats was criticized during his lifetime for being a "Cockney Poet," by which his detractors meant that he wrote like a lower-class person, a worker rather than a refined poet. Pick specific details about this poem that might have led them to this conclusion, and explain your choices.

- John Keats was only 26 when he died. Read about someone who was famous and died young and draw a chart that points out other aspects that their life had in common with Keats's.

provided gentle images of life, such as the lover's breathing and the hint of fertility in the "ripening" breast. This reversal should not come as too much of a shock, though, given that, by the fourteenth line, the speaker has already wedged himself into an unsolvable predicament. Some of the complexity of life that he is getting at here is implied in the poem's twisted language. For instance, lines 2 through 9, starting with "Not" and drifting from that thought until "No—," leave one idea after the next unfinished, so that the subject that began the poem, the speaker's actual life, is forgotten. It becomes difficult for the reader to follow the central idea as it loops off, one prepositional phrase leading from the last, until, like life, the poem's central unity is just a mass of knots that cannot be untangled at the end, just abandoned. The air of contradiction is captured in the last line: "And so live forever—or else swoon to death." Eternal life might logically be paired with a long life, or instant death considered beside dying soon, but mention-

ing these two ideas that are so opposite just does not seem to make sense. This is the nature of paradox, to drive readers to a deeper level of thought by canceling out their preconceived notions. As a matter of fact, death and eternal life do have something in common: they both last forever. This poem makes the point that at a moment of perfect bliss, this speaker could accept either death or eternal life, because either would freeze the moment and allow him to continue on in the same way forever—to be "steadfast."

Style

"Bright Star! Would I Were Steadfast as Thou Art" is a sonnet, a traditional poetic form characterized by its length of fourteen lines and its use of a set rhyme scheme. Although there are many variations on the sonnet form, most are based on the two major types: the Petrarchan, or Italian, sonnet and the Shakespearean, or English, sonnet. In different ways, "Bright Star!" resembles both. While its rhyme scheme is that of the Shakespearean form— three quatrains rhyming *abab cdcd efef,* followed by a couplet rhyming *gg*—its thematic division most closely follows the Petrarchan model. In this type of sonnet, the first eight lines, or the octave, generally present some kind of question, doubt, desire, or vision of the ideal. The last six lines, or the sestet, generally answer the question, ease the doubt, satisfy the desire, or fulfill the vision. In Keats's poem, the first eight lines explore the steadfastness of the star, which watches over nature "with eternal lids apart." The speaker longs to be just "as steadfast," yet, like the star, he needs something to watch over. In the sestet, he turns his attention to his love, the object of his eternal vigilance.

Historical Context

Discussion of English Romantic poets usually refers to the small handful who wrote in a short period of time around the turn of the nineteenth century. Three poets in particular—Keats, Lord Byron, and Percy Shelley—dominate the public's imagination of what a Romantic poet is like. All three were friends and associates, they were gifted and serious about artistry, and all three died relatively young, leaving their poetry to be associated with

Compare & Contrast

- **1819:** An iron cooking stove was patented by inventor John Conant. It was not a commercial success, however, because most housewives chose to cook food on their fireplaces, as they were accustomed.

  Today: Many cooks are impatient with the time it takes to heat food with fire, gas, or electric heat, so they use the microwave oven, using principles they do not understand.

- **1819:** The French Revolution was over: Napoleon had been defeated at Waterloo four years earlier, and King Louis XVIII was restored to the throne.

  Today: France is ruled by a president. It is one of the largest Western democracies to have elected a socialist leader in modern times (Francois Mitterand, in 1981).

- **1819:** The *Savannah* was the first steamship to cross an ocean.

  Today: Although the airplane has replaced steamship travel as a mode of transportation, luxury cruises are a popular vacation option.

- **1819:** Beethoven, who had been losing his hearing since 1801, was completely deaf.

  Today: Music aficionados find some of Beethoven's works composed after he went deaf, including his string quartets, to be among the most beautiful ever written.

---

the compelling blend of youth and doom. Romanticism, in fact, can be seen in almost all poetry, with stylistic strains going back at least to Shakespeare's peer Edmund Spenser (1553-1599), whose allegorical epic *The Faerie Queen* was to have a profound influence on Keats in the 1800's. It was the generation immediately preceding Keats's, though, that brought Romanticism into its own as a conscious artistic practice. A strong influence on those early Romantics was Thomas Chatterton, who killed himself in 1770, just before his eighteenth birthday, out of despair over the lack of critical reception for his works. Chatterton had a talent for mimicking the penmanship and language of the Middle Ages, and at age fifteen he published a collection of poems attributed to Thomas Rowley, a fifteenth-century poet he had made up. This nostalgia for the long-ago past became a key element of writing of the time, and is strongly evident in the works of the Scottish poet Robert Burns (1759-1796) who is usually considered a quasi-Romantic poet, and of Sir Walter Scott (1771-1832), who started his career writing mediocre poems but became an important part of literary history with historical romance novels. In the last years of the eighteenth century William Wordsworth and Samuel Taylor Coleridge began Romanticism as we talk about it today. Both poets were free-thinkers, somewhat radical, ready to change conventional assumptions.

A main influence on them, and on the Romantic movements all over the world and in all different branches of art and philosophy, was the French Revolution. The central force of the Romantic movement was the importance placed on individuality, and the French Revolution was the key moment in world history when the rights of individuals came to be recognized. It marked the shift from a feudal society, where citizens were locked into the social fate that they inherited. Previously, about three percent of the population had owned most of the land in France and held all of the political power, while the other ninety-seven percent worked to pay rent and taxes with no hope of social gain. The American Revolution from 1776 to 1783 prompted the citizens of France to act against this unfair system. It showed them an example of a society in which the monarchy was dismissed in favor of democratic elections that would enact the will of the common person. The French King, Louis XVI, had been supporting the Americans against his long-standing enemies, the British, and had tripled the amount that was due on the public debt. To cover the payments, greater taxes were levied, putting even more pressure on the taxpayers and pushing them even closer to revolution. The revolution began in 1789 when people panicked over the rumor that the nobility, in response to the growing political power being demanded by the commoners, planned to collect all of the nation's grain and ship it abroad, to starve the population. What started with ideals of liberty, equality and respect for all broke down into violence. Nobles, including the King and Queen, were captured and beheaded. Between 1793 and 1794 seventeen thousand people were put to death during a period that came to be known as the Reign of Terror. To take advantage of the violence and confusion in France's political system, enemy nations, Austria, Prussia, the Netherlands, Spain, Sardinia, and Great Britain stayed on the offensive. France was able to hold up against them by conscripting more and more people into the army. The new revolutionary government was turning out to be just as hard on the common citizens as the aristocracy had been. In 1799 a powerful military leader, Napoleon Bonaparte, rose up to lead the government: he disbanded the government of the people almost immediately, ruled with absolute authority, and in a few years proclaimed himself Emperor for Life, putting France back into the political inequality that had sparked the revolution.

Coleridge and Wordsworth had each witnessed the events in France and had been stirred by the early revolution's promise of respect for the individual but had been horrified by the bloody chaos that resulted. The two poets Coleridge and Wordsworth met and became friends in 1795, and they both ended up writing poetry that was private, that emphasized nature and history and personality, that looked sadly at the world without pretending that it could be made better with political solutions. In 1798 they published a collection of poems together, anonymously, called *Lyrical Ballads*. When it was reissued in 1800, it included a preface that outlined their theories of poetry, and that preface turned out to be one of the most influential poetic manifestos in history. In it, they rejected things that tied poetry too closely to the society the poet lived in; things like sophistication and elevated diction and current events were to be avoided, while a deep appreciation of the self and its relationship with nature were to be cultivated. By the late 1810s, their influence had evolved, in the works of Keats, Byron and Shelley, into a poetic stance that showed the Romantic poet as a lonesome, brooding soul who felt misunderstood, alienated within his own time and place, overcome by powerful desires that society wanted to repress.

Critical Overview

In her book *John Keats,* Aileen Ward discusses the conflicts Keats weighs in "Bright Star! Would I Were Steadfast as Thou Art." She believes that the poem represents a way for Keats to come to terms with contrasting elements that he addressed in other works. In the poetic odes that he wrote, including "Ode to a Nightingale" and "Ode on a Grecian Urn," Keats considered the difference, as Ward puts it, between "the timeless but unreal perfection of art and the time-bound realizations of life." In other words, Keats was enthralled by the beauty and permanence of art and nature, but he knew that the human experience was different, limited by time and self-awareness. To resolve this dilemma, "Bright Star!" considers, in Ward's words, an "ideal moment made actual." This moment is "a vision of death at the moment of supreme happiness" for the speaker. In other words, the way that the speaker is able to understand timelessness and perfection is to imagine dying when he is with his love, enjoying a perfect moment of calm.

Criticism

Jeannine Johnson

Jeannine Johnson received her Ph.D. from Yale University and is currently visiting assistant professor of English at Wake Forest University. In the following essay, Johnson demonstrates that although Keats's prayer in "Bright star!" goes unanswered, the poet is not disappointed but remains content.

In "Bright star! would I were steadfast as thou art," the object of John Keats's initial address is the North Star, or polestar. He speaks of it as existing "in lone splendour," referring to the unequaled brightness of this star. Navigators have long relied on the North Star to help them determine latitude and north-south direction in the northern hemisphere, and at the beginning of the poem, the poet is in the position of the navigator, observing the star and looking to it for guidance. Yet when Keats

What Do I Read Next?

- Both the Modern Library and Penguin Classics have versions available of *The Complete Poems of John Keats.*

- It is almost impossible to talk about Keats's poetry without encountering some discussion of the poet himself, and in particular the controversy between critics who thought he lacked talent and his friends who saw his genius. The debate is played out before readers' eyes in G.M. Matthews' collection of reviews and letters from Keats's time, called *Keats: The Critical Heritage* (published by Barnes and Noble in 1971).

- One of the most influential recent books about Romanticism is by influential critic Northrop Frye, whose short 1968 book *A Study of English Romanticism* gives an excellent quick background to the cultural movement that is almost always mentioned along with Keats's name.

- John Evangelist Walsh, whose earlier work includes a biography of Edgar Allan Poe, wrote the 1999 book *Darkling I Listen: The Last Days*

and *Death of John Keats,* available from St. Martin's Press.

- Keats's name is often mentioned in conjunction with his friend and peer, Percy Bysshe Shelley. The Modern Library edition of *The Complete Poems of Shelley* includes an introduction by his wife, Mary Wollstonecraft Shelley (author of *Frankenstein*).

- Keats was greatly influenced by the work of poet William Wordsworth, who is credited with being one of the founders of English Romanticism. W.W. Norton has made a book-length study of the different versions of Wordsworth greatest poem available in *"The Prelude": 1799, 1805, 1850.* This book includes critical essays.

- Probably the best poet to follow Keats and show his influence was Robert Browning. Browning was too prolific for all of his poetry to be collected in one volume, but the important works are available in Penguin Poetry Library's *Browning: Selected Poetry.*

---

invokes this relationship, he reverses the parties' normal positions: instead of a navigator looking at the star, the poet says that the star is "watching … / The moving waters" and everything on it. With this subtle reversal, the poet attempts to appropriate for himself the star's steadfastness, which is his aim in this piece. Although he is ultimately unsuccessful in obtaining this unchangeableness and reliability, the poet remains tranquil, knowing that his love is true, even if time is fickle.

The poet first tells us what he wants—steadfastness—and then he tells us why he wants it. He wishes to be forever linked in passion to his "fair love," a poetic figure inspired by Frances ("Fanny") Brawne, Keats's neighbor and, by 1819, his fiancee. Several of his poems—informally known as the "Fanny lyrics"—are associated with her. In addition to "Bright star!" these are: "The Day is Gone, and All Its Sweets Are Gone!" "I Cry Your Mercy, Pity, Love—Ay, Love!" "What Can I Do To Drive

Away," and "To Fanny." The ghoulish late poem, "This Living Hand, Now Warm and Capable," is also frequently linked to Fanny. Confusion and desperation characterize the other Fanny lyrics, as well as many of his letters to her. For example, in "I Cry Your Mercy" the poet pleads with his paramour, "Yourself—your soul—in pity give me all, / Withhold no atom's atom or I die," while in "What can I do to drive away" he revels in his agony, crying, "O, the sweetness of the pain!" (*The Complete Poems*).

However, in "Bright Star!" there is little, if any, of this extravagant agitation. The poem is an even-tempered prayer, made not out of distress but out of contentment. Further, the poet does not pray for affection: in contrast to the other Fanny lyrics, the speaker of this poem is fully certain that his feelings are returned by his beloved. Instead, the poet asks for "steadfastness." In the first line, he prays to be as constant and unchangeable as is the

North Star, but very quickly he qualifies his request. As the literary critic Harold Bloom succinctly puts it, "Keats wants to be as steadfast as the star, but not in the star's way of steadfastness" (*The Visionary Company,* Bloom's emphasis).

As Bloom points out, the poet goes on in lines 2-8 to describe the star's way of steadfastness (*The Visionary Company*). This "way" is above all one of solitude. The star hangs "in lone splendour," and the poet calls it an "Eremite," or hermit. Keats says that it rests "aloft the night," meaning both *in* the night sky and *above* the night sky. This ambiguity suggests that the star's distance from earth is so great that we cannot fix its position with any certainty. The star is "patient" but also "sleepless," implying that its calm condition is less desirable than it is stoical. The star's existence is an austere one, and it is associated with sacred observations. It oversees the oceans which are "priestlike" as they literally wash the shores of the land on which we live and figuratively purify our unholy lives. This link to the religious and spiritual further distances the star from the worldly concerns of the poet.

As he makes clear with the "Not" that introduces the second line, the poet desires another kind of steadfastness, which is described in lines 9-14. The "No" that begins line nine reiterates the poet's wish to qualify the type of unchangeableness that he seeks. The literary critic David Perkins explains that "In the drama of the poem, he discovers that his wish is not to be like the star after all, but rather to transpose the potentiality of the star for eternal awareness into the realm of human life and feeling, and that of the most intense variety" (*The Quest for Permanence*). The poet does not envy the star's temperate piety. He does not want the complete vision of a distant domain but an "eternal awareness" of his own immediate sphere of ardor and devotion. As Keats has it, he seeks to be "Awake for ever in a sweet unrest" and in the company of his beloved.

The problem with this aspiration is that it is not possible. John Barnard, a contemporary editor and critic of Keats, observes that "the sonnet's yearning for the star's 'steadfastness' and unchangeability admits that human love cannot attain its calm certainty or eternity. The long moment may feel like a kind of sensual eternity, but, unlike the star's lonely splendour, the mutual pleasure of human lovers is only attainable or meaningful in a time-scale which includes change" (*John Keats*). That is to say, Keats longs to experience an infinite romantic climax, but a climax implies a pro-

With this duplication, Keats creates in miniature the paradoxical state in which he hopes to remain forever: this is a moment in which change and passion are possible, but a moment that is also infinitely repeated, unchanging, and eternal."

gressive series of moments which have preceded it. This progression occurs in time, not out of time, and with time comes change, something which the poet wishes to forestall.

The poet's desire to resolve opposites is also reflected in the poem's structure. In this poem, Keats cleverly combines the English and Italian sonnet forms. The rhyming pattern (*abab cdcd efef gg*) creates three quatrains and a couplet, the form common to the English, or Shakespearean, sonnet. But the poem also is clearly divided between the first eight lines and the last six, establishing the octave and sestet split that characterizes the Italian, or Petrarchan, sonnet. In an Italian sonnet, a problem is posed in the first eight lines, and a response or solution to that problem is offered in the last six. In "Bright Star!" the problem, such as it is, is that the poet wants to be like the star in some respects but not in others. The response or solution, set forth in the last six lines, is to embrace some of the star's qualities and reject the rest. The poet addresses the star in the octave but then shifts to a third person address (speaking of "her") in the sestet. Similar vowel sounds in "breast," "rest," "breath," and "death" further mark the sestet as a single unit. However, the sonnet returns to a dominant Shakespearean form at the couplet. In the last two lines the poet provides a final statement that comments upon—and is separable from—the rest of the poem.

The purpose of the last six lines—whether viewed as a sestet or as a quatrain plus a couplet—is made more clear when we examine the revisions that Keats made in composing the poem. During the nineteenth century, "Bright Star!" was thought to be Keats's last poem, written in September 1820, when he copied it out in a volume of Shakespeare's poems. In the 1848 collection, *Life, Letters, and Literary Remains of John Keats,* for instance, this poem was given the simple title, "Keats's Last Sonnet." However, in the twentieth century, an earlier version of the poem, dated 1819, was discovered. Though there is continuing debate, most scholars believe the poem to have been composed in the late fall of 1819, by which time, as Keats's biographer Walter Jackson Bate reminds us, "the tuberculosis of the lungs that was to prove fatal to him had seriously begun (or suddenly moved into an active stage), bringing with it periods of immense fatigue and some fever" (*John Keats*).

The primary revisions involve the last five lines of the sonnet, and, with perhaps only one exception, they do not alter the substance of the poem's thought. The end of the earlier version reads: "Cheek-pillow'd on my Love's white ripening breast / To touch, for ever, its warm sink and swell, / Awake, for ever, in a sweet unrest, / To hear, to feel her tender-taken breath, / Half passionless, and so swoon on to death." In the 1820 version, Keats creates two more sensuous and deliberate lines in writing "Pillowed upon my fair love's ripening breast / To feel for ever its soft swell and fall." The repeated "f," "s," and "l" sounds roll gently through these lines, without the encumbrance of the rather brusque "ch," "k," and "t" sounds in the words "Cheek," white," "touch," and "sink."

In his revision, Keats slows the introduction of the couplet with the repetition of the word "Still." Here, "still" means both "always" and "unmoving." But it also means "again"—and in fact the word is stated once and then *again*—suggesting the movement of time and the variation of activity on which human life depends. With this duplication, Keats creates in miniature the paradoxical state in which he hopes to remain forever: this is a moment in which change and passion are possible, but a moment that is also infinitely repeated, unchanging, and eternal.

The repetition of "still" also underscores the break between the rest of the poem and this final statement. In the 1819 version, the poet equates his passionate summit with death: he speculates that he will be "Half passionless, *and* so swoon on to death" (emphasis added). It is a sweet transition from consummation to collapse. However, in the 1820 version of the poem, death is not the conse-

quence of, but the alternative to, passion: the poet hopes to lie on his lover's breast "And so live ever—*or else* swoon to death" (emphasis added). This more ominous line hints that neither possibility is completely desirable. Indeed, though Keats and Fanny Brawne were engaged, the poet was aware by 1820 when he revised the poem that he would not live long, and that, due to his illness and confirmed poverty, marriage would be impossible. The poet's situation was unenviable, and his attempt in "Bright Star!" to unite earthly desire with celestial privilege fails. Nevertheless, the overall tone of the poem is serene, and even in these final lines the poet's voice is relatively self-assured, a sign that, though Keats might ask for more time to live and to love, what he does have will suffice.

Source: Jeannine Johnson, in an essay for *Poetry for Students,* Gale, 2000.

Aviya Kushner

Aviya Kushner is the Contributing Editor in Poetry at BarnesandNoble.com *and the Poetry Editor of* Neworld Magazine. *She is a graduate of the acclaimed creative writing program in poetry at Boston University, where she received the Fitzgerald Award in Translation. Her writing on poetry has appeared in* Harvard Review *and* The Boston Phoenix, *and she has served as Poetry Coordinator for* AGNI Magazine. *She has given readings of her own work throughout the United States, and she teaches at Massachusetts Communications College in Boston. In the following essay, Kushner describes the sonnet as expressing Keats's desire to have the "steadfastness" and immortality of a star and of a Shakespeare, able to look upon one's love and to be remembered for one's verses for eternity.*

Sonnet Written on a Blank Page in Shakespeare's Poems

The oldest son of a stable-keeper, the great poet John Keats devoted himself to poetry at the age of twenty-one. Tragically, after five years of feverish writing and significant publication, Keats died at twenty-six—a victim of consumption.

The fact of his early death colors the reading of many of Keats's most accomplished poems, and even their rapturous moments tend to appear tinged with the sorrow of impending doom. Though he continued to write magnificent odes which address truth, beauty, and the lure of immortality, Keats was painfully aware that he would die. He wrote of what he would never get to see, both poetically and personally. The woman he loved and the words he loved were not to be his for long.

In the introduction to his lengthy and masterful poem "Endymion," Keats wrote movingly of the limitations of all beginning poets, and he was particularly humble when referring directly to his own work. He noted that "the reader ... must soon perceive great inexperience, immaturity, and every error denoting a feverish attempt, rather than a deed accomplished." What's more, Keats wrote that "the foundations are too sandy. It is just that this youngster should die away: a sad thought for me...."

Reading this description of the shortcomings naturally faced by a young man writing ambitious poems, it is hard not to imagine what such a self-aware young writer might have grown to achieve had he lived.

Keats wondered that too. In Sonnet 24, he looks at a bright star illuminating the night, and wishes that he were as "steadfast"—as lasting—as that heavenly resident. In many of his poems, Keats uses the conditional—"had I," or "if only I would"—to introduce a point. In a life cut so short, Keats unfortunately had many "what ifs" to write about. Sonnet 2, for example, details how he might be received by a woman if only he were better-looking:

Had I a man's fair form, then might my sighs / Be echoed swiftly through that ivory shell, / Thine ear, and find thy gentle heart: so well / Would passion arm me for the enterprise: / But ah! I am no knight whose foeman dies;

In Sonnet 2, Keats imagines that his "sighs" and other overtures would be more welcome if he had a "fair form." In the first line of Sonnet 24, Keats muses that his life would be better if he had another seemingly essential quality. In the opening line, punctuated by an exclamation point, the speaker looks longingly at the star and cries:

Bright star! Would I were as steadfast as thou art—

"steadfast" was what the illness-plagued Keats wanted to be but couldn't. He then takes a closer look at this star and details why it is fortunate:

Not in lone splendour bring aloft the night / And watching, with eternal lids apart, / Like Nature's patient, sleepless Eremite ...

With the phrase "eternal lids," Keats introduces the notion of immortality. The "steadfast" star has been there for a long time, and will remain there long after the speaker is gone. The star has eternal life, which is what the speaker most craves. The star also gets to look leisurely at the beauty of the natural world, which was one of Keats's great themes:

> *Unlike the speaker, the star has a chance to see the lovely girl sleep and watch her as she breathes in and out. By watching the beautiful girl and touching her moving, breathing body, the star has the capacity to 'live for ever.'*

The moving waters at their priestlike task / Of pure ablution round earth's human shores, / Or gazing on the new soft fallen mask / Of snow upon the mountains and the moors

With "moors," a word associated with the English landscape, Keats establishes this as a British poem, descended from the tradition of Shakespeare. Interestingly, this sonnet was written in a blank page in Shakespeare's poems, which certainly may have brought on thoughts of both a "bright star" and immortality. As a writer, according to many scholars of English literature, Shakespeare certainly stands in "lone splendour." But many critics would argue that Keats was also a writer of "splendour."

However, there is one key difference between Shakespeare and Keats. Shakespeare lived long enough to produce a wide array of plays and poems, both comedies and tragedies. In this devotion to writing and his consistent production of high-quality work, Shakespeare was certainly "steadfast." But by the time this sonnet was written, Keats knew that the steadfastedness born of longevity was beyond his grasp.

Keats does choose a "steadfast" form—the sonnet. The sonnet was around before him and is still around several centuries after his death. As is traditional for a sonnet, the first eight lines here form one thought, and the last six represent a break into another thought.

Here, the word "no" introduces a new idea. The poem here becomes personal. Instead of simply watching, the star is now directed at an individual sight—the fair love. Keats wrote numerous poems about his lady love, and here he expresses some jealousy because the bright star will be able to continue to look at this woman and feel her "ripening breast":

To feel for ever its soft fall and swell, / Awake for ever in a sweet unrest / Still, still to hear her tender-taken breath, / And so live for ever—or else swoon to death.

Unlike the speaker, the star has a chance to see the lovely girl sleep and watch her as she breathes in and out. By watching the beautiful girl and touching her moving, breathing body, the star has the capacity to "live for ever." Alternately, the star has the choice of dying brilliantly. While Keats coughed his way to an unglamorous end, the star can "swoon" to its death, flayed by beauty. For Keats, life—and death—were about beauty, and the opportunity to observe it and to sing its praises.

Source: Aviya Kushner, in an essay for *Poetry for Students,* Gale, 2000.

David Kelly

David Kelly is an instructor of Creative Writing at several community colleges in Illinois, as well as a fiction writer and playwright. In this essay, he examines the variations on human identity that John Keats explores in the sonnet "Bright Star!" and how death is the logical end.

In an October, 1818, letter to his friend Richard Woodhouse, John Keats wrote, "A Poet is the most unpractical of any thing in existence; because he has no Identity—he is continually for—and filling some other Body—The Sun, the Moon, the Sea and Men and Women who are creatures of impulse and are poetical and have about them an unchangeable attribute—the poet has none; no identity—he is certainly the most unpoetical of all God's Creatures." In the poem, "Bright Star! Would I Were Steadfast as Thou Art," we see the qualities that Keats gave to the poet projected onto the star. The poem's speaker expresses his wish to reach that same level of detachment from the things of the world. At the same time, though, he also praises the poetical experiences that he can have as a man—the manifestations of Identity that Keats says the poet does not have available to him. He wonders whether, if he could be just one, he would be the man or the poet. The complex interweaving of confidence and doubt regarding just who he is tilts, in this sonnet, first one way then the other. Where it ends is death, which, probably not by coincidence, Keats had experienced in recent events of his life and was aware

was coming for him all too soon. It is Keats's glory that he was able to see himself evenly suspended between the two sides that made up his Identity, between involvement and isolation, a conundrum that other poets claim to solve or else allow to drive them insane. To pin down with any degree of precision what each of these identities meant to Keats might lead to at least an understanding of the bigger puzzle of how he is able to present death as the same thing as eternal life.

Such a delicate balance was not always a part of Keats's worldview, but something that he grew into. In a long essay dissecting how he came to his theory of poetry, Walter Jackson Bate mentioned, among others, the influence of philosopher and literary critic William Hazlitt, whose depth of taste Keats listed, along with Wordsworth's *Excursion* (published 1814) and Benjamin Haydon's pictures, as "the three things to rejoice at in this age." According to Bate, Hazlitt thought of himself as a philosopher and psychologist (the two were closely linked in the years before psychology was recognized as a science). His book *Essay on the Principles of Human Action,* which he began in his early twenties, was not ready for publication until he was twenty-seven: if he had been more prolific he might be widely remembered today as a philosopher, but instead he is remembered for his brilliant and scathing essays of literary criticism. When Keats read *Essay on the Principles of Human Action,* his thinking about the role of the artist was changed. Hazlitt tried to contradict the widely-held assumption that human behavior was ruled only by self-interest, which was itself controlled by sensory input and memory. Memory and sensation could only account for behavior that was based on what had happened and what was currently going on: what, Hazlitt asked, about behaviors based on concerns for the future? Humans constantly make decisions to steer themselves from fates that they have observed happening to others. Hazlitt proposed that the mind forms empathy for others, even when the "other" is the self as one imagines ending up in the future. The mind acts according to what it thinks the other person's experience must feel like.

Hazlitt's theory of empathy shows up in much of Keats's later work, including "Bright Star!" The speaker of the poem is a human being, and as such has the ability to project himself into the position of the star, to imagine what its existence must be like. It is notable that the poem does not try to give the star any response to all that it sees transpiring beneath it, the waves and the snow and so forth. The inanimate star would of course hold no opinions about such things, but even when he imagines himself witnessing the same sights Keats expresses no reaction, no judgement. His empathy enables him to put himself in the star's place, but this human trait stops there: he is not empathetic as the star. In his imagination he takes the trip from the Earth up into the sky, but once there his imagination stays up there, isolated out in the cold, "in splendor held aloft."

It is evident that the speaker's desire to leave his earthly vantage point and experience vast landscapes is in fact his ideal of a poet who has reached perfection, no longer held down by a self, by any identity that would intrude upon the empathetic experience of seeing what it is like in other people's lives. This is such a lonely view of the artist's life that it almost raises the question for the reader about just why one would want to be a poet, except that Keats answers that by conjuring up wonders from an angle unseen before the Age of Flight, unavailable to the non-artist whose vision is cluttered with his own ego. With just the few simple lines that render the lapping waters and the soft-fallen snow, Keats draws the reader into his vision, making us jealous of the abstracted solitude of the star. It may be isolated from the world that we know, but the consolation of philosophy has always been that knowledge is a greater thrill than human companionship, and in this poem Keats gives us a glimpse from the ultimate position of knowledge: the all-seeing star, the poet. And if superior human knowledge is not enough to trade off against the fear of isolation, there is also the element of moral righteousness that is implied. The star/poet is presented as a quasi-religious figure, an Eremite, and from its unique vantage point is witness to the ocean's baptism of the shore. Intellectual and spiritual fulfillment are offered to fill the hole left within the artist who steps outside of the poetry of humanity to become "the most unpoetical of all God's Creatures."

But that whole case is presented first, in the octet, to upset the readers' preconceptions that humans would be happier in the company of their own and not, like poets, observing from afar. In the sestet, Keats reintroduces the pleasure of human companionship in graphic terms, to show that it is actually as important as distant observation. He gives to his view of humanity the life-filled images of love, breath, and budding breasts, which, both in the poem and in the common adage, bring him back to Earth. It is no coincidence that the rolling waves in the first stanza and the lover's soft breathing in the second resemble one another in their hypnotic

> *The right combination of love and libido changes the question a person is faced with. Life is no longer an issue of whether one should become distant and eternal through art, but rather how to use art's eternal quality in order to make a fleeting moment of life last."*

regularity, for they are both the living pulse of life. The waves, though, are only observed, not truly experienced, while the heaving chest is *felt,* flesh against flesh, and so its influence is difficult for the poem's speaker to ignore or rationalize away. From an imagined distance the speaker can think of himself as enlightened and heavenly enough, but it is plain that once the lover is introduced the cool remoteness that meant so much has a difficult time justifying itself.

And so Keats ends up at the very sharpest point of the artist's eternal dilemma. He is left to decide which is more important to him, being an artist or being a human. In other places, notably his "Ode On a Grecian Urn," Keats has marveled at the artist's power over time, over such simple things as human emotions. This time the "poeticness" of his lover draws him obsessively back toward life. The right combination of love and libido changes the question a person is faced with. Life is no longer an issue of whether one should become distant and eternal through art, but rather how to use art's eternal quality in order to make a fleeting moment of life last. The problem that Keats cannot solve, according "Bright Star," is that art makes a moment eternal by taking it away from life and making it into an artistic piece, and he can only be a successful artist absent from life. He finds no way for eternity and life to exist at the same time.

Hence, death. In the last line of this sonnet he is willing to accept death, even to "swoon to" it, using a word that implies both being dragged against one's will and also being intoxicated with pleasure. This meditation has shown the poem's speaker that living forever with his lover could be done, through the way an artist can freeze the world, but the true lesson of "Bright Star!" is that art is not life. Death, usually considered life's opposite, is more of a part of the process of life than emotional detachment is. It is human nature to struggle against death, and that may lead sometimes to a wish for eternal life, but Keats realizes the implications of what it would mean to stand outside the flow of life and live forever, and in the end this poem brings readers to understand that death could be no worse.

David Kelly, in an essay for *Poetry for Students,* Gale, 2000.

Nicholas Roe

In this excerpt, Roe argues that Keats's sonnet, although written to his beloved, is more than just a love poem. Rather, it contains the author's central themes of beauty and mortality.

… For Wordsworth as for Shelley, the star is a radiant emblem of imagination as the translated expression of political ideals. For Wordsworth and Shelley, too, the star was explicitly associated with Milton's political constancy, the lack of which Shelley "alone deplored" in Wordsworth. I want now to return to Keats, and offer a reading of one of his best-known sonnets that will draw upon the political and literary context that I've been exploring so far:

> Bright star! Would I were steadfast as thou art—
> Not in lone splendour hung aloft the night
> And watching, with eternal lids apart,
> Like nature's patient, sleepless Eremite,
> The moving waters at their priestlike task
> Of pure ablution round earth's human shores
> Or gazing on the new soft-fallen mask
>
> Of snow upon the mountains and the moors;
> No—yet still steadfast, still unchangeable,
> Pillowed upon my fair love's ripening breast,
> To feel for ever its soft fall and swell,
> Still, still to hear her tender-taken breath,
> And so live ever—or else swoon to death.

Keats's "Bright star" sonnet is frequently read as a love poem to Fanny Brawne, alongside other lyrics to her such as "The day is gone"; "To Fanny"; "I cry your mercy, pity, love"; and "Ode to Fanny." But as John Barnard recently pointed out, these "poems [to Fanny Brawne] are painful to read because they are private and desperately confused." "Only the 'Bright star' sonnet," he goes on "is in control of its emotions." That control derives from the imaginative priority of the poem as one more

effort to reconcile Keats's central themes of poetry and mortality; the permanence of art and the transience of life. This ballasts Keats's private feeling for Fanny, and generalizes the poem beyond personal intimacy to address the great presiders of Keats's art: Milton and Wordsworth.

A number of Keats scholars, among them Christopher Ricks, have linked the "Bright star" sonnet with Keats's letter to Fanny of 25 July 1819, particularly Keats's closing words:

> I am distracted with a thousand thoughts. I will imagine you Venus to night and pray, pray, pray to your star like a Hethen.
>
> Your's ever, fair Star, John Keats

However, as John Barnard again points out, in this letter "Fanny is … imagined as the evening star, Venus, and in the sonnet Keats is thinking of the North Star." And indeed, the sonnet does open as a prayer to be "constant as the northern star," but then withdraws from that remote, inhuman changelessness to admit the sensual intimacy of the lovers. Keats's symbolic wish is seemingly that his "Bright star" might simultaneously represent a polar constancy as well as the westering presence of Venus, the lover's evening star. This potential reconciliation takes one back to Keats's letter to Tom in June 1818, where he describes his response on seeing Lake Windermere for the first time. "There are many disfigurements to this Lake," he writes, "—not in the way of land or water. No; the two views we have had of it are of the most noble tenderness—they can never fade away—they make one forget the divisions of life; age, youth, poverty and riches; and refine one's sensual vision into a sort of north star which can never cease to be open lidded and stedfast."

The point here is not that the "Bright star" sonnet echoes the letter word for word, "north star … open lidded … stedfast"; "Bright star … steadfast … eternal lids apart." Keats's letter to Tom describes an imaginative process by which apprehended beauty—or "sensual vision"—is refined into a permanent ideal that Keats likens to the "north star." For Keats such a constancy assuages the mortal "divisions of life." Not only is this the wishful state of Keats's sonnet—"Awake for ever in a sweet unrest"—it is the distinctive ideal of all Keats's greatest poetry: the eternal yearning of lovers in the *Grecian Urn;* the ecstatic ceaseless ceasing of the *Nightingale Ode;* the patient prolonging of the moment in *To Autumn,* such that the season's passing is infinitely delayed, while "by a cyder-press, with patient look, / Thou watchest the last oozings hours by hours." Keats's desire to "re-fine … sensual vision into a sort of north star" is the imaginative pole to which all of these great po-ems move. In the letter to Tom, though, it is an immediate consolation for "the divisions of life" and for what he terms "the many disfigurements to [the] Lake." The source of this "disfigurement" is rather surprising. Keats's letter goes on: "The disfigurement I mean is the miasma of London. I do suppose it contaminated with bucks and sol-diers, and women of fashion—and hat-band igno-rance. The border inhabitants are quite out of keep-ing with the romance about them, from a continual intercourse with London rank and fashion. But why should I grumble? They let me have a prime glass of soda water—O they are as good as their neighbors." Yet this conceited tirade against Lon-don tourists—Keats was one of them himself—is actually a distraction from the focal point of "dis-figurement" Keats has in mind, and which imme-diately follows: "But Lord Wordsworth, instead of being in retirement, has himself and his house full in the thick of fashionable visitors quite convenient to be pointed at all the summer long." Keats's de-sire to resolve the "divisions of life" into perma-nence finds its ultimate cause in Wordsworth's for-saken retirement; his political orthodoxy; his fashionable popularity. And Keats's "north star which can never cease to be open lidded and sted-fast" represents a constancy that finds its deepest significance in Keats's disappointed recoil from a Wordsworthian mutability: "Sad—sad—sad … What can we say?"

Keats's "Bright star" sonnet is a love poem for Fanny Brawne that also draws upon this more dis-tant but enduring disenchantment with Wordsworth. In that "Lord Wordsworth's" orthodoxy was one outcome of Wordsworth's experience of revolu-tionary defeat, Keats's sonnet is a late approach to consolation for that failure and an attempt to com-pensate for the Miltonic task that Wordsworth had set himself in the "Prospectus" to *The Recluse*, and apparently failed to carry through. One can sub-stantiate this larger point by returning to the first poem in Wordsworth's "Sonnets Dedicated to Lib-erty":

Composed by the
Sea-Side, near Calais,
August, 1802

Fair Star of Evening, Splendor of the West,
Star of my Country! on the horizon's brink
Thou hangest, stooping, as might seem, to sink
On England's bosom; yet well pleas'd to rest,
Meanwhile, and be to her a glorious crest

> *In that 'Lord Wordsworth's' orthodoxy was one outcome of Wordsworth's experience of revolutionary defeat, Keats's sonnet is a late approach to consolation for that failure...."*

Conspicuous to the Nations. Thou, I think,
Should'st be my Country's emblem; and should'st wink,
Bright Star! with laughter on her banners, drest
In thy fresh beauty. There! that dusky spot
Beneath thee, it is England; there it lies.
Blessings be on you both! one hope, one lot,
One life, one glory! I, with many a fear
For my dear Country, many heartfelt sighs,
Among Men who do not love her linger here.

This sonnet was written at Calais during Wordsworth's visit in August 1802. It presents the translation of Wordsworth's political allegiance from France to England and—at another level—the shift in his affections from Annette Vallon to his future wife Mary. Hence the "Fair Star of Evening" is Venus, the lover's evening star about to "sink" in its evening splendor "On England's bosom." But as if to rescue the star from a wholly erotic decli-nation and preserve it as a national "emblem" of England, Wordsworth has it "well pleas'd to rest, / Meanwhile," apparently stationary over "[his] Country."

Wordsworth's "Fair Star" is an image of ar-rested incipience calculated to strike Keats, "stoop-ing … yet well pleas'd to rest." It provides a sym-bolic reconciliation of the sonnet's political and personal themes, an ideal poise that Keats believed Wordsworth had failed to sustain. Keats's "Bright star" sonnet retains the star as an emblem of stead-fastness, "watching, with eternal lids apart, / Like nature's patient, sleepless eremite"—but rejects its "lone splendour" in isolation for the erotic fulfill-ment that Wordsworth's sonnet had deferred,

No—yet still steadfast, still unchangeable,
Pillowed by my fair love's ripening breast,
To feel for ever its soft fall and swell,
Awake for ever in a sweet unrest.

For Wordsworth the star was associated with a Miltonic constancy that he had celebrated in *An Evening Walk* in 1794, and sought to emulate in *The Recluse* as projected in the "Prospectus." For Shelley the "lone star" had represented Wordsworth's former dedication to republican ideals, an eminence that he had lost in later years. But Keats's wish for "steadfastness" as a poet is conditional only upon "earth's human shores"; his "Bright star" sonnet admits human vulnerability and redeems it in the tender union of the lovers. In so doing the upheaval of revolution, "the weariness, the fever, and the fret," are resolved by the "sweet unrest" of their lovemaking. And the disappointed idealism of Wordsworth, Shelley, and of Keats himself finds a last, fully human consolation.

Source: Nicholas Roe, " 'Brightest Star, Sweet Unrest': Image and Consolation in Wordsworth, Shelley, and Keats," in *History & Myth: Essays on English Romantic Literature,* edited by Stephen C. Behrendt, Wayne State University Press, 1990, pp. 130–48.

Sources

Barnard, John, *John Keats,* Cambridge University Press, 1987.

Bate, Walter Jackson, *John Keats,* Boston: The Bellknap Press of Harvard University Press, 1963.

Bloom, Harold, *The Visionary Company: A Reading of English Romantic Poetry,* Cornell University Press, 1971.

The Columbia History of British Poetry, edited by Carl Woodring, New York: Columbia University Press, 1994.

Keats, John, *The Complete Poems,* edited by John Barnard, Penguin, 1988.

Perkins, David, *The Quest for Permanence: The Symbolism of Wordsworth, Shelley, and Keats,* Harvard University Press, 1959.

Reeves, James, *A Short History of English Poetry, 1340-1940,* American edition, New York: E.P. Dutton & Co., 1962.

Ward, Aileen, "Between Despair and Energy," in *John Keats,* Octagon Books, 1982, pp. 292-300.

For Further Study

Armstrong, Isabel, *Language as Living Form in Nineteenth Century Poetry,* New Jersey: Barnes and Noble Books, 1982.

This book examines the culture of the ear and discusses many of the literary figures associated with Keats, including Shelly and Wordsworth, but Keats himself is hardly mentioned.

Bernbaum, Ernest, *Guide Through the Romantic Movement,* New York: The Ronald Press Co., 1949.

Bernbaum gives brief biographies of all of the most notable authors associated with Romanticism, including many who are not usually recognized as being with the group.

Bostetter, Edward E., *The Romantic Ventriloquists: Wordsworth, Coleridge, Keats, Shelley and Byron,* Seattle: University of Washington Press, 1963.

Bostetter's chapter on Keats covers all of the major points of his philosophy and technique in an insightful if slightly stiff manner.

Jones, John, *John Keats' Dream of Truth,* New York: Barnes & Noble, Inc., 1969.

In analyzing the scope of Keats's poetry, Jones includes an interesting comparison of the use of the eternal in "Bright Star!" and "Ode on a Grecian Urn."

Sherwin, Paul, "Dying Into Light: Keats' Struggle with Milton in 'Hyperion,' " in *John Keats,* edited with an Introduction by Harold Bloom, New York: Chelsea House Publishers, 1985.

This essay finds "Bright Star!" to be a statement of how Keats's world view differed from that of the poet John Milton.

Eating Poetry

Mark Strand
1968

Mark Strand is one of the most prominent figures in contemporary American poetry, and yet his poems are often considered some of the most elusive. Much of his work encompasses dark themes and macabre scenarios that shift quickly from the physical to the metaphysical, usually placing people and animals in bizarre situations. Why, then, has Strand won numerous awards and fellowships for his poetry, been sought as a teacher, lecturer, and reader at universities across the country and across the world, and been selected Poet Laureate of the United States? The answer lies in how readers *approach* Strand's work, and "Eating Poetry" provides us ample opportunity to delve into it, get caught up in it, and come out knowing we have experienced something unusually intriguing. Strand's second collection, *Reasons for Moving* (1968) contains the poem "Eating Poetry," and this collection earned him national recognition as a poet.

Just the title "Eating Poetry" piques curiosity. The first assumption may be that this is only an interesting metaphor for the notion of really enjoying verse, but Strand does not stop there. This poem features a character *literally* eating poetry. All in the span of 18 lines, a man gobbles up poems in a library, mystifies the librarian, turns into a dog, and terrifies the librarian. This is obviously not a poem we go into looking for a concrete exploration of human experience. It is, however, an abstract and sensuous look at one experience in particular—that of truly and completely fulfilling an attraction, in this case, to poetry. "Eating Poetry" also exemplifies Strand's tendency to taint even light or comical situations with an eerie and gruesome flavor. For this reason, we are often left not quite sure of a poem's overall intent, but we are sure our minds have ventured some place new.

Author Biography

Although Mark Strand was born in Summerside, Prince Edward Island, Canada, in 1934, he moved with his family to the United States at the age of four and spent most of his childhood in New York, Philadelphia, and Cleveland. As a teenager, he lived in Colombia, Peru, and Mexico, most of the traveling due to his father's business in sales. His first education interest was in the visual arts, and he studied painting at Yale after completing his bachelor's degree at Antioch College in Ohio. During this time, he also became interested in writing and turned his attention full time to poetry and short fiction, eventually completing a Master of Fine Arts degree in the writer's workshop at the University of Iowa. Strand never lost his desire to paint and to study art and has published several articles and books on art criticism. He has written nine books of poetry, including the recent 1998 publication of *Blizzard of One,* as well as three illustrated children's books.

Reasons for Moving, containing the poem "Eating Poetry," was Strand's second collection and earned him national recognition as a poet. Published in 1968, this book established Strand's reputation as a writer of poetic "conundrums," or riddles, usually full of incongruous details, sometimes funny, always bizarre. The early work also presented Strand as a poet with dark, foreboding themes, often centered around death or the idea of negation. His popularity derived from an ability to stimulate a reader's intellect with exact language and surreal imagery, and the fact that the allusions, metaphors, and scenes were on the odd or macabre side only fueled interest in the work.

Because so much of Mark Strand's poetry takes place in an unreal world where anything can and does happen, there is little evidence to link it specifically to events in the poet's actual life. While some later pieces have drawn slightly from a more confessional bent, "Eating Poetry" represents the "true" Strand poem. *Reasons for Moving* and the third book, *Darker* (1970), put Strand on the path to prominence in American poetry. Over his career, he has received fellowships from the Ingram Mer-

Mark Strand

rill, Rockefeller, and Guggenheim foundations and from the National Endowment for the Arts; he has been honored with an Edgar Allan Poe Award, a MacArthur Award, the Bobbitt Prize for Poetry, and Yale's Bollingen Prize. Strand has taught at over 15 universities from New York to California to Brazil and currently teaches in the Committee on Social Thought at the University of Chicago.

Poem Text

Ink runs from the corners of my mouth.
There is no happiness like mine.
I have been eating poetry.

The librarian does not believe what she sees.
Her eyes are sad   5
and she walks with her hands in her dress.

The poems are gone.
The light is dim.
The dogs are on the basement stairs and coming
    up.

Their eyeballs roll,   10
their blond legs burn like brush.
The poor librarian begins to stamp her feet and
    weep.

She does not understand.
When I get on my knees and lick her hand,
she screams.   15

I am a new man.
I snarl at her and bark.
I romp with joy in the bookish dark.

Poem Summary

Lines: 1-3

From the outset of "Eating Poetry," the scene is peculiar, and it builds toward an even stranger, extraordinary climax at the end. The first line has us picture a man with ink running from his mouth. Notice that the verb Strand chose is not "drips" or "drizzles" or "seeps," but *runs*. It gives the impression of someone eating very hungrily, "shoveling it in," so to speak. We do not have to wait long to find out if this gluttonous act is painful for the speaker, for in line 2, he tells us, "There is no happiness like mine." Now we know that the ink running from his mouth is comparable to the juice of a thick steak on a beef lover's lips or a refreshing sports drink pouring down the chin of a happy athlete. But what causes such glee for the speaker here is not food or drink. Rather, his reason is: "I have been eating poetry." This line—as all the others—is very simply put, as though a common statement of fact. The *fact* here, though, is anything but common, and as we move through the next lines, the speaker acknowledges such.

Lines: 4-6

Line 4 introduces a second character in the poem, and she appears quite a bit more normal than the narrator. In learning that "The librarian does not believe what she sees," we are drawn back into a fairly realistic world—one in which we may have the same reaction and share the feeling of the person who has just witnessed something bizarre. Lines 5 and 6 depict the librarian's initial response to her unusual patron, portraying her as "sad." Her eyes apparently show sympathy, and by walking "with her hands in her dress," she demonstrates a helplessness to do anything about the situation. Resigning herself to pace with hidden hands also indicates cautious behavior and a desire to protect herself. While there is nothing strange about the librarian's responses at this point, she is still a part of an abnormal scene, and her own behavior will take a turn for the odd side as she becomes more and more caught up in the weird actions of the man who is eating poetry.

Lines: 7-9

The third stanza sends us back into the surreal world of the speaker. In this scene, he has finished devouring whatever pile of books he had in front of him, and states very simply, "The poems are gone." Just as simply, he tells us, "The light is dim," and it may be because the library is closing and someone is turning off the lights or it may refer to evening coming on with its loss of sunlight. Whichever "literal" meaning this line refers to, it also lends figuratively a gloomy, darkening aura to an already eerie setting. In line 9, Strand demonstrates his tendency to introduce further oddities into a poem by suddenly shifting to completely different characters (in this case, dogs) whose presence is incongruous to everything mentioned so far. "The dogs are on the basement stairs and coming up" is a puzzling statement that only evokes questions: What dogs? How does the speaker know the library has a basement? Why are there dogs in it? Why are they coming up? There are no answers offered to these questions, but the animals do become a part of the build-up toward the poem's bizarre ending and a metaphorical link to the speaker himself.

Lines: 10-12

The fourth stanza provides a description of the dogs much in the same way that the second did for the librarian. The dogs, however, are more difficult to grasp for the language is more unlikely, the scene more horrific. "Their eyeballs roll," indicates a sign of madness and portrays a wild or hysterical lack of control. While wild-eyed animals may not be all that far-fetched, line 11 ("their blond legs burn like brush") is unrealistic. But it does serve the purpose of heightened horror and unbelievable occurrence that fuel this poem with a macabre, comedic effect. The poem returns to the librarian in line 12, and she, too, is becoming more hysterical and behaving irrationally in light of the situation. While mad dogs run up the stairs with their legs on fire, the "poor librarian begins to stamp her feet and weep." This response makes the woman seem both childlike and foolish, considering that any "normal" person would most likely be running for the door instead of standing there stamping her feet. The scene, however, is somewhat funny and most certainly surreal, and this is the effect for which Strand is most noted.

Lines: 13-15

Line 13 is an obvious example of understatement. *Of course* the librarian "does not under-

Media Adaptations

- In 1978, Mark Strand recorded a 60-minute cassette containing the poems "From the Long Sad Party" and "Shooting Whales." He is introduced by fellow poet Gregory Orr.

- If you have audio access on the Internet, you can hear Mark Strand read his poem "From the Long Sad Party" on "The Academy of American Poets" website at http://www.poets.org/.

stand," and the speaker admits it. We have the impression, however, that he does not consider her feeling obvious nor that it should go without saying. The simplicity of the sentence underscores his own naivete, and the next line takes us even further into the strange mind of the man who eats poetry. It also renders a startling connection between the dogs and the man. Suddenly, he has become one, or, at least, begun to act like one. The man-dog in line 14 does not appear as ferocious as the animals that were charging up the basement stairs, but, metaphorically, the link between the images works. The man who is now on his knees is docile at this point and merely licks the librarian's hand. Finally, the woman returns to a more likely reaction: "she screams."

Lines: 16-18

The imagery in the final stanza is both ironic and contradictory. We learned in line 14 that the speaker had taken on the characteristics of a dog, but in line 16 he tells us "I am a new man." He immediately follows this statement with more canine allusions: "I snarl at her and bark." Bouncing back and forth between images that are incongruous and offering no ultimate explanation for the confusion is a technique that draws readers to this poet's work instead of driving them away. Strand piques curiosity and teases the intellect in such a way that we are prepared for such odd and delightful lines as the one that ends "Eating Poetry": "I romp with joy in the bookish dark." This line sustains the man-dog metaphor (dogs and people may both romp

with joy) and presents yet another paradoxical scene. The word "bookish" carries a dull, stuffy tone, most often connoting a studious, formal person or place. And in this case, it is "dark" as well. But this rather somber image is butted up against a reference to raucous, carefree play, as the speaker who has been eating poetry finally gives in to the overwhelming pleasure of doing so. We do not know what happens to the librarian nor whether the dogs in the basement are real, and by the end of the poem it doesn't matter much. The man who seems deranged at first has taken the reader from a bizarre beginning through a frightening episode and finally to a gleeful end in which we can celebrate his love of poetry along with him. We are not expected to analyze nor apply logic to the work. It is meant to entice, provoke, puzzle, and delight.

Themes

Realism vs. Surrealism

The most obvious element of Mark Strand's "Eating Poetry"—as well as much of his other work—is the surrealism that bombards and takes over the poem. As a twentieth-century artistic movement, surrealism is an attempt to express what the subconscious mind is thinking and how it works as opposed to the realities that we experience in the conscious mind. One way to grasp the nuances of what is "surreal" is to think about what dreams are like. Consider the fantastic imagery, the weird occurrences that could not happen in real life, and the ease with which they are accepted in the dream itself. We don't often halt the action in a bizarre nightmare to say, "Wait a minute. This isn't realistic." Instead, we simply follow the lead of whatever strange events take place without any idea of the outcome.

The speaker in "Eating Poetry" is caught up in a dreamlike, abstract world, and his behavior, in turn, draws the librarian into the same unreal circumstances. The entire premise of the poem—the idea of digesting so much paper that the ink runs from his mouth—is a surreal one, and, just as in dreams, each character plays a strange role. A brief synopsis of this poem is evidence enough: a man sits in a library eating books, the librarian paces, the lights go out, dogs run up from the basement with their legs on fire, the librarian cries, the man turns into a dog and licks her hand, the librarian screams, the man growls and barks and romps in a very unlikely place—a library. We cannot discern an exact reason that the events unfold in this manner any more than we can come up with a definitive analysis of odd dreams. There may be many theories, but the main point is the disturbing, thought-provoking surreal experience itself. As editor for the Winter 1995-96 issue of *Ploughshares,* Strand said in the introduction in regard to his selection of poems that "I am not concerned with truth, nor with conventional notions of what is beautiful." This sentiment is obvious in his own poems, which are usually neither "truthful" nor beautiful, but which intrigue the imagination and command attention just the same.

Dark Comedy

Sometimes we may become so distracted by the macabre and morbid imagery of a surreal work that we neglect to notice the humor in it. "Eating Poetry" presents such a deranged scenario that most people do not laugh while reading through it. On a second or third read, however, we may find some levity in picturing a fretful librarian keeping an eye on a patron shoving pages of a book into his mouth. We may also laugh at the notion of a grown man leaping and rolling about on the floor like a playful pup who has no regard for rules or protocol. On one level, the poem is actually a *happy* one, a clever metaphor for a true love of poetry. The speaker tells us from the outset that "There is no happiness like mine," and, yet, we don't tend to take his word for it. And this is where the comedy's "darkness" comes in. Although we are told very matter-of-factly that the man is happy and although we might really laugh if we saw someone acting so bizarre in a public place, there is enough of a sense of uneasiness and horrific details to keep this from being a "light" poem. The undercurrent of distress and puzzlement prevents it from being truly funny, but there is still an undeniable jocular element in the work. Strand surely had his own poetry in mind when he commented in the *Ploughshares* introduction that "Sense, so long as it's not too familiar, is a pleasure, but so is nonsense when shrewdly exploited." "Eating Poetry" is a good example of nonsense, but it also demonstrates a clever manipulation of the folly into a delightful exercise for the mind.

Simple Language

The language a poet uses may not always be "thematic" by itself, but often a recurring style or word selection can present a certain motif. In "Eating Poetry," the language is simple and precise, written (or spoken) in a very brief, controlled manner. What makes this especially interesting in Strand's poetry is that the simple language is juxtaposed against a complex, easily misinterpreted background of abnormal events. He describes these wild, uncanny circumstances with the conventional monotony of a recipe. And, yet, the poem is far from monotonous. The use of unpretentious words actually adds tension and absurdity to an already surreal situation. To state calmly such lines as, "I have been eating poetry," "The poems are gone," "I am a new man," and "I snarl at her and bark" makes their meanings more eerie than if they were screamed or shouted as though by a madman. The speaker does not "sound" mad, but his actions tell a different story.

Topics for Further Study

- Explain your opinion on whether a poem with surrealistic imagery is more interesting or less interesting to read than a one with conventional images and scenarios.

- Write about a scene you have witnessed or an experience you have had that was bizarre and seemed both real and unreal at the same time.

- Explain some of the similarities and differences between surrealist writing and surrealist art, using examples from both genres to support your points.

- If you saw a man sitting in a library shoving pages from a book into his mouth, what would your reaction be and how do you think other people around him would react? In answering, consider such particulars as social expectations and current laws.

Style

On the page, "Eating Poetry" appears very structured and uniform. It consists of six stanzas, each containing three lines. One line in each stanza (with the exception of the second) is obviously much lengthier than the other two, and most of the "lines" are simple, declarative sentences with a subject, verb, and period at the end. While it is common for poets to resort to illustrative language and use "flowery" words strung together in only pieces of thoughts and cryptic phrases, Strand typically does not employ such techniques. Read each line of "Eating Poetry" by itself, out of context, and it makes perfect sense. The *meaning* of the statement "Ink runs from the corners of my mouth" may be far-reaching or very odd, but we know exactly what the sentence tells us—and we can picture it. The same may be said for the description of the librarian, the dimness of the room, dogs running up the stairs, and even a man on his knees licking a woman's hand. It is only when we put all these lines together to form a poem that they suddenly become peculiar and difficult to understand.

There is only *one* simile in this poem: "their blond legs burn like brush." Most eighteen-line poems (as well as much shorter ones) contain several figures of speech, and the simile, or the comparison of two items typically using the word "like," is a very common one. But in Strand's "Eating Poetry," poetic devices are nearly nonexistent. There are two exact rhymes (understand/hand and bark/dark) and little alliteration. What like-sounds do exist are not all that obvious and seem to occur by happenstance: mouth/mine, sees/sad, dim/dogs, and so forth. Line 11 is the most poetically "devised" line in the poem, as it contains not only the one simile, but also the alliteration of three "b" words: blond/burn/brush.

As we can see, a discussion of Strand's poetic style usually involves talking about what is *not* there. He is a poet noted for an ability to turn everyday language and simple sentence structure into captivating verse, and his poems often leave readers puzzled even though we seem to have understood every word we read. That alone speaks for Strand's uniqueness as a contemporary poet.

Historical Context

Strand wrote "Eating Poetry" sometime during the mid- to late-1960s and published it in his 1968 collection *Reasons for Moving.* The setting for this poem is indeterminate, for we know only that the narrative takes place in a library, but we don't know in what city, state, or country, and there is no time period mentioned. Strand spent 1965 and 1966 as a Fulbright lecturer in Rio de Janeiro and returned to the United States afterwards to teach at Mount Holyoke College in Massachusetts in 1967. These two positions may not have had any bearing on the poems in *Reasons for Moving,* but the significance may lie in the amount of traveling the poet had already done and in his continuing to move about throughout his career.

The lack of a permanent or semi-permanent home during childhood and adolescence possibly contributed to Strand's tendency to write poems with "neutral" settings. There is no indication that his early life presented personal hardships, but frequent moving could have played a role in his frequent writing about absence and movement. One of his most well-known poems, "Keeping Things Whole," contains the lines "Wherever I am / I am what is missing" and "We all have reasons / for moving. / I move / to keep things whole." And, of course, he selected words from this poem to be the title of the entire collection.

Not much has been written about Strand's personal life nor his responses to the turbulent world of the 1960s. His poems at the time did not reflect the war in Vietnam, social and political movements, the drug culture, or environmental issues. When Bill Thomas interviewed him in 1991 for *Los Angeles Times Magazine,* Strand's comment on being a popular poet during that restless time period was, "Groupies were a big part of the scene. Poets were underground pop stars, and when we made the campus circuit, girls would flock around. It wasn't bad. I rather liked the uncertainties of my life then."

Strand's flippancy here should not be taken to mean that he was oblivious to or unconcerned about the turmoil that was happening throughout the United States and across the world during the 1960s. Although he often gave amusing or wry answers to interview questions, his poetry makes apparent a much more serious, even darker outlook. Perhaps the most revealing statement in Strand's response is his comment about liking the "uncertainties" of his life at the time. He was not alone in his feeling, of course, for there was much uncertainty not only in individuals but in institutions, political systems, and society in general. Mentioning specific locations or limiting a creative work to a particular time and place seems ineffectual for many of Strand's poems, and especially one such as "Eating Poetry." The bizarre nature of the scene itself would override the fact that it takes place in New York or Iowa or Hong Kong. The lack of set-

Compare & Contrast

- **1961:** American psychologist B. F. Skinner published his highly acclaimed book *Walden Two.* In it, Skinner advanced the theory of "behaviorism," which rejects the unobservable and the unconscious in favor of actual responses to actual events.

- **1966:** French writer and so-called founder of surrealism Andre Breton died at the age of 70. Breton wrote three manifestos on surrealism and opened a studio for "surrealistic research."

- **1989:** Spanish painter Salvador Dali died at the age of 85. Dali was a leader in surrealist visual art, using a precise style that enhanced the dreamlike effect of his work.

- **1990:** President George Bush and the 101st Congress declared the 1990s to be the "Decade of the Brain." Throughout the decade, scientific information and research about the brain has amassed at an enormous rate, thanks mostly to technological advances in computer imaging and brain mapping.

---

ting identity actually lends itself to the oddness and mystery of the poem. It says this macabre scene could happen in any place at any time.

Critical Overview

From the beginning, Mark Strand's work caught the attention and won the praise of critics and readers of poetry in general. His distinct style and odd subject matter were the major draw. The first two books, *Sleeping With One Eye Open* and *Reasons for Moving,* established his reputation as a poet caught up in morbidity and death, as well as self-absorption most often expressed through dreamlike events. That he was able to write clear, concise, brief poems that opened up a very complex world of distortions for the reader was a credit to his talent as a poet. Critic David Kirby, in his *Mark Strand and the Poet's Place in Contemporary Culture,* states that, "Many poems in Strand's first book show an uneasy preoccupation with the self, and the vehicle used to express that preoccupation is often a dream state in which the speaker is divided between two worlds and can locate himself comfortably in neither."

In Richard Howard's *Alone with America: Essays on the Art of Poetry in the United States Since 1950,* the critic comments that *Reasons for Mov-*

ing is "two dozen poems in which [Strand] not only raises his voice but rouses his vision with it, so that we do not again forget what we have seen, what we have heard." Addressing "Eating Poetry" in particular, Howard claims that "The poems Strand is eating are those of his first book, and the diet affords him a distinct playfulness, a grotesquerie unthinkable in the old forebodings."

Regardless of the specific interpretations and broad assumptions that critics have made and continue to make about Mark Strand's poetry, nearly all agree that its uniqueness is both stimulating and refreshing. His work is still well-received, and his latest collection entitled *Blizzard of One* elicited this anonymous online comment: [it is] "an extraordinary book—the summation of the work of a lifetime by one of our very few true masters of the art of poetry."

Criticism

Jonathan N. Barron

Jonathan N. Barron is associate professor of English at the University of Southern Mississippi. He has co-edited Jewish American Poetry *(forthcoming from University Press of New England),* Robert Frost at the Millennium *(forthcoming from*

What Do I Read Next?

- *Surrealist Women: An International Anthology* is a wide-ranging and delightful collection of essays compiled by editor Penelope Rosemont and published in 1998. The writers explore such diverse topics as racism in the 1930s, French poetry, and the tale of "The Golden Goose," all with a surrealistic twist.

- The question is whether creativity is a therapeutic, culturally enriching pursuit or only an outpouring of a dark unconscious full of dangerous, neurotic thoughts. An answer is offered by Kevin Brophy in *Creativity: Psychoanalysis, Surrealism and Creative Writing* (1999). Brophy uses theory, history, autobiography, and fiction to make his intriguing point.

- Little publicized in America, the poets and writers in *Another Republic: 17 European and South American Writers* provide a wonderful overview of international poetry that many Americans do not otherwise have the opportunity to read. This 1985 collection is edited by Mark Strand and Charles Simic.

- Whether you are already experienced in dream interpretation or haven't given it much thought, Anthony Shafton's *Dream Reader: Contemporary Approaches to the Understanding of Dreams* (1995) offers an interesting, intelligent, and accessible overview of the field of dream studies. This book is not a far-out, New Age diatribe, but a thoughtful and serious look at a some very odd phenomena.

- Psychiatrist J. Allan Hobson takes an unusual look at the human mind, using illustrative stories from his own life and the lives of his patients in *Dreaming as Delirium: How the Brain Goes Out of Its Mind,* published in 1999. Among other controversial theories, Hobson argues that there is a close similarity between the brain's chemical characteristics during the states of dreaming and psychosis.

University of Missouri Press), as well as a forthcoming collection of essays on the poetic movement, New Formalism. Beginning in 2001, he will be the editor-in-chief of The Robert Frost Review. *In the following essay, Barron examines "Eating Poetry" in relation to Surrealism and Deep Image poetry, and compares the eating of poetry to Communion.*

In his *Biographia Literaria* (1817), the great English Romantic poet, Samuel Taylor Coleridge famously distinguished between two mental faculties, "fancy" and "imagination." According to Coleridge, fancy is a rather mundane, even boring mental exercise where one thinks about things that do not exist. In other words, the fancy is not the mental faculty that allows us to conjure for supernatural things. The imagination, by contrast, is, according to Coleridge, "the living Power and prime Agent of all human Perception … It dissolves, diffuses, dissipates, in order to recreate." In other words, the imagination allows us to dream and envision the impossible, the wonderful, the bizarre. To make the distinction between fancy and imagination even more clear, Coleridge says that if fancy never allows us to think of anything unusual, the imagination insists that we only think of impossible, unusual things. As an example of what he means by "imagination" Coleridge says that Fancy is "the drapery" and "imagination the soul." To him, then, the essence of human creative endeavor is located in the imagination and its ability to link seemingly impossible things together: "sameness, with difference; … the general, with the concrete; the idea, with the image."

A little more than a hundred years later, in 1924, the French poet, Andre Breton, launched a poetic movement, "surrealism," that, through the use of Sigmund Freud's new discoveries in psychology, took Coleridge's idea of "the imagination" to even higher levels of bizarre and strange associations and conjunctions. Breton wrote: "Beloved imagination, what I most like in you is your unsparing quality." What he meant was that the imagination "knows no bounds" and so, in surrealism, he meant to free the imagination in order to allow for an ever more rich, more provocative literature. He defined surrealism as verbal or written expression made "in the absence of any control exercised by reason, exempt from any aesthetic or moral concern." In this way, Breton meant to challenge, combat, and stop the influence of realistic, straightforward literature. "I loathe it," said Breton about "the realistic attitude. "It is made up of mediocrity, hate, and dull conceit." That way of thinking, what Coleridge called the fancy, said Breton, is "a dog's life." In order not to be a dog, then, one must adopt the surrealist principle of a liberated imagination and tap into one's deepest unconscious, subconscious truth.

In the United States, it was not until the early 1960s that significant numbers of fine poets began to turn to such surrealistic ideas. In the 1960s in the books of such notable American poets as Robert Bly, James Wright, Galway Kinnell, W. S. Merwin, Louis Simpson, and Mark Strand one finds an abundance of surreal imagery the like of which had never before been included in such quantity and quality in America. In part, Robert Bly deserves a great deal of credit for this new interest in the power of surreal imagery. In the early 1960s, he wrote a powerful and influential essay, "A Wrong Turning in American Poetry." There, he attacks the great Modernist poets of the preceding generation for ignoring the "imagination" in favor of mere "fancy." In that essay, he calls for a renewed attention to the South American and Spanish poetic traditions which had been, in the 1930s, almost entirely overtaken by surrealism. What Bly most objected to in English poetry was its lack of imagination, its lack of what Coleridge called soul. Said Bly of such poetry, "it is first of all a poetry without a spiritual life." More troubling, however, was the fact that "the poetry we have had in this country is a poetry without even a trace of revolutionary feeling." For Bly the trouble with American poetry was that it "has been a poetry essentially without the unconscious," the very thing Breton had insisted enter European poetry. Eventually, Bly's demand that American poets make use of surreal imagery in their work led to a full-blown poetic movement, "deep image poetry." The poets associated with this movement include Mark Strand, and their work was notable particularly because it claimed to reveal, through the use of bizarre, unusual imaginative imagery, the depths of spirituality and religious feeling latent in the human soul. Deep image poetry was as a result of this group of poets' reading in their surrealist predecessors a spirituality that was also deeply anti-materialistic. Deep image poetry, however, often refused to traffic in the more frightening, even sinister themes surrealism opened up for poetry. In surrealism, for example, one finds a slight edge—a dark and sinister quality, a belief that an animalistic unrestrained power exists deep in every individual.

Of all the deep image poets, then, Mark Strand mined the surrealists dark and sinister vein the

> *From the fourth stanza to the conclusion of the poem, then, we enter the Coleridgean terrain of the imagination through the bizarre imagery of Surrealism. The poem, in other words, becomes decidedly outlandish."*

most. In Strand's witty and terrifying "Eating Poetry" (1968) one gets a wonderful sense of the disturbing and even beast-like energy released by a surrealist approach to the deep image. For the deep image here, the surprising, imaginative, strange image that becomes the focus of the poem is a dog, or, more accurately, a man who becomes a dog. As if turning the tables on Breton's own dismissal of dogs as totally unimaginative, Strand, in this poem, becomes a dog and in so doing creates a deep image for a wild, even revolutionary masculine energy.

"Eating Poetry" was published in Strand's second book, *Reasons for Moving* (Atheneum 1968), a book notably dark and violent. The poems of that book, however, and especially this poem invoke such imagery in order to make a case for the violent, transformative emotional power of poetry itself. In the late 1960s, this was an especially important message to make, and it was a continuation of the point Bly had made in his famous essay. The late 1960s, after all, were a time of great social unrest, of violence associated both with the African-American struggle for Civil Rights and with opposition to the war in Vietnam. In "Eating Poetry," which was published in perhaps the most violent year in the domestic history of the United States after World War II, Strand charts the dangerous power imaginative poetry can have on those who, metaphorically speaking, "eat" it.

The poem's scene, while strange, is easily summarized. In a library, a female librarian is confronted with someone who insists on eating the poetry contained there. Not only does the narrator eat the poetry but he also is joined by a pack of dogs.

> *Poetry is not ordinary stuff, and it changes its readers into 'new men' and new women. In order to transform, however, poetry's readers must realize that poems are not meant to be read. They are meant to be eaten, and eaten with gusto."*

In 18 lines, the poem, written in the first person as if spoken by the poetry eater, charts the terror felt by the librarian. It also records the transformative joy felt by the eater, a joy released in part by the fear of the librarian.

Examining the details of the opening lines one realizes that the eating, in an odd way, could easily refer to the sacred eating ceremony of communion in Christianity. In other words, poetry, in Strand's poem, becomes the sacred body, the wafer of Being, the essence of all that is holy. After all, both the Deep Image poets and the Surrealists argued that poetry was a shamanistic, supernatural art. To eat it, then, would be to participate in a spiritual renewal that might very well overthrow the mundane boring world of routines, fixed ideas, of what Coleridge labeled "the fancy," and what Breton called "realism."

In a weird (or, surreal) version of the communion ritual wafer and wine in Strand's poem are now paper and ink: the material body of a printed poem. With this allusion to Communion in mind look again at the language of the first stanza:

Ink runs from the corners of my mouth.
There is no happiness like mine.

I have been eating poetry.

While these lines do not yet include any explicit terror, or fear their aggressive tone, and the violence of the eating—a kind of ravenous attack—does stand in striking contrast to the happiness, love, and peace one finds in so much other Deep Image poetry of the time. Also, one cannot help but

notice that, in the violence of such eating, this speaker is happy. In this communion, a kind of savage beast is born. In the Surrealism of Breton, the awakening of the beast within, the liberation of the inner animal, was often a goal for poetry. Here, in Strand's poem, one sees that aspect of Surrealism dramatized.

The animalistic energy is depicted in contrast to the other principal character in the poem, the librarian. In the second stanza, we meet her and she is depicted as a conventional, institutional type—a stereotypical librarian. These first two stanzas, then, establish a symbolic story where the man who feeds on poetry grows wild with rebellion against the conformist rules of a book-controlling culture. The man, liberated through poetry, can now rebel and find the true source of his individuality. No one else, no librarian, will any longer control his access to information about his own life—the very stuff of poetry.

In fact, the pack of running beasts are let loose only after the opposition is established. The dogs, in other words, run up the stairs and are set free only after the man eats his poetry:

The poems are gone.
The light is dim.

The dogs are on the basement stairs and coming
    up.

So far, however, as odd as the speaker's behavior has been, it is not necessarily Surreal in that it is not necessarily impossible in the way that imaginative Surreal images are often impossible. Nothing here defies the laws of physics for example. The poem, so far, merely contrasts a man with a woman and introduces a pack of dogs.

In the fourth stanza, however, the speaker becomes a dog. As both Surrealism and Deep Image poetry would have us read, the speaker here literally becomes a dog; he does not merely act doglike. From the fourth stanza to the conclusion of the poem, then, we enter the Coleridgean terrain of the imagination through the bizarre imagery of Surrealism. The poem, in other words, becomes decidedly outlandish.

As the stanza develops, the intensity, fear, and even horror of the scene builds. First, the dogs are described as they enter the room. Then, we are told that "the poor librarian begins to stamp her feet and weep." This scene exaggerates the contrast between the savage instinctive truth of poetry and the decorum and safety of cultural institutions. Faced with such wildness, we are told, the librarian "does not understand." Just when reason is destroyed, just when it is impossible any longer to understand, the poem's most incredible moment occurs: "When I get on my knees and lick her hand, / she screams." It is one thing for a pack of running dogs to invade the library and quite another for this man, himself, to become one of those dogs.

In the final three lines of the poem, Strand celebrates the liberated masculine energy that eating poetry has set free:

> I am a new man.
> I snarl at her and bark.
> I romp with joy in the bookish dark.

These lines encourage a reading of genuine surreal, dreamlike transformation. The man who ate the poems here becomes a dog "romping," "snarling," and "barking." The bookish dark, the silent home of a culture of repressive rules, has now been successfully overcome. The strange communion that began this poem, the eating of the poetry, has now allowed for this incredible transformation, for the liberation of the animal within, to occur. The speaker is, by the end, a new man, a dog.

At this point, it might well strike most readers that an implicit sexism pervades the imagery of this poem. Repressive institutional culture is depicted as a female librarian while the wild freedom of art is depicted in terms of men and male animals. It may well be that this is the fundamental premise and assumption behind the poem. On the other hand, the tone of this poem is so arch that it is equally possible to read it as a mockery, a send up, of the very sexism so common to those who argued on behalf of the animal within—which usually meant liberating the male to further oppress women. In other words, one can easily read this poem with an ironic smile as a satire on an implicit sexism latent in the seemingly more gentle deep image poets.

However one chooses to read the politics of this poem's imagery, however, one cannot help but admire that imagery's force, and the claims it makes on behalf of the transformative power of poetry.

Source: Jonathan N. Barron, in an essay for *Poetry for Students,* Gale, 2000.

Aviya Kushner

Aviya Kushner is the Contributing Editor in Poetry at BarnesandNoble.com *and the Poetry Editor of* Neworld Magazine. *She is a graduate of the acclaimed creative writing program in poetry at Boston University, where she received the Fitzger-*ald Award in Translation. *Her writing on poetry has appeared in* Harvard Review *and* The Boston Phoenix, *and she has served as Poetry Coordinator for* AGNI Magazine. *She has given readings of her own work throughout the United States, and she teaches at Massachusetts Communications College in Boston. In the following essay, Kushner discusses the sensory qualities of the poem.*

Pulitzer Prize-winning poet Mark Strand is known for both his love of language and his love of food. An outstanding cook and a colorful conversationalist, he often uses culinary references in his attempts to explain the uncontrollable urge to write and perfect a poem. Food, like language, has texture, color, and weight. In fact, for Strand, poetry—like food—is a basic need.

Strand likes to say that poets "eat poetry, not meat loaf." He is a voracious reader of poetry in several languages, and is known to encourage his students to read widely and incessantly. He began to explore the idea of poems as almost physical sustenance in the fantastical poem "Eating Poetry," written in 1968 and included in his very first book. Throughout the poem, the speaker flips between mentions of food and mentioned of words. Beginning with the title, the speaker uses verbs associated with meals to describe his joy in reading and in fact, devouring poetry.

The opening line—"Ink runs from the corners of my mouth" —blurs the border between reading and eating. The first line also sets up a surreal, dream-like mood, which Strand employs in many poems. An avid reader and translator of South American poets who write about unlikely, outlandish, and absurd possibilities, Strand thrives on bringing the very strange into English. He has lived in Brazil and Italy, and he incorporates those literatures' focus on dreams and elaborate fantasy to his own writing.

Strand began his career as a painter, and earned an MFA from Yale's School of Art. He's also written extensively about art, especially on the mystery-laden paintings of the American artist Edward Hopper. Even in his taste in painting, Strand is drawn to the possibility of a surreal occurrence, a sudden drift into a dream.

Of course, dream sequences and riffs into fantasy can be a bit confusing for the reader. The first line here is a bit puzzling, but that is part of the dream set-up. The poem wants the reader to ask questions. Has the speaker eaten ink? Has he eaten a pen? Is he deranged?

These questions create mystery, and make the reader want to read on. The questions propel the poem, and the unanswered functions like gasoline, moving things along. The speaker only reveals a bit of what is going on, trying to hold on to as much suspense as possible:

There is no happiness like mine.
I have been eating poetry.

"There is no happiness" signals that this is a unique experience, and a very joyous one. Whether it is actual or imagined is unclear. But the ink running down the mouth is the remnant of the eaten poems. There is physical evidence of the happiness. Of course, as the reader reads this particular poem, he is also "eating poetry." And so, the experience is mutual—the speaker is letting the reader share in the joy.

What's more, this is a forbidden joy, since these poems belong in the library. The librarian is in shock, and "she does not believe what she sees." Unlike the speaker, elated from his meal of words, the librarian is sad. She walks "with her hands in her dress," an allusion to her loneliness—the loneliness of those who do not have poems.

The next stanza presents another turn:

The poems are gone.
The light is dim.
The dogs are on the basement stairs and coming
      up.

Suddenly, the poems have disappeared. This is another standard Strand feature—removing the subject. Strand is a poet who likes to think about absence, whether of other people or objects, or of himself. He has written long poems about loved ones who have died and the space they have left in his lives. Very early on, in "Keeping Things Whole," also written in 1968, he wrote:

Wherever I am I am what is missing.

Here, the jolting absence coupled with "the light is dim" weaves the dream possibility again. Maybe the ink is not real, maybe the dogs are imagined, and the librarian just a made-up character.

In the next line, there's an even bigger leap toward strangeness. In this library where poems are eaten and a sad librarian stares in disbelief, dogs appear, and they rush up the stairs. The librarian is at a complete loss as the dogs get closer:

Their eyeballs roll,
Their blond legs burn like brush.
The poor librarian begins to stomp her feet and
      weep.

The dream may be turning to nightmare, since "their eyeballs roll" and "their blond legs burn like brush" do not indicate the friendliest of dogs. The librarian, now referred to as "the poor librarian," is besides herself. She stomps her feet and weeps.

In this stanza, Strand lets sound propel the action "Blond legs burn with brush" uses the alliteration of the repeated "b"s to create a menacing sound which blusters forward. In the next line, the words "feet" and "weep" use assonance to emphasize the passage.

What is going on here? The librarian doesn't have a clue, and her bafflement may mirror the reader's. "She does not understand," the speaker says, and he proceeds to try and make her understand by touching her.

The speaker "gets on his knees and licks her hand," perhaps imitating the dog. She screams. But this speaker is not a dog. Instead, he states rather clearly in the last stanza:

I am a new man.
I snarl at her and bark.
I romp with joy in the bookish dark.

The speaker states that he is a new man, and the seventeen one-syllable words in a row add crisp authority to his claim. But is he really a new man? The next line explains how this "new man" acts:

I snarl at her and bark.
I romp with joy in the bookish dark.

"Snarl" and "bark" again use sound to create power, and the final "dark" capitalizes on this repetition. The snarling, barking man has something in common with the crazed dogs. He "romps with joy," returning to the earlier statement that "there is no happiness like mine."

The final description of the scene—"bookish dark"—brings everything together. This is a special kind of darkness, a new kind of dim space. It is the odd and promising darkness of books, the possibility presented by poems and the words in them. Those words can create eyeball-rolling dogs, and a romping snarling man out of a reader in some musty stacks. Poetry is not ordinary stuff, and it changes its readers into "new men" and new women. In order to transform, however, poetry's readers must realize that poems are not meant to be read. They are meant to be eaten, and eaten with gusto.

Source: Aviya Kushner, in an essay for *Poetry for Students,* Gale, 2000.

Sources

Amazon Books, http://www.amazon.com, accessed December 28, 1999.

Bly, Robert, "A Wrong Turning in American Poetry," in *American Poetry: Wildness and Domesticity,* New York: Harper and Row, 1990, pp. 7-35.

Breton, Andre, "Surrealist Manifesto" (1924), in *Manifestoes of Surrealism,* translated by Richard Seaver and Helen R. Lane, Ann Arbor: University of Michigan Press, 1969, pp. 1-48.

Coleridge, Samuel Taylor, *Biographia Literaria* (1817), edited by J. Shawcross, Vols. 1 and 2, London: Oxford University Press, 1907, vol. 1, pp. 202; vol. 2, pp. 12,13.

The History Channel, http://www.historychannel.com/, accessed December 27, 1999.

Howard, Richard, *Alone with America: Essays on the Art of Poetry in the United States Since 1950,* enlarged edition, New York: Atheneum, 1980, pp. 589-602.

Kirby, David, *Mark Strand and the Poet's Place in Contemporary Culture,* Columbia, MO: University of Missouri Press, 1990.

"Mark Strand: Blizzard of One," in Poetry Daily, http://www.poems.com/bliz2str.htm, accessed December 13, 1999.

Strand, Mark, introduction to *Ploughshares,* Winter, 1995-96.

———, *Reasons for Moving,* New York: Atheneum, 1968.

Thomas, Bill, Interview with Mark Strand, *Los Angeles Times Magazine,* January 13, 1991, p. 14.

For Further Study

Dali, Salvador and Haim Finkelstein, eds., *The Collected Writings of Salvador Dali,* London: Cambridge University Press, 1999.

> While Salvador Dali is remembered mostly for his surrealist painting, he was also a prolific writer. The essays in this book fall into the surrealist category as well (one review calls them "weird, wonderful, and poetic") and help us to understand the connection between dreamlike painting and dreamlike prose.

Strand, Mark, *Blizzard of One,* New York: Alfred A. Knopf, 1998.

> Strand's most recent collection continues to display his ability to provoke and amaze with short poems and everyday language. Many of the poems in this book relay a sense of happenstance in much of our lives—that most things just come and go regardless of our striving.

———, *Hopper,* Hopewell, New Jersey: Ecco Press, 1994.

> Strand's interest in painting continued even after he turned his career attention to poetry. In this book about the artist Edward Hopper, Strand explores the geometry of his paintings, showing how Hopper used negative space to elicit emotion much the same way Strand uses it in his poetry.

Elegy Written in a Country Churchyard

Thomas Gray
1751

Thomas Gray's "Elegy Written in a Country Churchyard" was first published in 1751. Gray may, however, have begun writing the poem in 1742, shortly after the death of his close friend Richard West. An elegy is a poem which laments the dead. Gray's "Elegy Written in a Country Churchyard" is noteworthy in that it mourns the death not of great or famous people, but of common men. The speaker of this poem sees a country churchyard at sunset, which impels him to meditate on the nature of human mortality. The poem invokes the classical idea of *memento mori,* a Latin phrase which states plainly to all mankind, "Remember that you must die." The speaker considers the fact that in death, there is no difference between great and common people. He goes on to wonder if among the lowly people buried in the churchyard there had been any natural poets or politicians whose talent had simply never been discovered or nurtured. This thought leads him to praise the dead for the honest, simple lives that they lived.

Gray did not produce a great deal of poetry; the "Elegy Written in a Country Churchyard," however, has earned him a respected and deserved place in literary history. The poem was written at the end of the Augustan Age and at the beginning of the Romantic period, and the poem has characteristics associated with both literary periods. On the one hand, it has the ordered, balanced phrasing and rational sentiments of Neoclassical poetry. On the other hand, it tends toward the emotionalism and individualism of the Romantic poets; most importantly, it idealizes and elevates the common man.

Author Biography

Born in the Cornhill district of London in 1716, Gray was the son of Dorothy Antrobus Gray, a milliner, and Philip Gray, a scrivener. Gray's father was a mentally disturbed and violent man who at times abused his wife. Gray attended Eton School from 1725 until 1734, when he entered Cambridge University. He left Cambridge in 1738 without taking a degree, intending to study law in London. However, he and childhood friend Horace Walpole embarked on an extended tour of Europe. The two separated in Italy in 1741 after a quarrel, and Gray continued the journey on his own. He returned to London later in the year, shortly before his father died. Gray then moved with his mother to Stoke Poges, Buckinhamshire, and began his most productive period of poetic composition. In 1742 Grey wrote his first major poem, "Ode on the Spring," which he sent to his close friend Richard West—unknowingly on the very day of West's death from tuberculosis. In the next three months Gray wrote "Ode on a Distant Prospect of Eton College," "Hymn to Adversity," and "Sonnet on the Death of Mr. Richard West." It is believed that he also worked on "Elegy Written in a Country Churchyard" during this time, though this poem was not published until 1751. Gray returned to Cambridge at the end of 1742 and received a Bachelor of Civil Law degree the next year. Gray lived at the university for most of the rest of his life, but he never took part in tutoring, lecturing, or other academic duties; instead he pursued his studies and writing, taking advantage of the intellectual stimulation of the setting. In 1757 Gray was offered the position of Poet Laureate, but he declined it. He moved to London in 1759 to study at the British Museum and remained there for two years. He read widely and earned a reputation as one of the most learned men in Europe. Except for regular trips back to London and elsewhere in England, Gray stayed in Cambridge from 1761 until the end of his life. In 1768 Gray was named Regius Professor of Modern History at Cambridge, an office he held until his death in 1771.

Thomas Gray

Poem Text

The Curfew tolls the knell of parting day,
    The lowing herd wind slowly o'er the lea,
The plowman homeward plods his weary way,
    And leaves the world to darkness and to me.

Now fades the glimmering landscape on the sight,   5
    And all the air a solemn stillness holds,
Save where the beetle wheels his droning flight,
    And drowsy tinklings lull the distant folds;

Save that from yonder ivy-mantled tower
    The moping owl does to the moon complain   10
Of such, as wandering near her secret bower,
    Molest her ancient solitary reign.

Beneath those rugged elms, that yew-tree's shade,
    Where heaves the turf in many a mouldering
      heap,
Each in his narrow cell for ever laid,   15
    The rude Forefathers of the hamlet sleep.

The breezy call of incense-breathing Morn,
    The swallow twittering from the straw-built
      shed,
The cock's shrill clarion, or the echoing horn,
    No more shall rouse them from their lowly bed.   20

For them no more the blazing hearth shall burn,
    Or busy housewife ply her evening care:
No children run to lisp their sire's return,
    Or climb his knees the envied kiss to share.

                      25
Oft did the harvest to their sickle yield,
    Their furrow oft the stubborn glebe has broke;
How jocund did they drive their team afield!
    How bowed the woods beneath their sturdy
      stroke!

Let not Ambition mock their useful toil,
    Their homely joys, and destiny obscure;   30
Nor Grandeur hear with a disdainful smile
    The short and simple annals of the poor.

The boast of heraldry, the pomp of power,
  And all that beauty, all that wealth e'er gave,
Awaits alike the inevitable hour.   35
  The paths of glory lead but to the grave.

Nor you, ye Proud, impute to These the fault,
  If Memory o'er their Tomb no Trophies raise,
Where through the long-drawn aisle and fretted
    vault
  The pealing anthem swells the note of praise.   40

Can storied urn or animated bust
  Back to its mansion call the fleeting breath?
Can Honor's voice provoke the silent dust,
  Or Flattery sooth the dull cold ear of Death?

Perhaps in this neglected spot is laid   45
  Some heart once pregnant with celestial fire;
Hands, that the rod of empire might have swayed,
  Or waked to ecstasy the living lyre.

But Knowledge to their eyes her ample page
  Rich with the spoils of time did ne'er unroll;   50
Chill Penury repressed their noble rage,
  And froze the genial current of the soul.

Full many a gem of purest ray serene,
  The dark unfathomed caves of ocean bear:
Full many a flower is born to blush unseen,   55
  And waste its sweetness on the desert air.

Some village-Hampden, that with dauntless breast
  The little Tyrant of his fields withstood;
Some mute inglorious Milton here may rest,
  Some Cromwell guiltless of his country's   60
    blood.

The applause of listening senates to command,
  The threats of pain and ruin to despise,
To scatter plenty o'er a smiling land,
  And read their history in a nation's eyes,

Their lot forbade: nor circumscribed alone   65
  Their growing virtues, but their crimes
    confin'd;
Forbade to wade through slaughter to a throne,
  And shut the gates of mercy on mankind,

The struggling pangs of conscious truth to hide,
  To quench the blushes of ingenuous shame,   70
Or heap the shrine of Luxury and Pride
  With incense kindled at the Muse's flame.

Far from the madding crowd's ignoble strife,
  Their sober wishes never learned to stray;
Along the cool sequestered vale of life   75
  They kept the noiseless tenor of their way.

Yet even these bones from insult to protect,
  Some frail memorial still erected nigh,
With uncouth rhymes and shapeless sculpture
    decked,
  Implores the passing tribute of a sigh.   80

Their name, their years, spelt by the unlettered
    muse,
  The place of fame and elegy supply:
And many a holy text around she strews,
  That teach the rustic moralist to die.
                                                     85

For who to dumb Forgetfulness a prey,
  This pleasing anxious being e'er resigned,
Left the warm precincts of the cheerful day,
  Nor cast one longing lingering look behind?

On some fond breast the parting soul relies,
  Some pious drops the closing eye requires;   90
Ev'n from the tomb the voice of Nature cries,
  Ev'n in our Ashes live their wonted Fires.

For thee, who mindful of the unhonoured Dead
  Dost in these lines their artless tale relate,
If chance, by lonely contemplation led,   95
  Some kindred Spirit shall inquire thy fate,

Haply some hoary-headed Swain may say,
  "Oft have we seen him at the peep of dawn
Brushing with hasty steps the dews away
  To meet the sun upon the upland lawn.   100

"There at the foot of yonder nodding beech
  That wreathes its old fantastic roots so high,
His listless length at noontide would he stretch,
  And pore upon the brook that babbles by.

"Hard by yon wood, now smiling as in scorn,   105
  Muttering his wayward fancies he would rove,
Now drooping, woeful wan, like one forlorn,
  Or crazed with care, or crossed in hopeless
    love.

"One morn I missed him on the customed hill,
  Along the heath and near his favorite tree;   110
Another came; nor yet beside the rill,
  Nor up the lawn, nor at the wood was he;

"The next with dirges due in sad array
  Slow through the church-way path we saw him
    borne.
Approach and read (for thou can'st read) the lay,   115
  Graved on the stone beneath yon agéd thorn."

The Epitaph

Here rests his head upon the lap of earth
  A youth to fortune and to fame unknown.
Fair Science frowned not on his humble birth,
  And Melancholy marked him for her own.   120

Large was his bounty, and his soul sincere,
  Heaven did a recompense as largely send:
He gave to Misery all he had, a tear,
  He gained from Heaven ('twas all he wished) a
    friend.

No farther seek his merits to disclose,   125
  Or draw his frailties from their dread abode,
(There they alike in trembling hope repose)
  The bosom of his Father and his God.

Poem Summary

Lines 1-4:

In the first stanza, the speaker observes the
signs of a country day drawing to a close: a cur-

few bell ringing, a herd of cattle moving across the pasture, and a farm laborer returning home. The speaker is then left alone to contemplate the isolated rural scene. The first line of the poem sets a distinctly somber tone: the curfew bell does not simply ring; it "knells"—a term usually applied to bells rung at a death or funeral. From the start, then, Gray reminds us of human mortality.

Lines 5-8:

The second stanza sustains the somber tone of the first: the speaker is not mournful, but pensive, as he describes the peaceful landscape that surrounds him. Even the air is characterized as having a "solemn stillness."

Lines 9-12:

The sound of an owl hooting intrudes upon the evening quiet. We are told that the owl "complains"; in this context, the word does not mean "to whine" or "grumble," but "to express sorrow." The owl's call, then, is suggestive of grief. Note that at no point in these three opening stanzas does Gray directly refer to death or a funeral; rather, he indirectly creates a funereal atmosphere by describing just a few mournful sounds.

Lines 13-16:

It is in the fourth stanza that the speaker directly draws our attention to the graves in the country churchyard. We are presented with two potentially conflicting images of death. Line 14 describes the heaps of earth surrounding the graves; in order to dig a grave, the earth must necessarily be disrupted. Note that the syntax of this line is slightly confusing. We would expect this sentence to read "Where the turf heaves"—not "where heaves the turf": Gray has inverted the word order. Just as the earth has been disrupted, the syntax imitates the way in which the earth has been disrupted. But by the same token, the "rude Forefathers" buried beneath the earth seem entirely at peace: we are told that they are laid in "cells," a term which reminds us of the quiet of a monastery, and that they "sleep."

Lines 17-20:

If the "Forefathers" are sleeping, however, the speaker reminds us that they will never again rise from their "beds" to hear the pleasurable sounds of country life that the living do. The term "lowly beds" describes not only the unpretentious graves in which the forefathers are buried, but the humble conditions that they endured when they were alive.

Media Adaptations

- J. Norton Publishers/Audio-Forum has produced an audiocassette entitled *How Shelley Died; Elegy in a Country Churchyard: Two Lectures* (1979) with Gilbert Highet.

- Caedmon has produced an audiocassette set (of 4 disks) entitled *Eighteenth Century Poets and Drama* (1970).

- Spoken Arts Corporation has produced an audiocassette set (of 6 disks) entitled *Great English Literature of the 18th Century* (1971).

- Perspective Films has produced a videocassette entitled *Elegy to Thomas Gray* (1980).

- Monterey Home Video has produced a videocassette entitled *The Poetry Hall of Fame: Volume IV* (1994) from the BBC series "Anyone for Tennyson?"

Lines 21-24:

The speaker then moves on to consider some of the other pleasures the dead will no longer enjoy: the happiness of home, wife, and children.

Lines 25-28:

The dead will also no longer be able to enjoy the pleasures of work, of plowing the fields each day. This stanza points to the way in which the "Elegy Written in a Country Churchyard" contains elements of both Augustan and Romantic poetry. Poetry that describes agriculture—as this one does—is called georgic. Georgic verse was extremely popular in the eighteenth century. Note, however, that Gray closely identifies the farmers with the land that they work. This association of man and nature is suggestive of a romantic attitude. The georgic elements of the stanza almost demand that we characterize it as typical of the eighteenth century, but its tone looks forward to the Romantic period.

Lines 29-32:

The next four stanzas caution those who are wealthy and powerful not to look down on the poor.

These lines warn the reader not to slight the "obscure" "destiny" of the poor—the fact that they will never be famous or have long histories, or "annals," written about them.

Lines 33-36:

This stanza invokes the idea of *memento mori* (literally, a reminder of mortality). The speaker reminds the reader that regardless of social position, beauty, or wealth, all must eventually die.

Lines 37-40:

The speaker also challenges the reader not to look down on the poor for having modest, simple graves. He suggests, moreover, that the elaborate memorials that adorn the graves of the "Proud" are somehow excessive. In this context, the word "fretted" in line 39 has a double meaning: on the one hand, it can refer to the design on a cathedral ceiling; on the other hand, it can suggest that there is something "fretful," or troublesome, about the extravagant memorials of the wealthy.

Lines 41-44:

The speaker observes that nothing can bring the dead back to life, and that all the advantages that the wealthy had in life are useless in the face of death. Neither elaborate funeral monuments nor impressive honors can restore life. Nor can flattery in some way be used to change the mind of death. Note here Gray's use of personification in characterizing both "flattery" and "death"—as though death has a will or mind of its own.

Lines 45-48:

The speaker then reconsiders the poor people buried in the churchyard. He wonders what great deeds they might have accomplished had they been given the opportunity: one of these poor farmers, the speaker reasons, might have been a great emperor; another might have "waked … the living lyre," or been a great poet or musician.

Lines 49-52:

The poor were never able to fulfill their political and artistic potential, however, because they were uneducated—they never received the "Knowledge" that would enable them to rule and to create. Instead, "Penury," or poverty, "froze the genial current of their soul." That is, poverty paralyzed their ability to draw upon their innermost passions—the very passions that could have inspired them to become great poets or politicians.

Lines 53-56:

In a series of analogies, Gray observes that the talents of the poor are like a "gem" hidden in the ocean or a "flower" blooming in the desert. Just as an unseen flower in the desert is a "waste," Gray suggests, the uneducated talents of the poor are also a "waste," because they remain unused and undeveloped.

Lines 57-60:

The speaker then compares these poor, uneducated people to three of the most famous and powerful people of the previous century: John Hampden, a parliamentary leader who defended the people against the abuses of Charles I; John Milton, the great poet who wrote *Paradise Lost* and who also opposed Charles I; and Oliver Cromwell, Lord Protector of England from 1653 to 1658. The speaker suggests that buried in this churchyard might be someone who—like Hampden, Milton, or Cromwell—had the innate ability to oppose tyranny, but never had the opportunity to exercise that ability.

Lines 61-64:

This person, the speaker reasons, with the proper education and resources, might have "commanded" the government as well as any great political leader. Note, however, that Gray gives us two ways in which to consider this power. On the one hand, a great ruler can receive applause and can ignore "threats of pain and ruin." A great leader can "scatter plenty," can offer prosperity, to a grateful nation. But on the other hand, if one governs, one is, in fact, exposed to dangerous threats. And simply governing to receive "applause" suggests a shallow and self-serving motive. Moreover, "scattering plenty" implies that the wealth of a nation can be squandered by its rulers. Gray may be suggesting that having power is not as desirable as it seems. Note that the final line of this stanza is enjambed; it continues into the following line—and in this case, the next stanza.

Lines 65-68:

The first line of this stanza continues the thought of the previous, enjambed line. It abruptly reminds us that the impoverished conditions of the poor "forbade" them from becoming great rulers. Gray underscores the abrupt shock of this idea by abruptly interrupting the flow of the line with a caesura. Building on the idea of the previous stanza, the speaker notes that if poverty prevented the country laborers from acquiring the "virtues" of great and powerful people, it also prevented them from committing the "crimes" often associated with those people—and especially with those people who hold political power. In particular, it prevented them from engaging in the bloody activity associated with the British Civil War.

Lines 69-72:

Because these farm laborers were not in positions of power, the speaker reasons, they never had to ignore their own consciences. Nor did they sacrifice their artistic talents (the gift of the "Muse") to "Luxury" or "Pride."

Lines 73-76:

The speaker continues his praise of the simple life of common people. They are "far from the madding crowd" of city and political life. "Madding" here can mean either "maddening" (that is, the source of madness or insanity) or it can mean "mad" (that is, the crowd is itself hatefully insane). In either case, the common country people were removed from this insane world; as a result, they never "strayed" into the immoral acts of the powerful. Instead, they kept steadily to their simple but meaningful lives.

Lines 77-80:

The speaker then reminds us that these common people are, in fact, long dead. He notes that even if they were not powerful or great, and even if they do not have an elaborate memorial of the sort mentioned in line 38, they still deserve homage or tribute. At the very least, he suggests, an onlooker should "sigh" on seeing their graves. Note here the multiple meanings we can attach to the word "passing." It can refer to the onlooker, who is simply walking or "passing by" these graves. It can mean "in passing"—that someone seeing these graves should take just a moment out of their busy lives to remember the dead. And "passing" itself is a euphemism for death. In a way, then, Gray is suggesting that there is no difference between the person "passing" by the grave and the person who has "passed" away—another reminder that all will eventually die.

Lines 81-84:

Instead of "fame and elegy," the people buried here have modest tombstones, which display only their names and the dates of their birth and death. These common people were not famous, and no one has written elaborate elegies or funeral verses for them. Still, the very modesty of their tomb-

stones testifies to the nobility and "holy" nature of their simple lives. As such, they provide an example not so much of how life should be lived, but how its end, death, should be approached. The term "rustic moralist" here is open to interpretation. It may refer to anyone who is in the countryside thinking about the meaning of death. But more likely, it refers to the speaker, who is himself moralizing—preaching or contemplating—about the nature of both life and death.

Lines 85-88:

The speaker reasons that most people, faced with the prospect of dying and ultimately being forgotten, cling to life. Note Gray's use of paradox in line 86: "this pleasing anxious being." On the one hand, "being" or living can be "anxious," filled with worries. On the other hand, just being alive—when faced with death—is itself "pleasing" or pleasant. The speaker is suggesting that even the troubles and worries of life are enjoyable in comparison to death.

Lines 89-92:

The dead rely on the living to remember them and to mourn for them. The speaker suggests that this need is so fundamental that even from the grave the buried dead seem to ask for remembrance. In fact, as line 92 suggests, the dead actually live on in our memories.

Lines 93-96:

In this stanza, the speaker addresses himself. He reasons that since he himself has been mindful of the dead, and has remembered and praised them in this poem, perhaps when he is dead someone will remember him. This person, he reasons, will necessarily be a "kindred Spirit," someone who is also a lonely wanderer in the country, meditating on the nature of death. The speaker then goes on to imagine his own death: he envisions this "kindred Spirit" seeing his (the speaker's) grave and wondering about his life and death.

Lines 97-100:

In the next five stanzas, the speaker imagines how an old farm laborer might remember him after his death. If, the speaker speculates, the "kindred Spirit" sees the speaker's grave and wonders about it, perhaps an old man might offer to describe the speaker. The old man would say that the speaker was often seen wandering about the countryside at dawn. Presumably, he was frequently out all night—as, no doubt, he has been in this very poem.

Lines 101-104:

At noon, the old man continues, the speaker would frequently stretch out under an old tree at noon, and stare at a nearby brook.

Lines 105-108:

The old man would have observed that the speaker's moods were changeable: sometimes the speaker would wander about in the nearby woods, "smiling scornfully" and talking to himself; other times, he would appear depressed; then again, sometimes he would look as though he were in anguish. Perhaps, the old man speculates, the speaker had been "crossed in hopeless love."

Lines 109-112:

The speaker continues to imagine this old man remembering him after his death. The old man would have noticed one morning that the speaker was absent: he was not in any of his favorite spots. Likewise, the old man would remember, the speaker did not appear the following day.

Lines 113-116:

The third day, however, the old man and his friends would have seen the speaker's body being carried to the churchyard for burial. (The speaker, then, is imagining himself buried in the very graveyard he once used to wander by.) The old man invites this curious passerby, or "kindred Spirit," to read the speaker's epitaph. Note the reminder that the old man is uneducated: he cannot read, although the passerby can do so.

Lines 117-120:

The last three stanzas are, in fact, the speaker's epitaph; the way in which the speaker imagines his epitaph will read. Through the epitaph, the speaker asks the passerby (and the reader) not to remember him as wealthy, famous, or brilliantly educated, but as one who was "melancholic" or deeply thoughtful and sad.

Lines 121-124:

The speaker asks that we remember him for being generous and sincere. His generosity was, in fact, his willingness to mourn for the dead. Because he was so generous, the speaker reasons, heaven gave him a "friend"—someone who would, in turn, mourn for him after his death. This friend is unnamed, but we can deduce that it is any "kindred Spirit"—including the reader—who reads the speaker's epitaph and remembers him.

Lines 125-128:

The speaker concludes by cautioning the reader not to praise him any further. He also asks that his "frailties," his flaws or personal weaknesses, not be considered; rather, they should be left to the care of God, with whom the speaker now resides. The poem, then, is an elegy not only for the common man, but for the speaker himself. Indeed, by the end of the poem it is evident that the speaker himself wishes to be identified not with the great and famous, but with the common people whom he has praised and with whom he will, presumably, be buried.

Themes

Death

Gray's "Elegy" is one of the best-known poems about death in all of European literature. The poem presents the reflections of an observer who, passing by a churchyard that is out in the country, stops for a moment to think about the significance of the strangers buried there. Scholars of medieval times sometimes kept human skulls on their desktops, to keep themselves conscious of the fact that someday they, like the skulls' former occupants, would die: from this practice we get the phrase *memento mori,* which we say to this day to describe any token one uses to keep one's mortality in mind. In this poem, the graveyard acts as a *memento mori,* reminding the narrator to not place too much value on this life because someday he too will be dead and buried. The speaker of the poem is surrounded by the idea of death, and throughout the first seven stanzas there are numerous images pointing out the contrast between death and life. After mentioning the churchyard in the title, which establishes the theme of mortality, the poem itself begins with images of gloom and finality. The darkness at the end of the day, the forlorn moan of lowing cattle, the stillness of the air (highlighted by the beetle's stilted motion) and the owl's nocturnal hooting all serve to set a background for this serious meditation. However, it is not until the fourth stanza that the poem actually begins to deal with the cemetery, mentioned as the place where the village forefathers "sleep." In the following stanzas, the speaker tries to imagine what the lives of these simple men might have been like, touching upon their relations with their wives, children, and the soil that they worked. They are not defined by their possessions, because they had few, and instead are defined by their actions, which serves to contrast their lives with their quiet existence in the graveyard. This "Elegy" presents the dead in the best light: their families adored them and they were cheerful in their work, as they "hummed the woods beneath their steady stroke." The speaker openly admits that they are spoken of so well precisely because they are dead, because death is such a terrible thing that its victims deserve the respect of the living. In line 90, the poet explains, "Some pious drops the closing eye requires," explaining that the living should show their respect for death with their sorrow.

Search for Self

The speaker of this poem goes through a process of recognizing what is important to him and choosing how to live his life (which leads to the epitaph with which he would like to be remembered). In stanza 8, the poem begins naming the attributes that are normally considered desirable but are now considered pointless when compared with the lives of the rustic dead in the country graveyard. Ambition and Grandeur, according to the speaker, should not think less of these people because of their simple accomplishments. He goes on to assert that Pride and Memory have no right to ignore them, and that Honor and Flattery will be as useless to the rich as to the poor when they are dead. The speaker, an educated person, gives much consideration to the subject of Knowledge, and whether the lack of it made the lives of these country people less significant. Their poverty blocked the way to knowledge, he decides, and the lack of knowledge separated them from vices as well as virtues, so that in the end he does not consider his education a factor in making him better or worse than them either. In the end, having eliminated all of the supposed benefits of the wealthy, educated world that he comes from, the speaker identifies himself with the graveyard inhabitants to such a degree that he winds up in this humble graveyard after his death. In contrast to the simple graves that he pondered over throughout his life, though, the speaker's grave is marked with a warm-hearted memorial, the "Epitaph" at the end of the poem. Assuming that such a thoughtful person would not have been so immodest as to write this epitaph for himself, there must have been some other literate person to remember him. He is also remembered by an illiterate member of the farm community, the "hoary-headed swain" who has to ask someone to read the epitaph. Before the death of the poem's narrator, this Swain established a nonverbal relationship with him, observing him from afar, won-

Topics for Further Study

- Do you think the speaker of this poem is sentimentalizing the forgotten people in the country churchyard, or is he giving them the recognition they deserve? Would this poem have the same meaning if it were written in a churchyard in a busy city?

- Visit a cemetery near you, pick the tombstone of a person that you do not know, and write a page about what that person might have been like, focusing on the social changes that person may have experienced. What does the length of that person's life tell you? What can you tell from where they are buried?

- It could be argued that people in modern society are more likely to remember the accomplishments of poor people than they were in Gray's time? It is just as possible, though, that we are as preoccupied with the famous and wealthy as people in seventeenth century England were with royalty. Explain what you think about this issue.

dering about him just as the narrator wondered about the country people buried there.

Class Conflict

A superficial reading of this poem might leave the impression that the author intends to present members of the lower class as being more worthy of praise than their upper-class counterparts. This would be a reasonable assumption, since so much of the poem is devoted to praising the simple virtues of the poor. In the larger scope, though, the position that Gray takes is that all people, poor or rich, are equal. This is a meditation on death, which has been called the "great equalizer" because no can avoid it. The reason that the poem seems to favor one class over the other is that it is working against the assumption that only those of the upper class are worthy of attention when they die. It is the humble condition of the country churchyard, with gravestones unmarked or possibly marked just with names by illiterate people unable to read, that draws attention to the virtues of the poor and un-educated (which society often forgets), and so much of the poem is spent praising their moral strength. The virtues of the wealthy and famous are not denied, they just are not explored in this poem because they are already so familiar. Evidence of the poem's evenhandedness about the different classes can be seen in the fact that, while praising the poor country people throughout, Gray also ac-knowledges that education, which may give them opportunity to develop moral excellence, may also lead them to corruption: as he says in stanza 17, the humble circumstances of the poor limited the growth not only of their virtues but also of their crimes. The poem thus leaves open the question of superiority. Society glorifies the rich, and the poem's narrator glorifies the poor, but, as he re-minds us, "The paths of glory lead but to the grave."

Style

"Elegy Written in a Country Churchyard" is writ-ten in heroic quatrains. A quatrain is a four-line stanza. Heroic quatrains rhyme in an *abab* pattern and are written in iambic pentameter. An iamb is a poetic foot consisting of one unstressed and one stressed syllable, as in the phrase "the world." Pen-tameter simply means that there are five feet in each line. Consider, for instance, the first line of Gray's "Elegy Written in a Country Churchyard":

The Curfew tolls the knell of parting day.

When we scan the line, or identify its stresses, it appears as follows:

TheCur / few tolls / the knell / of part / ing day.

Try reading the line aloud: its regular, steady rhythm helps to creates a calm and quiet mood—one appropriate to the meditative nature of this poem.

Historical Context

When Thomas Gray was writing this poem, the world was going through a period of intellectual development that thinkers of the time dubbed the "Age of Enlightenment." The Enlightenment was a philosophical movement that grew out of the great advances made by scientists in the seventeenth and eighteenth centuries. One key example which ended up having great influence on the Enlighten-ment was Sir Isaac Newton's theory of universal gravitation, which proposed laws that explained and predicted the behavior of matter in all circum-stances everywhere. Newton published this theory in his book *Philosophiae Naturalis Principia Math-ematica* in 1687, and it marked a turning point in the history of science. At the same time, this idea of the power of rationalism was growing in the area of philosophy. Thinkers such as Rene Descartes (1596-1650) and Baruch Spinoza (1632-1677) took up the idea of rationalism, attempting to apply the methods of scientific inquiry to the field of philos-ophy; Descartes' famous statement "I think, there-fore I am" represents his attempt to start with the one simple truth that he could be sure of about the world, which was that he himself existed. In polit-ical science, Thomas Hobbes (1588-1679) explored the interrelations of social interactions in such works as *The Elements of Law, Natural and Politic,* and John Locke (1632-1704) explained human in-telligence as being the sum of what is learned through experience, not the God-given right of a few.

By the start of the eighteenth century, intel-lectuals throughout the world were excited about the new Age of Enlightenment, which promised hu-manity new hope for controlling the world's prob-lems. At first, though, the Enlightenment's enthu-siasts were considered dangerous radicals. They rejected tradition that was not backed up with solid rational explanation, and tradition was the basis for most rulers' political power. Royalty ruled by re-lation to previous rulers, and landowners feasted while peasants starved because of rights based on inheritance, but rationalism served to undermine such rights and to blur class distinctions. In partic-ular, the Catholic Church, which had been a strong influence in European politics for centuries, was threatened by the skepticism of Enlightenment thinkers who felt society should be organized ac-cording to rational rather than religious principles. As religious explanations of the universe lost cred-ibility to scientific explanations that were based on observation, the Church took a defensive position, jailing free thinkers for heresy when they published theories that contradicted church tradition. In ear-lier times, Galileo, for example, was imprisoned for supporting the Copernican heliocentric view of the solar system. In the early 1700s, the church clashed frequently with Enlightenment theorists who made even minor claims about the nature of man and so-ciety that could be considered heretical. By the middle of the century, when Thomas Gray wrote

Compare & Contrast

- **1751:** Benjamin Franklin, flying a kite in a thunderstorm with a key at the end of the string, discovered the fact that lightning behaves like electricity and flows through conductive material.

  Today: Control of electricity is one of the fundamental principles of our society. Blackouts, when electricity becomes unavailable, create major disruptions.

- **1751:** Whaling was an important part of the economy of the New England colonies, with more than sixty whaling ships trolling the water off the coast.

  Today: Environmental organizations fight to protect the rights of endangered whale species, but the world has much less use for whale meat or for whale oil to light lamps.

- **1751:** English theologian and evangelist John Wesley was travelling almost 5000 miles every year to spread the word about Christianity, founding the denomination known as Methodism.

  Today: Methodism is recognized as one of the mainstream Protestant religions.

- **1751:** Approximately one-fifth of the people in New England, which was to become America after the war for independence in 1776, were slaves.

  1863: Abraham Lincoln issued the Emancipation Proclamation, which made slavery illegal in the United States. It was not accepted in the South until after their defeat in the Civil War in 1865.

  Today: Most of the world has laws against slavery, but there are still regular scattered reports of people, usually immigrants and females, who are forced into labor against their wills.

- **1751:** Denis Diderot published the first volume of the first modern encyclopedia, his *Encyclopaedie, ou Dictionaire raisonne des sciences, des arts et des metiers, par une societe de gens de lettres*. The work eventually spanned eleven volumes, with the last volume finished in 1772.

  Today: Many established encyclopedias, as well as uncollected information that is compiled into encyclopedias, is available from a computer terminal from anywhere on the globe via the Internet.

---

his "Elegy," Enlightenment rationality had gained enough public support to stand on its own. To some extent, the poem displays Enlightenment principles in the way that the speaker shows faith that the rural poor could be intelligent and successful if they had proper education, reflecting Locke's theory of the mind as a "blank slate" that is ready to grow. The pessimism he shows, though, regarding the potential for corruption if the poor were educated, is contrary to the standard Enlightenment optimism about the good that will result from education.

The high point for the Enlightenment was the American Revolution in 1776. This marked the beginning of a society based on rationality and fairness, not tradition. The basis for the American Revolution was that people living in North America would now be better able to decide what was best for them than a king living in England, reflecting a faith in the common person's ability to reason. The Declaration of Independence is a major philosophical work concerning the rights of human beings to determine their own fates. The end of the Enlightenment as an intellectual movement came soon after, however, with the French Revolution from 1789 to 1799. Like the revolution in America, the French Revolution was an attempt to let individuals control their own destinies, based on faith in reason, which Enlightenment thinkers had been advocating for nearly a hundred years. While the American Revolution created a new society, however, the French Revolution created chaos, a bloodbath of government suppression of revolutionaries and public executions of deposed government figures. In the end, the oppressive system of feudal land ownership was abolished, but only at the end of a bitter struggle that required both sides to focus their attention on jingoistic slogans. The ideal of rationality became lost with the emphasis on the rights of individuals and the belief that the simple, uncorrupt poor know better than the pampered rich. The Enlightenment gave way to the age of Romanticism, which emphasized an almost mystical belief in individuality and the goodness of nature.

Critical Overview

Over the years, Gray's "Elegy Written in a Country Churchyard" has received extensive critical attention. Critics have long recognized Gray's "Elegy Written in a Country Churchyard" for its restrained and dignified expression of simple truths. In *Lives of the English Poets,* Samuel Johnson praised the poem for its universal appeal and its originality: "The 'Churchyard' abounds with images which find a mirrour in every mind, and with sentiments to which every bosom returns an echo are to me original…. Had Gray written often thus, it had been vain to blame, and useless to praise him." Other writers, such as Samuel Coleridge and Matthew Arnold, also admired the work, although Arnold's criticism was somewhat cautious. Arnold noted in his *Essays in Criticism* that "the 'Elegy Written in a Country Churchyard' is a beautiful poem … But it is true that the 'Elegy Written in a Country Churchyard' owe[s] much of its success to its subject, and that it has received a too unmeasured and unbounded praise."

In the twentieth century, critics have often observed two competing "voices" or attitudes in Gray's writings. Joseph Wood Krutch, in his introduction to *The Selected Letters of Thomas Gray,* offers a useful comparison of the classical and Romantic tendencies in the "Elegy Written in a Country Churchyard." Krutch maintains that there are certainly strong romantic qualities in the poem, but that it is more clearly identifiable with the eighteenth century: "there is nothing mystical, at least nothing transcendental, in the 'Elegy Written in a Country Churchyard.' It is everywhere stubbornly rational, even in its melancholy. The simple life, even the life close to nature, is good because it is healthful and free from great temptation, not because God dwells in a sunset." In more recent years, critical attention has been focused on Gray's com-

plex use of language. Some critics have noted a degree of ambiguity in Gray's syntax. One critic, W. Hutchings, argues in an essay in *Studies in Philology* that this ambiguity tends to "undermine" the apparently secure or simple universe that Gray has depicted. Hutchings notes, "there is an extraordinary degree of instability about [the 'Elegy Written in a Country Churchyard'], one which often expresses itself by making its syntax fluid, even indeterminate. Far from being something to be amended or ignored, this quality is the key to the 'Elegy Written in a Country Churchyard.'" We notice, then, a transformation in the way in which this poem has been viewed: early critics tended to praise the poem for its simple truths; more recent critics, however, have begun to wonder if underneath these apparently simple truths there are more troubling questions.

Criticism

David Kelly

David Kelly is an instructor of literature and writing at several community colleges in Illinois, as well as a fiction writer. Here, he examines Gray's "Elegy" as a reflection of social conscience, finding it to be advanced in identifying the problems of a class-based society but lacking in solutions.

The most common interpretation of Thomas Gray's poem "Elegy Written in a Country Churchyard" is that it is an expression of sympathy and support for those who have the misfortune to be without money or social prestige. When critics do not approach it from this angle, they almost always look at it as a broader philosophical statement about how fortune in this world ends up being no help to the dead, an interpretation that rests almost entirely upon line 36, "The paths of glory lead but to the grave." These are both pertinent ideas that Gray does cover, but they're fairly obvious ideas to readers today, and either could have been adequately dispatched in a poem a third as long. We have to question how obvious such ideas about social rank would have been in the feudal monarchy of Gray's England, circa 1750. If Gray was a thinker ahead of his time, then the ideas that we take for granted may have been unheard of to his peers.

It would be almost impossible to believe that people before Gray wished anything but the best

What Do I Read Next?

- The most authoritative edition of Gray's poetry is the edition originally published by the Oxford Press in 1966, entitled *The Complete Poems of Thomas Gray: English, Latin and Greek.* H. W. Starr wrote the introduction and edited the book with J. R. Hendrickson.

- John Dyer is a Welsh pastoral poet who wrote at the same time as Gray. His greatest works, including "Grongar Hill," considered one of the first romantic pastoral poems, are included in the collection *Poems, 1761.*

- Samuel Johnson was the outstanding literary figure of Gray's time. Among his writings was the ten-volume *Lives of the Poets,* which includes a brief biography of Gray, as well as a number of poems that he wrote himself. He is best known today for the biography that James Boswell wrote about him, *The Life of Samuel Johnson,* considered one of the best biographies ever and an important source for readers who want to understand the British literary scene in the eighteenth century.

- Gray wrote during the Age of Enlightenment, a period of intense intellectual activity throughout the world. One of the leading thinkers of the time was French Philosopher Rene Descartes, who is often credited with adding humanity to the age of ideas. His *Discourse on Method and the Meditations* is still considered one of the world's most important philosophical works.

- Thomas Gray is often considered a poet ahead of his time, who predated the Romantic Movement that swept across the globe approximately fifty years later. More than his contemporaries, his contemplative style, and concern for humanity are often compared to the works of William Wordsworth, one of the founders of Romanticism. Wordsworth's "Lines Composed A Few Miles Above Tintern Abbey, on Revisiting the Banks of the Wye During a Tour, July 13th, 1798," has a much looser structure than Gray's "Elegy," but there is a similarity in the melancholy of both poems.

- Richard Gough's *The History of Myddle* was written between 1700 and 1706, chronicling the lives of people living in the small English town of Myddle in Shropshire. This rural history is probably as close as one can get to reading about the lives of the people discussed in Gray's "Elegy." A 1980 edition of Gough's book is available, with an introduction by Dr. Peter Razzell.

for victims of misfortune. After all, as the word itself indicates, misfortune has two significant characteristics: it is bad, and it happens because of luck or chance, fortune. By its basic definition, people with bad luck cannot be blamed, and that makes them innocent sufferers. To that extent, Gray seems to have brought nothing new to the question of human relations, just the circular argument that those who do not deserve misfortune do not deserve it. The fact is, though, that the issue has never been as clear-cut as that. There is the question of whether the poor, such as the struggling farmers that Gray talks about, have been cast their lot by random chance, or whether they might not actually be collecting exactly what they deserve.

We see this same question arise just as clearly, if not more so, in contemporary America. In our two-party system, the general attitude toward poverty and its related problems, such as poor education and health, shifts from one side of the spectrum to the other every generation or so. One party is dominant during a time when the general public believes that the poor are neglected, and as a result spending for social programs will increase; a few years later, the prevailing mood will hold that the poor are coddled and therefore lack the will to raise themselves out of poverty, and spending then decreases. The issue seems to balance on the question of just how much the people involved are responsible for their own positions as part of the

> *The 'Elegy' has an inconsistency in praising the inherent worth of the simple country people while pretending that their lives are somehow less for having not received the benediction of a poet before."*

underclass, and therefore how much sympathy they deserve.

"Elegy Written in a Country Churchyard" appeared at one of those cultural moments when change was in the air but had not quite arrived. In a piece celebrating the two hundredth anniversary of the "Elegy"'s publication, Carl J. Weaver provided an inventory of "the originality of Gray's democratic sympathy": the American Revolution was twenty-five years away, and the French Revolution forty; it was to be twenty years until Oliver Goldsmith would write of "a bold peasantry, their country's pride," and still another twenty-five after that until Robert Burns framed the simplicity of the democratic spirit with "A man's a man, for a' that." Ideas of equality may be at the core of the society we live in, but they were exceptional when Gray wrote.

This apparently was the reason why he felt the need to go to such lengths to help his readers know the simple country people he was writing about. They were not the lazy, stupid brutes his readers would have to believe they were in order to believe that they deserved to live in poverty and obscurity. They worked hard at "useful toil," their children loved them, and they asked for little in return. These were not easy people to ignore, by Gray's standard: their virtues should have made them stand out as society's finest, and he writes with bitterness that they were left to rot in obscurity in tiny churchyards while men and women not nearly as useful or loved rested under marble monuments.

As a vindication of the poor, this poem does excellent work: like all of the best works of social conscience, it knows how to handle its audience, making our hearts swell with pride for the virtues

of the downtrodden. This is where the regular rhythm and unyielding rhyme scheme fit in, by assuring readers of the inevitability of this view of the simple country folk and not just a limited view of one select group. The problem is that, having imagined the greatness of the "rude Forefathers" so well and rendered them so convincingly, Gray did not have any idea about what he should do about their descendants that labored on. He was hardly the revolutionary. As much as he opposed inequity, still he was not ready to call for some sort of Marxist social reorganization that would bring the intellectuals and civil servants to the farms and give plowboys their turn in the House of Lords. The best that Gray could come up with to compensate for the opportunities that had been denied these simple country people was the complaint that they should have memorials on their graves as nice as those that mark the remains of social luminaries, in acknowledgment of the fact that they could have been important too, given the chance.

The problem with having nothing to offer but praise and recognition is that the poem burns up the value of praise on its way to affirming the commoners' self-worth. "Can storied urn or animated bust / Back to its mansion call the fleeting breath?" the poem asks, and the answer, of course, is no. "Can Honor's voice provoke the silent dust, or / Flattery sooth the dull cold ear of Death?" Since they can't, then just what *are* we supposed to do about those who died without recognition? The poem expends much of its energy convincing readers that these people lived valuable, useful lives and that memorials are for the Proud and the Vain, but it also wants to stir our sense of pathos over the fact that they do not have grand memorials. As William Empson has pointed out, referring to the fourteenth stanza of Gray's "Elegy" in his essay "Proletarian Literature," "a gem does mind being in a cave and a flower prefers not to be picked." The occupants of the churchyard may have had bad lives, but that is not their own view, it is the judgement of an onlooker, the speaker of the poem: it is the same voice that simultaneously warns us not to be so arrogant as to assume that their lives are worthless.

In the end, there is nothing the speaker can offer but himself. Literary historians have gone back and forth for two-and-a-half centuries about who the young man elegized at the end is supposed to be: Gray, his recently deceased friend Richard West, a townsperson, or someone completely new. One thing that seems certain is the bond between him and the speaker of the first 116 lines; the melancholy of the nightfall in the first stanzas per-fectly matches the young man's "drooping, woeful wan" muttering as he looked out over the ceme-tery. The attitudes and sensibilities which take their effect on readers throughout the 29 initial stanzas have already affected the "youth to fortune" who is buried there, and so his way of dealing with so-cial inequity can be taken as the poem's result.

The answer this poem offers for the fact that good people who lack social prominence are left forgotten after death is for a prominent person to climb down into the grave with them, to be buried beside them and to raise up at least one large mon-ument with a lofty epitaph within that forsaken cemetery. It is a much more temperate solution than calling for a revolution to disrupt the social struc-ture (like the revolutions that were to come later in that century). It is at least more active than simply walking away from the problem and concluding that the downtrodden must somehow deserve the fate dealt them. Lacking a burning indignity about the way things are but unable to sit comfortably with it, Gray's young man, steeped in sadness, opts for a show of solidarity to mock the rules that say he is from a different "set" than the farm people.

Is it effective? There is no way to tell from the way the poem leaves things. Generally, rejection of one's class privileges and identifying with the downtrodden only produces the minimal effect of making one's relatives and former friends sigh and wink, unless the class advantage is used to pry some good out of the situation. A child of wealth from a gated suburban community who goes to live in the inner city in order to upset conventional assump-tions is likely to just make people think he or she has an inflated sense of importance, while a physi-cian who goes to an impoverished area to work is both an inspiration and a practical asset. The "El-egy" has an inconsistency in praising the inherent worth of the simple country people while pretend-ing that their lives are somehow less for having not received the benediction of a poet before. This is reflected in the egoism in believing that having the body of a beloved young man from a good home among them is somehow an enriching experience for the rural dead. Gray's heart was in the right place, far ahead of its time in terms of his thoughts on social equity, and with no models for him to draw from we shouldn't be surprised that his at-tempt to bridge the chasm of social class would re-flect the very prejudices he was trying to overcome.

Source: David Kelly, in an essay for *Poetry for Students,* Gale, 2000.

Aviya Kushner

Aviya Kushner is the Contributing Editor in Poetry at BarnesandNoble.com *and the Poetry Ed-itor of* Neworld Magazine. *She is a graduate of the acclaimed creative writing program in poetry at Boston University, where she received the Fitzger-ald Award in Translation. Her writing on poetry has appeared in* Harvard Review *and* The Boston Phoenix, *and she has served as Poetry Coordina-tor for* AGNI Magazine. *She has given readings of her own work throughout the United States, and she teaches at Massachusetts Communications College in Boston. In the following essay, Kushner describes the pastoral qualities of the "Elegy," which contribute "to the sense that it tells a universal story which spans both nations and centuries."*

One of the most famous poems in the history of the English language might never have been pub-lished if its author had had his way. Thomas Gray never tried to publish "Elegy Written in a Country Churchyard," and was quite dismayed to find that a journal he didn't like much chose to print it.

Once it was published—through a friend of Gray's who sent a copy in to the journal—the "El-egy" was a hit. The poem's grip on the readers of its time was no temporary fluke. Today, the "El-egy" still resonates with readers around the world. Much of that resonance is due to the great classic literary texts the "Elegy" borrows from, and the major human stories it manages to contain. The Book of Ecclesiastes, Dante's *Inferno* and *Purga-torio,* and the pastoral visions of Virgil all lie qui-etly beneath the poem, contributing to the sense that it tells a universal story which spans both nations and centuries.

Fittingly, the elegy of timeless topics begins in slow motion:

The Curfew tolls the knell of parting day,
The lowing herd wind slowly o'er the lea,
The plowman homeward plods his weary way,
And leaves the world to darkness and to me.

The words "toll," "lowing," and "slowly" physically decrease the speed of the poem. The nu-merous "l"s in the first stanza produce a lull, and the reader literally "plods his weary way" along with the poet.

As Henry Weinfield observes in his book *The Poet Without a Name: Gray's Elegy and the Prob-lem of History,* there are numerous opportunities for sound here. The plowman and the herd both make noise, and yet, the overwhelming impression

> *The poet then details the sounds of the countryside—the cock in the morning, the swallow, the echoing horn—which are not heard by the dead. While the opening stanza may have detailed a still silence, the dead and buried know an even stiller silence."*

of the first stanza is silence. It is this deep and carefully controlled silence, presented in exact rhyme and pristine pentameter, that gives the opening a timeless feel.

With its mention of the herd, the opening stanza also positions itself in the pastoral tradition—the line of poetry based on songs sung by shepherds. Pastoral poetry often involves nostalgia for a past, but that past doesn't necessarily exist. Instead, pastoral poems often look back longingly on an idealized time where purity and virtue supposedly ruled.

Musically, the second stanza maintains the silence of the first. Late afternoon is turning to evening:

Now fades the glimmering landscape on the sight,
And all the air a solemn stillness holds,
Save where the beetle wheels his droning flight,
And drowsy tinklings lull the distant folds;

The movement of the day, from afternoon to dusk to dark, is just one of the movements the "Elegy" will address. Day and night foreshadow life and death, along with labor and the end of labor, and the building and destroying of personal history.

The plowman is progressing on his journey as day turns into evening. And soon, he reaches the churchyard, where beneath "rugged elms" and the "yew-tree's shade," the "rude Forefathers of the hamlet sleep."

The poet then details the sounds of the countryside—the cock in the morning, the swallow, the echoing horn—which are not heard by the dead. While the opening stanza may have detailed a still silence, the dead and buried know an even stiller silence.

These buried forefathers not only don't hear anymore, they also don't see and feel. They don't see their children or their wives, and they don't gaze upon the fireplace. This inactivity doesn't mean they weren't active in their lives. In fact, they worked very hard:

Oft did the harvest to their sickle yield,
Their furrow oft the stubborn glebe has broke;
How jocund did they drive their team afield!
How bow'd the woods beneath their sturdy stroke!

At one time, these buried men had power over their animals and over the woods. Although they were only country laborers, the poet takes pains to make sure these achievements are not belittled:

Let not Ambition mock their useful toil,
Their homely joys, and destiny obscure,
Nor Grandeur hear with a disdainful smile,
The short and simple annals of the poor.

This addressing of powers like "Ambition" and "Grandeur" seems a bit reminiscent of the Platonic forms of the Good, the Beautiful, and the like. Plato tried to nail down a definition of the Good, and here the poet seems to question what Ambition and Grandeur are, anyway. After all, one thing is clear in a graveyard—it is the final resting-place for all social classes.

Power, beauty, and wealth, according to the poet, all "awaits alike th'inevitable hour." At the end, the wildly successful match the poor in one respect: "The paths of glory lead but to the grave."

In this country churchyard, the poet speculates about the talents of those buried here:

Perhaps in this neglected spot is laid
Some heart once pregnant with celestial fire,
Hands, that the rod of empire might have sway'd
Or wak'd to the ecstasy the living lyre.

Some of those buried here may have been outstanding ministers, rulers, or musicians. But destiny is often controlled by money, or what the poet calls "Chill Penury." This churchyard might have contained a Milton or a Cromwell, if only economics didn't play a part.

But despite the poverty and relative obscurity of those buried here, they still require the dignity of a proper place to rest:

Yet ev'n these bones from insult to protect
Some frail memorial still erected nigh,
With uncouth rhymes and shapeless sculpture
    deck'd,

Implores the passing tribute of a sigh.

The churchyard, according to the poet, protects the dead from insult. But it also performs an essential function—it "teaches" the living how to die.

The poem ends with a description of the death of one individual man, who wasn't seen on his usual hill, heath, and tree. He was also not "beside the rill" or "up the lawn." He had died, and was being carried to the churchyard.

The dead man is carried slowly through the church-way path, the motion mimicking the slow-motion opening of the poem. Although those in attendance can't read, an epitaph has been prepared for the dead man.

The epitaph acknowledges that this dead man was not lucky in Fame or Fortune. But in death, he is equal to all others, ready to relocate to "the bosom of his Father and his God."

Source: Aviya Kushner, in an essay for *Poetry for Students*, Gale, 2000.

R. J. Ellis

In this essay, Ellis investigates the central mystery in one of the best-known poems in the English language.

Gray's 'Elegy' is one of the better known poems in the English language. It is also one of those poems about which there is centred an enduring controversy. This can be referred to in shorthand as the 'stonecutter debate' and centres on a moment in the poem when, after an apparently serene enough progress into the pastoral mode, with an elegiac 'graveyard poets' edge to it, the poem suddenly introduces a startling complication. The 'Elegy' up until this moment seems to have a clear enough, and clearly centred, narrative voice, established emphatically in its very first stanza:

The Curfew tolls the knell of parting day,
The lowing herd wind slowly o'er the lea,
The plowman homeward plods his weary way,
And leaves the world to darkness and to me.

The first stanza thus ends on the word 'me'—announcing thereby a tone of personal, musing reflection. The 'me' is in fact quite heavily emphasised: the final word of the stanza, it is also underscored by the rhyme scheme. The poem thus seems to settle into a tone of first-person intimacy between the 'Poet,' that is to say the persona of the poem, and the audience. However, this apparent stability is ineradicably complicated by a sudden change of centre in lines 93–98:

> *On the other hand 'thee' is also a conventional multi-faceted portrait—stranding together West, Gray, the sensitive reader, the stonecutter/woodcarver, each one in slightly different ways safely locatable in all those pastoral traditions these identities reference, within which 'The Ignote' might be safely constrained...."*

For thee, who mindful of th' unhonour'd Dead
Dost in these lines their artless tale relate;
If chance, by lonely contemplation led,
Some kindred Spirit shall inquire thy fate,
Haply some hoary-headed Swain may say,
'Oft have we seen him at the peep of dawn ...'

These lines, in rapid succession, introduce a new cast of characters: a 'thee', a 'kindred spirit' and a 'hoary-headed Swain.' The last two exist in some imagined future, imagined apparently by the poem's 'me' as 'haply' meeting to discuss the 'fate' of 'thee.' And it is precisely this 'thee' which poses the problem: who exactly is 'thee'? This question is important because the voice of the 'Hoary headed swain,' speaking in this imagined future to the 'kindred spirit,' dominates the remainder of the poem, and speaks wholly of this 'thee,' who he regularly saw 'Mutt'ring ... wayward fancies' until he died. Indeed, crucially, 'The EPITAPH' at the end is apparently engraved on the headstone of the now deceased 'thee' in the imagined future created within the poem. The poem thus ends not by focusing on the reflections of the poem's narrator, 'me,' but on 'thee,' whoever this person is, on the fate of 'thee,' and on 'thee's' epitaph.

The question 'who is "thee"?' has been variously answered, and it is not my purpose fully to rehearse the resulting debate here. This has already often been done, for example in Herbert W. Starr's

Twentieth Century Interpretations of Gray's 'Elegy' 63. The dominant explanation is that 'thee' is in fact 'me,' either seen to be Gray, or the poem's persona (depending on how you view the relationship of 'me' to the poet in this poem). Briefly, this proposal depends on us understanding that Gray/the poem's persona has reached a point where his reflections are mature enough for him to distance himself from his own death, which he now imagines peacefully, having come to terms with his own mortality—even to the extent of imagining his own epitaph. A problem with this reading is the disconcerting smugness which now accrues to 'The EPITAPH':

> Large was his bounty, and his soul sincere...

Alternative proposals are fairly thick on the ground, however. Another popular suggestion is that the 'thee' is Gray's close friend Richard West, who had died not long before. The composition date of the 'Elegy' is not quite clear: one, largely discarded, suggestion is that it was commenced as early as 1742, which means it may have been begun just after West's death. Indeed the epitaph, for some critics, was one that Gray originally intended for West, an aspiring poet and Eton College schoolmate, whose career was abbreviated by his premature death. The 'Elegy,' however, hardly supports this suggestion (not least because West's background was not 'humble,' as line 119 seems to indicate), and anyway its composition date is now usually accepted to be rather later.

A third suggestion is that this 'thee' represents an imagined poet, or even an imagined personification, 'The Poet.' Most usually this 'poet' is seen as a *poeta ignotus*—an unknown poet of humble origins fated never to reach a wide audience—composing his poems, his 'wayward fancies,' in rural obscurity before dying, unrecognised and largely unread. But this idea, like the others, has to be imposed on the poem, since it is not overtly the case that this, or any of the other readings so far examined, is correct, though each can lay claim to some degree of plausibility. These readings each, in turn, offer the promise of coherence, but it is only a promise, for the text offers no implicit or explicit support for any of them.

This lack of plain support fuels the next, undeniably dramatic, development. This seeks to define an actual figure in the poem, to whom the pronoun 'thee' refers—the figure of the 'stonecutter.' This argument is difficult to summarise. Briefly, it depends on noting that an unknown poet—a *poeta ignotus*—of sorts has earlier been (at the very least

implicitly) introduced into the poem, namely in lines 79–81, which speak of 'uncouth rimes' decking the 'frail memorials' in the churchyard, with 'names and years' 'spelt by th' unletter'd muse.' This *poeta ignotus* is usually labelled the 'stonecutter poet,' who, according to this reading, is reverted to in line 93, becoming 'thee ... mindful of th' unhonour'd dead'—'mindful' in that he composes verses for the gravemarkers of these dead. But, again, there are problems with this reading: is this 'stonecutter' explicitly mentioned, by being described as the 'unletter'd muse,' or is the 'muse' here to be better understood as the personification of an abstract muse (as 'the muse of poetry' or, in my opinion more pertinently, as the 'muse of literacy'), rather than any individual. And, anyway, even if we accept that 'muse' refers to a person, we are only sure this 'muse' writes 'names [and] ... years,' the bare data that all gravestones carry. Whether he also writes the 'uncouth rhimes' is less certain. Furthermore, the grammatical connection between lines 79–81 and lines 93 ff. is at best remote. Farcically enough, even this attempt to render the 'Elegy' back into good order has led on to a subcontroversy; this occasioned by noting that the 'memorials' are 'frail' and thus more likely to be made of 'wood,' the usual material used for the gravestones of the poor: the 'stonecutter' must now become a 'wood carver'.

What we have ended up with is a plethora of proposed spokespersons, who all in their own way can be sensibly proposed as signifieds for the pronominal signifier, 'thee.'

> (a) Gray himself (thee = me) (real)
>
> (b) the persona of the poem (thee = me) (imagined)
>
> (c) someone else (e.g., West) (real)
>
> (d) a fictional (imaginary) poet ('*poeta ignotus*') (imagined)
>
> (e) a personification: The Poet (imagined)
>
> (f) an actual unknown poet (the stone cutter/wood carver) (real)

Now, I of course cannot resist adding one further plausible signified. It seems to me a further plausible reading could be that 'thee' denominates

> (g) the reader of the poem (thee = thee, the reader) (real)

—an idea depending on a scenario where the reader is reciting the 'Elegy,' to him or herself or actually aloud, and in this sense relating the tale told in the 'Elegy,' the tale of 'th' unhonour'd dead,' of which the reader is, *sui generis,* being 'mindful' whilst reading the poem. Here the sense of 'relate' being deployed is related to the (now obsolete) one, '4b: to adduce, cite (an authority (*OED*). This might seem to render up Gray's idea of his readership in an interesting way: a readership which is sensitive, but not especially exalted. A problem here could be the objection that, since Walpole was one of Gray's readers, these cannot really be seen as generically 'humble' in origins—but this problem can be dismissed to some extent by refusing to accept that 'me' and Gray can be equated and instead preferring to regard 'me' in the poem as a persona.

However, it is not my purpose to press this particular case. My point in proposing a seventh possible identity for 'thee,' which seems, perhaps, to stand up just as well as any other suggestion, is to dramatise the sudden decentering of the poem's narrational harmony. The centre of the poem is suddenly called in doubt by this question: 'who is "thee"?' and its refusal to be resolved. It will be my contention that this irresolution is thematically integral. To explain why I believe this will take me down two lines of analysis, which I will then need to relate together before returning to the question of 'thee' and his identity. Both these lines of analysis demand some reference out to history and part of my point is that the 'Elegy' has still to be fully located within its history. The critics Richard C. Sha and John Lucas have provided recent impetus to this process, which, perhaps, finds its most significant start in William Empson's *Some Versions of the Pastoral.* My analysis owes debts to all of these critics: hopefully what I am about to offer will represent a useful extension to their arguments.

The two lines of historical contextualisation I wish to address are, respectively, the chronological position of the 'Elegy' in the process of rural change generated by the development of enclosure and engrossment occurring during the seventeenth and eighteenth centuries, and the chronological position of the 'Elegy' in the process of transition from a society which was predominantly illiterate to one which was predominantly literate. These lines of contextualisation are worth careful examination because, I will contend, in the period during which Gray was working on the 'Elegy'—most generally reckoned to be 1746–1750—these two important historical processes had reached points of pivotal significance, which actively impinge upon the poem's thematic structure: their impact on the poem, I contend, is discursively constitutive. What follows are some outlines as to where considering these contextual aspects would lead, rather than a completed project, but I believe these outlines are broadly reliable and point out some interesting directions.

In the middle decade of the eighteenth century, 1746 to 1755, precisely when for much of the time Gray was at work on the 'Elegy,' the process of enclosure had reached a transition point. It has become increasingly recognised that the enclosure movement had a very long foreground: it had been occurring in a piecemeal, unlegislated and unsystematic way, for many decades in the seventeenth century; the early eighteenth century saw a general, but not consistently maintained, acceleration in this process. The 1750s saw the beginnings of a new dimension to this process, as landowners increasingly turned to private parliamentary bills to facilitate the process of enclosure. This change-over, to the use of private bills, only became fully functional as the 1760s commenced: thereafter the process was very rapid. In the period 1750 to 1810 Paul Langford estimates that nearly four thousand enclosure acts were passed, whilst C.P. Hill states that the period 1760 to 1793 saw 1,335 bills passed. What occurred was the ending of the open-field system and the large-scale absorption of common land into private ownership, as the enclosure movement entered its final, parliamentary phase. In this sense, the 'Elegy' appeared in print at this pivotal point: just as parliament began to become the main conduit for the processes of enclosure. Just as significantly, though, Buckinghamshire and Cambridgeshire were situated geographically in that part of the country still largely unenclosed, and thus poised for large-scale take-over by this new mode of parliamentary-authorised enclosure, which re-invigorated the whole trend. The process of enclosure and engrossment in East Anglia had been largely completed by the end of the seventeenth century, Cambridgeshire and north Buckinghamshire were brought fully under the processes of enclosure during 'the first generation of parliamentary enclosures,' which would be, precisely, 1750–1770. Thus Gray's country churchyard, whether one chooses to locate it conventionally in Stoke Poges, or, more freely, somewhere in the area between Stoke Poges and Cambridge is, from the point of view of the historical geographer, at the centre of the changing and accelerating enclosure and engrossment process, moving out of a piecemeal and unlegislated phase into one dominated by Parliamentary acts. These developments were the subject of extensive contemporary debate. Thematically, I contend, all this impresses itself on the poem, once one gives proper emphasis to the primary human impact of this rural change.

Historians now seem to be moving towards some sort of consensus concerning the human impact of engrossment and enclosure in one arena of their debate about this process. There is still the predictable disagreement about to what extent the rural population *as a whole* suffered from these changes: some economic historians insistently point to what they discern as rises in both productivity and levels of employment. However, there is widespread agreement that 'many individuals' losses may have been serious. Equally, it would seem to be generally agreed that there developed a clear 'tendency to replace farm servants with wage-paid labour hired for the purpose' because 'The new farms wanted wage labourers.' Quite simply, the loss of common land forced the rural population to turn to day labour, and day labour 'offered no equivalent security … [to] freehold, copyhold or … long lease.' This represented, then, a significant alteration in social relations. It has been called 'a crisis of paternalism,' and seems to have been the subject of substantial contemporary debate. Radical historians, such as Christopher Hill, reference contemporary mid-century documents exposing a discourse nakedly representing this shift towards day-labour as an ideological contrivance. Hill quotes 'official Board of Agriculture reports' which praise the enclosure of the commons 'because it forced labourers to "work every day in the year" … depriving the lower orders of any chance of economic independence … [so that] "the subordination of the lower ranks of society … would be thereby considerably secured."' Similarly Hill references 'a pamphlet of 1739' which asserted that 'The only way to make the lower orders temperate and industrious … was to lay them under the necessity of labouring all the time they can spare from rest and sleep in order to procure the necessities of life.'

I wish to propose that this 'crisis of [rural] paternalism,' gaining momentum in the middle decades of the eighteenth century, can be laid alongside a crisis in the poetic discourse of pastoralism. We are, after all, only two decades away from the publication of Oliver Goldsmith's *The Deserted Village* (1770). George Crabbe's *The Village* lies only just over one decade further off (1783). Goldsmith's and Crabbe's poems speak of the full impact of enclosure and engrossment in their different ways, and represent the tight squeeze within which the pastoral was constrained. Gray comes significantly earlier in this process, and his 'Elegy' feels around the edges of this gathering process. What else are we to make of the strangely unsta-

ble oscillation in the pattern of this poem's representation of country life?:

> The Curfew tolls the knell of parting day,
> The lowing herd wind slowly o'er the lea
> The plowman homeward plods his weary way,
> And leaves the world to darkness and to me.

Representing 'lowing herd[s] wind[ing] slowly o'er the lea' is idyllic enough—falling well within conservative expectations of the genre, but 'The plowman … plodd[ing] … wear[il]y' is far less reassuring, and much more in line with the sentiments of Hill's 1739 pamphleteer. In fact this disconcerting switching of mood is recurrent. I offer a partial list:

1.3: plods his weary
1.5: glimmering landscape
1.6: stillness
1.8: drowsy tinklings lull
1.14: mould'ring heap
1.15: narrow cell
1.16: rude Forefathers
1.16: hamlet sleep
1.17: incense-breathing Morn
1.20: lowly
1.21: blazing hearth
1.25: harvest
1.27: jocund
1.30: homely joys
1.30: destiny obscure
1.32: simple annals 1.32: short … poor
1.45: neglected spot
1.51: chill Penury
1.52: genial currents 1.52: froze
1.56: waste
1.65: forbad
1.74: sober
1.75: cool
1.76: noiseless tenor
1.79: uncouth … shapeless
1.81: unlettered

It should be observed that antithesis is one central rhetorical trope of this poem, and this has led to the suggestion that what Gray is aiming for here is a 'balance' which, correctly understood, is a guarantee of the poem's apoliticism. I find myself unable to go along with this representation of the poem. After all, the 'Elegy' purports, despite its eventual, disconcerting narrative decentering, to describe a real village graveyard around which real activity occurs: the 'plowman … plods' in the present tense to lend, exactly, a sense of immediacy. The disconcerting shuttle between negative and positive representations of this rural experience has thus, unsurprisingly, led this poem to be seen 'both as rightist and leftist propaganda.' Certainly, there is, virtually, an alternation: rural life being represented as fulfilling, then debilitating, rewarding, then chilling—which perhaps functions as a discursive analogue of the confusing social crisis borne within the processes of enclosure. In this respect it is crucial to note that the narrative is led in by a 'plowman,' and a 'weary' plowman at that: a representative, precisely, of the growing numbers of agricultural labourers coming to dominate the rural scene. In fact, the labours described are all potentially those of farm workers:

> Oft did the harvest to their sickle yield.
> Their furrow oft the stubborn glebe has broke;
> How jocund did they drive their team afield!
> How bow'd the woods beneath their sturdy stroke!

It is consistent with my argument here to note that two of these activities (the clearing of woods and the ploughing up of 'the stubborn glebe,' which the *OED* links to common land by quoting a source of 1598: 'Houses … he raseth, to make the common gleabe his private land' [T. Bastard, *Chrestoleros*]) could both quite well refer to the enclosure of common land: this is, perhaps, how Clare understood these lines, as witness this echo in his 'Helpstone' (even allowing for the deployment of stock pastoral imagery the parallelism is worth comment), in which Clare is plainly describing the process of enclosure: 'Accursed wealth …/Thou art the cause that levels every tree/And woods bow down to clear a way for thee.'

It is equally consistent to observe, however, that in the equivalent stanza of the 'Elegy,' though the second of these four activities strongly suggests hard labour, this is plainly set, once again disconcertingly, beside a more idyllic portrait of easy pastoral fulfilment, of 'yield[ing]' and 'bow[ing],' without Clare's sense of irony (his 'woods' bow to 'wealth'). Nevertheless, the impression recurrently is of labour and labourers rather than farming and farmers. This sense of a rural working class is perhaps reinforced by constant reminders in Gray's poem of their illiteracy. And this observation ushers in my second theme.

In exploring the relation of the 'Elegy' to actual processes in historical geography, what I am arguing is that the conventional pastoral discourse, as a mode of representing the rural English experience, is losing in this poem any monolithic integrity, and being riven by real contradictory inputs—the observable rural changes here suffuse the 'Elegy's' dramatic representations. In Foucauldian terms, the discourse is falling available, potentially, to seizure—or recuperation. Something similar, I believe, underlies the poem's apparent uncertainties about literacy. At one point late in the poem,

in line 115, 'thee' (here it definitely refers to 'some kindred Spirit' who by 'chance' may 'enquire thy fate') is invited by the 'hoary-headed Swain' to 'approach and read (for thou can'st read).' The clear implication is that the elderly rural inhabitant cannot read (else the clause is almost wholly redundant). This near-certainty about reading abilities ('hoary headed Swain' = non-reader, 'kindred Spirit' = reader) comes almost as a relief after a cluster of doubtful suggestions about levels of literacy. Previously, you will recall, we have had the disconcerting image of an 'unletter'd Muse' spelling 'names [and] … years.' The only way to grasp this image, before it disintegrates into unresolvable contradictions (how can someone who is 'unletter'd' spell?) is to understand that here the 'letters' in question must refer to the Classical education that would not have been available to any rural memorialist: the latter is 'unletter'd' in this sense: without the Classics. But, even as the issue of literacy recedes by understanding 'unletter'd' in this way, and thus apparently resolving the contradiction, it is replaced by the issue of education. The problematic status of this issue is well-captured by the near-oxymoronic juxtaposition of 'unletter'd' with 'Muse,' which must thereby be divested of its Classical associations and left simply as 'inspiration' (the 'Muse of inspiration', and not a Classical Muse), in a process of transference only just coming into the language (the *OED*'s first recorded example, 1d, dates from 1721). The terrain here is riddled with ironies, which Gray promptly compounds by offering us what can reasonably be described as a meta-textual irony, since we are reminded that we are reading an elegy at the very moment that we are being reminded that others cannot, else they would not need to rely on an 'unletter'd muse':

> Their names, their years, spelt by th' unletter'd
>   muse,
> The place of fame and elegy supply.

It will be my contention that, here again, these issues, and their problematic representation in the text, derive from the particular historical context investing Gray's 'Elegy.'

It is increasingly often argued by historians that the middle decades of the eighteenth century mark a transition point in the cultural valuation and significance of literacy:

> In the mid-eighteenth century about a third of men and two thirds of women were unable to sign their name, though the local incidence of illiteracy varied widely. But the acquisition of basic reading skills by those on the margin of middle- and lower-class life,

for whom they were coming to be an essential working asset, was a notable feature of urban society.

The sting lies in the tail of this analysis: that literacy was becoming of increasing cultural importance was particularly true for those living in towns and cities—but the dislocations occasioned by the processes of enclosure and engrossing had displaced segments of the rural population. Some of these were inevitably drawn into these urban areas (in a process of increasingly fluid interchange between country and city), as the position of the rural worker, now an agricultural labourer, was rendered far more precarious. Education, particularly education to provide literacy, was becoming increasingly necessary. This, too has been quite widely agreed on by historians: one basic sign of this was patterns of reading:

> There were many pointers to wide and growing readership in the mid-eighteenth century, including the production of both metropolitan and provincial newspapers, and the multiplication of new tract and book titles generally.

But these positive signs are counterbalanced by the way in which there was no decisive increase in the numbers signing parish marriage registers in the period 1754 to 1800. Indeed it is a significant sign of the growing importance of literacy that it was the year 1753 that had witnessed the introduction of Lord Hardwicke's act requiring the signing of parochial wedding registers (thus enabling us to know the percentage signing marriage registers). Literacy was plainly becoming increasingly important for the individual in his or her negotiations with society. Literacy, I am suggesting, and beside it, education, were two key issues of the middle decades of the eighteenth century, issues of decisive socio-cultural significance. Reading and writing were key terrains of cultural hegemony. To obtain these prizes was of real social significance throughout the eighteenth century:

> In the 1720s Mandeville had … [contended] that to secure the contentment of the poor with their lot, it is requisite that great numbers of them should be ignorant as well as poor.

John Clare, born in 1793, in his autobiographical writings, notes:

> As my parents had the good fate to have but a small family, I being the eldest of 4, two of whom dyed in their Infancy, my mothers hopfull ambition ran high of being able to make me a good scholar as she said she expirenced enough in her own case to avoid bringing up her children in ignorance, but god help her, her hopful and tender kindness was often crossd with difficultys … I believe I was not older than 10 when my father took me to seek the scanty rewards

> of industry … as to my schooling, I think never a year passd me till I was 11 or 12 but 3 months or more at the worst of times was luckily spared for my improvement …

Even allowing for the conventionality of Clare's sentiments, this determination maps onto the lack of opportunity to obtain schooling, on the one hand, and the increasingly high valuation being placed upon literacy in the market place as well as in polite society on the other. Indeed it is possible to contend that education became increasingly hierarchized, thus Gillian Sutherland claims that 'In the course of the eighteenth century, "plebeians," those whose fathers were not gentlemen, disappeared altogether' from Oxford and Cambridge.

These considerations bear sharply upon the constantly problematic introduction of the theme of reading and writing into Gray's 'Elegy':

> Let not Ambition mock their useful toil,
> Their homely joys, and destiny obscure;
> Nor Grandeur hear with a disdainful smile,
> The short and simple annals of the poor.

Annals are '1. A narrative of events written year by year, or 2. Historical records generally' (*OED*)—but in both cases, written records that the poor cannot keep. This is an issue of social status, as Gray's later reference, in stanza eleven, to a 'storied urn' in turn implies: the urn, is of course here a classical one, with a frieze on it narrating a story visually, for the viewer to 'read'—but this 'reading' is itself fundamentally dependent on knowledge of the classics, which 'th' unletter'd Muse' surely does not possess—and so we return to the oxymoron which served as the foundation of my argument. The fact is that these agricultural labourers possessed 'rude Forefathers'—uneducated forefathers, and their gravemarkers will bear 'uncouth rhimes.' But (and here the pendulum swings again) these gravemarkers also carry 'holy text,' and it was precisely the Church, and particularly the Nonconformist Church, with its insistence on reading the Bible, which operated as the main stimulus towards and conduit for what education was obtainable, and then only to a very limited number. Thus Clare, in his 'Shepherd's Calendar,' will write, in 1827, of the shepherd boy still struggling with his letters:

> He hears the wild geese gabble oer his head
> And pleasd wi fancys in his musings bred
> He marks the figured forms in which they flye
> And pausing follows wi a wondering eye
> Likening their curious march in curves or rows
> To every letter which his memory knows

Issues of literacy and education are here, as with Gray, interlinked with the issuings of the creative imagination, but far more explicitly, and from quite another perspective.

Gray's background may not be irrelevant here: he was the son of a scrivener and exchange broker (albeit one able to send his son to Eton), and in this sense slightly on the edge of the social circles in which he moved. Walpole confessed that 'insensible to the feelings of one I thought below me … I treated [Gray] insolently.' For Gray, therefore, issues of social rank, social order and the advantages of being lettered must have had a particular piquancy. It is tempting then, to identify him in the poem not with the suddenly introduced 'thee' in the poem, nor even with the 'me' that opens up the poem's reflections, but with the 'mopeing owl' in stanza three, located in 'yonder ivy-mantled tow'r,' high above the country churchyard, safe from the questions of literacy and class which in the graveyard down below press upon the consciousness.

All this comes to a climax in 'The EPITAPH' at the end of the poem, which contains one of the most difficult lines in the poem—'Fair Science frowned not on his humble birth'—difficult, because whilst it plainly serves as a key pointer to the identity of the individual being remembered in this epitaph, the 'thee' introduced in stanza twenty-four, this line also, ironically, enormously limits the range of identities assignable to this individual. This constraint results from conjoining the 'birth' of 'thee' with the words 'humble' and 'science.' Such a conjunction renders problematic the identity of 'thee,' since 'science'—in the sense of knowledge acquired by learning—rarely conjoined with humbleness at people's births in mid-eighteenth century England. And this observation precisely maps out for us the links between the 'Elegy's' uneasy treatment of rural labouring experience, its recurrent concern with levels of literacy and the problem of arriving at a satisfactory identification of 'thee.' Each possible identity for 'thee' stumbles up against the problem of who could plausibly conjoin 'humbleness' and 'science' in their origins. Hence, I believe, the resort to identifying 'thee' as a *poeta ignotus*—an unknown poet: it is, quite simply, a way out of this dilemma. This is in fact a pressing issue for Gray: he was much attracted by the idea that true Englishness resided in those marginalised by the Norman invasion and subsequent repressions: hence his interest in the fragments of 'Ossian,' his poems such as 'The Bard' (1757) and translations such as 'The

Triumphs of Owen' (1768). However, these beliefs and interests directed him away from the 'letter'd Muse' into a cultural terrain manifestly neglected and marginalised, full, indeed of unknown poets—such as Stephen Duck, 'a common thresher,' whose *Poems on Several Subjects* had appeared in 1730. It was indeed this period, the middle decades of the eighteenth century, that saw the irruption of vernacular poets into polite society—writers contesting, at least in part, how to understand the presence of 'fair science' at their births: the sense of 'science' would now need to shift to 'knowledge (more or less extensive) as a personal attribute' (*OED*).

This may be conjoined, I believe, to the crisis of pastoralism that I am proposing, twinned as it is with the crisis of paternalism: what is developing is a loss of confidence in the pastoral's discursive representation of a whole nation, and a recognition of cultural and social fragmentation and social division. This manifests itself in a recognition of what I shall describe as an 'Other,' a manifestation of cultural otherness—in this poem, 'thee'—to be desired (as Edenic), feared (as penury), and, indeed, killed off, after being described in terms of melancholic exclusion. In this sense, Gray opens the way towards the Romantics, as many critics have observed, but, I would claim, his accompanying recognition of cultural division, along lines of class and education, points out the way for the concerted development of other written cultural traditions, separate from that laid out by 'th' …letter'd Muse.' And this is one main element of the link between Gray and Clare. Clare's lines:

No, not a friend on earth had I
But my own kin and poesy

links clearly, in my mind, to the 'thee' as Other depicted by 'the hoary-headed Swain':

'His listless length at noontide wou'd he stretch
'And pore upon the brook that babbles by.
'Hard by yon wood, now smiling as in scorn,
'Mutt'ring his wayward fancies he wou'd rove,
'Now drooping, woeful wan, like one forlorn,
'Or craz'd with care, or cross'd in hopeless love.

One needs to be careful here: one needs to recognise the conventionalities investing these images, and I am not proposing that Gray's 'thee' is in some way equitable with Clare. There is a clear enough separation here, which may be related to John Lucas's depiction of Gray as 'muddled' in his handling of the politics involved in depicting 'Englishness.' What I certainly want to note here is that the portrait of 'thee' cannot be read off simply as 'a poet entirely unkown to fame, an Ignotus,' as suggested by Odell Shepard, but rather as a complex doppelganger: tradition and its fracturing is contained within him.

On the one hand 'thee' is not a *poeta ignotus* so much as quite literally 'The Ignote', the unknown—the Other, yet to be delivered by the cultural fragmentation sweeping across an enclosing, engrossing, urbanising and industrialising land, where literacy and class would become primary. On the other hand 'thee' is also a conventional multi-faceted portrait—stranding together West, Gray, the sensitive reader, the stonecutter/woodcarver, each one in slightly different ways safely locatable in all those pastoral traditions these identities reference, within which 'The Ignote' might be safely constrained: as the simple rural friend, as the poet (re-)discovering himself in bucolic reverie, as the urban(e) audience longing for rural retreat—as the pastoral rural bard is progressively superseded by the more complex and problematic figure of the peasant poet. Just as Clare came to regret his constraint within one of these categories, the 'peasant poet'—a category misrepresenting Clare, so 'The Ignote' in the 'Elegy' cannot adequately be contained within any of these categories, but plays disturbingly across them all, unsettling the pastoral's attempt to invest the countryside with order. Thus the answer to the question 'who can Gray have had in mind when he introduced 'thee' into his poem?' is quite literally that 'no answer fits *anymore.*' After all, we end up in a projected future set in tension with a counterpoint of intertextual allusions, borrowings and debts from the pastoral's past—Raymond Williams' backward moving escalator which seems to offer us the promise of establishing some identity, but always fails. However the 'Elegy' also disconcertingly moves from unsettled backward-looking pastoral generalisation towards the anxious future of an imagined, particular 'thee.' But this is only ever a seeming particularity, upon which each attempt to place an existing identity fails, and further reveals 'The(e) Ignote' as a void still to be filled. External to the poem, one good answer to the question 'who is "thee"?' thus *is* John Clare (whose close friend and fellow autodidact John Turnill wrote at least one epitaph, and who seriously considered a career as a monumental mason), but he is not yet born. In the poem's own terms, there perhaps is and can be no answer, so instead of seeking one, I think it is better to rephrase the question: the 'Elegy,' in generating the problem of who 'thee' is, is also raising the question, what on earth is descending upon the inhabitant of the changing English countryside—what identity has s/he got?—a question, I would argue, of very real penetration, and one bound up with shifting social relations and their definition in language, discourse and education—the very themes I see as central to the poem.

Source: R. J. Ellis, "Plodding Plowmen: Issues of Labour and Literacy in Gray's 'Elegy,'" in *The Independent Spirit: John Clare and the Self-Taught Tradition,* edited by John Goodridge, John Clare Society and Margaret Grainger Memorial Trust, 1994, pp. 27–43.

Andrew Dillon

In this essay, Dillon explores the reasons behind Gray's rewriting of the poem's ending.

The "Elegy Written in a Country Churchyard" can be read as a journey of recognition, conceived in dusk and worked out—not in a miasma of depression—but in the light of a symbolic self-destruction. The poem contains a drama of identification with the buried farmers of the village of Stoke Poges; however, this identification yields the poet a brief delivery from his rather narrow life. Moreover, the development of the poem has a quasi-heroic quality, for it grows out of a shorter early version that is a more emotionally distanced study of man's final destiny. When Thomas Gray returned to the Eton manuscript of the "Elegy," he filled the new ending with far more intimate feelings.

The poem opens with the speaker's evocation of the world immediately around the graveyard; it then focuses on a plowman, who "homeward plods his weary way." As if at home in the oncoming darkness, Gray clearly includes himself in the poem in stanzas that are full of a mournful music; suddenly, the verbs take on an almost independent energy: the turf "heaves" as the poet observes the graves as "many a mould'ring heap." As will be later developed, this heaving of the earth suggests a kind of life within.

A series of vital images follows as if the quiet, celibate scholar perceived the farmers' lives in moments of dreamy wistfulness. In spite of the need to point out that the cheerful aspects of the laborers' mornings exist for them no more, the speaker describes elements of dawn: "breezy," "twitt'ring," "the cock's shrill clarion." There follows a series of pictures of a very different end of day than Thomas Gray could know: the "blazing hearth," the "busy housewife," children, and their climbing of the farmer's knees. Finally, stanza seven depicts the farmer's daily life:

Oft did the harvest to their sickle yield,
Their furrow oft the stubborn glebe has broke;

How jocund did they drive their team afield!
How bow'd the woods beneath their sturdy stroke!

These verbs evidence virile strength; they portray a celebration of physical power in that stroke that bows the woods. This may have been merely an idealization of everyday life, but it does touch on what could have been a psychological problem for Gray; it evokes the pride that rises from earning one's own way.

Gray's fellowship at Cambridge gave him a life-long tenure for a somewhat elegant—if narrow—scholarly existence. He was never required to teach and never delivered a lecture. Clarence Tracy asserts that Gray "lived for years on public patronage" and goes on to say that "his friend, Mason, made it a virtue in him that he never dirtied his mind with any intention of earning his living." Tracy also quotes Mason as saying his "life was spent in that kind of learned leisure, which has only self-improvement and self-gratification for its object."

Gray's biographer, Ketton-Cremer, suggests, "the man of reading and reflection often feels an envious admiration for the man of physical skill." However, Gray modulates any such response into an identification—as well as a defense of the farmers against the putative disdain of the upper classes. When he honors the simple graves of the poor, he points out that the "storied urn" and "animated bust" of the aristocrat cannot bring back the dead, as if in an urgent exhortation of the prosperous—or that side of Thomas Gray that has enjoyed a life of leisure.

Gray goes on to suggest the possibility that here may lie "some heart once pregnant with celestial fire," but "chill Penury repress'd their noble range" because they lacked the good fortune of having an education. The farmers, then, were left in pastoral innocence like the famous flower "born to blush unseen." The poem is now near its first ending, which is preserved only in the Eton manuscript of Gray's "Elegy." Here, perhaps somewhat self-consciously, Gray implies that learning, worldly power, and leisure could do little but corrupt:

The thoughtless World to Majesty may bow
Exalt the brave, & idolize Success
But more to Innocence their Safety owe
Than Power & Genius e'er conspired to bless
And thou, who mindful of the unhonour'd Dead
Dost in these Notes their artless Tale relate
By Night & lonely Contemplation led
To linger in the gloomy Walks of Fate
Hark how the sacred Calm, that broods around
Bids ev'ry fierce tumultuous Passion cease

> *As the swain describes it, Gray's Romantic crisis becomes a self-immolation, a brief escape from his life, for he has moved on to a fearful insight: it is as if Gray and the deceased farmers share a complex species of mortality where the vital dead are more alive than the living speaker feels he is."*

In still small Accents whisp'ring from the Ground
A grateful Earnest of eternal Peace
No more with Reason & thyself at Strife;
Give anxious Cares & endless Wishes room
But thro' the cool sequester'd Vale of Life
Pursue the silent Tenour of thy Doom.

A close look at Starr and Hendrickson's rendition of the sixth line of the Eton manuscript excerpt shows an alteration to the word "their" from the original "thy." Of course, this "thy" might have been meant only to refer to the narrator of the poem as he possessed the poem—but it may very well have indicated a deeper involvement as if Gray were briefly identifying with the dead in a melancholic assessment of what his life had become.

The moment of ambiguity between whether "thy" referred only to the tale or to the life of the narrator is resolved when Gray struck out "thy" and rewrote "their," for the line now seems to concern no one except the dead farmers. However, the brief scratchings remain to suggest that the "Elegy" was for his own existence and that he had briefly included himself among the dead.

When he was much younger, Gray had written a four-line Latin fragment, "O lachrymarum Fons—O fountain of tears." Starr and Hendrickson's translation is: "O fountain of tears which have their sacred sources in the sensitive soul! Four times blessed he who has felt thee, holy Nymph, bubbling up from depths of his heart." This is a moving evocation of the ability to feel as if reaching out to the self's own source of tears; moreover, it suggests an earlier psychological breakthrough in response to depression. While Ian Jack asserts that Gray dropped the original four-stanza ending of his "Elegy" because "it preached a Stoic attitude to life that he could not accept," it is as likely a conjecture that the new ending was yet another breakthrough in understanding for Gray, since it formed an escape from the depressing aspects of merely pursuing what he called "the silent Tenour of thy Doom" (Eton ms. 88).

R. W. Ketton-Cremer has demonstrated Gray's depression; it seems likely to infer an etiology of that condition in "his father's brutality to his mother" and in Gray's subsequent dependence on his mother. David Cecil points out "by the easygoing University regulations of those days he could go on residing in the college free, for as long as he wanted." Cecil also quotes one early letter to a friend saying, "When you have seen one of my days, you have seen a whole year of my life. They go round and round like a blind horse in the mill, only he has the satisfaction of fancying he makes progress, and gets some ground: my eyes are open enough to see the same dull prospect, and having made four and twenty steps more, I shall now be just where I was."

When Gray took up the Eton manuscript to write the ending with which readers are familiar, the farmers are the ones who keep to the "sequester'd vale of life"—and keep "the noiseless tenor of their way." This last word, "way," is, of course, a significant change from Gray's term for himself in the earlier version: "of thy doom" (Eton ms. 88). Moreover, his new understanding is accompanied by a second major surge of energy:

> Far from the madding crowd's ignoble strife,
> Their sober wishes never learn'd to stray;
> Along the cool sequester'd vale of life
> They kept the noiseless tenor of their way.

Later, Gray united himself with the farmers and all mankind in tremendously original lines:

> For who to dumb Forgetfulness a prey,
> This pleasing anxious being e'er resign'd,
> Left the warm precincts of the chearful day,
> Nor cast one longing ling'ring look behind?
> On some fond breast the parting soul relies,
> Some pious drops the closing eye requires;
> Ev'n from the tomb the voice of Nature cries,
> Ev'n in our Ashes live their wonted Fires.

Dr. Johnson said of the two stanzas that contain the ashes line, "I have never seen the notions

in any other place; yet he that reads them here, persuades himself that he has always felt them" (Ketton-Cremer). The poet means to suggest that life is still speaking from the buried ashes—yet whose ashes are these? They are those of the safe dead, yet they also form a melancholic, personal estimation of the poet—alive but in the ashes of an entombed self.

When Gray asserts, "Ev'n from the tomb the voice of Nature cries," he must feel the strength of a tremendous moment of human projection; his living soul is speaking for the abstraction, Nature. Then, the idea is reinforced with, "Ev'n in our Ashes live their wonted Fires." In the "our" of this line, Gray achieves a kind of emotional closure and becomes more nearly one with the ironically vital dead.

Perhaps it is at this exact moment of desperate recognition that he becomes "the central figure of the poem and occupies that place until the end" (Ketton-Cremer). At any rate, in the next line, Gray speaks of "thee," who relates these lines. Of course, the "me" of the beginning of the poem and the "thee" here are the same being, for Gray suddenly distances his spirit from his everyday self. Moreover, this objectification of the soul is Gray's chance to take the whole journey of imagination—and the poem becomes his elegy, *his* storied urn" as Cleanth Brooks suggests.

Gray then invokes a "hoary-headed Swain" who would by chance ("haply") describe the poem's speaker, now depicted as a rather romantic youth, who is seen as pale and wandering, possibly "craz'd with care, or cross'd in hopeless love." Frank Brady suggests that "the swain's description of the narrator" shows that the narrator's "life is apparently unproductive and unfulfilled." Then, the Swain is to tell the reader, who is suddenly referred to as a "kindred Spirit," that the narrator is dead! He then invites the reader to read the narrator's epitaph, where an offering of the soul to God is recorded. We must understand that Gray—as narrator—has imaginatively entered the local society and has been long known to the swain, who is the second living farmer in the poem. In fact, he is the older parallel of the earlier rustic who "homeward plods his weary way." That previous figure may have given Gray the first intimation of the farmer's warm reception at home as this imaginary swain yields Gray his escape from mere static contemplation.

The poet has now managed to stage a symbolic death so that his epitaph can be read in the churchyard. It is an unusual conception that allows Gray to break through the natural terror of dying in order to forge a relationship between a fear of death and an acceptance of that death. As the swain describes it, Gray's Romantic crisis becomes a self-immolation, a brief escape from his life, for he has moved on to a fearful insight: it is as if Gray and the deceased farmers share a complex species of mortality where the vital dead are more alive than the living speaker feels he is. Their very ashes contain a fire of life that the speaker senses he is missing, and, thus, they are the object of his sympathetic projection.

Perhaps Gray's personal sense of a buried life can be best approached from the end of the epitaph in which we are earlier told that "Melancholy mark'd him for her own":

> No farther seek his merits to disclose,
> Or draw his frailties from their dread abode,
> (There they alike in trembling hope repose)
> The bosom of his Father and his God.

His frailties are undefined, but they are seen as existing along with his merits in a trembling condition lodged in "the bosom of his Father and his God." It is a strange view of eternal love that reposes the deceased one's attributes only in trembling hope—forever. Indeed, it is depressing, for it pictures God as a stern, judgmental father who holds this split youth (merits and frailties) in eternal abeyance like a bird in winter.

Gray's "Elegy," then, is as much about depression as it is about other species of entombments. Moreover, three years before his death in 1771, in the "Ode for Music," Gray once again referred to melancholy:

> Oft at the blush of dawn
> I trod your level lawn,
> Oft woo'd the gleam of *Cynthia* silver-bright
> In cloisters dim, far from the haunts of Folly,
> With Freedom by my Side, and soft-ey'd
>   Melancholy.

Ketton-Cremer suggests that the lines reflect Gray's life at Cambridge "remotely but unmistakably."

However, the "Elegy" works because of the exquisite beauty of its language and the psychic complicity of the minds of readers with that of Thomas Gray. Our guide has disappeared; however, that is not an idiosyncratic moment of desertion but a great release of the imagination. Nevertheless, the vitality we project to the farmers and the buried speaker, is, of course, our own. Moreover, the poem serves as Gray's self-wrought myth,

where life's verve is celebrated, a descent into the earth is recorded, yet a resurrection is shown. In fact, the "Elegy" presents the reader with the "moment of awareness, the essential substance of myth" (Aldus). Therefore, readers return to the poem to take a journey underground while still in "this pleasing anxious being." However, the "Elegy"'s exchange for our energy is a delight which turns us back to the world as we depart the poem's mimetic twilight with our own "wonted fires."

Source: Andrew Dillon, "Depression and Release: The Journey of the Spirit in Thomas Gray's 'Elegy,'" in *North Dakota Quarterly,* Vol. 60, No. 4, Fall, 1992, pp. 128–34.

Richard C. Sha

In the following essay, Sha encourages the reader to look beneath the surface for meaning in Gray's poem.

Thomas Gray ends his *Elegy Written in a Country Churchyard* with an injunction to his readers not to look beyond the confines of the poem. As part of the poet's own epitaph, the enjoinder takes on the force of lapidary inscription and we are made to hear, as it were, the voice of the dead or one who speaks for the dead.

> No farther seek his merits to disclose,
> Or draw his frailties from their dread abode,
> (There they alike in trembling hope repose)
> The bosom of his Father and his God.

But Gray also cleverly projects his future audience in the role of a sympathetic reader of the elegy; we readers, who are now "mindful of the unhonoured dead" and are the poet's "kindred spirits," inquire about the poem and about the swain's and Gray's fates, but only insofar as we avoid topical issues and confine ourselves to thinking about the poem in terms of universal truths. The poet, moreover, practically commands his readers to "relate" to this "artless tale." As Peter Sacks has argued, Gray employs a kind of "posthumous ventriloquism" by putting "words into the mouths of his survivors." It is therefore not altogether surprising that the interpretative history of the poem largely testifies to the fact that readers have heeded the poet's ghostly admonitions. However, we need now to exorcise this ghost fully by looking at the material history imbedded within and surrounding the poem: historical particularities demand that we look beyond the poem's universalizing rhetoric. Moreover, that history bids us to ask: why is the mid-eighteenth-century an appropriate moment for an elegy about the poor? Why exactly does Gray praise the poor? On what issues concerning the peasants

> *A politicized reading of Gray's elegy, then, indicates that although the poet is sympathetic to the poor, Gray's compassion is contingent upon the silent and cheerful penury of the lower classes."*

is the poem conspicuously silent and what are the specific causes of this silence? What ideological pressures does Gray confront in his treatment of the poor? My aim here is to formulate possible answers to these questions.

Although no poem escapes history, Gray's *Elegy* is most often talked about as if it has—a fact that attests to the power of Gray's rhetorical strategy. Samuel Johnson spoke for generations of critics when he praised the poem's universal appeal and claimed that the elegy "abounds … with sentiments to which every bosom returns an echo." In perhaps the most famous essay on the poem, Cleanth Brooks sees the "the total context of the whole poem" as the ironies and paradoxes of "Gray's storied urn"; that is, the elaborate personifications are contrasted ironically with the simple churchyard. Death, therefore, becomes the great leveller, and brings "the proud and the humble together in common humanity." Much more recently, Wallace Jackson aptly characterizes the tendency of Gray criticism as, on one hand, governed by the belief that Gray was unhappily separated from his age, and, on the other, centered on the problem of voice in the elegy. The few critics who have delved into the poem's material history include William Empson, F. W. Bateson, Frank Ellis, and John Barrell. Insofar as Empson argues that Gray compares "the social arrangement" of the poor and the elite "to nature" in order to make this hierarchy seem natural, he anticipates some of my remarks. And Barrell's study of the representation of the rural poor throughout the eighteenth century is important to my project. A sustained archeology of the material history of the poem, however, needs to be done.

Let us first acknowledge that Gray's attitude towards the poor is somewhat sympathetic. As the son of a scrivener, Gray's upper-class affiliations were tenuous; this made the poet more sympathetic to the plight of the beleaguered, but it also perhaps made him anxious to bury his class identification with them. Indeed, in much the same way that a farm laborer worked for his lord, Gray depended upon the upper class for patronage. Closer scrutiny of Gray's treatment of the poor reveals this ambiguity. As I will argue below, the poet's compassion is strongly predicated both on the cheerful industry of the poor, and on their acceptance of their place. The poet's upper-class affiliations must have exerted ideological pressures on his attitudes to the poor; not only was Horace Walpole, Gray's friend and patron, the elegy's initial private audience, but Walpole circulated the poem among his coterie. Gray could thus remain sympathetic to the poor as long as he depicted them as somewhat abstract and distanced. If the poor got too close, the elite typically grew uneasy. In a letter to Montagu, Walpole, a member of the House of Commons, demonstrated just such discomfort. Referring to a mob of electors—a group of even a higher economic and social class than Gray's rustics—Walpole wrote with disdain,

> Think of me, the subject of a mob, who was scarce before in a mob, addressing them in the town hall, riding at the head of two thousand people, dining with above two hundred of them, amid bumpers, huzzas, songs, and tobacco,… I have borne it all cheerfully.

Walpole's attitude towards the common people seems exemplary of a leisured class which preferred not to get too close to the lower sorts.

We can witness this patronizing attitude towards the poor in many of the contemporary debates concerning them; these debates in turn inform Gray's poem itself. The upper classes grew anxious about the rapid proliferation of the poor and vigorously argued about possible solutions to this problem. When Gray refers to "the poor," and their "short and simple annals" he elliptically suggests such controversy. In the eighteenth century, the very term, "the poor," was charged with political significance to which we today are less sensitized; Samuel Johnson records in his 1755 *Dictionary* that the "poor" refers to "Those who are in the lowest rank of community; those who cannot subsist but by the charity of others.…" Johnson's definition, of course, accounts for both the idle and laboring poor. As I shall argue later, the absence of any overt reference to charity in Gray's poem is telling. "The poor," moreover, were the subject of much legislation; during the years 1732–50 alone the House of Commons heard 17 bills or petitions for bills concerning them. Members of Parliament argued about how to remedy the defects of antiquated poor laws of Queen Elizabeth's reign, how to regulate the choice of church wardens and overseers of the destitute, and how to raise funds for workhouses to keep these people from being idle.

Many of these bills were motivated less by a sense of compassion for the poor and more by a desire to protect propertied interests from possible harm. As early as 1733, for example, representatives from Middlesex sought to "Ease" the "Tranquility of the Inhabitants" by erecting a workhouse for the "Employment and Maintenance of the Poor." Apparently the "clamorous Proceedings and irregular Behaviour" of the "great Multitude" who attended the Vestry not only discouraged the town's "principal Inhabitants from attending," but also so alarmed these inhabitants that they sought to keep the poor better employed. The "clamouring" multitude were not confined to Middlesex, however. Two years later, representatives from Westminister demanded more "Night Watchmen" to protect the "Security of Lives and Properties." Petitioners from Colchester, Essex, also lamented the "extremely numerous poor," and spoke of "the Failure of Part of the Administration of Justice to the unspeakable Detriment and Danger of the petitioners" themselves. Others argued in 1736 before the House for the "better Relief and Employment of the Poor" and for "more effective punishment of Rogues and Vagabonds." Brought again in 1743, that bill was emended to include the punishment of "other idle and disorderly Persons."

One year later, Parliament issued an act which deemed all who begged or received alms idle and disorderly; moreover, these legislators declared that those who refused to work could be sent to a house of correction where they would be put to hard labor. Because the poor were held responsible for their own condition, legislation became increasingly punitive. Such a hardened attitude is epitomized by a bill of February 1747, in which representatives complained that "the Poor of Suffolk do daily multiply." "Idleness and Debauchery amongst the meaner Sort do greatly increase," petitioners warned, "for want of Workhouses to keep them employed." When Gray alludes to "the poor," then, he addresses one of the more vexing political issues of his time.

Insofar as Gray speaks to this issue, what might he mean by referring to the poor's "short and simple annals?" As Cleanth Brooks has pointed out, the poor do not, properly speaking, have "annals." "Annals" record the history of the gentry or monarchy; Gray would later use the term more appropriately when he asked Horace Walpole about the "annals of Strawberry Hill." That Gray calls the poor's annals "short and simple" might be an ironic reference to the brevity of peasants' lives and thus the rustic grave markers themselves. Perhaps this description is even an unconsciously euphemised version of Hobbes's "nasty, brutish, and short." If we construe the term literally, moreover, the extant "annals" of the eighteenth-century poor are largely the aforementioned bills, poor house and workhouse rolls, and parish registers which recorded the relief administered to the peasants: records not of the poor's acts but of acts against them. In fact, in "The Parish Register" of 1805, George Crabbe explicitly calls such registers "annals" of the poor. Given that the site of the "Elegy" is at the center of the parish (Churchyard), that the clergy would have been responsible for dispensing poor relief, and that payments for burial and grave-digging expenses were especially common forms of such relief, we find the material history upon which the poem is based effectively "buried" beneath the poem's rhetoric. If the elegy can be viewed as Gray's "annals" of the poor, then we must ask why Gray seeks to superscribe his "annals" upon the actual ones, thereby, almost effacing them.

To arrive at possible answers to this question, we might examine the poem's relative silence on certain issues. As David Simpson has argued, a genuinely historical method should include an inquiry into the "allusions that they [texts] do not make, but would arguably have been expected to make." I would suggest that although there are no direct references either to the legislation concerning the poor or to charity within the poem, the elegy's epitaph takes on important resonances when considered in terms of the politics of such benevolence. The historian W. A. Speck would perhaps agree that such silence is telling: he writes that "charity was at the very interface between the propertied classes and the dispossessed in early modern England." Likewise, John Barrell argues that the eighteenth-century poor "took on the status of an undifferentiated class"—one distinguished only by its need for charity. Yet in seeking both to align his persona—a "youth to fame and fortune unknown"—with the buried peasants and also to isolate that persona, Gray suggests that the poor are more interested in the upper class's sympathy than their economic aid.

Large was his bounty, and his soul sincere,
Heav'n did a recompense as largely send:
He gave to Mis'ry all he had, a tear,
He gain'd from Heav'n ('twas all he wished) a
    friend.

Here, an aura of Christian *caritas* threatens to obfuscate an economic register of earnings and losses. The subject of the epitaph earns heavenly "recompense" through his sincere bestowal of "bounty"; indeed, recompense is not only contingent upon the rustic's giving of his bounty, but is also directly proportional to (i.e., "as large" as) that bounty. He also "gains" a friend for a tear. In as much as these lines evenly alternate between sums and losses—the first and third stress the latter, the second and fourth foreground the former—the very structure of the stanza helps to reinforce a sense of economic balance and equal distribution. Gray presumes to speak for the poor, moreover, by suggesting that friendship from above is all the youth wishes in return for his spiritual "bounty." Gray even circumscribes his desire within a parenthesis: a typographical maneuver that prefigures the peasants' ultimate confinement to "rude and narrow cells." Since Gray's lines acquire the force of epitaphic inscription, this parenthesis could be a kind of grammatical (not to mention economic) coffin. If we accept the logic of this stanza, the poor are well off and perhaps even better off than those who have money. Tears are a more valuable form of currency than the finest gold, for a single one can be exchanged for friendship. I might add that the poor would have had no shortage of tears to shed. Because God has already given "recompense" to the poor, and because the poor do not desire economic aid, readers of the poem need no longer be so concerned with almsgiving or charity. What could the affluent do that God had not already done? In displacing material economics by a spiritual one, Gray makes poverty a theological rather than political or economic issue. Gray's aestheticized "annals" thus potentially render the parish registers and poorhouse rolls obsolete.

The word "bounty" deserves further comment. Johnson defines "bounty" as "generosity, liberality, and munificence." Moreover, while elaborating the meaning of the term, Johnson takes great pains to distinguish between "bounty" and alms; the former is "used when persons, not absolutely necessitious, receive gifts … and the latter refers specifically to charity." Not only are the poor idealized as generous (one might ask what they might have to be generous with), but also the choice of "bounty" for "alms" is suggestive. Certainly, the

latter is more appropriate. "Bounty," however, neither calls to mind the systems which support the poor, nor reminds the wealthy who read the poem of the reasons why the poor need charity. It is, after all, the peasantry's "useful toil" that the middle-to-upper classes exploit. The fact that the poor do not receive material bounty, but *give* it is also curious. Rather than moving the reader of the elegy to social action, the poem allows the elite to remain complacent because the poor do not need much charity. "Mis'ry" has already conditioned the poor to be spiritually generous; thus, the obtrusion of economic assistance would serve only to make them greedy and self-indulgent.

The elegy is also quietly suggestive about the contemporary controversy concerning the education of the poor. We are told that "Knowledge" neither unrolls her scrolls nor teaches the peasants how to read her inscriptions. Moreover, before the epitaph is placed before our eyes, we are asked to approach and "read (for thou can'st read)" it. And yet the poem effaces the material cause of the poor's illiteracy: the machinations of the elite, who thought that the educated poor might no longer accept their penury. In *The English Common Reader*, Richard Altick traces the politics of literacy in the seventeenth and eighteenth century. After the Interregnum,

> …the opportunity for the children of the poor to read was sharply curtailed…. Since the power of the press had been so dramatically revealed during the Puritan regime, one vital way of insuring the nation's stability was to keep masses ignorant of their letters.

In his "Free Inquiry into the Origin and Nature of Evil" (1757), Soame Jenyns spoke for propertied interests when he pronounced that "ignorance is the appointed lot of all born to poverty and the drudgeries of life….the only opiate capable of infusing that sensibility, which can enable them to endure the miseries of [life] … It is the cordial administered by the generous hand of Providence…." Indeed, it is possible that Gray, who was reading Jenyns's poetry as early as January of 1748, might have also read this essay. Yet while men like Jenyns sought to keep the poor as ignorant as possible, others such as members of the Society for the Promotion of Christian Knowledge as well as Methodists insisted that "reading Christians will be knowing Christians." Through charity schools and the dissemination of cheap literature, these Christians sought to inculcate the masses with piety and a sense of duty. Such indoctrination would ensure that the poor would learn their place. Both sides were united by their common perception of the poor as a class to be feared and by their desire to preserve the social hierarchy.

In the context of this debate, the line "Their sober wishes never *learned* to stray" (emphasis mine), takes on distinctly repressive overtones. The poor accept their "chill penury" and remain "jocund" in their domestic bowers only because they do not know any better. Furthermore, although these laborers cannot be taught how to read, they can be taught how to die; in lines 83–84, Gray points to the "holy texts" of the graveyard "That teach the rustic moralist to die." The main speaker of the elegy subtly aligns himself with those who would keep the poor ignorant in order to preserve the social hegemony. And insofar as the act of reading becomes literally associated with burial, the elegy itself seems, at least rhetorically, to require the demise of the poor. Even more disturbing, however, is the poem's naturalizing of the political reasons for the poor's illiteracy and the reifying of the boundaries between those who can and cannot read. The elegy insists upon the division between "thee" (the reading audience) and "their": "their lot forbade," their unlettered muse "strews" holy texts, and "their crimes" are circumscribed. Gray appropriates the abstracted and personified concepts of "Knowledge" and "lot" to account for the inability of the poor to read. Men like Jenyns, as it is made to seem, have no role in this. Illiteracy, therefore, becomes a natural and unquestioned condition of the poor.

Perhaps Gray's awareness of the important role literacy and pamphleteering played in the English Civil War compels him to speak of a "mute inglorious Milton"; a silent and unknown Milton would neither have written a defense of the regicide of King Charles nor have published praise of Cromwell. Insofar as Gray links Milton with other English radicals who brought much turmoil to England—namely, Hampden, and Cromwell—he provides his readers with a lesson in exemplary history. The poet's conviction that the masses must remain illiterate leads him to reflect upon what might have happened in terms of the English Revolution had the poor had greater access to knowledge. And if we recall that the putative topography of the poem is Stoke Poges, Buckinghamshire, this history becomes even geographically immediate to Gray, who is putting the finishing touches on his Elegy at Stoke. For even without the widespread literacy of the poor, the Buckinghamshire Levellers had managed to publish and disperse a 1648 pamphlet entitled "More Light Shining in Buckinghamshire," which called for the levelling of all social distinctions and for the equal distribution of all property. The Levellers demanded not only "the removall of the kingly power" in order "to free all alike out of slavery," but also denounced the self-interest of "Richmen [who] cry for a King … and of the Lord's Barons" who "cry for a King, else their tyrannical House of Peers falls down." Not only were the Levellers active during the revolution, but Buckinghamshire was also the site of a Digger community—a group which also published pamphlets denouncing private property. Because the causes of their discontent were still active in the eighteenth century, might it not be these specific "crimes" that Gray alludes to when he refers to the poor's "circumscribed crimes," and could not the allusions to Hampden, Milton, and Cromwell potentially recall the rebels that the poor almost became and still, as I will argue later, could (and did) become? Only ignorance prevents the poor from "wad [ing] through slaughter to a throne" and "shut[ting] the gates of mercy on mankind." If the poor cannot read, then they cannot "learn to stray"; that is, they cannot yearn for equality and position. The poem thus actively buries or silences their desires.

Leisured classes not only sought to infuse the poor with the opiate of ignorance by prohibiting reading as a form of recreation, but also they tried to suppress rural sports. Throughout the eighteenth century men of property thought that popular recreation encouraged the poor to become idle; even worse, the carnivalesque atmosphere of these festivities had the potential to undermine the social order. Robert Malcolmson summarizes this strategy: "The more popular diversion could be controlled and restrained, the more would the national economy be strengthened and expanded; habits of leisure had to be brought into line with the requirements of efficient and orderly production." If we consider that the churchyard was a favorite playground for the lower classes in the eighteenth century, the complete absence of popular recreation within the elegy is perhaps important. In fact, the churchyard of the poem seems to have been taken over by leisured upper-class sentimentalists who have presumably earned the right to such leisure. By contrast, even within the speaker's imaginative projections of the lives of the poor, leisure is conspicuously absent. In much the same way that John Barrell argues that paintings in the mid-eighteenth century sought to represent the poor as working blithely, Gray seeks to convert the poor to an industrious poor. Thus Gray exclaims:

> Oft did the harvest to their sickle yield,
> Their furrow oft the stubborn glebe has broke;
> How jocund did they drive their team afield!
> How bowed the woods beneath their sturdy stroke!

Not only do these peasants labor diligently, they are perfectly content in doing so. Because they labor cheerfully, Gray seems to say, they deserve our respect and sympathy. Indeed, the poet himself left ten pounds to be distributed to "honest and industrious poor Persons" in the Parish of Stoke Poges.

To the ends of making the poor industrious and of suppressing recreation, propertied interests sought to discourage all forms of public assembly for the poor and attempted "to confine their recreation, when necessary, to domestic pleasures....The home was a refuge from the world; here amusement could be rational, regulated, uplifting, and subservient to the laws of religion." We note accordingly that Gray's portraits of rural life do not suggest any form of public life on the part of the poor; rather, his peasants are "far from the madding crowd's ignoble strife." The emphasis here, I suggest, is on "far." Similarly, the poet perhaps displaces representations of recreation with moments of domestic tranquility:

> For them no more the blazing hearth shall burn,
> Or busy housewife ply her evening care:
> No children run to lisp their sire's return,
> Or climb his knees the envied kiss to share.

Without question, Gray here devalues the public realm for the poor and seeks to confirm familial values of privacy and domestic autonomy. Furthermore, the poet's choice of "sire," that is, "a lord, master, or sovereign" (*OED*), hearkens back to an age of feudalism when a "sire's" rule was entirely capable of instilling order. Perhaps the initial solitary figure of Gray's poetic landscape, the ploughman who "homeward plods his weary way," returns to such a domestic bower to uphold this order. Indeed, this rustic farmer becomes a universal type of a domesticated and industrious laborer. The poet denies this figure of all potential radical action. Might Gray have stripped this farmer of topicality because local farm laborers had a history of revolt? We might recall here that the Buckinghamshire community of Diggers were a radical group so named because they subsisted by digging and cultivating common land.

The suppression of popular recreation did not, however, end with the reinculcation of familial values and the discouragement of all forms of public assembly. Nothing but the doctrine of necessity would ensure that the poor remained industrious. If the poor had to work continually to provide for their basic necessities, then productivity would be maximized. In 1757 William Temple, a strong advocate of this doctrine, wrote:

> The only way to make them [the poor] temperate and industrious is to lay them under a necessity of labouring all the time they can spare for meals and sleep, in order to procure the common necessities of life.

While scarcity facilitated industry, abundance would lead to idleness and crime. If we briefly look again at the stanza of the epitaph which details what the "youth to fortune and to fame unknown" must give in order to receive God's recompense, we find, not surprisingly, that he must give "all he had" before he can receive, and that those lines add up to a zero-sum gain. Furthermore, Gray's virtual redefinition of charity within the poem would ensure that the poor never rise above necessity. Too much aid given to the peasants might leave them with a surplus; that in turn would lead to idleness and debauchery. The poet is thus understandably relieved that the poor do not have the power "to scatter plenty o'er a smiling land." In as much as "plenty" suggests abundance and, according to Johnson's *Dictionary*, "more than is necessary," might this line be an oblique reference to charity? Indeed, the choice of "scattering" implies a completely indiscriminate manner of distribution. The line "Chill Penury repressed their noble rage," then, potentially recalls the doctrine of necessity. Not only have the actual causes of poverty been mythologized through abstract personification, but it is also that very penury that enables the poem to maintain its elegiac tenor; that is, their poverty makes the poor worthy of an elegy. Had the poor not been completely destitute, Gray suggests, their "noble rage" might have become "ignoble strife." The poor might have diverted their energies from labor to popular revolt.

Both the poet and men of propertied interests had good reason to believe that the poor would rise up against them; although Gray desperately seeks to marginalize the crowd by placing it "far" away in his elegy, the "madding crowd" was closer to the poet's Buckinghamshire home and to the country churchyard of Stoke Poges than anyone there would have liked. As I have already noted, Buckinghamshire had had a history of popular uprisings. And although E. P. Thompson argues that eighteenth-century crowds were ruled by the "remarkable restraint" of a "moral economy," "crowd" was a terrifying word for the established order: "crowd" implied either "a multitude confusedly pressed together" or a "promiscuous medley, without order or distinction" (Johnson's *Dictionary*). Moreover, as Eveline Cruickshanks has argued, "Large crowd demonstrations and violent riots could not be ignored by an elite devoid of an effective professional police force or a large standing army." As if the use of the word "crowd" were not adequately alarming, Gray also calls attention to their "ignoble strife" and to the fact that they are "madding" or furious. The issuance of a Riot Act in 1715 by Parliament, specifically to put an end to "tumults and riotous assemblies, and for the more speedy and effectual punishing of rioters," suggests that eighteenth-century crowds were an extremely disruptive force; indeed, under the Act's provisions, crowds of twelve or more which unlawfully assembled for an hour after the reading of a proclamation were guilty of a felony, and were subject to capital punishment. Despite the act, however, rioting was not contained. The prime minister, Sir Robert Walpole (father of Gray's friend and patron), himself witnessed just how unruly a crowd could be; in response to his attempt to postpone the unpopular 1733 Excise Bill, the crowd outside the House mobbed Walpole and his friends, and even though the Riot Act was read, blows and abuse were exchanged.

That the crowd was threatening to the established order is confirmed by their disruptiveness and virtual ubiquity. I will list only a few examples germane to the elegy. In Charnwood Forest, Leicestershire, in 1748, crowds demanded rights to the common and destroyed warrens in the presence of troops, constables, and gameskeepers. Apparently this crowd was taken seriously; their demands were met. At Bristol, between July and August 1749, farmers and laborers who feared the extra charges on produce brought into the area destroyed toll-gates on roads leading to that city. By August 3rd, almost all turnpikes and turnpike houses there were razed. These highway disturbances were not uncommon and were noted in 1727, 1731, 1734, and in 1735–36 in Bristol, Gloucester, Ledbury, and Herefordshire. And according to a 1750 eye-witness account, "a crowd of people assembled" in Walsall and proceeded to shout treasonable expressions and to fire shots at an effigy of King George II. In 1751, the year that Gray's *Elegy* first appeared in print, moreover, rioters at Cannock Chase slaughtered 10,000 of the Earl of Uxbridge's rabbits. The most common form of protest, however, were food riots with nationwide waves in 1709–10, 1727–29, 1739–40, and in 1756–57. All of this strongly suggests that crowds would have been very much on the minds of those who read the poem.

If we accept the idea that Gray may have had specific crowd disturbances in mind, then the lines, "The cock's shrill clarion or the echoing horn / No

more shall rouse them from their lowly bed," may allude as well to the mob's rebellions. Although as Roger Lonsdale has noted, "echoing horn" perhaps recalls Milton's "Hounds and Horn" which "Chearly rouse the slumbring morn" ("L'Allegro"), and thus refer to the hunting horns of the gentry, E. P. Thompson informs us that crowds in the mid-eighteenth century were often mobilized by horns and drums. Agreeing with Thompson, John Stevenson writes: "Mobs were frequently headed by someone blowing a horn." The fact that this horn is "echoing" suggests that rural rebellion was not an isolated phenomenon. Indeed, when Gray writes that the Poor have "kept the noiseless tenor of their way," might he not be actively silencing the peasants? In the four rejected stanzas of the Eton Manuscript which originally appeared immediately before the lines referring to their "noiseless tenor," Gray extols the "sacred calm" of the graveyard which now fortunately "Bids every tumultuous Passion cease." The "cock's shrill clarion" may recall another sound which the gentry would have shuddered to hear. According to Johnson's *Dictionary,* "cock" could suggest a "conquerer or leader of men," and "clarion" was the sound of a trumpet—"a wind instrument of war." The poet's choice of the verb "rouse," then is fitting; although the overt meaning of the term is clearly "wake," the word, taken as an imperative, would suggest incitement to action. One need only think here of the commanding and manifesto-like call with which Blake would later begin his epic, *Milton:* "Rouze up O Young Men of the New Age! set your foreheads against the ignorant Hirelings!" As long as Gray's poem keeps the poor buried, the peasants can thankfully no longer be "roused" to such revolution.

But the reference to the crowd's "ignoble strife" may be even more historically specific. Food riots were extremely common in 1740: just a few years before Gray would begin writing his elegy. To cite only a few instances, crowds rose in New-castle-upon-Tyne protesting the high price of corn, and plundered granaries. When a rioter was killed, the crowd "ransacked" the town hall and carried away 1,800 pounds of the town's money. In the process, the crowd "wounded most of the gentlemen." And in Norwich, the rabble fixed notes upon bakery doors in the city demanding that the price of wheat be lowered. When the mayor committed the leaders to prison, the crowd became so incensed that they stormed the prison and released their companions. Elsewhere, villagers pulled down mills, protested rises in prices, and began stopping the transport of any grain to be for exportation. As the historian R. B. Rose aptly put it, "Where simple hunger riots are concerned, no part of England seems to have been immune."

What precipitated the riots of 1739–40 was severe frost—one of the coldest winter seasons on record—and the ensuing miserable harvests. According to William Ellis, a farmer in Buckinghamshire,

> The Hard Frost that began about Christmas of 1739, and ended the 23rd of February following, was deemed the sharpest in the Memory of Man; for it occassioned the Death of many poor people who wanted Heat and Victuals.…

Another account reads:

> An unheard of frost seized with extraordinary severity on the world and the elements, so that it is scarcely possible to number or relate the many strange occurences that took place through its violence.…This extraordinary weather was followed by an equally uncommon spring. In May no sign of verdure was yet to be seen; it was still cold in July, and the vegetation was still then further hindered by drought.…

Although Gray's grand tour to France and Italy with Walpole lasted from March 1739 to September 1741, Gray knew about the severe weather; in a letter to his wife dated March 1740, the poet writes, "I hope at present … that all your frosts, and snows, … are, by this time, utterly vanished." Indeed, the bitter cold would remain a major topic of conversation in England; scattered throughout the January, March, and July issues of *Gentleman's Magazine* (1740), for example, are numerous letters, articles, and even poems about the weather. Not surprisingly, the frost triggered enormous increases in wheat and coal prices. For example, at Oxford in the first few months of 1740, wheat prices rose from twenty to fifty nine shillings per bushel. Coal prices in London also trebled from January to March. Because the poor relied upon bread as their main source of nourishment and coal for a cheap form of fuel, many died. In response to the growing hardships of the peasants, those who could afford to do so began thinking about how to help them. *The Craftsman* of January 26, 1740, contained the following editorial note:

> We have many dismal Accounts from all Parts of the great Damages done by the severity of the Weather, and of the Hardships the Poor undergo from the extravagant Price of Firing and Coal, and We receive likewise many satisfactory Advices of the charitable Benevolence of well-disposed Christians to assist them in this calamitous Season.

There are reportedly so many letters that the editors cannot print them all. Perhaps it can be safely said that the frost did focus more public attention on the poor than there otherwise would have been.

Given this context, it is quite possible that Gray's lines about the "Chill Penury" which "repressed their noble rage" and which "froze the genial current" of the peasant's souls either are direct references to the frost of 1739–40 or would have been taken in that sense. And there was another unusual frost from the first of February to the middle of March in 1746 which may have helped to remind readers of the earlier "chill." Quite literally then, the poor lie in a "mouldering heap" because their "genial currents" have been frozen. If the peasants, moreover, were as potentially militant as I suggest, their currents are hardly "genial" but were more accurately termed "violent." For the established order, the deaths of the peasants were perhaps the best that could be hoped for. Insofar as their confinement to "narrow cells" was no longer temporary—that is, there would be no more need for prison cells to contain these potential rioters—but now permanent, the elite might rest more comfortably. As if to lend authority to the poem, Gray concludes the elegy proper with "the voice of nature" which demands that the peasants be so confined.

A politicized reading of Gray's elegy, then, indicates that although the poet is sympathetic to the poor, Gray's compassion is contingent upon the silent and cheerful penury of the lower classes. Much more than critics of the poem have recognized, Gray's attitudes towards these peasants were conditioned by the contemporary debates concerning them. Because the very hegemony of the propertied classes was at stake, Gray sought to place the poor "far from the madding crowd's ignoble strife" even if that meant inflicting upon them intellectual, economic, social, and finally, physical death. Because the *Elegy Written in a Country Churchyard* actively suppresses the rebellious history of the poor, the poem both memorializes and anticipates the burial of English peasants whose "trembling hopes" must be contained within the safe walls of Gray's parenthetical coffins.

Source: Richard C. Sha, "Gray's Political *Elegy:* Poetry as the Burial of History," in *Philological Quarterly,* Vol. 69, No. 3, Summer, 1990, pp. 337–57.

Sources

Arnold, Matthew, "Thomas Gray," in his *Essays in Criticism,* 2nd ser., The Macmillan Company, 1934, pp. 69-99.

Brady, Frank, "Structure and Meaning in Gray's *Elegy*," in *Thomas Gray's Elegy Written in a Country Churchyard*, edited by Harold Bloom, Philadelphia: Chelsea House Publishers, 1987.

Ellis, Frank Hale, "Gray's *Elegy:* The Biographical Problem in Literary Criticism," in *Twentieth Century Interpretations of Gray's "Elegy,"* edited by Herbert W. Starr, Englewood Cliffs, NJ: Prentice-Hall, Inc., 1968.

Empson, William, "Proletarian Literature," in *English Pastoral Poetry,* New York: New Directions, 1935, pp. 4-5.

Hutchings, W., "Syntax of Death: Instability in Gray's 'Elegy Written in a Country Churchyard,'" in *Studies in Philology,* Vol. LXXXI, No. 4, Fall, 1984, pp. 496-514.

Johnson, Samuel, "Gray," in his *Lives of the English Poets,* Vol. II, 1781; reprinted by Oxford University Press, 1967, pp. 453-64.

Krutch, Joseph Wood, "Introduction," in *The Selected Letters of Thomas Gray* by Thomas Gray, edited by Joseph Wood Krutch, New York: Farrar, Strauss and Young, Inc., 1952, pp. ix-xxxii.

Weaver, Carl J., "The Bicentenary of Gray's 'Elegy,'" in *Colby Library Quarterly,* Series III, No. 1, February, 1951, pp. 9-12.

Weinfield, Henry, *The Poet Without a Name: Gray's "Elegy" and the Problem of History,* Carbondale: Southern Illinois University Press, 1991.

For Further Study

Brooks, Cleanth, "Gray's Storied Urn," in *The Well-Wrought Urn,* New York: Harcourt Brace, 1947, pp. 96-113.

Brooks, one of this century's most esteemed literary critics, examines the layers of complexity in this seemingly simple poem, which he likens to "a tissue of allusion and half-allusion."

Glazier, Lyle, "Gray's *Elegy:* "The Skull Beneath the Skin," in *University of Kansas Review,* Vol. XIX, Spring, 1953, pp. 174-180.

Glazier interprets this as a poem of equality, favoring no class over another. He reminds readers that it is not merely about the virtues of the poor, but a declaration that all persons, rich and poor, are mortal.

Golden, Morris, *Thomas Gray,* New York: Grosset & Dunlap, Publishers, 1964.

This book-length overview of Gray's life and career provided students with a good general background of the poet's importance.

Hutchings, W., "Syntax of Death: Instability in Gray's *Elegy Written in a Country Churchyard,*" in *Thomas Gray's Elegy Written in a Country Churchyard,* edited by Harold Bloom, Philadelphia: Chelsea House Publishers, 1987.

This essay gives a focused, scholarly look at Gray's use of language and punctuation, with ample references to other poems and other critics' thoughts.

McCarthy, B. Eugene, *Thomas Gray: The Progress of a Poet,* Madison, NJ: Fairleigh Dickinson University Press, 1997.

McCarthy examines the development of Gray's life and thought, giving special attention to his translations and, of course, the "Elegy."

The Exhibit

Lisel Mueller
1986

"The Exhibit" (contained in Lisel Mueller's collection *Second Language* [1986]) blends history and mythology to express the lingering grief and denial that still haunt an elderly man who survived being a prisoner of war. Using the unicorn metaphor, the poet shows how the horrible *public* event of world war has a lasting detrimental effect on *private* life and how our present lives are determined and shaped by the past. Mueller often writes autobiographical poems which include members of her family, and "The Exhibit" is about an uncle living in East Germany many years after the world wars of the twentieth century. The poem does not specify whether the uncle was a prisoner during the first or second world war, but his age could well place him in WWI. We know, however, that Lisel Mueller's own life was directly affected by WWII and that many of her poems stem from the events of the Holocaust. Regardless of which world war is the reference here, the meaning is the same—war takes its toll not only on the body, but on the mind, leaving decades of appalling memories for survivors and often causing them to turn to imagination and myth for comfort.

"The Exhibit" implies the atrocities of war without ever mentioning particular acts. Mueller is able to convey the horrors of conflict essentially by talking about its opposite. As a symbol of both strength and gentleness, the unicorn exemplifies the world as it *should* be. By highlighting the mythical creature's virtuous behavior and its undeniable purity, the poet actually signifies everything that the real world is not.

Author Biography

Lisel Mueller was born in 1924 in Hamburg, Germany, and moved to the United States with her parents in 1939. Both parents were teachers, and her father was a political dissident as well. Escaping Nazi Germany, he settled his family in Evansville, Indiana, where Lisel quickly learned to speak English, earning American citizenship six years later. As an extremely bright student, she spent only one year in an American high school before attending the University of Evansville, graduating in 1944 at the age of twenty.

Although she dabbled in some adolescent poetry while in school, Lisel did not begin to write serious poetry until after the death of her mother in 1953. At that time, she began a self-taught course of study, including both traditional forms and free verse, eventually settling into her own simple, unadorned poetic style. Determined to combine her love of the creative arts with a "normal" life, she also married, had children, and found employment over the years as a social worker, receptionist, library assistant, and freelance writer. Her first collection of poems, *Dependencies,* was published in 1965, twelve years after she began to study and write poetry. In 1977, she became an instructor in the Master of Fine Arts writing program at Goddard College in Vermont.

Growing up in Germany in the 1920s and 1930s and eventually fleeing that country undoubtedly had an obvious and profound effect on anyone who lived through it. For writers, poets, painters and all others who turned to creative outlets, the influence of the turmoil and countless horrors is understandably evident in their work. Much of Lisel Mueller's poetry reflects her memories of and feelings toward her homeland and the friends and loved ones she left behind after escaping to the United States. "The Exhibit" is a typical, yet powerful, example of how this poet learned to blend world history with personal history and how even something as overwhelming as world war can be captured in simple words and simple style and still carry the impact of something complex and terrifying. Even though Lisel has lived in America for over sixty years, she has never lost her feeling of identity with Europeans. When she was interviewed by fellow poets William Heyen and Stan Sanvel Rubin in 1989, she admitted feeling more at home in the United States than anywhere else. She went on to say, however, that, "At the same time I am not a native; I see the culture and myself in it—with European eyes, and

Lisel Mueller

my poetry accommodates a bias toward historical determinism." Perhaps no other events in recorded history could make one feel more "determined" by the past than the world wars that destroyed so many lives and forever changed those who survived them. Lisel Mueller's work is a compelling portrayal of that concept.

Poem Text

My uncle in East Germany
points to the unicorn in the painting
and explains it is now extinct.
We correct him, say such a creature
never existed. He does not argue,   5
but we know he does not believe us.
He is certain power and gentleness
must have gone hand in hand
once. A prisoner of war
even after the war was over,   10
my uncle needs to believe in something
that could not be captured except by love,
whose single luminous horn
redeemed the murderous forest
and, dipped into foul water,   15
would turn it pure. This world,
this terrible world we live in,
is not the only possible one,
his eighty-year-old eyes insist,
dry wells that fill so easily now.   20

Media Adaptations

- In 1979, Lisel Mueller recorded a 60-minute tape of eleven poems, with an introduction by Tom Mandel. Poet/novelist Clarence Major joins Mueller as a co-reader on some poems. This tape is difficult to find, but may be back-ordered from some online booksellers, such as amazon.com.

- In 1995, the Illinois Association of Teachers of English (IATE) recorded an interview with Lisel Mueller. It is available by contacting: IATE, English Building, 608 South Wright Street, Urbana, IL 61801.

Poem Summary

Lines 1-2:

The first two lines in "The Exhibit" give us the setting for the poem and confirm the obvious implication of the title. It takes place in an art museum in East Germany. While the country may not seem significant at this early point in the poem, it becomes paramount to our understanding the mindset of the uncle, who will turn out to be the central "character" in the work.

The mention of the unicorn in the painting may also seem minor in the second line, but the mythological creature will become the metaphor used as the major theme throughout the poem. Unicorns have a long history in the legends of various peoples around the world. They have appeared in assorted forms in Roman, Greek, Norse, and other mythologies, sometimes portraying the features of a small goat and sometimes of a large horse with a flowing white mane and white hooves. Regardless of the predominant physical shape the unicorn takes in the tales, one feature is common across cultures and time periods: the white spiral horn protruding upright from its forehead. Also in all legends, unicorns are emblems of purity, and stories center around their lives among virgin goddesses. Although the unicorn would fight ferociously when cornered, it could be tamed by the loving touch of a virgin. Their horns were said to offer protection against poison and could purify a contaminated stream when dipped into it. Overall, the unicorn symbolizes a beast with strength and power who can be—and most often is—very gentle.

Line 3:

The third line gives us our first glimpse into the mind of the uncle who explains to those around him that the unicorn "is now extinct." The initial reaction here may be amusement at the naive mistake made by a man who apparently believes unicorns actually existed once and are now extinct, as other real animals have become over time. By the end of the poem, however, we understand that simple naivete does not justifiably explain the uncle's notion that these creatures once lived on earth.

Lines 4-6:

In line 4, the speaker and whoever else is present correct the uncle, telling him that "such a creature / never existed." Even though he does not dispute their words, they know that "he does not believe us." At this point, we may still assume that the man is innocently ignorant of the unicorn's existence only in legends and that his belief in them does not stem from any *need* or *preference*. Rather, he simply appears not to have his zoological history in order.

Lines 7-8:

Lines 7 and 8 introduce a new possibility into the uncle's thoughts and indicate that something much more than simple naivete or ignorance is going on in his mind. While the words "power and gentleness" are a direct reference to the attributes of the unicorn, the unicorn, in turn, becomes a two-fold metaphor for the rest of the poem. In these two lines, it represents the manner in which a world leader or political figure should rule—with strength, but also with gentleness and kindness. This, of course, is in direct contrast to the corrupt dictatorship of Adolph Hitler in Europe during the early twentieth century. The uncle is "certain power and gentleness / must have gone hand in hand (once)" because he cannot allow himself to believe that humankind has *always* been victimized by tyrants whose strength emanates not from gentleness, but from selfishness and cruelty.

Lines 9-12:

Line 9 helps us further understand the emotional plight of the uncle: he has survived the horrors of being a prisoner of war. Line 10 signifies the lasting grip that the physical and emotional strain still has on his mind. Even though the actual fighting is over, the uncle is yet a "prisoner" of its terrible toll, and he will never emotionally escape from those grim memories. Lines 11 and 12 make up the second part of the unicorn's twofold metaphor. Here, the uncle himself is the reference because he "needs to believe in something / that could not be captured except by love." Recall that the unicorn could fight savagely when it had to, but was then calmed by the touch of a virgin. During the war, the uncle had been captured by the enemy, a source of great bitterness and pain. He needs to know that there exists a creature—if not a man— who could remain free from persecution and not fall "victim" to anything but the love of a gentle, pure woman. The idea of "love" here, however, does not mean only the romantic affection shared between two people. Instead, it encompasses a world-love, or a general peace and friendship among masses of people and between nations.

Lines 13-16:

These lines refer to the legendary single horn of the unicorn, so brilliantly white that it appeared "luminous." It was so pure in nature that it could bring peace to any calamities in the forests, whether they were battles between men, between beasts, or between men and beasts. Lines 15 and 16 reiterate the magical power of the horn that "dipped into foul water, / would turn it pure."

Line 17:

In line 17, "this terrible world we live in" is diametrically opposed to the make-believe world of the unicorn. Here, the speaker acknowledges her own awareness of and grief over the terrible suffering that so many people have endured (or not survived) at the hands of diabolic leaders.

Lines 18-19:

These two lines connect directly to line 17 but are presented from the perspective of the uncle again. He cannot believe that the "terrible world"— the one he has been told is *real*—is "the only possible one." His denial, however, does not come in the form of verbal protest or in any words at all. The speaker knows that her uncle clings to the possibility of a better world only because "his eighty-year-old eyes insist." This line, of course, is the first mention of the uncle's age. We have likely assumed that he was an older man, but now we know that the grief brought on by world war has been

with him for not only many years, but for *decades,* and that he will carry that sorrow to his grave.

Line 20:

The last line of the poem also refers to the uncle's eyes and indicates simply that his tears come easily now. The word "now" seems to imply that the older he gets the more he cries. We may assume, then, that the longer he lives in "this terrible world" the more he must resign himself to accept that a world in which "power and gentleness" go "hand in hand" has never existed, and, most likely, never will.

Themes

Historical Determinism

Historical determinism is an idea implying that what has occurred in the past has a direct impact on what occurs in the present, in both personal lives and in society in general. Lisel Mueller was born in a time and place that will fill the pages of history books for decades, probably centuries, to come. World War II not only *affected* the lives of millions of people around the globe, but also helped to *shape* those lives into whatever they would become over the years. Whether that tumultuous time inspired creative outpourings or brought survivors to the brink of suicide, the fact that it altered life on earth is undeniable. The theory of historical determinism is common in Mueller's poetry. In a 1985 interview with author and Michigan State University professor Nancy Bunge, she stated, "I'm partial to history. To me a sense of what has gone on in the past is very important to one's view of the world."

"The Exhibit" is an obvious example of historical determinism. The uncle, who spent at least part of the war as a prisoner, has built a belief in a mythological "hero" of sorts in order to insulate his mind from having to accept only the harsh realities of the world he lives in. In much the same way that we build walls to protect ourselves from natural elements or enemies, the uncle has constructed a frame of thought—one that allows him to temper the cruelty he suffered by thinking about the kind, gentle world that must have existed before. The poem indicates that most of this very elderly man's life was determined by war, that he has endured decades of grief and turned to fantasy for comfort, perhaps so fervently that he now cannot separate fact from fiction. While we do not

Topics for Further Study

- Select a member of your family whom you believe has been changed in some way by an event in history, either a worldwide, national, or local occurrence. Write an essay on how this individual's mind-set or personality has been partly shaped by the event.

- If you were going to believe in a mythological creature or person, which one would it be and why? Explain the reasons for your choice in an essay.

- Write two brief poems on the same topic, using two different styles. For one poem, use a "Germanic" style and for the other, use language that is more indicative of a "Latinate" style. Which one do you prefer and why?

- Andersonville Village in southwest Georgia is the sight of a notorious Confederate prison used during the Civil War. After researching the topic, write an essay on what conditions at the prison led to the deaths of nearly 13,000 Union soldiers.

know anything about the uncle's life previous to the war, we can safely assume that he did not believe in unicorns or, more importantly, that he did not feel a *need* to.

Poetry and Politics

Not many American poets take on the task of making social statements in their poetry. Political activism may be prevalent on American streets, but in verse form it doesn't occur on a regular basis. Lisel Mueller, as a European-born American, has never shied away from putting her views on social issues, war, equal rights, and other matters of the political conscience in her work as a poet. In the 1985 interview with Nancy Bunge, she had this to say in regard to the difference that nationality seems to make in poets: "There is a problem with finding subject matter in our society, partly because there is a great bias among young writers against

political writing…. That seems to me a uniquely American and English tradition of disassociating writing from what goes on in the world because it's certainly not true of European writers and it's not true of South American writers."

In "The Exhibit," Mueller uses both allusion ("… to believe in something / that could not be captured except by love") and straightforward commentary ("This world, / this terrible world we live in") to make her point about the private horrors of a very public war. She uses the personal story of a relative to depict what so many other survivors of the war must have struggled with throughout their own lives. While it may be true that keeping historical events in mind may help prevent a repeat of the bad ones, memories also take their toll on the emotions, and this poem clearly displays the unending sorrow that is often born of political tyranny.

Myth and Reality

Myth plays a major role in "The Exhibit" in two different ways. First, it is the emotional shield that the uncle takes up to protect himself from a total resignation to the real world. As we go through the poem and learn more about his reasons for believing in unicorns, we come to understand that those reasons are quite valid. Just as children turn to their imaginations for comfort or companionship, adults, too, often use a fantasy world or a belief in something incredible in order to bring a positive aspect to an otherwise dismal world. The uncle in Mueller's poem may be only pretending to believe in mythological unicorns, but it is better for him to pretend than to give in completely to his very real memories.

The second role for myth in "The Exhibit" is that it serves as a juxtaposition to reality. For the unicorn, "power and gentleness / must have gone hand in hand," which is in direct opposition to the power and *corruption* that often go hand in hand in the real world. In this particular instance, the "power" alluded to is likely Adolph Hitler and/or any of the other Axis Power leaders during WWII. The description of the forest as "murderous" is also worth noting here. We know that the virtuous unicorn could bring peace and justice to beasts fighting in the woods, but the word "murderous" implies a human factor. Animals may kill, but only human beings commit murder, essentially a legal term. By setting myth against reality, Mueller makes a strong statement about "this terrible world we live in."

Style

When interviewer Nancy Bunge asked Lisel Mueller to comment on her style of writing, the poet had this to say: "My poetry is largely Germanic in the sense that I usually use strong, short words and not many Latinates because they sound weaker to me—conversational, essayistic." The "Latinates" that Mueller refers to are words derived from the ancient Roman and Latin languages, including those we now call the Romance languages, such as Italian, French, Portuguese, and Spanish. Words in these languages tend to be lengthier than the terse, sharper-sounding Germanic words, and, therefore, may sound more "conversational."

"The Exhibit" demonstrates Mueller's use of Germanic style in that its language is simple, yet powerful in delivering the message, and the lines are compact, fairly even in length, giving the poem the look of a short, neat rectangle on the page. There is no obvious rhyme and little alliteration (the repetition of consonant or vowel sounds, especially at the beginnings of words, such as "points" and "painting," "explains" and "extinct," or "correct" and "creature"). The poem is essentially a series of six complete sentences, the first four being rather brief, taking up only eight full lines, and the last two seeming more "poetic," spanning the remainder of the 20-line poem.

The first half of "The Exhibit" sets the scene for us, stating in simple, declarative sentences that it takes place in an East German museum where at least three people are looking at a painting of a unicorn. One of them believes the creature used to exist but the others do not, and they say so. Simple enough at this point, but in the second half of the poem we span decades, going back in time to a world war and illuminating the particular horrors of one of its prisoners. The fifth "sentence" is lengthy (beginning in line 9 with "A prisoner of war ..." and ending in line 16 with "... would turn it pure"), and the words are perhaps the most "complicated" in the poem, with "luminous," "redeemed," and "murderous." However, in lines 13 and 14, the words "luminous" and "murderous" are not only an effective near-rhyme, but also play well off one another to maintain the metaphor of a gentle, virtuous creature ("luminous" refers to the unicorn) versus the realities of mankind ("murderous"). While this metaphor is extended throughout the poem and the unicorn alluded to in a variety of instances, the final line contains the only "simple" metaphor in the poem: "dry wells" representing the uncle's eyes.

Historical Context

"The Exhibit" is contained in Lisel Mueller's *Second Language* collection, published in 1986. But regardless of the year or even the decade in which her poetry was written, much of the historical influence on it comes not from the time she was writing it, but from the earlier part of the twentieth century. In her 1989 interview with Rubin and Heyen, she stated that, "There's no way anymore for the individual to escape from history, the public life we all share. Being European born, I felt this very strongly. That is the story of my parents, who were born shortly before World War I, and their whole life was determined by history. Everything was imposed on them from the outside because the twentieth century in Germany was catastrophic."

Although Mueller left Germany in 1939, she lived there long enough to experience Adolph Hitler's rise to chancellor of the country, his creation of the Third Reich, the elimination of all political parties other than National Socialism, and the opening of the first concentration camp at Dachau. In the year she and her family fled their homeland, Hitler invaded Poland, and France and Great Britain declared war on Germany. At fifteen, she was very aware of the social and political atrocities taking place around her, and she witnessed the pain and stress inflicted on citizens and soldiers alike, as well as on her own loved ones.

By the time "The Exhibit" was published in the 1980s, Lisel Mueller had been a naturalized American for over 40 years. No industrial nation, however, is isolated from events happening around the world. Even as a citizen of the United States, the poet experienced the strain of social unrest in the 1960s, the civil rights movement, the war in Vietnam, and the Cold War, which spanned decades before coming to a symbolic end with the crumbling of the Berlin Wall in 1989. The turbulent times of the 1960s and 1970s had a profound effect on Mueller herself, and, subsequently, on the work she produced afterwards. In her 1985 interview with Nancy Bunge, she commented on her life during the years of the Vietnam War: "Those were bad years for me, not in terms of my private life, but in terms of being involved in the shame and guilt and wrongness of this country.... I took it all very personally, and perhaps the history of Nazi Germany in the back of my mind made me feel involved with it."

Obviously, what is in the *back of one's mind* plays a significant role in "The Exhibit." The hor-

Compare & Contrast

- **1982:** The Vietnam War Memorial, designed by Maya Lin, is dedicated in Washington D.C.

- **1982:** Helmut Kohl becomes chancellor of West Germany. Over the following decade he would be a major factor in the country's unification with East Germany.

- **1987:** Nazi leader Klaus Barbie is convicted of World War II crimes.

- **1991:** The Persian Gulf War begins as the United States and its allies drop bombs on Iraq and Kuwait.

- **1993:** The movie *Schindler's List,* centering on the real life events of a German man who helped hide Jews during the Holocaust, wins the Oscar for Best Picture, and the Holocaust Memorial Museum is dedicated in Washington D.C.

- **1995:** U.S. Army veteran Timothy McVeigh is arrested for the bombing of a federal building in Oklahoma City. The blast killed 169 people and remains the worst terrorist attack on U.S. soil.

rors associated with war and with being a prisoner of war are constantly in the back of the uncle's mind. He portrays a classic example of "post-traumatic stress syndrome" (PTSS), a term referring to a cluster of symptoms experienced by survivors of especially traumatic events in their lives. According to the "Sleep Disorders: Post Traumatic Stress Syndrome" Web site, PTSS derived from an earlier attempt to describe the effects of war upon war survivors in the twentieth century. "Shell shock" and "battle fatigue" were previous terms that psychologists used to describe the common symptoms, including recurring nightmares, hypersensitivity, and intrusive thoughts, feelings, and memories. While there is no direct mention of the uncle having nightmares, the implication is there, and the memories of his life during the war frequently intrude upon his mind. His heightened sensitivity is evidenced in the last line which tells us that his eyes are "dry wells that fill so easily now." He is so sensitive to the "terrible world" that he has invented a make-believe one in which unicorns once ruled with kindness and gentleness, and he insists that this mythological land and time must be "possible."

Critical Overview

Lisel Mueller did not publish her first book of poems until she was 41 years old. The first collection, *Dependencies,* was well-received by critics, although Mueller herself later claimed the poems in it were too decorative and metaphorical. Her second book showed more evidence of the brief, sharp Germanic style she would become both comfortable with and known for. This collection, *The Private Life* (1976), was a Lamont Poetry Selection of the Academy of American Poets. Four years later, she published *The Need to Hold Still,* which was awarded the American Book Award for Poetry in 1981.

During the 1980s, Mueller was also noted for her work in translating the work of German poet Marie Luise Kaschnitz and of German novelist W. Anna Migutsch. These translations forced Mueller into looking very closely at how her proficiency in two languages affected her choice of words in her own writing. *Second Language* (in which "The Exhibit" first appeared) was a direct result of that examination, and this book was recognized for its particular focus on the blending of public and private lives and the interconnectedness of history and present-day life. It presents very complicated subjects in her typical clear, precise language that appeals to poetry "experts" and novices alike. Her ability to evoke emotion and paint vivid pictures with plain, simple language (whether English or German) helped make *Second Language* one of her most widely read collections.

Criticism

Adrian Blevins

Adrian Blevins, a poet and essayist who has taught at Hollins University, Sweet Briar College, and in the Virginia Community College System, is the author of The Man Who Went Out for Cigarettes, *a chapbook of poems, and has published poems, stories, and essays in many magazines, journals, and anthologies. In the following essay, Blevins argues that Lisel Mueller's lyric poem "The Exhibit" is more complex than it may first appear to be.*

After a single reading, Lisel Mueller's "The Exhibit" seems to contest, out of its own apparent simplicity, any real need for comment. What useful remark can be made about a straight-forward account of a poet's memory of a small disagreement with her uncle, or about the portrait of an old man whose war experience has made him either unable or unwilling to recognize the difference between an extinct animal and a mythological one? Even Mueller's language in "The Exhibit" is economical, or written in what American poet and critic Alice Fulton, in review of Mueller's *Second Language,* calls "the plain style"—a language nearly lacking in the musical devices that make most poetry full and sensual and audacious enough to bind. Yet one of "The Exhibits'" glories is that it only seems simple. Fulton says:

> … reading Lisel Mueller … is a bit like gazing at a lake or a tree. At first you think nothing new here: another wave, another leaf. But if you bring your full attention to bear, you're amazed at the implication and activity of an apparently simple surface.

All literature, because it exists both in the moment the reader encounters it and in another one the writer recalls, imagines, pretends, or craves, commits a miracle: a semantic violation of the laws governing the nature of time. But many lyric poems, because they forsake the world's abundance by narrowing their focus into a single instance or theme, are especially able to heighten or enrich our perceptions of even the simplest of experiences. Many lyric poems can be likened to still-life paintings: because there's no competing landscape in a painting of a bowl of apples (let's say), we are often able to see the fruit better—to witness it glisten and shine or resemble a bruise or a face. Mueller's talent and proclivity for the lyric has made her a master of this sort of poetic still-life. *Second Language,* the book from which we take "The Exhibit," is full of poems much like it—po-

ems in which small memories and observations become more conceptional meditations on topics as wide-ranging as the experience of exile, the cost and weight of experience, and the imagination's power to redeem and even heal us.

On the most basic level, "The Exhibit" describes the speaker's memory of a conversation with her uncle. The speaker, her uncle, and an unnamed companion are in East Germany looking at a painting of a unicorn that is hanging in what we assume, because of the poem's title, to be an art museum. The poem's tension is revealed when the speaker tells us that her uncle says the unicorn in the painting is "now extinct." Although the speaker tells her uncle that "such a creature never existed," she says she knows "he does not believe [her]." The poem advances on the axis of this conflict between what the speaker knows to be true and what her uncle thinks ought to be true, which in turn leads the speaker to realize that her uncle "needs to believe in something / that could not be captured except by love." The poem's poignancy comes from the speaker's empathy, which rises out of her recognition that her uncle, "a prisoner of war / even after the war was over," chooses to believe that the unicorn in the painting is real because he needs to believe that "this world, / this terrible world we live in, / is not the only possible one." Thus the poem's most basic argument— that there is, at least in the mind of an old man, more than one world—reinforces the duality that lyric poems themselves actualize. Although this is not precisely an example of organic form (this term describes a poem whose technique seems to mimic and enhance its own topic), it does reveal a complexity in the poem that is not immediately obvious, suggesting even on this most rhetorical level that there's more to "The Exhibit" than we first realize.

It also seems important, if not altogether serendipitous, that the speaker and her uncle are looking at a unicorn, rather than a dragon or some other mythological creature. In Western literature unicorns symbolize virtues innocent people (children, victims of war) embody. They can only be caught and tamed by young, unmarried girls. The uncle's belief that unicorns are real suggests that he longs for the kind of innocence they symbolize, while his belief that unicorns are extinct suggests that the world has destroyed or even murdered this virtue. The contrast Mueller establishes between the uncle's beliefs and what we know about him— that he's eighty years old and "a prisoner of war / even after the war was over"—presents the idea that experience and the knowledge that accompanies it are often very costly commodities, not only

What Do I Read Next?

- Though part of Lisel Mueller's *Learning to Play by Ear* contains poems from her first collection, *Dependencies,* it also includes essays and interviews not found anywhere else. In this book, she discusses everything from syntax and diction to memory and the writing life.

- *Driven into Paradise: The Musical Migration from Nazi Germany to the United States* (1999) is a collection of essays concerning a result of Nazi Germany that is not often considered. Editors Reinhold Brinkmann and Christoph Wolff have gathered writings by and about the forced migration of German musicians and the flood of artists and intellectuals who entered the United States from 1933 to 1944. The essays reveal the impoverishment of Germany that turned into enrichment for America.

- Written by a prisoner of war, Sidney Stewart's *Give Us This Day* was first published in 1957. Stewart was the only survivor among a group of American soldiers captured by the Japanese during WWII, and his story is told in a plain narrative that is both fascinating and revealing of the strength of the human spirit.

- Paul Celan was one of the most important poets to come out of Nazi Germany only to commit suicide decades later in 1970. John Felstiner's *Paul Celan: Poet, Survivor, Jew* (1995) is the first critical biography of the poet and highlights the connection between Celan's own experiences and his poetry. Celan's work attempted to expose the truth in a world that wanted to silence him.

- Roy Wilkinson's *Are You a Unicorn? The Meaning and Mission of Unicorns* (1998, 2nd edition) explores the possibility that some human beings are actually "unicorns" trapped in a world of violence and selfishness. Written on an adult level, the author poses provocative questions about certain people who exhibit the characteristics of the mythological creatures and may well be unicorns on earth.

- James Randi is noted for his books and lectures exposing fraud in so-called paranormal events—everything from ESP to haunted houses to a belief in unicorns. *Flim Flam! Psychics, ESP, Unicorns, and Other Delusions* (1998) is a fun and interesting look at a wide range of both off-the-wall and widely accepted beliefs, as told by one who thinks it's all nonsense.

---

to the people of the world, but also to the world itself.

This theme is reinforced in several ways. First there's the closing image of the uncle's eyes, which the speaker calls "dry wells that fill so easily now." This image likens the uncle to a child, and children are, of course, the ultimate symbols of innocence and purity. The poet's repetition of the word "world" in the lines "this world, / this terrible world we live in" mimics both the sound and repetition of the word "war" earlier in the poem, placing emphasis on the unfortunate truth the old man's belief in unicorns is meant to challenge. Thus we can see a duality, or another complexity, at work in Mueller's poem: first, there's the real world, which is so "terrible" it con-

tains the "murderous forest," and the "foul water," and, second, there's the imagined, fantastic, or mythological world in which a unicorn's "single luminous horn" can "[redeem] the murderous forest." These two realities sit side by side for most of the duration of "The Exhibit." One of the questions we might ask ourselves, then, is which world the speaker of this poem might prefer. Perhaps a look at Mueller's technique will tell us.

Mueller risks sentimentality at almost every turn in "The Exhibit." Her diction is dangerously abstract and conceptual (she uses "power," "gentleness," "love," and "pure" in what by any standard is a very short poem) and her rhetorical method—the use of the unicorn as a central figure—is both overtly symbolic and potentially trite. But the gradual movement of the poem downward toward the more archetypal setting of the forest and the unicorn's "luminous horn" within it saves the poem, if just barely, from sentimentality. The movement, or progression, of "The Exhibit" into this central image in which the unicorn's horn "redeemed the murderous forest / and, dipped into the foul water, / would then turn it pure ..." redeems by both the increasing speed of the lines and the use of more concrete images the power and importance of the mythological forest, which has been set up in contrast to the civilized, and more plain, landscape of the art museum. That Mueller uses a more discursive, prosaic, or matter-of-fact line in her description of her conversation with her uncle and then shifts into more imagistic and rhythmic lines describing the forest and the unicorn sets up a dichotomy that pitches itself, lyrically, in favor of the imagined world.

In "The Image as a Form of Intelligence," American poet and critic Robert Bly argues that the image is a poetic device that can "fill the gap between ourselves and nature." He says: "a human being can reach out with his left hand to the world of human intelligence and with his right hand to the natural world, and touch both at the same time." The speaker of "The Exhibit" and her uncle can be said to represent the world of human intelligence on the one hand and the natural or mythological world on the other. But this is not to suggest that the speaker of "The Exhibit" embraces the world of logic and reason. It is important to note that the speaker of this poem does not really argue with her uncle; she not only allows him to believe in the extinct unicorn, but, by way of a series of realizations and observations about the way he suffered in the war, understands why he must. "The Exhibit" closes on a note of extreme empathy. The last line is one of the few images in the poem, and for this reason brings as much attention to itself as do the earlier images of forest and unicorn horn. The drawn-out affect of the closing anapest, especially in contrast to the energy of the iambs of "dry wells that fill"—produces a sound like a sigh of resignation. The musicality and physicality of this closing line makes it especially emotive, and thus reinforces the speaker's realization that the worlds we imagine (and even invent) for ourselves are not only as important as the real world we find ourselves living in, but are perhaps as well metaphorical necessities, rising as they do from the kind of imaginative thinking that would redeem us from the cost and weight of living in a world so terrible

> *Set within this emotional scene, the uncle is like a child who is old enough to know there is no Santa Claus, but who is not ready to accept the loss of the comfort of believing in him."*

it could produce, among other horrors, the Holocaust.

American poet and critic Dick Allen, in a 1977 discussion of Mueller's third book, *A Private Life,* argues in his conclusion to an overall complementary review that "the only thing I miss is ... the drive toward the core, the steady deepening." This seems a reasonable enough request, and one Lisel Mueller seems to have heard. As our look at "The Exhibit" has shown, often there is more to Mueller's minimalist poems than we first might think. Though the ocean may at first look like a desert—all flat and steady and fixed—we know it isn't one, but rather the commonplace surface of deep body of water within which dwells a whole second universe. It is thus like many of the best lyric poems—a creation whose plenty we need only dive in for.

Source: Adrian Blevins, in an essay for *Poetry for Students,* Gale, 2000.

Pamela Steed Hill

Pamela Steed Hill has had poems published in close to a hundred journals and is the author of In Praise of Motels, *a collection of poems published by Blair Mountain Press. She is an associate editor for* University Communications *at The Ohio State University. In the following essay, Steed Hill discusses the idea that the detrimental effects of war remain with survivors long after the battles have ended, often causing them to take comfort in a world of make-believe.*

For individuals who have never been directly touched by war or by any other catastrophic event, the idea of "historical determinism" may seem far-fetched. Many of us want to believe that we have complete control over who we are and why we have certain feelings or behave in particular ways. But there are those whose lives have been greatly altered by experiences with the horrors of war, especially the world wars that affected millions of human beings all over the globe during the first half of the twentieth century. Born in Germany in 1924, Lisel Mueller was an eyewitness to the atrocities of political tyranny and the persecution of select groups of people. She would physically escape the Second World War at the age of fifteen when she and her family fled to the United States. She would never, however, be emotionally free from the suffering she left behind and the loved ones who stayed to endure it.

"The Exhibit" explores the effects that war—and that being a prisoner of war—has had on the mind and spirit of an elderly man, identified in the poem as Mueller's uncle who lives in East Germany. The setting for the poem is an art museum, and, specifically, it takes place in front of a painting of a unicorn. This serene, pleasant, and most likely quiet atmosphere is in sharp contrast to the environment revealed later in the poem through the use of metaphor and allusion. Mueller presents a striking juxtaposition of emotions by taking us into the mind of the uncle who may appear to be on a casual outing with family members, but who is still haunted by the grief and pain of events that took place many decades earlier.

The poem begins innocently enough, with the uncle explaining to his listeners that the unicorn "is now extinct." When he is told that unicorns cannot be extinct because they never lived in the first place, he does not argue the point, but neither does he believe it. In this opening third of "The Exhibit" we may assume the uncle is simply naive in thinking that the mythological creature—typically presented as a white horse with a long white mane and a white spiral horn protruding from the front of its forehead—actually roamed the earth at one time. As the poem develops, however, we learn that his belief in a being that represents both "power and gentleness" is actually a kind of protection against having to accept the world as it really is. More importantly, his imagination is a shield against the memories of war and of being a prisoner of war. Mueller expresses the lingering pain of the uncle's experience in describing him as "A prisoner of war / even after the war was over."

What life was like for the uncle prior to the conflict we don't know. He was presumably a young man when it started, and Mueller focuses her poem on how the later decades of his life were shaped by the war years. He probably did not believe in unicorns when he was younger, and, of course, the irony here is that childish naivete would not have been uncommon for him then. But the experience of world war caused his emotions to do an about-face, so to speak, luring him into the comfort of fantasy and make-believe as he grew older. A very revealing point in the poem is in lines 11 and 12, which tell us that the uncle "... needs to believe in something / that could not be captured except by love." The key word here is "needs." It's not that the war veteran simply believes in something or necessarily wants to, but that he essentially requires it. He must believe in a world other than the real one in order not to be swallowed up by the memories of how horrible it all can be.

This poem speaks very strongly on the terrible human cost of war. Mueller doesn't address the number of actual deaths that occurred during the world wars, but, instead, focuses on the toll they took on the mind. This is a common theme in her poetry, and it often pairs with the corresponding idea of historical determinism. What an individual witnesses or experiences on a grand scale has a direct impact on the smaller, personal scale. This poet's own frame of reference stems from WWII in particular, but the sentiments she presents in poetic form would apply to all national or global conflicts. When she was interviewed by author and professor Nancy Bunge in 1985, Mueller commented on her belief in the vital role that history plays in our lives, stating that "what has gone on in the past is very important to one's view of the world." She also stated that during the Vietnam War, she felt personally the "shame and guilt and wrongness" of America in that conflict. Although she had been a naturalized citizen of the United States for over twenty years at that point, she still attributed some of her outrage to having the "history of Nazi Germany in the back of my mind."

That same history, of course, is what is on the uncle's mind in "The Exhibit." It has caused him to turn to a belief in the unicorn because the legends surrounding this gallant mythological creature portray it as both strong and gentle, much unlike the human leaders that the uncle suffered under who were strong and tyrannical. When he was captured during the war (we don't know exactly by whom), he had yet another burden to bear and was unfortunate enough to see war from a different cruel perspective—that of a prisoner. The unicorn became an appealing "hero" to the uncle because it could not be captured except by the tender touch of a virgin woman, or, in other words, by love. This he sees as a "good" kind of captivity, directly opposed to being taken by an enemy. Lines 13-16 of the poem rely on allusion to the typical characteristics of the unicorn and on the metaphor in reference to the real world as a "murderous forest" and as "foul water." Legend tells us that the unicorn could be a vicious fighter, but it was supposedly a "just" fighter, and its enemies were truly evil. Therefore, its "single luminous horn / redeemed the murderous forest / and, dipped into foul water, / would turn it pure." During the Nazi years in Germany, the atmosphere was surely "murderous" and "foul," and the uncle needed to believe in something that could bring about redemption and purity for the human race.

In the next-to-last line of "The Exhibit," we learn that the uncle is eighty years old. While we may have assumed he was an elderly man, it is important to know just how elderly because it helps to amplify the long-term effects of history. We are not told the year in which his captors actually released him, but for decades he has been a "psychological" prisoner of war. He is apparently still prone to tears of grief since Mueller describes his eyes as "dry wells that fill so easily now." But this sentimentality cannot be dismissed as the emotional tendencies of the aged because it is derived from a very real and a very distressing source.

Perhaps the most provocative question that remains at the end of the poem is whether the uncle really believes that unicorns once existed and that their ability to be both powerful and gentle was true. There is evidence for both a yes and a no answer, though each is subtle and ultimately inconclusive. The fact that the uncle brings up the subject in the first place indicates that he does believe in the creatures. If he realized his feelings were based solely on imagination and that revealing them would only bring teasing from his family, if not ridicule, it seems unlikely that he would confess to his fantasy world while touring a museum. The sixth line supports the notion that his belief in unicorns is real because the speaker acknowledges that "he does not believe us"—this in regard to his being told the creatures never existed. But one word near the end of the poem throws this hypothesis into doubt.

In line 19, the word "insist" implies a forced argument, one that is built on a desperate attempt to deny what one simply does not want to accept. In this case, the uncle cannot accept that "this terrible world we live in" is the "only possible one." The last four lines of the poem paint a picture of the old man that is very vivid. He stands in front of a painting that contains an image he has come to consider sacred—that of the beloved unicorn. While pondering the rejection of its existence by his family members and remembering the atrocities of the "terrible world," he begins to cry, or, at least, his eyes fill with tears. Set within this emotional scene, the uncle is like a child who is old enough to know there is no Santa Claus, but who is not ready to accept the loss of the comfort of believing in him. "Insist" here connotes urgency and need, but not necessarily honest conviction. The impression is that the overwhelming realization that the real world—the terrible one—truly is the only possible one is more than the uncle can take. His response is simply to insist, silently, that it isn't true.

Much of this poem's strength lies in its portrayal of complex human emotions and catastrophic events in simple, easy-to-understand language. Often, the most horrific subjects are only cheapened by an attempt to dramatize or elaborate on their shocking aspects. As in "The Exhibit," however, a matter-of-fact, unadorned manner of relating a story can produce an even more chilling impression than if the "blood and guts" were spelled out in gruesome detail. The uncle does not scream his suffering throughout the galleries of the museum, and it is safe to assume that he has kept his pain to himself for his entire adult life. In the same way, the poem does not shriek its purpose or themes at the reader. Instead, it quietly and methodically takes us into the weary mind of a war veteran who did indeed survive the Holocaust, but who will always be its victim.

Source: Pamela Steed Hill, in an essay for *Poetry for Students,* Gale, 2000.

Sources

Allen, Dick, "To The Wall," in *Poetry,* September, 1977, p. 347.

Bly, Robert, "The Image as a Form of Intelligence," reprinted in *A Field Guide to Contemporary Poetry and Poetics,* Oberlin College Press, 1997, p. 109.

Bunge, Nancy, *Finding the Words: Conversations With Writers Who Teach,* Athens, Ohio: Swallow Press, 1985, pp. 96-105.

Fulton, Alice, "Main Things," in *Poetry,* January, 1988, p. 360.

"The History Channel," www.historychannel.com, accessed February 2, 2000.

Mueller, Lisel, *Second Language,* Baton Rouge: Louisiana State University Press, 1986.

Rubin, Stan Sanvel and William Heyan, "The Steady Interior Hum," in *The Post-Confessionals: Conversations With American Poets of the Eighties,* edited by Earl G. Ingersoll, Judith Kitchen, and S. Rubin, Cranbury, New Jersey: Associated University Presses, 1989.

"Sleep Disorders: Post Traumatic Stress Syndrome," http://dreamdoctor.com/sleep/disorders/ptss.html, accessed January 31, 2000.

For Further Study

Carlson, Lewis H., *We Were Each Other's Prisoners: An Oral History of World War II American and German Prisoners of War,* New York: Basic Books, 1997.

Based on over 150 interviews with prisoners of war during WWII, this book tells the stories of the survivors in their own words. It includes the tale of an anti-Nazi German soldier who refused to fight for Hitler and another prisoner who escaped from his captors three times.

Mueller, Lisel, *Alive Together,* Baton Rouge: Louisiana State University Press, 1996.

This is a collection of Mueller's new and selected poems, including some of those contained in *Second Language* and her four other books. It compiles 35 years worth of her best work and, as the title suggests, its theme is the miracle of human love, despite all odds.

For An Assyrian Frieze

Peter Viereck
1948

Although his work is not read much today, Peter Viereck was one of the leading American poets of the 1950s and 1960s. But Viereck did not limit himself to writing poetry; he also became an important voice as a cultural critic, arguing for a sophisticated, intellectual model of conservatism. As a poet, Viereck was conservative: he opposed what he viewed as excessive experimentation and obscurity, and advocated a return to form, to rhyme, and to simple lyrics. In this, he was going against the dominant movement in poetry at the time—the allusive, free-verse modernist verse written by such poets as T.S. Eliot, Ezra Pound, and William Carlos Williams. "For An Assyrian Frieze" appeared in 1948, in *Terror and Decorum,* Viereck's first volume of poetry and one that won him the Pulitzer Prize for poetry. "For An Assyrian Frieze" takes a cue from Pound in that the poet immerses himself in a long-ago time, but, unlike Pound, Viereck narrates this picture of Assyrian society in a very regular, formal verse. The portrait of the violent bloodlusting Assyrian society, synechdochized as the "lion with a prophet's beard," is ironic, given the calm regularity of the verse form. Such techniques characterize not only Viereck's poetry but also his ideas of cultural conservatism.

Author Biography

Peter Viereck was born in New York City in 1916. He attended the elite Horace Mann School

Peter Viereck

for Boys and Harvard, from which he graduated *summa cum laude* in 1937. While at Harvard, he won both the Garrison medal for the best undergraduate poetry and the Bowdoin prize for the best philosophical prose—one of the few Harvard students ever to accomplish that. After doing some graduate work at Oxford University in England, Viereck returned to the United States and completed a Ph.D. in history in 1942. He enlisted in the U.S. Army after completing his Ph.D. and worked in the Psychological Warfare Intelligence Branch, earning battle stars and also helping to monitor the wartime broadcasts that the eminent poet Ezra Pound made from Italy.

Upon returning to the United States, Viereck began teaching, first at Harvard and Smith and then, in 1948, at Mount Holyoke, a women's college in South Hadley, Massachusetts. He was an active member of Mount Holyoke's faculty until his retirement in 1987 but continued teaching as an emeritus professor until 1997.

Viereck continued to write poetry from his school days well into his retirement. His first book, *Terror and Decorum,* won the 1949 Pulitzer Prize for poetry. He continued to write poetry throughout the 1950s and 1960s, had his poems appear in a number of anthologies, and even published a "poem and a play (first of all a poem)," *The Tree*

Witch (1961). Many of his earlier poems are collected in *New and Selected Poems: 1932-1967.* In the 1990s he experienced another burst of creativity, publishing a number of books that dealt with questions of death. In addition, Viereck has written books on philosophy, political science, and history, including *Conservatism Revisited: The Revolt Against Revolt, 1815-1949* (1950) and *Shame and Glory of the Intellectuals* (1953).

Poem Text

"I, the great king, the powerful king, king of the
    world, King of Assyria, the king whose path
    was a cyclone, whose battle was a flaming
    sea, I am powerful, all-powerful, exalted,
    almighty, majestic, all-important in
    power,"—inscription of 670 B.C.

Sometimes, a lion with a prophet's beard
Lopes from a bas-relief to stretch his claws.
His bestial eyes are wonderfully sad.

Then he grow wings, the terrible king grows wings,
And flies above the black Euphrates loam,   5
Hunting for enemies of Nineveh.

His names are Shamshi and Adadnrari,
Tiglath-Pileser, Assurbanipal,
And the first Sargon of Dur-Sharukin.

"The day my chariots stormed the town, I waxed   10
My beard with oil of rose and waterlily,
And freed nine pearl-caged nightingales, and built

A pillar of skills so high it stabbed the sun."
(Was that the tomb's voice, or the desert-wind's?
Or ours?—what ghost is still our roaring priest?)   15

The scribes shall say: his will outflew his wisdom.
The saints shall say: his was the sin of pride.
The skulls say nothing. And the lizards grin.

This is the rapture that the Gentiles feared
When Joshua made music masterful.   20
Each sinew is a harp-string crouched to twang.

The treble of such bloodlust if he pounced
Would shriek an anti-social kind of beauty
Like parrots in a gypsy carnival.

Then back to stone. In stone he sleeps the least.   25
It's not with love his brooding glitters so.
Earth spawns no gangrene half so luminous

As the contagion of those molten eyes.

Poem Summary

Stanzas 1-3

In the first stanza, Viereck introduces the subject of his poem, a bas-relief (or a sculpture in which figures are carved so that they protrude out of a stone background) from ancient Assyria. Assyria was an ancient kingdom, very powerful in Biblical times (it flourished especially from 1000 B.C. to 606 B.C.) that stretched from the Tigris and Euphrates basin to modern-day Syria, Lebanon, and Israel. The bas-relief shows "a lion with a prophet's beard" with "wonderfully sad" eyes. To the narrator, the lion appears to be coming out of the bas-relief to stretch its paws, just before "the terrible king grows wings." At this point, the narrator is imagining rather than simply transcribing what is in the sculpture. He sees the lion fly "above the black Euphrates loam, / Hunting for the enemies of Nineveh." Nineveh was an important city in the heart of the Assyrian territory in present-day Iraq. In the third stanza of this section, the narrator calls out some of the names of this lion; the names are the names of the powerful kings of the Assyrian empire, culminating with "the first Sargon of Dur-Sharukin." Sargon was one of the greatest kings of Assyria, ruling from 722 B.C. to 705 B.C, and built his palace at Dur-Sharukin, near Nineveh.

Stanzas 4-5

In these stanzas the narrator hears the voice of the lion—the lion who channels the spirits of the dead Assyrian kings—and begins to understand the character of Assyrian life. This lion speaks of luxuriating while his "chariots stormed the town" and of building "a pillar of skulls so high it stabbed the sun." Here, the poet is drawing a contrast between the personal luxury that the king enjoys and the savagery that was the hallmark of the Assyrian empire. The poet, after hearing this, questions himself: "Was that the tomb's voice, or the desert-wind's? Or ours?" He does not know where these vioces come from, and fears that perhaps he will awaken this spirit of savagery and bloodlust in his own time (drawing an ironic parallel with the unimaginable, industrialized killing perpetrated in particular by the Nazis and carried out in general during the Second World War that had just ended).

Stanza 6

This stanza makes the central contrast of the poem—between the events of the past and how later people understand them—explicit. The poet talks about how four groups of "commentators" interpret the actions of this lion, the representation of the Assyrian empire. The "scribes" explain them as a political act; the "saints" see his actions in religious terms and condemn him; the "skulls" of his victims simply sit in silent witness; the "lizards," representing the unchanging nature of the desert, "grin."

Stanzas 7-10

The final stanzas of the poem bring the poet's own voice to the fore. Here, he explains how he understands the historical legacy of this dumb, yet eloquent, bas-relief. The narrator attempts to come to grips with the kind of violence that characterized the ancient world, but is unable to. He refers to the "rapture that the Gentiles feared / When Joshua made music masterful," alluding to the Biblical story of Joshua destroying the city of Jericho. In stanzas 7 and 8, the narrator compares the "sinews" of a warrior to musical instruments, again emphasizing the foreignness of the bloodlust of the ancient world. But even he is attracted by the primitive energy of this will to violence, saying that "Earth spawns no gangrene half so luminous / As the contagion of those molten eyes." The counterpoint of the terms "gangrene" (a blood infection that causes limbs to rot, and one of the most revolting conditions a human can contract) and "luminous" (an almost always positive term, referring to a lovely glow given off by something) epitomizes the combination of disgust at and attraction to violence and bloodlust that the bas-relief inspires in the poet.

Themes

In "For An Assyrian Frieze," Peter Viereck presents the reader with a work of ancient art, a piece of silent desert stone on which is carved a "lion with a prophet's beard." The work causes him to imagine the mindset, the ethos, of the Assyrian empire that produced the sculpture. Thinking about Assyria's gleeful bloodlust, he is both repelled and fascinated.

The Ancient World

The remnants of the ancient world have always been an important topic in Western literature. For centuries after the fall of the Roman Empire, Europeans marvelled at the ruins left behind, not understanding how such structures could have been built because the knowledge of engineering and artistic techniques of the Romans had been lost. The Renaissance and Enlightenment were spurred on by continued discoveries of ancient artifacts—Egyptian, Greek, and Roman.

Western literature springs largely from the Greeks, and for many readers a poet could not be considered "great" without somehow engaging in a dialogue with the father of Western poetry,

Topics for Further Study

- Research the Assyrian Empire. Where was it? What were the characteristics of its culture and society? Who were its important leaders? What legacies did it leave to the modern world?

- Dante's *Divine Comedy,* Shelley's "The Triumph of Life," and Viereck's "For An Assyrian Frieze" all use a similar verse form—three-line stanzas. How does this verse form help the poem to move along? What does the rhyme in Dante's and Shelley's poems contribute that Viereck did not want in his poem? Why do you think Viereck made that decision?

- John Keats's poem "Ode on a Grecian Urn" and Percy Shelley's poem "Ozymandias," both written at approximately the same time, express very different impressions that a speaker obtains by looking at an ancient artifact. What does each speaker get out of his artifact? Viereck's poem also involves an observer gazing upon an ancient artwork and having particular feelings and ideas evoked in him by this artifact. How does his poem express an image of ancient civilization different from that of Keats or Shelley?

- In the poem, Viereck's speaker looks upon a "frieze" that he also calls a "bas-relief." What are each of these kinds of sculptures? What are some famous examples of friezes and bas-reliefs? What cultures made these kinds of sculptures? Can you find examples of friezes or bas-reliefs at your school or in your town?

Homer. During the Romantic period of the early nineteenth century, many of the most important poets took as their main topic the confrontation between ancient civilizations and the modern world. Goethe wrote a book on his time discovering the ruins in the city of Rome, while Keats's famous "Ode on a Grecian Urn" uses the decoration on an ancient Greek amphora to meditate on the fleeting nature of beauty and to suggest that the classical world put a greater premium on love, beauty, and pleasure than does modern society. But the most

important precursor for Viereck's poem is Percy Bysshe Shelley's 1817 sonnet "Ozymandias." "Ozymandias" describes a half-destroyed statue in "an antique land," most likely in the Middle East or Egypt. Shelley's poem examines the transitory nature of arrogance and power. In his poem, Viereck goes even farther back, looking at a remnant of one of the first civilizations on earth, the Assyrian. Viereck is certainly responding to Shelley, saying that while the power may not last, the violent impulses that help individuals obtain and maintain power do not die out.

Poets and Violence

Poets seem to be noted for pacifism. Especially in modern America, we have a hard time thinking of poets as violent people. Our stereotypical image of them represents them as contemplating the beauties of nature, lost-in-thought, sensitive, and artistic. Artists are seen in much the same way in our popular imagination. In fact, we often oppose art and violence; the two have little to do with each other except that art often protests violence (as in Picasso's masterpiece *Guernica* or Matthew Arnold's poem "Dover Beach"). But, in the not-too-distant-past, poets were closely associated with violence. Rudyard Kipling's nineteenth century verse advanced the imperial project and glorified combat. In revolutionary America and France, poetic odes were written to stir people to fight against governmental power. If we go even farther back, to classical times, poets were almost always conscripted to help incite warlike feelings among the populace of a given nation—Virgil's great epic the *Aeneid* was written specifically to glorify the Roman state and its warlike ways. And finally, Homer, in the *Iliad* and the *Odyssey,* celebrates the valour of men in combat.

Viereck's poem examines these conflicting emotions in the poet. Confronted by the implacable foreignness of this bas-relief, in which a "lion with a prophet's beard" represents all of the cruelty and bloodthirstiness of ancient societies, the narrator falls into a reverie, imagining the lion to be speaking to him. The lion is the stone embodiment of all of the warlike rulers of the Assyrian empire, from the early "Shamshi," who reigned in the eighteenth century before Christ, to Sargon, who held the throne one thousand years later. The narrator imagines this lion—who is a metonym for the whole Assyrian culture—to be speaking to him, telling him about the way he preened himself while his armies were slaughtering thousands. The narrator cannot understand this love for violence, but when the lion speaks of it he remembers that other people of that foreign time and land also gloried in violence and slaughter—even the Israelites who are the predecessors to the pacifistic early Christians. By describing the lion as having a "prophet's beard," Viereck makes this difficult-to-understand combination even more explicit. We must confront the fact, Viereck argues, that even those who followed the Hebrew God engaged in this sort of violence. It was not just the Assyrians, those villains of the Old Testament, but it was the Hebrews themselves who slaughtered on a massive scale. And, he concludes the poem by saying that "luminous" "gangrene" still lives on this earth—certainly a reference to the war just ended when this poem was written, a war that killed hundreds of times more people than were killed in any Assyrian war.

Style

"For An Assyrian Frieze" makes use of a regular line structure. The poem is constructed as a series of three-line stanzas of loose iambic pentameter. For the most part, each line has five feet that each consist of an unstressed syllable followed by a stressed syllable, but as is customary today even among the most conservative practitioners of traditional verse, some lines will have eleven syllables and some might have even twelve, but almost every line has only five stressed syllables.

There is no end-rhyme in the poem. Had there been, this poem would have potentially been in the Italian verse form terza rima, in which the poet uses three-line stanzas with the rhyme scheme *aba bcb cdc* and so on. This would have been an especially appropriate choice, because the two best-known examples of terza rima are Dante Aligheri's *Commedia Divina* and Percy Shelley's "The Triumph of Life," two poems in which the poet examines the aftermath of a violent past. But terza rima can also sound like a singsong, and perhaps for that reason Viereck avoids actually using it while also gently suggesting it.

The poem can be broken into three parts. The first part is a description of the frieze and how it begins to speak to the narrator; the second part is what the lion has to say; and the third part is the narrator's interpretation and understanding of the importance of the lion's words. This tripartite division of content is mirrored in the three-line structure of the verses. Dante, also, used a tripartite structure in his lines and content, but for Dante that

structure was also the structuring principle of the poem as a whole—after all, the tripartite structure was inspired by the Holy Trinity, which is the real subject of Dante's poem. In the *Commedia Divina,* there are three sections: the Inferno, the Purgatorio, and the Paradiso. The first two sections have thirty-three "cantos," or chapters, while the third has thirty-four, so the poem has 100 cantos in total. Viereck does much the same thing here: he has nine stanzas of three lines each, emphasizing the tripartite structure, but adds a final one-line stanza to bring the total number to 10.

Historical Context

In 1949, poetry was a major issue in the public arena. Ezra Pound, one of the most famous and best-respected English-language poets in the world, was languishing in a Washington, D.C., mental hospital, having been found mentally unfit to stand trial on treason charges. During World War II, Pound had made broadcasts on Italian state radio, and many people felt that this was a treasonous act. (Pound argued that the content of his broadcasts was never determined by the Fascist authorities.) Disgraced, depressed, and shamed, Pound seemed to have departed the public eye, perhaps for good.

But that year, Pound published the latest installment of his long poem, *The Cantos.* This book, called *The Pisan Cantos* because much of it had been written while Pound was incarcerated in an Army detention camp in Pisa, Italy, won the first Bollingen Prize for Poetry, an award sponsored by the Library of Congress. Immediately a furor was sparked. How could Pound be given an award for a book of poetry that, on its first page, mourns Mussolini? How could a traitor be given an award by the same government that had so recently wanted to execute him?

The controversy soon stopped focusing on Pound and became a debate about the proper way to look at poetry, or art in general, and about what the relationship of art and politics should be. The Bollingen judges defended their decision, saying that the aesthetic value of the book was their only criteria. Others, such as the poet and critic Robert Hillyer, shot back that it was impossible for vile political sentiments not to detract from a book's aesthetic value. Hillyer, writing in the *Saturday Review of Literature,* argued that a new poetic orthodoxy, epitomized by T. S. Eliot, wanted to make poetry hermetic, closed, and to take it out of pub-

Compare & Contrast

- **1949:** As Europe reorganizes itself after the mayhem of World War II, the United States and the Soviet Union become the world's dominant powers. The Soviet Union installs puppet governments in Eastern and Central Europe while the United States works desperately (and often covertly) to influence elections and the political climate in countries such as Greece and Italy.

  2000: The Soviet "empire," having fallen in 1989-1991, has become Russia. By the year 2000, the transition to capitalism has impoverished Russia, transferring much of the wealth that was previously held by Communist officials to corrupt officials of the new government and mobsters. The countries of Eastern and Central Europe fare better.

- **1949:** Because of the G.I. Bill, veterans returning from World War II are entitled to a college education. Swelling university enrollments change American society forever, and a college education comes within reach of families that could never have afforded one before.

  2000: In the new economy, a college education now serves the same purpose as a high-school diploma used to: it is the bare minimum educational achievement required to enter most professions. More Americans than ever attend college.

- **1949:** Ezra Pound, incarcerated in St. Elizabeth's mental hospital in Washington, D.C., after being found incompetent to stand trial on his treason charges, wins the first Bollingen Prize for poetry for his book *The Pisan Cantos*. The award ignites a controversy when many other poets and large segments of the public object to a man who made broadcasts on Italian state radio during the war being given an award by the Library of Congress. In the same year, Peter Viereck wins the Pulitzer Prize for poetry for his book *Terror and Decorum*.

  2000: Poetry's public profile is increasing for a number of reasons. U.S. Poet Laureate Robert Pinsky travels the country promoting poetry, and, on this trip, compiles a CD of Americans reading their favorite poems aloud. At the same time, the performance-oriented "slam poetry" movement is gaining in popularity.

- **1949:** President Harry S. Truman takes office after winning a surprising election victory over Thomas Dewey the previous year.

  2000: Vice-President Al Gore contests the Democratic nomination for president with former Senator Bill Bradley of New Jersey. Among the Republicans, the leading candidates are Texas governor George W. Bush—son of former President George Bush—and Arizona Senator John McCain.

---

lic life by drowning it in obscurity. Hillyer's "common-sense" approach to poetry came under fire by both left-and right-wing partisans, who felt that art must be given leeway to examine and express all political opinions.

Viereck's *Terror and Decorum* came out that same year, was probably also considered by the Bollingen committee, and ended up winning the year's Pulitzer Prize for poetry. Viereck also joined in the debate. He contributed a fifteen-page prose statement to the poems he included in John Ciardi's anthology of *Mid-Century American Po-ets,* laying out his opposition to the T. S. Eliot model of poetry. "Mine ... is a classicism of the industrial age," he wrote, "with an ivory tower built where the subway rumbles the loudest. Being classicist means that my poetry is equally interested in shaking off the vague sentimentalities of the pre-Eliot romanticism and the hermetic ingenuities of the post-Eliot version of neo-classicism. The former contains (1) no fun and (2) no humanness." This accusation of a lack of humanity was a common one levelled against both Eliot's and Pound's poetry. In a 1951 lecture, Viereck attacked the "debatable" *Pisan Cantos* and defended those poets, such as himself, who neither saw the value in such a book nor objected to it simply out of know-nothing middle-class Babbittry. "I am thinking," he says, "of good students or good writers or good readers, who approach such a work with a completely open mind about the Pound-Eliot schools but who with the best will in the world cannot find it beautiful." He characterizes the worst excesses of the "Pound-Eliot schools" as "too much revolt … the irresponsible cult of obfuscating for the sake of obfuscating and of shocking for the sake of shocking, whether in art, ethics, or politics." And in an article published in the conservative magazine *Commentary* in 1951, Viereck attacked Pound in particular.

The Pound-Eliot orthodoxy ruled the American poetry scene for decades, largely because the most influential cultural critics and literature professors had grown up in the era when Pound and Eliot were revolutionizing the literary world. These revolutionaries, as Viereck points out, became the institutions they had rebelled against. Viereck's lack of recognition is almost certainly a result of the enduring Pound-Eliot orthodoxy that he rebelled against—an orthodoxy that has softened but certainly still remains, in a residual form, today.

Critical Overview

"For An Assyrian Frieze" appeared in 1948 in *Terror and Decorum,* Peter Viereck's first volume of poetry and one that won him the Pulitzer Prize for poetry. *Terror and Decorum* was not Viereck's first published book, however; in 1941, while still a graduate student at Harvard, Viereck published *Metapolitics: From the Romantics to Hitler.* Critics and readers have understood Viereck's work to be a reaction against the modernist orthodoxy represented most forcefully by T.S. Eliot, and this is largely because Viereck explained his own work, over and over again, as being such a reaction.

Notwithstanding his opposition to the dominance of Eliot, Viereck's first volume of poetry was instantly hailed as the work of one of America's most promising poets. In the *Saturday Review of Literature,* Selden Rodman wrote that although none of the individual poems in the book was immediately remarkable for its brilliance, "his book as a whole is so rich in experimental vigor, so full of new poetic attitudes toward civilization and its

discontents, so fresh and earthy in its re-animation of the American spirit, that it seems to offer endless possibilities of development." Rodman remarks that Viereck's main themes are the war and the poet in America.

The *New Yorker,* in its anonymous review, was less glowing. Identifying Viereck's aim as "to attempt reconciliation between 'heart and head, Id and Edo, love and law,'" the reviewer feels that Viereck "does not effect this reconciliation, because he is only too sympathetic toward the emotional terms of these oppositions and strongly on the side of decorum." Rolfe Humphries, writing for the *Nation,* felt that Viereck was promising but "has, I hope he knows, a great deal to learn." "He gives it too much of the old college try, shows off, I think, an awful lot; parades his information, sometimes his cleverness; offends against detachment, sometimes against taste." But Humphries did feel that Viereck had a "lushness" in his vocabulary. Viereck responded to his critics in his contribution to John Ciardi's anthology of *Mid-Century American Poets* in 1950: "Several critics of *Terror and Decorum* beamed upon what they called 'its wit'; others frowned upon 'its frivolous clowning around' … The element of so-called wit or buffoonery is a means, not an end … it is my means for expressing the tragedy inseparable from living and the terror inseparable from the shock of beauty."

Later critics have often used Viereck's own terms to analyze his poetry, looking at the poems in terms of his political ideas. John Lawlor, writing in a French journal in 1954, noted Viereck's "sense of historical timing" and his "conviction that poetry must achieve 'a difficult simplicity.'" Borrowing Viereck's own words, Lawlor remarks that the book is "Viereck's means of expressing the tragedy inseparable from living and the terror inseparable from the shock of beauty." In 1968, on the occasion of the publication of his collection *New and Selected Poems, 1932-1967,* Josephine Jacobson wrote for the *Massachusetts Review* that "Viereck's work has three qualities essential to any good poet. He has an individual, sustaining style … poetic convictions, flexible in approach but durable in essence … and an affinity for themes of inherent scope and power."

In recent years Viereck has been almost forgotten, even as he has begun again to produce new verse. In 1980, Idris McIlveen wrote about him in the *Dictionary of Literary Biography,* remarking that "Viereck argues for the importance of traditions and values that have functioned positively to protect man against his own irrational appetites and ego ... [his] political and poetic theories intersect and support one another, for he believes that man's salvation is through his cultural heritage, especially his literature and his imagination." Viereck, today an old man writing about how he is facing death, continues to be a model of the poet as an integral element of his culture's public life.

Criticism

Greg Barnhisel

Greg Barnhisel holds a Ph.D. in American literature. In this essay, he discusses how Viereck uses "For An Assyrian Frieze" to respond to some of his most important predecessors in poetic history.

Poets have always responded to works of art, and written poems about their responses. But ever since the Romantic era of the late eighteenth and early nineteenth century, the discussion of or response to another work of art has become an extremely common topic in English-language poetry. The fact that this topic became so widespread in the Romantic era is partially due to that era's rediscovery of many lost works of Greek and Roman art from the classical period. The excavation of Pompeii and Herculaneum, beginning in 1748, and the slow rediscovery of the "Domus Aurea" (Golden House) of the emperor Nero in Rome (ongoing since the Renaissance, but in the Romantic period such writers as Goethe and Byron visited the half-excavated rooms and even wrote graffiti on ceilings) exposed artists and poets to the artistic accomplishments of prior ages. This often made these artists and writers consider not only the formal qualities of the artwork itself but also the difference between the mindsets of the people of the ancient time and the people of their own day.

Today, it is hard to find a poet who does not respond to artworks in his or her poems. William Carlos Williams, for instance, wrote an entire book of responses to *Pictures from Brueghel.* But the most famous responses to artworks in the entire history of English-language poetry are almost certainly two poems written within two years of each other: Percy Shelley's 1817 "Ozymandias" and John Keats' 1819 "Ode on a Grecian Urn." In his own "For an Assyrian Frieze," Peter Viereck is not only taking the same basic topic as Keats and Shelley did, but is in the process engaging in a con-

versation with them, a conversation that had specific aims given the poetic climate of the time.

In 1949, the world of Anglo-American poetry was dominated by one figure: T. S. Eliot. Although Eliot did not produce much poetry, many of the poems that he did write had become very popular and influential, and had also come to represent the entire era, an era defined later as "modernist." "The Love Song of J. Alfred Prufrock," "Marina," "Sweeney Among the Nightingales," the "Four Quartets," and especially "The Waste Land" came to define the twentieth century. Their employment of different, often conflicting voices; their experiments with chronology, sequence, and structure; their extensive use of allusion, especially to medieval and Renaissance works; their portrayal of a world in which all certainties had been shattered and human beings wandered in a futile search for meaning; their fundamental pessimism about the state of human beings in a world that had seen two unimaginably destructive wars within thirty years of each other; all of these qualities came to be understood as the qualities of the time itself. Eliot, and Ezra Pound who came before Eliot and used many of the same techniques but never found as much success in his lifetime, became the inspirations for almost every poet in the period from 1920 to 1950.

The modernist method and ideas had become almost an orthodoxy. Eliot had founded and edited a magazine, the *Criterion,* that powerfully spread his ideas. He also served as the managing editor for one of England's most important trade publishing firms, Faber and Faber. His influence dominated poetry and academia, and even left-wing cultural critics who loathed Eliot's conservative politics felt that his artistic innovations were brilliant. Novelists such as James Joyce and Virginia Woolf were having success translating "modernist" techniques and ideas into fiction, and in painting, the cubists and surrealists and other movements were expressing ideas about their own art that were strikingly similar to Eliot's ideas about poetry and literature.

But there were dissenters. There were still poets writing who were optimistic about humanity, poets who wished to celebrate the good things about being alive rather than to bemoan man's folly. There were also poets who were unsure about the value of the formal innovations of the modernists. However, the dissenters lacked the strong public voice and following of the modernists.

The dissenters, having been largely shut out of the business of cultural criticism, had to strike back through their verse, writing poetry that did not fol-

What Do I Read Next?

- "For An Assyrian Frieze" first appeared in Viereck's first book, *Terror and Decorum* (1949). Viereck continued to publish poetry for decades; an excellent compendium and introduction to his body of work is 1967's *New and Selected Poems, 1932-1967*.

- To see what other, similar poets were writing at this time, look at John Ciardi's 1950 anthology *Mid-Century American Poets*. In this book, both poetry and prose by poets such as Theodore Roethke, Robert Lowell, and Elizabeth Bishop are included.

- Although somewhat dated, A.T. Olmstead's massive 1923 *History of Assyria* provides a great, and detailed, introduction to the subject. An even older book, George Stephen Goodspeed's *A History of the Babylonians and Assyrians* (1915) tells the same story but is aimed at readers familiar with the Bible's stories of these cultures.

- Viereck's poem responds to two of the most famous poems in the English language, both of which are structured as a modern man's meditations caused by gazing upon a work of art from the ancient world. John Keats's "Ode on a Grecian Urn" stresses the importance of beauty: "Beauty is truth, truth beauty, —that is all / Ye know on earth, and all ye need to know." Percy Shelley's "Ozymandias" takes a very different lesson from the artifact: his speaker, looking upon the crumbling statue that boasts the omnipotence of its subject, learns of the vanity and futility of the most ambitious human aspirations.

- One of Viereck's best-known works of social and political commentary is his 1953 work *Shame and Glory of the Intellectuals*. Although this book centers on the challenges that the Soviet and Communist threat posed to conservatism (and is therefore a little dated), Viereck's ideas about the place of art in a truly conservative society still are interesting today. American conservatism has traditionally ridiculed intellectuals and been ashamed of intellectual achievement among its own members; Viereck suggests a way that conservatism can welcome intellectuals. Viereck's earlier book on conservative ideas, his 1949 work *Conservatism Revisited: The Revolt Against Revolt, 1815-1949*, is also an important source for his political ideas.

---

low Eliot's lead. On the one hand, the modernists, in their implacable drive to (in Pound's words) "make it new," had even prescribed which poets readers should read and which formerly "great" poets should be excised from the canon. Eliot privileged what he called the "Metaphysicals," or such poets as Sidney, Marvell, Herbert, and Ben Jonson, who were writing before Milton, during the English renaissance. Ezra Pound advocated the work of the medieval troubadours of northern Italy and southern France. On the other hand, the modernists had no love for the Romantics—the group that had been the inspiration for the poets of the late 1800s, against whom the modernists were most directly rebelling. Viereck, then, by simply joining in a conversation with Keats and Shelley, was committing a small act of insurrection.

But Viereck was not afraid of a confrontation with the Eliot-Pound orthodoxy. In a number of essays from this time, Viereck lays out the difference between his kind of poetry and what he calls the "irresponsible cult of obfuscating for the sake of obfuscating and of shocking merely for the sake of shocking." The poetry of Eliot's admirers (and, we are to understand, Eliot himself) has "no fun" and "no humanness." For Viereck, the cardinal sin of Eliot and the modernists is that they revile humans. They see no value in human pleasures, whereas the Romantics privileged the experience of the individual above all.

Dissenters, such as Viereck, also questioned the modernist attitude toward the value of art. Ezra Pound, for example, in a poem cursing the senseless destruction of World War I, sarcastically de-

> *For Viereck, the cardinal sin of Eliot and the modernists is that they revile humans. They see no value in human pleasures, whereas the Romantics privileged the experience of the individual above all."*

scribed cultural heritage as "an old bitch gone in the teeth," and dismissed the artworks of a culture as "two gross of broken statues [and] a few thousand battered books." However, the dissenter Viereck adopts the veneration of artwork of previous eras that was a particular characteristic of the Romantics, who were attracted to ruins, to palimpsests, to fragments that could send the viewer into a reverie. Viereck responds to this and initiates a conversation with his poetic predecessors. Shelley's poem "Ozymandias" is a short poem, in 14-line sonnet form, about a "traveller in an antique land" who came upon "two vast and trunkless legs of stone" and a "shattered visage" in the desert. The pedestal reads "My name is Ozymandias, king of kings: / Look upon my works, ye Mighty, and despair!" For Shelley, these words represent the pure vanity of Ozymandias's ambition. All of the greatness of Ozymandias's works have become nothing but a pair of sculpted legs and a broken face. But also for the poet, the term "despair" is doubly meaningful. Where Ozymandias wished the "Mighty" to look upon his works and despair because they could never equal them, the words now mean something entirely different: the "Mighty," looking upon Ozymandias's works, will now see the inevitably temporary nature of even the most permanent-seeming accomplishments.

Keats takes an entirely different lesson from his artwork, a "Grecian urn," or a Greek amphora. On this amphora is painted a pastoral scene, with a lover pursuing a beloved, musicians playing, and a religious sacrifice about to occur. Keats is sent into a rapture by gazing upon the beauty of the scene. He lovingly describes the figures painted on the vase, then says, addressing the vase, that "when old age shall this generation waste, / Thou shalt remain, in midst of other woe / Than ours, a friend to man, to whom thou say'st, / 'Beauty is truth, truth beauty.'" For Keats, the artworks of the past do not emphasize the temporary nature of human strivings but rather the eternity of beauty. Humans themselves decline and suffer "woe," but a beautiful artwork is unchanging, always expressing the same "truth" to people.

Viereck's frieze also tells him something about eternal things, but it is not the eternity of truth or beauty that he learns from this Assyrian sculpture. Rather, Viereck sees the horrific blood-lust of the Assyrians, epitomized in the reference to "a pillar of skulls so high it stabbed the sun." Although it seems to be the sculpture speaking, after the statement in italics in the middle of the poem the narrator asks himself who, actually, has been talking: "Was that the tomb's voice, or the desert-wind's? / Or ours?" The "scribes" and "saints" both explain the Assyrian's motivations and downfall in their own terms, but the poet seems to feel differently than they do. From this frieze, Viereck takes the lesson that blood-lust is eternal, that it is a "contagion" from which no civilization—not the civilization of the Israelites, and certainly not the civilization of the twentieth century!—is immune.

The literary critic Harold Bloom theorizes that "great" poets engage in "agon," or competition, with each other, wrestling for the title of Great Poet. Competitors use various strategies, Bloom says, most of which derive from Freudian psychological tendencies in the human mind. The most important of these is the Oedipus complex. A poet with ambitions must symbolically "slay" his immediate predecessor (his father-figure), either by directly attacking him, by intentionally "misreading" his work, or by simply ignoring him. Yet, Bloom notes, the "son" poet will always bear traces of his predecessor's work, even if he desperately wishes to expunge those traces.

Viereck's "For an Assyrian Frieze" demonstrates Bloom's theory brilliantly. Viereck sees Eliot as his most important immediate predecessor; he feels smothered by Eliot, feels that only by symbolically "slaying" Eliot's poetic influence can he express himself. For this reason, he rejects Eliot's formal experimentation, and he responds not to Eliot but to the predecessor poets—the Romantics—that Eliot himself had rejected in his own bid for greatness. But Viereck's poem bears the marks of Eliot nevertheless. Like Eliot did when choosing, in "The Waste Land," to allude to Sanskrit literature rather than to a more traditional, classical predecessor, Viereck chooses to respond to an Assyrian artwork rather than to that of the Romans or Greeks (like Keats) or that of the Egyptians (like Shelley). Viereck also sees not beauty in the work, as Keats found in the urn, nor the futility of human vanity, as Shelley understood the "vast and trunkless legs of stone" to represent. Rather, like Eliot, he conservatively and pessimistically sees the ancient evidence of human beings' bloodthirstiness in the "luminous" "gangrene" of the "contagion" of the frieze's "molten eyes." Even in attempting to rid himself of the pernicious influence of Eliot, Viereck cannot help but reproduce some of the qualities of Eliot's verse.

Source: Greg Barnhisel, in an essay for *Poetry for Students,* Gale, 2000.

Sources

Ciardi, John, *Mid-Century American Poets,* New York: Twayne, 1950.

Henault, Marie, *Peter Viereck,* New York: Twayne, 1969.

Humphries, Rolfe, "Verse Chronicle," review of *Terror and Decorum* by Peter Viereck, in the *Nation,* November 13, 1948, pp. 556-7.

Jacobson, Josephine, "Peter Viereck: Durable Poet," review of *New and Selected Poems 1932-1967* by Peter Viereck, in the *Massachusetts Review,* Vol. 7, 1968, pp. 591-5.

Lawlor, John, "Peter Viereck, Poet and Critic of Values," in *Etudes Anglaises,* Vol. 7, No. 3, 1954, pp. 280-93.

McIlveen, Idris, "Peter Viereck," in *Dictionary of Literary Biography,* Volume 5: *Twentieth-Century American Poets,* edited by Donald J. Greiner, Detroit: Gale Research, 1980, pp. 340-347.

Review of *Terror and Decorum* by Peter Viereck, *New Yorker,* January 22, 1949, p. 75.

Rodman, Selden, "Against Barracks and Classroom," review of *Terror and Decorum* by Peter Viereck, in the *Saturday Review of Literature,* October 9, 1948, pp. 29-30.

For Further Study

Bradley, Sculley, ed., *The Arts in Renewal,* Philadelphia: University of Pennsylvania Press, 1951.

This anthology collects statements on art by a number of writers and critics who were "against the grain" of the 1950s. At a time when the experimentation of modernism dominated the serious literary world, these writers argue for a return to conservatism and to art that appeals to a more popular sensibility.

Lawlor, John, "Peter Viereck, Poet and Critic of Values," in *Etudes Anglaises,* Vol. 7, No. 3, 1954, pp. 280-93.

This discussion of the symbolic geography of Laguna mythology is crucial to any understanding of the philosophical underpinnings of the symbols in Viereck's writing.

Four Mountain Wolves

Leslie Marmon Silko

1975

"Four Mountain Wolves" by Leslie Marmon Silko is an excellent example of the work that has emerged from the recent "Native American Literary Renaissance." Silko, along with Louise Erdrich, N. Scott Momaday, Gerald Vizenor, and others, is a representative figure of this renaissance, in which the writers meld Western and Native American literary techniques, themes, and subject matter. Silko's poem, which originally appeared in the anthology *Voices of the Rainbow: Contemporary Native American Poetry* (1975), immerses the reader into nature. In the wintry mountains of New Mexico, the narrator of the poem watches four different wolves, each representing different aspects of the natural and spiritual world, travel from the northeast. The poem combines a modernist-influenced free verse structure with a quiet, almost chant-like feel. Silko's Laguna Pueblo heritage comes out both in the form and the content of the poem, but the poem is not only interesting for its "Native Americanness": it is a poem that beautifully evokes a natural setting and gives us a close, almost frightening, but still respectful perspective on an animal that has always represented fear and threat to humans.

Author Biography

Leslie Marmon Silko was born in Albuquerque, New Mexico in 1948, to a family of mixed

Leslie Marmon Silko

white and native blood. Soon afterward she moved to the Laguna Pueblo of northern New Mexico. Her great-grandfather Robert G. Marmon had come to the pueblo in 1872, and took as his wife a Laguna woman, Marie Anaya. Silko's Marmon ancestors, Protestants from Ohio, had served terms as pueblo governors, and had had some part in undermining traditional ways in the Laguna pueblo. As a child, Silko grew up speaking Keresan, but her formal education—first at a Bureau of Indian Affairs school on the pueblo and then at Catholic schools in Albuquerque—immersed her in Anglophone culture and the English language. She attended the University of New Mexico, graduated in 1969, attended law school, and began teaching at Navajo Community College in Tsaile, Arizona.

In 1969 Silko published her first story, "The Man To Send Rain Clouds," in the *New Mexico Quarterly*. Through the 1970s she continued to teach and write, living for two years in Ketchikan, Alaska, and then moving to Tucson, Arizona, where she lives today. Readers and critics began to notice her stories and poems in the early 1970s, and today she is considered perhaps the central figure of the "Native American Renaissance" of that period. In 1974, Silko's stories appeared in the first important Native American anthology, and also that year, she published *Laguna Woman*, a collec-

tion of poetry. In 1977 *Ceremony* appeared, a novel about a Native American veteran's return from World War II. Silko's *Storyteller* was published in 1981. This book, a hard-to-categorize combination of Native American storytelling, traditional Western fiction, nonfiction, poems, and photographs. Also that year, Silko received a prestigious MacArthur Foundation "genius" grant, which she used to work on her next book, *Almanac of the Dead,* which came out in 1991. Recently, she has produced a collection of reminiscences entitled *Sacred Water,* a book that she binds by hand, and a collection of essays entitled *Yellow Woman and a Beauty of the Spirit: Essays on Native American Life Today.*

Poem Text

(Chinle, late winter, 1973, when the wolves came) 1

Gray mist wolf
   from mountain frozen lake
traveling southwest
   over deep snow crust singing
   Ah ouoo 5
   Ah ouoo
   the fog hangs belly high
   and the deer have all gone.
   Ah ouoo
   Ah ouoo 10

Gray mist wolf 15
   following the edge of the Sun.
wirling snow wolf
   spill the yellow-eyed wind
   on blue lake stars
   Orion 20
   Saturn.

Swirling snow wolf
   tear the heart from the silence
   rip the tongue from the darkness
   Shake the earth with your breathing 25
   and explode gray ice dreams of eternity.

Mountain white mist wolf
   frozen crystals on silver hair
   icy whiskers
   steaming silver mist from his mouth 30

Gray fog wolf
   silent
   swift and wet
   howling along cliffs of midnight sky,
   you have traveled the years 35
   on your way to Black Mountain.

Call to the centuries as you pass
   howling wolf wind

their fear is your triumph
they huddle in the distances   40
weak.

Lean wolf running
    where miles become faded in time,
    the urge the desire is always with me
    the dream of green eyes wolf   45
    as she reached the swollen belly elk
    softly
    her pale lavender outline
    startled into eternity.

Final Stanza

The final stanza of the third section brings these two different embodiments of the wolf—the physical and realistic, and the cosmic or temporal—together. In this last stanza, the "lean wolf running" combines the physical—"green eyes," "lean"—with the abstract—"miles become faded in time." This last wolf, the one that brings together all of the aspects of the wolf of the poem, becomes a representation of the eternal physicality of nature as it kills a "swollen belly elk" and startles that animal "into eternity."

Poem Summary

Section 1

In the first section of the poem the narrator is observing a "gray mist wolf" who is travelling to the southwest "over deep snow crust." We hear a howl, "Ah ouoo," but are not sure whether it is the howl of the wolf or of the narrator. The wolf treks through the fog and the cold. "All the deer have gone," the narrator tells us, and the "wild turkey" are "all flown away." This wolf is looking for food.

Section 2

The second section of the poem shows us a "swirling snow wolf." This wolf is not hungry like its predecessor; rather, he is an image of cosmic violence, "spill[ing] the yellow-eyed wind / on blue lake stars / Orion / Saturn." The narrator characterizes this wolf with very violent imagery, commanding it to "tear the heart from the silence / rip the tongue from the darkness." This wolf seems to represent the violence and power of nature and the ways that nature has to remind us of the real, physical world when we are contemplating the infinite.

Section 3

The third section presents us with two wolves: one, "mountain white mist wolf," is described only in terms of his snowy, frozen fur and the steam rising from his panting mouth, while the second, a "gray fog wolf," is simply "silent / swift and wet." This wolf has come a long way, and has travelled for years on its way to Black Mountain. The gray fog wolf becomes a symbol of the passing of time when the narrator tells it to "call to the centuries." This wolf is similar to the wolf in the second stanza in that both are described in abstract, spatial, and temporal terms, while the first wolf and the mountain white wolf are both purely physical, realistic beings.

Themes

In "Four Mountain Wolves," Leslie Marmon Silko presents the reader with a natural setting: in a particularly cold, harsh, winter, a number of wolves journey from the north to the southwest in search of the prey that is scarce in their own habitats. These wolves represent not only the brutality, ferocity, and amorality of nature, but also the cosmic truths of being a living creature in the universe.

Nature

The natural world dominates the poem. Most of the descriptive words used in the poem draw the reader's attention to qualities in the landscape. Words such as "frozen," "deep," "belly high," "swirling," "icy," and "howling" all call attention to the wintry scenes through which the wolves travel. The wolves are driven to leave their native habitat by the particular harshness of the winter of 1973, when their usual prey—turkeys, deer, even elk—become scarce. The poem asks the reader to think about the vicissitudes of nature and especially about the cruelty of nature. Can one consider any natural process cruel? What is more cruel—the weather that forces the wolves from their homes, or the wolf that kills the pregnant elk?

Time

In the Euro-American tradition, time is something that is measured, parcelled out, and used to precisely pinpoint events and occurrences. In much Native American thought and literature time is a much more amorphous, fluid entity. This is largely because of the much greater importance that is given to nature. As Silko herself said in an interview with Laura Coltelli, "I grew up with people who followed, or whose world vision was based on a different way of organizing human experience, natural cycles." Time, in nature, is not measured with the regularity of hours, minutes, and seconds; rather, it is changing, contingent, dependent upon the seasons.

However, in "Four Mountain Wolves" time is not measured in terms of days. Instead, time here is seen in a much broader context. The wolves represent what has always been, what time does not change. The second wolf "explode[s] gray ice dreams of eternity," while the gray fog wolf has "traveled for years" and calls "to the centuries." These wolves remind the narrator of what does not change. Native American storytelling generally takes place in an unspecified time period very similar to the Euro-American concept of "once upon a time." These wolves are representatives of that mythic time, but the poet reminds us of how she exists in both specific and unspecified time by telling us that this poem takes place exactly in the winter of 1973. The tension between the unspecified mythic time of the wolves and the precise time of the modern American world mirrors the Native American writer's predicament, suspended between two worlds with profoundly different ideas of knowledge and reckoning.

Cruelty/Violence

This theme is closely related to the theme of nature discussed above, but this theme can be more specific. The wolf has been almost throughout human history the embodiment of human fears in regions in which the two species have come into contact. The wolf is a fearsome animal, resembling both the annoying but rarely dangerous coyote and the friendly dog, but can be an implacable foe of man.

The wolf represents the ferocity of nature and the cruelty and violence inherent in the natural world. Like all animals, the wolf must consume life to survive, but unlike most other animals, the wolf will stalk and attack humans. Especially among groups of humans who live in close contact to nature or in small, isolated societies, the wolf is the most dangerous face of nature. But the wolf also forces people to confront their own cruelty, for like the wolf humans, too, stalk and kill prey and eat almost any living creature. And whereas some other predatory animals who occasionally confront humans—the lion or the bear, for instance—might overawe humans, the wolf is very similar to a human. It is approximately human size and is almost a match in a fair fight. In the poem, the narrator melds with the wolf near the end: "the urge the

Topics for Further Study

- Landscape is an important element of Silko's poem, and the specific landscape of the New Mexico mountains is a fundamental part of the tribal lives of the pueblo Indians. Research the natural environment of such New Mexico peoples as the Taos, Jemez, and Laguna pueblos. What is the land like? What natural resources did the people use to survive? What animals did they use, and which did they fear?

- The wolf is an animal that figures in much of Native American writing, both contemporary and traditional. Research the importance of the wolf as a metaphorical, mythical, and actual figure in the literatures of the Indians of North America. How does the wolf's role differ in the literatures of peoples from different areas? You might want to look at such tribes and groups as the Sioux, the Iroquois and Algonquins, the Indians of the northwest coast, and the pueblo peoples of the Southwest.

- Do some research on Native American literature, especially the oral literature of traditional storytelling and chants. What purposes do these stories and chants serve? What forms do they take? What are some recurring characters and figures in these stories? How do the stories differ from tribe to tribe and region to region?

dream is always with me," says the narrator, telling the reader that the same violent predatory needs that drive the wolf also drive the human.

Style

"Four Mountain Wolves" makes use of an innovative combination of modernist free verse and traditional American Indian chant forms. Free verse, which was developed as a poetic style in the 1800s and pioneered by such figures as Walt Whitman, was an attempt to allow the poet's emotions to drive the length and form of a line of poetry. For almost

all of human history and in almost every human society, poetry was characterized by regularity in its
lines. As an oral form, poetry needed to have such
regularity in order for performers to more easily
memorize the poems and for audiences to be drawn
in by the rhythm and sound of the words. But
largely because of the Romantic movement of the
late 1700s and early 1800s, poets began to believe
that they should be allowed to use any form, or
even no form, to express themselves, because purity of self-expression was the ultimate goal.

Free verse caught on quickly, and by the 1920s
became the most popular form of verse among the
leading innovators of the day, especially among
English-language poets. Such poets as Ezra Pound,
T. S. Eliot, and William Carlos Williams allowed
the mood and the subject matter to determine the
length and rhythm of lines. This does not mean that
traditional verse structures were abandoned; on the
contrary, poets continue to employ them today.
Even Eliot and Pound wrote poems using verse
structure. But this group—known as the "modernists"—demanded the right to use them at will,
and even to move in and out of them in the same
poem.

Silko's poem is a perfect example of free verse.
The subject matter determines the length of the line;
she generally gives one complete thought in each
line. In addition, the poem, read aloud, bears a distinct resemblance to the kinds of chants used in traditional Native American ceremonies. We do not
have here the short lines of a poet like Williams,
nor do we have the lengthy, declamatory lines of
Whitman or Pound. These lines are quiet, respectful. They give equal weight to a long description
with many adjectives as they do to the representation of the wolf's howl. They demand a pause at the
beginning and the end, but at the same time they
have a singsong quality that helps them interlock.

Historical Context

Silko's writing is saturated with the facts and traditions of her Laguna Pueblo heritage. As well,
Silko's writing also exhibits the influences of contemporary American society. She does not live separated from the world; rather, even as she has
delved mentally and spiritually into the roots of her
native heritage, she remains deeply involved with
the outside world, and currently teaches at the University of Arizona in Tucson.

But to understand Silko's writing it is necessary to briefly outline the historical place of the
New Mexico pueblo tribes. The groups of American Indians collectively known as the Pueblo
groups inhabit the Southwest, particularly the present-day states of New Mexico and Arizona. These
tribes built permanent structures as their community dwellings. These "pueblos" are in essence
apartment buildings in which tribe members live.
In addition, each pueblo had at least one "kiva," an
underground room in which religious ceremonies
and tribal governance took place.

These pueblo groups have been in close contact with Europeans for much longer than many
other American Indian tribes. The New Mexico and
Arizona territory was once part of Mexico, and
Spanish explorers and Franciscan missionaries
were familiar with these peoples before the American Revolution. Mexico encouraged settlement in
these lands, and so before these tribes knew the An-
glo settlers of the United States they were living in
close proximity to Mexican citizens.

The United States took over this land as a result of the Mexican-American War of the 1830s,
but for a long time it remained simply territory.
New Mexico did not become a state until after
World War II. When the United States took over
the New Mexico territory, it recognized the independence of these pueblos. Today, small independent pueblos can be found all over the state. Silko's
home, the Laguna Pueblo, is one of these. These
pueblos are officially reservations, yet they are
dwarfed by the vast Navajo Reservation that
stretches over much of New Mexico and Arizona.
The pueblos are self-governing entities with their
own police forces and social services. Tourism has
begun to encroach on some of the pueblos—the
Taos Pueblo, located as it is next to a very popular ski resort town, is a particular example—but the
pueblo dwellers (the pueblo structures themselves
do not house the majority of the residents, who live
on the reservation's territory) maintain their independence and distinctiveness even as they occasionally encourage tourists to view the pueblo and
some of their ceremonies.

Like other Native American peoples, the
pueblo tribes have a close and intertwined relationship with the natural world. In her essay on
"The Psychological Landscape of [Silko's novel]
Ceremony," Paula Gunn Allen writes that "the fundamental idea of Native American life [is that] the
land and the People are the same." The landscape,
the seasons, and the animals that inhabit the world

Compare & Contrast

- **1973:** President Richard Nixon, just re-elected in November 1972, comes under fire for his possible involvement in the Watergate scandal. In the following year, Nixon's impeachment is recommended and he resigns from office.

  1998-1999: President Bill Clinton comes under fire for lying under oath and covering up his sexual relationship with a White House intern, Monica Lewinsky. The Senate does not find him guilty of the "high crimes and misdemeanors" necessary to remove him from office.

- **1973:** The social movements for civil rights and against the war in Vietnam engender other related movements. One is the feminist movement. Another is the environmental movement. For the first time in U.S. history, Congress debates laws intended to protect natural resources such as clean air and water from corporate and individual polluters. President Nixon supports some of these ideas.

  2000: Both Democratic candidates for President, Al Gore and Bill Bradley, wholeheartedly endorse an environmental agenda. The leading Republican candidates, George W. Bush and John McCain, pay their respects to the environmental movement but are criticized by environmental groups.

- **1973:** Pressure from the oil-producing countries of the Middle East, political instability in the region, and (many suspect) machinations by American oil companies cause oil and gasoline prices to skyrocket. In response, Americans begin demanding smaller, more fuel-efficient cars.

  2000: Lasting economic good times and steadily low gas prices cause many Americans to buy large "sport-utility vehicles" that consume a great deal of gasoline. The Japanese companies that produced small, fuel-efficient cars in the leaner 1970s and 1980s join in the rush to make the popular "SUV"s. But in early 2000, the highest gasoline prices in ten years cause many Americans to think about buying smaller cars again.

- **1973:** The "Cold War" between the United States and the Soviet Union has begun to thaw slightly because of Nixon's policy of "detente." Still, the countries eye each other suspiciously.

  2000: More than ten years after the Soviet "empire" fell, Russia is unstable. Its transition to a capitalist economy has primarily enriched corrupt officials and organized-crime figures; it is engaged in brutal war against Chechnya, a breakaway territory; and its constitutional system of government seems susceptible to a charismatic dictator. Moreover, the poverty that has Russia in its grip is also affecting the scientists and officials with control over the old Soviet weapons of mass destruction, and Western diplomats and politicians fear that these impoverished scientists and bureaucrats might sell those weapons to terrorists.

---

are all integral parts of Native American life. "Four Mountain Wolves" is a description of wolves migrating south in search of food, certainly, but the animals represent more than just predation. Wolves were important to many tribes. The Pawnee, when on the warpath, would simulate wolves and wear wolf skins. A Cheyenne war song speaks of leaving the tribe's opponents for the wolves to eat, but also talks about how warriors must be as the wolf.

One northern Mexican tribe continues to protect the wolf even as ranchers in the area seek to make the animal extinct.

If Native American tribes rhetorically constructed their closeness to nature in general and the wolf in particular, the U.S. government, in its drive to "tame" and settle the vast Western territories, argued the opposite. In the United States during the late 1800s and early 1900s, government-organized campaigns to wipe out the wolf—using poison, especially strychnine—in recently-settled areas were largely successful, and at the same time wolf-hunters rhetorically portrayed wolves as evil, cowardly, treacherous beasts that must be exterminated. Ironically, much the same rhetoric was being used at the same time to argue for one solution to the "Indian problem." Today, the U.S. Department of the Interior seeks to reintroduce the wolf to the West—with mixed results.

Critical Overview

Appearing in one of the first books that presented the work of the burgeoning Native American Renaissance, "Four Mountain Wolves" received almost no attention when it initially was published, and has, in fact, almost never been mentioned in any discussion of Silko's work as a whole. Although her first published book, *Laguna Woman*, was a collection of poetry, Silko is best known as a prose writer. Her novel *Ceremony* and her two later books *Storyteller* and *Almanac of the Dead* are the cornerstones on which her considerable literary reputation rest. Criticism of those works often focuses on how Silko melds Euro-American literary traditions with traditional Native American and specifically Laguna forms.

But this is not to say that no critic has written about Silko's poetry. William Clements remarks, in an overview of Silko's career that appeared in the *Dictionary of Literary Biography* that "Silko's poems reflect her roots in Laguna culture and the landscape of the Southwest. They also reiterate her theme of the adaptability and dynamism of Native American traditions." Elsewhere, Clements also notes that "The brevity of the poems [of the *Laguna Woman* collection], the visual effects of short stanzas and indentations of individual words or short phrases that often trail across the page, and the avoidance of conventional stanza length, meter, and rhyme all suggest the influences of the modernist lyric poem expressed in free verse. Silko does, however, use repetition occasionally in combination with indentation and separation of words and phrases to create a chantlike drive and urgency in her poems."

Silko herself perhaps provides the most telling explanation of her techniques and her location at the crossroads of cultures in the biographical note she provided for *Voices from the Rainbow*, the anthology in which "Four Mountain Wolves" appears. "My family are the Marmons at Old Laguna on the Laguna Pueblo Reservation where I grew up. We are mixed bloods—Laguna, Mexican, white—but the way we live is like Marmons, and if you are from Laguna Pueblo you will understand what I mean. All those languages, all those ways of living are combined, and we live somewhere on the fringes of all three. But I don't apologize for this any more—not to whites, not to full bloods—our origin is unlike any other. My poetry, my storytelling rise out of this source."

Criticism

Greg Barnhisel

Barnhisel holds a Ph.D in American literature. In this essay, he discusses the mythical and symbolic underpinnings of "Four Mountain Wolves" and about its themes of melding and combination.

Leslie Marmon Silko's poem "Four Mountain Wolves" is at first glance a simple poem. It appears to be merely a description of a number of wolves who travel from the northeast to the southwest during a particularly harsh winter. But the poem is much more than this. The poem represents the close relationship with nature characteristic of Native American cultures. The wolf is violent, threatening, but portrayed almost flatly. Its threat is represented as something profoundly natural and normal. Rather than representing an imminent threat to humans, these hungry wolves are simply manifestations of the primal drives of nature.

The poem is also deeply involved with the symbolic geography and the cosmology of the Laguna people. Silko, of mixed heritage (white, Native American, and Mexican) grew up in the Laguna pueblo. Her grandmother Lillie and her "Aunt Susie" (another relative) knew the old stories, and passed them on to Silko at an early age. In *Storyteller,* Silko says that they gave her "an entire culture by word of mouth." The wolves in the poem and the narrator's attitude toward them represent Native Americans' relation to nature, certainly, but they also represent much deeper and more specific elements of Laguna thought and spirituality.

Just who these wolves are, and even how many wolves there are, can be confusing. The poet muddles the numerology of the poem: although the title is "Four Mountain Wolves," five wolves are described. Moreover, there are three sections to the poem. The poem begins simply enough, with the first numbered section entirely devoted to a description of one animal, the "gray mist wolf." This leads readers to expect there to be four sections, each devoted to a description of one discrete wolf. And the second section, entirely devoted to the "swirling snow wolf," continues with this structure.

But Silko confounds our expectations. The third and final section of the poem describes three distinct wolves: the "mountain white mist wolf," the "gray fog wolf," and a "lean wolf running." How many wolves are there? Are there five—these three and the two from the previous stanzas? Or perhaps is the "mountain white mist wolf" and the "swirling snow wolf" the same animal, the "gray mist wolf" and the "gray fog wolf" the same, and the "lean wolf running" a different wolf? In that case, there are only three. Silko is apparently blurring the easy distinction between the wolves on purpose, perhaps in a way that mirrors her melding of the Western and native traditions.

But in one way of reading the poem, there are indeed four wolves. To arrive at this conclusion we must start by looking at the specific attributes of the wolves as Silko describes them. We learn the most specific information about the first wolf. It is travelling over the wintry landscape from the northeast—the poem takes place in Chinle, Arizona, a town in the middle of the Navajo reservation near the Canyon de Chelly, so the wolves are most likely coming from southern Utah or southwestern Colorado—and is journeying over "deep snow crust" because of hunger. This wolf is described in terms of specific, physical details. The next wolf, though, is characterized much more in symbolic, metaphorical terms. The narrator calls to the swirling snow wolf to "tear the heart from the silence / rip the tongue from the darkness / Shake the earth with your dreaming / and explode gray ice dreams of eternity." This wolf's attributes are cosmic; the narrator sees it as the manifestation of nature's power, threat, and potential violence.

The final stanza combines the two types of wolf—the real and the metaphorical. The "mountain white mist wolf" is purely physical, pictured with "frozen crystals on silver hair" and "icy whiskers," while the "gray fog wolf" has been "traveling the years." Finally, the "lean wolf running" combines the two—it is physical in that it eyes a pregnant elk, but it also runs "where miles become faded in time." The poem's four wolves—two physical, two metaphorical—become one.

But it is not only the wolves that meld in the final stanza. The last section of the final stanza

> *How can a creature that brings death and violence represent life and regeneration? It is here that the Native American belief structures about nature come into play. Death does not only represent death in this poem: as an integral part of nature, it also brings life, keeps life going. Things are circular."*

brings all of the elements of the poem—the narrator, the wolves, the physical world, the metaphorical world, the cosmos, and even the elk—together. The narrator addresses the wolf but also becomes it—"the urge the desire is always with me," the narrator says, referring to the wolf's predatory urges and its need to migrate. As the physical world and the cosmic world are combined in the "lean wolf running," the elk also takes part in this: it is "startled into eternity." The poem even suggests the Einsteinian impossibility of separating time and space when the narrator says that the wolf is running "where miles become faded in time."

The poem is about the melding of things. It also melds elements even in its structure. The poem is clearly influenced by the technique of free verse that was developed by nineteenth century poets such as Walt Whitman and that gained great popularity with the writings of the modernist poets of the 1910s and 1920s. Free verse allows the subject matter of a line to dictate its length and rhythm, and in "Four Mountain Wolves" Silko uses this to imitate the rhythm of a traditional Native American chant and the sounds of a wolf howl. In the way that its sound attempts to arrive at a place somewhere between animal and human, "Four Mountain Wolves" is reminiscent of poems like Ezra Pound's well-known "The Return," a poem about the tentative steps taken by the Greek demigods as they come back to life. In its quiet, re-

What Do I Read Next?

- Barry Lopez's 1978 study *Of Wolves and Men* is an eloquent, lyrical study of the animal that inspires a primitive fear in humans. Lopez's book is not quite a monograph, not quite an expressive essay, and not quite a scientific study; rather, it is a meditation on this animal, both its real and mythical characteristics.

- *Native American Renaissance* by Kenneth Lincoln was one of the first, and remains one of the most important, studies of the flowering of writing by Native American authors in the late 1960s and the 1970s. Lincoln looks at large themes and specific authors, and spends much time discussing Silko's work.

- *The Crossing* by El Paso-based novelist Cormac McCarthy is primarily a story of a young New Mexico cowboy who travels back and forth across the Mexican-U.S. border. However, the novel begins with an unforgettable story of how this main character traps a female wolf that has come onto his family's land from Mexico. After trapping the wolf, the protagonist frees her and takes her back to her home in Mexico. Especially memorable is a passage early in the book told from the wolf's point of view.

- Silko's best-known work is her 1977 novel *Ceremony,* the story of a Native American World War II veteran who returns to his homeland only to feel out of place. The character, Tayo, must rediscover the spiritual and mythical roots of his people in order to reorient himself. Another important work by Silko is her encyclopedic *Storyteller,* a combination of a novel, a compilation of traditional stories, a poetry collection, and a book of photographs.

---

spectful, yet encouraging tone, Silko's poem echoes Pound's.

Silko uses these Western techniques in order to describe a scene that is profoundly American Indian in spiritual resonance. The details of the poem

derive from Silko's deep understanding of the cosmology of her people. The literary critic Edith Swan, writing in *American Indian Quarterly,* describes in detail the symbolic geography of the Laguna world. For the Laguna, the four cardinal directions each represent a color, and these equivalencies come from the mythology of the underworld. "Folklore," Swan writes, "depicts the gradual upward progress of the people who still appear in their supernatural form. They climb from one world to the next, successively going from the white to the red, blue, and yellow worlds … This sequence of colors provides a code synonymous with the cardinal directions of east, south, west, and north; both series signify upward movement." The world moves, according to Laguna cosmology, counterclockwise: from north to west, and this first movement is the same path that the gray mist wolf travels. The northeast represents the winter solstice. In this cosmology, things will then move to the south and then back up to the east, which is the direction that also represents the wolf and the coyote.

Although this system is complicated and applying it to this poem is difficult, Silko seems to be using it. Her wolves travel from the north (the winter, the beginning of things) in a southwesterly direction, toward the Laguna people and toward the warmer seasons. They will return to the east, the direction whose attributes include the autumn and the color white. Her wolves' journeys mirror the cosmic organization of the Laguna world.

The colors of the poem also drive the meaning. Swan notes the way that colors are connected with the cardinal directions and with particular animals, seasons, and natural elements. In her interview with Laura Coltelli, collected in *Winged Words,* Silko discusses the importance of color to her novel *Ceremony,* a discussion that also applies to this poem. White and gray dominate the poem. Frost, snow, ice, the fur on a snow wolf, all suggest whiteness. Referring to *Ceremony,* Silko said that "the key figure is the field of white, if you want to talk about the field of white like a painter, the blank or whatever." And in this poem, white dominates both the animals and the snowy landscape.

But in the second section the narrator describes the wind as "yellow-eyed." Yellow, Silko has stated, "in the Pueblo culture is an important color. It's a color connected with the East, and corn, and corn pollen, and dawn. So I don't think we can go too far in a traditional direction, with what yellow means." In the poem, the wolf, characterized by the wintry, northern color white, travels to the southwest (as the sun does in the winter). But it is not only associated with cold, winter, bleakness, and death, as it would be if it were only characterized by whiteness. The "yellow-eyed wind" that blows around the wolf gives it attributes of life. How can a creature that brings death and violence represent life and regeneration? It is here that the Native American belief structures about nature come into play. Death does not only represent death in this poem: as an integral part of nature, it also brings life, keeps life going. Things are circular. Even the wolf's journey is circular; the Laguna mythic structure suggests that it will eventually return to the east, where journeys end.

Source: Greg Barnhisel, in an essay for *Poetry for Students,* Gale, 2000.

Dean Rader

Dean Rader is Assistant Professor of English at Texas Lutheran Univerity in Seguin, Texas. In the following essay, Rader uses the importance of the number 4 in Navajo culture to offer four different interpretations of Silko's "Four Mountain Wolves."

In "Thirteen Ways of Looking at a Blackbird," Wallace Stevens suggests there are numerous ways (in this case thirteen) of looking at the world around us. In the poem, he creates a kind of trinity among the speaker, the landscape, and a blackbird to show the multiple options for interpreting one's relationship to nature, the imagination, and the self. The number thirteen is a somewhat random number for Stevens—the poem could just as easily have been about twenty-two or seven ways of looking at a blackbird—but that's not the case for the number four with Leslie Marmon Silko. In her poem "Four Mountain Wolves," Silko grounds her poem around the number four, a sacred number for the Navajo and in so doing, raises her poem above mere randomness. Just as Stevens uses the number thirteen to suggest that there are at least thirteen different ways of reading the world, I would like to use the number four to suggest four possible readings of Silko's "Four Mountain Wolves," the combination of which offers important insight into the world view of American Indian cultures of the Southwest.

I. The Navajo Landscape

"Four Mountain Wolves" is set in Chinle, Arizona, in the middle of the Navajo reservation. Although Silko is not Navajo, (she is from the Laguna Pueblo in New Mexico), she is intimately

> *If we think of the origination of the poem at Canyon de Chelly, at the site of the Anasazi, whose name means, 'Ancient Ones,' then the poem functions as an allegory, and the wolf represents the Native journey from the past through the centuries to the present."*

familiar with the Navajo nation, or Dine, as they call themselves, which means "The People." Navajo lies about 200 miles northwest of Laguna and is the largest Native American nation in terms of sheer geographical space. One could also argue that Navajos take up the most cultural space in Native American imaginations, as they enjoy a distinguished reputation as warriors, survivors, farmers, and artisans. Additionally, Chinle is the sight of one of the most famous American Indian ruins, Canyon de Chelly, a gorgeous labyrinth of red rock and steep sedimented walls. This canyon was the home of the Anasazi, and most anthropologists believe that the Navajo and Pueblo people, of which Laguna belongs, are descendants of the Anasazi. So, the wolves in Silko's poem move through one of the most sacred spaces in one of the most important Native American nations in the world. In other words, this setting is not coincidental.

Neither is the number of wolves. As was stated earlier, the number four is a holy number for the Navajo: their nation is defined by four sacred mountains; they have four major colors; and both are associated with the four cardinal directions, the four seasons, and what the Dine believe are four different worlds. For the Dine, as for most Native Americans, there exists a strong and intrinsic relationship between humans, animals, and the natural world. All are alive; all have spirits; all need each other for survival. In her article about Silko, "The Psychological Landscape of Ceremony," fellow Laguna poet Paula Gunn Allen underscores this view: "We are the land. To the best of my under-standing, that is the fundamental idea of Native American life; the land and the People are the same." Indeed, in "Four Mountain Wolves," the land takes on human and animal characteristics, for instance, "yellow-eyed wind" and "howling wind." In section two of the poem, it seems as though the wolf hunts and kills nature as though it were its prey:

> tear the heart from the silence
> rip the tongue from the darkness
> Shake the earth with your breathing
> and explode the gray ice dreams of eternity.

Note the similarities in this stanza and in the entire poem with another early poem by Silko, "In Cold Storm":

> Out of the thick ice sky
> running swiftly
> pounding
> swirling above the treetops
> The snow elk come,
> Moving, moving
> white song
> storm wind in the branches.

In both texts, we see animals moving among a snowy landscape; yet these are no ordinary animals and this no ordinary landscape. The urgency of both poems creates a sense of motion and tur-bulence. The landscape is alive, like the animals, and is moving, changing, growing, thriving. The landscape is not static and is not a backdrop for hu-man epiphanies as one might find in much Ro-mantic poetry. On the contrary, the environment is energy and life itself.

Thus, the poem serves as a kind of holy text—it canonizes the vitality and sanctity of the Navajo world and consecrates the exchange of animal and nature.

II. Autobiography: The Wolf as Self and Artist

If, as Allen claims, the people are the land and the land are the people, we should assume the same kind of symbiotic relationship regarding animals and people. In fact, there are long traditions in Na-tive American mythology of animals turning into people and vice versa. Sometimes, animals are peo-ple, though they are masking as animals. Tradi-tionally, wolves are not major players in Navajo mythology and religion. Wolf's younger brother, Coyote, is the more popular canine mammal. How-ever, wolves do carry important characteristics. For instance, in the Paiute story "Wolf Creates the Earth" Wolf possesses god-like abilities to create,

an ability that might seem an attractive power for a writer who sees her role in life as creating worlds on the page. Similarly, Wolf is perceived to be more stable, more dependable than Coyote, who carries an infamous reputation as a trickster. In Navajo country, though, it is always possible that Wolf is a skinwalker, or in Navajo, a *yenaldlooshi*. Literally, "*yenaldlooshi*" means "he who trots along here and there on all fours" but culturally, a *yenaldlooshi* is a human that wears the skin of a coyote or wolf and travels at night. Skinwalkers, or shapeshifters as they are sometimes called, have the ability to turn from animal to human; thus, they in-habit both worlds.

Given this information, how could this seem-ingly innocuous poem about four wolves also be about Silko herself? There are several likely re-sponses to this question, all of which presuppose a connection between the wolves and Silko herself; in fact, one might argue that the wolves are Silko. One way in which Silko might identify with the wolf is in terms of solitude. Writers often feel as though they live on the margins of society, alienated from mainstream society. In the poem, the "lone wolf" is indeed alone. It can rely on no one and must sus-tain itself. Its only trace is its voice, a realization a writer might also share. No doubt Silko is aware of Wolf's ability to shout the world into being, as in the Paiute story. And, as a writer and as a story-teller, she appreciates and reveres the primal power of words to make worlds. In this sense, the wolf's singing in stanza one might be her own.

Perhaps Silko relates to the *yenaldlooshi* as-pect of the wolf. For her, the wolf could function as a powerful embodiment of the belief that we share the *spiritus mundi* with animals, that on some level, there is no distinction between human and animal.

On a more literal level, the poem might also be about the concerns of aging. The Navajo peak to the North, which is most likely Black Mountain, is associated with both old age and death. Simi-larly, the four different wolves might suggest, for Silko, four different stages of life. The energetic vi-olent wolf of section two evokes the volatility of youth, whereas the "silver hair[ed]" and "icy whisker[ed]" wolf that has "travelled the years" and "Call[ed] to the centuries" intimates a feeling of age. The "Lean wolf running" in the final stanza might suggest a kind of spirit wolf, a timeless be-ing for whom miles and years fall at the feet of "urge" and "desire." Perhaps like this wolf, Silko's words will themselves endure "into eternity."

III. Wolf and Song as Ritual

In *The Sacred Hoop: Recovering the Feminine in American Indian Traditions,* Paula Gunn Allen correctly notes that many Indian writers "derive many of their structural and symbolic elements from certain rituals." While "Four Mountain Wolves" could very easily be a poem describing four different wolves among four different landscapes, it could just as easily be a creative play on a Native American ritual in which a shaman embodies or becomes a wolf in a ceremony. In a Native American ceremony, and in particular, a Navajo chant, a singer not only narrates a story but in so doing, actually becomes that which he is ritualizing. In her important book *Navajo Religion: A Study of Symbolism,* G. A. Reichard, a scholar of Navajo folklore and mythology, claims that Wolf plays an important role in the Flint chant, a ritual for healing in which "Dark wolf represents Bear; White Wolf, Wolf himself; Yellow Wolf, Mountain Lion; Pink Wolf represents all these … as well as Otter." Though the wolves in Silko's poem do not, by color, correspond to the wolves in the Flint chant, it is possible that the various wolves are not wolves at all but other animals, such as the mountain lion, bear and otter.

Just as the poem articulates an interchange between human and animal, so might it engender an interchange between animal and animal.

Furthermore, return to the singing in lines 4-6:

over the deep snow crust   singing
Ah ouoo
Ah ouoo

Silko does not tell us who is singing. Is it a wolf? Is it Wolf himself? Is it a singer in a chant, mimicking the wolf, ritualizing his voice through ceremony?

Rituals also move in a cycle in that they contain circular structures that suggest a wholeness, unity. Silko's poem possesses similar circularity. Notice how the words used to describe the wolves suggest a kind of incantation, a repetition befitting a ritual. Also, the poem ends with the wolf moving again, a gesture that reinscribes him into the flux of nature and positions him among the sacred mountain.

Finally, if the poem is a sort of ritual, then the purpose of the poem would be to heal or to restore the wolf. This happens. The lonely, hungry wolf, driven by wind and hunger, ultimately finds a "swollen belly elk" that will provide him nourishment and sustenance that initiates both the elk and the wolf back into the cycles of life.

IV. Survival: Wolf and American Indian Resistance

Though each of the above readings offer tenable access to Silko's text, the reading that may be the most useful and the most provocative is a reading that acknowledges the ever-important motif of survival. Over the past 40 years, one of the most pervasive and most critical themes of American Indian expression is the ability of Native American peoples to survive. Despite government orders of removal, the Trail of Tears, the smallpox blankets that killed thousands, the massacres of women and children, and the government bounty on Native American heads, American Indians have managed not only to endure but to endure with dignity, authenticity and cultural relevancy. It might be suggested that in "Four Mountain Wolves" Silko aligns the wolves with the station of contemporary American Indians. Like the wolf, Native Americans often find themselves cut off from the "America," yet, through spiritual and natural renewal and through cultural practice and preservation, they manage not only to survive, but to keep moving with power and authority.

In her poem "Indian Song: Survival," written about the same time as "Four Mountain Wolves," Silko uses the journey motif to connect Indian survival with landscape and progress:

Mountain forest wind travels east and I answer:
taste me,
I am the wind
touch me,
I am the lean gray deer
running on the edge of the rainbow.

The technique of locating the self and a culture in an individual animal occurs not only in this poem but also in "Four Mountain Wolves." Just as the deer follows the edge of the rainbow, so does the wolf "follow the edge of the sun." For Native Americans, cultural survival is incumbent upon reclaiming and rejuvenating their connection to nature.

If we think of the origination of the poem at Canyon de Chelly, at the site of the Anasazi, whose name means, "Ancient Ones," then the poem functions as an allegory, and the wolf represents the Native American journey from the past through the centuries to the present. The fact that time (and perhaps white people) are rendered frozen, afraid (their fear is your triumph / they huddle in the distances / weak), is a testament to the ability of Native American people to persist.

The final stanza might symbolize a union be-tween Native American visions of the future and the simple abundance of the American dream. American Indians want not merely to survive but to live well. Silko dreams of the green-eyed wolf who eats the swollen elk, who, well fed, well nour-ished, and reinserted into the forces of nature runs wild, free, into eternity.

V. Integration

By themselves, the above readings are a bit re-ductive. However, if one sees them as interrelated, as part and parcel of each other, then they open up Silko's text and Native American expression to possibility and interpretation in interesting ways. In fact, because Laguna and Dine, people cannot sep-arate the self from animals from nature from cul-tural history, neither should the reader. Perhaps like the sacred Navajo mountains, the four peaks of this essay will outline a matrix of interpretive inter-change between you, Silko, and everything in be-tween.

Source: Dean Rader, in an essay for *Poetry for Students,* Gale, 2000.

Sources

Allen, Paula Gunn, "The Psychological Landscape of Cer-emony," in *American Indian Quarterly,* Vol. 5, 1979, pp. 7-12.

————, *The Sacred Hoop: Recovering the Feminine in American Indian Traditions,* Boston: Beacon Press, 1992.

Clements, William M., "Leslie (Marmon) Silko," in *Dictio-nary of Literary Biography,* Volume 143: *American Novel-ists Since World War II, Third Series,* edited by James R. Giles, Detroit: Gale Research, 1994, pp. 196-205.

Coltelli, Laura, *Winged Words: American Indian Writers Speak,* Lincoln: University of Nebraska Press, 1990.

Manley, Kathleen, "Leslie Marmon Silko's Use of Color in *Ceremony,* in *Southern Folklore,* Vol. 46, No. 2, 1989, pp. 133-146.

Rosen, Kenneth, ed., *Voices of the Rainbow: Comtemporary Poetry by American Indians,* New York: The Viking Press, 1975.

Reichard, Gladys, *Navajo Religion: A Study of Symbolism,* Bollingen Series, No. 18, Princeton: Princeton University Press, 1974.

For Further Study

Allen, Paula Gunn, "The Feminine Landscape of Leslie Mar-mon Silko's *Ceremony,* in *Studies in American Indian Lit-erature,* edited by Paula Gunn Allen, New York: Modern Language Association, 1983, pp. 127-33.
    Allen looks at the close relationship between Native American ideas of nature and Silko's writing. She particularly focuses on how Silko uses feminine at-tributes of landscape.

Manley, Kathleen, "Leslie Marmon Silko's Use of Color in *Ceremony,* in *Southern Folklore,* Vol. 46, No. 2, 1989, pp. 133-146.
    Manley looks at the symbolic value of various col-ors in Silko's most famous novel. Her insights about the importance of colors in Laguna mythology, though, apply to Silko's poetry, as well.

Nelson, Robert M., *Place and Vision: The Function of Land-scape in Native American Fiction,* New York: Peter Lang, 1993.
    Nelson examines the uses that Native American writ-ers have for landscape and nature. Although Nelson's subject is specifically fiction, the importance of na-ture and landscape is perhaps even greater in Amer-ican Indian poetry.

Swan, Edith, "Laguna Symbolic Geography and Silko's *Ceremony,*" in *American Indian Quarterly,* Vol. 12, No. 3, 1988, pp. 229-249.
    This discussion of the symbolic geography of Laguna mythology is crucial to any understanding of the philosophical underpinnings of the symbols in Silko's writing.

In Memory of Radio

Amiri Baraka
1961

"In Memory of Radio" appears in Baraka's first collection of poetry, *Preface to a Twenty Volume Suicide Note,* published in 1961. Baraka was then known as LeRoi Jones. Although the poems in this collection express disaffection with conventional social values and mores, they do not embody the often strident political views Baraka became known for later in his career, when he embraced Black nationalism and then international Marxism. The third poem in the collection, "In Memory of Radio" comes just before a poem to his wife, "For Hettie." It is not, however, about memory or, necessarily, radio. Rather, Baraka uses these subjects to explore ideas of taste, technology, imagination, identity, and the poet's role in society. Written in free verse and employing a conversational, sometimes humorous voice, the poem uses the speaker's memory of radio shows to ostensibly evoke a sense of nostalgia and loss. In actuality, the poem comments on the very insidiousness of radio itself, and how the medium commands human attention and creates a reality separate from the one in which human beings live. The central image in the poem is a superhero from comic books and radio shows called The Shadow. Under the cloak of invisibility, The Shadow hunts down and roots out evil in the world. The words he uttered after he transformed himself from Lamont Cranston, a millionaire playboy, to The Shadow have become a part of popular culture: "Who knows what evil lurks in the hearts of men? The Shadow knows."

Amiri Baraka

Baraka's early writing was very much influenced by Beat writers such as Jack Kerouac and Allen Ginsberg, both of whom wrote spontaneously and championed the immediacy and the authenticity of human experience. Like much of Beat literature, Baraka's poem offers a critique of mid-century American culture and society. The poem questions middle-class tastes, popular culture, and America's seeming unquestioning acceptance of technology. Like much Beat writing it is more process than product, and hence difficult to summarize or paraphrase.

Author Biography

Amiri Baraka, who was born Everett LeRoi Jones in Newark, New Jersey in 1934, has been one of the strongest African-American voices for political change in the last thirty years. The son of Coyette ("Coyt") LeRoi Jones, and Anna Lois Jones, Baraka is widely recognized as a leading playwright, poet, essayist, and cultural historian as well. By his own account, Baraka cultivated his imagination as a child in playgrounds and on the streets of Newark, as well as from comic books and radio, which he listened to regularly. His favorite shows included *The Lone Ranger, Sam Spade, In-*

ner Sanctum, I Love a Mystery, The Shadow, Let's Pretend, and *Escape.* From these he developed strong images of evil and the heroes who defeated evil. These images later formed a central part of his writing, both in his poetry and his plays such as *What Was the Relationship of the Lone Ranger to the Means of Production?.*

After three years in the Air Force, Baraka moved to Greenwich Village, the center of bohemian life in the 1950s and 1960s, and subsequently earned a degree from Rutgers University. In his early years in New York, he cultivated his passion for writing and along with Hettie Roberta Cohen, his first wife, published two influential Beat magazines, *Yugen* and *Floating Bear,* which showcased influential writers such as Allen Ginsberg, Frank O'Hara, and Gilbert Sorrentino. His first volume of poetry, *Preface to a Twenty Volume Suicide Note,* appeared in 1961, the same year he was awarded a John Hay Whitney Fellowship for his fiction and poetry. In 1959 Baraka visited Castro's Cuba, which opened his eyes to politics, and specifically the ways in which art and writing can be political. This awakened consciousness also provided him with new themes for his writing. After winning an Obie award in 1964 for his provocative play about racial conflict and identity, *Dutchman,* Baraka founded the Black Arts Repertory Theatre/School (BART/S), which dedicated itself to fostering racially focused art in Black communities, specifically Harlem. In the mid-1960s, he divorced his wife and moved to Harlem, changing his name from LeRoi Jones to Amiri Baraka, a Bantuized Muslim name meaning "Blessed Prince." This began the "Black Nationalist" phase of Baraka's life, which saw the writer championing Black political and cultural groups, including the Black Panthers. In the mid-1970s Baraka renounced nationalism and declared himself an international Marxist. He has since devoted himself to speaking and working for the oppressed and against capitalist exploitation throughout the world.

In addition to his prolific writing output, Baraka has held a number of teaching positions. In 1999 he retired from his last teaching position—Professor of African Studies at the State University of New York at Stony Brook.

Poem Text

Who has ever stopped to think of the divinity of
      Lamont Cranston?

(Only Jack Kerouac, that I know of: & me.
The rest of you probably had on WCBS and Kate
  Smith,
Or something equally unattractive.)

What can I say?   5
It is better to have loved and lost
Than to put linoleum in your living rooms?

Am I a sage or something?
Mandrake's hypnotic gesture of the week?
(Remember, I do not have the healing powers of   10
  Oral Roberts …
I cannot, like F. J. Sheen, tell you how to get saved
  & rich!
I cannot even order you to gaschamber satori like
  Hitler or Goody Knight
& Love is an evil word.
Turn it backwards/see, what I mean?
An evol word. & besides   15
Who understands it?
I certainly wouldn't like to go out on that kind of
  limb.

Saturday mornings we listened to Red Lantern &
  his undersea folk.
At 11, Let's Pretend/& we did/& I, the poet, still
  do, Thank God!

What was it he used to say (after the   20
  transformation, when he was safe
& invisible & the unbelievers couldn't throw
  stones?) "Heh, heh, heh,
Who knows what evil lurks in the hearts of men?
  The Shadow knows."

O, yes he does
O, yes he does.
An evil word it is,   25
This Love.

Poem Summary

Stanza 1:

The title sets the tone for the poem. We expect an elegy to the radio, a nostalgic reminiscence about its effect on the speaker. We get that and more. Lamont Cranston is the alter ego of the Shadow, a black-cloaked crime fighter with an eerie laugh. *The Shadow* was the subject of hundreds of pulp novels and a radio show which ran in the 1930s and 1940s. The speaker wants us to think about how a figure from popular culture can also be divine. He also, consciously or not, sets himself apart from others who listen to radio, declaring that radio stations such as WCBS (a New York City station) and singers such as Kate Smith (a popular crooner who immortalized the song

Media Adaptations

- The University of Northern Iowa released a video of Baraka's 1994 Keynote speech to the International Conference on the Short Story in English. Baraka speaks about the relationship between the short story and poetry in his own work.

- The University of San Francisco's Poetry Center released a video called *Color,* an anthology of contemporary African-American poetry. Baraka reads on the video, which was scripted by poet Al Young.

- New Letters On the Air issued an audio cassette of Baraka reading his poetry in 1988.

- Everett/Edwards issued an audio cassette of Baraka reading his poems in 1976.

- Baraka plays a visionary homeless prophet in the 1998 Hollywood film, *Bullworth,* starring Warren Beatty and Halle Berry.

"God Bless America" and who had her own radio show on CBS) are "unattractive." The speaker aligns his taste with Jack Kerouac, one of the leading authors of the Beat movement of the 1950s and 1960s who wrote about jazz and blues and his experiences in the gritty American counterculture in novels such as *On the Road, Dharma Bums,* and *The Subterraneans.* The tone of this stanza is smug, almost arrogant, as he lumps the reader in with "the rest of you."

Stanza 2:

Like the first stanza, this one begins with a rhetorical question. There is nothing to say, the speaker suggests. He underscores this with a play on these famous lines from Lord Alfred Tennyson's poem "In Memoriam": "'Tis better to have loved and lost, / Than never to have loved at all." Making these lines part of a non-sequitur also illustrates the Beat sensibility, which set itself apart from high art and saw sacredness in the everyday. His references to linoleum and living rooms, though apparently nonsensical, underscore the inferiority and shallowness of middle-class tastes.

Stanza 3:

Baraka continues with the playful tone of the poem, again beginning a stanza with a question. He is obviously not a sage, but he also wants to point out that neither are public figures who often lay claim to sage status. Mandrake is Mandrake the Magician, the hero of a comic strip of the 1940s and 1950s written by Lee Falk and Fred Fredericks. Oral Roberts is an evangelist well known for soliciting funds over the radio and television.

Bishop Fulton J. Sheen delivered the first radio message from Radio City, and was the first to host a regular series of religious radio broadcasts. His national NBC show was called "The Catholic Hour." Hitler, of course, was the genocidal German leader of World War II responsible for the systematic extermination of Jews and others in death camps. Baraka uses the phrase "gaschamber satori" ironically to emphasize the moral murkiness with which we perceive public figures, and how bad is often seen as good and good as bad. A "satori" is a state of spiritual enlightenment in Zen Buddhism, itself a popular religion among some of the Beats.

Stanza 4:

The reader is told what has only been suggested so far, that good and bad, evil and love exist dialectically. That is, one cannot exist without the other. To attempt to understand love is folly, the speaker implies. Not even a poet can understand love.

Stanza 5:

These two lines elaborate on the kinds of shows that the speaker listened to as a child. *Red Lantern* was a character from the children's show *Land of the Lost*. He was a fish who led kids down below the sea to search for their lost toys. *Let's Pretend,* also a children's show, dramatized the Grimm's fairy-tales for radio. The speaker makes the link between his childhood activities of pretending while listening to these shows with his activities as a poet, where he also uses his imagination and "pretends."

Stanza 6:

This stanza refers to the Shadow, first mentioned in the opening stanza. To combat evil, the Shadow had the ability to make himself invisible ("the transformation"). "The transformation" also echoes a religious idea, the transformation of bread

and wine into the body and blood of Christ during the act of communion. Indeed, by describing the Shadow in terms of his adversaries, the "unbelievers" who would throw stones, Baraka ascribes to him a religious quality, which is reinforced by the Shadow's ability to see into the hearts of men.

Stanza 7:

The rhythm of these last lines and the rhyme "does/love" end the poem on a breathy and whimsical note. Baraka has used his memory about radio as a vehicle for commenting on a bigger theme: the inherent duality of the world and of human nature.

Themes

Appearances and Reality

"In Memory of Radio" examines the idea of appearance and reality, suggesting that the world of phenomena or appearances is not to be trusted. In the Western world, Plato was one of the first to popularize this idea in his "Allegory of the Cave," claiming that human beings mistakenly believe that the world as we see or experience it is the real world. Plato believed that the things or objects of the given world were merely imperfect copies of the real, which existed in the realm of ideas. Baraka also calls into question the reliability of what we see, or in this case hear and read. He questions his own authority as poet in the third stanza when he asks, "What am I a sage or something?"—implying that readers would do well not to necessarily trust the page. He then likens his own poetic authority to that of Mandrake, a fictional character who performed magic tricks as well as hypnosis. Not only should we not put our trust in the poet (an idea that Plato also endorsed in *The Republic*), but we should not trust radio either, as it too creates a fictional world, as evidenced by the shows and personalities he lists: *Let's Pretend, Red Lantern,* Mandrake, Hitler, F. J. Sheen, and Oral Roberts, all proselytizers of a particular world view. His lumping of characters from radio shows, a seemingly benign form of entertainment, with religious figures, and the world's most infamous mass murderer, emphasizes the degree to which the poet believes society has been duped by what they see, hear, and read. The character of The Shadow himself is a symbol for the invisible world of ideas. As such he personifies the "real" in his ability to see into the hearts of men. By using The Shadow as the poem's central symbolic image Baraka ties to-

Topics for Further Study

- Think about the television shows you watched, books or comics you read, or films you viewed as a child. Write an essay exploring the influence of characters from those shows or comics on your adult life. Has your image of heroes or villains been shaped by such characters? How?

- The Internet is to many of today's children what radio was to those of Baraka's generation. Write a speculative essay from a future point of view describing the kind of technological nostalgia someone writing thirty years from now might have.

- Make a list of your favorite foods, restaurants, magazines, books, television shows, movies, kinds of music, art, and activities. Freewrite about what these things might have in common (if anything). Then write an essay exploring what your tastes might say about you and your class status or aspirations.

gether ideas of metaphysical reality and moral reality, implying that because human beings act upon what their senses tell them, they act incorrectly. In this way, love, a concept we conventionally associate with good, can be "seen" as evil.

Culture Clash

"In Memory of Radio" presents a contradictory and, ultimately, unresolved stance towards mid-century American popular culture. Although the poem criticizes middle-class bourgeois tastes, it does not provide a clear-cut alternative to those tastes. The poem begins by praising Lamont Cranston, the alter ego of The Shadow, a crime-fighting hero of radio, comic books, and novels, and condemning Kate Smith, a popular singer, star of her own radio and television show who was known for her fierce patriotism and traditional values. By aligning himself with Jack Kerouac, Beat icon and countercultural hero, the speaker sides with those who experimented with new forms of art and experience. Kerouac and the Beats were known for their oppositional stance towards the sta-

tus quo. They loved jazz and blues, celebrated sexuality, and often smoked marijuana and took speed, hallucinogens, and other mind-altering substances. The poem takes another jab at a symbol of traditional Western culture in the second stanza when the speaker butchers Tennyson's famous lines "'Tis better to have loved and lost / Than never to have loved at all." The substituted lines are telling, for they yoke together the hackneyed sentiment of a canonical poem with a status symbol of the growing middle class: linoleum. The third stanza skewers popular radio and television evangelists, Oral Roberts and Bishop Sheen, and Mandrake the Magician, suggesting that those who listen and believe what these figures have to say are being duped. But comic book and radio show characters also belong to middle-class tastes, and it is here that the poem's oppositional stance towards bourgeois tastes falls short. Perhaps, however, in positioning children's shows and characters such as The Shadow, *Red Lantern* and *Let's Pretend* as somehow more wholesome, Baraka is making the point that these shows foreground their "pretend" qualities, whereas adult celebrities do not, claiming reality as their province.

Style

"In Memory of Radio" is written in a very loose conversational free-verse style using associative logic. Its use of informal punctuation and speech rhythms show the influence of Projectivist verse, a kind of poetry based on theories articulated by Charles Olson, among others. Unlike more conventional strains of poetry, Projectivist verse does not attempt to illustrate one central idea through imagery or statement but rather to evoke a mood or "circle" an issue through spontaneously recording the writer's thoughts as he or she writes. Such composition is also linked to the improvisatory processes of jazz, which heavily influences Baraka's writing. The poem's use of sometimes incongruent images, as in "I cannot order you to go to the gaschamber satori like Hitler or Goody Knight" shows the influence of Dadaism, an early twentieth-century art movement which rebelled against traditional subject matter, conventional forms, and often common sense itself.

Mood is the atmosphere or emotional tone of a poem which helps to configure a reader's expectations. Through his at times contradictory reminiscences of the past, Baraka establishes a mood of

Compare & Contrast

- **1920:** The first commercial radio broadcast takes place August 20, on station WWJ in Detroit.

  1922: Network broadcasting begins when WJZ and WGY in New York broadcast the World Series.

  1926: The Radio Corporation of America (RCA) begins the first national network which helps connect the entire nation.

  1931: Kate Smith's own radio show airs.

  1932: *The Shadow,* a radio drama, is first broadcast, and lasts until 1954. Other shows that aired this year include *Buck Rogers, The Adventures of Charlie Chan, The Ed Sullivan Show, The Marx Brothers,* and *Tarzan.*

  1934: *Let's Pretend* is first broadcast, and lasts until 1954.

  1952: Bishop Fulton J. Sheen moves to television from radio. His show, "Life is Worth Living," is the first religious television show in New York when there are very few television sets in the city.

  1954: Bishop Fulton J. Sheen reaches 25 million people on television. In 1955, Sheen is broadcast across 170 stations in the United States and seventeen in Canada. From 1952 to 1953, Sheen is paid $10,000 per telecast by Admiral Corporation. In successive seasons, Admiral pays $12,000 and $14,000 per appearance. In 1955, Sheen draws $16,500 per show. Sheen sends all these fees to the Propagation of the Faith for the poor overseas.

  1950-1960: The Kate Smith Hour (1950–54) airs on National Broadcasting Company television. She returns with CBS's Kate Smith Show in 1960.

  1970: Radio historians often mark this year as the beginning of the "Modern" era of radio.

  1990s: The popularity of old radio shows remains strong, as Hollywood produces new film versions of old shows such as *Tarzan, Buck Rogers,* and *The Shadow.*

- **1957:** Jack Kerouac publishes *On the Road,* a novel about young intellectuals' exploration of personal identity and search for meaning in a spiritually bankrupt America.

  Today: *On the Road* is considered a classic work of American literature and required reading in many college classrooms.

---

resignation and despair, what we might expect for a poem about loss. However, because of the speaker's offhanded, erratic way of presenting information, his unwillingness to develop a thought, and his use of The Shadow's own signature tag line (i.e., "Who knows what evil lurks in the hearts of men? The Shadow knows.") followed by his creepy snicker, it is hard to take the poem seriously.

Historical Context

For poets and writers, the 1960s were a time of experimentation and prolific output. Inexpensive offset, letterpress, and mimeograph machines allowed almost anyone to become a publisher. Those at the margins of society—minorities, the poor, the disenfranchised, the "oddball," or simply those with different visions of society—took advantage of the "mimeograph revolution," producing countless newsletters, journals, pamphlets and other publications. Baraka himself was integral in a number of publishing ventures including Totem Press, and the magazines *Yugen* and *The Floating Bear.* With Totem Press Baraka published poets such as Frank O'Hara, Carol Berg, Gilbert Sorrentino, Diane Wakoski, Jack Kerouac, Paul Blackburn, and Gary Snyder. Corinth Books co-published and distributed many of Totem's titles in the late 1960s. In

1958 Baraka, along with his first wife, Hettie Cohen, edited and published *Yugen,* a "zine" devoted to New York writers, as well as minority voices. Many of the writers in *Yugen* also appeared in Donald Allen's groundbreaking anthology, *The New American Poetry,* published in 1960 largely as a response to the 1957 anthology *New Poetry of England and America,* a collection edited by Louis Simpson, Donald Hall, and Robert Pack which emphasized what Allen called "academic poetry." *Yugen* also became known for publishing theoretical essays spelling out the critical stances of many experimental writers and groups. *The Floating Bear,* co-edited with poet Diane di Prima, was a mimeographed newsletter which circulated solely through a mailing list. Named after Winnie-the-Pooh's boat made of a honey pot, the newsletter came out monthly for the first two years. In a study of the history of the small press in America during this time, *A Secret Location on the Lower East Side,* Diane di Prima attributes the success of the newsletter to Baraka's (then LeRoi Jones) work habits: "LeRoi could work at an incredible rate. He could read two manuscripts at a time, one with each eye. He would spread things out on the table while he was eating supper, and reject them all—listening to the news and a jazz record he was going to review, all at the same time," she said. Di Prima also gives credit to their many friends who helped to collate, staple, edit, and stuff envelopes in all-night "publishing parties."

Many of these writers were associated or came to be associated with the Beat movement which rebelled against the perceived moral and cultural bankruptcy of middle-class American life. They loathed what they saw as the crass materialism of American life and its emphasis on conformity and living a "safe" life. Beats loved the bebop jazz of Dizzy Gillespie and Charlie Parker, whose improvisatory methods of composition they frequently followed in their own lives and art. In art they praised the abstract expressionists such as Jackson Pollack and Willem DeKooning, whose non-representational paintings celebrated color and movement and asked viewers to make their own meaning out of what they saw. The word "Beat" itself signified both exhaustion and beatification; in their writing and performances Beats such as Jack Kerouac and Allen Ginsberg expressed their disgust with the shallow commercialism and conformist attitudes of society, often choosing to heighten their own experiences through the use of stimulants and hallucinogens such as marijuana, peyote, and speed. Jack Kerouac's own best-selling novel *On the Road,* published in 1957, told the story of rebellious hipsters who lived spontaneously, crisscrossing the country while high on Benzedrine and alcohol, always ready for a sexual (mis)adventure.

Critical Overview

Critics have praised Baraka's first volume of poetry, *Preface to a Twenty Volume Suicide Note,* in which "In Memory of Radio" appeared, many claiming that it contains some of his very best poetry. M. L. Rosenthal says that the collection shows that Baraka "has a natural gift for quick, vivid imagery and spontaneous humor, and his poems are filled with sardonic or sensuous or slangily knowledgeable passages." Theodore Hudson similarly applauds the volume, writing "All things considered 'Preface' was an auspicious beginning for LeRoi Jones the poet." "In Memory of Radio" can be read as a critique of the ways that American society unquestioningly believes what they hear on radio and see on television. However it can, and has, also been read as an endorsement of the fantasy life. Calling the piece "a typical beat Poem," critic William J. Harris writes that Baraka "not only valorizes 'pretending,' he also rejects the role of poet as an active agent in the world." Lloyd W. Brown, though, sees more complexity in the poem, reading it as an indictment of "the culture's destructive dichotomies between reason and feeling." Brown sees Mandrake as Baraka's symbol of rationalism, a force which blocks society's capacity to see itself clearly. "Baraka's poem defines the 'magic' of radio as a symptom of the irrational basis on which the culture perceives the achievements of technological reason. On both counts Mandrake therefore represents the scientific logic that made possible the technological 'magic' of radio."

Criticism

Chris Semansky

Chris Semansky's poetry, essays, and stories appear regularly in literary magazines and journals. In the following essay, Semansky examines the idea of loss in Amiri Baraka's poem, "In Memory of Radio."

Traditionally, elegies have addressed the idea of loss. Sometimes that loss is physical, as in the death of a loved one, and sometimes the loss is

> *The self-knowledge of the speaker of 'In Memory of Radio' stems in part from his recognition that his childhood love of radio shows and his memory of such shows are not uncomplicated."*

emotional, as in the loss of love, or metaphysical, as when the poet meditates on human mortality itself. Amiri Baraka's poem, "In Memory of Radio," adds another subject: the loss of self. His poem signals not the loss of a particular time when radio shows had emotional clout or entertainment value but the loss of a part of the speaker who has moved from innocence to a kind of experience which implicitly undermines his previous response to radio.

Baraka opens the poem by using a convention which often appears in pastoral elegies, the invocation of the muses. Baraka's muse, however, is not one of the Greek goddesses cavorting on Mount Helicon, but Lamont Cranston, the alter ego of the Shadow, a crimefighting superhero of pulp novels, comic books, and radio shows from the poet's childhood. The Shadow only assumed the identity of Lamont Cranston, a millionaire playboy not unlike Batman's Bruce Wayne or Superman's Clark Kent, when he felt he could gain more information as Cranston. In reality The Shadow was Kent Allard, an adventurer and pilot who crashed deep in the tropical jungles of South America shortly before The Shadow appeared in New York City. It is the speaker's memory of Cranston that spurs him to think about other radio performers, specifically Kate Smith, the patriotic singer who built her reputation belting out "God Bless America" and helping to sell war bonds and entertain the troops during World War II. Smith's songs were often carried by WCBS, a New York City radio station catering to mainstream tastes. By claiming Jack Kerouac as ally against the tacky tastes of the hoi-polloi, the speaker skirts arrogance. But as he himself says in the very next stanza, "What can I say?" This willingness to undercut his own statements marks the

beginning of a self-questioning in the poem, which is never fully resolved.

Part of this poem's confusion lies in the difficulty of its tone, or stance towards its subject. When the speaker asks "Am I a sage or something?" does he mean "Look at me, I know what I'm talking about"? Or does he mean "You are a fool to believe me"? The speaker's cockiness in the opening stanza would seem to argue for the former, but a case could also be made for the latter when he compares himself to Mandrake the Magician, another icon of mid-century popular culture and, seemingly, a metaphor of one of poets' historical roles to construct make believe worlds. The speaker himself seems to endorse this role when he comments on the radio show *Let's Pretend*. Yet another view is that of critic Lloyd W. Brown, who in his study of Baraka's life and writing has this to say about Mandrake:

> The figure's familiar attributes (the hypnotic gesture and the powers of invisibility) reinforce that sense of a wonderful ("magical") emotional intimacy which is intrinsic to the experience of listening to radio: the listener develops private relationships with radio characters precisely because the latter's invisibility demands an imaginative participation from the listener, and thereby enhances the intimacy of the relationship.

This magic, this intimacy, Brown continues, is also a fraud, "a pretended closeness, which does not really compensate for the isolation and divisiveness that the culture encourages by virtue of its fearfully puritanic and narrowly rationalistic responses to love and involvement."

It is not necessary to resolve the meaning of Mandrake or, indeed, the poem as a whole. At this point in his career Baraka himself was exploring his beliefs, testing out ideas and ways of being in the world. He was also more interested in the idea that poems say more than their writers could possibly know. In the mid-1960s, when the poet's own politics were beginning to cohere, he would write poems which were clearer (though not necessarily better) in their meaning, more diatribe and rant than lyrical self-exploration. Combined with the image of The Shadow, the Mandrake figure foreshadows Baraka's future image of himself as a harbinger of White death / destruction. Both images are echoed in his poem "State/meant" published five years after "In Memory of Radio" at the start of the poet's Black nationalist phase:

> We are unfair, and unfair.
> We are black magicians, black art
> s we make in black labs of the heart.

The fair are
fair, and death
ly white.

The day will not save them
and we own
the night.

The "black labs of the heart" are themselves present in "In Memory of Radio." By focusing on popular public figures such as Bishop Fulton J. Sheen and Oral Roberts, who began their careers proselytizing on radio, the narrator underscores the idea that people are gullible. Not only do we fall for what we are told (e.g., the promise of religious or economic salvation or, in Hitler's case, genetic and national salvation), but we have been trained to be so since childhood. What the speaker once thought were good things, radio shows and characters such as *Red Lantern* and *Let's Pretend,* turn out to be inherently evil, for they condition him, and by implication the public, to live in the world of make believe. The Shadow is an attractive figure for the speaker because he contains within himself both good and evil. He knows the evil that lurks within the heart of men because that same evil is in his own heart. Baraka scholar William J. Harris describes the writer's relation to his fantasies as follows:

> In Baraka there has always been a battle between the imagination and the real world. Baraka was attracted to the world of the imagination because there he could be anyone and have anything he wanted. In his Beat days, the late 1950s and early 1960s, the propensity for fantasy displaced history and ethnicity from his work; feeling kinship with the other Beats, he could say that he was 'as any other sad man here / an American.'

Harris misses the mark with the word "displaced," as history and ethnicity became subjects for the poet only *after* he immersed himself in the world and ideas of Beat culture. A more accurate way of describing Baraka's change would be to say that he could only embrace the radical poetics of first Black nationalism and then international Marxism once he had rejected the radical poetics of the counterculture Beats.

The self-knowledge of the speaker of "In Memory of Radio" stems in part from his recognition that his childhood love of radio shows and his memory of such shows are not uncomplicated. Though this love helped to form the adult self he speaks from, the poet who can (seemingly) construct whole worlds from scratch, it also helped to put him in touch with his (potentially) evil self. There is no mistaking that the speaker of this poem sees himself as a kind of Shadow figure. Just as lis-

What Do I Read Next?

- *The Autobiography of LeRoi Jones,* by Amiri Baraka, details the author's life up to his fortieth birthday in 1974. Baraka recounts his experiences from his participation in post-World War II counterculture and his role in Black nationalism after the assassination of Malcolm X to his conversion to Islam and his commitment to an international socialist vision.

- Baraka's 1995 book, *Transbluesency: The Selected Poems of Amiri Baraka/LeRoi Jones (1961-1995),* edited by Paul Vangelisti, pays homage to blues and jazz greats Thelonius Monk, Miles Davis, Sonny Rollins, and John Coltrane. The collection includes many out-of-print and limited edition chapbooks and broadsides.

- Komozi Woodard's recently released study, *A Nation Within a Nation: Amiri Baraka (Leroi Jones) and Black Power Politics,* closely examines Baraka's politics and activism during the 1960s and 1970s, when Baraka was an outspoken advocate for Black nationalist causes.

- For a stronger sense of Baraka's pre-Black nationalist Beat poetry, read his first collection, *Preface to a Twenty Volume Suicide Note,* published in 1961 by Totem Press and Corinth Books.

teners cannot see The Shadow on radio, readers cannot see the writer of poetry or know what is in his heart, the intentions behind the making of the poem. The shadow/Shadow is an apt image for Baraka the poet, for it can symbolically accommodate many of the themes and subjects Baraka mines in his poetry: African-American identity, the relationship between the real and the imaginary, invisibility, good and evil, social justice. That sometimes evil is necessary to bring about good is a claim Baraka himself makes in his more militant writings. This seeming contradiction is evident in his statement that "The Black Artist's role in America is to aid in the destruction of America as he knows it." For LeRoi Jones/Amiri Baraka, that destruction also entails a destruction of one self to give birth to another.

Source: Chris Semansky, in an essay for *Poetry for Students,* Gale, 2000.

Tyrus Miller

Tyrus Miller is an assistant professor of comparative literature and English at Yale University, where he teaches twentieth-century literature and visual culture. His book Late Modernism: Politics, Fiction, and the Arts Between the World Wars *is forthcoming. In the following essay, Miller discusses the various functions of the poem, such as to memorialize Baraka's life and death, to reflect on the loss of one's innocence and the realization that such innocence might be a kind of blindness, and to reveal the morality associated with the concepts of color and race.*

"In Memory of Radio" dates from the late 1950s and appeared in a book entitled *Preface to a Twenty Volume Suicide Note …,* the first collection of poems by the African-American writer Le Roi Jones (now named Amiri Baraka). Spanning the end of the radio age and the emergence of television, Jones's poem is a lament for the radio as a vanishing medium once capable of entrancing its listeners with spellbinding dramas. This magic power of radio, the "divinity" once radiated by such fictional heroes as Orson Welles's Lamont Cranston in the radio drama *The Shadow,* has now faded into thin air. Like a gathering of howling ghosts, "In Memory of Radio" evokes disembodied voices coming over the airwaves, invisible men and laughing shadows, part of the child's lost world conjured back momentarily by poetic memory.

The titles of both the poem and the collection in which it appeared suggest Jones's powerful preoccupation with death. The poem's title reveals that "In Memory of Radio" will be a sort of elegy, a memorial for the dead, for a cultural experience definitively lost from the world of everyday reality and only to be revisited through a special act of imagination. The book's title, in contrast to that of the poem, evokes a death yet to come and a labor of writing leading towards that death while desperately attempting to forestall it. Jones's "preface," his volume of poems, lies one step before the extraordinarily long "suicide note" that itself must proceed and explain the act of suicide. Figuratively, then, Jones is treating his first book as the initial step into a lifelong work of writing that will sum up his life and show how it led up to and justified his death.

Jones's book as a whole thus points forward towards his ultimate death, following the fulfillment of his task as a man and as writer. In contrast, his poem "In Memory of Radio" acknowledges that even this first entry into writing, this "preface" to the long "suicide note" of his oeuvre, is already steeped in death. For it emerges out of the death and remembrance of his childhood's most intense imaginative experience, the long hours a boy spent seated before the radio.

Jones's poem also suggests, however, that the disappearance of the radio world has its parallel in the child's maturing beyond the state of unthinking belief on which his imaginative play with the radio depended. As the radio age yielded to the new technology of television, so too the poet has emerged into a new "shadowed" complexity of adult emotional and social vision. The radio thus carries a double significance in Jones's poem. It symbolizes an "innocence lost"; yet now seen from the perspective of adulthood, its content never was so innocent. The child's innocence, which the adult poet seems to mourn as a more authentic and undivided state of imaginative power, was also a form of blindness, a failure to grasp the real world's truth. This metaphorical blindness, however, was in turn conditioned by the literal invisibility of the radio personages, who appeared only through the magical conjurings of their voices. The imaginative pleasures of the radio, Jones implies, was like a kind of hypnosis, making him close his eyes to what was in front of him in order to animate the fantasy voices of the airwaves.

The radio, the adult poet realizes, always lay under the shadow of politics, class and racial divisions, state power, and sexuality, even as it nourished the child's imagination and allowed the poet within him to develop. The child's seemingly innocent fascination with the radio world was, all the while, unknowingly leading him down into the obscure regions of the heart, the twisted paths of love and evil deeply entwined in his inner nature. And as he recognizes only now, the heroes of the child's radio mythology already "knew" all that and were whispering the unhappy truths in his ear all along. Thus, as an invisible man of the modern city, taking on the shape and shade of night in order to defeat the criminal that is at home there, the Shadow divines "what evil lurks in the hearts of men." For Jones, everything has been transmuted by this sobering recognition of his own double nature. Not even his childhood myths, he confesses, will allow him any longer to sustain the mythology of his own childhood innocence, which to his now-opened eyes appears as no more than the guilt of a willed blindness.

Jones begins the poem by laying claim to a special experience and insight gained through his radio listening. As boys, he and the Beat novelist Jack Kerouac, he writes, shared an enthusiasm for the fictional character of Lamont Cranston, the daylight form of The Shadow. For them, Cranston was a kind of god, an invisible sacred figure who spoke to them through the radio. No one else, he suggests, understood the power of these figures of imagination. Others listened to the mainstream popular music of Kate Smith, unable to rise to the religious zeal of these imaginative boys one day to become poets. But already by the second stanza, Jones ironically undercuts this romantic priesthood of the radio god, weighing the loss of his beloved hero against the suburban triteness implied by the figure of Kate Smith. He reluctantly admits that his awed absorption in The Shadow may have been no better than the gullibility of an adult consumer's hooked by a radio advertisement into buying a product: "What can I say / It is better to have loved and lost / Than to put linoleum in your living room?"

In the third stanza, Jones sets his radio experience apart from the adult one in which race, politics, and religion are more openly the content. Yet he also offers a litany of radio figures that serve as the sinister mirror of his own "religion" of the radio deity Lamont Cranston. In the opening lines of the stanza, for example, he mentions "Mandrake the Magician," whose program was broadcast several times a week from 1940 to 1942. Mandrake was a master magician, accompanied by a servant named Juano Hernandez and a powerful giant named Lothar. He would invoke a magical spell and hypnotize his adversaries. Jones implies that he once identified with these figures, wishing to share in their omniscience and omnipotence. But now he questions that same childish desire as impossible and ridiculous: "Am I a sage or something? / Mandrake's hypnotic gesture of the week?"

In the lines that follow, this desire for magical potency by means of the radio becomes still more dubious, as Jones recalls a series of real-life figures who used the radio to pursue religious, political, and financial power. The poet denies that he can duplicate the healing spells of Oral Roberts, a fundamentalist faith healer and preacher, and he disavows the promises of earthly happiness and salvation that the Catholic evangelist Fulton J. Sheen

> *Jones, however, does not simply intend a moral allegory with his figures of darkness and evil. His self-conscious acceptance of the 'dark side' as a space of moral insight refers as well to his dawning recognition of the politics of race in America."*

regularly made over the radio. In the last line, in the climax of the stanza, he presents the most evil form of "hypnosis" through the radio, the political exploitation of its magic to evil ends: "I cannot even order you to gaschamber satori like Hitler or Goody Knight." Here Jones alludes to Adolf Hitler's use of the radio to spread his message of war, conquest, and genocide. And he associates the recent phenomenon of Nazism with a domestic barbarity, the use of the gaschamber not only in the Nazi death camps, but also in the State of California's prisons since 1938. "Goody Knight" refers to Goodwin Knight, the Governor of California from 1953-1959, who appeared often on radio and television: on Jack Benny's radio show in 1957, for example, and on the *I Love Lucy* television show inaugurating the opening of Disneyland in 1955. If Lamont Cranston and, perhaps, Mandrake the Magician were the good deities of Jones's radio pantheon, he reminds us that they nonetheless shared the radio sky with real men of power, men whom Jones had come to see as the evil sorcerers of the mass media.

As Jones suggests, the child's dreams of superhuman powers to do good, fantasies fed by radio listening, are uncomfortably close to the bogus promises of power and moral rightness sold by evangelists and demagogues. He implies that for every fictional radio hero fighting evil with special powers in the 1930s and 1940s, the radio also allowed a fascist manipulator of the medium like Charles Coughlin or Martin Luther Thomas to spread messages of hatred and intolerance. In

> *Behind the facade of social stability and harmony, the poem asserts, there is really little altruism or love. Love spelled backwards is 'an evol word,' and no one knows that more surely than Blacks.*"

his own love for the radio and its moral heroes, Jones is forced to recognize this love's potential to be perverted into its opposite, hatred and evil. Accordingly, the next stanza makes explicit this reversibility of love, now not just in reference to Jones's childhood love for the radio, but as an elemental capacity of his own nature and of human nature in general: "Turn it backwards / see, see what I mean? / An evol word. & besides / who understands it?" This sudden loss of moral bearings makes it difficult for the poet to risk loving, the way he once spontaneously and wholeheartedly embraced his heroes in his radio days. If love and evil are so nearly mirror images of one another, so intertwined in the human heart, the poet implicitly asks, how can we know whether we are falling in love or falling into sin? "I certainly wouldn't like to go out on that kind of limb," Jones writes.

In the next two stanzas, however, he turns this negative insight back around into a positive potential for moral knowledge. If moral good does not lie with secret powers, perhaps at least awareness of the danger of self-deception is itself a kind of moral stance: an ethic of self-scrutiny. In turn, the imaginative capacities cultivated by the radio, by the children's shows "Red Lantern" and "Let's Pretend," allow a new form of identification to emerge in the poem. It is not the *power* of the Shadow that Jones now wants to take upon himself, but the Shadow's penetrating *knowledge* of the evil side of human nature, an insight that is also self-knowledge, the recognition of oneself as a figure of night and shadow: "What was it he used to say (after the transformation, when he was safe / & invisible & the unbelievers couldn't throw stones?) "Heh, heh, heh, / Who knows what evil lurks in the hearts of men? The Shadow knows." The Shadow folds evil back into self-consciousness: himself having the form of darkness and shadow, he can see into the hidden depths of the human heart. So too, in terms of his physical presence as a figure on the radio, he is paradoxically characterized by a double invisibility, an invisibility made self-conscious. Not only, as a radio voice, is he invisible to his listeners, but even within the world of the radio fiction, he also passes unseen among his fellow characters, themselves of course invisible to their listeners.

Jones, however, does not simply intend a moral allegory with his figures of darkness and evil. His self-conscious acceptance of the "dark side" as a space of moral insight refers as well to his dawning recognition of the politics of race in America. For Jones, being black, having a skin color that this racist society has traditionally feared and despised, becomes a special vantage point from which to see through the facade of America's constitutional promises to the social and psychological evils lurking in its heart. Suggestively, the radio figures that Jones holds up for scorn are primarily real white personages—Kate Smith, Oral Roberts, Archbishop Sheen, Adolf Hitler, Goody Knight—but figures whose race society takes as a given, neutral fact, because the radio conveys only their voices. In contrast, although the existence of such fictional characters as "Red Lantern" and "The Shadow" is only imaginatively derived from the actors' invisible voices, their fictive visual presence, their "color," is specially remarked and emphasized. Subtly, then, Jones implies that the very capacity to imagine race in America and to make visible the evils perpetrated in its name may be the ambiguous privilege of people of color, the terrible good of that evil they suffer under racism. Identification with radio heroes "of color"—the red or black figures of the radio dramas—may thus foreshadow a more fundamental *self*-identification of the poet with his blackness, a moral stance at once "evil" in racist eyes and a hard-won "love" of a self shrouded in the shadow of blackness. It is this, ultimately, that the radio hero teaches the poet, how to transmute the stigma of his own darkness, the darkness of his skin and the moral darkness within him, into a self-conscious affirmation of love: "O, yes he does / O, yes he does. / An evil word it is, / This Love."

Source: Tyrus Miller, in an essay for *Poetry for Students*, Gale, 2000.

John E. Hakac

In this brief essay, Hakac discusses the hidden meaning in the language of the poem.

Imamu Amiri Baraka (LeRoi Jones) was fond of disguising racial themes in some of his early poetry. For example, "In Memory of Radio" has no trace of explicit racial reference, yet the poem is easily read as a statement that Blacks living in a white society have a special ability for the divination of evil. The poet's use of jive and the reader's conversion of a brief passage into Black English reveal Baraka's oblique theme.

Structurally the poem begins with a reference to Lamont Cranston and ends with one to him as the Shadow, jive for Black. It develops the poet's pre- and post-World War II assumption that radio heavily, through optimism and fantasy, purveyed the view that God's in His Heaven, All's Right with the Status Quo. The mention of Hitler and Goody Knight in line 11, however, contradicts that view by alluding to violence and death. Goodwin J. Knight was governor of California for six of the twelve years Caryl Whittier Chessman lived on Death Row awaiting execution. Chessman's prison term spanned the administrations of governors Earl Warren, Knight, and Edmund G. Brown. Convicted of sexual kidnapping in 1948 and ultimately executed on May 2, 1960, Chessman received four of his eight stays of execution from various state and federal courts while Knight was in office, although Knight himself did not issue any of the stays. By 1959, when the poem appeared in the *White Dove Review,* the Chessman case had ignited an international clamour protesting the death penalty and the inhumanity of keeping a man on Death Row for over a decade. Later, bowing under pressure from the U.S. State Department, Governor Brown granted Chessman a sixty-day reprieve on February 18, 1960, designed to ward off hostile demonstrations and possible riots during President Eisenhower's upcoming visit to South America.

Behind the facade of social stability and harmony, the poem asserts, there is really little altruism or love. Love spelled backwards is "an evol word," and no one knows that more surely than Blacks. Baraka cleverly sets up the idea by quoting Lamont Cranston, now become the Shadow, uttering his famous words from invisibility: "Heh, Heh, Heh, / Who knows what evil lurks in the hearts of men?"

At this point, reading lines 22–24 in Black English illuminates the poet's concealed meaning:

"'De Shadow know!' / O, yeah he do / O, yeah he do." A shadow, Baraka feels, has the keen insight, the "divinity," to detect evil unerringly like the Shadow—perhaps because a "shadow" too, ironically, is an invisible man.

Source: John E. Hakac, "Baraka's 'In Memory of Radio,'" in *Concerning Poetry,* Vol. 10, No. 1, Spring, 1977, p. 85.

Sources

Allen, Donald and George F. Butterick, eds., *The Postmoderns: The New American Poetry Revised,* New York: Grove Press, 1982.

Baraka, Amiri, *The Autobiography of LeRoi Jones,* New York: Freundlich Books, 1984.

———, *Transbluesency: The Selected Poems of Amiri Baraka/LeRoi Jones (1961-1995),* edited by Paul Vangelisti, Marsilio Publishers, 1995.

Brown, Lloyd W., *Amiri Baraka,* Boston: Twayne Publishers, 1980.

Harris, William J., *The Poetry and Politics of Amiri Baraka: The Jazz Aesthetic,* Columbia: University of Missouri Press, 1985.

———, *The Leroi Jones/Amiri Baraka Reader,* New York City: Thunder's Mouth Press, 1991.

Horowitz, David A., Peter N. Carroll, and David D. Lee, eds., *On the Edge: A New History of 20th-Century America,* Los Angeles: West Publishing Co., 1990.

Hudson, Theodore R., *From LeRoi Jones to Amiri Baraka,* Durham, NC: Duke University Press, 1973.

Jones, Hettie, *How I Became Hettie Jones,* New York: E. P. Dutton, 1990.

Jones, LeRoi, *Preface to a Twenty Volume Suicide Note,* New York: Corinth Books, 1961.

Rosenthal, M. L., *The New Poets: American & British Poetry Since World War II,* New York: Oxford University Press, 1967.

Sollors, Werner, *Amiri Baraka/LeRoi Jones: The Quest for a "Populist Modernism,"* New York: Columbia University Press, 1978.

Woodard, Komozi, *A Nation Within a Nation: Amiri Baraka (Leroi Jones) and Black Power Politics,* Chapel Hill: University of North Carolina Press, 1999.

For Further Study

Allen, Donald, ed., *The New American Poetry: 1945-1960,* New York: Grove Press, 1960.

This anthology was published to showcase those poets writing against the grain since Wolrd War II, in style and forms aligned with movements in music and painting such as abstract expresionism and jazz. Allen organizes the poets into categories which are still used today to identify particular poetic traditions: New York School, Beat, Black Mountain School, and the San Francisco Renaissance.

Allen, Donald, and Warren Tallman, eds., *The Poetics of the New American Poetry,* New York: Grove Press, 1973.

This book is meant to accompany Allen's anthology, *The New American Poetry: 1945-1960.* Here the poets themselves provide statements on their own poetics and writing processes. This book is essential for understanding the theories behind the practices of Allen's poets.

Clay, Stephen and Rodney Phillips, *A Secret Location on the Lower East Side: Adventures in Writing, 1960-1980,* New York: Granary Books/The New York Public Library, 1998.

This book documents the intense and experimental publishing activities of poets and writers from 1960-1980, when Amiri Baraka, then LeRoi Jones, and his wife edited and published *Floating Bear* and *Yugen.* An indispensable resource for learning about small-press publishing during this period.

The Missing

Thom Gunn

1997

Completed in 1997, Thom Gunn's "The Missing" takes its place among the most eloquent and poignant testaments to have arisen from the literature of AIDS. Part elegy, part rueful meditation, the poem is told from the perspective of the survivor, one who has been left behind in the wake of a string of senseless deaths. Here, the speaker faces an uncertain and sorely compromised future stripped of the loving support of the friends on whom he has come to rely so heavily. And yet, more than a confrontation of the mystery and irrationality of death, the poem explores the extent to which society influences and shapes the individual. It celebrates the meaningful connections and lasting ties that punctuate a life and often outlive it in the realm of memory.

"The Missing" first appeared in Gunn's 1992 collection, *The Man with Night Sweats.* As its title declares, the AIDS crisis is one of its central preoccupations. Night sweats are one of the symptoms of AIDS and often come as a harrowing harbinger of a yet undiagnosed disease that has already taken up residence in the body. Clearly, this grim and visceral detail indicates a book that is honest in its unsentimental portraits of lives cut short and of people languishing in their prime.

In addition, the poem displays another hallmark of Gunn's poetry: a complex and seamlessly rendered formal structure. Written in iambic pentameter and adopting an *abab* rhyme scheme, "The Missing" is a unique example of a traditional, formal poem taking a contemporary theme as its subject. "Rhythmic form and subject-matter are locked

Thom Gunn

in a permanent embrace," Gunn writes in an essay expressing his theories of poetics, and the embrace is an image that recurs throughout Gunn's work and figures centrally in "The Missing." It is an image of both friendship and desire, two sources of empowerment and identity. But it also an image with the dark shadow of death looming over it, suggesting the infection, the tragedy to which desire can lead.

Author Biography

Thompson William Gunn was born in Gravesend, Kent, England, on August 29, 1929. His parents, both journalists, relocated to the London suburb of Hempstead Heath, where they outlasted the Blitz and the rigors of the war. His late teens saw a stint in the British Army and a brief period living and working in Paris. It was there that Gunn made his first serious foray into writing, reading the French masters and trying his hand at fiction. In the early 1950s, he attended Trinity College at Cambridge and published his first collection of verse, *Fighting Terms,* while still an undergraduate. A creative writing fellowship at Stanford University brought him to the San Francisco Bay Area

in 1954. In 1958, Gunn accepted an offer to teach at the University of California at Berkeley, all the time keeping one ear tuned to the sexual and cultural revolution sweeping through San Francisco and the nation. After a year in London, Gunn gave up the university post in 1966, teaching briefly at Princeton University and immersing himself in the rhythms of New York City's bohemian enclave, Greenwich Village.

Despite the move to the East Coast, Gunn would not stray from San Francisco for long. His more than thirty books of poetry and prose bear witness to an ever-evolving style of clarity and emotional honesty. Gunn could be best described as an Anglo-American poet, known for his interest in both traditional and free verse and the facility with which he moves between the two. A recipient of numerous accolades, including a MacArthur Fellowship and the Lenore Marshall Poetry Prize, he still resides in San Francisco, where he continues to teach part-time as a senior lecturer at the University of California at Berkeley.

Poem Text

Now as I watch the progress of the plague,
The friends surrounding me fall sick, grow thin,
and drop away. Bared, is my shape less vague
—Sharply exposed and with a sculpted skin?

I do not like the statue's chill contour,   5
Not nowadays. The warmth investing me
Led outward through mind, limb, feeling, and more
In an involved increasing family.

Contact of friend led to another friend
Supple entwinement through the living mass   10
Which for all that I knew might have no end,
Image of an unlimited embrace.

I do not just feel ease, though comfortable:
Aggressive as in some ideal of sport,
With ceaseless movement thrilling through the   15
        whole,
their push kept me as firm as their support.

But death—Their deaths have left me less defined:
It was their pulsing presence made me clear.
I borrowed from it, I was unconfined,
Who tonight balance unsupported here,   20

Eyes glaring from raw marble, in a pose
Languorously part-buried in the block,
Shins perfect and no calves, as if I froze
Between potential and a finished work.

—Abandoned incomplete, shape of a shape,   25
In which exact detail shows the more strange,
Trapped in unwholeness, I find no escape
Back to the play of constant give and change.

Poem Summary

Lines 1-4:

From the onset, the speaker is established as an observer, watching the spread of an unnamed "plague"—the AIDS epidemic. As the speaker helplessly witnesses, his friends wilt and expire. Their bodies, unable to resist the spread of the disease, "grow thin." They become foreign and altered as they succumb to the virus, vulnerable, or as the speaker puts it, "bared." This slow yet sudden expiration prompts the speaker to examine his own state. Is health something the speaker can still rely on without question? Will he be able to avoid this dissipation, in which the body grows more and more "vague"? Though his "shape" can be "sculpted," though the body can be built up and strengthened, ultimately there is no real cure for chronic diseases like AIDS.

Lines 5-8:

While steeling the body's exterior, growing tougher in the face of tragedy may seem like a logical strategy, it is a response the speaker ultimately rejects. "I do not like the statue's chill contour" he asserts, as it is equated with an emotional coldness, an indifference to or denial of the terrible reality of the epidemic. Self-defense or self-protection could result in a dangerous isolation at a time when the action and togetherness of community are needed. It is a mode of response the speaker feels is no longer appropriate, "not nowadays." What is needed instead is the unification of all the body's reserves, combining the intellect, physical strength, and emotion ("mind, limb, feeling") into a greater and more powerful whole. Only then can this strength be projected outward in a vital connection with others. In the stanza's final line, the speaker effectively employs the literary device alliteration, or the repetition of initial sounds. "In" is echoed in "involved," which once again repeats its sound with "increasing." Here the poet has found a way to match form and content. The specific choice of words and sounds mirrors and validates the poem's argument, the specific point it is trying to establish. Thus, the connection formed in the repetition of sounds is an aural way of demonstrating the connectedness of the speaker's ever-growing "family."

Lines 9-12:

In this sharply observed and delicately phrased stanza, Gunn injects a dark irony into the poem. The onslaught of the disease has spurred a mobi-

lization, as friends, both the stricken and the concerned, unite for support and action. First described in the second stanza, the third extends and deepens the portrayal of this process of coming together. In the face of the grim realities of the epidemic, fellowship and community have prevailed, spreading from "friend ... to ... friend." These close bonds grow and replicate, moving from a "supple entwinement" to "an unlimited embrace." And yet upon closer examination the bonds are the source of something far more insidious. Gunn's words are filled with dark intention and double meanings. While the diction fittingly conveys the rallying spirit spreading among the speaker's friends, it also chillingly describes the pathology of the disease as well, spreading out in a lengthening chain of infection. In this light, the line "Contact of friend led to another friend" takes an ironic turn as the means

of this growing camaraderie and growing intimacy becomes the very means through which the disease is transmitted. The joy and endless possibility of this brotherhood, "which for all that I knew might have no end" is subverted, turning to fear and helplessness when the world is faced with a virus that researchers and scientists have been unable to conquer.

Lines 13-16:

The double face of the language extends into the fourth stanza, although less overtly than before. On the surface, Gunn is still describing the spirit of unity, building and growing not only in his group of immediate acquaintances but far beyond. They are a source of comfort, "aggressive as in some ideal of sport." Here, the poem returns to the imagery of the first two stanzas, borrowing from the figure of the statue. While there its presence unsettled the speaker, by the fourth stanza the image of the physical body has been transformed. Now, the self-contained strength has been brought out of isolation and is firmly rooted in this new context of friends. Thus, only when power is linked with others can its true potential be unleashed. Only then can the strength be sustained and made truly "firm." This support is necessary, for just as its power grows so does the potency and effect of the disease, "aggressive" in its own right, infecting and claiming countless numbers. When the shadow of disease is cast on the stanza, Gunn's words, "with ceaseless movement ... through the whole," take on a chilling impact in hinting at the unchecked devastation the "plague" may have on an unsuspecting population.

Lines 17-20:

In losing his friends to AIDS, the speaker feels he has also lost part of his identity. It is death that ultimately unsettles and topples his sense of community and wholeness. The end of line 17 mirrors the end of line 3 in answering the question posed in the first stanza. "Less vague" has given way to "less defined," as the speaker relied on the "pulsing presence" of others to make him more "clear." Now those sparks are dwindling. By the end of the stanza, Gunn's words once again echo the first two stanzas. Unlike the statue, the speaker was once "unconfined." But now that is changing, as he "[balances] unsupported here." In less than a stanza, "support" (line 16) has been transformed into its opposite and the freedom and fellowship, "the warmth investing me" (line 6) have devolved to the solitude of the opening.

Lines 21-24:

The sixth stanza continues to revisit the imagery of the opening. The speaker is still watching, "eyes glaring," but this time he observes "from raw marble," an imaginative space into which he has projected himself. He is reverting back to the statue's pose, a form he rejected in the first line of the second stanza. This stanza is rife with contradictions and unresolved tensions. The speaker seems to be in the process of emerging from the marble and yet his body is positioned "languorously," a word that elicits connotations of softness and suppleness, in stark contrast to the hard rock. His body is "part-buried in the block," a symbol of his contrary stance. He wants to shield himself from the stark reality of a circle of friends devastated by AIDS. But he cannot. The disease will not go away, no matter how steeled, how posed, he makes himself. The third line furthers this contradictory stance. The shins are "perfect," but there are "no calves." He is incomplete, the one part elegantly formed, but negated by the absence of another, by the lack of a whole. The last line is another example of the complex, double nature of Gunn's language. The speaker could be talking of his own loss, by the death of friends and supporters, or directly referencing the lives claimed by AIDS. Here, fear and grief partially paralyze him and limit his own potential, just as disease has cut short the potential of the others. In other words, in the world of irony and contradiction the disease has occasioned, he is torn between the world of the living and the realm of the dead.

Lines 25-28:

In the final stanza, the notion of lives left incomplete is overtly stated. His friends have been robbed of the chance to realize the full arc of their existence. As a result, the speaker's life will suffer as well in the wake of this loss, and thus, it becomes clear why Gunn has adopted his verbal strategy of doublespeak. Though ostensibly focusing on himself, the speaker is really addressing, at the same time, the countless lives that have fallen victim to AIDS. As their lives have been "abandoned incomplete," so too has the poet been abandoned, left feeling incomplete as he has lost all the things these friends would have contributed to his own existence. Thus, this loss of a sense of community has ultimately narrowed the speaker's sense of self. The disease has symbolically and indirectly infected him as well. Again he returns to the worries voiced in the question at the end of the first stanza and provides yet another answer. No, the speaker seems to have resolved, now he is more vague, a "shape of a shape." To make matters worse, he is "trapped in unwholeness." He cannot proceed, feeling so ill-defined and bereft of the strength and support which once surrounded him. And yet he cannot go back, cannot "escape / Back to the play of constant give and change." The joy of interacting with these friends and the unknown, unpredictable future they would have shared is lost to him forever.

Themes

Community vs. Solitude

In "The Missing," the speaker assumes a terrible responsibility as a voice forced to speak not only for itself but the countless others whom death has silenced. It is the way the speaker solves this dilemma of representation that makes the poem a unique achievement. In speaking of the self, the sudden unexpected condition of loss and loneliness in which the speaker is suddenly entrenched, he is able to address the grave plague that has threatened any sense of community. Thus, a vibrant and living link is established between the living and the dead that otherwise would be impossible.

The arc of the poem moves from solitude to a vital sense of community, and then back to the sole voice devoid of these social connections. In the first stanza, the speaker's friends have begun to "fall sick, grow thin, / And drop away." He finds himself confronting his own body, and thus his own mortality in light of this development. In the second through fourth stanzas, this self-consciousness is temporarily postponed by the "involved increasing family" that had once assembled around him. But this comfort was fleeting. The community assumes an ironic, if not paradoxical, presence in the poem. It was this very assembling of a group of friends and lovers that has allowed the disease to spread. By the fifth stanza, the poem begins its retrograde, its backward, movement. The speaker remains, "[balancing] unsupported here." Without the love and support of his friends, the speaker feels he is something less, "a shape of a shape," that can resort only to the slim comfort of memories. At its end, the poem does not offer any solutions, any realizations this pain has offered the speaker. In losing others, the speaker, "trapped in unwholeness," has ultimately lost part of himself as well.

Exposure vs. Self-Protection

The poem takes as its subject the spread of the deadly AIDS virus, a modern plague that has claimed millions of people worldwide. In lieu of a cure for the disease "Which for all I knew might have no end," the speaker presents the solidarity of those whose lives have been touched by the epidemic. Their unity is the one source of comfort and strength staving off the inevitable fate of those infected with the virus. And yet, in describing this community of the concerned, the poem assumes a hint of irony. "Contact of friend led to another friend," the speaker offers, presenting the story of his growing chain of acquaintances. But the diction here, the specific word choices, makes the speaker's true intent unclear. Is he describing this growing group of friends or the silent, unchecked progress of the disease? Opening oneself to others, to an intimate, sexual love, possibly means opening oneself to infection. Here, exposure to this thrilling "unlimited embrace" has a potentially deadly element.

An image central to this theme is the figure of the statue. To counteract or diffuse this threat of infection, the speaker assumes the static form of a man partially trapped in a block of marble. In one sense, it is a posture of self-protection. If his body becomes rigid, if his exterior is steeled to both the physical threat of infection and the emotional pain the AIDS crisis has occasioned, then the speaker can ensure his safety, can create a haven. But, again, Gunn's treatment of this image invests it with a double nature. While mimicking a statue may be an attempt at self-preservation, ultimately it threatens and unsettles the speaker's well-being, and thus, the strategy becomes unacceptable: "I do not like the statue's chill contour." Metaphorically turning the self into stone only results in blocking "the warmth investing" the speaker that has ultimately led to this thriving network of friends. In this light, the statue becomes an image of cowardice and isolation. But despite how hard the speaker attempts to resist this solitary life of hiding, at the end of the poem he cannot escape it. Half-finished, only partially chiseled from the block, he is "Abandoned incomplete."

Loss of Identity

In the wake of such tragedy, the speaker is threatened with a loss of identity. "Their deaths have left me less defined: / It was their pulsing presence made me clear." The speaker has grown to rely on his family of friends, these close ties empowering him and keeping him "firm." "But death" has taken this all away, and the speaker is left to "balance unsupported" and alone. In light of this, another dimension to the image of the statue have rendered him a living person trapped in a life-less form.

Topics for Further Study

- Research the origins of the children's nursery rhyme "Ring around the Rosie." Explain its imagery in terms of how it relates to the Black Plague. Compare the tone of the poem with that of Gunn's "The Missing." How does the singsong rhythm of the nursery rhyme compare with Gunn's meter and rhyme scheme?

- Investigate Patient Zero, the mythical man once believed to have introduced AIDS to the United States, and Typhoid Mary, the cook who was allegedly the cause of 51 cases of typhoid. Focus specifically on the distinction between myth and reality in their stories. What would be the purpose of inventing such a figure as Patient Zero? Why would there be such legend and infamy surrounding the life of Typhoid Mary? What does the existence of these figures reveal about the nature of fear and misinformation surrounding disease?

- Write a poem in the voice of one of the above-mentioned figures or a mythical "disease carrier" of your own invention.

emerges. The speaker feels as if his body were "part-buried in the block." His reaching out to a community of friends can be likened to the figure starting to take shape, breaking free of the heavy block of stone. But despite the "Shins perfect," there are "no calves." They have not yet been formed. In other words, he is incomplete, lacking some essential parts. The balance between the self and the community that surrounds and supports it has been compromised. This external source is diminishing, and in its absence the speaker lacks an essentially complete and fully integrated wholeness. While a statue may embody strength and physical perfection, it is devoid of an inner life or a true identity. While it resembles a human form, it is nothing more than the "chill contour" of stone. Thus, the speaker is "Trapped in unwholeness," his eyes peering out from behind the "raw marble." The seemingly endless deaths that surround him

Style

The first line of a poem is considered by many to be its most important. It is the reader's entry into the poem, introducing the work and establishing both expectation and the desire to delve further. In addition, it presents language in a pattern that is either puzzling or familiar, that mimics everyday speech or is foreign in its sound and arrangement. With "The Missing," the reader is immediately presented with a blend of these two different modes. The diction, or specific word choices, is simple (plain words that are easily recognizable). And yet as the first quatrain (four-line stanza) unfolds, a certain pattern emerges, a rhythm strikes the ear. There are ten syllables in every line, laid out in an almost regular pattern of stressed and unstressed syllables. In the first line, for example, the stresses alternate, falling on "Now," "watch," the first syllable of "progress," "of," and "plague." This meter, or recurring pattern of beats, acts like an engine driving the poem and propelling the reader rhythmically through it. It is called iambic pentameter, meaning there are five ("penta") two-beat units in each line.

In addition, there is another formal device Gunn employs in "The Missing": an *abab* rhyme scheme. That means the last words of the first and third lines, and the second and fourth lines, respectively, match each other in their sounds. Most of Gunn's lines end with perfect rhymes as in "plague" and "vague." Others end on slant rhymes in which the sounds are similar but not precisely paired: "mass" and "embrace." Either way, these rhymes, in combination with the meter, are the glue that holds each stanza and ultimately the poem together.

These formal elements employed by Gunn achieve other effects as well. Gunn's poem of mortality and the death of friends never swerves toward the maudlin or overtly sentimental. The rhyme and meter help prevent this by imposing a regimen of strict control on the poem. Thus, the chaos and senseless loss the poem takes as its subject is counterbalanced, reined in by its form. The formal devices impose a sense of order and logic in the face of a threat and a reality against which the speaker is otherwise powerless. Here form attempts to tame the wild disorder of the speaker's world.

Compare & Contrast

- **1347-1350:** Black Death sweeps across Europe, introduced into the bloodstream of its victims by a bacillus carried by the Oriental rat flea. When it is over, the epidemic has claimed more than 30 million people, approximately one-third of the continent's population.

  1918: A worldwide influenza epidemic leaves 20 million dead.

  1939-1945: World War II results in the loss of more than 50 million lives.

  2000: To date, the AIDS virus has claimed approximately 17 million victims.

- **1926-1946:** Controversial theories of the origin of AIDS abound. Some scientists believe the virus spread from monkeys to humans some time during this period.

  1959: A man dies in Africa's Congo in what researchers say was the first proven AIDS death.

  July 31, 1981: Under the headline "Rare Cancer Seen in 41 Homosexuals," the *New York Times* reports that a "rare and often rapidly fatal form of cancer" has been diagnosed in gay men in San Francisco and New York City. For the first time, the American public is informed of the disease that would come to be known as AIDS.

  1997: The approximate worldwide death count from the disease tops off at 6.4 million. An estimated 22 million people worldwide are HIV-positive, more than the population of Australia.

  1980: There are 422 diagnosed cases of AIDS in the United States, resulting in 31 deaths.

  1992: Although estimates place the number of cases in the United States at more than a million, there are 257,750 diagnosed instances of the disease and 157,637 AIDS-related deaths.

  1998: This year sees a total of 665,357 diagnosed U.S. cases with a total of 401,028 deaths.

  1985: Women represent 7 percent of all cases.

  1996: As the disease spreads farther and farther into the heterosexual population, that number jumps to 20 percent.

Historical Context

AIDS (Acquired Immune Deficiency Syndrome) first crept into the world's consciousness in the early 1980s as the death toll started mounting. And yet, initially the seemingly scattered and random deaths were no indication of the millions the disease claims to this day. At its onset, the medical community was stunned and unprepared, fearing they had the makings of a modern plague, a virus of which they knew little and for which they had no cure. AIDS is a disease transferred through the exchange of bodily fluids, and it is commonly, though not exclusively, sexually transmitted or introduced through a blood transfusion. In light of such a pathology, experts predicted that the rate of transmission would skyrocket worldwide. Their fears proved true.

In the wake of growing fears, activists and medical professionals raced not only to dispel misconceptions about the disease, but to disseminate accurate information in the belief that public awareness was the best means of prevention. Initially, among those hardest hit by AIDS were homosexual men. After the *New York Times* reported early findings of the disease in 1981, AIDS was dubbed the Gay Cancer. While opportunistic diseases have little prejudice or preference for whom they strike, the epidemic presented a daunting setback to a community of activists fighting for societal acceptance and equal rights. Those involved in the gay community and the gay rights movement now had added responsibilities: advocate the allotment of research money, fight for the rights of the infected, and all the while care for the sick and dying.

At the time Thom Gunn's "The Missing" was completed in 1987, although a wealth of information was known about the disease when compared to the early 1980s, the relentless spread of AIDS continued unchecked. Similarly, the fear of infection was not on the decline either. AIDS had cut an especially wide swath through major urban centers, such as New York City and San Francisco, Gunn's hometown, where gay populations were high. Significant numbers of diagnosed cases began to emerge as well in people of all races, genders, and sexual orientations. Action and organization were needed.

On the local level, the "involved increasing family" Gunn cites in "The Missing," refers to his immediate group of friends. To him the disease was at its most tragic and most personal when it claimed those closest to him. But this cohesive unity also has a wider scope, possibly including the highly organized and unified gay community of San Francisco as well as AIDS activists and researchers everywhere. Within the first few years of the onset of the crisis, a collaborative network of city and state agencies, hospitals, health care providers, and community-based organizations (CBOs) began to develop. A large array of services evolved to help people who tested HIV-positive (usually a harbinger of the development of full-blown AIDS). This complex network became known as the San Francisco model of AIDS care. Long considered an exemplary approach, the San Francisco methods of care spread as people from around the world visited the city, interested in helping remove the stigma of AIDS and developing models of treatment. This increasing family turned out to be a passionate group of caring and talented individuals with a commitment to wipe out the disease.

The contributions of these various advocates and medical health professionals have resulted in significant strides not only in the treatment of AIDS but in its public perception as well. New medicines and new treatments aimed at staving off AIDS-related illnesses have extended and improved the lives of patients and significantly altered the strict death sentence a positive diagnosis once was. In the United States in 1997, AIDS deaths dipped for the first time since the onset of the epidemic. However, like the common cold and the various types of cancer, forms of prevention and treatment improve, but a cure remains elusive.

Critical Overview

Hugh Haughton in *The Times Literary Supplement* praises the *The Man with Night Sweats* for its "somewhat scaresome lucidity" and feels the poem "seeks to render permanent the transitory embraces through which we play out our need for each other and shield ourselves." Haughton also notes that "Gunn's verse has always been marked by a strange combination of intimacy and detachment ... Gunn's lyrics hold experience and the reader at arm's length." In "The Missing," Haughton detects a poet "poignantly facing his physical vulnerability," as "the speaker constructs a kind of bounding shield out of the tightly interlaced ... rhymed ... quatrains." The reviewer sees the poem in terms of the embrace, a recurring image in the collection and Gunn's work in general. "Seeking to define his need for solidarity, he adopts another very different image of an 'embrace.' ... Of course the 'supple entwinement' of that 'unlimited embrace,' the source of his sense of belonging within the 'increasing family,' has, of course, become the source of his crisis, leaving the poet precariously 'unsupported' and 'incomplete.'"

Henri Cole in *The Nation* comments on the form fitting such a poem "of mortality, where metrical patterns help control elegiac emotions, like the steady drum tap accompanying a coffin to its cemetery." He cites Gunn's collection as an "[example] of art produced at the historical moment it depicts and standing as a monument to the human spirit in the face of appalling suffering."

William Logan in *The New York Times Book Review* observes of Gunn, "Here his formal distances, his comforts in the methods of literary detachment, give him a purchase not available to poets more weakly personal. The poems are written in a measured voice of despair, every word a vain effort of memory, a memory that is the only memorial to these abbreviated lives." Although the collection is given a less than favorable review, Logan concludes, "Mr. Gunn's best poetry is a resistance to the beautiful, a withholding or withdrawing in the formality of the verse moment...."

Criticism

Robert Bee

Robert Bee is a freelance writer who teaches at Rutgers University. He has published over 20 short stories and a number of book reviews. In this essay, he focuses on how "The Missing" fits within the dominant themes of Thom Gunn's career and responds to the affect of the AIDS crisis within the gay community.

Thom Gunn's poem "The Missing" is taken from his 1992 book, *The Man with Night Sweats,* a series of poems responding to the AIDS crisis. Gunn, a gay poet living in San Francisco, responds to the crisis in unsentimental, unflinching verse. As Deborah Landau points out in her essay, "How to Live. What to Do: The Poetics and Politics of AIDS": "By exposing the anguish and suffering brought on by AIDS, Gunn chooses an aesthetic strategy that might inspire empathy from readers who have never had a direct experience with the disease." Although other writers, such as the contemporary gay poet Paul Monette, have responded to the AIDS crisis through political rage, Gunn chooses a realistic portrayal of the ravages of the disease on the victims and their loved ones.

The poem's themes rest on a series of oppositions, beginning with the structure. "The Missing" is written in a rigorous, traditional form with rhymed couplets. The controlled form and restrained emotion contrasts with the horror and powerlessness the poet feels in the face of the ravaging disease. Gunn may need to write in a rigorous form to control or deal with such painful emotions and subject matter.

The poem contrasts the narrator's memories of the time before AIDS with the effect the disease has on his community. In the second and third stanza, Gunn describes a time before the plague in almost utopian imagery. He seems to have found a romantic freedom after the gay rights movements of the late 1960s, when gay men and women could more openly explore their sexuality. He points out, "Contact of friend led to another friend, / Supple entwinement through the living mass / Which for all I knew might have no end, / Image of an unlimited embrace." He envisions a community so close that it becomes one "living mass," possibly embracing all humanity.

This passage resembles the utopian imagery of some of Gunn's earlier poetry. In his essay "My Life Up to Now," reprinted in *The Occasions of Poetry,* he describes the freedom he felt in the 1960s and 1970s in London and especially San Francisco. For example, in "My Life Up to Now," he describes the Golden Gate Park in San Francisco, the scene of so many mass gatherings in the 1960s: "The first field of a glistening continent / Each found by trust-

> *In 'The Missing,' Gunn combines his interest in freedom with humanism. The humanism of the poem deepens the tragedy, for the narrator's loss is not just personal, it includes the loss of a community."*

ing Eden in the human." The "unlimited embrace" in "The Missing" involves trusting "the Eden in the human." Merle E. Brown in *Double Lyric: Divisiveness and Communal Creativity in Recent English Poetry* points out, "Gunn wants ... to become one with the very quick of life itself .... he wants to experience complete emotional, bodily oneness with other human beings." Thus, within a bleak poem exists an oasis of utopian sentiment, a remarkably optimistic view of human possibility.

The second and third stanzas also promote an ideal of freedom, for the remembered times before AIDS were characterized by "ceaseless movement" in which the poet was "Aggressive as in some ideal of sport." This passage is reminiscent of the notion of freedom, movement and aggression so controversial in Gunn's early work. As Alan Bold points out, in his book *Thom Gunn & Ted Hughes,* Gunn was known as being a poet "wallowing in violence" who writes about "motor cyclists and predatory birds." Yet Gunn's interest in the bikers and toughs did not really celebrate violence; he was intrigued with the freedom and ceaseless movement of the bikers. Movement and freedom have become interconnected in Gunn's adopted country of America where cars and the open road have become forms of independence. His most famous poem, "On the Move," describes a biker gang in California and admires their ceaseless movement and their embrace of the animal in the human. "On the Move" also demonstrates a concern with the issue of identity, the fact that, as Alan Bold points out in *Thom Gunn & Ted Hughes,* "man's ability to act positively and with purpose is handicapped by his habit of personal reflection." He admired the unreflecting action of the toughs, who are freer than an introspective intellectual.

What Do I Read Next?

- Thom Gunn's *Collected Poems* appeared in 1994 to critical acclaim. Compiling the highlights of a prolific thirty-five-year career, the volume is essential to those seeking a fuller understanding of Gunn's work: his points of departure, the evolution of his style, and the consistent, yet evolving presence of metrical and rhythmic forms. The collection includes a generous sampling from Gunn's major volumes and displays his inventiveness, shimmering diction, and democratic range of subjects.

- In addition to his poetry, Thom Gunn enjoys a burgeoning reputation as a literary critic. His collection of essays, *The Occasions of Poetry,* reissued in 1999, offers insightful critical assessment of some of his greatest influences, from William Carlos Williams and Gary Snyder to Thomas Hardy and Robert Duncan. Also included are five autobiographical essays, which offer a firsthand account of Gunn's development as a poet and chart his reactions to the prevailing literary trends of the times. An essential volume for those interested in accessing a fuller perspective of Gunn's times and career.

- Its broad scope and variety of genres are just two of the hallmarks of *The Columbia Anthology of Gay Literature: Readings from Western Antiquity to the Present Day* (1998). Selections begin with Sumerian lore, span classical Greek and Latin texts, continue through European, English, Latin American, and American literary periods and end with the modern-day golden age of gay literature. General editor Byrne R. S. Fone's comprehensive introduction to each featured writer helps provide an understanding of the important role homosexual love has played in the history of Western literature.

- Those interested in reading the work of other writers who have also chosen AIDS as their theme should consult the anthology *Poets for Life: Seventy-Six Poets Respond to AIDS* (1992). Editor Michael Klein has brought together the poetry of writers representing a broad range of backgrounds, experiences, and attitudes. In ad-

dition to Thom Gunn, the work of such notable poets as Adrienne Rich, James Merrill, Heather McHugh, Deborah Digges, and Mark Doty is included. Now considered an important work in the history of AIDS literature, the volume offers a comprehensive look at the poetics of mortality and disease.

- In 1721, with the Black Death once again threatening Europe, Daniel Defoe penned *A Journal of the Plague Year* to alert the indifferent population of England to the grave danger threatening them and to remind them of the ravages of the Great Plague of 1665. Set in that year, Defoe's unique brand of fictive journalism takes the form of a tale told through the eyes of a survivor—a saddler who has chosen to remain while multitudes flee the disease-stricken city. When it first appeared, readers mistook Defoe's vibrant and irresistible realism as an eyewitness account. The lively, if not chilling, details bring the horrors of the times dramatically to life, as the weak prey on the dying and the pious administer to the sick. Terrified residents wonder who will be the next to succumb, as the death carts rattle along the streets of London to the cries of "Bring out your dead!"

- One of the many obstacles activists and health officials faced in fighting the spread of AIDS was educating the public and combating the wild rumors and misinformation that circulated in all communities. The essay collection *Writing AIDS: Gay Literature, Language, and Analysis* (1993) examines the role language and writing played in representing and reporting the realities of the crisis. The volume offers a wide-ranging look at the implications the disease has had for activism, literature, film, journalism, and culture, and the role writers have played in responding to the disease. Also explored are the varying moralistic interpretations of the disease and the sexual acts that, in some cases, transmitted the virus. The collection concludes with an extensive annotated bibliography of AIDS literature.

In "The Missing," Gunn combines his interest in freedom with humanism. The humanism of the poem deepens the tragedy, for the narrator's loss is not just personal, it includes the loss of a community. The death of any member of the community diminishes the narrator, leaving him unsupported and alone. The narrator is part of a larger human mass dying piece by piece.

The poem undercuts the pleasant memories of the second and third stanza with bitter irony. The contact of friend with friend, which so appeals to the narrator, spreads the disease, making it more insidious. The utopian unlimited embrace degenerates into a potential apocalypse.

On several occasions in the poem, the narrator compares himself to a statue in his grief. In the first stanza, he writes "my shape [is].... / Sharply exposed and with a sculpted skin." Near the end of the poem, he develops the haunting image of self as statue: "Eyes glaring from raw marble, in a pose / Languorously half-buried in the block, / Shins perfect and no calves, as if I froze / Between potential and a finished work." To create a sense of immobility, Gunn compares himself to a statue so immobile that its calves and feet are unfinished. The pain of immobility gains further significance if one considers that praise of action characteristic of most of Gunn's verse, as in the poem "On the Move."

Gunn describes the statue as "froze / Between potential and a finished work"—thus emphasizing not just the immobility but also the fact that the narrator feels incomplete now that so many friends have died. Without the community, the "Supple entwinement," he feels unfinished, "Trapped in unwholeness."

The statue imagery furthermore brings into the poem the contrast between introspection and violent action, an important theme in Gunn's career. Gunn stands out as an intellectual who admires the unreflecting, decisive tough. Yet the narrator of "The Missing" can do nothing as he watches "friends … fall sick, grow thin, / And drop away." There is no clear action to take. Incapable of action or even movement, the statue only ruminates over its anxieties.

The poem closes on a bleak note, "I find no escape / Back to the play of constant give and change." There is no way for the narrator to return to the lost world of ceaseless movement and the unlimited embrace. As Deborah Landau points out, Gunn's AIDS poems end with "no consolation, transformation, or epiphany." The only hope rests in surviving difficult circumstances. Despite the bleakness, the poem ultimately impresses because of its high aesthetic accomplishment, its ability to bring together so many of the themes of Gunn's work, and the empathy it produces in readers, who witness the suffering of the dying and the sorrow of the survivors.

Source: Robert Bee, in an essay for *Poetry for Students,* Gale, 2000.

Marisa Anne Pagnattaro

Marisa Anne Pagnattaro, J.D., Ph.D. in English, is a freelance writer and a Robert E. West Teaching Fellow in the English Department at the University of Georgia. In the following essay, Pagnattaro explores Gunn's attempt to come to terms with the loss of friends who died from AIDS.

When Thom Gunn was unanimously awarded the Lenore Marshall/Nation poetry prize for *The Man with Night Sweats,* U.S. Poet Laureate Robert Pinsky described Gunn's talent as "distinctive genius—clear, direct but always with something in reserve, generous toward weakness, dryly deflating of cant, a purely focused flame of perception." *The Man with Night Sweats* was widely hailed for its deft treatment of the AIDS epidemic from the perspective of an insider in San Francisco's gay community. Born in England, Gunn moved to California in 1954 for a creative writing fellowship at Stanford University. Gunn studied under the well-known literary critic Yvor Winters, who once remarked that many of Gunn's early poems exist "on the narrow line between great writing and skillful journalism." Gunn continues this tradition in *The Man with Night Sweats,* a collection of poetry about friends he lost to AIDS. In an interview with Jim Powell, Gunn acknowledged this aspect of the book:

> It seems to me that one of my subjects is friendship, the value of friendship. It is a subject that has preoccupied me in recent years. This shows especially in *The Passages of Joy,* though nobody noticed it. Everybody noticed the gay poetry, but there are many poems about friendship in that book and a great many more in a new one that have to do with friendship, or imply it as a value, as indeed it is for me.

Passages of Joy, which was published ten years before *The Man with Night Sweats,* addresses homosexuality in an almost uncomplicated and celebratory way. Many of the first poems in *The Man with Night Sweats* similarly embrace physical pleasure and the power of seduction. The final poems, however, reflect how the AIDS crisis eclipsed earlier carefree days. In point of fact, they are pre-

> *Echoing his mentor, Yvor Winters, Gunn has defined poetry as 'a statement in words about a human experience ... with moral import.' "*

ceded by a dark epigram from Charles Hinkle: "Rain punishes the city, / like raw mind that batters flesh, / ever saddened by what fails." The title poem "The Man With Night Sweats," which is found within this final section, jars readers into the grim reality of the present. Through its opening stanza Gunn brings the reality of AIDS to the surface: "I wake up cold, I who / Prospered through dreams of heat / Wake to their residue, / Sweat, and a clinging sheet." Night sweats can be an indication of an AIDS infection even before a blood test identifies the disease. The resulting insidious sense of terror is seen throughout the poem and is ultimately encapsulated in the futility of the speaker's final gesture: "Stopped upright where I am / Hugging my body to me / As if to shield it from / The pains that will go through me, / As if hands were enough / To hold an avalanche off."

This visceral reaction creates a feeling of suffocation as the weight and implications of the disease inevitably descend. Living in San Francisco, Gunn saw the effect of AIDS firsthand. In the Powell interview, Gunn further elaborated on the impetus for writing these poems:

> ... if you're a writer and you have a lot of friends who suddenly die, then you're going to write about it. And then, one of the oldest subjects is how you face the end. One thing I've been greatly struck by in the people I've watched die is the extraordinary bravery with which people face death. So many of one's values—for humanist atheists like myself, as opposed to religious people—arise in confrontation with death.

One of the final poems in the collection *The Missing* reflects this desire to come to terms with loss; even the title suggests a lack of resolution, an absence of closure.

The speaker in "The Missing" watches "the progress of the plague," standing idly by, unable to take any action as the deadly disease spreads. By using the word "plague," Gunn summons the horror of the deadly bubonic plague in Europe. The speaker looks on as the disease begins to consume his friends who "fall sick, grow thin, and drop away" like withering vines and rotting vegetables. He also expresses his own vulnerability, questioning "Bared, is my shape less vague / Sharply exposed and with a sculpted skin?" Here the speaker implicitly questions the risk to his own statuesque "sculpted"—ostensibly robust and healthy—body.

Although Gunn has expressed cynicism about the phrase "gay community," AIDS shifted his perspective as he witnessed the interconnectedness of so many men. Appropriately, the next images in the poem suggest the human entanglement with an "increasing family" of victims: "Contact of friend led to another friend / Supple entwinement through the living mass / Which for all that I knew might have no end, / Image of an unlimited embrace."

The speaker feels a connection with those around him in an all-encompassing sense of humanity. In an interview with Clive Wilmer, Gunn explained the "Image of an unlimited embrace" as meaning "partly friends, partly sexual partners, partly even the vaguest of acquaintances, with the sense of being in some way part of a community." This sentiment extends into the next quatrain: "I do not just feel ease, though comfortable: / Aggressive as in some ideal of sport, / With ceaseless movement thrilling through the whole, / their push kept me as firm as their support." Quoting this stanza, Gunn elaborated: "Take that image of sport. (Somebody pointed out that I constantly use the word play in *The Man with Night Sweats,* which is—again—something I wasn't completely aware of.) If you use the idea of sport, you think of the violence of the push, yes, but there's an ambiguity: an embrace can be a wrestler's embrace or it can be the embrace of love. There's a tremendous doubleness in that image, which I have used elsewhere in fact: the idea of embrace which can be violent or tender. But if you look at it in any one moment, if it's frozen, it could be either, and maybe the two figures swaying in that embrace are not even quite sure which it is. Like Aufidius and Coriolanus [two Shakespearian enemies who bitterly join forces]: they embrace, they're enemies. They embrace in admiration at one point. It's ambiguous because the two things are connected. It could turn, at any moment, from the one to the other, I suppose." Inasmuch as Coriolanus died as a result of joining forces with Aufidius, this allusion deeply complicates the poem with a sense of great ambivalence.

The final three stanzas underscore the speaker's fear, exacerbated by having seen his friends die. Ironically, he claims "Their deaths have left me less defined," as if to say that because he lacks the finality of death, he is not clear about his place in life. He now lacks the "pulsing presence" of friends which gave his life definition, as if he could define his own existence through the lives of these lost friends; without them, he feels "unsupported."

The statue imagery that runs throughout the poem is further emphasized in these lines: "Eyes glaring from raw marble, in a pose / Languorously part buried in the block, / Shins perfect and no calves, as if I froze / Between potential and a finished work." It is not entirely clear whose eyes are glaring. The image calls to mind the speaker surrounded by the corpses of his friends who were robbed of their potential in life and became untimely "finished work." Yet, the image could also refer to the speaker, as a self-conscious reflection of his own eyes glaring from his perfect body. He feels part buried by the dead friends, frozen in a timeless hiatus between life and death.

The final stanza, however, returns readers to the speaker's fears and sense of powerlessness: "Abandoned incomplete, shape of a shape, / In which exact detail shows to more strange, / Trapped in unwholeness, I find no escape / Back to the play of constant give and change." Deserted by friends, lovers, and acquaintances, his entire being is permeated with the sense of being unfinished, and lacking the grounding to be complete. Defenseless, he has no hope of flight from his predicament and will be continually subjected to the random ebb and flow of life. "The Missing" is a statement of loss, not only of friends, but also of one's sense of self-definition—all caused by the epidemic we have come to know as AIDS. By the end of the poem, it becomes apparent that what seemingly began as a kind of elegy for lost friends, has evolved into a self-absorbed statement of personal loss. In one sense, the speaker mourns the passing of his friends, not for the loss of their lives, but for the void which he now feels.

Like all of Gunn's poetry, "The Missing" is technically masterful. Influenced by great poets such as John Donne and Basil Bunting, many of the poems in *The Man with Night Sweats* are written in traditional forms, cross-rhymed pentameter quatrains and pentameter couplets. Save one exception, the seven quatrains in "The Missing" are pleasingly iambic, flowing from line to line with

great ease. The one line with an extra beat, "I do not just feel ease, though comfortable" seems like a calculated attempt to create a subtle underlying feeling of uncomfortableness, a nagging addition to underscore the speaker's agitation. When asked by Powell if he "can think in rhyme" Gunn responded: "I suppose there are times when it's easy and so you could say that I'm moving comfortably within the form, but those times are extremely rare. What I find more to the point is that in looking for rhyme, or in trying to get the meter right, you are often having to delve deeper into your subject so that you discover things about it, your reaction to it, that you didn't know before … As you get more desperate, you actually start to think more deeply about the subject in hand, so that rhyme turns out to be a method of thematic exploration."

Echoing his mentor, Yvor Winters, Gunn has defined poetry as "a statement in words about a human experience … with moral import." He even went so far as to say that in poems like "The Missing," he makes "moral evaluations of a life that many people would consider totally immoral." Indeed, this is yet another example of the way in which Gunn's poetry provokes readers to reflect on their sense of humanity and the interconnectedness of all of human life.

Source: Marisa Pagnattaro, in an essay for *Poetry for Students,* Gale, 2000.

Sources

Bold, Alan, *Gunn & Hughes: Thom Gunn and Ted Hughes,* New York: Barnes and Noble Books, 1976.

Brown, Merle E., *Double Lyric: Divisiveness and Communal Creativity in Recent English Poetry,* New York: Columbia University Press, 1983.

Cole, Henri, "Sketches of the Great Epidemic," in *The Nation,* September 7, 1992, pp. 221-23.

Contemporary Literary Criticism, Vol. 81, Detroit: Gale, 1994.

Contemporary Poets, 6th ed., Detroit: St. James, 1996.

Corn, Alfred, "Review of The Man with Night Sweats," in *Poetry,* February, 1993, pp. 291-95.

Gunn, Thom. "My Life Up to Now," in *The Occasions of Poetry: Essays in Criticism and Autobiography,* London: Faber and Faber, 1982.

Haughton, Hugh, "An Unlimited Embrace," in *The Times Literary Supplement,* May 1, 1992, pp. 12-13.

Landau, Deborah. "How to Live, What to Do: The Poetics and Politics of AIDS," in *American Literature,* Vol. 68, No. 1, March, 1996, pp. 193-225.

Logan, William, "Angels, Voyeurs, and Cooks," in *The New York Times Book Review,* November 15, 1992, pp. 15-16.

Pinsky, Robert, "The Lenore Marshall/'Nation' Poetry Prize-1993," in *The Nation,* December 6, 1993, pp. 701-02.

Powell, Jim, "An Anglo-American Poet," Interview by the author, in *PN Review,* Vol. 70, 1989, reprinted in *Shelf Life: Essays, Memoirs and an Interview,* London: Faber and Faber, 1993.

Scammell, William, "Not Quite Concentrating into Passion," in *The Spectator,* March 7, 1992, p. 32.

Wilmer, Clive, "Thom Gunn: The Art of Poetry LXXII," interview by the author, in *Paris Review,* Vol. 37, No. 135, Summer, 1995.

Winters, Yvor, "Early Gunn," in *Forms of Discovery: Critical and Historical Essays on the Forms of the Short Poem in English,* Chicago: Swallow, 1967.

Wood, Michael, "Outside the Shady Octopus Saloon," in *The New York Review of Books,* May 27, 1993, pp. 32-34.

For Further Study

Bold, Alan, *Gunn & Hughes: Thom Gunn and Ted Hughes,* New York: Barnes and Noble Books, 1976.

> Thom Gunn and Ted Hughes first established a foothold in 1950s England, and this study offers a thoughtful review of each poet's aesthetic origins and the themes that preoccupied the writers in their earliest works. Although the focus on Hughes will be of less value to the reader interested in a deeper appreciation of Gunn, Bold's volume nonetheless presents the similar and increasingly divergent currents present in their subsequent works. Long considered an expatriate living and writing in the West Coast, Gunn's debt to the long British literary tradition from which he arose is presented here, firmly placing him as an inheritor of and rebel to that legacy.

Dyson, A. E., ed., *Three Contemporary Poets: Thomas Gunn, Ted Hughes, and R. S. Thomas,* London: Macmillan, 1990.

> Another study considering the work of Ted Hughes (and the lesser-known R. S. Thomas), the essays here present Thom Gunn within the context of his British contemporaries. These writers are viewed as important transitional figures with a foot in both the formalist tradition and the somewhat wilder freedoms of what is loosely labeled "contemporary poetry." Sometimes these competing influences imbue Gunn's poetry with an unresolved tension. Most often, though, the synthesis results in poetry that is bold and utterly new.

Woods, Gregory, *Articulate Flesh: Male Homoeroticism in Modern Poetry,* New Haven, CT: Yale University Press, 1987.

> Woods's study takes as its point of departure the fact that gay men have been among the seminal figures of modern poetry. Thus, homoeroticism is a recurring, if often overlooked, theme. This thoughtful survey remedies this, identifying themes of homoeroticism that have been present in literature since its inception but focusing particularly on the amplified presence of homosexual themes in contemporary literature.

Old Ironsides

Oliver Wendell Holmes

1830

In 1830, the U.S. Navy made plans to scrap the 44-gun frigate *Constitution,* the nation's most celebrated warship. Launched in 1797, "Old Ironsides" had earned her nickname during the War of 1812, defeating a number of fabled British vessels including the HMS *Guerièrre.* Though the war as a whole ended indecisively, from it the young republic drew many symbols of its recent independence. One such symbol was "The Star Spangled Banner," written in 1814 to memorialize the shelling of Fort McHenry. Another symbol profound to many Americans was the *Constitution* itself, which represented the nation's freedom on the seas, an issue that had initially sparked the conflict with the British. When the young Holmes read a Boston newspaper account of the proposed dismantling of the *Constitution* in 1830, he penned "Old Ironsides," a sentimental poem remembered mostly for its role in saving the frigate from decommission. In the poem, Holmes offers emotional reminiscences of the ship's past glory, of her deck "red with heroes' blood" and of her "victor's tread." In the last stanza, which makes the leap to the universal theme of death, Holmes insists that the frigate's most fitting grave is "beneath the waves," that she should be given "to the god of storms" rather than suffer the ignoble fate of the scrapheap. Although the present-day reader might find the poem's patriotic tone a bit maudlin, "Old Ironsides" still provides a good example of poetry's ability to sway public sentiment: the *Constitution* was preserved in 1830 and again several

Oliver Wendell Holmes

times subsequently, and today students of poetry and history alike can find her docked just north of Boston, the U.S. Navy's oldest commissioned vessel.

Author Biography

Holmes was born August 29, 1809, in Cambridge, Massachusetts. He graduated from Harvard in 1830, and after a year spent studying law, decided to follow his wishes and pursue a career in medicine. He went to France to study at the Ecole de Medicine in Paris, considered one of the finest medical schools of its day. Holmes returned to the United States in 1835 and the following year received his medical degree from the Harvard Medical School. On June 15, 1840 he married Amelia Jackson and established a practice in Boston. During this time he was also a prolific writer of medical essays, a researcher, a professor at Harvard, a practicing physician, and a poet.

Holmes also became a member of the intellectual elite of Boston society, a group known as the Boston Brahmins, which included Ralph Waldo Emerson, James Russell Lowell, and Henry Wadsworth Longfellow, among others. Holmes named the new literary magazine Lowell was to

edit *Atlantic Monthly,* and in the magazine's debut issue, Holmes published the first installment of the series of essays that would establish him as the dominant force in intellectual life in Boston and Cambridge: *The Autocrat of the Breakfast-Table.* The series was published as a book to critical and popular success in 1858 and was followed by *The Professor at the Breakfast-Table* in 1860.

Holmes's first novel, *Elsie Venner,* was published in 1861. Although initially compared favorably to Hawthorne's *The House of the Seven Gables,* Holmes's novels failed to achieve the critical or popular success of his essays and poetry. Throughout his career, Holmes fought for the humane treatment of the insane and the criminal, arguing that, contrary to Calvinistic belief that the mentally disturbed were evil, they suffered from a medical condition. After Holmes retired from his medical practice in 1882, he continued to write until his death at his Boston home on October 7, 1894.

Poem Text

Ay, tear her tattered ensign down!
    Long has it waved on high,
And many an eye has danced to see
    That banner in the sky;
Beneath it rung the battle shout,   5
    And burst the cannon's roar;—
The meteor of the ocean air
    Shall sweep the clouds no more!

Her deck, once red with heroes' blood,
    Where knelt the vanquished foe,   10
When winds were hurrying o'er the flood,
    And waves were white below,
No more shall feel the victor's tread,
    Or know the conquered knee;—
The harpies of the shore shall pluck   15
    The eagle of the sea!

O better that her shattered hulk
    Should sink beneath the wave;
Her thunders shook the mighty deep,
    And there should be her grave;   20
Nail to the mast her holy flag,
    Set every threadbare sail,
And give her to the god of storms,
    The lightning and the gale!

Poem Summary

Lines 1-4:

The first stanza meditates on the ship's "ensign," or the naval flag that flies upon its mast, as a symbol of the *Constitution* herself. Though not invented by Holmes, "Old Ironsides" is a metaphorical nickname—ironclad vessels did not come into use until the Civil War—and like the "tattered" flag, the ship has survived much adversity. Also like the flag ("Long has it waved on high"), the ship occupies a lofty position—not physically, of course, but in the imagination. Because of its role in history, the *Constitution* is in the national consciousness a symbol for the "higher" virtues for which the republic is thought to stand. One such virtue is freedom, and in the early days of the United States the concept of freedom was closely associated with the two wars against Britain. Thus the ship is an important symbol to the many Americans whose eyes have "danced to that banner in the sky."

Lines 5-8:

In lines 5 and 6 the flag aloft is contrasted with sounds of battle below. These sounds are conveyed through the use of alliteration, or the repetition of initial consonant sounds as in "beneath," "battle" and "burst." By using this sonic device, Holmes appeals directly to the senses, helping the reader not only to understand but to feel the contrast between the symbolically significant flag and the visceral reality of those battles that helped preserve the nation. Having done this, Holmes appeals to the reader's emotions, lamenting the passing of the symbol: the flag "shall sweep the clouds no more!"

Lines 9-16:

Again note the alliteration in lines 11 and 12. As in the first stanza, the device is used here to convey the sounds and feel of the sea: the "winds" and the "waves … white below." But while in the first stanza the poet employs sound to enhance a philosophical contrast, in these lines the intent of both sound and image is primarily emotional. The images presented are highly romanticized—the "heroes' blood," the "vanquished knee," the "victor's tread"—and their appeal is directly to the reader's patriotic heart. Philosophy here barely invades the domain of sentimentality and only in the most simplistic way: Holmes compares a past full of glory with a future in which that glory will be "no more." Finally, the poet takes direct and emotional aim at those officials behind the proposed scrapping of the *Constitution,* calling them "harpies of the shore," (foul malevolent creatures from Greek mythology that are part women and part bird) who wish to "pluck the eagle of the sea." Since the eagle was at that time and is still a sym-

Media Adaptations

- Spoken Arts has produced an audiocassette entitled *Anthology of 19th Century American Poets* (1989).

- Imperial Productions has produced an audiocassette entitled *Oliver Wendell Holmes* (1965).

- Caedmon has produced a record album entitled *Three Hundred Years of Great American Poetry, from Anne Bradstreet through Stephen Crane* (1962).

- Encyclopedia Britannica Films has produced a 16mm film entitled *Oliver Wendell Holmes* (1950).

- Encyclopedia Britannica Films has produced a filmstrip entitled *American Authors* (1958).

bol of the United States, and since to "pluck" a bird is to rob it of its grandeur, the implication of lines 9 and 10 is that those who want to dismantle the *Constitution* are in fact unpatriotic. This is intended to raise the reader's indignation as well as to give that indignation a specific target.

Lines 17-24:

In these lines the poem takes a romantic twist. Rather than suggest that "Old Ironsides" be preserved, as the reader might expect, Holmes proposes that a fitting "grave" for the ship is the sea itself, the "mighty deep" that the *Constitution's* "thunder shook." In this manner the poem takes on a more universal theme: since death is inevitable, it is better to die as one lived rather than to have life prolonged by artificial or unnatural means. This philosophy seems to have reached beyond Holmes's poetry: as a noted physician and medical essayist, he later opposed the overuse of drugs to keep patients alive and advocated letting nature run its course. In the final lines, the poem shifts to the imperative and takes on a spiritual resonance. Holmes commands the reader to "nail to the mast her holy flag" and to "give her to the god of storms." The implication is that the manner of

Topics for Further Study

- Think of an object that you are familiar with and try to write a poem about its history. Mention the people who have used it, the events it has been part of, and its significance in society.

- Click on to the *Constitution*'s web site at www.ussconstitution.navy.mil and find some event in the ship's history that interests you. Then report on that event and on other things that were going on in the United States at the same time.

- What happens to ships that are decommissioned today? Make a chart showing which ships go where, and where their various components go when they are scrapped.

- Why does the speaker think this ship would be better off sinking? Point to specific images from the poem that support his idea that destruction is better than decommissioning for a warship.

death, like the manner in which we live life, is a combination of divine intent and free will, the former demanding faith but the latter requiring action.

Themes

Pride

For the most part, this poem evokes pride by evoking battle imagery, which is fitting because it was in battle that the *Constitution* distinguished itself. The images, even the ones that are drawn from nature, are loud and fierce: "the battle shout," "the cannon's roar," "her thunders shook," and of course "the lightning and the gale." All of this activity sets the reader's heart to racing, as it is commonly said pride does. The second stanza in particular describes the situation in terms of winners and losers: the heroes and the victor, the vanquished and the conquered. Absent here is a sense of the complex causes of the War of 1812 or the compromises that

were made to secure peace, which would weaken the sense of pride by making the ship's military victories seem less necessary. The pride this poem attaches to the *Constitution* is based in reality, but it is attained by ignoring details and by heightening sensory associations.

Permanence

This poem is a lament for the battleship *U.S.S. Constitution,* which was faced with fading from public memory after being dismantled. As such, it is also a warning about the changes in values that the author perceived had made the *Constitution*'s destruction possible. The ship is associated in this poem with images of strength and courage: not just the abstract sensory images like the "cannon's roar" and the waving of the tattered flag, but specifically such ideals as "the hero's blood" and "the victor's tread" and the deck "where knelt the vanquished foe." According to the poem, all of the glory that is thought of with the ship is about to be replaced by its opposite: cowardice, pettiness and weakness, represented by "the harpies of the shore." Certainly, the decision to retire the *Constitution* was a financial one; the Navy would not throw away equipment that still could be used. Holmes's point is that, while the ship's financial value may have faded, its emotional worth is permanent. Another poem might have concentrated on the ship's history as part of the ongoing growth of the country, or on the use that was to be made of the timbers when it was broken up, giving life to new ships, rather than raising the fear that all it had stood for would be obliterated once the ship itself was gone. America was a relatively new country at the time, not yet fifty years old. Not only was it necessary for Americans to grab ahold of what proud traditions they could find, but it was also easy to believe that great and heroic achievements could slip away and be lost to history if people neglected the tangible symbols of those achievements. Similar fears exist throughout history, including today, as people wonder what aspects of human nature will fade away with the rise of each new generation.

Apathy and Passivity

Holmes takes an ironic stance in this poem, stating a position with his words that is clearly the opposite of how he feels. When he says, "Ay, tear her tattered insignia down!" what he really means is that it should continue to fly, just as he suggests sinking the ship when his true desire is to save it. Using this approach, he was able to stir readers out of their apathy regarding the ship's destruction and let them see their own lack of will reflected in the his attitude. In modern, post-Freudian times, we have come to call this technique "reverse psychology": manipulating someone to agree with your position by pretending to want the opposite. In "Old Ironsides," Holmes plays off of the passivity of the general public in two ways. By claiming so fervently that the *Constitution* should not only be decommissioned but should be dumped out into the middle of the ocean, he stirs any emotions for the old ship that might still remain within people who had forgotten how much they cared. By using vibrant, thundering imagery, he raised the sense of excitement that the passive public had allowed to fade away over years of peacetime. The issue is cast as a struggle between the villainy of the land-bound harpies of the shore and the heroism that is represented by the eagle of the sea. By taking the stance that all is lost, that they might as well give in to the forces of cowardice, Holmes was able to make his audience approach the idea of saving the *Constitution* as if they had thought of it themselves.

Freedom

Because the *Constitution* was successfully used to battle the British, who had held America as a colonial subject until the War of Independence, it naturally became a powerful symbol of the nation's freedom. Oliver Wendell Holmes built upon this association by using images in the poem that suggest freedom, particularly images of flight. He draws readers' attention skyward from the very first line, with the mention of the ship's flag, "That banner in the sky." The *Constitution* is then compared to a meteor that sweeps through the clouds and to an "eagle of the sea." In the last stanza the poem favors cutting the ship loose and setting it to sink to the bottom of the ocean rather than reusing what can be salvaged of it, presenting this as a more dignified ending for something that has stood for freedom.

Style

"Old Ironsides" is written in three, eight-line stanzas, but each stanza really consists of two quatrains (four-line units of verse) consisting of alternating tetrameter and trimeter lines. This means that each first and third line has four stressed syllables, or beats, while each second and fourth line has three stressed syllables. Quatrains written in this manner are called ballad stanzas. Since ballads often ad-

dress heroic and romantic themes, Holmes may have chosen this form to capture the reader's emotions.

The dominant meter of the poem is iambic, which means the poem's lines are constructed in two-syllable segments, called iambs, in which the first syllable is unstressed and the second is stressed. If we divide the iambs from one another and mark the unstressed and stressed syllables in line 6, for example, it appears like this:

Andburst / thecan / non'sroar;—

The reader will notice the emphasis on the stressed syllables. This pattern exists most regularly in the trimeter lines of the poem, lines which most often finish the thoughts begun in the tetrameter lines. This regularity serves to emphasize every other line, giving the poem a forceful as well as a musical feel.

Historical Context

The War of 1812

This poem is about the battleship *U.S.S. Constitution,* which became a symbol of American pride when it was triumphant over the ships of the British fleet during the War of 1812. In a sense, the conclusion of the War of 1812 represented the true moment of independence from Britain for the new country, because it settled issues and lingering grievances that had been left incomplete at the end of the Revolutionary War. When that war ended in 1783, Americans distrusted the British and the British disliked the Americans, as would be expected after any violent separation. The two countries had mutual financial interests, though, especially in the West Indies of the Caribbean Sea, which were close to the United States but were still British colonies. Upper Canada was a British colony as well, and from there the British supplied Native Americans with goods and weapons with which to fight Americans on their own land. By 1793, Britain was at war again, this time with France. During this war America remained neutral, even though France had been a valued ally during the Revolution, and as a result of this neutrality and the strife in Europe the new nation was able to prosper greatly. Hostilities against Britain were cooled in 1794 by a treaty negotiated by Supreme Court Justice John Jay. Hostilities between France and England ended briefly in 1801, but when they resumed on 1803 the British were not willing to let

Compare & Contrast

- **1830:** The *U.S.S. Constitution* is mentioned in a newspaper article as one being considered for decommission, having served the for over thirty years.

  Today: The *Constitution* has been preserved for the last 170 years, thanks to Holmes's poem, and is on view at the Boston Navy Yard.

- **1830:** At the site of Fort Dearborn, on the shore of Lake Michigan, the town of Chicago is planned.

  Today: Chicago has three million people and is the country's third largest city. It was the second largest from the end of the nineteenth century until the 1990 census, when Los Angeles overtook it.

- **1830:** The trip from Boston to New York takes thirty-six hours by steamboat and stage.

  Today: The trip from Boston to New York takes less than an hour-and-a-half by airplane, but travel time to and from major metropolitan airports can double or triple that time.

- **1830:** Illustrator John James Audubon publishes the first edition of his book of paintings, *Birds of America.*

  Today: The organization named in honor of John James Audubon, The Audubon Society, is one of the preeminent conservation societies in America.

- **1830:** President Andrew Jackson signs the Indian Removal Act, authorizing the general displacement of Indian populations to the west of the Mississippi River.

  Today: Most Americans now find Jackson's anti-Indian policies a source of national shame, although these policies were popular in their day.

- **1830:** The Church of Jesus Christ of Latter-Day Saints is founded by twenty-six-year-old Joseph Smith. Smith explains that the *Book of Mormon,* which is the basis of the church, has been written on golden tablets buried near where he lives in Palmyra, NY, and been translated for him by an angel named Moroni.

  Today: With almost five million members, the Mormon church is among the most influential in America.

American ships trade with France. British ships boarded American ships regularly, at gunpoint when necessary, to make sure that they were carrying no supplies that the French could use in the war. The British naval fleet was understaffed because many sailors had walked away from their military duty to prosper on American trading vessels. To get their truant sailors back, the British boarded American merchant ships and took back British sailors, even if they had become naturalized American citizens. These outrages on the seas, in addition to the hostilities along the Canadian border, led to the outbreak of war in 1812. When Britain refused to end their blockade of Europe, war broke out.

The war did not go well for America at first. A U.S. invasion of Montreal was thwarted, and the British took Detroit. The British Royal Navy blockaded the eastern seaboard, displaying naval superiority, although some individual ships, such as the Constitution, were victorious, giving Americans cause for hope. By 1814, the Americans were doing their best to hold off the British, when Napoleon's army was defeated at Waterloo, freeing more British troops to fight the American war. Washington D.C. was conquered, and many government buildings, including the White House, were burned. When peace talks began in 1814, both sides came to the negotiations with unrealistically high expectations. The Americans wanted Britain to give up the Canadian territory, while Britain wanted an independent state for Native Americans between the United States and Canadian borders. Finally, peace was achieved when both sides agreed to go back to the provisions that were agreed upon with the Treaty of Paris, which had ended the Revolutionary War in 1783.

America in 1830

Oliver Wendell Holmes was a member of upper Boston society, which was referred to as the Boston Brahmins (the word denotes the highest caste in the rigid Hindu social structure). At the time, the country had fewer than thirteen million citizens. The population was concentrated along the Eastern Seaboard, where three-fourths of the citizens lived—the area west of the Appalachian Mountains had some settlements and a few large cities, but those were considered the frontier. Progress into the wide-open heart of the country had come from the south and from New England. New Orleans, for instance, had a population of 46,000, and Cincinnati had 24,000, while Chicago, later to be the country's second largest population, was just a wilderness outpost. By comparison, the country's largest city, New York, had 200,000 citizens, and Holmes's Boston, relatively small for an established eastern city, had 60,000. Most of the country's population lived on farms, taking advantage of the fertile soil and open space available in the relatively new country, on land that they or their parents had settled.

In the election of 1828, the country favored Andrew Jackson, a populist with a reputation for being a man of the people. Jackson was one of the few heroes to emerge from the War of 1812, having won an important victory against the British in the Battle of New Orleans. Nicknamed "Old Hickory," he was the first president to come from beyond the New England states, and his election was a sign of the country's bold, strong, brave self-image, which is evident in "Old Ironsides." Despite his image as an outsider to the political establishment, Jackson actually did little that was helpful to the common people. He increased his power as President by initiating the policy of appointing political supporters to his Cabinet and he opposed the rights that states claimed to hold independently of federal law: when South Carolina threatened to refuse to pay several federal tariffs, Jackson was prepared to send federal troops to collect the money before a new compromise measure was drawn up. In addition, Jackson was brutal with the Native Americans who stood in the way of the United States' expansion. During the War of 1812 he had wiped out the Upper Creek and had forced the Creek to give up twenty three million acres of land to the government; after the war he led raids against

the Seminole; as President, he ignored a Supreme Court ruling that prohibited moving the Cherokee off of their land in Georgia. Eventually, his administration was responsible for resettling almost all of the indigenous tribes to west of the Mississippi River. Through all of this, Jackson maintained his image as a man of the people, and he easily won re-election in 1832.

Critical Overview

"Old Ironsides" was first published in 1836 in *Poems*. The volume, Holmes's first, earned the young poet a reputation as a humorist, but critics also noticed what several termed the "manly sentiment" of his more serious poems. "He knows how to be sentimental without silliness, and vigorous without violence," an anonymous reviewer commented in *The Yale Literary Magazine* in 1837. The reviewer notes that Holmes avoids the "sin" of clever writers: "a disposition to run as near to mawkishness as possible without falling into it." On the contrary, the reviewer gently accuses Holmes of failing to exploit the more serious side of his vision. If anything, the reviewer suggests, "there is too little sentimentality; and we could wish he had allowed himself more latitude where he shows himself most capable." Another anonymous critic, writing in a 1837 volume of *The North American Review,* remarks upon the "easy and natural flow" of Holmes's lyrics. Discussing "Old Ironsides," the critic says that "the strain upon the plan by the Navy Department for breaking up the Frigate *Constitution,* an unhappy suggestion of some one who was probably more familiar with national shipyards than national feelings, will rank among the best martial songs of England."

Criticism

David Kelly

David Kelly is an instructor of literature and writing at several community colleges in Illinois, as well as a fiction writer and playwright. Here, he examines the unique qualities of "Old Ironsides" and why the poem cannot be judged by ordinary poetic standards.

Given that there does not seem to be anything tricky or complex about Oliver Wendell Holmes's

What Do I Read Next?

- *Around the World in Old Ironsides: The Voyage of U.S.S. Constitution, 1844-1846* is an illustrate and meticulously researched book published by the Norfolk County Historical Society, in 1993, to commemorate the voyage.

- The authoritative source for all of Holmes's poetry is *The Complete Poetical Works of Oliver Wendell Holmes,* published in a hardcover edition by Cambridge Press in 1992.

- Holmes was at least as well-known for his essays as his poetry. Soon after "Old Ironsides" catapulted him to fame, he wrote two columns for *New England Magazine* called "The Autocrat at the Breakfast Table." He used that title for his regular column in *The Atlantic* twenty-five years later. The light-hearted columns collected in the book *The Autocrat of the Breakfast Table* (originally published in 1858) represent some of his best writing.

- One of the most notable biographies of the poet is Eleanor M. Tilton's *Amiable Autocrat: A Biography of Dr. Oliver Wendell Holmes,* published by Schuman in 1947.

---

love poem to an old battle ship, it hardly makes sense that "Old Ironsides" has lasted as long as it has in the standard corpus of American literary classics. However, the poem (as well as the ship that is its focus) has proven to be indestructible. This is unique. It upsets all expectations of how things generally go. It isn't a very good poem by conventional measures, nor is the ship useful, and yet both have stayed with us, capturing the imaginations of new audiences year after year. We are left to reconsider what it is that a poem should do, what a war vessel is good for, and why these two have been able to survive nearly two centuries when anything similar has long since passed from anyone's concern.

When Holmes wrote this poem, the *Constitution* was old, not necessarily ready to be taken out of commission but being considered for it, along with most of the navy's other ships. It may well have been of more use to the country's defense for the timbers that would have been salvaged from it (no, it did not actually have iron sides). If it had any further use as a fighting vessel, its days were certainly numbered, having had a good long run for a wooden battleship and having taken on its share of enemy fire and navigation accidents. The Naval board that planned to decommission the *Constitution* certainly had no idea that any sort of controversy would arise from it. Every tool becomes obsolete eventually.

Historical preservation was not then and still is not a prominent trait of the American psyche. In this country we are resistant to giving too much attention to an object's historical significance, and are usually willing to consider the ways that preservation is not economically viable. Venerable buildings that serve for a time as a source of civic pride are often demolished, even in spite of opposing protests. New buildings are raised on the sites of old ones—this is close to the heart of the American way of thought. It is not necessarily the way in older countries, where history has taught the benefits of being aware of cultural heritage and buildings have survived, often refurbished when necessary, for a century or two or more. America's history is short, and was even more so during Holmes's childhood, and this country's strength is economic, not cultural. Leaving things the way they are impedes economic growth. There is no shame in this: The American character, based on the almost endless resources available for most of our history, has had a tradition of renewal, not reflection. And yet, even with these prevalent attitudes, the country has insisted on keeping the *Constitution,* now docked in Boston, even though it is more than a hundred and fifty years past its expiration date.

At the risk of sounding callous about a national treasure, one of the things that favors keeping the *Constitution* around is that it is relatively inexpensive. The ship has only been used for ceremonial purposes for the past hundred and fifty years, and has only been out on the open ocean once since the 1880s. It has been supported by private donations, such as the admission charge for boarding it or the fees for renting it for corporate functions, or the "Pennies" campaign in the 1920s that collected nearly $31,000 from schoolchildren around the nation for the ship's upkeep. Under a 1954 law, the Secretary of the Navy is authorized to use public funds to maintain the *Constitution* in her original condition, but not for active service. Still, the nation is not in need of the ship's raw materials, and the space that it takes to keep a boat dockside is minimal, and it can be moved to a less expensive place if necessary. Compared to the cost of maintaining a landmark building, which becomes a greater liability if the property it rests on increases in value, the cost to the Navy of keeping this ship are hardly noticeable.

Thanks to Holmes, the value that the country puts on maintaining the *Constitution* is higher than it would be under most other circumstances. This was a young country in 1830, with no Taj Mahal, no Parthenon, no sphinx to remind Americans of their national identity. The nation's sense of self was still developing. The defining characteristics were that America had fought its way free from the British twice, in the Revolution and in the War of 1812, and that it still had the "wilderness" of the land beyond the Mississippi to grow into. War and trailblazing and the conquering of indigenous people were rugged pursuits: it seems natural, from our perspective of this distance in time, that a symbol of military strength would strike the public's imagination as a good national emblem. Judging by the way that the general population responded to Holmes's poem "Old Ironsides"—it sped from local publication to newspapers across the country to privately-printed leaflets in little more than a week—it would seem that Americans were ready for a symbol of their country's greatness. Holmes's masterstroke was the fact that the *Constitution* captured the sense of independence from Europe so thoroughly.

The poem's success as a popular piece is therefore understandable—it was perfectly placed in time, coming along just when it was needed, earning the sort of widespread recognition that thousands of new ventures strive for every day, although the secret recipe only seems to come together for those who are not trying. As the story goes, Holmes, who was twenty-one at the time he wrote "Old Ironsides," did not think of himself as a serious artist, just a dabbler in clever verse, as were all well-bred college students of the time. He dashed the poem off the very afternoon that he heard the Navy was considering retiring the *Constitution,* and it was published in the Boston paper the next day. Though it is rare, it is believable that one could spontaneously capture the public mood in one quick burst of sincerity, that one young man could, with a little bit of skill but mostly with luck,

> *The ironic stance, too, is very well-handled, very appropriate for his purpose. It somehow manages to help readers take the prose seriously, dampening the more feverish excesses."*

channel the Zeitgeist of the time. What this story does not account for, though, is artistic integrity. It would be almost impossible to believe that the poem could have survived this long without it, though; if its only virtue were its timeliness, it would have been left behind decades ago, irrelevant as yesterday's news.

The poetic imagery Holmes used was certainly sound: "tattered ensign"; "meteor of the ocean air"; "the conquered knee"—he did a good, though not overwhelming, job of turning his ideas into tangible objects that readers could appreciate with their senses, and in that way created a more gripping experience than would have been yielded by simply tossing around high-minded ideas. The ironic stance, too, is very well-handled, very appropriate for his purpose. It somehow manages to help readers take the prose seriously, dampening the more feverish excesses. It is in the poem's rhythm and rhyme, though, where students of poetry generally part ways with the general public. The structure should be appropriate to the function, and this either is or isn't, depending on what you think the poem's function is intended to be.

If this is supposed to be a serious expression of the poet's rage and concern, then the tightness of the metered verse and the rigidity of the rhyme scheme trivializes that. It is difficult to reconcile heartfelt expression with slavish devotion to structure. Assuming that one's deepest personal feelings are specific and individualized, then writing about feelings within an unyielding pattern is like using a kit from the store marked "Individuality" to show what makes you unique. If, on the other hand, we think his goal was to write a poem for mass appeal, to bring the widest possible audience to his "cause" of rescuing the *Constitution* from demolition, then certainly a formulaic structure would be most fitting. When dealing with great numbers of people with different backgrounds and expectations, it would be best to use one innocuous, standardized form so as not to distract them from the message. The vast public is not trained in understanding poetic form and is most interested in content, so the best thing about the pattern Holmes uses is that one hardly has to think of it.

It is difficult to say that this is art. It is certainly hugely successful, stirring pride across different subcultures and generations, and in that respect we can call it an artistic performance. What's lacking is the personal element that we associate with artistic expression. The emotions in this poem probably are the ones that Oliver Wendell Holmes was feeling on that afternoon in 1830 when he sat down and wrote out "Old Ironsides," but they are the simple emotions of a young man angry at government incompetence. It would be a little pretentious to say that angry young men cannot create art from their emotions but we can at least wish for some careful display of the details, not just broad strokes of anger and patriotism. Still, the combination of the poem with the ship itself has proven to create a synergy of American pride that is greater than either of the two could separately, making a sort of performance art that goes beyond the media of either ship-building or poetry. We cannot judge the "Old Ironsides" phenomenon by any known standards because there has never been anything quite like it.

Source: David Kelly, in an essay for *Poetry for Students,* Gale, 2000.

Sources

"Holmes' Poems," in *The North American Review,* Vol. XLIV, No. 94, January, 1837, pp. 275-7.

"Poems," in *The Yale Literary Magazine,* Vol. II, No. 4, February, 1837, pp. 113-24.

Remini, Robert V., *The Revolutionary Age of Andrew Jackson,* New York: Harper & Rowe, 1976.

Turner, Frederick Jackson, *The United States, 1830-1850: The Nation and Its Sections,* Gloucester, MA: Peter Smith, 1958.

For Further Study

Hickey, Donald R. *The War of 1812: A Short History.* Chicago: University of Illinois Press, 1995.
    For students who are interested in the circumstances surrounding the *Constitution*'s claim to fame, this brief book packs in a clear and concise overview.

Horsman, Reginald. *The Causes of the War of 1812.* Philadelphia: University of Pennsylvania Press, 1962.
    Horsman's analysis of the age sets aside many myths and explains the true circumstances under which the *Constitution* earned its fame.

Psalm 8

King James Bible

A psalm is a sacred song, hymn, or poem; usually, the term is associated with the Book of Psalms, a book in the Bible containing 150 of these sacred works. Most of the psalms were originally believed to be written by David, the Hebrew king who lived around 970 B.C. Biblical scholars of recent centuries, however, have come to agree that the psalms are, at least in part, the work of many authors. The Old Testament of the King James Version of the Bible contains the most famous English translation of the psalms. Although the King James Version was finished in 1611, the original Hebrew psalm texts are thought to date between the thirteenth and the third centuries B.C. The predominant theme of the Book of Psalms is the expression of faith in God, but the individual poems have been classified into many forms, including hymns, laments, songs of confidence, and songs of thanksgiving.

"Psalm 8" is a hymn, or a song of praise. In it, the poet meditates upon the grandeur of the night sky and man's seeming insignificance in comparison with it. But the speaker's faith reminds him that man is made in God's image and is thus greater than the rest of God's natural creations. For this reason, man is given dominion over the natural world, but only at a price. Man's first and last thoughts, as they are in the psalm, must be of God. Without such faith, man would be humbled by nature into hopeless insignificance.

Poem Text

O Lord our Lord, how excellent is thy name in all
    the earth! who hast set thy glory above the
    heavens.
Out of the mouth of babes and sucklings hast thou
    ordained strength because of thine enemies,
    that thou mightest still the enemy and the
    avenger.

When I consider thy heavens, the work of thy
    fingers, the moon and the stars, which thou
    hast ordained;

What is man, that thou art mindful of him? and the
    son of man, that thou visitest him?

For thou hast made him a little lower than the   5
    angels, and hast crowned him with glory
    and honour.

Thou madest him to have dominion over the works
    of thy hands; thou hast put all things under
    his feet:

All sheep and oxen, yea, and the beasts of the
    field;

The fowl of the air, and the fish of the sea, and
    whatsoever passeth through the paths of the
    seas.

O Lord our Lord, how excellent is thy name in all
    the earth!

Poem Summary

Line 1:

The first and last verses of the psalm frame the rest, giving the congregation both a part to sing and a means of expressing the key ideas the psalm develops. Those ideas are God's glory and man's closeness to God. The latter is evident in the first line of the verse: The word "Lord" is from the Hebrew *Yahweh,* both a more sacred and a more intimate way of addressing God than *Elohim* (literally, "God"), which appears in other psalms. Though this may reflect the psalm's authorship (some biblical writers consistently chose one name for God over the other), it also expresses the genuine sentiment of the poem. God here is not a distant being, but one with whom man feels an intimate devotion.

When applied to God in the Old Testament, the word "glory" usually refers to God's visible manifestation to humans. The psalmist reflects on

Media Adaptations

- Dove Entertainment presents *The Book of Psalms* with Michael York on audio compact disk (1995).

- Modern Library/BBC Audio Books have produced the audiocassette entitled *The Book of Psalms and the Book of Proverbs: The Authorized Edition* (1996) with David Suchet and Hannah Gordon.

- Victory Technology has produced a CD-ROM entitled *Psalms: Book I* (1999) as part of the Bible Savers series.

- Treehaus Communications has produced a videocassette entitled *Psalms of Joy* (1986).

- Fresno Pacific University has produced an audio compact disc entitled *O Lord Our God, How Excellent Is Thy Name* (1999) with the Fresno Pacific University Concert Choir.

- Zondervan publishers have produced *The Old Testament from the New Revised Edition* as tape 23 of a 36 audiocassette set (1983).

- Caedmon has produced an audiocassette entitled *The Psalms and The Tale of David* (1956) with Dame Judith Anderson.

- Marty Goetz Ministries has produced an audiocassette entitled *Psalm Enchanted Evening* (1998) with Marty Goetz.

this idea in later verses of "Psalm 8," beholding God's creation (the "heavens" in verse 3) and perceiving God's infinite power. But the relationship between God and creation is clear from the outset of the poem: God is "above" everything in nature—even the heavens themselves.

Line 2:

The second verse expresses the belief that God's power is evident in the least as well as in the greatest of his creations. It also predicts the relationship between man and God described in the third and fourth verses. Just as man perceives God with awe, so "babes" look upon adults. Yet as children are created in the image of adults, so man is in the image of God. Even though they cannot understand the nature of adults, children still possess the same "ordained strength" God has instilled in his creations. Further, that strength is especially apparent because children, like nature, are innocent, as yet uncorrupted by the evil of "the enemy and the avenger." Adults' strength, the psalmist implies later, exists in a similar type of innocence. By experiencing his own humility in the face of the vast universe, man throws himself before God the way a child submits to the authority of adults.

Lines 3-4:

In the third and fourth verses the psalmist experiences what might be called in modern times an "existential crisis," but the cosmic uncertainty inspired by the heavens is hardly limited to modern humans. One might be reminded of the French philosopher Blaise Pascal's conclusion: "The eternal silence of these infinite spaces frightens me." Observing the night sky, the "moon and the stars," the speaker is forced to ask himself, "What is man?" The question suggests its own answer, one at which most people have arrived while looking into the stars. In comparison with the vast order of the cosmos, man seems finite and insignificant—so insignificant, in fact, that the psalmist wonders why God would trifle with such a creature. While the question is never directly answered in the poem, the moment of potential despair resolves itself through other natural observations. Man might seem small compared with the heavens, but he is large compared with the other creatures of earth. In this the psalmist takes faith that God is indeed "mindful" of man. Thus the heavens, which are an indication of God's "glory," are not so much daunting as they are an indication of the grace granted by God to man.

Lines 5-8:

The "glory" in verse 5 is a different type than that in verse 1, coming from a different Hebrew word. When applied to man in the Old Testament, glory usually means "importance," and in verses 5 through 8 the psalmist contrasts man's importance on earth with his seeming insignificance under the stars. Though he is "a little lower than the angels," man is dominant over the other "works of [God's] hands": the domestic and wild animals, the fish and fowl, and the seas themselves. This arrangement recalls the biblical creation story in which God grants man dominion over nature because man is

created in God's likeness. In this psalm, man's authority is symbolized by regal trappings: man is "crowned in glory and honor." But importantly, this authority is derived specifically from God. Unlike classical Greek thought, which suggests that man has dignity and authority unto himself, the Hebrew philosophy holds that man's value comes only through God. Why God has granted such value or even created man at all—"What is man?"—are questions the psalmist leaves unanswered.

Lines 19-20:

Note that the refrain, though a repetition of the first verse of the psalm, lacks the line "who hast set thy glory above the heavens." Some argue that this suggests the psalmist now puts earth above the heavens or considers the heavens less relevent. Another possibility is that the psalmist's meditation has eased his fear of the vastness of the cosmos, that he now wishes to acknowledge God's presence on earth and in man.

Themes

God and Religion

One of the main themes recurring throughout the Book of Psalms is God's awesome power. In this particular poem, the first stanza sings about God's greatness and glory. The praise does not continue unabated throughout the following lines, however. By the second line, the poem begins to balance the power of God against the power of God's enemies. It is significant that the power that God ordains, or decrees, in the world comes out of the mouths of humans. It would be impossible for God to have enemies who are more powerful than Himself, because God is omnipotent, but this poem accepts the enemies of God as those who could oppose Him by swaying humans' minds, by turning the human race against Him. God is therefore credited here with instilling humans with an innate sense of His glory, with a sense of him already within "babes and sucklings." The enemies of God are therefore thwarted by humans' worship of Him.

Casting God as a triumphant figure is less important to modern sensibilities than it would have been for the original audience of this psalm centuries ago. The God of the New Testament is characterized as a loving deity whose message is that humans should learn to live together with love, but the people this psalm was written for were more concerned with assuring their own safety against

Topics for Further Study

- Rewrite this poem as a business memo, explaining each point to your associates.

- Why do you think this psalm is addressed to God, who would presumably be aware of all of the accomplishments the writer ascribes to Him?

- Choose some of the marvels of the modern world that you would praise God for in a psalm that you would write. Make a collage, either with pictures or with recorded sounds, that puts these wonders on display.

- Compose a musical tune that you think would be appropriate for singing this psalm, and record your version.

---

aggression from their own enemies. Overall, Psalm 8 assures the support of God's omnipotent power for his people by offering Him the love of his people. For this reason, it is significant that the poem begins and ends with the phrase "How excellent is thy name … " This form of praise, in addition to the obvious recognition for God's countless achievements, stresses the fact that God is spoken well of by His people, that His name itself is revered. As stated in the first line, He is, to the singers of the psalm, to those who honor His name, "*our* Lord."

Nature and Its Meaning

In contemporary American thought we are used to viewing human accomplishment as a violation of nature, or at least as a contrast to it. One basic example of this sort of thinking is the way that products are considered better if they are made with natural ingredients instead of artificial ones. "Psalm 8" also makes a distinction between things that are natural and those that are made by humans, but instead of waxing nostalgic for some forgotten time long ago when humans did not dominate nature, this psalm glorifies human dominance. This may be seen as a reflection of the fact that this psalm was written at a time when humans did not control their physical world, or at least when our

ability to control our environment was still an open question. The more we have succeeded in fighting hunger, predators, and diseases, the more we have become conscious of what has been lost even as we have won, while the author or authors of "Psalm 8" would only have the struggle against nature's frightening vastness to consider. As a conscious being, the speaker of this poem considers humanity to be given a right to rule all of nature, a right given by the authority of God Himself. It not only records the situation at the time of its writing by mentioning man's right to rule over the animals that had already been domesticated, the "beasts of the field," it also claims rights over all of the creatures that humanity had not yet been able to control, the ones that still flew or swam freely. The psalm does not question whether it is God's will that humanity dominate the universe, but instead that right is assumed without further examination. Other religions may have developed with a consideration of nature, and Western civilization (which is strongly influenced by the Judeo-Christian tradition) only developed a widespread "back to nature" ethic within the last two centuries, as the Industrial Revolution has made humans' domination of nature complete.

Identity

This psalm represents humanity's continuing struggle to understand its significance, to see where it fits between the glorious achievements of God and the baseness of common life on Earth. The answer offered here is that humans are "a little lower than the angels" while still being "crowned" with "glory and honor." The poem conveys some of the psalmist's awe of the vast wonders which God put into place in the universe by leaving the thought addressed in line 3 as an incomplete thought, as if the facts themselves are so incredible that there is no way to finish the idea that is started: the line begins with "When I consider …," but this thought trails off without ever saying what the speaker does when considering. God's immense power, which is emphasized in the first half of the psalm, is connected to humans in line 4. The relationship may be thought of as slight—the relationship is that God thinks of humans—but it is presented as greatly significant that we get any of God's attention at all. Being thought of by God, the poem implies, must mean that humanity is itself significant. One interesting phrase from this section of the psalm is "the son of man" in line 4. This phrase is generally used to refer to Jesus Christ, although Biblical scholars estimate that the psalms were written five hundred to one thousand years before Christ's birth. The use of this phrase may reflect the influence of later translators, who used these words to fit the rest of Biblical history, or it may have been a forecast of Christ's coming, as is seen in many Old Testament writings.

While identifying humanity with God's greatness, this psalm also identifies humans with the Earthly animals. The questions in line 4 lead the poem forward into thoughts about the animals that God created to live in this world. Although humans are considered to "have dominion" over them, we still live among them, and are in some ways more like them than like God. Humanity can be identified as either God-like or animal-like, and this poem is a meditation on which part of the human identity is more significant. It concludes that the heavenly side dominates: humanity fits closely into line with God and the angels but hovers over the things of the Earth, like them but not really of them.

Style

"Psalm 8" consists of two distinct parts, each playing a precise liturgical role in the ritual in which the poem was meant to be sung. One part was intended to be sung by the entire gathering of worshipers, while the second part was intended to be sung by a soloist. This can be seen in the shift in point of view in the psalm: verses 1 and 9 are written in the first person plural ("O Lord *our* Lord"), but verse 3 is written in the first person singular ("When *I* consider thy heavens"). Also, the repetition in the first and ninth verses have led scholars to believe that these parts must have been sung collectively.

The verse is the basic unit of ancient Hebrew poetry. Each verse generally completes a thought or reflects on a single aspect of the poem. A chief poetic feature of the verse is rhythm. Though we do not know precisely how ancient Hebrew was pronounced, we can observe that the translated verses contain a rough pattern of stressed syllables. As an example of this, consider the following translated verse from the psalm. When the stressed and unstressed syllables are marked, the verse appears as follows:

Thefowlof theair, and thefish ofthe sea,
And whatso everpas seththroughthepaths of theseas

The reader must remember that the translations of the Psalms can give only an approximation of the original Hebrew rhythms and that tight scansion is often impossible. Still, the artful renderings of the King James Version of the Bible give a good idea of the sound of the original versions. It should also be noted that the rhythm of the verses is enhanced by the repetition of certain phrases. In other words, not only do the syllable stresses fall into a certain pattern, the words themselves repeat to create rhythmic sound. In the above example, the phrase "of the" appears three times in the verse, giving the passage a hypnotic sound that is somewhat like a chant.

Historical Context

Many of the Psalms of the Bible, including Psalm 8, are attributed to David, king of Judah and Israel, who ruled approximately three thousand years ago. David is revered as one of the greatest figures of the Old Testament and is often referred to in later books, which sometimes use the phrase "the House of David" to refer to the Jewish people as a whole and refer to the Messiah as the "Son of David." He was born to a poor rural family, but at an early age he became well-known for his courage and musical skills, and was asked to live in the household of the king of Israel, Saul I, and be his armor bearer. One of the best-known stories in Western history is young David's slaying of the giant Goliath, who was a member of the Philistine tribe that were the enemies of the Israelites. David grew up in Saul's court, became a close friend of Saul's son Jonathon, married Saul's daughter Michal, and led the Israelites to victory in wars against the Philistines. His successes made Saul jealous, though, and he was banished, spending his early adult years wandering the land, gaining the friendship and support of many people, eventually being made king of Hebron in 1000 B.C. After Saul's death David was able to use the army of Hebron and the good will he had gained to defeat Saul's son Ishbosheth and become king of Israel. He was a powerful military leader, leading the army to victory against the Philistines, Moabites, Aramaeans, Edomites, and Ammonites. He captured and built up the city of Jerusalem.

While David is remembered reverently for making Israel a powerful nation for centuries to come, he was also a flawed leader. During the procession that brought the Ark of the Covenant to the resting place he had made for it in Jerusalem, he danced openly and without inhibition, and his wife Michal complained about such vulgar behavior for

Compare & Contrast

- **1611:** English explorer Henry Hudson disappeared after sailing into the interior of the wilderness in the Northeast part of the continent, trying to find a passage into the interior. He only made it into a shallow strait before being icebound and then abandoned by mutineers who took over his ship.

  Today: Hudson's name is known across the globe because his name was given to the famous Hudson River, which borders New York City.

- **1611:** William Shakespeare, who died in 1616, was in the last phase of his career, creating complex, mature tragicomedies such as *Cymbeline, The Winter's Tale,* and *The Tempest.*

  Today: Shakespeare's reputation as a playwright has yet to be surpassed.

- **1611:** England's King James I is a supporter of the doctrine of the divine rights of kings. This doctrine maintains that royal personages had to answer to no one but God for their decisions.

  Today: The British royalty has only symbolic significance. Real political power is held by the elected Parliament. With their personal lives under scrutiny of the media, members of the British royal family are constantly the subject of ridicule.

- **1611:** The settlers of Jamestown, Virginia, the first permanent English settlement in America, tried to recover after the devastating winter of 1609-1610, referred to as the "Starving Time."

- **Today:** The hardships of the Jamestown Colony are remembered at Thanksgiving, when Americans celebrate the later time, in the 1620s, when the colony began producing bountiful harvests.

- **1611:** The Virginia colony started growing tobacco for the first time.

  Today: At almost six billion pounds produced annually, tobacco is such an important part of the American economy that the government is reluctant to regulate its production, even as associated health risks become evident.

God's chosen one. Also, one time he stayed home after sending his army into battle, and he became infatuated with Bathsheba, the wife of one of his soldiers; he had an affair with her, then ordered her husband into the front lines of battle, where he was killed almost immediately. After that, David's life fell apart. His daughter Tamar was raped by her half-brother Amnon, who was, in turn, killed by his half-brother Absalom. Absalom then went into exile, as David did, and when he returned he too raised a rebellion to take the throne of Israel. The rebellion did not succeed, but David's power over his kingdom diminished as he aged. In the end, the rest of his family abandoned him when he named Solomon, his son by Bathsheba, to follow him instead of his first-born son Adonijah.

Many historians have expressed doubts that David was the author of the Psalms that are ascribed to him. They consider the Psalms to be part of the Pseudepigrapha, which are writings in the Bible that were falsely credited to ancient authors. These historians point out that the phrase that is commonly translated from ancient Hebrew to say "A Psalm of David" may be wrongly translated, or misunderstood. The Hebrew part of speech *le,* which is commonly translated as "of," has many meanings, so that the phrase might better be translated as "a song in the manner of David." Or the authors of the Psalms may have given credit to David as a matter of reverence, to show their deference to his great reputation as the Old Testament's great musician.

There is no way of actually knowing who wrote the psalms that are in the Bible, or when they were written. The psalm form is tightly structured and clear-cut, so historians cannot guess much about a psalm's age from its style. Most of the Near Eastern literatures that we are aware of show some forms of psalms, some dated centuries before the events of David's time. It is clear that the writers of the Biblical psalms used imagery and phrases from other cultures. The Davidic Psalms (those thought to be written by David) may be the oldest, and may date to within a century or two of David's lifetime (he died circa 960 B.C.), although other psalms refer to events as late as 586 B.C.

The English translation of the Bible that is most well-know today is the Authorized Version that was translated by Bible authorities between 1604 and 1611 under the commission of King James I of England (it is commonly called the King James Version). Although Christianity had come to England in the Third Century A.D., the Bible had been available only in Latin until the 1300s, when Protestant reformer John Wycliffe set about translating it, to make it more widely available to people who read English. Over the next two hundred years, different versions were made, reflecting the decisions made by their translators and the sources that the translators used. The King James Bible reflects an attempt to standardize the language, and is noted for the success of its translators in capturing the poetic spirit as well as the meaning of the ancient scriptures. Several other translations have been made in the latter part of this century, attempting to give an accurate rendering of the original Hebrew and Greek languages in modern and easy-to-understand idiom: the Revised Standard Version (1952), the New American Standard Bible (1971-1977), and the New International Version (1978), for example.

Critical Overview

Many critics have commented on the relationships among man, God, and nature in "Psalm 8." Lynn Harold Hough argues that the psalm's depiction of man as sovereign over nature demonstrates a "humanism gloriously free from the tendency to sink into the life of the beast which is below man or to try to be the God who is above him." Hough writes that this psalm is an articulate example of a view of man "from which Old Testament writings never deviate." In his discussion of this psalm, John Patterson brings a scientific perspective to bear. Humans, he argues, have always been terrified by the seemingly infinite cosmos, but never more so than in modern times: "Has not the astronomer told us that he has searched the skies and finds no need of the 'God-hypothesis'?" Patterson contends that the psalmist took a more peaceful view toward the

stars. "They brought him comfort and blessing," he writes. "The stars spoke of divine greatness; they revealed God's majesty and power. They were the work of his fingers—and what fingerwork!" Finally, the psychoanalyst Erich Fromm writes about the final verse's omission of the phrase "Who hast set thy glory above the heavens." In the beginning of the psalm, he argues, the poet equates God's glory on earth and in heaven. "The psalm ends in the full confirmation on *this life* and man's strength on earth," Fromm writes. "The thought of heaven is eliminated in order to emphasize fully this earth, and man on it, is full of God's glory."

Criticism

Emily Archer

Emily Archer holds a Ph.D. in English from Georgia State University, has taught literature and poetry at several colleges, and has published essays, reviews, interviews, and poetry in numerous literary journals. In this essay, Emily Archer explores the implications for the way sacred texts are read, focusing on the Judaic commentaries known as midrash.

According to one Jewish creation story, when God resolved to create human beings on the sixth day, he sought the counsel of the angels before mixing the appropriate amounts of dust and breath. "The angels were not all of one opinion," says this legend from Louis Ginzberg's collection of *midrash.* The Angels of Love and Truth were at odds, as were the Angels of Peace and Justice. In the foreknowledge with which they are endowed in these stories, the angelic host are under no illusion that humankind's crown "of glory and honor" would be prone to slip and crack. Thus, some of the angels were less than enthusiastic, but managed to ask politely, "What is man, that Thou art mindful of him, and the son of man, that Thou visitest him?" Those, God could placate with a simple reply: "The fowl of the air and the fish of the sea, what were they created for? Of what avail a larder full of appetizing dainties, and no guest to enjoy them?" Other angels posed the question in jealous scorn: "What is man that Thou art mindful of him? And the son of man that Thou visitest him?!" To those, God's reply was swift and simple: he "stretched forth His little finger" and set them aflame. Raphael's band of angels took note of such a fate and wisely decided instead to affirm the

What Do I Read Next?

- Thomas Merton, one of the best-read writers on religious matters of this century, wrote a brief book in 1956 called *Praying the Psalms* that is still in print. It reflects Merton's thoughtful blend of Christianity with Zen Buddhism.

- Dover Thrift Editions published a copy of *The Book of Psalms* that is available for under one and a half dollars.

- Poet Stephen Mitchell translated fifty of the best-known psalms from their ancient Hebrew sources and published them under the title *A Book of Psalms* in 1994. His interpretations are graceful and enlightening.

- Gwendolyn Sims Warren's 1998 collection *Ev'ry Time I Feel the Spirit: 101 Best-Loved Psalms, Gospel Hymns and Spiritual Songs of the African-American Church* (published by Henry Holt) draws the connection from the Book of Psalms to contemporary religious music.

- *The Abbey Psalter: The Book of Psalms Used by the Trappist Monks of the Genesee Abbey* was published by the Paulist Press in 1981. It is a large, artistic book rendered in calligraphy.

- In 1997 Priests for Equality published a new translation of the Psalms, carefully avoiding wording that is biased against women. The result of their work is *The Inclusive Psalms*, offering a modern interpretation that is more in-tune with today's sensibilities.

- Hermann Gunkel, one of the twentieth century's most respected Biblical scholars, was working on his book about the Psalms at the time of his final illness in 1931, so he turned over his work to one of his students. The resulting work, *Introduction to Psalms: The Genres of the Religious Lyric of Israel* is available today with Gunkel, Joachim Begrich, and James D. Nogalski listed as authors.

- Nahum M. Sarna, Professor Emeritus of Biblical Studies at Brandeis University, examines the Psalms in perspective in his 1995 book *On the Book of Psalms: Exploring the Prayers of Ancient Israel.*

Almighty's plan: "Lord of the world, it is well that Thou has thought of creating man."

The original setting of "What is man … ?" is Psalm 8. The angels in this story have simply "borrowed" it to take their various stands on the proposed creation of human beings. In its text of origin, the question expresses David's humble wonder at his honorable place in the order of creation. In all its reverent playfulness with the Torah (the sacred Hebrew scriptures), the story from the *midrash* takes David's question "out of context" and puts it into the mouths of the angels. Re-imagined and re-located in this way, the question "What is man … ?" serves the rabbinic storyteller anew in his sacred purpose: to keep the story of God's covenant with creation alive through re-imaginations of the scriptures, through fresh interpretations of the relationship between humanity and divinity.

"What is man … ?" is a question as old as human consciousness itself, and has been asked, in various ways, in every time and place. In Psalm 8, the question and its answer belong "first" to the consciousness of the ancient Hebrew, to a Jewish cosmology, to the Torah and its commentaries. But the psalm portrays a cosmic beauty and a human dignity hard for other peoples and religions to resist. Christianity, for one, has "borrowed" not only Psalm 8, but the Hebrew Bible itself, calling it the Old Testament. Through its account of the appearance of Jesus Christ in history, the New Testament, as some Christians would say, "fulfills" or "completes" the Old. In Paul's letter to the Hebrews, one of the "epistles" of the New Testament, the words of Psalm 8 are borrowed outright to delineate the features of this new world and its Lord. The "one in a certain place" below is, of course, the poet

David, contemplating the starry sky of the Near East. But Paul suggests that David's words "testify" not simply to David's God, Yahweh, and his own wondrous present, but to the "new" Adam, Jesus Christ, and the age he would usher in:

> But one in a certain place testified, saying, What is man, that thou art mindful of him? Or the son of man, that thou visitest him? Thou madest him a little lower than the angels; thou crownedst him with glory and honor, and didst set him over the works of thy hands; Thou hast put all things in subjection under his feet. For in that he put all in subjection under him, he left nothing that is not put under him. But now we see not yet all things put under him. But we see Jesus, who was made a little lower than the angels for the suffering of death, crowned with glory and honor…. (Hebrews 2:5-9)

Once borrowed, no text stays the same. Words do new work in new settings. Christian theology and its world-view are heavily indebted to its Jewish roots, but the departures from Judaism are also profound, and too complex and extensive to begin to assess here.

The *midrash,* however, provides a glimpse into the way Jewish scriptural tradition has borrowed texts from itself, not necessarily with an eye toward "completing" anything; rather, to take a narrative detail, character, passage, or word in as many directions as Judaism's essential theology will allow. Both the poet of Psalm 8 and his words thus appear in other contexts worth examining, settings that help profile the shape of Jewish cosmology and bring interpretations within its own imaginative traditions into focus.

Midrash is a term for those commentaries on the Torah which flourished from the third to the twelfth centuries A. D., but which continue, in new and eclectic forms, to be created in the present day. In the early twentieth century, Louis Ginzberg collected *midrash* from its classical period and assembled them into four volumes called *The Legends of the Jews* (1909). Volume One begins with the creation, and Volume Four concludes with Esther and the return of the captivity. In her ongoing work with "visual theology," artist Jo Milgrom today describes *midrash* in her essay in *Parabola: Crossroads* as "both a method and a genre of literature in which imaginative interpretation discovers biblical meanings that are continually contemporary." The *midrash* are highly "intertextual," to use a recent term in literary criticism. Intertextuality is one way of describing what happens when texts speak with, gossip about, or otherwise refer to other texts. Sometimes the purpose is to enhance, embroider, elaborate, or fabulate a text; other times

> *But the context is now the whole of creation, rendering the 'enemy' more than natural or political. The enemy is cosmic. It is chaos, in its many guises. If Psalm 8 is essentially a praise for cosmic order, the enemy would therefore be anything that threatens a return to disorder and formlessness."*

to subvert, deny, expose, or make ironic. Thus, intertextuality is all about the dynamic relationships between, within, and among passages of writing.

The *midrash* displays all those rich possibilities. In their endless play upon the Torah, no one *midrashic* interpretation or legend is definitive, decisive, or "correct." No one rabbi, theologian, school, or sect has the final word. Jewish tradition believes that it takes every interpretation, in every place and time, to keep the sacred powers of the text alive. With every commentary or story comes fresh understanding of God's unfolding design both for the Jewish people in history and for creation. "Midrash is to the Bible what imagination is to knowledge," Jo Milgrom suggests. The Torah stands firm, but not static, at the center of the imaginative company of words that dance around it.

The impulse to perform *midrash* is as old as the Hebrew scriptures themselves. In fact, the Torah contains its own *midrash,* as one can clearly see in numerous instances of one passage of scriptural referring to another, and for a variety of purposes: to bolster the authority of a prophecy, to remind God of his help in the past in order to ask for a favor in the present, to borrow an image that elevates the beauty of a praise, or the poignancy of a lament. David's Psalm 8 is itself a kind of *midrash* on the creation story in the Book of Genesis. It comments on Genesis in poem form, condensing the ordered sequence of the creation described in the first chapter, day one through day six, into lyrical praise for the Creator and the whole design of the cosmos. "Like many lyric poems," says Robert Alter in *The Art of Biblical Poetry,* "[Psalm 8] is the complex realization of one moment of perception," as though the poet arrests time and perceives all the divinely ordained cosmos at once.

The writers of *midrash* capitalized on this strong connection between David the King who tended sheep, and Adam the "crown" and caretaker of creation. In fact, as one legend goes, in a measure David was indebted for his life to Adam. At first only three hours of existence had been allotted to him. When God caused all future generations to pass in review before Adam, he besought God to give David seventy of the thousand years destined for him. A deed of gift, signed by God and the angel Metatron, was drawn up. Seventy years were legally conveyed from Adam to David, and in accordance with Adam's wishes, beauty, dominion, and poetical gift went with them. Thus, in this story, not only do the animals pass in front of the first man to receive their names, but all future generations of human beings as well. This story attributes to Adam a power greater than that which the Torah's text explicitly states, but which it implicitly permits to the writer of *midrash.* In this expansion of his privilege and responsibility, Adam petitions God to grant the shepherd-king both longer life and those very gifts that made the writing of a poem such as Psalm 8 possible: "beauty, dominion, and poetical gift." As if in gratitude, not only to God, but to Adam, David writes a song in which beauty and dominion are the content, and in which poetical gift dictates the language and form.

But as that particular *midrash* proceeds, we learn that "Beauty and talent, Adam's gifts to David, did not shield their possessor against hardship." Legend complicates David's birth-status, rendering his father Jesse pious, but vulnerable to temptation. As a result of a series of deceptions, David is born the "supposed son of a slave," and therefore consigned to the lowly, lonely position of tending Jesse's sheep in the desert. There in the wilderness, David proves not only his intelligence in shepherding, but his physical prowess as well: "one day he slew four lions and three bears, though he had no weapons." So the *midrash* continues, in stories of David's trials with dangerous beasts, jealous kings, embittered court scholars, and, of course, with the giant Goliath. Both in humble tasks and feats of brave wit and strength, David proves himself worthy of becoming king of Israel. The story of his anointing in the *midrash* is embroidered with

magic and miracle, as the drops of oil in the horn flowed of their own accord and "on his garments changed into diamonds and pearls."

Yet, while this human has been made "a little lower than the angels" and "crowned … with glory and honor," there is also the undeniable presence of the "enemy and the avenger" in Psalm 8, as well as in the sacred stories. David may have the upper hand as he engages in battle with the mammoth "reem," a beast he mistakes at first for a mountain. But the "enemy" is also grievously, intimately human in the person of his own son Absalom, who ultimately dies at the hands of David's army. The "avenger" is politically dangerous in the form of jealous king Saul, whose son Jonathan befriends David and nearly dies for doing so.

God has enemies, too, as the second verse of Psalm 8 suggests. But these are enemies of a different order, and the means of their conquest is not what one would expect: "Out of the mouths of babes and sucklings hast thou ordained strength because of thine enemies." How might the babbling of an infant vanquish an enemy, we may ask skeptically. But David's God often turns the tables of power, and catches human assumptions by surprise. The psalmist somehow recognizes that within this paradox, strength does not belong solely to the physical realm. By extension, perhaps, neither does "dominion." "Babes and sucklings" are the perfect image of innocence, in all the strength of new-made perfection. The profound strength of innocence is suggested in the words of Gerard Manley Hopkins' poem "God's Grandeur": despite the fact that "all is seared with trade; bleared, smeared with toil; / And wears man's smudge and shares man's smell," yet "There lives the dearest freshness deep down things."

The next verses in Psalm 8 proceed, in part, as an elaboration of that paradox of strength-in-weakness. Humankind is as tiny and powerless as an infant in contrast to the "work of thy fingers, the moon and the stars," the vast spangled heaven, which "thou hast ordained." But the context is now the whole of creation, rendering the "enemy" more than natural or political. The enemy is cosmic. It is chaos, in its many guises. If Psalm 8 is essentially a praise for cosmic order, the enemy would therefore be anything that threatens a return to disorder and formlessness.

The inescapable darkness of the world-as-it-is is implied in Psalm 8 by the presence of enemies. Were it not for this shadow, Psalm 8 would deliver an image of the created cosmos in its purity and original blessing. But the poet David was well aware of the suffering and loss that being human necessarily entails. The question he wails in Psalm 22 is the opposite of the question he sings in Psalm 8: "My God, my God, why hast thou forsaken me? Why art thou so far from helping me, and from the words of my roaring?" This is the cry of the human being in exile from home, the misery of feeling abandoned by God. The poignancy of being so forsaken is all the more keen in light of the intimacy intended between human and divine, the relationship at the heart of the Jewish world view. The Torah declares that human beings are made *imago Dei,* in the image of God, and their purpose on earth is to participate in, reflect, and return divine glory:

> And God said, Let us make man in our image, after our likeness; and let them have dominion over the fish of the sea, and over the fowl of the air, and over the cattle, and over all the earth, and over every creeping thing that creepeth upon the earth. So God created man in his own image, in the image of God created he him; male and female created he them (Gen. 1: 26-27).

In Psalm 8, the *imago Dei* is not limited to its expression in humankind; God's name is "excellent … in all the earth." The psalmist praises God in terms of language itself, the omnipresence of the divine name. From star-studded sky to ocean depths, no element of creation is excluded from David's exaltation; the poet "reads" the signature of God in "all." But the first verse suggests that while the Creator's glory is certainly reflected within creation, it is important to see that its origin is somehow also beyond creation," *above* the heavens." God's name, or presence, is both imminent and transcendent. "Thy name" both opens and closes Psalm 8, symbolically enveloping all of creation. In this psalm and the cosmology it reflects, the name of God is both the first word and the last.

Jewish tradition teaches that the world is created through words. God created the world by uttering "Let there be … ", and "it was so"—light, darkness, birds, fish, seas, plants, dry land. For the Hebrew, the word precedes all. Language constitutes reality. According to one *midrash,* there was a beginning prior even to the beginning of "heaven and earth" related in Genesis, and it consisted of "seven things." The first of those seven is "the Torah written with black fire on white fire, and lying in the lap of God." Here the sacred scripture is embodied as a feminine being from whom God, her intimate, seeks counsel when he "resolved upon the creation of the world." The letters of the alphabet

likewise take human form in their descent from God's crown "whereon they were engraved with a pen of flaming fire." "Create the world through me!" each letter entreats in the *midrash,* each supplying a reason to be the agent of divine design. One by one, the twenty-two Hebrew letters present their case, and one by one nearly every one is refused. For example, "*Pe* had *Podeh,* redeemer, to its credit, but *Pesha',* transgression, reflected dishonor upon it…. *Yod* at first sight seemed the appropriate letter for the beginning of creation, on account of its association with *Yah,* God, if only *Yezer ha-Ra,* the evil inclination, had not happened to begin with it, too. One by one each is discredited, except for the humble *Alef,* "who had refrained from urging its claims." But ultimately, God grants the place of honor to *Bet,* as *Bet* begins the primary words of praise, "blessed be": "Blessed be the Lord forever. Blessed be he that cometh in the name of the Lord." In Psalm 8, the poet "considers" and praises this state of cosmic blessing.

Besides the emphasis on the creative power of language, Psalm 8 also praises the power of craft, of making. God's craftsmanship is evident in both his handwork in the earth, and in the glory he has "set" above the heavens. The phrase "work of thy fingers" implies not only a shaping, but a refined, even delicate, finishing. In this theophany, or divine manifestation, God proves to be a craftsman of great manual dexterity, on intimate terms with his tools and materials. In their Greek origins, the words "chaos" and "cosmos" were opposites, the one being "formless disorder," and the other, "harmonious order." God the craftsman brings cosmos out of chaos with the materials at hand; God the poet makes a world out of words of blessing. Thus, the creation David praises is distinguished by a beauteous order, a shining display of letters that descend through the "chain of being" in which every living thing has its divinely ordained place. In its innocent state, creation is filled with "handmade" harmonies among every sphere of life.

Humankind's "ordained place" is between animal and spirit, "just a little lower than the angels," yet a little higher, the psalm implies, than the "sheep and oxen, yea, and the beasts of the field." Adam and Eve are a curious mixture of earth and heaven, a balance of the humble and exalted, both frail and wondrous. The Jewish world-picture is clear about the earthiness of human origin. "Why," asks David, "would God 'visit' the human creature"; after all, as David knows, "the Lord God formed man out of the dust of the ground" (Gen. 2:7). The name "Adam" itself comes from the Hebrew *adamah,* or ground. One *midrash* asks why "God created man on the sixth day and not earlier," and its answer is, "to teach him the lesson of humility, for even the lowly insect, which was created on the fifth day, preceded man in the order of creation." Psalm 8 expresses this dual nature strategically by asking "What is man … ?" Positioned between the celestial beauty over which he has no power and the beasts in his care, the psalmist can only ask a humble, if not somewhat rhetorical, question. That the same God who fashioned the constellations with his "fingers" would not only "visit" a being made of dust, but also "crown him with glory and honor" is cause for great wonder.

But as the angels knew, humans would not stay "in place," and would soon betray the glory that distinguished them in the grand, original scheme of things. After Adam and Eve reintroduce chaos into the world, the gift of "dominion" becomes troublesome. "Dominion" quickly degenerates into "domination," and to an irrevocable link in history with crusades of political oppression and ecological disaster. There is no escaping the fact that for modern, ecologically-minded readers of the Bible, "dominion" calls up a consumptive, adversarial role with nature. The "bad" definitions of "dominion" seem to have become license for human arrogance and greed, with consequences far more extensive than dying coral reefs, smog alerts, and retreating wetlands can even begin to suggest. "Dominion" comes originally from the Latin "dominus," "Lord" or "king." In the original psalmic utterance, being granted "dominion" was part of being created *imago Dei.* Humankind would be "lord" in relation to "all things under his feet." The original design of human lordship was to be a reflection of the Lord God. And human "dominion" would mirror the "Dominus Deus" whose divine power seeks the welfare of each created thing in its relation to the entire cosmic order. Unfortunately, "lordship" has also been corrupted in its associations with slavery, oppression, and human rights abuses. And "dominion" smacks of a decidedly feudal worldview sanctioned by interpretations of Genesis which lead to power for the benefit of an elite few, and oppression for the rest.

The cosmogonies of other ancient peoples offer quite a different relationship among divinity, humankind, and nature. According to the Australian Aboriginal creation story, the eternal ancestors slept beneath the surface of the earth, until they awoke and wandered the bare plain. As they journeyed, they found unfinished human beings, half-formed of animals or plants. It was the ancestors'

task to finish their making, and then return to sleep in the shape of a rock, hill, water-hole, or tree. The Aborigines believe, therefore, that every human being is a transformation of nature; thus each has an intimate allegiance to his or her "totem," animal, plant, or rock. In Aboriginal cosmology, there is no higher or lower form, no vertical chain of descent from more divine to less.

Native American traditions understand nature as an interdependent democracy of being, a fragile and intricately interconnected web, rather than a descending chain in which one life form is less sentient of God than another. In the words of Chief Seattle, "We did not make the web; we are merely a strand in it." At the beginning of Leslie Marmon Silko's novel, *Ceremony,* the main character, a Laguna Indian, holds in his damaged psyche the seemingly irreconcilable clash between the Native American worldview and that of post-World War II United States. Tayo returns home from the horrors of war in the Pacific nearly destroyed in mind and body, yet finds himself mysteriously "ordained" to help heal his homeland and restore the spiritual life of his people. In the process, his own healing occurs. The journey to wholeness begins as Tayo is reminded of his relationship to the earth and its creatures, evident even in the ceremony that follows the killing of a deer: They sprinkled the cornmeal on the nose and fed the deer's spirit. They had to show their love and respect, their appreciation; otherwise, the deer would be offended, and they would not come to die for them the following year …. He felt humbled by the size of the full moon, by the chill wind that swept wide across the foothills of the mountain. They said the deer gave itself to them because it loved them, and he could feel the love as the fading heat of the deer's body warmed his hands. It is not difficult to see the poet of Psalm 8, like a double exposure, standing behind this image on his own foothills in the Near East night, crafting praise for the presence of love within creation, even in the practice of "dominion."

In an interview with Bill Moyers, Joseph Campbell, the popular scholar of world mythology, has this to say of the "biblical" relationship of man and nature:

Moyers: Don't you think modern Americans have rejected the ancient idea of nature as a divinity because it would have kept us from achieving dominance over nature? How can you cut down trees and uproot the land and turn the rivers into real estate without killing God? *Campbell:* Yes, but that's not simply a characteristic of modern Americans, that is the biblical condemnation of nature which they inherited from their own religion and brought with them, mainly from England. God is separate from nature, and nature is condemned of God. It's right there in Genesis: we are to be the masters of the world. But if you will think of ourselves as coming out of the earth, rather than having been thrown in here from somewhere else, you see that we are the earth, we are the consciousness of the earth. These are the eyes of the earth. And this is the voice of the earth.

Campbell's response is not actually to the text of the Bible itself, to Genesis or Psalm 8. It is a response to the way the biblical words have been interpreted, to the way the text has been "inherited," and to the consequences of that interpretation in the world. The text in Genesis indeed commands the first pair to have dominion over all things, and David borrows it for the purposes of his psalm-poem. Those words, taken out of original context, have often become license under "the authority of God" to conquer and divide, rather than cooperate and protect "the beasts of the field" and "the fish of the sea." It would have been more accurate for Campbell to lament that certain appropriations of the text "condemn" nature.

The Torah tells a story of original blessing, not condemnation. "Let there be …. and it was good" is the enduring refrain of the world's beginnings. The devout Jew prays at the beginning of every day, "O God, the soul which you have implanted in me is a pure one—you created it, you molded it, you breathed it into me…." Jews believe that because the human soul is derived from the breath of God, humankind is inherently pure and good. The *midrash* expresses this in its high praise for Adam's newly-created perfection: His person was so handsome that the very sole of his foot obscured the splendor of the sun. His spiritual qualities kept pace with his personal charm, for God had fashioned his soul with particular care. She is the image of God, and as God fills the world, so the soul fills the human body…. The perfections of Adam's soul showed themselves as soon as he received her, indeed, while he was still without life.

To stay alive, texts depend on readers. And readers in turn, have responsibility for the ways their interpretations, which are also "texts," continue creation, or destroy it. Words make the world. In a recent "psychological" interpretation of the Gospel of Matthew, *Creation Continues,* Fritz Kunkel urges a direction for human consciousness that shares the essential paradoxes and humility of the ancient Psalm 8:

> The way up is the way down; to grow mature means to become like children…. Not the egocentric arrogance of the human mind which stresses our superiority over animals and plants, but humble open mind-

edness allowing us to admire, discover, and learn their secrets, is the helpful attitude. 'Behold the birds … consider the lilies.' That means to spend many hours of meditation on the mysteries of animal and vegetal life. We might then discover that we share their mysteries.

At the turn of the new millennium, the world seems hungry for stories that may somehow reverse the tide of "dominion" gone wrong, for new *midrash* that, in their imaginative power to transform, may "still the enemy and the avenger" of the world's health and peace.

Source: Emily Archer, in an essay for *Poetry for Students,* Gale, 2000.

David Kelly

David Kelly is an instructor of literature and writing at several community colleges in Illinois, as well as a fiction writer and playwright. In the following essay, he considers the structure of "Psalm 8" to see what it can tell us about the values of the people who wrote it.

Like much great writing of ancient times, from the epic of Gilgamesh to the Old Testament, "Psalm 8" can be read as serving dual religious and social functions. It can be seen as a prayer, and there is no doubt that it is this function that has enabled it to survive throughout the generations. Even readers who lack religious sentiment, though—who take the "God" that prayers refer to as a personification of humanity's greatest fears and ambitions—can see in "Psalm 8" a snapshot of the human psyche as it was in the process of developing, and compare it to the way that the world is experienced today.

As a prayer, this psalm is a song of praise, with no particular overt request made of God, just an expression of His excellence. This method of speaking to God and telling him that He is great might seem a little pointless at first, since God certainly would not need humans to verify His greatness, but it is effective as an exercise in focusing the attention of large groups who are praying. It might be wrong to think of the psalm as being so presumptuous as to offer human goodwill or some kind of affirmation to the Creator of the Universe, who has presumably gotten along fine without it, but the praise and affirmation in the psalm do serve the function of making the people who speak or sing it more conscious of God's greatness. A line like "the moon and the stars, which thou hast ordained," is effective because it makes the person saying it, not God, think about God's achievements. This

> *Domain over the domesticated beasts of the fields was of course the most important thing for people of an agrarian culture, and could perhaps have been highlighted more prominently in this psalm. But a more thought-provoking concept is the dominion over the creatures of the sky and sea as well."*

may be the only way that the human mind can hope to grasp achievements of such magnitude.

Since the prayer is one of praise, then it is best that it sets forth a list of specifics about God's greatness, rather than filling the air with vacant superlatives that just repeat the idea of greatness over and over. In general, the Psalms of David follow this pattern, making a broad claim in the first few lines and then commencing to provide vivid, sense-related details throughout the long middle segment, finally closing with a repetition of the opening declaration or exclamation, often using the same words. For converts and children who were first being brought into the faith, this type of poetry helped keep the goals of religion within focus and provided a general outline that could be filled in by stories of Yahweh's interactions with the chosen people in earlier books.

The reader can see a reflection in the concerns expressed in "Psalm 8," of a community bound by their religion. They felt themselves to be God's chosen ones and yet were at the same time uneasy enough and self-conscious enough (when talking to Him) to take an accounting of their own position. Tribes of the ancient Biblical times survived by thinking of society, and not the individual, as the most important human unit. While people in the modern world conceive of society as a tool, here to serve people and make their lives among other people work out more smoothly, the flow of re-

sponsibility would have gone in the other direction for the people who originally created and repeated "Psalm 8." Looking at this psalm, the reader can tell that all of humanity was not what was meant when "man" was referred to: although the psalm uses the word "man" in the way that modern people usually do to indicate all human beings, it also mentions a separate category of enemies who do not seem to be counted among the same group of people as those who were reciting the psalm.

This psalm, conspicuously, reveals a hierarchy in the universe as it marvels at things that have come to be that way (but shows little interest in how or why things came to be so, other than accepting it as God's will). In the King James version, the poem specifies that man is "a little lower" than the angels. Angels are mentioned nowhere else in this cosmology, and their sudden introduction seems forced, as if they were added at a different time by a different author. The Revised Standard Version, published in 1952, was put together using the King James Version, more recent discoveries of ancient Hebrew texts, and nearly three hundred and fifty years of additional scholarship. In the Revised Standard Version (RSV), man is said to be "little less than God," leaving the angels out of the picture altogether. This approach does help streamline the cosmology by removing the distracting and perhaps unnecessary element, but it also removes the sense of gradation that makes readers feel that humanity is being specifically located in the universe. In the RSV, the universe has become more of a duality, with God and man against everything else. This seems to fit more comfortably with contemporary thought, but it loses the fullness of the King James version where angels added to the abundance of life in the universe.

The modern worldview does not emphasize the fact that God has "crowned (humanity) with glory and honor." One of the most interesting aspects of "Psalm 8" is the litany of creatures between lines 7 and 8 that serve as a reminder of humanity's greatness. The range suggested in these two brief lines is a staggering example of poetic compression, covering all animal life while at the same time managing to be specific. Domain over the domesticated beasts of the fields was of course the most important thing for people of an agrarian culture, and could perhaps have been highlighted more prominently in this psalm. But a more thought-provoking concept is the dominion over the creatures of the sky and sea as well. Like everything else in this psalm, there is the implication of the natural order that determines what is important by way of relationships. In this case, that order is centered around the sea and having access to the sea, which might naturally occupy the minds of people who had lived in the desert. The variety and magnificence of land-locked creatures who lived in, say, a jungle or forest, might not have occurred to the psalmists. Their eyes turned from desert to sea, from nomadic culture to the relatively recent developments of agriculture—the free-roaming creatures of the earth would probably have been out of their field of vision.

The cosmology of "Psalm 8" is thorough, and goes in descending order: God, moon and stars, angels, humans, domesticated animals, fish and fowl, and then the wild animals that appear now and then, drawn to the water. The high ranking of humans is an acknowledged mystery, according to the questions in line 4, but it is nonetheless accepted. More perplexing is the power that the psalm ascribes to enemies. Line 2 specifically states that it is God's enemies being discussed, but it does not specify who these enemies of God would be. It is possible that the enemy facing God is of a different category than man, except that the phrase "still the enemy and the avenger" implies that God's enemy is indeed human. These two ways of reading it present widely different implications for both the worldview of the poem and its structural integrity. If God's enemies are other celestial beings, such as the hoards of daemons mentioned elsewhere in the Bible and perhaps closely associated with the early formative days of the Hebrew religion, then a place can be found for them in the order of the universe, most likely in the vicinity of angels but above humans. If God's enemies are human, though, the measurements of God's awesome power are turned backward in a way that reads almost like farce. Power over human enemies, which should hardly need mentioning, is given precedence over His ability to create the moon and stars and to delegate power to humanity. The question "What is man, that thou art mindful of him?" changes from a humble, slightly proud recognition that humans might be important enough to warrant some of God's attention to an arrogant claim that God feels human enemies enough of a threat to keep an eye on them.

"Psalm 8" represents a primitive people's attempt to juggle the difficult tasks of praising God, assuring themselves that their enemies represent little threat, and define their place in the spectrum of life in the universe. Because of different translations and different possible interpretations, it sometimes seems to address itself to different concerns: read casually, this psalm might appear to have two

or three subjects. The key value, of course, is what this poem tells us about ourselves. Like the ancient Hebrews, modern humans are nervous about those who wish them harm but are confident about their ability to dominate the universe. They do not judge ourselves in relation to angels, but they do still find themselves the favorites of heaven. Perhaps even more today than in ancient times, people are inclined to jump from considering the magnificence of the universe to reflecting, "What is man?"

Source: David Kelly, in an essay for *Poetry for Students,* Gale, 2000.

Sources

Alter, Robert, *The Art of Biblical Poetry,* New York: Basic Books, 1985.

————, "Psalms," in *The Literary Guide to the Bible,* edited by Robert Alter and Frank Kermode, Cambridge: The Belknap Press of Harvard University Press, 1987.

Campbell, Joseph, with Bill Moyers, *The Power of Myth,* New York: Doubleday, 1988.

Fromm, Erich, "The Psalms," in *You Shall Be as Gods: A Radical Interpretation of the Old Testament and Its Traditions,* Holt, Rinehart and Winston, 1966, pp. 201-24.

Ginzberg, Louis, *The Legends of the Jews,* 4 vols., Philadelphia: The Jewish Publication Society of America, 1909-1938.

Gottcent, John H., *The Bible: A Literary Study,* Boston: Twayne Publishers, 1986.

Hough, Lynn Harold, "The Battle with Doubt and the Lyrical Voices," in *The Meaning of Human Experience,* Abington-Cokesbury Press, 1945, pp. 119-35.

Kunkel, Fritz, *Creation Continues,* New York: Paulist Press, 1987.

Milgrom, Jo, essay in *Parabola: Crossroads.*

Patterson, John, "The Divine Revelation," in *The Praises of Israel: Studies Literary and Religious in the Psalms,* Scribner's, 1950, pp. 170-91.

Silko, Leslie Marmon, *Ceremony,* New York: Viking Press, 1977.

For Further Study

Dahood, Mitchell, *Psalms I: 1-50,* Garden City, NY: 1956.
    This is Volume 16 of the thirty-eight volume Anchor Bible commentary set. In this book Psalm 8 is accompanied by four pages of notes that refer to previous translations, cross-references, and related literature.

Fosdick, Harry Emerson, *A Guide to Understanding the Bible: The Development of Ideas Within the Old and New Testament,* New York: Harper Torchbooks, 1956.

Fosdick offers a chronology of the ideas according to categories: "The Idea of Right and Wrong," "The Idea of Man," "The Idea of God," etc.

Frye, Northrop, *The Great Code: The Bible and Literature,* New York: Harcourt, Brace Jovanovich, 1982.

Frye, one of the most respected literary critics of modern times, examines the Bible, not *as* literature, but as a historically significant document that uses many literary techniques.

Gabel, John B., and Charles B. Wheeler, *The Bible as Literature: An Introduction,* New York: Oxford University Press, 1986.

This book gives short treatment to the Apocrypha and the Pseudepigrapha, which the psalms may belong to, but it is thorough in its information.

Gordon, Cyrus H., and Gary A. Rendsburg, *The Bible and the Ancient Near East,* 4th ed., New York: W. W. Norton & Co., 1997.

This largely historical work examines the ancient world that the Psalms emerged from, relating the style and structure of the Psalms to non-Biblical sources of the same time period.

The Oxford History of the Biblical World, edited by Michael D. Coogan, New York: Oxford University Press, 1998.

This large, illustrated volume is intended for use as a reference. It is a comprehensive source regarding the way that Biblical thought developed from its earliest history.

Reactionary Essay on Applied Science

Phyllis McGinley
1951

"Reactionary Essay on Applied Science," with its blend of light domestic humor and social satire, is characteristic of much of McGinley's best poetry. First published in the *New Yorker* in 1951, it was included that same year in *A Short Walk from the Station,* as well as in *Times Three,* the 1961 Pulitzer Prize-winning volume of poetry which spanned three decades of her work. Many of McGinley's poems were based on her experiences as a suburban housewife and mother. She used this perspective, one frequently scorned by more serious writers, to comment on the ironies she found in the world around her. In this poem, she presents a "reactionary" view of the world of inventions. The poem satirically compares several minor discoveries which have practical importance in the speaker's life, such as the safety match, paper towels, and window screens, with highly praised inventions and inventors such as the Wright Brothers with their airplane and Eli Whitney and his cotton gin.

Like most writers of light verse, McGinley uses both complex rhythm and rhyme with technical virtuosity. Her language is clever and witty; in fact, she is sometimes compared to Dorothy Parker for her sophisticated use of humor. However, McGinley never employs Parker's caustic, at times bitter, overtones. Underlying even her most serious social criticism is an optimistic thread.

McGinley's work is accessible to a large and varied audience because her subjects and themes revolve around ordinary domestic life. In a 1965

Phyllis McGinley

interview in *Time* magazine, McGinley noted, "At a time when poetry has become the property of the universities and not the common people, I have a vast number of people who have become my readers. I have kept the door open and perhaps led them to greater poetry."

Author Biography

McGinley was born on March 21, 1905 in Ontario, Oregon, but moved to a ranch near Iliff, Colorado, when she was only three months old. Her father, David McGinley, speculated in real estate, usually unsuccessfully, which caused the family to move frequently. She didn't enjoy her early childhood on the ranch where she and her brother felt isolated and friendless. After her father's death in 1917, her mother, Julia Keisel McGinley, took the two children back to her home in Ogden, Utah, where they moved in with Julia's sister. McGinley liked this stable new environment where she felt secure, enjoying for the first time the sense of having a permanent home.

McGinley attended the University of Utah. After graduation, she taught school, first in Utah and then in New Rochelle, New York. Soon she began

submitting poetry to magazines; this early material was serious and romantic. McGinley compared her style to that of the pre-Raphealite poet, Charles Algernon Swinburne. At the urging of an editor at the *New Yorker,* however, she turned to light verse, which had the advantage of paying more than serious poetry. When the principal of the New Rochelle high school where she was teaching learned that her work was being published, he criticized her moonlighting. She decided to quit her job and move to New York City where she began working at an advertising agency. A few months later, she became poetry editor of *Town and Country* magazine, a job which gave her time to write.

In 1934, she met Bill Hayden, a Bell Telephone employee who was also a jazz musician. Since McGinley wanted a regular domestic life, she worried that his musical background would involve too wild a lifestyle. However, when he surprised her by having their wedding banns announced at church, she agreed to marry him. The couple moved to Larchmont, a New York City suburb. McGinley adapted easily to her role as a housewife and mother. When the first of her two daughters was born in 1939, she described herself as euphoric. She enjoyed almost every aspect of her life and the world around her. At the same time, she continued submitting poetry to a wide range of magazines. The domestic bliss and woes of her life were translated into verse. Some of her finest and most serious poetry deals with the relationships between mothers and daughters: the stages of their growth, the difficulty of letting go, and learning to cope once they are gone.

During the 1960s, McGinley took on the role of defending the joys of domesticity against feminists such as Betty Friedan, whose *The Feminine Mystique* labeled the role of housewife dangerous, stagnating, even a type of mental illness. McGinley's 1964 collection of essays, *Sixpence in Her Shoe,* was written in part as a rebuttal to attacks on the role of woman as homemaker. When she was featured on the cover of *Time* magazine in 1965, the caption across the cover quoted, "I rise to defend the quite possible She."

That same year, McGinley was invited to read at the White House Festival of the Arts. Throughout her life, McGinley received many honors, including the Edna St. Vincent Millay Prize for poetry. She was also a member of the National Institute of Arts and Letters. In addition to poetry, McGinley also wrote very successful children's stories. Her last work was a collection of essays humanizing the saints. After her husband died in 1972, McGinley moved to an apartment in New York City. She died in 1978.

Poem Text

I cannot love the Brothers Wright,
   Marconi wins my mixed devotion.
   Had no one yet discovered flight
   Or set the air waves in commotion,
Life would, I think, have been as well.   5
That also goes for A. G. Bell.

What I'm really thankful for, when I'm cleaning up
   after lunch,
Is the invention of waxed paper.

That Edison improved my lot,
   I sometimes doubt; nor care a jitney   10
Whether the kettle steamed, or Watt,
   Or if the gin invented Whitney.
Butter the world, I often feel,
Had nobody contrived the wheel.

On the other hand, I'm awfully indebted   15
To whoever it was dreamed up the elastic band.

Yes, Pausing grateful, now and then,
   upon my prim, domestic courses,
I offer praise to lesser men—
   Fultons unsung, anonymous Morses—   20
Whose deft and innocent devices
Pleasure my house with sweets and spices.

I give you, for instance, the fellow
Who first had the idea for Scotch Tape.

I hail the man who thought of soap,   25
   The chap responsible for zippers,
Sun lotion, the stamped envelope,
   And screens, and wading pools for nippers,
Venetian blinds of various classes,
and bobby pins and tinted glasses.   30

DeForest never thought up anything
So useful as a bobby pin.

Those baubles are the ones that keep
   Their places, and beget no trouble,
Incite no battles, stab no sleep,   35
   Reduce no villages to rubble,
Being primarily designed
By men of unambitious mind.

You remember how Orville Wright said his flying
   machine
Was going to outlaw war?   40

Let them on Archimedes dote
   Who like to hear the planet rattling

I cannot cast a hearty vote
   For Galileo or for Gatling,
Preferring, of the Freaks of science,   45
The pygmies rather than the giants—

(And from experience being wary of
Greek geniuses bearing gifts)—

Deciding, on reflection calm,
   mankind is better of with trifles: 50
With Band-Aid rather than the bomb,
   With safety match than safety rifles.
Let the earth fall or the earth spin!
A brave new world might well begin
With no invention   55
Worth the mention
Save paper towels and aspirin.

Remind me to call the repairman
About my big, new, automatically defrosting
   refrigerator with the built-in electric eye.

Poem Summary

Lines 1-4:

The poem begins with a sextet introducing an ironic critique of modern technology, the "applied science" of the title. The speaker declines to join in the widespread praise of major scientific advances. The first four lines are balanced; one and three refer to the Wright brothers and their airplane, while two and four refer to Guglielmo Marconi, the inventor who sent the first transatlantic wireless signals. The poem's description of his accomplishment as setting "the air waves in commotion" illustrates both McGinley's brand of humor and the speaker's attitude. While a commotion isn't a catastrophic event, the statement pictures air waves crowded with a jumble of discordant sounds. Clearly, peaceful and undisturbed air would be more pleasant.

Although the poem uses the first person, a speaker who like the author appears to be a suburban housewife, McGinley adopts this persona to present a satiric view of the modern world. At times during the poem, McGinley even encourages the reader to view the speaker, as well as the subject, with humor.

Lines 5-6:

Each sextet, except the final one, ends with a couplet. Here Alexander Graham Bell and his telephone join the Wrights and Marconi on the poem's list of dubious achievers. The fifth line sums up the

Media Adaptations

- McGinley's poems are included in Volumes 2 and 4 of *The Poetry Hall of Fame,* a 1993-94 release of the PBS series *Anyone for Tennyson* by Monterrey Home Video

- In 1986, The Library of Congress produced an audiocassette *Nine Pulitzer Prize Poets Reading Their Own Poems*

- Some of McGinley's work is heard in *A Quip with Yip and Friends,* a 1990 video released by Monterrey Home Video.

- *The Year Without a Santa,* McGinley's popular Christmas tale was re-released in 1999 by Warner Studios.

poem's main idea: the world would do just as well without the tinkering of these men.

Lines 7-8:

Much of the poem's charm and humor comes in the use of conversational asides between each stanza. This is a technique McGinley has used in several poems. The chatty, informal tone introduces the type of invention the speaker finds truly useful: waxed paper, which was popularly used during the 1950s for wrapping up leftovers.

Lines 9-12:

This segment illustrates both the poem's wit and one of its weaknesses. Writers of light verse have often been accused of sacrificing meaning to the poem's rhyme scheme or rhythm. The use of jitney in line ten is an example. A jitney is a small bus or informal type of transportation. Its main role in the poem is to rhyme with Whitney; the word's meaning is irrelevant. However, the rhythmic flow of these lines allows McGinley to indulge in some of the most clever wordplay in the poem. James Watt developed an improved steam engine. McGinley connects the steam engine with a steam kettle, states her indifference to it, and then creates a play on Watt's name, using "or Watt" instead of "or what." The fact that watt is also a measurement of

energy only adds to the complex wordplay. Line twelve continues this. Eli Whitney invented the cotton gin, a machine which cleans and removes the seeds from cotton. McGinley inverts the idea, allowing the reader to consider another meaning of gin, as an alcoholic beverage. The machine, of course, did not create the inventor, but what (or watt) role might gin, the drink, have had in aiding Whitney's creativity.

Lines 13-14:

The couplet sums up the meaning once again, suggesting that even the wheel might have been a mistake.

Lines 15-16:

This aside praises the unknown inventor of the rubber band. Notice the use of casual, even cliched, transitional phrases such as "on the other hand" to introduce several of the asides. This helps to quickly establish the break in rhythm and mood which marks the switch from the formal poetic pattern to the conversational line.

Lines 17-18:

These lines create a portrait of the speaker, which in itself is slightly mocking, with the description of "prim, domestic courses."

Lines 19-22:

The speaker's heroes produce practical inventions designed to make daily life more pleasurable. There is an implied contrast between their "innocent devices" and the potentially more dangerous or disturbing ones of the previously mentioned famous inventors.

Lines 23-24:

The break leads into the next stanza, which contains a list of the type of the inventions the speaker admires.

Lines 25-30:

The use of a list or catalogue of items is another technique McGinley often uses in her poems. This stanza enumerates admirable inventions. It is made entertaining, however, through the interesting word choices. Hail, usually a formal or impressive term, is paired with soap. Line 26 blends three similarly disparate words: chap, responsible, and zippers. Venetian blinds, which are simply window blinds, are given varying degrees of social status. While the reader is unlikely to analyze this use of language, it contributes to the poem's ironic tone.

Alliteration, the use of words which begin with the same letter, contributes to the flowing rhythm: deft and devices, sweets and spices, prim and praise. Pausing in the first line and pleasure in the last bracket the sextet.

Lines 31-32:

Lee DeForest, a pioneer in electronics, created a vacuum tube which was essential to the development of radio and television. He also helped set up the United States Naval communication system.

Lines 33-38:

Until this stanza, the speaker merely expressed her own preference for minor inventions. Now the dangerous quality of major inventions, which was first implied by contrast in line 21, is specifically demonstrated. Domestic inventions improve the world. However, many major inventions are altered for use in war; several have enormous potential for destruction. Here alliteration is used for emphasis in phrases such as "stab no sleep", and "reduce … to rubble."

Lines 39-40:

The irony in this aside fully develops the point of the last stanza. Even though Orville Wright had noble goals for the airplane, World War II demonstrated how impossible his dream proved to be. Instead of outlawing war, the airplane enabled armies to destroy entire cities, becoming weapons of mass destruction.

Lines 41-44:

This stanza contrasts the values and attitudes of those who hold the traditional views on scientific accomplishments with those of the speaker. Praise for Archimedes the mathematician is also praise for the inventor of some of the most ingenious weapons of destruction of his period, the Second Punic War. Richard Gatling, the inventor of the Gatling Gun, a forerunner of the modern machine gun, will never receive the speaker's approval.

Lines 45-46:

The couplet harshly labels the developers of applied science as freaks. Use of the capital letter emphasizes this judgement.

Lines 47-48:

The use of the parentheses gives these lines an additional level of distance from the formal sextets. The topic both refers back to Archimedes, the Greek genius, and reminds the reader of the story of the Trojan Horse from Homer's *Iliad*. The Greeks, pretending to retreat from Troy, left behind a gift of peace, a large wooden horse. After the people of Troy brought the peace offering into their city, they went to sleep, only to discover that it was filled with Greek soldiers. Troy was destroyed. The aside hints that when modern society welcomes these fantastic inventions, devastion may be a hidden consequence.

Lines 49-52:

The sextet form is abandoned for a concluding nine-line stanza. These lines again restate the poem's theme. Man is better off with simple, practical domestic inventions. McGinley again uses alliteration to emphasize the contrasts in lines 51 and 52.

Lines 53-57:

The speaker predicts how a better world might develop with only minor innovations on hand. The reference to "a brave new world" is designed to remind the reader of Aldous Huxley's 1931 novel, *Brave New World*, which presents a futuristic society where technology has created a nightmare world.

Lines 58-59:

The final lines provide another slightly mocking view of the speaker who is, after all, primarily concerned with her marvelous new appliances.

Themes

The Dangers of Modern Technology

"Reactionary Essay on Applied Science" contrasts the benefits of minor domestic inventions with the major scientific accomplishments of famous inventors. Even though the work is lightly humorous, the underlying satire contains a serious premise: many so-called technological advances are in fact dangerous and destructive.

McGinley uses contrast throughout the poem to illustrate her thesis. Many of the asides, as well as the third and fourth stanzas, focus on inventions by "unsung" creators. These are small innovations which serve a single positive purpose. Yet these small purposes can collectively make daily life easier. Imagine a world without soap, window screens, and zippers. However, the poem's theme notes that the most important quality of these inventions may

Topics for Further Study

- Write your own reactionary poem or essay in which you challenge a popularly held opinion or attitude.

- Over the centuries, many idealists dreamed of creating utopias. Writers such as Aldous Huxley forewarned of dystopias. Report on the origins of both terms, and trace their development in society and literature.

- Contrast the inventions you find indispensable with those you wish had never been created.

- Working in a group, develop a set of criteria, a rubric, for judging contemporary satire. Then choose one such satire (an essay or editorial, a cartoon, a video of a standup comic), and evaluate it according to your standards.

---

be something other than their ability to make life more pleasant and convenient. What is truly relevant is that they cannot be put to destructive ends. In spite of the Biblical tale of David who killed Goliath with a type of slingshot, the elastic band is unlikely to plunge the world, or even the neighborhood, into war.

The other stanzas present those troublesome inventions which make the speaker uneasy. McGinley carefully selects incidents to build her case. The use of the Wright brothers in both the first stanza and in the fifth aside perfectly illustrates the theme. The airplane seemed miraculous when it was first invented. In fact, Orville Wright thought that it could perform a true miracle, the establishment of world peace. However, in a few years, the airplane was converted all too easily into a weapon of mass destruction. Pearl Harbor, Hiroshima, Dresden, Nagasaki: all provide testimony to this fact. Many other inventions also have their destructive side. While modern methods of communication may, at first, seem only beneficial, advanced communication systems have been turned to sophisticated military purposes.

McGinley uses historical references to illustrate the fact that the potential for destruction has

often accompanied lofty scientific thought. Archimedes, the most brilliant mathematician of his age, invented the catapult and several other devices of war, including a devastating burning mirror. Some of Galileo's discoveries underlie the science of ballistics.

The title of the poem implies that its viewpoint runs counter to most popular opinion. However, McGinley's perceptions are shared by several other writers. In his introduction to *Times Three,* W. H. Auden prefaced a quotation from the poem with the statement that "ten minutes with a newspaper leave me with the conviction that the human race has little chance of survival unless men are disenfranchised and debarred from political life: in a technological age, only women have the sense to know which toys are dangerous." As early as 1931, Aldous Huxley envisioned a *Brave New World* where technology and medical research had eradicated love, home and family, and man existed only to serve machine rather than the opposite. Interestingly, in this society, time was measured A.F., or after Henry Ford. McGinley's reference to this work in her poem helps to underline the distinction she makes between the pygmies of modern science whose products make daily life more convenient and the giants whose inventions contain ominous potential.

Woman's Role in the Home

A major theme in McGinley's work revolves around the differences between male and female attitudes and activities. It is important to remember that she is writing about a separation in roles which was considered natural by a large segment of society during the first half of the twentieth century. While such a strict division may seem unacceptable to a modern reader, during the 1950s, when "Reactionary Essay on Applied Science" was written, the traditional woman's role was in the home. W. H. Auden described McGinley's art as innately feminine: "What, in fact, distinguishes Phyllis McGinley's poems from those of most light verse poets is that no man could have written them.... She speaks up bravely for her sex." This comment was intended both as a valid critical comment and a statement of praise.

In fact, McGinley does present the values of the housewife of the 1940s and 1950s. An underlying issue in the poem stresses the importance of the women's role in creating a healthy, happy environment for her family. The speaker's concerns are centered around the home. What occupies her is cleaning up after lunch and making sure the children can play in the wading pool, safe from sunburn thanks to the invention of sun lotion. Although there is a hint of humor in McGinley's portrayal of the speaker, there is no mockery of either the person or the role. This contrast between the nurturing quality of the speaker and the destructive ethos of modern science is clear.

It is important to note that the poem never suggests that being a housewife is limiting. Clearly the speaker is extremely well-educated and intelligent. In fact, McGinley was in favor of a liberal arts education for all women, since she believed that this education could be put to good use in the home. She made this point clearly in her 1965 interview in *Time* magazine: "We who belong to the profession of housewife hold the fate of the world in our hands. It is our influence which will determine the culture of coming generations. We are the people who chiefly listen to the music, buy the books, attend the theater, prowl the art galleries, collect for charities, brood over the schools, converse with the children. Our minds need to be rich and flexible for those duties."

Style

A major characteristic of light verse is the use of regular rhyme and rhythm, although the pattern may be broken or exaggerated in places for emphasis or humorous effect. This is true of "Reactionary Essay on Applied Science." The verses are sextets, which means they contain six lines each. This pattern is altered by the use of conversational lines between the stanzas. These are not lines of verse. Instead McGinley adopts a casual tone which sounds as if she is interrupting the poem in order to address the reader personally. Part of the humor in the poem comes from the contrast between these two styles. The final stanza also varies the pattern since it runs nine lines long.

The verses are written in iambic tetrameter. Iambic means that the lines are broken into two syllable units; the first syllable is unstressed, the second stressed. Tetrameter indicates that each line contains four of these units. Even though the second and fourth lines frequently contain nine syllables, the poem may still be described as iambic tetrameter because only four of the syllables are stressed. This usually occurs in the poem because McGinley ends the nine-syllable lines with a feminine rhyme: two rhyming syllables where one is

stressed and other unstressed, courses and Morses, jitney and Whitney, for example.

Another technique McGinley uses is the list or catalogue. However, her lists are never simple compilations. Through careful use of clever word combinations, striking adjectives, and assonance and alliteration, these rosters help to develop the poem's humor and theme. In "Reactionary Essay on Applied Science," McGinley develops her theme through the use of two contrasting catalogues of inventions.

Historical Context

During the middle years of the twentieth century, the "American Dream" for many people became a dream of suburbia. This consisted of many components, including safe tree-lined streets filled with privately-owned single family homes, often surrounded by white picket fences. This area retained enough characteristics of the countryside to allow children to roam freely in constructive and healthy play. Convenient transportation took Dad to work, while Mom stayed home and baked cookies. The dream had a strong materialistic component. Maintenance of the ideal was expensive and required cars, swimming pools, and a wide range of household and garden machinery, such as the frost-free refrigerator of "Reactionary Essay." McGinley was, in many ways, an advocate of the suburban lifestyle, defending it in prose and poetry, as well as in her own personal life.

The idea of the suburb, a community centered around an urban center, was certainly not unique to the twentieth century. Both ancient Greece and Rome had areas that could be considered suburbs. Several scholars trace more recent suburban development to seventeenth century London where the plague of 1665 and the great fire of 1666 forced large numbers of the populace to settle in tracts surrounding the central city. The Industrial Revolution of the eighteenth and nineteenth centuries, however, created a new impetus to develop communities outside the central core of cities. When workers abandoned their farms and flocked to the manufacturing centers, the population of urban areas throughout Europe and North America grew dramatically. In 1850, New York City's population was under 700,000. By the turn of the century it had grown to over 3,000,000. This enormous growth created many problems. The number of

Compare & Contrast

- **1951:** Julius and Ethel Rosenberg were sentenced to death for passing information about the nuclear bomb to the Soviet Union. Two years later, they were executed.

  1999: Wen Ho Lee, a scientist at Los Alamos, was accused of giving the United States' nuclear secrets to the Chinese. Although both the press and the FBI drew comparisons between this case and that of the Rosenbergs, Wen Ho Lee has not been charged.

- **1951:** Color television was made popularly available, and in June CBS began producing color broadcasts.

  1975: Sony introduced the first practical VCR to the United States, radically expanding the role of television.

  1997: DVD players reached the American market, providing cinematic viewing quality at home.

---

people seeking work in the cities caused living conditions to deteriorate. Slums grew up across the industrialized world: in New York, London, Chicago, Brussels, and Manchester. Living conditions were often appalling, with six to ten people frequently sharing a single, small, dark room with no access to clean water. Noise, filth, and crime proliferated.

Partly because of these conditions, which affected both wealthy and impoverished urban dwellers to varying degrees, several nineteenth century writers created a romanticized view of a suburban ideal, far from the noise and confusion of the city. One of the most prominent was Catherine Beecher, the sister of Harriet Beecher Stowe, author of the celebrated antislavery novel, *Uncle Tom's Cabin.* Beecher published several books on domestic life. In her opinion, the home should be a place of security and nurturing. Therefore, the location of the household became extremely important. A suburban lifestyle would provide an environment where the wife and mother could reign, free from the harmful influences of city life.

Frederick Law Olmstead, the creator of New York City's Central Park, developed sixteen suburban areas in the late nineteenth and early twentieth century. His goal was to combine the advantages of town life with the joys of a rural wilderness. His planned communities were refuges for the affluent middle and upper classes who were now moving to exclusive suburbs across the country. In time, however, suburbs were also designed

for workers as well. Industrialists such as Henry Ford helped to develop suburban areas to house their employees. However, all of these communities tended to be homogenous, very much segregated by class, ethnicity, and race.

Developing working-class suburbs was not Ford's only contribution to the growth of outlying areas. The widespread ownership of automobiles helped to create a suburban explosion during the 1920s. The years after the first world war were the first "boom" period for the suburbs. This was in large part due to the fact that developments in technology and transit allowed middle-class suburban dwellers to genuinely have the best that both city and countryside had to offer. Transportation became quick and inexpensive, eliminating the long, cumbersome commutes of the past. A suburban area was able to tap into the nearby city's utilities. However, since suburbs were setting up their own government and school systems, they were able to avoid some of the heavy tax burdens associated with urban areas. Several suburbs of this period bore a strong resemblance to the romanticized ideal espoused by Beecher in the nineteenth century, and then later adopted by many women's magazines in the 1920s and 1930s.

The Depression brought an end to the development of these communities. However, several initiatives established by the Roosevelt administration to combat poverty had a significant impact on future growth. The Federal Housing Authority

(FHA) and the Home Owners Loan Corporation (HOLC) helped many working-class families obtain homes.

After World War II, the stream of movement to areas outside the cities became a torrent. Soldiers returning from war were desperate for housing. Developers began creating suburban communities to answer their needs. The most famous of these developers were the Levitt brothers who applied the principles of the assembly line to setting up neighborhoods. Since each member of the crew performed only one task, production moved quickly. A single crew could set up as many as 150 houses in a single week. These were not the gracious, carefully designed homes of many early communities. They were tract homes, all looking very much alike, laid out in uniform rows, rather than winding streets. However, they quickly answered a desperate need.

The prosperity that came after the war helped to bring a middle-class lifestyle to most suburban areas. McGinley's world of deft devices and many pleasures was fairly widespread. During the 1950s, popular magazines such as *Life, Time,* and *The Saturday Evening Post* joined politicians and civic leaders in proclaiming that millions had truly attained the American Dream. Voices of criticism against this new lifestyle were muted. However, the period of grace would only last a few years. By the end of the decade, suburbia and its values were under attack by intellectuals and sociologists. The pleasant world was now called shallow, mindless, and spiritually deadening.

Critical Overview

During her lifetime, McGinley received great popular acclaim, being one of the few poets in the twentieth century to find a place on the *New York Times* best-seller list. She also received the praise of many contemporary poets, such as W. H. Auden, who wrote the introduction to *Times Three.* During the last decades of the twentieth century, however, McGinley's work has received little attention although she is still included in several anthologies. This is in part because light verse has traditionally failed to receive serious critical analysis. In addition, humorous verse is no longer as popular with readers as it was during the first half of the century. Finally, because much of McGinley's humor is topical, many specific details in her work are dated. This is true even in "Reactionary Essay on Applied Science."

Linda Welshimer Wagner's *Phyllis McGinley* is the only book-length study on the poet. Wagner emphasizes McGinley's mastery of poetic techniques, emphasizing her skill and dedication to her craft. This technical excellence enabled McGinley to experiment with innovative forms with effective and striking results. Wagner mentions the use of the conversational lines in "Reactionary Essay on Applied Science" as a successful example of such experimentation. Wagner also describes the characteristics of light verse, categorizing it into four levels, with one being the simplest and four the most thematically complex. She then compares some of McGinley's Level IV poems with other contemporary writers such as Denise Levertov.

In his article, "The Poetry of Phyllis McGinley," Louis Hasley also discusses the variety and complexity of McGinley's style. He analyzed several sections of *Times Three* in order to demonstrate the different verse patterns in her work. The article includes a set of standards for judging light verse; these help to indicate the range of McGinley's artistry. Hasley believes that her work has more in common with the wit and style of the Cavalier poets of seventeenth century England than with her contemporaries.

In "The Light Touch," Bette Richart is slightly more critical in her evaluation of McGinley's poetry. Although she admires the technical virtuosity of the poems, she is at times critical of McGinley's tone and subject matter, finding her work coy or immature in places. Richart is not totally comfortable with the addition of suburbia to the topics for light verse, believing that the subject matter helps to create an attitude of complacency. Richart finds this weakness in striking contrast with the brilliant, philosophical artistry of several works dealing with age and youth, including poems such as "The Dollhouse," which she would rank far above the finest light verse.

Criticism

Chris Semansky

Chris Semansky's poems, essays, and criticism appear regularly in literary journals and magazines. In the following essay, Semansky explores the relationship between gender and technology in

What Do I Read Next?

- McGinley's 1961 Pulitzer Prize winning collection of poetry, *Times Three,* demonstrates the wit, variety, and technical virtuosity of her poetry.

- In *The Feminist Mystique,* Betty Friedan's groundbreaking 1963 feminist manifesto, she challenges the traditional view of the happy housewife as dangerous and dehumanizing, accusing successful women, including McGinley, of denying their roles as individuals.

- McGinley's *Sixpence in Her Shoe* is a collection of essays defending the joys of domesticity and womanhood, written in part as a rebuttal to Friedan's book.

- *This Fabulous Century, 1950-1960,* vividly conveys the culture, values, and personalities of the decades in words and pictures, including a segment on suburbia.

- The 1979 anthology, *The Oxford Book of American Light Verse,* presents a wide range of humorous poems including works by such usually serious writers as T. S. Eliot and Tennessee Williams, as well as traditional humorists like McGinley.

- *No More Masks: An Anthology of Poems by Women,* edited by Florence Howe and Ellen Bass in 1973, attempts to explore the range and uniqueness of women's voices ranging from a radical feminist perspective to the more traditional views of poets such as McGinley.

Phyllis McGinley's poem "Reactionary Essay on Applied Science."

W. H. Auden said that when Phyllis McGinley was confronted by things and people who did not please her, she did not—like other satirists—show shock or temper, but merely observed the case with deadly accuracy. McGinley's "Reactionary Essay on Applied Science" takes its initial power from this dispassionate view. It examines

the nature of invention and its dubious assistance in increasing human health and happiness. The poem is an adulterated sextilla, juxtaposing stanzas written in this poetic form with single lines of free verse, as if the speaker is interrupting her own highly organized attack against "progressive" inventions with stage-whispered asides. This breached form carries the poet's meaning clearly: the "reactionary" free verse is set against the traditional rhymed stanzas in the same way that the speaker in the poem uses her defaming criticism against the traditional and esteemed positions of the inventors.

The first stanzas of the poem establish these oppositional forces, pitting derisive commentary about discoveries the speaker could have done without against the more domestic, less glittery innovations for which she is thankful. Accordingly, she tells us that the Wright Brothers can keep their airplane and Marconi his wireless telegraphy, but the waxed paper with which she covers leftovers at lunch is a hugely useful tool for which she feels real gratitude. Likewise, neither Edison's light bulb nor Whitney's cotton gin leave her even vaguely impressed, but she calls herself "awfully indebted to whoever it was dreamed up the elastic band." While the speaker does not explicitly draw our attention to the fact, the inventors about whom she gripes are all men, and her appreciation of simple domestic inventions is a female slap in the face to their "planet rattling" but ultimately painfully uncontrollable discoveries.

From the start, the speaker situates herself firmly outside the quest for technological progress, telling us that she pauses, "now and then / upon my prim, domestic courses," to "offer praise to lesser men." Among those men she wishes to offer praise to are the inventors of such homely devices as soap, zippers, sun lotion, tinted glasses, and Venetian blinds. It is notable, however, that the speaker does not mention the names of the inventors of these varied apparatuses she claims to praise, while she is careful to attach the names of more consequential inventors firmly to their creations. This fact leads the reader to a tension within the poem: although the speaker declares herself unmoved and unimpressed by the milestones of supposed progress, she nevertheless cannot completely separate herself from the momentous nature of those forces. Galileo's revered name is uttered so that he can be renounced, but the inventor of the bobby pin languishes in neglectful anonymity from the start. Notable, as well, is the utter absence of women inventors. The only female presence in the poem is the speaker herself. But she attempts to critique the technological world even while it encompasses her, despite her apparent understanding that her protestations against masculine ideas of progress cannot hope to have any effect. Like the poems of Dorothy Parker, McGinley's poem relies on the acerbic wit of a female speaker gazing at the world with perfect vision as she is pulled under by the greater strength of contrary opinion.

In the fifth rhymed stanza the speaker gives her reasons for rejecting what the world at large seems to applaud, noting that the simple, practical devices good for everyday household use "beget no trouble / Incite no battles, stab no sleep / Reduce no villages to rubble." It is at this point in the poem that we can see that the speaker is troubled more by the consequences of invention than by the inventions themselves. Where does it all lead? she seems to ask, and cites Orville Wright's perplexing claim that his flying machine was going to outlaw war. She charges the reader with the question, asking, by this particular, if we can bear to remember the innocent, hopeful claims which accompany every new discovery, no matter what destruction or pandemonium ensues from them. The old-fashioned term "flying-machine" underscores the changes in form a given invention makes (from the short, exciting first lifts away from gravity to skies crossed by swarms of planes bombing cities beneath them) as well as reminding us that our innocently spoken-of machines, while harmless at their inception, "fly" out of our control with some consistency.

By the sixth rhymed stanza, the speaker moves into an offensive against all who show ambition, and states her preference for "the pygmies rather than the giants," bringing the division she set about making in the beginning stanzas to its highest pitch. Through the surface we can see the poet's suggestion that this division also stand for the one that exists between inhabitors of the traditionally female domestic world, and those in the masculine world, who are cast here as being in perpetual revolt against imagined deprivations that they redress with disastrous and monstrous inventions. That the word "pygmies" is used to connote the gentler, more female approach to life, and "giants" connoting those who act upon life, rather than bear its consequences—is in keeping with the general tone of the poem to this point. The speaker, handicapped by both her sex and her practical turn of mind, must learn to get by the best she can in a world in which she does not feel she fits, and in which she is surrounded by "giants" and those who revere them:

> *The speaker finishes by being as trapped by her addiction to homely, burden-relieving inventions as others have been to Gatling guns. In the end, only the machine is left to perceive, all others having given up their right to see with any clarity or wisdom."*

the inventors and their supporters, who enjoy appreciable practical advantages over the pygmies.

In the seventh rhymed stanza, McGinley alludes to Huxley's *Brave New World:* "Let the earth fall or the earth spin! / A brave new world might well begin / with no invention / worth the mention / save paper towels and aspirin." The final word of this stanza, "aspirin," is a slant or approximate rhyme, and its effect is to bring levity to this manifesto. At the same time that McGinley's poem concurs with Huxley's harrowing vision of a dystopic future in which the needs of human beings are subsumed by larger machinations of progress, it also laughs at the idea of any future capable of being salvaged by aspirin and paper towels.

This lightness at the end of this stanza is the turning point in the poem, for "Reactionary Essay on Applied Science" is not content, ultimately, to do no more than call sides in a gender war and advise, in cautionary whispers, against a way life that is already in existence. McGinley does not let the speaker in her poem rest in the position of elevated ethical and philosophical insight into which she has been placed. Although the speaker's last breath comes at the reader in the form of lines of free verse "reacting" against the sextilla's scheme, the content of those lines dissolves the line between the safe and practical world of domesticity and the wider, wilder world of constant progress and invention: "Remind me to call the repairman / About my big, new, automatically defrosting refrigerator with the / built-in electric eye."

By the end of the poem the speaker is strangely bedded with those she has been judging, and the firm, practical ground of female sensibility has given way beneath her feet, dissolved not by a hunger to fly or bomb or re-imagine orbiting planets, but through the simple, pernicious belief that those inventions that pleased her most were somehow least harmful; were so innocuous, in fact, that their humble presence could never lead anyone astray. The speaker is revealed as having fallen down a slippery slope of convenience devices, from waxed paper to elastic bands to bobby pins, and finally to an automatically defrosting refrigerator. The refrigerator takes its place in her life by striking a simple bargain: it defrosts itself so she doesn't have to, but in return it gets to look out at her with its single eye. The eye, as the poem states, is not an optional device, but "built-in," and from this we can infer that the poem professes that each piece of technological change we let into our lives comes with its own "built-in" power over us. The speaker finishes by being as trapped by her addiction to homely, burden-relieving inventions as others have been to Gatling guns. In the end, only the machine is left to perceive, all others having given up their right to see with any clarity or wisdom. The speaker, who began by contextualizing and judging the world around her, has disappeared into that context irretrievably. And the gaze of the refrigerator's single eye looks out at the reader with the innocence of a cat who has just swallowed a canary.

Source: Chris Semansky, in an essay for *Poetry for Students,* Gale, 2000.

Sources

Auden, W. H., Foreward to *Times Three,* by Phyllis McGinley, New York: Viking Press, 1961.

Blain, Virginia, *The Feminist Companion to Literature,* New Haven: Yale University Press, 1990.

Hasley, Louis, "The Poetry of Phyllis McGinley," in *The Catholic World,* August, 1970, pp. 211-215.

McGinley, Phyllis, *Times Three,* NYC: Viking Press, 1961.

Palen, John J., *The Suburbs,* New York: McGraw Hill, 1995.

Richart, Bette, "The Light Touch," in *Commonweal,* December 9, 1960, pp. 277-279.

"The Telltale Hearth," in *Time,* June 18, 1965, pp. 74-78.

Wagner, Linda Welshimer, *Phyllis McGinley,* New York: Twayne, 1971.

For Further Study

Allen, Everett S., *Famous American Humorous Poets,* New York: Dodd, Mead & Co., 1968.
    The chapter on McGinley provides a good introduction to her work, including a biography, evaluation of McGinley's stature as a poet, and a discussion of her themes and style.

Doyle, Lewis, "The Poems of Phyllis McGinley," in *America,* December 18, 1954, pp. 320-322.
    The article places McGinley in the tradition of such Celtic satirists as Jonathan Swift, Oscar Wilde, and G. B. Shaw.

Jackson, Kenneth T., *Crabgrass Frontier,* New York: Oxford University Press, 1985.
    This is intriguing and very readable account of the growth of suburban areas.

"Life with a Poet: The Lady from Larchmont," in *Newsweek,* September 26, 1960, pp. 120-122.
    In this interview, McGinley discusses both her role as a poet and as a public figure.

McCord, David, "She Speaks a Language of Delight," in *Saturday Review,* December 9, 1960, p. 32.
    McCord describes the cleverness of McGinley's poetic technique over the decades, noting both her unique voice and her models.

Sullivan, Kay. "From Suburbs to Saints: Phyllis McGinley," in *Catholic World,* September, 1957, pp. 420-425.
    This article is a source of rich biographical detail.

Sonnet 19

William Shakespeare
1609

Shakespeare's Sonnet 19 is about the destructive power of time which consumes everything in its path. Eventually, time will also destroy the poet's beautiful young friend. However, although the poet can do nothing to prevent this, he defies time by asserting that the friend will live forever through his verse.

The sonnet is one of a collection of 154 sonnets by Shakespeare that were first published in 1609. Probably written in the early to mid-1590s, when the sonnet was a fashionable literary form, these poems are generally regarded as the finest sonnet sequence in the English language. The collection as a whole appears to tell a story, of the love of the poet for a young man of great beauty and high rank, and the frustration and anguish, as well as the joy, the poet experiences as a consequence of his love. The young man is unnamed, but many scholars believe he may have been Henry Wriothesley, the 3rd Earl of Southampton, to whom Shakespeare dedicated his long poem, *Venus and Adonis,* in 1593.

Other characters who appear in the sonnet sequence are the poet's mistress, a dark woman who seduces the poet's friend, and a rival poet, who competes with the poet for the friend's attention. Attempts to identify the "Dark Lady" have proved fruitless; the "Rival Poet" may have been Shakespeare's contemporary, Christopher Marlowe, but this cannot be known for certain.

Perhaps more important than trying to identify any historical characters that Shakespeare may have had in mind is to appreciate the sonnets as

William Shakespeare

sustained meditations on the human emotions and aspirations aroused by intense love. These include the appreciation of beauty and the longing to make it permanent; affirmations of the transcendent power of art; and emotions ranging from elation to jealousy, guilt, forgiveness, sorrow and desire.

Author Biography

William Shakespeare's exact birthdate is unknown, but he was baptized on April 26, 1564, in Stratford-upon-Avon, the eldest son of John Shakespeare, a glove maker and wool merchant, and his wife, Mary Arden, the daughter of a prominent landowner. Details of Shakespeare's early life are conjectural, since no records exist. He probably attended the local grammar school and may have studied there until the age of sixteen, during which time he would have received a thorough grounding in the Latin classics. Documents show that in 1592, at age eighteen, Shakespeare married Anne Hathaway, a woman eight years his senior. The following year, Shakespeare's first child, Susanna, was born. Two years later came twins, Judith and Hamnet.

Sometime in the mid-1580s, Shakespeare left Stratford and eventually came to London. Legend has it that he was forced to flee his hometown be-cause he was caught poaching deer, but this cannot be verified. Nothing is known for certain of this period of Shakespeare's life until 1592. In that year, Robert Greene, a university-educated playwright, warned his friends of an "upstart crow," an actor who had turned to playwriting and was "in his own conceit the only Shakes-scene in a country." It is clear from this reference that Shakespeare had already made an impact on the London theatre business.

Within two years, Shakespeare published two long poems, *Venus and Adonis* (1593) and *The Rape of Lucrece* (1594). It was also during this period, perhaps 1592 to 1595, that the sonnets were probably written. Shakespeare's chief work, however, was for the theatre. In 1594, he was a charter member of the Lord Chamberlain's Men, which became the King's Men in 1603. Shakespeare continued to act as well as write. The roles he played are not known, although legend has it that he played the ghost in *Hamlet* and the servant, Adam, in *As You Like It*. He also acted in two of Ben Jonson's plays.

Shakespeare was also, it appears from the records, an astute businessman. From 1599, he held a one-tenth interest in the Globe Theatre, where the Lord Chamberlain's Men performed and therefore had an influence on the policy of the company. He prospered financially, making investments in Stratford real estate. These included the purchase of New Place, the second largest house in town, in 1597.

Shakespeare remained a member of the same theatrical company until his retirement to Stratford in about 1612. Over a period of twenty years he had become the most popular playwright in London, writing a total of thirty-seven plays.

Shakespeare died in Stratford on April 23, 1616, and was buried within the chancel of the Holy Trinity church.

Poem Text

Devouring Time, blunt thou the lion's paws,
And make the earth devour her own sweet brood;
Pluck the keen teeth from the fierce tiger's jaws,
And burn the long-lived phoenix in her blood;
Make glad and sorry seasons as thou fleets,   5
And do whate'er thou wilt, swift-footed Time,
To the wide world and all her fading sweets;
But I forbid thee one most heinous crime:
O, carve not with thy hours my love's fair brow,
Nor draw no lines there with thine antique pen;   10
Him in thy course untainted do allow
For beauty's pattern to succeeding men.
Yet, do thy worst, old Time: despite thy wrong,
My love shall in my verse ever live young.

Poem Summary

Lines 1-2:

The entire sonnet is in the form of an apostrophe to Time, which is capitalized to establish it as an immensely powerful, all-consuming force. (An apostrophe is a direct address to an inanimate entity, such as a force of nature, or to an absent person.) Time eats up ("devours") everything. In line one, the poet chooses an animal of great power, the lion, in order to highlight the fact that Time eventually reduces even the strongest, the fiercest, the kingliest of creatures to powerlessness. This is conveyed in the image of the lion's sharp claws becoming blunt: Time will take away his ability to hunt and therefore to survive. In line two, the theme of the destructive nature of Time is expanded; it now applies not only to one specific creature but to everything in nature. The poet, still speaking directly to Time, instructs it to compel the earth to take back into herself everything that she has produced ("her own sweet brood") however beautiful and delightful ("sweet") those products may be. In these two lines, for reasons that he will later explain, it is as if the poet is egging Time on to perform the work that he knows Time will do anyway, without any encouragement from him.

Lines 3-4:

In line 3, the poet further builds on the idea expressed in the first two lines. He selects another powerful wild creature, the tiger, and urges Time to pull out its teeth, thereby reducing to impotence the creature that most embodies the raw power and energy of the life force. In line 4 the poet shifts his thought from the natural world to the mythological realm. Referring to the phoenix, a mythical bird, he urges Time to burn her alive ("in her blood" means while the blood still courses through her veins). The phoenix is referred to as "long-lived" because it was said to live about five hundred years. In these first four lines then, neither immense power, embodied in lion and tiger, nor mythical longevity, are any match for time. Nothing escapes; everything is felled by Time eventually.

Lines 5-7:

The poet now moves to a more general invitation to Time to carry out its work. Since it is time that produces all change and fluctuation in the world, the poet urges Time to go ahead and produce through its passing the different, "glad and sorry" seasons. Glad seasons refers to spring and summer, which are associated with renewal, hope

Media Adaptations

- The sonnets have been recorded on audiotape and there are a number of different versions available. *Sonnets by William Shakespeare,* issued in 1988 by Caedmon, features the eminent British Shakespearean actor Sir John Gielgud reading 120 of the sonnets.

- All 154 sonnets are available on the CD, *The Sonnets,* by William Shakespeare, with Alex Jennings as reader, issued by Naxos Audio Books in 1998.

- Another unabridged version is the audiocassette, *The Complete Shakespeare Sonnets,* read by Jane Alexander, Patrick Stewart, and Alfred Molina. This was issued by Airplay Inc. in 1999.

- *Shakespeare's Sonnets,* by William Shakespeare, read by Simon Callow, an audiocassette issued in 1996 by HighBridge Company.

and love, when the sun rises high and blesses all things with life. The "sorry" seasons are those of fall and winter, which are associated with decline, loss and death. ("Sorry" is used in the sense of miserable or dismal.) In line 6, the poet encourages Time to do whatever it chooses and addresses it as "swift-footed." This is a reference to how quickly time seems to pass, how soon summer turns to fall, and youth to age. In line 7, the poet gives his permission to Time to act on everything under the sun ("the wide world"), letting nothing escape, not even earth's "fading sweets," a phrase which suggests flowers in the process of losing their beauty. The emphasis on the fragile beauty of a flower leads into the surprising plea that the poet makes in the lines that follow.

Lines 8-10:

Having in the previous seven lines allowed Time to do what it will—all the while speaking as if Time needed his permission—the poet suddenly changes tack. He has only been appearing to accept everything that Time does. In allowing Time to do its destructive work throughout the world, the poet has in fact been hiding his true intention, which is to set up the initial conditions for a bargain with Time. In lines 8-10, the poet attempts to strike this incredible, impossible bargain. He states that Time can do whatever it wants except for one hateful ("heinous") act which the poet would regard as a crime. This act, which the poet implores Time not to do, is Time's carving of its marks on the forehead ("brow") of the poet's dear friend. In other words, the poet is asking that his friend's face should never bear the wrinkles that are the marks of age. The poet repeats this in line 10, referring to Time's "antique pen." Antique means old—Time has been doing its work for as long as there has been creation—and may also carry the sense of "antic," which means a prank. Time therefore wields a pen that plays a prank on beauty by despoiling it.

Lines 11-12:

In these lines the poet continues his plea that his friend be spared the ravages that time inflicts on everything else. As time runs its course, it must allow the friend to remain "untainted," that is, untouched or unblemished. The poet desires this not for his own selfish pleasure, but so that his friend can be seen by all subsequent generations ("succeeding men") as the true model of beauty ("beauty's pattern"), a kind of template of human beauty for others to follow.

Lines 13-14:

The point of the sonnet now makes a rapid turnaround. It is as if the poet is now ready to acknowledge the impossibility of what he has demanded. Time is not a force that can be bargained with. It is impersonal; its progress cannot be halted or even modified. Time cannot be petitioned for mercy as a person might petition God. No one, not even the poet's friend, is going to be untouched by time. The poet now appears to accept this hard fact, but at the same time he manages to sound defiant ("Yet do thy worst, old Time"), thus developing the more muted challenge he first expressed in line 6 ("And do whate'er thou wilt"). In the last line, the poet has a surprise for Time: in spite of the harm that Time will inflict ("despite thy wrong") the poet's friend will indeed live forever, as beautiful and as youthful as he is now, through the poet's verse in praise of him. Thus the destructive "antique pen" of Time in line 10 is contrasted with the creative pen of the poet which can bestow a kind of immortality.

Themes

Time

The main theme of Sonnet 19 is the destructiveness of Time. Time lays waste to all things: the powerful, the beautiful, the long-lived. Shakespeare develops this theme relentlessly through the first seven lines of the sonnet, the effect building up through repetition and variety. Particularly when read aloud, these seven lines leave no listener or reader in any doubt about the universal power of Time—the formidable last enemy. It is a theme that is universal in its relevance and needs no sophistication to grasp, since everyone at some point in their lives experiences the ravages of time and contemplates what time has taken from them.

Sometimes referred to as mutability (which means change), this theme was a common one in Renaissance literature. Everything is in flux, nothing is stable or permanent, but all is subject to change and decay. In this particular sonnet, Shakespeare appears to have been inspired by the ancient Roman poet Ovid, since the phrase "Time the devourer destroys all things" occurs in Ovid's *Metamorphoses,* which was one of Shakespeare's favorite sources.

Shakespeare explores the same theme of the destructiveness of time in many other sonnets, including numbers 15, 16, 59 and 60.

Beauty

Although the beauty of the friend is mentioned in only one line, and the poet gives no specific details about the nature of this beauty, it is clear that he regards his friend's beauty to be of a special nature. It is this that makes the conflict in the sonnet between beauty and time so poignant. The concept of beauty that the poet presents is a very high-minded one: The friend is not beautiful in any ordinary way; he is "beauty's pattern to succeeding men" (line 12). The friend is thus presented as the archetype of beauty; in his physical form the friend embodies the perfection of creation that can never be surpassed. In the friend, the process of creation has reached its summit, and all that is necessary now is to preserve it or copy it. Nothing new is required.

This is not an isolated theme in the sonnets. Shakespeare employs it frequently in others, such as numbers 1, 104, and 106. In sonnet 14, the poet writes of the friend, "Thy end is truth's and beauty's doom and date." In other words, when the friend dies, all truth and absolute beauty dies with him. As in sonnet 19, the friend is beauty itself, the model of beauty to which all creation aspires.

Art

The final couplet of the sonnet proposes a solution to the destruction wreaked by time. It promises that although time will cut the friend down like everything else, he will attain immortality through the poet's verse ("My love shall in my verse ever live young.") It should be noted that the poet does not propose a religious solution to the devastating effects of time. He does not take refuge in the Christian promise of an afterlife for all those who believe in Christ. Nor is there any reference to the eternity of the soul. In this sense, the sonnet is somewhat bleak, for there will be no personal survival of the friend, either as body or spirit. He will age and die like everyone else. Whatever eternal life there may be is bestowed entirely by art.

This gives to art a very high status indeed, and it is one that has been echoed by poets and artists throughout the ages. Not only did some of Shakespeare's contemporaries among the Elizabethan sonneteers, such as Michael Drayton, employ the same theme, it can be found in the fourteenth-century Italian sonnets of Petrarch as well as in the work of ancient writers such as Horace and Ovid. The same theme can be found in more modern poetry, such as the Romantic poet John Keats's "Ode on a Grecian Urn" and in the twentieth-century work of W. B. Yeats, including his poem, "Sailing to Byzantium." Shakespeare himself employed the same theme on a number of occasions throughout the sonnet sequence, including sonnets 18, 100-108, and elsewhere.

Style

A sonnet is a fourteen-line poem that follows certain well-established conventions in its rhyme scheme. The Shakespearean sonnet is composed of three quatrains (a verse of four lines) which develops the thought or argument, followed by a concluding couplet (two lines), which resolves the issue, often with a witty or unexpected turn in the thought. The rhyme scheme is *abab cdcd efef gg*. That is, line 1 rhymes with line 3, line 2 with line 4, line 5 with line 7, and so on.

Shakespeare's sonnets are written in iambic pentameter, which means that each line consists of five metrical feet, each foot made up of an unstressed syllable followed by a stressed syllable. A

Topics for Further Study

- On the World Wide Web, go to http://www.bluemountain.com/eng/shakespeare/index.html, a site which sends out e-greetings cards made up of Shakespeare's sonnets. Compare Sonnet 116, which the site selects, to Sonnet 18, another favorite sonnet. Which would be more suitable to send to a beloved friend as a greeting, and why? Would these sonnets be a better choice than Sonnet 19?

- Describe some of the many ways that individuals and societies memorialize their loved ones and their heroes. Which ways are the most effective and long-lasting?

- Is it easier or more difficult to express emotions and ideas in a 14-line sonnet, with its rigid structure, than in free verse? To find out, write a sonnet, and then express the same feelings and ideas in a poem written in free verse.

- America is a society that tends to value youth and beauty at the expense of age. Do all societies around the world value youth in this way, or do some view the later stages of life differently? What advantages might age possess that would compensate for the loss of youth and beauty?

foot consists of two beats. However, Shakespeare makes many variations on this basic metrical rhythm. The result is a counterpoint between the fixed metrical base (what we usually hear and are expecting to hear) and the variable element (what we actually hear). The variations create subtle emphases and effects that would not otherwise be present.

Sonnet 19 has many examples of metrical variation. In the third foot of line 1, the poet has substituted a trochaic foot, which is a stressed syllable followed by an unstressed syllable, for the regular iambic foot. The expected rhythm has been reversed so that the word "blunt" is emphasized. The effect is to give more force to the actions of time. A similar inversion occurs in line 3, in which the first foot consists of a trochee rather than an iamb. The effect is that the word "Pluck" stands out strongly against the metrical base, once more emphasizing the destructive actions of Time. These two words, "blunt" and "pluck," are linked still further by another poetic device: assonance, the repetition of vowel sounds.

Yet another variation in the metrical rhythm occurs in line 3. The second foot ("keen teeth") is a spondee, which means it has two stressed syllables. Following so soon after the inversion that emphasized "pluck," the effect is to drive home Time's act of pulling out even the sharpest of teeth. This effect is further emphasized by the assonance of the long vowel sounds, and the fact that in the act of pronouncing these two words, the teeth are bared.

The metrical rhythm settles down into a more regular iambic pattern with the beginning of the third quatrain. As the poet recalls his friend, the smoother rhythm and the absence of harsh consonants convey a sense of calm. The most notable metrical variation is at the beginning of line 11, in which the inversion of the first foot produces the trochee, "Him in," in which the stress falls on the first word. This clearly brings out the importance and significance of the poet's friend.

Alliteration, the repetition of consonants, is another device used in this sonnet to reinforce meaning. In line 4, for example, the repetition of "b" sounds in "burn" and "blood" serve to link the destructiveness of time with the full vigor of life (expressed in "blood"). A second example is in the alliteration of the "c" sound in the last word of line 8, "crime," with "carve" in the following line, a device which reinforces the poet's view that it is a crime for time to create lines on a person's face. Finally, the "b" sound in "beauty" in line 12 harks back to "burn" and "blood," (line 4), which serves to underline one of the sonnet's main themes: the transience of beauty.

More examples of assonance provide further evidence of the subtle meanings that the use of such poetic devices can convey. In line 1, the long vowel sound in "Devouring" is repeated in "thou." Given the fact that in the act of pronouncing the vowel, the mouth must open wide, as if ready to consume something, the assonance emphasizes the consuming nature of time. Finally, in the concluding couplet, the assonance of the vowel sound in the repeated "thy" (line 13) with the repeated "my" of line 14 emphasizes the contrast between time as destroyer and the poet as creator.

Historical Context

As a literary genre, the sonnet originated in Italy and is associated with the name of Francis Petrarch (1304–1374). Petrarch was inspired by the first sight of a woman he referred to as "Laura," and whom he loved and worshipped from afar for a period of twenty years until her death in 1348, and for ten years after that. The poems Petrarch wrote describing his hopeless love for Laura inspired a vogue that lasted for centuries in Western poetry.

The characteristic Petrarchan sonnet consists of an octave (eight lines) in which the subject is described and developed, and a sestet (six lines) in which the thought takes a turn and there is a solution to the problem or an easing of it.

This sonnet form reached England two hundred years after Petrarch. The first English sonneteers were Sir Thomas Wyatt (1503–1542) and Henry Howard, the Earl of Surrey (1517–1547). Many of their sonnets were virtual translations of Petrarch, but eventually a new sonnet form evolved, which became known as the English sonnet. In the English sonnet (also called the Shakespearean sonnet) the argument or thought is presented and developed over three quatrains and then resolved in a concluding couplet.

By the time Shakespeare wrote his sonnets in the 1590s, the sonnet was the latest literary fad. It must have seemed at the time that almost every poet in England was turning out sonnets by the sackload. Sonnet cycles became fashionable. These told a story of how the poet first met his love and the trials and tribulations he has endured as a consequence. Sometimes the sonnet cycles were based on autobiographical situations, but others were simply literary inventions. The most well known sonnet cycle was *Astrophil and Stella* (1591), by Sir Philip Sidney. Once that became popular, it spawned many imitations, such as Samuel Daniel's *Delia* (1592), *Ideas Mirrour*, by Michael Drayton (1594), and Edmund Spenser's *Amoretti* (1595). The sonnet fad was quite short-lived, however, and by 1597, with the publication of Robert Tofte's *Laura*, it had virtually played itself out.

With the exception of Sidney's work, few of these sonnets are read today, and then mostly by scholars of the period. To the modern reader, many of them seem dull, artificial, and trite. But it is important to remember that this is the literary background against which Shakespeare wrote his own sonnets. He was working in a traditional form, with rigid requirements and conventions. Some of the

Compare & Contrast

- **1590s:** Writers who were not courtiers or nobles had to find a wealthy patron to support them financially. The writer would dedicate his work to the patron and praise him lavishly, in the hope that the nobleman would be sufficiently flattered to further advance the writer's career. Sometimes writers would be admitted to the patron's literary or intellectual circles.

  Today: Rather than cultivating private patrons, poets and writers often seek sponsorship in the form of grants from government-funded organizations such as the National Endowment for the Humanities. They may also receive advances against future royalties from publishers, or be employed as professors of creative writing by colleges and universities.

- **1609:** Shakespeare's sonnets were published apparently without his permission. In Elizabethan and Jacobean England the author held no copyright to his work, and a publisher was under no obligation to seek the author's permission to publish it. After publication, the copyright belonged to the publisher. Authors did not receive royalties from the sales of their books. All pub-

lished books had to be approved by the political and ecclesiastical authorities.

Today: Strict copyright laws ensure that a writer's work cannot be published without his permission. Legally enforceable contracts between author and publisher uphold the rights of both. Authors are paid royalties based on sales. In the United States and most other democratic countries, neither the government nor religious organizations have any control over what a commercial publisher may publish.

- **1564-1616:** During every year of Shakespeare's lifetime, Europe was engaged in war. From 1585 onwards, England was at war in the Netherlands, in Ireland, and at sea. In 1588, England defeated the Spanish Armada, and for much of this period England held the balance of power between the great powers of France and Spain.

  Today: England, France, and Spain are all members of the European Community; economic and political ties between the nations of Western Europe are so close that war between them is unthinkable.

---

subject matter was fixed. The poet would confess his love and praise his beloved in exaggerated language that included the use of "conceits," or unusual comparisons. But he would also complain about her "cruelty" in dismissing or ignoring him, and lament the sighing, the sleepless nights, and the pain that he suffered because of his separation from her. He would also worry about losing her to a rival suitor, and would frequently assert the immortality of his verse.

However, Shakespeare was no slave to convention. His sonnets differ in important ways from the work of his predecessors and contemporaries. The majority of Shakespeare's sonnets are addressed to a young man, not a woman, and the young man appears to belong to a higher social class than his admirer. Also, the black-eyed, black-haired Dark Lady who is addressed or referred to in over twenty

sonnets is very different from the conventional sonnet lady. Shakespeare says as much in Sonnet 130, which is a parody of the customary ways that sonneteers described the object of their love:

> My mistress' eyes are nothing like the sun / Coral is far more red than her lips' red / If snow be white, why then her breasts are dun / If hairs be wires, black wires grow on her head.

"Dun" is a dull grayish-brown, and is hardly a complimentary term. And the blackness of the lady's hair is the opposite of the traditional golden hair of the loved one.

This sonnet is often thought to be a parody of a sonnet published by Thomas Watson in 1582, which begins:

> Hark you that list to hear what saint I serve / Her yellow locks exceed the beaten gold / Her sparkling eyes

in heaven a place deserve / Her forehead high and fair of comely mould.

Shakespeare further departs from tradition when he makes it clear that the Dark Lady is not a paragon of virtue. Even though, almost against his will, he is in love with her, he does not regard her as a woman of sound moral character. On the contrary, he presents her as promiscuous and untrustworthy, unlike the usual chaste and virtuous sonnet lady.

In the descriptions of the range of emotions the poet experiences as a result of his relationships with the friend and the Dark Lady, Shakespeare's sonnets attain a psychological complexity that his contemporaries could not match. Taking themes and a poetic form that already permeated Elizabethan literary culture, Shakespeare's creative and deeply probing mind took them to heights not attained before or since. Ironically, by the time Shakespeare's sonnets were published in 1609, the sonnet craze that had inspired them was over.

Critical Overview

The sonnets appear to have attracted little attention when first published in 1609, and they have not always enjoyed the high reputation they do today. Indeed, the sonnets were reprinted only once during the seventeenth century, and it is possible that the original edition was withdrawn by Thomas Thorpe, the publisher, perhaps after a complaint by members of the aristocracy about the intimate nature of the love portrayed in some of the sonnets. However, this cannot be known for certain.

In the eighteenth century most readers regarded the sonnets as inferior to the plays of Shakespeare, and editions of Shakespeare's works sometimes omitted them. In the nineteenth century, the poet William Wordsworth dismissed the sonnets as "tedious and obscure," although he later changed his mind.

During the nineteenth century scholars mainly occupied themselves with trying to identify the characters in the sequence with actual people that Shakespeare may have known. It was generally assumed that the sonnets were autobiographical. Opinion was sharply divided as to their merit.

Modern critics have been less willing to assume that the sonnets tell an autobiographical story and have been more inclined to analyze them simply as literature, assuming that whether they are truth or fiction can never be known for certain. Crit-

ics today have no doubt about the high quality of the sonnets, and not since John Crowe Ransom's *The World's Body* (1938) has there been a major dissenting view.

Sonnet 19 has not attracted as much comment as some of the more famous sonnets. This may be because it does not present any interpretive difficulties. Its meaning is plain, and it has little complexity either in form or thought. However, the sonnet has had its admirers. It appealed to the Romantic poet John Keats, who quoted from line 10 ("Nor draw no lines there with thine antique pen") in a letter of 1817. Keats also seems to have been recalling Sonnet 19 in his phrase "fast-fading flowers" in "Ode to a Nightingale" (1819), which echoes the "fading sweets" of Shakespeare's sonnet (line 7). Keats's ode, like Sonnet 19, deals with beauty and time.

Another appreciation of Sonnet 19 came from the mid-twentieth-century poet Edith Sitwell, who described it as

> "one of the greatest sonnets in the English language, with its tremendous first lines … The huge, fiery, and majestic double vowel sounds contained in 'Devouring' and 'Lion's' (those in 'Lion's' rear themselves up and then bring down their splendid and terrible weight)—these make the line stretch onward and outward until it is overwhelmed, as it were, by the dust of death, by darkness, with the muffling sounds, first of 'blunt,' then of the far thicker, more muffling sounds of 'paws.'"

Several other critics have commented favorably on the exquisite musical effects of the first quatrain.

Opinion has not been unanimous, however. In 1964, A. L. Rowse called Sonnet 19 a "somewhat laboured poem," contrasting it unfavorably with the sonnet that precedes it ("Shall I compare thee to a summer's day?"). Philip Martin complained that the sonnet lacked profundity and the couplet was "unsatisfactory." The latter point echoed the view of C. L. Barber, who commented that the claims made in the concluding couplet "have not weight enough to make a satisfying balance."

Criticism

Chris Semansky

Screenwriter, poet, and essayist Chris Semansky's most recent collection of poems, Blindsided, *has been published by 26 Books of Portland, Oregon. In the following essay, Semansky examines how Shakespeare's Sonnet 19 suggests that art transcends time.*

The idea that human beings can immortalize themselves in their art is popular among artists and writers and serves as an alternative to notions of immortality rooted in an afterlife or in one's progeny. In antiquity, Horace and Ovid held this belief, just as today many poets do. Shakespeare also subscribed to this idea of creative immortality, and made it the topic of many of his poems. In Sonnet 19, one of a number of sonnets which praise the beauty of the Earl of Southhampton, the speaker desires that the young man he writes about never age. The speaker explicitly addresses Time, asking it to spare his beloved, and then, after acknowledging the impossibility of that, states that his love will live on in his poetry regardless of Time's effects.

We can think about the desire to have our creative work live on past our deaths as a feature of evolution. That is, our work functions in a way like our children. It comes from us, and after we die we have no say in how it will behave or how others will respond to it. The first four lines of the sonnet remind us not only of our mortality but of our *animal* nature, and how it, rather than our souls, minds, or the work that we produce, is the real enemy of time.

> Devouring Time, blunt thou the lion's paws, And make the earth devour her own sweet brood; Pluck the keen teeth from the fierce tiger's jaws And burn the long-lived phoenix in her blood;

By focusing on what Time does to the fiercest of animals—the lion and the tiger—the speaker by extension suggests what it will also do to human bodies. Ironically, Time is figured as a predator and predators presented as prey. The very tools of hunting—paws and jaws—are rendered useless by Time. Time makes the earth itself, represented as an animate creature, into a being which is self-destroying, a reluctant cannibal. This image suggests the Greek myth of Kronos, the god of time, who had been warned that one of his children would overthrow him. To preempt this he swallowed them when they were born. But how are we to make sense of the Phoenix as a predator or prey? A mythical creature, the Phoenix performs a ritual every five hundred years in which it builds itself a nest of fragrant herbs and spices and then dies in that nest. A new Phoenix is born just as the old Phoenix dies, and in five hundred years the ritual is repeated. By using this bird as an example of the devastation that Time can wreak, Shakespeare sug-

> *But warning Time not to use 'thine antique pen' is unusual in that it matches the speaker's own weapon against time ... this metaphor also suggests that Time has the capacity to 'rewrite' the speaker's love, to represent him in a way the speaker did not intend, as 'tainted.' "*

gests that even seemingly immortal beings are subject to death and annihilation. Rather than being reborn, the Phoenix is burned in its own blood. The cycle of time itself stops.

Time is sinister, these first lines proclaim, a killer who can demolish the real and the mythical alike. Emphasizing this contempt is the speaker's use of apostrophe. Apostrophe is a rhetorical technique in which someone or thing is explicitly addressed. Use of apostrophe often draws attention to the tone of the poem, as an explicit address makes more concrete, more tangible the speaker and audience. We can make judgements about the speaker, his motivations and character, because we know to whom he speaks and the context of his words. Many poems using this device apostrophize *things,* personifying them. Personification can dramatize action, as it assigns human qualities to abstract entities or non-human beings. Shakespeare represents Time in a similarly malicious vein in "The Rape of Lucrece":

> Mis-shapen Time, copesmate of ugly Night,
> Swift subtle post, carrier of grisly care,
> Eater of youth, false slave to false delight,
> Base watch of woes, sin's pack-horse, virtue's snare;
> Thou nursest all and murd'rest all that are:
> O, hear me then, injurious, shifting Time!
> Be guilty of my death, since of my crime.

Here Time is a freak, a demon, messenger, and assassin. Shakespeare continues his catalogue of invective in Sonnet 19, making time into a malevolent force, a relentless hunter and destroyer, a lawbreaker.

What Do I Read Next?

- Shakespeare's plays, *A Midsummer Night's Dream* and *Romeo and Juliet,* were both written at about the same time as the sonnets, and they both deal with the many different aspects, both positive and negative, of romantic love. *Romeo and Juliet* begins with a sonnet ("Two households, both alike in dignity") and when the lovers meet their first dialogue forms a sonnet ("If I profane with my unworthiest hand").

- Later writers have used the sonnet form to explore subjects other than love. Some of the most notable examples are John Donne's "Holy Sonnets," which are expressions of religious faith; sonnets by William Wordsworth ("Composed upon Westminster Bridge," "It Is a Beauteous Evening," "London, 1802," and "The World Is Too Much With Us" are some of the best known); and John Milton's sonnet on his blindness ("When I Consider How My Life Is Spent").

- *Metamorphoses,* Book 15, by Ovid (43 B.C.- A.D. 17), particularly the section given to Pythagoras to explain his philosophy. This contains a number of passages that inspired Shakespeare's sonnets, especially sonnets 19, 59, and 60.

- The subject of beauty has occupied philosophers as well as poets. In *The Symposium,* Plato investigated the ultimate nature of beauty, which he finally located, not in human form (unlike

Shakespeare in Sonnet 19), but in a timeless, absolute, eternal dimension of existence.

- Like Sonnet 19, "Ode on a Grecian Urn" (1819), by John Keats, and "Sailing to Byzantium" (1927), by William Butler Yeats, both deal with the themes of transience, eternity, and the nature of art. "Oxymandias" (1817), a sonnet by Percy Bysshe Shelley, and "The Old Men Admiring Themselves in the Water" (1903) by Yeats, are both powerful evocations of the remorseless passage of time.

- *Einstein's Dreams,* by Alan Lightman (1993) is a fascinating series of fables that play with the nature of time. In the fables, which are presented as if they are the dreams of Albert Einstein immediately prior to his discovery of the special theory of relativity, time can manifest in many ways, or not at all—time may not always or inevitably be the all-consuming "devourer" of Sonnet 19.

- In "The Biology of Beauty" (*Newsweek,* June 3, 1996, pp. 60-69), journalist Geoffrey Cowley explores what we consider to be beautiful in humans. He finds among other things that beauty is related to symmetry, and that certain criteria of beauty are applied with remarkable consistency, even in cultures that differ widely from each other.

The speaker, however, is not cowed by Time's prowess as a killer but rather, seeks to duel with Time, addressing it with hostility, daring it to "do whate'er thou wilt." Exhibiting confidence that his own powers are greater than Time's, the speaker addresses his adversary as if it were a criminal, forbidding it "one most heinous crime." That crime is making his beloved grow older. The speaker tells time:

O, carve not with thy hours my love's fair brow,
Nor draw no lines there with thine antique pen;
Him in thy course untainted do allow
For beauty's pattern to succeeding men.

What is interesting here is not that the speaker represents one of Time's weapon as "hours"; that is predictable. But warning Time not to use "thine antique pen" is unusual in that it matches the speaker's own weapon against time. A wrinkled brow shows the ravages of physical aging, and that the speaker fears his love's beauty would be diminished. But this metaphor also suggests that Time has the capacity to "rewrite" the speaker's love, to represent him in a way the speaker did not intend, as "tainted." That Time itself is subject to its own processes is evident in the speaker's characterization of the pen as "antique." It has worked its evil upon others before and continues to do so. The speaker is disingenuous, however, in asking Time not to taint his love so that his love can remain "beauty's pattern to succeeding men," for it is not succeeding men's beauty that concerns the speaker, but his *own* love's beauty and the speaker's representation of that love. By suggesting that his motivations are for the better of all men, the speaker presents himself as altruistic, someone who would willingly sacrifice self-interest for the good of others. This makes it easier for readers to see the speaker in heroic terms, and hence assist him in his quest to immortalize his love in verse.

After twelve lines of bluster, accusation, and false praise, the speaker relents, saying "do thy worst, old Time / My love shall in my verse ever live young." The tone here changes. The speaker sounds almost resigned that regardless of his own efforts, Time will take his love's beauty and, eventually, his love's life. What consoles the speaker in the face of this loss is his belief that his love will live on in his poetry. The last line, however, is ambiguous. Does "love" here mean an idea of the person he loves, or does it mean the affection he holds for that person? The former would be in keeping with the speaker's representation of himself as an enemy of Time, someone committed to preserving the image of someone else. The latter would tell us that perhaps the speaker's motivations are not as selfless as he would have readers believe. The irony is that in ending the poem on an ambiguous note, the protagonist of the poem adopts some of the characteristics of his proclaimed antagonist. Time, in Shakespeare's case, has been his ally, not his foe, as a virtual industry dedicated to figuring out just what he *did* mean, in his poems as well as his plays, has grown throughout the years.

Source: Chris Semansky, in an essay for *Poetry for Students,* Gale, 2000.

Sources

Booth, Stephen, *Shakespeare's Sonnets,* Yale University Press, 1977.

Hardin, Craig, Ed., *The Complete Works of Shakespeare,* Scott, Foresman and Company, 1973.

Martin, Philip, *Shakespeare's Sonnets: Self, Love and Art,* Cambridge University Press, 1972.

Muir, Kenneth, *Shakespeare's Sonnets,* George Allen and Unwin, 1979.

Rowse, A. L., *Shakespeare's Sonnets,* Harper and Row, 1964.

Sitwell, Edith, *A Notebook on William Shakespeare,* Beacon Press, 1961.

Smith, Hallett, *The Tension of the Lyre: Poetry in Shakespeare's Sonnets,* Huntingdon Library, 1981.

For Further Study

Auden, W. H. "Introduction," in *Shakespeare: The Sonnets,* edited by William Burto, Penguin, 1999.

A lively, opinionated essay on the sonnets by one of the finest twentieth century poets. Auden pours scorn on the attempt to identify the real life characters in the sonnets, but he does argue that the primary experience that gave rise to the sonnets was a mystical perception of what he calls the Vision of Eros.

Bloom, Harold, Ed, *William Shakespeare's Sonnets,* Modern Critical Interpretations, Chelsea House, 1987.

This is a collection of six critical essays on the sonnets. The essays are of varying difficulty; the most useful for the beginning student is C. L. Barber's "An Essay on Shakespeare's Sonnets," in which he argues that Shakespeare uses the sonnets as a vehicle for the transformation of suffering into passion.

Blomquist, Eric, Sonnet Central Web Site. http://www.sonnets.org/

This is an excellent collection of sonnets from all periods, including a large selection of Elizabethan sonnets, as well as some critical essays. The essays are somewhat dated (date of publication ranges from 1885 to 1917) but are still useful. In addition, users may post their own sonnets and vote in a sonnet v. sonnet contest.

Fussell, Paul, Poetic Meter and Poetic Form, Revised edition, Random House, 1979.

This is a very clearly written guide to the varieties of meter and poetic forms in English poetry. It includes a chapter on the sonnet which explains the structure of the Shakespearean sonnet and how it differs from the Petrarchan form.

Leishman, J. B., *Themes and Variations in Shakespeare's Sonnets,* Harper, 1963.

Leishman explores the theme of immortalization by means of poetry from Roman authors such as Pindar, to Petrarch, the French poet Pierre de Ronsard, and Shakespeare's English predecessors. Leishman also examines the theme of "devouring time and fading beauty" from the ancient Greeks to Shakespeare. What emerges from the study is that Shakespeare's treatment of these themes was subtly different from those of his predecessors.

Lever, J. W., *The Elizabethan Love Sonnet,* Methuen, 1956.

Lever includes chapters on the Petrarchan sonnet and Elizabethan sonneteers such as Wyatt, Surrey, Sidney, and Spenser. He follows this with a masterful and readable exposition of Shakespeare's sonnets, which he sees as the finest examples of lyric poetry in the Elizabethan age.

Saint Francis and the Sow

Galway Kinnell
1980

"Saint Francis and the Sow" appeared in *Mortal Acts, Mortal Words* in 1980. With its sensuous language of "touch" and blessing of earthly existence, this poem has become a signature piece for Kinnell's work in the last two decades. Nine years elapsed between *The Book of Nightmares* (1971) and this volume. In the "silent" interval between the two books, Kinnell took a new direction, sensing in 1972 that "a door has been closed on something." When it opened again, Kinnell's approach to mortality took fewer paths through the surreal and cosmic images that filled *The Book of Nightmares,* and more through ordinary rooms lit by day. This "Franciscan" poem and numerous others in *Mortal Acts, Mortal Words*—"After Making Love We Hear Footsteps," "Brother of My Heart," "Goodbye," "There are Things I Tell to No One"— are composed out of Kinnell's keen awareness of death-in-life.

What makes a poem such as "Saint Francis and the Sow" different from those in earlier volumes is a stronger sense that mortality is not an occasion for despair but for affirmation of life. Poet Donald Hall observes the crucial difference between simplistic affirmation, and the life-affirmation at this poem's center. "Saint Francis and the Sow," Hall asserts, has nothing to do with the uncritical cheerfulness of the "Booster Club," nor does it belong to the "Nice Doggie School of Contemporary American Verse." Rather, here is a poet, Hall says, "who understands that we live by emptying our-

selves," and that in Kinnell's poetic cosmos, "*up* always summons the implication of *down*."

This "transcendence downward" is especially evident in Kinnell's numerous animal poems, with their grounding in earthy particulars. Those particulars become violent and gruesome in "The Porcupine" and "The Bear," two poems from *Body Rags* in which poet and animal are closely identified. "Saint Francis and the Sow" evokes all the senses—sight, sound, touch, and smell—in its attention to the sow's "creased forehead" and "earthen snout," the "fodder and slops" and the noisy sucking of shoats. But there is also a bit of mystery infused in this barnyard scene, in the "spiritual curl" of the sow's tail, and in the "blue milken dreaminess" that feeds her young. The realms of heaven and earth are co-mingled in Kinnell's poems, and the mundane is nearly always the seat of mystery. In a later poem, "The Angel," Kinnell inverts the usual chain of being so that a dog, not a supra-human spirit, becomes the angel "who mediates between us / and the world underneath us."

"Saint Francis and the Sow" invokes the legendary Francis who revered all animals, even the lowly housefly. Francis was thus a natural choice for the bearer of blessing in Kinnell's "pig" poem. By his own admission, Kinnell's art is a "poetics of the physical world," not of "theology and philosophy, with their large words, their formulations, their airtight systems." Rather, as he says, "the subject of the poem is the thing which dies," but not before the mortal acts of word and touch can call forth its essential loveliness.

Galway Kinnell

Author Biography

Galway Kinnell was born on February 1, 1927, in Providence, Rhode Island, the fourth child of James and Elizabeth Mills Kinnell, immigrants from Scotland and Ireland. Galway turned five the year the Kinnell family moved to nearby Pawtucket so that his carpenter father could continue to earn a living during the Great Depression. "How I came to practice poetry is a little bit of a mystery to me," says Kinnell in a recent interview, but he does remember that "I came to love poetry when I discovered, in a little anthology in my parents' bookshelf, the poems of Edgar Allan Poe in particular." Poe's language provided a counterpoint to the "rather unpoetical" accent of Rhode Island. "It's a very charming and loveable accent, but not very musical," Kinnell admits, and "to discover that this

language could sing like that—'It was many and many a year ago in a kingdom by the sea …'—thrilled me." Kinnell describes his childhood as "particularly lonely," and his personality, "shy to the point of mutinous." By age twelve he knew he wanted to write poems himself, because it was the only way he had of saying the things he "couldn't express in ordinary life." Poetry was the key to "that inner life," he says, whose "weight of meaning and feeling … has to get out."

As Kinnell became more serious about writing poetry, encouraging influences came his way—an English teacher at Wilbraham Academy, and at Princeton, his roommate, the poet W. S. Merwin. But most important was a teacher, Charles G. Bell, who astutely recognized Kinnell's gift at "first sight." Bell remembers in a memoir that

> "In the winter of 1946-47, when I was teaching at Princeton University, a dark-shocked student, looking more like a prize fighter than a literary man, showed me a poem, maybe his first. I remember it as a Wordsworthian sonnet, not what the avant-garde of Princeton, Blackmur or Berryman, would have taken to—old diction, no modern flair. But the last couplet had a romantic fierceness that amazed me. The man who had done that could go beyond any poetic limits to be assigned. I was reckless enough to tell him so."

Kinnell gives Charles Bell credit for mentoring his work through its youthful use of traditional forms into a distinctive voice that seemed to flower "from within" and come to full expression in free verse. And even as a mature poet, Kinnell continued to turn to Bell for trustworthy critiques of his work. Bell proclaims Kinnell "of all the poets born in the twenties and thirties … the only one who has taken up the passionate symbolic search of the great American tradition," and describes the poet with words such as "passionate," "volcanic," "lyrical," "transparent," "intuitive," and "death-haunted."

Hardly a better set of adjectives is available for Kinnell since his entry into American poetry in 1960 with *What a Kingdom It Was.* This volume and its famous long poem "The Avenue Bearing the Initial of Christ into the New World," reflects Kinnell's gypsy-like decade after graduating *summa cum laude* from Princeton in 1948. Having earned an M.A. in English from the University of Rochester, he then spent time at the University of Chicago, the University of Grenoble (France), in New York City, at Juniata College (Huntington, Pennsylvania), Colorado State University, Reed College (Portland, Oregon), University of California at Irvine, the University of Iowa, and in Iran as a Fulbright lecturer. In 1961, Kinnell bought an abandoned farm in rural Sheffield, Vermont, and before 1968 had published two more volumes of poetry and translations of the French poets François Villon and Yves Bonnefoy.

During the sixties, Kinnell became a social and political activist. He was jailed briefly for his work on behalf of the Congress of Racial Equality in Louisiana, and protested along with other American poets against the Vietnam War in numerous readings. Poems such as "The Last River" and "Vapor Trail Reflected in the Frog Pond" articulate Kinnell's passionate engagement in these national crises. In 1965, Kinnell married Inés Delgado de Torres, and two children, Maud and Fergus, soon followed. The children inspired several of Kinnell's well-known poems, such as "Under the Maud Moon," in which he remembers Maud's birth and the "agonized clenches making / the last molds of her life in the dark." With its eulogistic litany, "Fergus Falling" opens *Mortal Acts, Mortal Words* (1980) by paying homage to a pond "from which many have gone" and which his son Fergus "saw … for the first time" just before a dangerous fall from a tree.

For the next twenty years, Kinnell's growing renown as a poet, reader, and teacher took him to posts in Spain, France, Australia, Hawaii, and even-

tually to New York City in 1985, where he still holds the post of Samuel F. B. Morse Professor of Fine Arts at New York University. Honors and prizes have followed nearly every volume, even when his work moved in new directions after the publication in 1971 of the critically acclaimed *Book of Nightmares.* This long meditation on death in a ten-part sequence muses finally whether it should be called a poem, or a "concert of one / divided among himself, / this earthward gesture / of the sky-diver." Despite his transition after that volume to more affirmative poems and shorter lyrics, Galway Kinnell continues to be preoccupied with the "poetics of the physical world," (after an essay by that name), in books such as *Mortal Acts, Mortal Words* (1980), *The Past* (1985), *When One Has Lived a Long Time* (1990), and most recently, *Imperfect Thirst* (1994). For forty years, Galway Kinnell has written and read poems which, to use his own words, "cling to the imperfect music of a human voice."

Poem Text

The bud
stands for all things,
even for those things that don't flower,
for everything flowers, from within, of self-
    blessing;
though sometimes it is necessary   5
to reteach a thing its loveliness,
to put a hand on its brow
of the flower
and retell it in words and in touch
it is lovely   10
until it flowers again from within, of self-blessing;
as Saint Francis
put his hand on the creased forehead
of the sow, and told her in words and in touch
blessings of earth on the sow, and the sow   15
began remembering all down her thick length,
from the earthen snout all the way
through the fodder and slops to the spiritual curl of
    the tail,
down through the great broken heart
to the blue milken dreaminess spurting and   20
    shuddering
from the fourteen teats into the fourteen mouths
    sucking and blowing beneath them
the long, perfect loveliness of sow.

Poem Summary

Lines: 1-2

"The bud / stands for all things," are the first two lines of this poem, and in a few, simple words, makes a profound claim. It declares that this single phenomenon of nature, the bud, has an elemental, omnipresent power, and that "All things" incorporate something of its essence. Yet, powerful as "the bud" is in the universe of this poem, it stands small and vulnerable on a line by itself. There is an infant tenderness to the two-syllable line that is itself quite bud-like. Flower images are common to poetry, so it is not the presence of a "bud" that is surprising. Rather it is the unfolding juxtaposition of bud with sow, and it is on this pairing that the metaphorical power of the poem rests.

Lines: 3-4

The next lines explore the meaning of "all things," and help explain the symbolic power of the bud. A bud contains within itself all that is needed for full flowering. It is pure potential, a flower fully present, but yet-to-be revealed. Some things, for whatever reason, do not ultimately flower, at least visibly. The bud "stands" for those things too, says the poem, because a certain kind of flowering still occurs—"from within." And the agent of such inner unfolding is "self-blessing." If "bud" is the kernel of all nouns in this poem, "blessing" is the essential verb. The capacity to flower, whether without, or from within (an ability "everything" has) is a matter of being blessed.

Lines: 5-11

The poem continues to unfold this connection between bud and blessing in a somewhat abstract way, using the unspecified noun "thing" as the object of blessing, and the one performing the blessing, also unnamed. The dialogue between inner and outer also continues. Everything, being bud-like, has the capacity to bless itself. But "sometimes it is necessary / to reteach a thing its loveliness," because it may have forgotten how to flower "from within, of self-blessing." Some other presence or power comes with "words and touch" to affect the healing. Even though both the one giving and receiving such a "reteaching" are kept vague in these lines, the manner of touching is quite specific and concrete; it is necessary "to put a hand on its brow / of the flower / and retell it in words and in touch / it is lovely."

Line: 12

Were it not for concrete words such as "bud," "hand," "brow," and "flower," the first half of the poem would be largely conceptual. The second half of "Saint Francis and the Sow," however, introduces us to a particular human and specific animal, the giver and receiver of blessing who together

Media Adaptations

- *Hard Prayer* (1991) compiles recordings of Kinnell reading his work over the past 30 years in a retrospective, 63-minute audio tape. With only one exception, the tape does not duplicate any other Kinnell recordings, according to its producers, Watershed Tapes. It is available through The Writer's Center on-line at www.writer.org/poettapes.

- Kinnell reads from *The Book of Nightmares* in a 1975 Caedmon studio recording, *The Poetry and Voice of Galway Kinnell,* also available from The Writer's Center at www.writer.org/poettapes.

- By entering the "Listening Booth" in The American Academy of Poets online site, www.poets.org, you can hear Kinnell reading "After Making Love We Hear Footsteps" in RealAudio. Kinnell also reads this poem (and others) at the Dodge Poetry Festival in Bill Moyers' most recent PBS series on poetry, *Fooling with Words.* Audio-visual clips of the programs can be accessed at www.wnet.org/foolingwithwords.

- Galway Kinnell is also featured in Bill Moyers' *The Power of the Word,* a documentary series that looks at how poets are "the keepers of language" and "the stewards of honest emotions." In the first program of the six-part series, "The Simple Acts of Life," Kinnell and Sharon Olds conclude the hour with a "conversation in poems" about sexual love. The series is available from PBS Video, circulates in many public and university libraries, and can be ordered from Films for the Humanities, 1-800-257-5126.

- A 1973 Franco Zeffirelli film, "Brother Sun, Sister Moon," dramatizes the life and times of Saint Francis of Assisi, played by Graham Faulk. The music is a re-arrangement of ancient melodies composed and performed by Donovan. In 1994, Mickey Rourke and Helena Bonham Carter star in what has been described as a more "hip" film version of the Saint's life, "Francesco." Both videos are available at www.amazon.com.

flesh out the teaching introduced in the first half of the poem. In the context of Kinnell's broader poetics—"a poetics of the physical world"—it makes perfect sense that Francis of Assisi would appear as the conveyor of blessing and transformation.

Born into a wealthy Italian merchant family in 1182, the young Francis Bernadone turned his back on prosperity and adopted a life of poverty and radical simplicity. The barefooted beggar-monk showed compassion and respect not only to every person, peasant or pope, but to every creature, whether petted or reviled. Paintings and frescoes show the Saint preaching to the birds or miraculously taming the devouring wolf of Grubbio. He showed no hesitation in kissing and laying hands on the lepers outside the city wall in gestures of love and compassion, and showed no more fear in converting a murderer than a scholar. He is well-known for his practice of oneness with all creation. In his famous song of praise, "Canticle to the Sun," Francis addresses the sun, moon, wind, water, earth, and fire as "brother" or "sister." His many followers founded the Franciscan order, still active today, and Francis is now considered the patron saint of ecology.

Line: 13-15

The legends surrounding Saint Francis, especially those recorded in *The Little Flowers of St. Francis of Assisi,* make this poem's "historical fiction" entirely plausible. Given Francis's radical gestures of blessing, it is easy to imagine his putting a "hand on the creased forehead / of the sow" and helping her flower again "from within."

The association of pig with earth is strong. Fewer animals seem more "earthy" in their habits and habitat. Despite their intelligence, pigs are the inspiration for so many insults. Yet in these lines, the sow's very earthen nature is the root of her blessing. "In words and in touch" the Saint helps her remember her elemental home and being as a blessing.

Lines: 16-18

The sow responds to the blessing quite physically and completely, from "the earthen snout" to the "spiritual curl of the tail," and through all the "fodder and slops" in between. The poem refuses to "prettify" the pig in the process of describing her response to the Saint's touch. She seems to become more "pig," more herself, not less. The poem's diction, or choice of words, keeps the "blessings of earth" grounded, quite literally, in the actual details of the sow's body and her pen.

Lines: 19-23

The continued repetition of "from … through … to … " in the description of this sow and her "flowering" emphasizes both the wholeness of the blessing and the completeness of the creature. In the preceding lines the description followed the horizontal axis: from nose to tail. Here it follows the vertical axis: from the spine, "down" through the heart, to the teats below. The axes cross in the "great broken heart," whose suffering remains a mystery.

This sense of completion is furthered by the perfect match between fourteen teats and fourteen mouths. Not one shoat is missing, and the mother's ample ability to nourish them all is conveyed by the vivid physicality of verbs, "spurting and shuddering," "sucking and blowing." The portrait is also enriched by the paradoxes of "hard spininess and "milken dreaminess." Through this close attention to the sow's actual creatureliness in all its completed dimensions, the poem becomes an antidote to the pigs of cartoons, caricatures, toys, and slang.

Line: 24

The first line of this poem began with a simple noun phrase; so does the last. In between is one single, complex sentence that journeys metaphorically from "bud" to "sow." "The bud" begins this poem as a symbol of the potential perfection and loveliness of all things. "Saint Francis" bends in compassion at its very center (line 12). The sow, at its end, embodies the blessing that has flowered to perfection. As a result of the poem's careful "reteaching," from concept, down through concrete particulars, to actual embodiment, the reader can reach an understanding of perfection and loveliness quite different from the teachings of modern media and mass culture.

Themes

Innocence and Guilt

The "bud" may stand "for all things" in this poem, but one of its most common associations is with "innocence." A bud is a flower in its infancy, both vulnerable to the elements and powerful in its potential beauty. Like any infant being, it is unblemished, whole, and pure in its emergent form. Seventeenth-century poet Thomas Traherne exalted the delights of infancy and childhood throughout his work, and expressed innocence in images of light:

No darkness then did overshade, But all within was pure and bright; No guilt did crush nor fear invade, But all my soul was full of light.

Some poets explore the condition of innocence through its contrasts. In the late eighteenth century, William Blake composed pairs of "songs" such as "The Lamb" and "The Tyger" whose seeming simple dualisms are challenged by a poetic voice who asks the tiger, "Did he who made the lamb make thee?" Innocence is unselfconscious by definition. It is in one's conscious "remembering" that a regeneration of loveliness and purity occurs. In his book on Galway Kinnell, *Intricate and Simple Things,* Lee Zimmerman compares Kinnell to Wordsworth, who "recognizes memory's power to evoke an early or original state of completion or grace and thereby replenish the present."

The infant state is "innocent" in the original (Latin) sense of the word, *in + nocens,* not-hurt. To lose one's innocence is to be "hurt," at some level, by knowledge and experience. To be innocent also means, in many contexts, to be found blameless of hurting another. John Milton's unforgettable portrait of Adam before the Fall in *Paradise Lost* (1667) provides a poignant example of mythic human innocence. In the epic's traditional Judeo-Christian theology, disobedience and an improper desire for power cause humankind's fall from innocence, and creation along with it, into a condition of guilt and division called "original sin." In the context of this theology, no one can remain innocent, because no one can retain the divine wholeness of being, blamelessness, and harmony with creation that characterized life in the "first garden."

Innocence, thus, is an original, but transient condition, the very character of infancy. A certain kind of innocence is attributed to so-called "primitive" cultures who have yet to acquire the technology and economics of "civilized" cultures. Primitive peoples are closer, we might say, to their own, and the earth's, origins. Our own culture generally understands children to be innocent until they have reached a certain age of accountability for their own moral behavior, and are able to act upon society's standards for right and wrong.

Kinnell's poem explores an innocence which both includes and transcends morality. It approaches what is called a "deep morality" (as opposed to moralism) that is more spiritual than sociological. Saint Francis's gesture restores the creature to harmony with the particulars of its own createdness, the "blessings of earth." The sow's "remembering" is a return, figuratively speaking, to her own "first garden," that state of innocence

Topics for Further Study

- Numerous fairy tales, such as "Beauty and the Beast" and "The Frog Prince," involve the magical transformation of ugliness into beauty, and occasionally vice-versa. Under what circumstances are fairy-tale characters transformed? What is the difference between transformation by "magic" and by "blessing"? What definition of "beauty" emerges from fairy tales? How does it compare and contrast with modern cultural notions of beauty?

- Collect advertisements which feature pigs as part of the product's name, appeal, or persuasion from different decades in the twentieth century. What images of pigs emerge? How does that image change over time?

- Research a saint's life, and (a) write a one-act play, or (b) produce a short film which dramatizes both the extraordinary and the ordinary features of that person's character and life.

- Write a poem, story, or memoir about something you either witnessed or experienced which involved remembrance and blessing.

where she is "not hurt" by human arrogance and perfectionism gone awry. Theologian Matthew Fox might see Francis' compassion toward the sow as an embodiment of "original blessing," a cosmology which counters the doctrine of "original sin" by assuming that creation is radically ("at root") good, not corrupt.

In a sense, it is not just the sow who is retaught "loveliness" in Kinnell's poem, but also potentially the reader. As Saint Francis blesses the sow, one's perception is also returned to a "blessed" state, "unhurt" by the negative associations the animal has acquired and freer to accept the "perfect loveliness" not only of sow, but of self and others.

Flesh vs. Spirit

Many of Galway Kinnell's poems have a spiritual dimension that occasionally surfaces in religious or liturgical language, as one can see in such titles as "The Avenue Bearing the Initial of Christ into the New World," "Prayer," and "Last Holy Fragrance." Yet these poems never "preach" any particular religion, doctrine, or theology. They are not religious poems, per se. The spirituality of "Saint Francis and the Sow" and many other Kinnell poems, avoids religious clichés and pious sentimentality in favor of a close attention to the actual, the seemingly unlovely realities of mundane, mortal existence. Francis is a saint in the context of this poem not only because the Church has canonized him, but because he has met the pig completely, and blessed her in all her earthy dimensions.

Kinnell has said on more than one occasion that his aesthetic depends on the "physical world." "The subject of the poem is the thing which dies," Kinnell explains, and "poetry is the wasted breath," not the ethereal music of the gods: "This is why it clings to the imperfect music of a human voice, this is why its verbs are imitative of bodily motions, why its prepositions pile up like crazy longings, why its nouns reverberate from the past as if they spoke for archetypes of earthly life, this is why the poem depends on adjectives, as if they were its senses, which want only to smell, touch, see, hear, taste, to press themselves to the physical world." ("The Poetics of the Physical World") The words of such poems will make some connection to the body and its senses, and by extension, to the body of the world. In "Saint Francis and the Sow," there is no artificial distinction between flesh and spirit. For blessing to effect its transformations, "all down her thick length," spirit and flesh must touch. The spirit cannot simply transcend "the fodder and slops" but passes through the rich stench on the way to the humblest place of all: the pig's tail. Even there, heaven and earth meet in its "spiritual curl." There is no regeneration in Kinnell's poems without this conversation between flesh and spirit, the visible and invisible, the immanent and the transcendent. The syllables of religious language acquire an earthiness heavy as the sow in Kinnell's sacramental relationship with the world. "It is typical of Kinnell," comments poet Donald Hall, this "having it both ways at once." Hall is referring to the horrible glory of "The Porcupine," but he could be speaking as well of the play of flesh and spirit in "Saint Francis and the Sow."

Animals

Anthropomorphism is a word which originally meant "human form" in Greek. When an animal or object is given human characteristics, we say its appearance is "anthropomorphic." There is an ele-

ment of anthropomorphism in "Saint Francis and the Sow": the sow has a "great broken heart" and an ability to "remember" her own loveliness, traits and abilities normally attributed to human beings. Even Saint Francis' act of compassion is a kind of anthropomorphism, since blessings, in a religious context, are typically bestowed on human beings. Not only does he put his hand on the pig's forehead, but the saint also speaks "blessings of earth" upon her, to which she responds in a very physical sort of "remembering." In the liturgical calendar, St. Francis' feast day is celebrated in early October in ritual blessings of animals.

Many writers and poets are leery of giving animals human attributes for fear of engaging in a preciousness characteristic of stuffed animal toys, or of denying animals the "rights" of their distinct differences from the human. Galway Kinnell struggled over this issue in the process of revising and re-revising "Saint Francis and the Sow" for re-publication in two later volumes. At the time he was choosing poems for *Selected Poems* (1982), Kinnell remembers thinking "'Can a pig really have a broken heart?' and I changed 'broken' to 'unbreakable.'" But for *Three Books: Body Rags; Mortal Acts, Mortal Words; The Past* (1993), he restored the poem's original wording, because

> Now I think I was right in the first place, and that my earlier scruple came from the harmful and surely false idea, carefully nurtured by our kind, that there is no resonance between our emotional life and that of the other animals.

It is important to notice that Kinnell says the "other" animals, thereby including the human in the animal realm. Animals are central subjects of several Kinnell poems. Their strong presence reflects that dimension of his aesthetic which is earthy and physical. In an interview for *American Poetry Observed,* Kinnell's comment about animals has Franciscan overtones: "When you sense the brotherhood between creatures, you are in touch with some kind of primal, natural event—your creatureliness, or whatever it might be." In a conversation with Gregory Fitzgerald, Kinnell suggests that the presence of animals in his poems comes from an "act of the imagination" and a desire "to see them in themselves and also to see their closeness to us." Kinnell's empathy with animals exemplifies the attitude in an earlier time and place described by Richard White as now at once recognizable and utterly strange. "Remembering it, we may feel like Dorothy remembering Oz. Because once, when animals were persons, the West was a biological republic. The sow in this poem is neither more human nor less animal for having been given a "broken heart." It is the human reader who is given the opportunity to become enlarged through this intimate identification with another creature."

Style

This poem is an example of the free verse style that characterizes much American poetry from the mid-fifties to the present. In free verse, there is no dependence on formal patterns of meter or rhyme for the poem's structure. Instead, the poem's content and emotional textures often determine line length and line breaks, the interior patterns of sounds, and the texture of images. Like many poets of his generation, Galway Kinnell wrote at first in "strict" forms. But long before he composed "Saint Francis and the Sow," his work had taken on the "old" free verse style that has its roots in the poetics of Walt Whitman, the "grandfather" of American free verse. In discussing his own style with Wayne Dodd and Stanley Plumly, Kinnell observes that Whitman "seeks in the music of his verse what he calls the 'perfect rectitude and insouciance of the movements of animals,' and his lines have that—they are exactly right yet there's no way to systemize them."

A Whitmanesque "rectitude and insouciance" is palpable in "Saint Francis and the Sow." There is a certain "insouciance" or nonchalance to the lack of stanza breaks, uneven line lengths, and discursive voice. But there is also a definite "rectitude" or discipline that guides the 24 lines into one coherent, logically-structured sentence. The poem's deductive reasoning, from general to specific, takes place almost invisibly through a strategic placement of images and punctuation. The more abstract first half of the poem is actually two independent clauses. The first four lines introduce the concept of self-blessing. A semicolon then introduces a qualification of that idea and an elaboration on the central image of the bud, all of which prepare the reader for the illustration of that concept in the poem's second half.

Like an icon, Saint Francis stands at the very center of the poem on a line by himself, just as the bud and sow similarly, and significantly, occupy the very first and last lines of the poem. The act of blessing then ripples along the second half of the poem through prepositional phrases minimally punctuated by commas, as though not to disturb the flow of healing energy. At the end of the penulti-

mate, or next-to-last line, a colon announces at last what the sow "began remembering": her own "long, perfect loveliness."

The description of the mother pig is quite sensuous, not only because Kinnell uses words that employ sight, sound, smell, and touch, but because the very patterns of sounds within and among words become physical things-in-themselves when read aloud. The explosive "sp" sounds of line 19 thrust their way into the portrait much like the spine itself. The "ur" sound which begins in "earth," the pig's elemental home, occurs over and over, in "earthen," "fodder," "curl," "spurting," and "shuddering." The dark vowels in "fodder and slops" are at one with the character of compost, and the ordinarily unlovely "uh" sound becomes "perfectly lovely" when repeated in the context of the sow's motherly abundance, her milk "shuddering" into the mouths of "sucking" piglets. As Kinnell's poem reveals, "free verse" is not liberation from form and discipline. It requires an ear trained to the rhythm and resonance of language, and an imagination awake to the power of both reason and emotion.

Historical Context

"Saint Francis and the Sow" appeared in *Mortal Acts, Mortal Words* in 1980, just as Ronald Reagan was elected President of the United States, and the nation entered what has been called the "decade of greed." Prosperity increased exponentially for a few, while poverty claimed unprecedented numbers of Americans, especially children.

Yet not everyone who could afford to blur the distinction between "want" and "need" did so. A growing number of Americans have reacted to consumerism and the excesses of "me-ism" by practicing voluntary simplicity, refusing or reusing products that deplete the earth's resources, and avoiding practices that contribute to the vast discrepancies between rich and poor in the world economy. By 1995, the Trends Research Institute had cited "simplifying" as one of the nation's leading cultural movements, and Elaine St. James uses that research to encourage her readers not to feel they are alone in their desire to change their lives.

In the vocabulary of "voluntary simplicity," Saint Francis has become a kind of icon. Biographies of the Saint, such as Green and Heinegg's *God's Fool,* show that Francis Bernadone was quite human and fallible, both as the privileged young son of a wealthy cloth merchant who loved raucous

Compare & Contrast

• **1726:** The poorer residents of Philadelphia, Pennsylvania, took part in a riot that culminated in destruction and fire. The governor put the uprising down, but over the next twelve years several more such riots occurred in response to economic discrepancies and laws that hindered labor.

1850: In New York City, the homeless represented a new and growing class. Over 18.5 thousand people were forced to seek shelter in little over 8 thousand city cellars. Tenements were built by 1856 to house some of these poor, but the majority remained homeless.

1928: America's prosperity following World War I meant a decline in the number of poor from 14 million at the turn of the century to 4 million. Shortly before Herbert Hoover was elected President of the U. S. that year, he announced that "we shall soon ... be in sight of the day when poverty will be banished from the nation."

1929: On October 29, called "Black Tuesday," the stock market crashed and plunged the nation into its worst-ever economic depression, known as the Great Depression. The number of jobless, homeless, and poor increased exponentially over the next several years, and by 1932, national wages were 60% less than in 1929.

1964: President Lyndon Johnson signed the Economic Opportunity Act in August to address the nation's poverty and joblessness. The bill authorized $947.5 million for youth programs, rural poverty relief, small business loans, and the establishment of training programs such as the Job Corps for youth.

1968: Not quite a month after the assassination of Dr. Martin Luther King, Jr., the "Poor People's March on Washington," planned by Dr. King before his death, got underway. Three thousand marchers camped near the Washington Monument on a muddy site dubbed "Resurrection City."

1987: In March several well-known actors and politicians took part in the "Grate American Sleep-Out," a protest in Washington D. C. designed to publicize the distress of the growing numbers of homeless people in the nation's capital.

1992-1993: Within one year, the number of people considered statistically poor increased by 1.2 million.

Today: Poor children in the United States are worse off than the poor children in 16 other industrialized nations.

• **1206:** While at prayer in the decaying church of San Damiano, Francis of Assisi heard a voice speaking "Francis, repair My house." In response, Francis became voluntarily poor, stripping himself (literally) of his clothes and his father's money. Despite the great embarrassment to his wealthy family, a barefooted Francis began begging throughout the region of Umbria, collecting money to restore St. Mary Major and many other churches which had crumbled through neglect or earthquake.

1228: Work began in Assisi on the Basilica of San Francesco (Saint Francis) on July 17th, the day after Pope Gregory IX canonized Francis a saint.

1997: Two separate devastating earthquakes in the Umbria region of Italy seriously damaged the Basilicas of Saint Francis and Saint Clare, Saint Mary Major Church, and numerous religious houses. Ironically enough, the first quake occurred on the date thought to be Francis' birth, September 26th, and the other on the date of his death, October 3rd. The Upper Basilica of Saint Francis was especially hard-hit, and many medieval frescoes (paintings on plaster) shattered to the ground into thousands of pieces. People came from around the world to help sift through the rubble to recover the missing fragments. The quakes also left thousands of people homeless.

1999: In early December, Pope John Paul II reconsecrates the main altar at the Basilica of Saint Francis.

Today: Many of the *terramotati* or "earthquake victims" remain homeless. Income generated from the many visitors and pilgrims expected in the year 2000 will be used to help restore homes and businesses. Meanwhile, the area's financial resources have been given largely to rebuilding the basilicas and shrines. Specially designed computer software is being used to map the millions of details in the thousands of color-coded bins of fresco fragments so that the invaluable art of Assisi can be restored.

---

parties and bloody battles; and later as the barefooted beggar who offered a radical love for all, human and animal, heedless of their status. He is famous, moreover, among those with an ecological consciousness for dispensing "blessings of the earth" and living in harmony with Brother Sun and Sister Moon. Francis was not born in poverty; he chose it. But he was not converted to such a life overnight. As accounts of his life attest, his spiritual visions and yearnings took years to penetrate the habits of excess and wealth acquired by birth and social position.

Likewise, many in the latter half of the 20th century who grew up near the mall-lined boulevards of most American cities, wealthy by the world's standards, are turning voluntarily to ways of living that recall "blessings of the earth," both in word and practice, and many are also engaged in political, social, and religious movements that foster peace and justice. The much-revered Mother Teresa of Calcutta, who died in 1997, was a contemporary "saint" whose life of voluntary poverty and far-reaching mission to the poorest of the poor has set an example of extraordinary compassion. Familiar are the photo images of her holding a starving infant or leprous cast-off. While few people exhibit the radical compassion and self-denial of a Mother Teresa, many are nevertheless converting to practices suggested by such books as Duane Elgin's 1981 *Voluntary Simplicity: Toward a Way of Life that is Outwardly Simple, Inwardly Rich*. Elgin's book draws upon the contrasts between a consumerist society and a sustainable society in order to suggest patterns for transformation.

Those skeptical of the "voluntary simplicity" movement argue that it is simply another inflection of a middle and upper-class economics of choice, just another lifestyle among lifestyles. They quickly point out the irony that merchandising has found a lucrative market along the borders of the movement, belying its original intent through a complex proliferation of natural, organic, and recycled goods and self-focused "natural" health products. This version of the "simple" life seems to bear little similarity to, or sympathy for the truly poor, those who know poverty by birth or accident, not by choice.

In *The New American Poverty* (1984), activist Michael Harrington asserts that the war on poverty proclaimed in the sixties has not only been lost, but that "new structures of misery" are strengthening poverty's tenacious, systemic hold. "The national vision has been impaired" for a number of complex reasons, Harrington says in the wake of the 1982-83 recession. The resulting "new" poverty cannot be understood, much less fought, apart from serious awareness and analysis of the economic and social structures that support it: It is not enough to demand sympathy for women from the Caribbean working a fourteen-hour day for a pittance in the New York City borough of Queens. To open our eyes today, it is also necessary for us to know why those women are there, to see not merely the exploitation they endure, but the structures that cause it as well. For it is precisely those structures that impair our vision in the first place. Numerous programs nationwide are taking these structures into account in their practical advocacy for the poor. Among the most effective are Habitat for Humanity, YouthBuild, City Year, Job Corps, Farmworker Justice Fund, Families First, and PraireFire. But it is clear that, despite its technological advances, twentieth-century America has proved Herbert Hoover's prophecy of 1928 wrong, and has been unable to "banish poverty from the nation," whether in its old or new forms. Nothing short of a world-wide revolution in consciousness and compassion is required to topple those "structures of misery." That is why Kinnell's poetic invocation of Saint Francis is both timely and timeless. What seems to be called for—not only on the part of poets, priests, and political activists, but urban planners and corporate executives, educators and health care workers—is a vision that transforms society by seeing into the essential, and potential, loveliness of every life.

Critical Overview

"Saint Francis and the Sow" is one of Galway Kinnell's most anthologized and often-read poems. For critic Howard Nelson, this poem stands "for the physical brilliance and weight in Kinnell's poetry," and the sow becomes, magically, "almost the earth herself." Hank Lazer also finds "Saint Francis and the Sow" a "remarkable poem," not only because it is "fit to join company with Kinnell's finest animal poems," but because it contains what Lazer considers to be at the heart of Kinnell's work, the "understanding that 'sometimes it is necessary / to reteach a thing its loveliness.'" We are to take the poem's method of blessing "in words and in touch" seriously, as the key to Kinnell's work, suggests Nancy Lewis Tuten, and look not to an inward-seeking spirituality for the pulse of his aesthetic, but to "the physical touch of another being." Liz Rosenberg's enthusiastic review of *Selected Poems* calls Kinnell "a poet with the flame of greatness," and unreservedly suggests that "Everyone—happy or unhappy, confirmed lover of poetry or despiser—should read Galway Kinnell," simply because "he may be the only great poet still writing great poems in America today."

Not every reader shares such glowing assessments of Kinnell's work. Donald Davie sums up his poetics as a "slogging for the absolute," and argues that Kinnell has created "a blowsy nineteenth-century titanism in which he has snared himself." Robert Peters's scathing review of *The Book of Nightmares* concludes that in 1970 Kinnell "seems to have reached the bottom of his bag of tricks .... Consider his diction, for example: certain words [darkness, light, bone, grave] appear with the inevitability of Cher Bono's navel." Kinnell's most pervasive flaw, suggests critic Harold Bloom, in his review of *Mortal Acts, Mortal Words,* is "a certain overambition that makes of each separate poem too crucial an event," related, no doubt, to the intense diction of "dying" that Peters noticed. Bloom's review concludes that Kinnell has generally not continued to live up to the "grand beginnings" augured by a much earlier, long poem, "The Avenue Bearing the Initial of Christ into the New World."

Poet Donald Hall negotiates a balanced route between these poles of appreciation and detraction. In his essay "Text as Test," Hall neither over-praises nor over-blames Kinnell's artistic habits. A respected poet in his own right, Hall approaches Kinnell's work from the vantage of practicing the art himself, and therefore can say with a credible hon-

esty—"I was unimpressed ... when I read the early poems." But he is also aware of the ways Kinnell's work has been since received, and therefore counters Harold Bloom's critical "condescension" to *Mortal Acts* which implies, Hall says, "that Kinnell's poetry ended with the Avenue C poem, where I claim it began." He also defends Kinnell against Davie's charge of restless spiritual "titanism":

> I find him less of a tourist among spiritual things than many of his contemporaries-subscribers to the God-of-the-Month-Club, worshippers at brief shrines like Castenada's Don Juan .... And I find Kinnell less restless and more settled ... than most contemporary American poets; more settled in a landscape, a loved place that holds him to the earth.

As much a comment on the current state of literary criticism as it is an article on Kinnell's poetry, Hall's essay concludes that these readers "miss" Kinnell because "our leading critics of the contemporary read without leg-muscles or tongues, read without bodies." Hall finds "Saint Francis and the Sow," in all its embodied earthiness, a good example of what he finds best about Kinnell's work, an "affirmation in death's face because of death's face."

Criticism

Jonathon N. Barron

Jonathan N. Barron is associate professor of English at the University of Southern Mississippi. He has co-edited Jewish American Poetry *(forthcoming from University Press of New England),* Robert Frost at the Millennium *(forthcoming from University of Missouri Press) as well as a forthcoming collection of essays on the poetic movement,* New Formalism. *Beginning in 2001, he will be the editor-in-chief of* The Robert Frost Review.

In a powerful defense of poetry's nobility, the contemporary American poet, Mary Oliver, wrote: "No poet ever wrote a poem to dishonor life, to compromise high ideals, to scorn religious views, to demean hope or gratitude, to argue against tenderness, to place rancor before love, or to praise littleness of soul. Not one. Not ever." To demonstrate the truth of Oliver's views, one need look no further than Galway Kinnell's marvelous and poignant poem, "Saint Francis and the Sow," from his 1980 collection *Mortal Acts, Mortal Words.* This poem—just as Oliver claimed all genuine poetry would—honors life, high ideals, and a religious view. It does all this by describing the poet's caress of a simple plant, a bud that may or may not flower. Although unnamed the plant is certainly common, perhaps even a weed.

In the first eleven lines, Kinnell depicts his caress. Then, in the lines that follow, he compares this gesture to the moment when St. Francis caressed a sow. The comparison, however, takes on a life of its own. Like a bud, it, too, blossoms into a set of vivid images. In turn, these images teach a spiritual lesson about the sanctity of all life. But more than that, in the comparison of Kinnell's touch to Saint Francis's, the poem reveals just how important a sense of self-respect, and self-pride must be. Ultimately, Kinnell's poem, through its extended metaphor, affirms the particularly American faith in absolute self-reliance, and self-worth. This theme, self-reliance, owes its greatest debt to the poetic tradition first heralded by the great nineteenth-century New England poet, essayist, and thinker, Ralph Waldo Emerson. In his famous essay (actually a small book) *Nature* (1836), Emerson summed up his natural theology in a now famous syllogism: "1. Words are signs of natural facts. 2. Particular natural facts are symbols of particular spiritual facts. 3. Nature is the symbol of the spirit." In these brief sentences, Emerson tells us that divinity, the soul, exists not just in people but in all nature as well. This thing called soul, or spirit, says Emerson, links people to nature. As a result, according to Emerson, the world is not a constant struggle and contest between matter and spirit. To his mind, there is no conflict because spirit, he tells us, is part of the very fabric of nature. This view—that one's soul is but a facet of a universal spirit that exists as well in nature—is in theology called "immanence." Simply defined, "immanence" means that spirituality emerges from within any given object. According to Emerson, then, both the natural world and human beings are vessels out of which the spirit blossomed. While this view about the location of divinity is not necessarily original to Emerson, it did lead him to draw a conclusion expressed in Nature and in subsequent essays that is very much unique to him. Simply stated, the view insists on a radical equality, a genuine democracy where people are equal to each other and where all nature itself is equal to people.

As fine a poet as he was an essayist, Emerson also expressed this sentiment in a wonderful poem from the 1830s, "The Rhodora." In that poem, Emerson comes across the fallen petals of the rhodora plant floating in a brook in the woods. Seeing them, he cannot resist celebrating their beauty,

> *In these lines, Kinnell, acting on the faith that, as William Blake said, 'everything that lives is holy,' teaches even the plants to know themselves. In so doing, he eradicates the spiritual hierarchy that would make a man's soul worth more than a plant's. In his poem, Kinnell combats the temptation to find a spiritual inequality in creation."*

their obvious soulfulness. In the last line of the poem, he links himself to the petals—"The self-same Power that brought me there brought you." The audacity of this in the early 19th century cannot be underestimated. For why would one ever think to equate the human with so simple and mundane an object as a flower? Yet this is precisely what Emerson does. In this line, Emerson meant literally to say that the flower and he were both divine, both equal, both possessed of the same "Power."

By the early 1840s, Emerson began to insist more overtly on the importance of such equality. It proved, he argued, that each individual was worthy and that, what he termed, "self-reliance" was the central principle for a well-lived life. In his great essay, "Self Reliance," Emerson tells his readers that self-respect is the only way to be fully human, the only way to acknowledge the divine in one's self: "Whoso would be a man must be a nonconformist." According to Emerson, one had, as it were, to bless oneself: "What I must do, is all that concerns me, not what people think." This does not degenerate into a celebration of mere selfishness because, said Emerson, there is a "deep force" in which "all things find their common origin." As he said in Nature, "the currents of the Universal Be-

What Do I Read Next?

- The writing of saints' lives is known as "hagiography" in Christian theology. In light of the current interest in ancient religions and pre-modern spiritual practices, numerous writings by saints and mystics have been edited and reissued, and new kinds of "hagiographies" published with a more diverse, contemporary reader in mind. Saint Francis of Assisi has especially received renewed attention because of his popularity among those engaged in the issues of poverty, simplicity, and ecology. He appears, for example in Carole Armstrong's beautifully illustrated *Lives and Legends of the Saints,* whose one-page biographies of Cecilia, Francis, Jerome, Martin, Peter, and many others, are accompanied by reproductions of some of the world's most famous paintings, such as a fresco by Giotto of St. Francis preaching to the birds, and Raphael's painting of St. George slaying the dragon. One of the most readable, very human accounts of St. Francis is by Julien Green and Peter Heinegg, *God's Fool* (1987).

- Susan Michaels looks at the Saint's life through the lens of Jungian psychology in *Journey Out of the Garden: St. Francis of Assisi and the Process of Individuation* (1997).

- Coincidence or not, it is interesting that Galway Kinnell introduces St. Francis and the sow by way of a "little flower," because the legends attributed to Francis's life and works are called *The Little Flowers of St. Francis.* A thirteenth-century Franciscan friar, Ugolino di Monte Santa Maria, compiled these 53 narratives of "miracles and devout examples," the first half of which concern St. Francis and his companions; the second, of stories related to the Franciscan brethren. It is the first half that contains the legends of St. Francis preaching to the birds (#16), converting the fierce wolf of Grubbio (#21), and taming the wild turtle doves (# 22). A recent Vintage edition of *The Little Flowers* (1998) is prefaced by Madeleine L'Engle, author of the award-winning novel, *A Wrinkle in Time.*

- Animals are the ostensible subjects of countless poems in contemporary American poetry; to name a few, James Dickey's "The Heaven of Animals," Elizabeth Bishop's "The Moose," Robert Lowell's "Skunk Hour," Richard Wilbur's "The Death of a Toad," "A Blessing" by James Wright, and "The Fox" by Philip Levine. Denise Levertov composed a sequence of seventeen poems called *Pig Dreams: Scenes from the Life of Sylvia* (1981) which reveal the great intelligence and emotional sophistication of a real Hampshire pig from North Eastern Vermont. Sylvia's "outlook on life" is illustrated in pastels by her owner, the artist Liebe Coolidge, "a Human," Levertov says, "with an unusual capacity for understanding the Piggish utterance." Levertov herself had an abiding interest in pigs, animals whom she felt are wrongly portrayed and "maligned." Poems such as "Her Destiny," "Winterpig," "Her Secret," "Her Nightmare," and "Her Lament" show this particular "pig-person" (to put it in Levertov's words) to be a creature capable of great rapport and identification with her human companions as well as with those of other species, namely John the Cat and Kaya the Cow. While the book's format and its folk-art illustrations would seem to appeal to young readers, the emotionally sophisticated, violent, or sensual content of several poems suggests otherwise. Levertov adamantly denied, and rightly so, that this is a "cute animal" book for children.

- In his portrait of a fearful "whisky priest" who runs for his life and forsakes his religious duties in war-torn Mexico, novelist Graham Greene offers a stark contrast to the stereotypes of saintly purity and holiness. *The Power and the Glory* (1940) dramatizes the struggle of a tortured soul, and in the process, blurs the ordinary distinctions between saint and sinner.

- *The Book of Nightmares* (1971) is possibly Galway Kinnell's most critically acclaimed volume of poems, and the most aesthetically controversial. Of the ten poems that compose the book, several are often separately anthologized, such as "Under the Maud Moon," and "Little Sleep's-Head Sprouting Hair in the Moonlight." As the title suggests, these poems reveal the darkness and terrors of the poet's soul, often under the guise of the ordinary images of daylight.

ing circulate through me; I am part or particle of God." Eventually, in another landmark essay, "The Poet," Emerson went so far as to claim that poets are the people most qualified to tell us these truths about our own inner-divinity, our own need for self-respect. Poets, said Emerson, could rekindle our knowledge of the divine flame that always flickers within us. "The poets," said Emerson, "are thus liberating gods."

Within twenty years of these essays, in 1855, America would see the publication of the first such fiery poet, Walt Whitman. Amazingly, however, both Emerson and Whitman eventually fell out of favor, out of the general literary tradition. By the 1940s and early 1950s, Whitman was all but erased from American literature by a new trend in literary study that dismissed such talk of self-reliance, soulfulness, and spirituality as so much hokkum and silliness. To poets who went to college in these years, as the scholar Alan Golding explains in a book on the subject, Whitman was a marginal figure, rarely taught, and rarely even mentioned as important or significant. In fact, both his free verse poetry, and Emerson's ideas of radical equality, and spiritual immanence were often scorned in the 1940s and early 1950s. As a result, it took a great deal of struggle against their teachers for poets of Kinnell's generation to return to Whitman and Emerson: it took a lot of courage for such poets to want to further their goals, and to insist that those goals were necessary, essential, and important.

James Wright was among the first poets of Kinnell's generation to turn to Whitman and Emerson. In 1963, he wrote perhaps the single most important and moving poem on these matters in American poetry, "A Blessing." There, Wright recounts the moment when, driving along the road in southern Minnesota, he stopped his car, walked over to a set of ponies, and caressed one's ear. His powerful conclusion states: "suddenly I realize / That if I stepped out of my body I would break / Into blossom." In these lines, Wright awakens to his own inner spirit thanks to the benevolent touch of another creature. By contrast, in Galway Kinnell's poem, one man blesses a plant, while another man blesses an animal. In both poems, however, the touch across the species barrier is meant to rekindle the major Emersonian belief that all life is sacred, that all life is interconnected, that all life is individual and worthy of self-respect. Indeed, the major message of Walt Whitman's poetry, that self-respect is the highest of ideals, returns with renewed vigor in the work of poets born in the late 1920s and early 1930s, the poets of James Wright's

and Galway Kinnell's generation. For example, in Wright's poem, the pony allows Wright to blossom and know himself better. Similarly, in Kinnell's poem, the poet, through his touch, allows a plant to blossom with a sense of inner spiritual importance. Kinnell even equates that touch with Saint Francis's caress of a sow as if to insist on the importance of communicated to each and every individual life its own innate self-worth. Interestingly, in both Wright's and Kinnell's poems the species barrier is crossed as one creature reminds the other of its inherent dignity. In these poems, as in Emerson's philosophy, no life form, on a spiritual, ethical plane is better than any other. And, as with Whitman, the poetic form for such a message is free verse: a set of line breaks that are meant to conform to the actual spoken breath of the poet.

Looking more closely at Kinnell's poem, then, one finds that in its first half (the first 13 lines) Kinnell, like Emerson, Whitman, and Wright before him, argues against the seemingly insurmountable hierarchies of less, better, best that separate life forms from one another. But unlike his three predecessors, Kinnell also turns to a specifically Christian source to make this same point. It is as if Kinnell wants to reconcile a more obviously Christian sensibility to the natural theology embraced by Emerson, Whitman, and Wright. In other words, when Kinnell compares his touch to that of Saint Francis, he implicitly compares an Emersonian naturalism to the specific theology of Christianity. When Kinnell, in the second half of his poem, turns to this Christian saint it is as if he were speaking across the gulf of time to Emerson himself. It is as if Kinnell were saying, you know, not only is all life radically equal but so too are all spiritual creeds. On the one hand there is the natural divinity celebrated by Emerson on the other there is the specifically Christian theology of Saint Francis. Rather than claim one is better, more pure than the other, Kinnell, in his poem shows them to be the same in their goals, in their implicit faith in self-reliance and self-respect. In the beginning of his poem, Kinnell makes a straightforward Emersonian message plain: The bud stands for all things, even for those things that don't flower, for everything flowers, from within, of self-blessing.

In these opening lines, Kinnell fully enters the tradition of immanence where "everything flowers, from within." He also reminds us of that tradition's ethical dimension, of the idea that, if all things are holy, than all things deserve equal respect. Through the metaphor of the bud, Kinnell is able to tell us that even the most banal of plants—even those plants which don't actually blossom—have an inner spirit. He also tells us that this spirit can go dormant. Even the simplest of life forms needs to be reminded that it, too, deserves respect for itself. In this small way, through a set of four free verse lines, Kinnell recasts Emerson for the contemporary period. Through the use of plain language, readily accessible imagery, and the free verse line Kinnell makes Emerson new. In the next seven lines, Kinnell focuses on the individualistic dimension of Emerson's theology, on Emerson's principle of self-reliance: sometimes it is necessary to reteach a thing its loveliness, to put a hand on its brow of the flower and retell it in words and in touch it is lovely until it flowers again from within, of self-blessing.

Note that Kinnell echoes, and nearly repeats one of his opening lines: "flowers again from within, of self-blessing." This notion of "self-blessing" is at once an allusion to James Wright's marvelous poem and a restatement of Emerson's major ideas. But more than that these lines focus on the word "reteach." Notice that, according to Kinnell, when he teaches the bud to find "the blossom within" he is actually only "reteaching" a lesson the bud itself had known but had evidently forgotten. This was Emerson's major point about the poet. The poet, in effect, was a catalyst reminding us of what we always knew but had somehow forgotten. In these lines, Kinnell, acting on the faith that, as William Blake said, "everything that lives is holy," teaches even the plants to know themselves. In so doing, he eradicates the spiritual hierarchy that would make a man's soul worth more than a plant's. In his poem, Kinnell combats the temptation to find a spiritual inequality in creation. Rather than claim to be better than anything, or anyone, Kinnell, in a moment of genuine spiritual self-effacement, gestures to a lowly bud and tells it that it contains its own blessing. In many ways this echo of James Wright's great poem is also a modern version of Emerson's "The Rhodora."

Where the poem becomes entirely original, however, is in the second half when Kinnell compares his touch to that of Saint Francis. In this second half, Kinnell develops a simile where his hand touching the bud becomes, in his imagination, the hand of Saint Francis touching a sow. In twelve lines developing this image, Kinnell focuses the reader's gaze on the specific details of the sow and of its little suckling at its teats. Few animals could be more lowly than this, few scenes more animalistic. We are put, through these details, as far from the human world as we can be. Kinnell, in effect,

rubs our noses in the dirt and smell of swine. And, as the piglets suckle, Saint Francis, in his caress, declares this scene holy and necessary not for the sake of humanity but for the sake of the sow herself. It is her self-respect, her worth as a creature with young giving life and feeding that life that Saint Francis, and now Kinnell, celebrates: "the long, perfect loveliness of sow." We, as readers, are not meant to find some use, some farming function, some domestic rationale in this loveliness. Rather, we are meant to see the sow as Saint Francis would have her see herself. If, as another poet of Kinnell's generation, Mary Oliver, declares, poetry is the art of "honoring life," "high ideals," and "religious views," if, as she insists, real poetry is an art of "hope," "gratitude," "tenderness" and "love" than both this poem, and this poet are the real thing.

Source: Jonathon N. Barron, in an essay for *Poetry for Students,* Gale, 2000.

Sources

Atkinson, Ed Brooks, *Selected Writings of Emerson,* Modern Library, 1950.

Bell, Charles, "Galway Kinnell," in *On the Poetry of Galway Kinnell: The Wages of Dying,* edited by Howard Nelson, Ann Arbor: The University of Michigan Press, 1987, pp. 25-28.

Bellamy, Joe David, ed., "Galway Kinnell," in *American Poetry Observed: Poets on Their Work,* Urbana: University of Illinois Press, 1984, pp. 134-142.

Bloom, Harold, "Straight Forth Out of Self," in *On the Poetry of Galway Kinnell: The Wages of Dying,* edited by Howard Nelson, Ann Arbor: The University of Michigan Press, 1987, pp. 104-106.

Carruth, Gorton, *What Happened When: A Chronology of Life and Events in America,* New York: Harper Collins, 1996.

Davie, Donald, "Slogging for the Absolute," in *On the Poetry of Galway Kinnell: The Wages of Dying,* edited by Howard Nelson, Ann Arbor: The University of Michigan Press, 1987, pp. 143-156.

Emerson, Ralph Waldo, "Self-Reliance," "The Poet," and "The Rhodora," in *Nature.*

Golding, Alan, *From Outlaw to Classic: Canons in American Poetry,* Wisconsin University Press, 1995.

Hall, Donald, "From 'Text as Test,'" in *On the Poetry of Galway Kinnell: The Wages of Dying,* edited by Howard Nelson, Ann Arbor: The University of Michigan Press, 1987, pp. 157-168.

Harrington, Michael, *The New American Poverty,* New York: Holt, Rinehart and Winston, 1984.

Howell, A. G. Ferrers, "Introduction," in *The Little Flowers of St. Francis of Assisi,* by Ugolino di Monte Santa Maria, edited by W. Heywood, New York: Vintage Books, 1998, pp. xix-xxxi.

Kinnell, Galway, "An Interview with A. Poulin, Jr., and Stan Sanvel Rubin," in *Walking Down the Stairs: Selections from Interviews,* Ann Arbor: The University of Michigan Press, 1978, pp. 20-32.

————, "An Interview with Wayne Dodd and Stanley Plumly," in *Walking Down the Stairs: Selections from Interviews,* Ann Arbor: The University of Michigan Press, 1978, pp. 41-57.

————, "An Interview with William Heyen and Gregory Fitzgerald," in *Walking Down the Stairs: Selections from Interviews,* Ann Arbor: The University of Michigan Press, 1978, pp. 1-6.

————, *The Poetics of the Physical World,* Annual Writer in Residence Lecture, No. 5, Fort Collins: Colorado State University, 1969.

————, *Three Books: Body Rags; Mortal Acts, Mortal Words; The Past,* Boston: Houghton Mifflin Co., 1993.

Lazer, Hank, "That Backward-Spreading Brightness," in *On the Poetry of Galway Kinnell: The Wages of Dying,* edited by Howard Nelson, Ann Arbor: The University of Michigan Press, 1987, pp. 107-118.

Nelson, Howard, ed., "Introduction," in *On the Poetry of Galway Kinnell: The Wages of Dying,* edited by Howard Nelson, Ann Arbor: The University of Michigan Press, 1987, pp. 1-18.

Oliver, Mary, *Rules for the Dance: A Handbook for Writing and Reading Metrical Verse,* Houghton, Mifflin, 1998.

Rosenberg, Liz, "A Poet with the Flame of Greatness," in *On the Poetry of Galway Kinnell: The Wages of Dying,* edited by Howard Nelson, Ann Arbor: The University of Michigan Press, 1987, pp. 119-121.

Peters, Robert, "On Climbing the Matterhorn: Monadnock," in *On the Poetry of Galway Kinnell: The Wages of Dying,* Ann Arbor: The University of Michigan Press, 1987, pp. 88-95.

St. James, Elaine, *Living the Simple Life,* New York: Hyperion, 1996.

Traherne, Thomas, "Innocence," in *Seventeenth-Century Prose and Poetry,* 2nd ed., edited by Alexander M. Witherspoon and Frank J. Warnke, New York: Harcourt, Brace & World, Inc., 1963, p. 1022.

Tuten, Nancy Lewis, "Galway Kinnell," in *Dictionary of Literary Biography Yearbook: 1987,* edited by J. M. Brook, Detroit: Gale, 1988, pp. 257-264.

White, Richard, "Animals and Enterprise," in *The Oxford History of the American West,* edited by Clyde A. Milner II, Carol A. O'Connor, and Martha A. Sandweiss, New York: Oxford University Press, 1994, p. 236.

Worth, Richard, *Poverty,* Lucent Overview Series, San Diego: Lucent Books, Inc., 1997.

Wright, James, *The Branch Will Not Break,* Wesleyan University Press, 1963.

Zimmerman, Lee, *Intricate and Simple Things: The Poetry of Galway Kinnell,* Urbana: University of Illinois Press, 1987.

For Further Study

Kinnell, Galway, "Poetry, Personality, and Death," in *A Field Guide to Contemporary Poetry and Poetics,* Rev. ed., edited by Stuart Friebert, David Walker, and David Young, Oberlin, OH: Oberlin College Press, 1997, pp. 203-223.

As the title of this essay suggests, Kinnell examines the relationships between the poem and the mortal human behind and within the poem. In an age of self-absorption, he says, "poetry has taken on itself the task of breaking out of the closed ego," but that requires a "death of the self." He defines this concept further, as "a death out of which one might hope to be reborn more giving, more alive, more open, more related to the natural life." Along with "The Poetics of the Physical World," it is considered to be one of Kinnell's most important, and controversial, aesthetic statements.

————, *Walking Down the Stairs: Selections from Interviews,* Ann Arbor: The University of Michigan Press, 1995.

The eleven interviews composing this book reveal much about Kinnell's personality, writing life, and artistic convictions. Conversations range from particular poems, changes in style, influences, and his role as teacher and translator, to personal habits, affections, and dislikes. The interviews cover the period between 1969 and 1976, representing a mere slice of the poet's forty-year career; an important one, nevertheless, since Kinnell was in the midst of significant aesthetic changes in the decade between 1970 and 1980.

Nelson, Howard, ed., *On the Poetry of Galway Kinnell: The Wages of Dying,* Ann Arbor: The University of Michigan Press, 1987.

This is an essential collection of Kinnell criticism, balanced and thorough, covering the first 25 years of the poet's career, from *What a Kingdom it Was* (1960) to *The Past* (1985). It is organized into five sections: overviews, book reviews, appraisals of his career, attention to individual poems, and a colorful reminiscence at the end by Anne Wright, wife of the late poet Charles Wright, one of Kinnell's closest friends.

Tuten, Nancy Lewis, ed., *Critical Essays on Galway Kinnell,* Boston: G. K. Hall & Co., 1997.

With its additional decade of coverage, Nancy Tuten's selection of reviews and essays complements Howard Nelson's earlier volume of criticism. Much like other volumes in the series Critical Essays on American Literature, this book features numerous reviews (here 28), only a few of which overlap with selections in Nelson's book. The essays of part two, written by both critics and poets, focus both on single books and on large themes such as transcendence, transformation, dualism, music, love, and death.

"Trouble with Math in a One-Room Country School"

Jane Kenyon
1986

"Trouble with Math in a One-Room Country School" first appeared in 1986 in Jane Kenyon's second volume of poems, *The Boat of Quiet Hours,* and again in her collection of new and selected poems, *Otherwise* (1996). In both prose and poems, Kenyon readily confesses that math was her weakest subject. This poem recalls a humiliating moment in elementary school when academic difficulty leads to punishment, not help. In her case, it also leads to an inner change, a heart newly "hardened against authority." In the short span of this three-stanza, 25-line poem we learn much about the settings, both outer and inner, for the change that takes place.

Aside from the title, the poem does not specifically identify the nature of her trouble, nor does it directly track the processes of her inner transformation. The poem delivers this "information" obliquely. As a result, the context of her "trouble with math" expands in the widening rings of sensory details, such as "the smell / of sweeping compound," the startling image of Christ on Ann's blue bookmark, and the sound of a Haydn melody hummed in the furnace closet. These indirections help tell a story far larger than the central issue or event itself. "Trouble with Math in a One-Room Country School" is typical of Kenyon's attention to a single moment, and of her ability to make it present through sensory detail and clear, spare language. The poem provides insight into the mind of a child: what she perceives, and how she copes with adult perceptions.

Author Biography

When Jane Kenyon died from leukemia on April 23, 1995, one month short of her 48th birthday, she had lived nearly twenty years in rural Wilmot, New Hampshire, with her husband, poet Donald Hall. "Eagle Pond" had been the home of Hall's family for generations, and it became the setting from which her mature poetry emerged. The farmhouse and countryside around Wilmot reminded Kenyon of her Michigan childhood before its landscape became paved over and subdivided: "The move to New Hampshire was a restoration of a kind of paradise," she told an interviewer.

Kenyon was born on May 23, 1947, and grew up in an old house "crowded with pictures, books, and music" on the rural outskirts of Ann Arbor, Michigan, home of the University of Michigan. Her parents were freelancers, according to Donald Hall's afterword in *Otherwise*. Reuel Kenyon was a jazz pianist, and Polly Kenyon a singer, seamstress, and sewing teacher. Jane attended a one-room country school until the fifth grade, and thereafter walked two miles along gravel roads to the annexed Foster School, Ann Arbor Township, No. 16 Fractional. In an interview with Bill Moyers, Kenyon speculates that "growing up in the country far from friends made me an inward child," and a lover of the natural world. This love and capacity for solitude rings dominant both in her poetry and in *A Hundred White Daffodils* (1999), a posthumous collection of Kenyon's miscellaneous prose, interviews, and translations of the Russian poet Anna Akhmatova.

"Childhood, when you are in it, seems to last forever," Kenyon begins an unfinished essay from that volume. She goes on to recall that "the central psychic fact" of her own seemingly endless childhood was "Grandmother's spiritual obsession, and her effort to secure me in her religious fold." Jane and her brother Reuel spent a great deal of time in their paternal grandmother's big boarding house near the University of Michigan. There her grandmother, Dora Kenyon, talked endlessly of the Second Coming of Christ, using apocalyptic language which Jane sometimes interpreted whimsically: "Jesus would come out of the clouds, or, as my imagination had it, he'd walk down a sunbeam like a ramp, to judge us—rather like Santa Clause, as I understood *him*." But more often, she was fearful. After all, God might come as "a thief in the night" to judge the world, and those not found in the Book of Life were bound for a violent, fiery end. As she imagined the Second Coming, "I was quite certain that Jesus would not wait while I fumbled with curlers and pajama buttons," and "it was hard for me to fall asleep at 925 South State Street." Grandmother Dora's authoritative spirituality and Kenyon's adolescent rejection of it is a kind of paradigm for several key images in "Trouble with Math in a One-Room Country School." "I grew contemptuous of religion and the people I knew who practiced it," says Kenyon, "although I took great pains to hide this development from Grandmother."

Besides the authority of her intense grandmother, the authority of public schooling was also a persistent source of "trouble" for Jane Kenyon. She confesses in "Dreams of Math," a column for the *The Concord Monitor,*

> It troubled me throughout my education that I had to obey and perform for teachers whose judgment I didn't respect. I had a few teachers whom I respected enormously, a middling group of ordinary mortals, and finally an index of teachers I thought ill of, who nonetheless had the power to determine the course of my education and my life.

"Trouble," in particular, took the form of math anxiety. In elementary school she

> discovered early on that letters, reading, spelling made sense to me, but numbers had such strange proclivities. That zero times four was zero, canceling the existence of the four, seemed dubious at best.

And in high school, "even geometry, which my friends told me I'd be able to master, bollixed me.... I turned to arts and letters, where I felt on safer ground."

From high school in Ann Arbor, Kenyon went on to the University of Michigan, earning a B.A. in 1970 and an M. A. in English in 1972. That same year, she married Donald Hall, a poet and English professor 19 years her senior. Hall gave up his academic position in 1975 and the two moved to the New Hampshire farmhouse in Wilmot, near the foot of Mt. Kearsage. Grudgingly at first, Kenyon also began attending church with Hall in Danbury where his family had been longstanding members. There she heard pastor Jack Jensen's well-crafted, intelligent sermons about "a God who overcomes you with love, not a God of rules and prohibitions." Gradually she found belief displacing fear.

In 1978, Alice James Books published Kenyon's first volume of poetry, *From Room to Room,* which critic Robin Latimer calls "the poetic diary of a honeymoon." The volumes that follow, *The Boat of Quiet Hours* (1986), *Let Evening Come* (1990), *Constance* (1993), and the posthumous

Otherwise (1996), chronicle Kenyon's lucid attention to New Hampshire's fickle weather and staid inhabitants, the seasonal cycles of garden and town life, Don's cancer, her constant bout with depression, and eventually, her own imminent death. "Trouble with Math in a One-Room Country School" departs from the here and now of Kenyon's adult life to recall a formative moment in her past. It bears her characteristic clarity and ability to embrace transformation in the midst of continuance: "She led me, blinking / and changed, back to class."

Poem Text

The others bent their heads and started in.
Confused, I asked my neighbor
to explain—a sturdy, bright-cheeked girl
who brought raw milk to school from her family's
herd of Holsteins. Ann had a blue bookmark,   5
and on it Christ revealed his beating heart,
holding the flesh back with His wounded hand.
Ann understood division....

Miss Moran sprang from her monumental desk
and led me roughly through the class   10
without a word. My shame was radical
as she propelled me past the cloakroom
to the furnace closet, where only the boys
were put, only the older ones at that.
The door swung briskly shut.   15

The warmth, the gloom, the smell
of sweeping compound clinging to the broom
soothed me. I found a bucket, turned it
upside down, and sat, hugging my knees.
I hummed a theme from Haydn that I knew   20
from my piano lessons …
and hardened my heart against authority.
And then I heard her steps, her fingers
on the latch. She led me, blinking
and changed, back to the class.   25

Poem Summary

Lines: 1-3

The title provides many of the "facts" for this poem at the outset, informing the reader just what the "trouble" is and where it will take place. In the context of the title, therefore, the meaning of the first line is clear: the poem's speaker is a student left behind while all the rest have begun working their math problems, perhaps for a quiz. The scene is a familiar one to many students, and so is the method for coping. The girl resorts to seeking help from her "neighbor," a word traditionally used for a student who sits adjacent to another. If we identify the "I" with Jane Kenyon herself, the farm girl could also have literally been a "neighbor," since the Kenyon family lived across the street from a large working farm in rural Michigan.

Lines: 3-8

In the middle of the third line, we begin to follow the "confused" girl's path of perception, which strays momentarily from the trouble at hand to keen observation of her "neighbor." With a few very deft strokes, we know by implication that this "neighbor" is a ruddy, healthy farm girl whose family is likely quite religious. She brings not only "raw milk" to school but also the "raw" image of Christ baring his heart and wounds. In any poem, particularly a short lyric, each and every word must have a role in conveying sound, sense, or image. One may wonder at first why the poem seems to wander from the trouble at hand—why is this description necessary? Perhaps that is the point. It is a foray with purpose, in the poem's context, in part explaining why the girl has trouble with math, as Kenyon did in her own life. A child like Kenyon is more likely to be absorbed in the details of person, place, and moment than in the abstractions and rote applications of numbers.

The description also touches upon a key feature of Kenyon's own biography, the authoritative presence of her rigidly religious grandmother, who spoke relentlessly and frighteningly about the Second Coming of Christ. But it is dangerous to ascribe biographical details too closely to a poem's reading, thereby distorting or reducing a detail or image by pressing it into biographical service. Here, the passionate and wounded Christ on the blue bookmark is juxtaposed with the fact that "Ann understood division." Kenyon could have placed "Ann understood division" on line three, and it would have made perfect sense that she would ask a student who "understood division" to "explain." The fact is still present. But in its actual position in the poem, this line gathers meaning that resonates with the image on the blue bookmark. Ann is not the only one who understood division; so does that "wounded hand," but in much more than a mathematical context. The stanza ends in an ellipsis, a technique of punctuation Kenyon used often. Here it directs the reader into the "something more" that could be said, yet isn't. It asks us to consider the various ways "division" could be understood in light of the images that have gone before.

Lines: 9-11

In the second stanza, the girl's reverie is interrupted abruptly. Miss Moran catches her "ask-

Media Adaptations

- Jane Kenyon reads three poems, "Man Eating," "Gettysburg: July 1, 1863," and "Happiness," in a CD recording, *The New Hampshire Writers' Project Sampler: Ten Years of Literary Performance, 1988-1998*. The CD also features two poems by Donald Hall.

- On October 26, 1995, a celebration of Jane Kenyon's life and work took place at the University of New Hampshire's Dimond Library. Three New Hampshire poets, Charles Simic, McKeel McBride, and Donald Hall, read selections from Kenyon's work and gave personal accounts of their connection with Kenyon and her poetry. A videotape and audio recording of the entire reading are available for on-site use in the Special Collections department of the University of New Hampshire library (phone 603-862-2714). A website for the Kenyon exhibit—www.izaak.unh.edu/specoll/exhibits/reading.htm—also makes several recorded excerpts of the celebration available online.

- You can listen to Donald Hall read two Kenyon poems, "Drawing from the Past" and "Surprise," in RealAudio, at *The Atlantic Monthly's* online site—www.theatlantic.com/unbound//poetry/anthology/Kenyon/2poems.htm.

- *A Life Together: Donald Hall and Jane Kenyon* is a video recording first broadcast in December of 1993 on *Bill Moyers' Journal*. Primarily an interview of the couple in their home in Wilmot, the Moyers film also includes footage of Kenyon and Hall reading to audiences at the Geraldine R. Dodge Poetry Festival and to neighbors in Wilmot. The video can be obtained from Films for the Humanities, 1-800-257-5126.

- At least two composers have set the poetry of Jane Kenyon to music. J. Mark Scearce wrote a score in 1997, *American Triptych: For Soprano, Flute, Clarinet/Bass Clarinet, Violin, Cello, Piano, and Percussion: On Three Poems by Jane Kenyon*. This piece features the poems "At the Store," "Down the Road," and "Let Evening Come." *Briefly It Enters* (1997) is a cycle of songs for voice and piano based on nine poems by Kenyon, composed by William Bolcom. It is published by E. B. Marks and distributed by H. Leonard, ISBN 0793591325.

- Bellarmine College in Louisville, Kentucky, hosted "The First Jane Kenyon Conference," April 16-18, 1998, and has made four audiocassette recordings of the conference readings and remembrances available.

---

ing" a neighbor for help, and obviously thinks she is cheating. Whether Miss Moran herself is large in actual stature or small seems irrelevant; her authority is obviously massive. The poem indicates that fact obliquely, not directly, through a *synecdoche* for that authority, "her monumental desk." A *synecdoche* is a figure of speech in which a part is used for a whole. "Throne," for example, is a familiar *synecdoche* for "king" or "queen," as in "You must lay your complaint before the throne." The adjective "monumental" modifies "desk," but by extension gives the teacher's authority a sense of massiveness, of towering institutional rigidity. Miss Moran acts swiftly to dispense discipline, but like a monument, performs it silently, "without a

word." The verbs speak for Miss Moran instead, telling all in the way she "sprang" from her desk and "led me roughly through the class." Clearly unused to being punished, Kenyon recalls, "My shame was radical." "Radical" carries here not only its usual sense of "extreme," but also, in the word's oldest meaning, of "coming from the root," in Latin, the *radix*. Her shame arose from the very root or foundation of her being.

Lines: 12-15

One can easily imagine the mortified, red face and averted eyes of this young girl, as her teacher "propels" her to the hellish "furnace closet," a place reserved only for the worst offenders, usually the older boys. That realization not only increases her shame, but also propels her ever more intensely toward decisive change. The stanza ends as abruptly as it began, with the closet door swinging "briskly shut."

Lines: 16-19

The incarceration doesn't have the desired effect, however. Strangely enough, the girl's shame is soon "soothed" inside the closet by the warmth and clean, familiar "smell/of sweeping compound," even by the "gloom." As she quietly fashions a makeshift seat and hugs her knees, we learn that this young girl has a peculiar strength and capacity to comfort herself.

Lines: 20-22

There in the semi-darkness she comforts herself with a phrase of music, calls upon her inner resources, and decides not to acquiesce to such injustice. Authority, she has just learned, is to be questioned, and if necessary, resisted: "I … hardened my heart against authority." Among other things, the ellipsis at the end of line 21 gives the illusion of time passing in reflection and eventual resolve, which is named in line 22.

Lines: 23-25

The anecdote, or brief story, concludes with the girl's release from her punitive cell. The poem provides us the "inside view" from the closet where, along with the girl, we hear Miss Moran's "fingers / on the latch" and we know what Miss Moran cannot know: the girl's "change" has nothing to do with the penitence Miss Moran intended. The girl is "blinking" not only because her eyes are adjusting from dark closet to bright classroom, but because she is also adjusting, figuratively, to the new light of her resolve.

Themes

Education

Few people living today have ever experienced education in a "one-room country school." But many can identify with the first half of this poem's title, "Trouble with Math." These days we say such people suffer from "math anxiety." There's hardly anyone who cannot recall having some sort of trouble in school: with a particular subject, in being misunderstood and suffering the consequences, in finding oneself "alien" to the approach of a particular teacher, with the social dimension of school,

or even with conventional schooling in general. This poem is not the only one in Kenyon's corpus that expresses her unhappiness with school. "Three Songs at the End of Summer" ends with a memory of standing scrubbed and neat in new clothes, "waiting for the school bus / with a dread that took my breath away,"

> holding … the new books—words, numbers, and operations with numbers I did not comprehend—and crayons, unspoiled by use, in a blue canvas satchel with red leather straps. Spruce, inadequate, and alien I stood at the side of the road. It was the only life I had.

The "white indifferent morning sky" arching overhead reminds us of Miss Moran's "monumental desk," both metaphors for the remote indifference of teachers to Kenyon's particular intelligence. The young Kenyon recognizes this more serious "trouble" early on, according to "Learning in the First Grade." In that poem, she yields to the teacher's authority, grudgingly supplying the answer expected, not the one she knows to be true:

> Oh, but my mind was finical. It put the teacher perpetually in the wrong. Called on, however, I said aloud: "The cup is red." "But it's not," I thought, like Galileo Galilei muttering under his beard….

There's a wry humor in this comparison of a savvy little girl to the famous Renaissance genius. But it also suggests a painful truth about many educational systems and their widely varying abilities to recognize and nurture the native genius of children, especially when those children don't conveniently conform to the theoretical model of a "good student." In the place and time Jane Kenyon attended elementary school, few formal resources existed for helping children with difficulties, or "learning issues," as we now say. Often a child's "problem" was judged to be moral, and the correction to her perceived laziness, dishonesty, or disobedience was simply punishment. Miss Moran obviously thought the little girl was cheating. Rather than explore her confusion and need for help, this teacher consigned her to academic purgatory, where it was assumed she would become contrite and penitent.

"Trouble with Math in One-Room Country School" has little to say, ultimately, about a child's difficulty comprehending operations with numbers. Instead, it is a story about the unintended learning that occurs in school. The child in this poem learns very little about math that day. Rather, it is her heart and will that have been educated, in the oldest sense of the word educated, "led out." She has been "led out" from the furnace closet having forged a new relationship to authority, and a new comprehension of her own strength. Meanwhile, with the quiet self-containment characteristic of Jane Kenyon and her poetry, this child would continue to endure school as though in a little boat:

> "All day in my imagination my body floated Above the classroom, navigating easily between fluorescent shoals … …. and no one knew I was not where I seemed to be…. "("The Little Boat" *Otherwise* 98-99).

Enclosures and Freedom

The second half of this poem's title tells where the trouble takes place: in the small confines of a "one-room country school." This setting is a variation on another theme recurring both in this poem and in Kenyon's work at large: the paradoxes of enclosure and freedom, confinement and release, binding and letting go. Rooms, closets, drawers, and other enclosed spaces often garner the attention in a Kenyon poem. In "Trouble with Math in a One-Room Country School," the fact that the school consists of "one room" is significant. All that can happen happens in that one enclosure, a microcosm where the drama between child and teacher, perception and truth, intention and outcome, is played out. If "all the world's a stage," according to Shakespeare, then the opposite is also true. This one-room stage is also a world where a suffering Christ "confined" in an image on a narrow blue bookmark finds dramatic parallel in the dark closet from which a suffering child emerges "blinking" in the new light of her transformation. Room within a room, the furnace closet or school "jail" becomes the unlikely place where inner freedom is wrought. Thus, this poem finds its place among other more famous expressions of freedom-in-confinement, notably Martin Luther King, Jr.'s "Letter from the Birmingham Jail," and John Bunyan's *Pilgrim's Progress*.

It doesn't take long, reading through Kenyon's poems, to notice how often they feature small rooms or closets as the locus for revelation and transformation. *From Room to Room* is the title of Kenyon's first collection of poems, in large part reflecting the experience of moving to her husband's family home in New Hampshire early in their marriage, and taking on a new life with its new enclosures and freedoms: "I move from room to room, a little dazed, like the fly. I watch it bump against each window." She feels "clumsy here" among the artifacts of her husband's ancestral past, and disembodied, "Out of my body for a while, / weightless in space." Another poem notes, in contrast, that

Topics for Further Study

- Design an oral history project that engages older members of your family or community in reconstructing a typical school day in their elementary school years. Focus your questions to evoke stories and vivid descriptions.

- Research the history of education in your own town, city, or county in the past 50 years. How have demographic, political, or economic trends influenced the patterns of growth and change in schools? Do these mirror broader national trends? How so?

- Write a thank-you letter to a teacher who has had a positive influence on your life. Include specific memories of classes or conversations or personal encouragement. Send it if you wish.

- Many powerful writings have emerged from enforced confinement in a concentration camp, prison, hospital room, or even a "furnace closet" at school. Sometimes enforced isolation can lead to transformation, through imaginative thinking, reflection, or decisions. Write a poem or story, serious or comic, in which your own experience of confinement led to change.

her husband "always belonged here…. certain as a rock," while she's "the one who worries / if I fit in with the furniture / and the landscape." It doesn't take long, however, for Kenyon to feel what writer Simone Weil calls "gravity and grace" take hold, as she refreshes the cliche "putting down roots" with a new image: "I feel my life start up again, like a cutting when it grows the first pale and tentative root hair in a glass of water." In "From to Room to Room," Kenyon expresses the paradox of freedom-in-bondage, the necessity of being tethered in order to explore, of being bound in order to be freed:

> "Blessed be the tie that binds … " we sing in the church down the road. And how does it go from there? The tie … the tether, the hose carrying oxygen to the astronaut, turning, turning outside the hatch, taking a look around.

By telling the story of her "trouble with math" with an emphasis on the room that holds the dynamic mix of feeling, action, perception, and change, Jane Kenyon's poem shows us the importance of the settings for our own life-stories. Finally, the poem explores an aspect of freedom—the paradox of great-in-small-that poet Langston Hughes also recognized when he wrote: Freedom is a strong seed planted in a great need.

Style

If you were to hear Jane Kenyon read aloud "Trouble with Math in a One-Room Country School" and not know it is broken into 25 lines and divided into three stanzas, it might sound like a well-crafted brief story, or *anecdote.* Yet, Kenyon did set her experience within the "confines" of a poetic form, the style called "free verse." Like the thematic paradox of freedom and enclosure that shapes this poem, "free verse" is not freedom *from* form. It is freedom *within* the discipline of well-chosen words, sensory details, images, combinations of sounds within and among words, and punctuation, all of which contribute meaningfully, not haphazardly, to its existence as a poem.

Much the way chapters help organize the narrative elements of fiction, or paragraphs signal a change in the focus of an essay, the stanza breaks in a poem can also signal a shift in perception, feeling, or action. To use another analogy, the space at the ends of lines and stanzas in a poem is like a "rest" in a musical score. The "white space" created between the end of one stanza and the beginning of the next allows a measure of reverberation from the images and sounds that have gone before. Then what follows, like the various movements in a sonata or symphony, creates a contrast in mood, tone, or pace, usually while maintaining a unifying *motif,* a thread of image, feeling, or experience.

If we examine Kenyon's poem with an eye and ear toward the beginnings and ends of its stanzas, we can notice, for example, the contrast between open and closed punctuation. The first line of the first stanza is a complete sentence, and ends in a period. The sense of closure is therefore very strong, and is a perfect match to this child's sense of being closed off from the rest of the class, shut out of the relative comfort with which the other students perform "operations with numbers."

But the last line of stanza one ends in an ellipsis, an "antonym" (or opposite) to the period. An ellipsis indicates that there is more, that something is not finished, and any completions or conclusions are left unresolved or unexpressed. Kenyon's ellipses (which occur consistently throughout her work, in nearly every poem) are a kind of invitation to the reader to suspend or delay the urge to *finish* the thought or experience; instead, to court possibility. Even though "Ann understood division" is a complete sentence, Kenyon chose, paradoxically, to "punctuate" it with an ellipsis. As a result, both line and stanza reverberate with several possible meanings: perhaps Ann understands more than division; or, division itself is more than a mathematical operation; or, there is no end to division in this world. The ellipsis is a form of punctuation that engages the reader more intensely in the poem and its possibilities.

Besides its collaboration with mystery and incompletion, the ellipses in this poem heighten the contrast with whatever comes next. And what comes next, in stanza two, is the opposite of a child's dreamy meditation on her classmate's blue bookmark and "bright cheeks." It is the sudden, vehement response from the stony cold (read "monumental") Miss Moran who has studied neither the particulars of this child's behavior, nor her need as a student. The stanza ends, fittingly enough, with another complete sentence, ending in a period: "The door swung briskly shut." In this way, the stanza is punctuated in accord with Miss Moran's brand of authority: judgmental, conclusive, unilateral. Even the word "shut" ends in a hard, closed, "t" sound. What reverberates in the musical "rest" between stanza two and three is the tuneless, muted slam of involuntary confinement, of being shut off, physically, in parallel to being shut away, mentally, from the rest of the class.

The third stanza opens with a line that is not punctuated, but which continues into the next line. Such a technique is called *enjambment.* An enjambed line creates a sense of fluidity and incompletion. In this poem it offers a contrast with the cold, decisive action and sound that has gone before. The flexibility of the enjambed line is in accord with the flexible strength of this child and her refusal to be daunted by punishment. Instead, she takes comfort where and how she can, changing a bucket into a chair, humming her way into a new "place" in relation to Miss Moran in particular, and authority in general.

The last two lines of the poem are also enjambed, and even though there is no hard stop at the end of such a line, the "white space" created between one line and the next allows a natural pause or breath. It also puts a slight emphasis both on the last word of line 24, "blinking," and the first phrase of line 25, "and changed." The entire poem concludes with the child having been led "back to class," and the sentence ends in the way we expect most poems to end, in a period. However, since the poem has created other options for closure, such as the ellipsis, this period assumes more than a mechanical responsibility. Periods and ellipses in many Kenyon poems often bear a stronger-than-ordinary burden of meaning. "Reading" the period in this way, we can accordingly interpret the paradox of the child returning, but changed, as a decisive moment in her life.

Historical Context

Jane Kenyon was an elementary school student in the mid-1950s. In United States educational history, these years were characterized by "Cold War" anxiety. "Cold War" is the term used to describe the antagonistic relations between the Soviet Union and the United States after World War II, when political and economic struggles mounted between capitalist, democratic nations and those under communist control. While both sides built up massive military power, there was no actual military combat, hence the term "cold." In 1957, the Soviet Union launched the world's first manmade satellite, Sputnik I. The U.S. responded to this event with some alarm, and intensified the emphasis on math and science in schools in order to give the country a competitive edge in this new dimension of the Cold War, the space race. Both rural and urban schools nationwide responded as they could to this new national "crisis." Those having "trouble with math" were a liability in the wake of accelerated pressure to do well in the subjects that would help the U.S. win the race against Sputnik and communism.

Cold War anxiety was not the only influence on the character of education in the 1950s, however. The decade was also marked by a kind of cultural conservatism that seemed to interpret the ideal democracy as dutiful and conforming, not critically engaged and diverse. Most public schools shaped their students accordingly.

Numerous advances made earlier in the century by John Dewey and proponents of "progressive education" diminished in the face of these cultural forces. Dewey's ideas opposed educational elitism and upheld notions of individual giftedness.

He didn't believe that a few students (usually from upper-class families) should receive an academic education, and the rest be assigned to vocational training. Nor did he believe that the curriculum should begin and end with the "3 R's"—"reading, writing, and 'rithmetic," but that the emotional, artistic, and creative potential in children also requires attention. Thus, music, drama, and art are intrinsic to the curricula of that broad spectrum of schools called "progressive." In so-called "traditional" schools, the arts are usually considered "specials" or "extras" and their funding is often the first to go in a budget cut.

Opponents of progressive education in the fifties, such as University of Chicago historian Arthur Bestor, called it "regressive education" on the grounds that "instead of advancing, it began to undermine the great traditions of liberal education and to substitute for them lesser aims, confused aims, or no aims at all" (*Education Week*). The controversial Navy admiral Hyman Rickover, who directed the construction and launching of the first atomic-powered submarine, spoke out stridently against progressive education in *Education and Freedom* (1959):

> Dewey's insistence on making the child's interest the determining factor in planning curricula has led to substitution of know-how subjects for solid learning …. Our young people are therefore deprived of the tremendous intellectual heritage of Western civilization which no child can possibly discover by himself; he must be led to it. (*Education Week*)

A new generation of "progressives" entered the educational forum in the 1960s. Among them was social critic Jonathan Kozol, whose telling title *Death at An Early Age* (1967) spared no one his scathingly honest examination of schools as "a crazy place to learn." John Holt, "grandfather" of the unschooling movement and author of such books as *How Children Fail* (1964) seems to have been a witness of the drama in Kenyon's one-room school when he suggests that for such children, school for them is a kind of jail.

> Do they not, to some extent, escape and frustrate the relentless, insatiable pressure of their elders by withdrawing the most intelligent and creative parts of their minds from the scene? Is this not at least a partial explanation of the extraordinary stupidity that otherwise bright children so often show in school? The stubborn and dogged "I don't get it" with which they meet the instructions and explanations of their teachers—may it not be a statement of resistance as well as one of panic and flight (*Education Week*)?

The vignette of the classroom in "Trouble with Math" seems cut from the template of a typical

Compare & Contrast

- **1847:** Lyman Cobb's *The Evil Tendencies of Corporal Punishment as a Means of Moral Discipline in Families and Schools* was published. The book argues against the practice of flogging as an educational practice. Cobb was also opposed to requiring students to do tedious reading.

  1899: The publication of John Dewey's *The School and Society* ignited a revolution in the theory and practice of American education.

  1923: The Iron Hill School, a one-room school, was constructed in rural Delaware for African-American children as part of philanthropist Pierre du Pont's "Delaware experiment." Even though the school was small, it incorporated many concepts and practices of progressive education.

  1975: The U. S. Supreme Court rules that teachers are permitted to spank students if the students are made aware in advance of the behavior that warrants such an action.

  1989: According to the Educational Testing Service, American students (age 13) rank last in math and science among students of the same age from South Korea, Great Britain, Ireland, Spain, and Canada.

  1997: The U. S. Supreme Court ruled that the Constitution does not prohibit school districts from sending teachers into religious schools to provide remedial services to needy students.

- **1946:** The Leukemia Research Foundation was founded in Chicago.

  1975: The five-year survival rate for adult patients with acute leukemia was 38%; for children, 53%.

  1988: The five-year survival rate for patients with acute leukemia improved to 55% in adults and 78% in children.

  1999: Over 22,000 adults and children in the United States died from leukemia.

  Today: A new experimental therapy involving the injection of an immunotoxin known as LMB-2 is found to be useful in treating the rare blood cancer known as HCL (hairy cell leukemia).

1950s school. As such, it would provide little room, so to speak, for an imagination as expansive, and a temperament as artistic as that of Jane Kenyon.

Critical Overview

By most accounts, Jane Kenyon was flourishing as a poet when she died from leukemia, barely 48 years old. She had written four volumes of poems, and showed no signs of flagging in her work, despite husband Donald Hall's struggle with cancer and her own relentless bouts with depression. Her poetry was recognized both locally and nationally: she was honored with several awards; was named Poet Laureate of New Hampshire; received several fellowships from the National Endowment for the Arts; and her poems appeared frequently in the annual series *The Best American Poetry*.

Many readers use words such as "accessible," "earnest," "contemplative," "spare," "reticent," and "full of common things" to describe the character of Kenyon's work. Scott Hightower of the *Library Journal* finds her writing "devoid of urbane ironies," and even though he was speaking specifically about her prose in *A Hundred White Daffodils,* the same is also true of her poems. That may be why her art does not easily yield to the strategies and language of most "schools" of literary criticism. In the *New Criterion,* Robert Richman recognizes that Kenyon "refuses to be tempted to any form of poetic cliche," and that in this "age of the pigeonhole," Kenyon shows a strong "resistance to easy categorization." Thus, there is relatively little criticism of Kenyon's work beyond book reviews, and no specific attention to "Trouble with Math in a One-Room Country School."

Kenyon's detractors are few, but their criticisms are consistent: her language is too simple, her concerns too enclosed. As Robin Latimer points out, Kenyon was criticized negatively after her second book for a pattern of "failing to flirt excess," and for keeping her subject matter too closely tethered to the boundaries of her daily routines and chores. Latimer herself finds that "dog-walking is alarmingly recurrent" in the sixty poems comprising *Let Evening Come* (1990), but concedes that "this simple image of coping" may be affirming for some readers. David Barber counters such criticism by arguing that Kenyon's "modesty of means is not the same thing of course as simplicity of apprehension"; that is, her images may partake of the mundane, but the weight of feeling and depth of attention they reveal is profound.

Kenyon selected "Trouble with Math in a One-Room Country School" to appear in *Otherwise,* the collection of poems published after her death. Because there was so much regret for her passing by fellow poets and readers alike, *Otherwise* received more attention than any volume before it. In his review of the posthumous volume, Robert Richman calls her death "a significant loss to American poetry." Paul Breslin concludes that "a significant expansion in Kenyon's range had just begun when her last illness cut it short." His essay review for *Poetry* observes the opening of Kenyon's gift from what he perceives as an early tendency to be somewhat closeted and "self-limited," to her later pieces which move away from private concerns into more "public" themes. Elizabeth Lund, writing for the *Christian Science Monitor,* suggests that reading *Otherwise* is a strong remedy for the feeling that contemporary poetry is "little more than a wasteland." "That's why it's important for aspiring writers—or any true poetry fan" to become familiar with poets like Jane Kenyon, says Lund. In her review of *Otherwise* for the *Women's Review of Books,* Adrian Oktenberg says, "When I think of her I think less often of other poets than of the modern artists of spirituality … who pursue an ideal of perfection with every fiber." By the end of her life, Kenyon had obviously traveled quite a distance from the childhood closets of religious and academic fear to a landscape that could liberate both an affirmative spirituality and her art.

Criticism

Alice Van Wart

Alice Van Wart is a writer and teaches literature and writing in the Department of Continuing Education at the University of Toronto. She has published two books of poetry and has written articles on modern and contemporary literature. In the following essay, Van Wart examines the sensitivity and intellect of the poet expressed in the poem.

Born in 1947, Kenyon's life was cut short by cancer in 1995. Throughout much of her life she suffered the crippling effects of a clinical depression, the shadow of which hovers over much of her poetry and accounts for a consistent theme in it: the redemption of suffering through an appreciation of beauty in the world of art and music and, most particularly, in the natural world. In a poem titled "Having It Out With Melancholy," Kenyon, experiencing a moment of intense happiness at her awareness of the beauty in life, rhetorically asks, "What hurt me so terribly / All my life until this moment?" Undoubtedly there is no one answer to this question, but in her poem "Trouble With Math in a One-Room Country School," there is the suggestion of the poet's acute sensitivity and a suble intellect, qualities that will set the poet apart at an early age.

Kenyon's poem "Trouble With Math in a One-Room Country School," first published in *The Boat of Quiet Hours,* is typical of much of Kenyon's poetry in that it conveys complex feeling and emotional clarity through deceptive simplicity of form and diction. Yet despite its surface acessibility the poem dramatizes a complex transformative moment in the poet's life to evoke the process of thought and shifting emotions. The poem is autobiographical, based on an incident that occurred when she attended a one-room country schoolhouse between the grades of one to four. In the poem the poet recalls a particular incident from childhood that changed her fundamentally. The incident occurred when she innocently asked another student, her neighbor Ann, to explain division, a concept the teacher had been teaching, but which she had not grasped. The teacher expelled the young Kenyon from the class for talking and punished her by putting her in the furnace closet. If the teacher's intention in her punishment was to embarrass her young student and make her respect authority, the teacher badly miscalculated. Far from breaking

As an adult the poet is aware that when she returned with the teacher to the classroom she is 'blinking' not just because her eyes are adjusting to the light, but because she sees the classroom in a new light. The poet experiences her first awareness of the hierarchical nature of authority and its power to dole out punishment, just or unjust."

down and becoming repentant for her action, the young Kenyon remained angry at the teacher's actions and "hardened" her heart "against authority."

Though the young girl may not have been aware of the true significance of the event at the time, the adult knows it was at that moment that something "changed" within her. The poem, written from the first-person point of view in three stanzas of free verse, is also an initiation poem. In the first stanza the poet describes the incident; in the second she shows the teacher's response to it; and in the third she shows the lasting response to her punishment. Kenyon crafts her poem using structure and diction in such a way that she recreates the perspective of childhood through the unwavering voice of an adult. This dual perspective works to show both the progression of the thought and the emotions of the girl from the moment she is caught asking for help to the moment she walks back into the classroom, and the thoughts and feelings of the adult as she looks back on the event, interpreting and finding in it significant meaning.

The poem begins *in medias res*. The students are assembled in class and told to work on a mathematics exercise. While the other students "bent their heads and started in," the poet remains "confused" about what she should be doing and asks

her "neighbor / to explain." The poet remembers Ann, as "a sturdy, bright cheeked girl / who brought raw milk to school from her family's herd of Holsteins." Remembering Ann reminds the poet that "Ann had a blue bookmark." The reason she remembers the bookmark is because on it was a picture of Christ, which "revealed his beating heart, / holding the flesh back with His wounded hand." Clearly the description of Ann as "a sturdy, bright-cheeked girl" is the adult's and the image of Christ is one that has stayed in the poet's mind.

The abrupt shift from the image on the bookmark to the cryptic last line of "Ann understood division" is initially startling, but the poet is making an associative connection between the image and the meaning of division, which will be fully clarified in the final stanza. The poet understands something about Ann's nature that the child would not have comprehended. In the context of the preceding lines of the first stanza that contain the image of Ann as a sturdy farm girl and the wounds of Christ, the line carries complex association. First, the young poet asked Ann to help her because Ann understood "division," which the young poet did not. Second, the adult sees there was already in Ann a a division or separation between her identity as a girl who brings raw milk from her family's farm to school and a smart student capable of understanding the mathematics of division.

In the second stanza the poet recalls the teacher's response as the teacher "sprang from her monumental desk" and led the young poet "roughly" out of the class. The poet's description clearly shows the child's perspective of the event. The teacher's reactions are imbued with a sense of force and anger as she "propelled" the young poet to the furnace closet, where the door "swung briskly shut." At the same time the poet conveys her feelings that the teacher's punishment was extreme, if not unfair, at least in accordance with the action that provoked it. Recalling the incident, the poet states how she felt at that moment; her shame, she says, "was radical." The poet's sense of shame suggests her own painful awareness of being guilty, as well as feeling disgraced in front of her schoolmates. The use of the word "radical" to describe her shame conveys the extent of her feelings and suggests other far-reaching consequences. The poet makes clear that part of her shame comes from being singled out as the first girl to be put into the furnace room for punishment. Previously, the poet explains, "only the boys" were put there, and, moreover, only "the older ones at that." By being placed in the furnace closet where "only the boys

What Do I Read Next?

- Donald Hall's *Without: Poems* appeared in 1998, three years after Jane Kenyon's death. The book's title refers to life "without" his wife. It is a sequence of elegiac poems that chronicle Kenyon's diagnosis, illness, and death, even while it gives a glimpse into the unusual marriage of two artists. Most importantly, perhaps, it tells the story of a profound grief. *Without* finds a prose parallel in *A Grief Observed* by British writer C. S. Lewis, who lost his wife, Joy Davidman, to cancer. The film version of Lewis's book, *Shadowlands* became a popular success in the mid-1990's.

- Just as *Without* poetically narrates the end of Kenyon and Hall's life together, Kenyon's first book of poems, *From Room to Room* (1978) relates the early years of their marriage as she tries to settle into Hall's family home in Wilmot, New Hampshire. Kenyon first wanders "from room to room" rather disembodied, musing over the artifacts of Hall's ancestors—a thimble, a long gray hair, a rusting cast-iron stove—until by the end of the book, in a poem about a church potluck, she has somehow "found myself among people trying to live ordered lives." The images in the book gradually change from rootlessness to a sense of belonging that frees her to look around with a different, more expansive per-

ception, revealed in the last poem "Now That We Live."

- Feminist critics Sandra Gilbert and Susan Gubar are co-editors of *The Norton Anthology of Literature by Women* (2nd ed. 1996), a vast survey of women's writing that begins with Julian of Norwich in the Middle Ages and concludes with contemporary writers such as Alice Walker and Lucille Clifton. Both British and American women are represented in this collection of prose, fiction, and poetry. In creating the anthology, Gilbert and Gubar attempted to "recover a long and often neglected literary history," and trace the dynamic contours of the tradition of women's writing in English.

- When Donald Hall returned to New Hampshire with Jane Kenyon, he said in *Here at Eagle Pond* (1990) that "for me, it was coming home, and it was coming home to the place of language." Eagle Pond was where Hall began to write poems at age eleven or twelve. In this book, illustrated by Thomas Nason, Hall supplies good reasons, often humorous, for "why we live here." Among other things, he discusses New Hampshire's "one thousand" seasons, why he hates Vermont, and why he loves the Red Sox and his satellite dish.

---

have gone before, the young poet felt singled out and isolated."

Ann may have understood something about the mathematics of "division," but the adult poet realizes it was at this point that she began to understand the meaning of division in another sense. In the final stanza the poet remembers her feelings in the closet. Compared to the previous fear and shame she had experienced before the door "swung briskly shut," the young poet finds herself "soothed." The transition between the girl's response to her teacher in the second stanza and her response to being locked in the closet in the third

stanza is unexpected. Rather than experiencing fear of the darkness or self-pity at her shame, the young poet finds "the warmth, the gloom, the smell / of sweeping compound clinging to the broom" calming and relieving. She finds herself a bucket on which to sit and begins drumming on her knees "a theme from Haydn" that she knew from her "piano lessons."

Now remembering this moment the poet realizes that during this time that something else occurred: that she "hardened" her "heart against authority." The poet's uses of the active rather than passive voice to describe her reaction suggests volition on her part; her hardened heart was not something that happened unconsciously but something she herself determined. The double use of the compound coordinating conjunction "and" in lines 20 and 22 shows the simultaneous occurrence of the young poet hardening her heart against authority and the teacher's return to the closet. The young poet hears the teacher's "steps, her fingers / on the latch," before she opens the door to lead her student "blinking / and changed, back to the class." During her time behind the closed door the young poet is not only isolated from the others in her class, but she is also aware of the indignity of her situation and experiences a sense of injustice. She understands the power the teacher has over her to compel obedience and inflict pain.

As an adult the poet is aware that when she returned with the teacher to the classroom she is "blinking" not just because her eyes are adjusting to the light, but because she sees the classroom in a new light. The poet experiences her first awareness of the hierarchical nature of authority and its power to dole out punishment, just or unjust. At that moment she sees the division authority engenders between those who have power and those who don't in the division between teachers and students and between boys and girls. Further, the poet's hardened heart recalls the image on Ann's bookmark of Christ's open and "beating heart." The "wounded hand" with which Christ holds back the flesh of his heart is in Christian terms a symbol of his forgiveness in the face of his betrayal and crucifixion. The poet, however, unlike Christ, has hardened her heart in the face of her punishment. The change that has come about as a result of her experience in the furnace closet rests in her future inability to accept or forgive the ruthlessness of authority. At the moment the young poet walked back into the classroom she is unconsciously aware that she has been singled out and set apart; she has become an outsider, a condition that she continues to feel as an adult.

The final stanza expands and clarifies the real meaning of the "division" in the last line of the first stanza. The tone of the poem resonates with the anger of the young girl, still felt by the adult poet as she recalls the incident. Although the locus of the shame and the sense of isolation resides initially within the incident itself, the poet's use of a dual perspective, the association of the images between the first and third stanza, and her use of diction convey both a sense of the complexity of her feelings as a child and the clarity of her emotions as she recalls the incident and understands its sig-

nificance. In this respect Kenyon's understanding of the incident is one of a loss of innocence. The feelings of shame she experienced have not been mitigated with time, but her understanding of herself has sharpened in her recollection of a seminal event in her life.

Source: Alice Van Wart, in an essay for *Poetry for Students,* Gale, 2000.

Aviya Kushner

Aviya Kushner is the Contributing Editor in Poetry at BarnesandNoble.com and the Poetry Editor of Neworld Magazine. *She is a graduate of the acclaimed creative writing program in poetry at Boston University, where she received the Fitzgerald Award in Translation. Her writing on poetry has appeared in* Harvard Review *and* The Boston Phoenix, *and she has served as Poetry Coordinator for* AGNI Magazine. *She has given readings of her own work throughout the United States, and she teaches at Massachusetts Communications College in Boston. In the following essay, Kushner discusses the factors, such as dialogue and action, that make this poem untypical of Kenyon's style.*

Jane Kenyon is generally a poet of quiet moments, a woman who writes of walks alone with the dog in winter, who details scrubbing floorboards and finding a long gray hair among them. Her poems rarely contain overt action and instead focus on thought—a subdued but firm revelation.

A classic example of a Kenyon thought poem is "The Suitor," which begins with a couple peacefully sleeping back to back as the wind rushes through a nearby tree. Then the poem veers:

> Suddenly I understand that I am happy / For months this feeling / has been coming closer, stopping / for short visits, like a timid suitor.

Like many Kenyon poems, there is no dialogue in "The Suitor." There is also no loud crashing action, which reflects the poet's daily routine of writing. Kenyon spent most of her life living in the New Hampshire countryside with her husband, the well-known poet Donald Hall. Many of her poems are about the natural landscape and her own domestic landscape as a bride in the Hall ancestral home and a younger poet married to an older, famous writer. In both her newspaper columns and her poetry, topics like a grandmother's tablecloth, daffodils, and the kindness of nearby neighbors repeat.

But Kenyon wasn't always the wife of Hall or a resident of the Hall home. She was not always a newcomer to a New England town. In "Trouble With Math in a One-Room Schoolhouse," she details the cold farm country she came from—where she lived as a little girl. The poem differs from standard Kenyon fare in more than just its location. Unlike those quiet, thought-filled poems which take place internally, it contains both dialogue and action, and it consciously tries to tell a story. But in the poem's head-on discussion of country morals, shame, knowledge, and God, clues to the Kenyon of serene lyric poems are to be found.

The title is long for Kenyon, and unusually direct. The poem will clearly take place in the country and in a schoolhouse, and the word "trouble" signals that problems lie ahead. But that's where the simple narrative ends and the twists begin.

The first line starts off on a confusing note. "The others bent their heads and started in." Which others? Starting in on what? The next line begins with a reflection of what the reader is probably thinking. "Confused, I asked my neighbor / to explain."

Through this inclusive opening sequence, Kenyon brings the reader into what otherwise might be a personal anecdote. The speaker is as lost as the reader is. The speaker then describes her neighbor, a bright-cheeked farm girl who brought raw milk to school from her family's herd of Holsteins. Ann's distinguishing feature is her blue bookmark, which had a very graphic description of Jesus Christ. In fact, on that blue bookmark, "Christ revealed his beating heart, holding the flesh back with his wounded hand."

Kenyon often referred to religion in her writing, especially her hesitancy in attending her husband's church and later, her joy in it. Here, the speaker comments simply: "Ann understood division." Division in this case can mean not just math, but the divisions of Christ's heart and his flesh. It can also be a humorous comment on the division between those who know and those who don't know math.

After this graphic and rather bloody description—very rare for the graceful Kenyon—the second stanza begins with a proper noun, which is also an unusual move for this poet. As for action, it's a big leap from the quiet request to a neighbor for some help with math. In fact, the stanza springs with movement:

> Miss Moran sprang from her monumental desk
> And led me roughly through the class without a word.

The speaker is about to be punished, and she knows it. The alliteration of "m" helps create that sense of knowing helplessness. Miss Moran appears so mad that she is actually speechless. In an

> *Kenyon often referred to religion in her writing, especially her hesitancy in attending her husband's church and later, her joy in it. Here, the speaker comments simply: 'Ann understood division.' Division in this case can mean not just math, but the divisions of Christ's heart and his flesh. It can also be a humorous comment on the division between those who know and those who don't know math.*

effort to match that horror, the speaker uses an odd adjective to describe her own embarrassment. Her "shame was radical / as she propelled me past the cloakroom to the furnace room …"

Kenyon uses internal rhyme to give the poem its own music. "Monumental," "radical," and "propelled" have similar endings, as do "put" and "shut." The clipped tone of "the door swung briskly shut" is followed by long, comma-filled descriptive lines.

> The warmth, the gloom, the smell
> Of sweeping compound clinging to the broom
> soothed me.

Here again, Kenyon uses like sounds—"gloom," "broom," and "soothed," repeating the "oo." In the furnace closet, the speaker finds a bucket and turns it upside-down so she can sit on it. She tries to hum a little, and "hardens her heart" against authority, using the Biblical phrase from Pharaoh's reactions to the Jewish slaves' cries.

"She led me, blinking / and changed, back to the class." After that spell in the hot, dark closet, the speaker blinks from the light. She has changed, though she doesn't specify how. It seems likely that authority is what the speaker has grown to despise. Even in a space as small as a one-room school, there are the powerful and the powerless. The speaker would grow to write about powers we have little control over—love, depression, and death—but this power is more disturbing, because it is simple human arrogance and desire to rule. While the healthy-looking Ann may "understand division," the speaker does not understand the need for division—between furnace-closet and classroom, between chastised students and classmates. This lack of understanding is the one connector between this poem and the rest of Kenyon's work.

As an older poet, she would later probe the subjects of understanding and lack of understanding repeatedly. She wrote of the death of a young man, and tried to understand his widow's state of mind. She wrote of the awful grip of depression, and tried to understand how it controls its victims. Of course, she also wrote numerous poems about being married and tried to understand how individual female identity is both lost and expanded within marriage's borders. In her probing, Kenyon often produced beautiful, clear poems of pure thought. What's fascinating about this fear-filled, action-packed poem is that it offers a glimpse into the headstrong girl who grew into one of our nation's most eloquent and elegant poets of the countryside.

Source: Aviya Kushner, in an essay for *Poetry for Students*, Gale, 2000.

Sources

Barber, David, "Body and Soul," in *Poetry*, June 1994, Vol. 164, Issue 3, pp. 161-164.

Breslin, Paul, "Four and a Half Books," *Poetry*, July 1997, Vol. 170, Issue 4, pp. 226-229.

Carruth, Gorton, *Student Handbook: What Happened When,* Vol. 4, The Southwestern Co., 1996.

Education Week (on-line magazine), Vol. 18. See: www.ed-week.org/ew/vol-18.

Hightower, Scott, a review of *A Hundred White Daffodils,* *Library Journal,* Sept. 1, 1999, Vol. 124, Issue 14, p. 191.

Latimer, Robin, "Jane Kenyon," in *American Poets Since World War II,* 3rd series, *Dictionary of Literary Biography,* Vol. 120, Gale Research, Inc., 1992, pp. 172-175.

Lund, Elizabeth, "Poems of an Age That Shuns Adornment," *Christian Science Monitor,* August 29, 1996, Vol. 88, Issue 193, p. B1.

Kenyon, Jane, *A Hundred White Daffodils,* Graywolf Press, 1999.

Kenyon, Jane, *Otherwise: New and Selected Poems,* Graywolf Press, 1996.

Oktenberg, Adrian, "In Solitude and Sorrow," in *Women's Review of Books,* July, 1996, Vol. 13, Issue 10-11, pp. 27-28.

Richman, Robert, "Luminous Particulars," in *New Criterion,* Vol. 14, Issue 9, pp. 76-80.

For Further Study

Kenyon, Jane, *A Hundred White Daffodils,* Graywolf Press, 1999.

Beyond those who read her columns in *The Concord Monitor* (New Hampshire), few were acquainted with Jane Kenyon the prose writer. *A Hundred White Daffodils* brings this dimension of her work to light with a collection of columns, miscellaneous prose pieces, transcripts of interviews, a handful of aesthetic statements, and her translations of the Russian poet Anna Akhmatova. The volume is introduced by Donald Hall, and concludes with Jack Kelleher's thorough bibliography of works by and about Kenyon, as well as audio and video recordings, and musical scores based on her poems.

Kenyon, Jane, *Otherwise: New and Selected Poems,* Graywolf Press, 1996.

In the weeks before her death, Kenyon selected poems from her four previous volumes and from among her new pieces to appear in this collection. The afterword by Donald Hall provides a brief portrait of his wife, her last days, and her last poem, "The Sick Wife."

Holden, Jonathan, "American Poetry: 1970-1990," *A Profile of Twentieth-Century American Poetry,* ed. Jack Myers and David Wojahn, Southern Illinois University Press, 1991, pp. 254-274.

Even though Jane Kenyon is not mentioned in this brief survey of American poetry from 1970-1990, it is helpful for reading her work (or that of any other contemporary poet) in this broader context. Holden explains clearly the various trends affecting and affected by American poetry, with a focus on the charge that poetry has become an "industry" at the expense of art.

One of the best ways to keep up with the trends in American poetry is to become acquainted with the series called *The Best American Poetry,* published annually since 1988. Each year's anthology is edited and introduced by a different poet, such as John Ashbery, Donald Hall, Jorie Graham, and Charles Simic, among others. Only one poem per poet is published in the anthology, thus allowing for an expansive range of well-known and emerging writers. The editors' introductions themselves reveal much about the state of poetry in America, and can be read as a kind of "weather report" of changes in and predictions for the art. David Lehman, editor of the series, says in the foreword to the 1995 volume, "Modern American poetry is a cultural glory on the level of jazz and abstract expressionism. It is constantly renewing and refreshing itself...."

War Is Kind

Stephen Crane
1899

"War is Kind" is the first poem of Stephen Crane's second collection of poems, *War is Kind and Other Lines,* published in 1899, less than a year before he died. The poem is sometimes referred to by its first line, "Do not weep, maiden, for war is kind." The subject of the poem is war and its effects. In this way it echoes the stories and scenes from Crane's Civil War novel, *The Red Badge of Courage.* Though Crane had been turned down because of poor health when he volunteered to enlist in the U.S. Navy, he saw his share of war and death as a journalist, covering conflicts in Greece, Puerto Rico, Cuba, and Spain. When Crane published *War is Kind and Other Lines* he and his wife, Cora, were deeply in debt. Having already established his literary reputation at 23 as the author of *The Red Badge of Courage* and many newspaper stories on wars around the globe, Crane was able to secure an advance for the collection.

Many of the short parable-like, densely imagistic lyrics in the collection deal with God's absence, the indifference of nature, the ironies of war, and the vagaries of love. "War is Kind" itself is a 26-line poem in five stanzas focusing on the emotional loss of three women whose lover, father, and son, respectively, have died in war. Crane's detailed snapshots of the fallen men in the first, third, and fifth stanzas evoke the savagery of war and its inherent cruelty. The indented second and fourth stanzas function as the poem's chorus, and provide more generalized images of war and cutting statements about the military. The poem's speaker, si-

Stephen Crane

who influenced Crane's style. Later, he also met and became fast friends with William Dean Howells, a champion of realist writing and a leading American literary critic. Although both his parents wrote (primarily religious articles) and two of his brothers were journalists, Crane was mostly a self-taught writer. After his aborted formal education he took newspaper jobs in New Jersey and New York, writing sketches and a novel, *Maggie: Girl of the Streets,* about the urban poor and, eventually, writing the novel *The Red Badge of Courage,* a psychological portrait of Henry Fleming, a fictional soldier during the Civil War, which made Crane famous. Crane is not considered a major poet, but did publish a few volumes including *The Black Riders* and *War is Kind and Other Lines.* His *Collected Poems* also include "Three Poems," discovered in 1928 in Jacksonville, Florida. Crane, who once commented that all life is war, covered many wars as a journalist, reporting on the Spanish-American war, the Greco-Turkish war, and the Cuban insurrection, primarily for the Hearst and Bachellor news syndicates. Always in poor health, Crane suffered a tubercular hemorrhage and died in 1900, just 29 years old.

multaneously sympathetic with the victims of war and cynical about the purposes of war, implicitly criticizes the image of the romantic hero, showing in graphic scenes the realities of battlefield death and the emotional torment it causes for those left behind.

Author Biography

Born in Newark, New Jersey, on November 1, 1871 to Mary Helen Peck Crane, Stephen Crane was the last of fourteen children. His father, the Reverend Dr. Jonathan Townley Crane, was an elder in the District of the Methodist Episcopal Church of Newark and, later, the Methodist pastor in Port Jervis, New York. After his father died in 1880, Crane and his mother moved to Asbury Park, New Jersey, where during the summers he helped his brother, Townley, with his news service.

At fifteen, Crane enrolled at the Hudson River Institute, a lightweight military prep school, but he never developed a fondness for formal education, flunking out of Lafayette College as an engineering student and then dropping out of Syracuse University after one term. At Syracuse, however, Crane met Hamlin Garland, the well-known realist writer

Poem Text

Do not weep, maiden, for war is kind.
Because your lover threw wild hands toward the sky
And the affrighted steed ran on alone,
Do not weep.
War is kind.   5

  Hoarse, booming drums of the regiment,
  Little souls who thirst for fight,
  These men were born to drill and die.
  The unexplained glory flies above them,
  Great is the battle-god, great, and his kingdom   10
  —
  A field where a thousand corpses lie.

Do not weep, babe, for war is kind.
Because your father tumbled in the yellow trenches,
Raged at his breast, gulped and died,
Do not weep.   15
War is kind.

  Swift blazing flag of the regiment,
  Eagle with crest of red and gold,
  These men were born to drill and die.
  Point for them the virtue of slaughter,   20
  Make plain to them the excellence of killing
  And a field where a thousand corpses lie.

Mother whose heart hung humble as a button
On the bright splendid shroud of your son,
Do not weep.   25
War is kind.

Poem Summary

Stanza 1:

The title alerts us to the ironic tone of the poem, as it is very difficult to imagine war being kind in any way. The opening stanza confirms that tone, as it addresses the lover of a soldier who has died in battle, telling her not to weep at his death. We are then presented a melodramatic image of that death, with the dying soldier throwing his "wild hands towards the sky/ And … [his] affrighted steed … running on alone." Since this poem was originally published, the image of the riderless horse galloping away from its fallen owner has become a staple of Western movies.

Stanza 2:

The speaker now presents more generalized images and statements about war, as opposed to the close-up image in the opening stanza. These lines convey a sense of the soldiers' exhaustion, futility, and resignation, as they fight with the flag ("unexplained glory") flying overhead. The speaker continues with his bitter irony when describing the battlefield "where a thousand corpses lie." The "great" battle-god alluded to might be Mars, the god of war in Roman mythology. This stanza, along with the fourth, functions as a refrain, as its third and sixth lines are repeated in each, and as a chorus. In Greek tragedies the chorus comments on characters and events, frequently making moral judgements about them. These lines underscore the senselessness of war and also touch on Crane's attitude towards the stupidity and insidiousness of the military. He adopts a condescending tone towards the soldiers as well, describing them as "little souls." By saying that "These men were born to drill and die," the speaker at once draws attention to the soldiers' (and by extension, all of humanity's) lack of choice in life, and the futility of the purpose that *has* been given to them. It is important to note that in this stanza the speaker condemns the military as a whole, while in the first, third, and fifth stanzas, he remains sympathetic to individual victims, themselves part of the military.

The rhythm and rhyme of this stanza and the fourth also underscore the ironic nature of the poem, as the chaotic experience of war and of dy-

Media Adaptations

- Project Gutenberg contains the entire texts for *Maggie, Girl of the Streets* and *The Red Badge of Courage:* http://promo.net/pg/_authors/i-_crane_stephen_.html

- The University of Texas at Austin maintains a website dedicated to Stephen Crane, his critics, and his admirers: http://www.cwrl.utexas.edu/~mmaynard/Crane/crane.html

- In 1951 John Huston directed the film version of Crane's novel *The Red Badge of Courage* for Metro-Goldwyn-Mayer. Narrated by James Whitmore, and starring Audie Murphy and Bill Mauldin, the film went through heavy editing after negative previews.

- Alan Oskvarek's search engine (www.good-net.com/thewall/) lets you search the Vietnam Veterans Memorial by name, hometown and branch of service. When a name is returned, it tells you at which panel and line the person's name can be found, along with the birthdate, length of service and how they died.

- The following site, sponsored by the Public Broadcasting System, allows you to view sheet music covers, listen to popular songs from the Spanish-American War era, and read 1890s sheet music: http://www.pbs.org/crucible/music.html

ing and mourning, are represented in an orderly structure. Lines one, four, and five are examples of imperfect rhyme which utilize the consonants "m" and "n," in "regiment," "them," and "kingdom." Lines three and six employ true rhyme, as the correspondence of the sounds is exact in "die" and "lie." Line two is an imperfect rhyme with three and six, as the word "fight" echoes the "i" in "die" and "lie."

Stanza 3:

In this stanza the speaker implores a daughter whose father has been killed in war not to cry. Again, we are presented with a close-up and graphic image of the dying soldier, this time tumbling "in the yellow trenches," and pounding his chest desperately before dying. "Yellow" can be read a number of ways in this passage. First, it may denote the life-affirming image of sunlight, underscoring the tragic irony of the soldier's death. But yellow also suggests sickness and disease, and it is quite easy to see the soldier falling among the jaundiced bodies of his comrades. Thirdly, it is a color associated with cowardice, a theme which Crane explores in *The Red Badge of Courage.* Given the ironic tone of this poem, the first reading seems most appropriate. The tactile images here (tumbling, gulping, raging) also emphasize the physicality of war and its toll on the human body.

Stanza 4:

As in the second stanza, we are presented with an image of the flag, this time "swift" and "blazing." The fierceness of this description leads into the refrain that "These men were born to drill and die," underscoring not only the brutal nature of war but of a society, a world, which programs human beings for particular malicious purposes. Crane believed that in large part human beings' destinies are determined by biological as well as social determinants, and that free will plays only a small role in our lives. Crane emphasizes the cynical view that the men will do what they are told is right when he says "Point for them the virtue of slaughter, / Make plain to the excellence of killing." The tone is not only ironic here, but despairing, as the speaker describes something he thinks can be no other way.

Stanza 5:

The simile in the first line—"Mother whose heart hung humble as a button"—connects the mother's mourning with the smallest detail of her son's clothing, filling the comparison with pathos. A button is humble because it is small and unassuming. This comparison also emphasizes what Crane sees as the unimportance or "smallness" of victims of war to the powers that be. The poem ends with the mourning of a mother for her fallen son because this relationship, perhaps more than any other, carries the highest degree of emotional resonance. There is no consoling the mother.

Themes

Natural Law

In "War is Kind" Crane emphasizes the psychological torment that dying soldiers and their loved ones endure instead of focusing on their heroic or patriotic behavior. He desires to present the world as he sees it rather than the way he wants it to be. Much of Crane's poetry and fiction depict how human beings behave in extreme circumstances, whether that be how the impoverished survive on the streets of New York City, how men in a lifeboat interact when faced with the prospect of drowning, or how soldiers behave while bullets and shrapnel flies around them. His deterministic philosophy, a feature of naturalism, is evident in the graphic ways he represents the soldiers' deaths. They die alone, fearful and full of rage, in a field "where a thousand corpses lie." Unlike some of his prose work which attempts to render humanity with a more detached, scientific eye, "War is Kind" also makes a moral judgement about the seeming "naturalness" of war, the speaker implicitly ridiculing the regiment which teaches the soldiers "to drill and die" and "Point[s] for them the virtue of slaughter." This judgement suggests that in this work, at least, Crane sees the possibility that things could be different. Although sympathetic with the suffering of the dying, he is outraged at the institutions which sanction war, in this case the military itself, represented by the regiment, which "make[s] plain … [to the soldiers] the excellence of killing." He expresses this outrage in his bitterly ironic refrain that "war is kind."

Patriotism

"War is Kind" implicitly questions the usefulness and validity of patriotism as an attitude and an ideology. The flag, an emblem of national pride which the speaker calls "the unexplained glory," flies above the soldiers marching to their deaths on the battlefield. Its "unexplainedness" points to the speaker's belief that it cannot be explained because there is nothing rational about men fighting and dying for a symbol. As a symbol of national identity and military authority, the flag commands respect. However, Crane represents it as a marker of fascistic might which demands total allegiance. Under the flag, soldiers are taught "the excellence of killing" and "the virtue of slaughter." Assigning such sinister motives to a country furthers the idea that patriotism is not only an act of blind obedience, but that it is reserved for those who do not have the ability or capacity to questions what being loyal to one's country really means. Crane highlights this idea when he says that such adherents to the flag "were born to drill and die," suggesting that there was never any other choice for them. Patriotism was a strong influence in Crane's time as

Topics for Further Study

- Find women who have lost a husband, lover, father, brother, or son in a military conflict and interview them. Write a description of the ways in which they have or have not accommodated their loss.

- After viewing a few popular war movies, for example, *The Thin Red Line, Forest Gump, Full Metal Jacket, Platoon,* etc., compose an essay comparing and contrasting the ways in which Crane's description of battlefield suffering and death match up with late twentieth-century visual depictions of the same.

- Choose a military conflict or war from the nineteenth century and research the material ways in which families who lost someone in the war suffered as a result. For example, what happened to the economic lives of women who lost husbands in war?

- Rewrite Crane's poem, but without the irony. Also, update the imagery to represent a twentieth-century military conflict. Discuss the changes you made and why you made them.

it is today. In its extreme and most public form, it fosters an almost militaristic devotion to the decisions a country makes, wrong or right. Many U.S. citizens chastised Jane Fonda during the Vietnam War, for example, when she publicly questioned the United States' involvement in that conflict. However, Fonda was also acting in a patriotic manner (which she has often claimed), for she wanted her country to do the morally correct thing. Crane fashions the United States as not only sinister but as uncaring and cruel, as it offers those who died fighting for it no solace.

Style

"War is Kind" is Crane's free verse meditation on war and loss. The poet utilizes concrete imagery and irony to compose a portrait of the cosmic futility of war. Concrete imagery describes the world in terms of the senses, what we experience with our sight, taste, touch, smell, and hearing. By appealing to our senses, Crane can more effectively show the horrors of war directly. Tactile imagery is especially prevalent in the poem and highlights the horrific effects of battle on the human body. The tone of his descriptions is ironic, that is, he does not mean that war is kind, but that it is cruel and unjust. Another example of irony occurs in the second stanza when the speaker says "Great is the battle-god, great, and his kingdom … " It is also ironic that war's "kindness" means that the soldiers' deaths bring them release from their suffering.

The poem employs two levels of diction, or word choice. The language of the first, third, and fifths stanzas is plain and closer to everyday speech, while the language of the indented second and fourth stanzas is embellished and inflated, and uses more formal verse conventions such as end rhyme. The contrast between these two styles adds to the poem's complexity, and furthers the author's intention to deflate the idea of romantic heroism in all of its guises.

Historical Context

Although Crane never served in the United States military, as a journalist he covered a number of conflicts for various newspapers and news services during the mid-to-late 1890s, including the Greco-Turkish War and the Spanish-American War. On page 91 of his study of Crane's life and work, Stephen Cady discusses Crane's compassion and empathy for the everyday suffering of war victims and quotes from an article Crane wrote about refugees: "There is more of this sort of thing in war than glory and heroic death, flags, banners, shouting, and victory." Crane's compassion transcended national identity, as he saw suffering resulting from war as a universal human problem rather than a primarily political one. Thus the flag in "War is Kind," though associated with a particular country, actually stands for all countries.

The Spanish-American War, which Crane covered for the *New York World,* lasted less than a year from declaration to treaty. However, the conflict between Cuba and Spain, which precipitated the war, was simmering when Crane was sent as a reporter to Cuba in 1896. In 1898 President McKinley ordered the battleship *Maine* to Havana harbor

Compare & Contrast

- **1895:** Jose Marti and Maximo Gomez lead Cuban revolution against Spanish colonialists.

  1896: Filipino nationalists revolt against the Spanish rule that has controlled the Philippines since the sixteenth century.

  1898: Months of tension between the United States and Spain climax in war.

  1899: The Treaty of Paris is ratified by the Senate in a 57-27 vote. Under the terms of the treaty, the U.S. gains possession of Cuba, Puerto Rico, Guam, and for $20 million, the Philippines.

  Today: Although Guam and Puerto Rico remain U.S. territories, the Philippines and Cuba are independent countries.

- **1890s:** Just as newspaper stories promoted the conflict, popular songs celebrate the Spanish-American War by honoring its heroes and victories. Songs like "Brave Dewey and His Men" and "The Charge of the Roosevelt Riders" laud war heroes Commodore Dewey and Theodore Roosevelt. Other songs, like 'Ma Filipino Babe" and "The Belle of Manila," sentimentalized the struggles abroad and romanticized the idea of intervention.

  Today: Films such as *Platoon, Hamburger Hill,* and *Full Metal Jacket* are explicitly critical of America's military interventions abroad, while other films such as *Rambo* and *Missing In Action* romanticize such interventions.

- **1892:** The People's Party, sometimes known as the Populists, pushes for reforms to make government institutions more responsive to the public. Their candidate for president, General James Weaver, a former Union army officer, wins 8.5 percent of the popular vote.

  1992: Ross Perot, a Texas billionaire businessman and a third party candidate for president, wins almost twenty percent of the popular vote.

---

in Cuba as a show of American might and as tacit support of the insurgents' position. Shortly after its arrival the ship was destroyed by a mysterious bomb blast and 250 men were lost. Although questions remain as to the source of the blast, it was enough of a reason for the United States to declare war on Spain, which the American public supported wholeheartedly. Spain capitulated within three months, and as a condition of the Paris Peace Treaty of 1898 gave up control of Cuba and ceded the Philippines, Guam, and Puerto Rico to the United States. The Hawaiian Islands had been annexed by an act of congress earlier that year, and now the United States stood as an imperial power with substantial overseas territories. Many inhabitants of these territories, however, grew to disdain the United States' interference in their domestic affairs and fought against them. In the Philippines, for example, rebel leader Emilio Aguinaldo led insurgents against Americans, who responded by destroying villages and forcing large numbers of peasants and rebels into concentration camps. All told, more than two hundred thousand Filipinos were killed in the uprising.

Crane is often cited as saying that all life is war, and biographers point out Crane's obsession with war, some suggesting that he had a death wish. As evidence of this, they recite the story of Crane in Cuba, strolling among soldiers along San Juan Hill. He wore a long white coat and refused to duck down even amidst a hail of sniper fire. Cady links Crane's behavior to the writer's desire to prove himself as a *true* war correspondent, someone who was a participant in what he wrote about, not just an observer. But Crane's behavior also seemed to signal that he was fated to die early, which is apropos of someone who believed that humanity's destiny was in its genes and immediate environment. Critic Daniel Hoffman agrees. In his article "The Many Red Devils upon the Page: The Poetry of Stephen Crane," Hoffman suggests that Crane's fascination with danger was in part a result of his rebellion against the religious orthodoxy of his family: "Not to make too much of genetic determinism, there does yet seem a thread of predestination in Stephen Crane's fascination with war (and with other perilous situations)," Hoffman writes.

Various strains of determinism were in the air in the late nineteenth century, as thinkers such as Karl Marx and Charles Darwin conceived of human behavior as a result of economic circumstances and biological imperatives, respectively. In literature Crane is often cited as being one of the first American naturalist writers. Naturalism is the term used to describe such deterministic thinking. Naturalist literature tends to present characters who are controlled by their passions or material environment, and who have very limited choices in their lives. In addition to Crane, late nineteenth- and early twentieth-century American practitioners of literary Naturalism include Frank Norris, Theodore Dreiser, Jack London, and John Dos Passos.

Critical Overview

Bettina L. Knapp writes that *War is Kind* is a both a gloomy and an emotionally charged collection of poems "replete with scenes of martyrdom and bone-hard metaphors." Knapp writes: "Despair, a morbid presence, permeates the world as individuals are forced to endure the agony of war." Knapp calls the title poem of the collection "one of the most extraordinary war poems of all time." Commenting on the historical reception of Crane's poetry in his book-length study of Crane's verse, Daniel Hoffman observes that "Crane's critics have often asserted that his verse did not develop at all. Such critics apparently have been content to regard as typical of his second book the nine or ten poems which correspond in method to those of the first." Hoffman, however, disagrees with these critics, claiming that Crane's poetry had indeed evolved from *The Black Riders* to *War is Kind*. Hoffman claims that poems from *War is Kind* express Crane's shift from allegory to symbolism, and that the subject matter of the latter poems represent "experiences and states of feeling more complex than the simple attitudes of the allegorical poems." Of the poem "War is Kind," Hoffman praises Crane's use of juxtaposition and repetition, claiming that "The power of the poem is in its style. Crane's style was a more flexible instrument than most critics of his poetry have allowed." Writing in a more recent article, "Many Red Devils Upon the Page: The Poetry of Stephen Crane," Hoffman waxes even more admiringly, claiming that "In American poetry Crane's poem ['War is Kind'] is worthy to stand beside those in Whitman's Drum-Taps (e.g., 'Come Up from the Fields, Father') and Melville's Battle-Pieces (e.g., 'The Portent,' 'Shiloh'). Despite the nation's experience of two world wars, Korea, and Vietnam, no twentieth-century American poet has written of war's illusions and sufferings with like authority."

Criticism

Chris Semansky

Screenwriter, poet, and essayist Chris Semansky's most recent collection of poems, Blindsided, *has been published by 26 Books of Portland, Oregon. In the following essay Semansky examines the imagery in Stephen Crane's "War is Kind," linking it to the Imagist movement of the twentieth century and to the poetry of World War I.*

Stephen Crane's title poem from his second collection, *War is Kind and Other Lines,* is representative of his best work. It prefigures many of the modern imagist poets such as Amy Lowell and William Carlos Williams in its concise and hard-edged descriptions and focus on the "thingness" of the world, yet retains some of the didactic and sentimental qualities of nineteenth-century verse. Combined with a piercing ironic tone, these qualities add layers of complexity to a poem which on first reading appears relatively simple.

Imagism emerged at the beginning of the twentieth century, just a little more than a decade after Crane's death. Formulated and popularized by writers such as Ezra Pound and T. E. Hulme, Imagism was a revolt against mannered and overly emotional verse. Writing in her Preface to the imagist anthology, *Some Imagist Poets (1915-1917),* Amy Lowell spells out some of the features of Imagism. These include an openness to all subject matter, the use of everyday speech, and the presentation of a concentrated image. Ezra Pound's "In a Station of the Metro" is perhaps the best-known Imagist poem. Pound relies on juxtaposition to present his vision of people at a train station:

> The apparition of these faces in the crowd, Petals on a wet, black bough.

Implicit in these two images is how faces look like petals. The comparison is implied, and readers must make the connection. Crane employs a similar strategy in "War is Kind," only he juxtaposes

The acid cynicism in these lines burns. Using patriotic pride and the myth of heroism to sanction men's natural tendencies toward violence, the military, the government are condemned, though not named."

showing with *telling,* that is, he gives us an image and then comments on it, rather than giving us two diverse images that suggest similarity. The imagery of Crane's first, third, and last stanzas can most profitably be seen in cinematic terms as rotating among medium shots, close-ups, and long shots. Directors use medium shots to frame the body from the waist up, emphasizing gestures. Close-ups usually frame the body from the chest up and emphasize facial expressions. Long shots often feature figures against landscapes, but from a distance. The first stanza, then, can be read as moving from a close-up, in which we can imagine the desperate look on the dying soldier's face as his hands flail about in a final gesture of surrender, to a long shot, in which we can see the dying soldier's horse galloping away, the distant figure of the falling soldier's hands in the sky, which dominates the background.

Framed by the speaker's seemingly faux consolation to the soldier's lover, this opening stanza prepares us for an elaboration of the bitterness and irony to follow. It is important to understand the comma in this first stanza. If we miss it, we miss the irony, and the pathos of the image. The second time the speaker tells the maiden not to weep, he says so for a reason: *"Because* [italics mine] your lover threw wild hands toward the sky / And the affrighted steed ran on alone ..." How are we to read this as a reason? Some critics see the irony in the contrast between the women's tears and the fact that death will soon relieve the dying man of his suffering. But the irony is in the reason, which is *not* a reason. War is *not* kind. But does that mean that the speaker is being glib in imploring the

maiden not to weep? Quite the contrary: rather, the speaker is encouraging the maiden to share in his own bitterness towards the forces that perpetuate war. The details of the dying soldier heighten the pathos of the scene and are meant to arouse readers' indignation.

The indignation of the speaker becomes even more apparent in the second stanza, which functions both as a chorus of sorts, and, in cinematic terms, as a "long shot":

Hoarse, booming drums of the regiment,
Little souls who thirst for fight,
These men were born to drill and die.
The unexplained glory flies above them,
Great is the battle-god, great, and his kingdom—
A field where a thousand corpses lie.

We see the regiment from a distance, bodies strewn everywhere, and then we get commentary on the scene, as if from a voice-over narrator. The language is more inflated than the three stanzas detailing individual deaths, and more abstract. We are given more statement than description, and more transparent irony, in case we missed the irony of the first stanza. In his study of Crane's poetry, critic Daniel Hoffman points out that these lines, which he says are spoken by an "intercalary chorus," are thick with "compelling rhythmic regularity—and rhyme." Hoffman writes: "There are rhymes 'die' and 'lie' in the set-in stanzas; wild, sky, affrighted, flies, bright; just these, and they ought to make a high lament. But of course they do nothing of the sort....The poem takes place in the successful war of the prose ('unexplained,' 'gulped,' and so on) against the poetic appearance of lament." This formal quality of the lament, then, provides an almost hypnotic backdrop to the poem, as readers are told of the lemming-like behavior of the soldiers and the "[battle]field where a thousand corpses lie."

Alluding to the party responsible for the horror, the speaker smirks "Great is the battle-god, great, and his kingdom." This description, possibly an allusion to the Roman god of war, Mars, lends an almost epic quality to the passage. In its depiction of how war uses soldiers, Crane's poem also foreshadows some of the great antiwar poems of the first world war, chief among them Wilfred Owen's "Dulce et Decorum Est." Owen's poem, which came towards the end of the war, is that of a soldier whose responsibility is to fight, whereas Crane's poem is that of a correspondent whose job is to report. Both use bitter irony to comment on the ways in which governments perpetuate lies about the nature and purposes of war. Here is the last stanza of Owen's poem, in which the speaker addresses the author of children's books which romanticize war:

> If in some smothering dreams you too could pace
> Behind the wagon that we flung him in,
> And watch the white eyes writhing in his face,
> His hanging face, like a devil's sick of sin;
> If you could here, at every jolt, the blood
> Come gargling from the froth-corrupted lungs,
> Obscene as cancer, bitter as the cud
> Of vile, incurable sores on innocent tongues,
> My friend, you would not tell with such high zest
> To children ardent for some desperate glory,
> The old lie: Dulce est decorum est
> Pro patria mori.

Literally translated from Latin, these lines read "It is sweet and meet to die for one's country." Owen's poem can be read as an elaboration of Crane's in its graphic depiction of war death, its critique of romantic heroism, and its implicit denunciation of the institutions which sponsor war. Both explicitly question those who would see fighting for one's country as a glorious act.

We can see Crane's dying soldier, who "tumble[s] in the yellow trenches" in the third stanza in Owen's soldier dying from poison gas. Although chlorine gas was not yet used as a weapon of mass destruction in Crane's time, the concrete details that each poet provides gives a clear picture of the physical and psychological suffering soldiers endure. If anything, Crane is more accusatory than Owen in his tone and his words. The fourth stanza of "War is Kind" makes this plain:

> Swift blazing flag of the regiment,
> Eagle with the crest of gold,
> These men were born to drill and die.
> Point for them the virtue of slaughter,
> Make plain to them the excellence of killing
> And a field where a thousand corpses lie.

The acid cynicism in these lines burns. Using patriotic pride and the myth of heroism to sanction men's natural tendencies toward violence, the military and the government are condemned, though not named. The last stanza, an image of a mother weeping over the body of her fallen son, is the most heart-wrenching of all, as it underscores the hopelessness of victims, both living and dead. Hoffman says about "War is Kind" what many have said or would like to have said to those who have lost loved ones in war: "A domestic, terrible poem, what it whispers is: 'I would console you, how I would console you! If I honestly could.'"

Source: Chris Semansky, in an essay for *Poetry for Students,* Gale, 2000.

Sources

Beer, Thomas, *Stephen Crane: A Study in American Letters,* Knopf, 1923.

Berryman, John, *Stephen Crane,* William Sloane Associates, 1950.

Cady, Edwin H., *Stephen Crane,* G. K. Hall & Co., 1980.

Crane, Stephen, *The Red Badge of Courage,* Buccaneer Books, 1990.

Davis, Linda H., *Badge of Courage: The Life of Stephen Crane,* Houghton Mifflin, 1998.

Follet, Wilson, ed., *The Collected Poems of Stephen Crane,* Knopf, 1930.

Gilkes, Lillian, *Cora Crane: A Biography of Mrs. Stephen Crane,* Indiana University Press, 1960.

Hoffman, Daniel, "The Many Red Devils upon the Page: The Poetry of Stephen Crane," in *Sewanee Review,* Vol. 102, No. 4, 1994, pp. 588-604.

———, *The Poetry of Stephen Crane,* Columbia University Press, 1957.

Knapp, Bettina L., *Stephen Crane,* Ungar, 1987.

Lowell, Amy, ed., *Some Imagist Poets (1915-1917),* Houghton Mifflin Company, 1915.

Stallman, Robert W., ed., *Stephen Crane: An Omnibus,* Knopf, 1952.

———, *Stephen Crane: A Biography,* George Braziller, 1968.

Zara, Louis, *Dark Rider: A Novel Based on the Life of Stephen Crane,* World, 1961.

For Further Study

Crane, Stephen, *The Selected Poems of Stephen Crane,* Knopf, 1930.

This collection contains poems from *The Black Riders and Other Lines, War is Kind and Other Lines,* and *Three Poems.*

Hoffman, Daniel G., *The Poetry of Stephen Crane,* Columbia University Press, 1957.

Hoffman's study of Crane's poetry remains the best such study done to date.

Wertheim, Stanley and Paul Sorrentino, eds.,*The Correspondence of Stephen Crane,* Columbia University Press, 1988.

Sorrentino and Wertheim correct previous errors made in reporting Crane's letters and illuminate the personality of Crane. This collection is indispensable reading for those interested in Crane's life.

Glossary of Literary Terms

A

Abstract: Used as a noun, the term refers to a short summary or outline of a longer work. As an adjective applied to writing or literary works, abstract refers to words or phrases that name things not knowable through the five senses.

Accent: The emphasis or stress placed on a syllable in poetry. Traditional poetry commonly uses patterns of accented and unaccented syllables (known as feet) that create distinct rhythms. Much modern poetry uses less formal arrangements that create a sense of freedom and spontaneity.

Aestheticism: A literary and artistic movement of the nineteenth century. Followers of the movement believed that art should not be mixed with social, political, or moral teaching. The statement "art for art's sake" is a good summary of aestheticism. The movement had its roots in France, but it gained widespread importance in England in the last half of the nineteenth century, where it helped change the Victorian practice of including moral lessons in literature.

Affective Fallacy: An error in judging the merits or faults of a work of literature. The "error" results from stressing the importance of the work's effect upon the reader—that is, how it makes a reader "feel" emotionally, what it does as a literary work—instead of stressing its inner qualities as a created object, or what it "is."

Age of Johnson: The period in English literature between 1750 and 1798, named after the most prominent literary figure of the age, Samuel Johnson. Works written during this time are noted for their emphasis on "sensibility," or emotional quality. These works formed a transition between the rational works of the Age of Reason, or Neoclassical period, and the emphasis on individual feelings and responses of the Romantic period.

Age of Reason: See *Neoclassicism*

Age of Sensibility: See *Age of Johnson*

Agrarians: A group of Southern American writers of the 1930s and 1940s who fostered an economic and cultural program for the South based on agriculture, in opposition to the industrial society of the North. The term can refer to any group that promotes the value of farm life and agricultural society.

Alexandrine Meter: See *Meter*

Allegory: A narrative technique in which characters representing things or abstract ideas are used to convey a message or teach a lesson. Allegory is typically used to teach moral, ethical, or religious lessons but is sometimes used for satiric or political purposes.

Alliteration: A poetic device where the first consonant sounds or any vowel sounds in words or syllables are repeated.

Allusion: A reference to a familiar literary or historical person or event, used to make an idea more easily understood.

Amerind Literature: The writing and oral traditions of Native Americans. Native American literature was originally passed on by word of mouth, so it consisted largely of stories and events that were easily memorized. Amerind prose is often rhythmic like poetry because it was recited to the beat of a ceremonial drum.

Analogy: A comparison of two things made to explain something unfamiliar through its similarities to something familiar, or to prove one point based on the acceptedness of another. Similes and metaphors are types of analogies.

Anapest: See *Foot*

Angry Young Men: A group of British writers of the 1950s whose work expressed bitterness and disillusionment with society. Common to their work is an antihero who rebels against a corrupt social order and strives for personal integrity.

Anthropomorphism: The presentation of animals or objects in human shape or with human characteristics. The term is derived from the Greek word for "human form."

Antimasque: See *Masque*

Antithesis: The antithesis of something is its direct opposite. In literature, the use of antithesis as a figure of speech results in two statements that show a contrast through the balancing of two opposite ideas. Technically, it is the second portion of the statement that is defined as the "antithesis"; the first portion is the "thesis."

Apocrypha: Writings tentatively attributed to an author but not proven or universally accepted to be their works. The term was originally applied to certain books of the Bible that were not considered inspired and so were not included in the "sacred canon."

Apollonian and Dionysian: The two impulses believed to guide authors of dramatic tragedy. The Apollonian impulse is named after Apollo, the Greek god of light and beauty and the symbol of intellectual order. The Dionysian impulse is named after Dionysus, the Greek god of wine and the symbol of the unrestrained forces of nature. The Apollonian impulse is to create a rational, harmonious world, while the Dionysian is to express the irrational forces of personality.

Apostrophe: A statement, question, or request addressed to an inanimate object or concept or to a nonexistent or absent person.

Archetype: The word archetype is commonly used to describe an original pattern or model from which all other things of the same kind are made. This term was introduced to literary criticism from the psychology of Carl Jung. It expresses Jung's theory that behind every person's "unconscious," or repressed memories of the past, lies the "collective unconscious" of the human race: memories of the countless typical experiences of our ancestors. These memories are said to prompt illogical associations that trigger powerful emotions in the reader. Often, the emotional process is primitive, even primordial. Archetypes are the literary images that grow out of the "collective unconscious." They appear in literature as incidents and plots that repeat basic patterns of life. They may also appear as stereotyped characters.

Argument: The argument of a work is the author's subject matter or principal idea.

Art for Art's Sake: See *Aestheticism*

Assonance: The repetition of similar vowel sounds in poetry.

Audience: The people for whom a piece of literature is written. Authors usually write with a certain audience in mind, for example, children, members of a religious or ethnic group, or colleagues in a professional field. The term "audience" also applies to the people who gather to see or hear any performance, including plays, poetry readings, speeches, and concerts.

Automatic Writing: Writing carried out without a preconceived plan in an effort to capture every random thought. Authors who engage in automatic writing typically do not revise their work, preferring instead to preserve the revealed truth and beauty of spontaneous expression.

Avant-garde: A French term meaning "vanguard." It is used in literary criticism to describe new writing that rejects traditional approaches to literature in favor of innovations in style or content.

B

Ballad: A short poem that tells a simple story and has a repeated refrain. Ballads were originally intended to be sung. Early ballads, known as folk ballads, were passed down through generations, so their authors are often unknown. Later ballads composed by known authors are called literary ballads.

Baroque: A term used in literary criticism to describe literature that is complex or ornate in style or diction. Baroque works typically express tension, anxiety, and violent emotion. The term "Baroque Age" designates a period in Western European literature beginning in the late sixteenth century and ending about one hundred years later.

Works of this period often mirror the qualities of works more generally associated with the label "baroque" and sometimes feature elaborate conceits.

Baroque Age: See *Baroque*

Baroque Period: See *Baroque*

Beat Generation: See *Beat Movement*

Beat Movement: A period featuring a group of American poets and novelists of the 1950s and 1960s—including Jack Kerouac, Allen Ginsberg, Gregory Corso, William S. Burroughs, and Lawrence Ferlinghetti—who rejected established social and literary values. Using such techniques as stream-of-consciousness writing and jazz-influenced free verse and focusing on unusual or abnormal states of mind—generated by religious ecstasy or the use of drugs—the Beat writers aimed to create works that were unconventional in both form and subject matter.

Beat Poets: See *Beat Movement*

Beats, The: See *Beat Movement*

Belles-lettres: A French term meaning "fine letters" or "beautiful writing." It is often used as a synonym for literature, typically referring to imaginative and artistic rather than scientific or expository writing. Current usage sometimes restricts the meaning to light or humorous writing and appreciative essays about literature.

Black Aesthetic Movement: A period of artistic and literary development among African Americans in the 1960s and early 1970s. This was the first major African American artistic movement since the Harlem Renaissance and was closely paralleled by the civil rights and black power movements. The black aesthetic writers attempted to produce works of art that would be meaningful to the black masses. Key figures in black aesthetics included one of its founders, poet and playwright Amiri Baraka, formerly known as LeRoi Jones; poet and essayist Haki R. Madhubuti, formerly Don L. Lee; poet and playwright Sonia Sanchez; and dramatist Ed Bullins.

Black Arts Movement: See *Black Aesthetic Movement*

Black Comedy: See *Black Humor*

Black Humor: Writing that places grotesque elements side by side with humorous ones in an attempt to shock the reader, forcing him or her to laugh at the horrifying reality of a disordered world.

Black Mountain School: Black Mountain College and three of its instructors—Robert Creeley, Robert Duncan, and Charles Olson—were all influential in projective verse. Today poets working in projective verse are referred to as members of the Black Mountain school.

Blank Verse: Loosely, any unrhymed poetry, but more generally, unrhymed iambic pentameter verse (composed of lines of five two-syllable feet with the first syllable accented, the second unaccented). Blank verse has been used by poets since the Renaissance for its flexibility and its graceful, dignified tone.

Bloomsbury Group: A group of English writers, artists, and intellectuals who held informal artistic and philosophical discussions in Bloomsbury, a district of London, from around 1907 to the early 1930s. The Bloomsbury Group held no uniform philosophical beliefs but did commonly express an aversion to moral prudery and a desire for greater social tolerance.

Bon Mot: A French term meaning "good word." A *bon mot* is a witty remark or clever observation.

Breath Verse: See *Projective Verse*

Burlesque: Any literary work that uses exaggeration to make its subject appear ridiculous, either by treating a trivial subject with profound seriousness or by treating a dignified subject frivolously. The word "burlesque" may also be used as an adjective, as in "burlesque show," to mean "striptease act."

C

Cadence: The natural rhythm of language caused by the alternation of accented and unaccented syllables. Much modern poetry—notably free verse—deliberately manipulates cadence to create complex rhythmic effects.

Caesura: A pause in a line of poetry, usually occurring near the middle. It typically corresponds to a break in the natural rhythm or sense of the line but is sometimes shifted to create special meanings or rhythmic effects.

Canzone: A short Italian or Provencal lyric poem, commonly about love and often set to music. The *canzone* has no set form but typically contains five or six stanzas made up of seven to twenty lines of eleven syllables each. A shorter, five- to ten-line "envoy," or concluding stanza, completes the poem.

Carpe Diem: A Latin term meaning "seize the day." This is a traditional theme of poetry, especially lyrics. A *carpe diem* poem advises the reader or the person it addresses to live for today and enjoy the pleasures of the moment.

Catharsis: The release or purging of unwanted emotions—specifically fear and pity—brought about by exposure to art. The term was first used by the Greek philosopher Aristotle in his *Poetics* to refer to the desired effect of tragedy on spectators.

Celtic Renaissance: A period of Irish literary and cultural history at the end of the nineteenth century. Followers of the movement aimed to create a romantic vision of Celtic myth and legend. The most significant works of the Celtic Renaissance typically present a dreamy, unreal world, usually in reaction against the reality of contemporary problems.

Celtic Twilight: See *Celtic Renaissance*

Character: Broadly speaking, a person in a literary work. The actions of characters are what constitute the plot of a story, novel, or poem. There are numerous types of characters, ranging from simple, stereotypical figures to intricate, multifaceted ones. In the techniques of anthropomorphism and personification, animals—and even places or things—can assume aspects of character. "Characterization" is the process by which an author creates vivid, believable characters in a work of art. This may be done in a variety of ways, including (1) direct description of the character by the narrator; (2) the direct presentation of the speech, thoughts, or actions of the character; and (3) the responses of other characters to the character. The term "character" also refers to a form originated by the ancient Greek writer Theophrastus that later became popular in the seventeenth and eighteenth centuries. It is a short essay or sketch of a person who prominently displays a specific attribute or quality, such as miserliness or ambition.

Characterization: See *Character*

Classical: In its strictest definition in literary criticism, classicism refers to works of ancient Greek or Roman literature. The term may also be used to describe a literary work of recognized importance (a "classic") from any time period or literature that exhibits the traits of classicism.

Classicism: A term used in literary criticism to describe critical doctrines that have their roots in ancient Greek and Roman literature, philosophy, and art. Works associated with classicism typically exhibit restraint on the part of the author, unity of design and purpose, clarity, simplicity, logical organization, and respect for tradition.

Colloquialism: A word, phrase, or form of pronunciation that is acceptable in casual conversation but not in formal, written communication. It is considered more acceptable than slang.

Complaint: A lyric poem, popular in the Renaissance, in which the speaker expresses sorrow about his or her condition. Typically, the speaker's sadness is caused by an unresponsive lover, but some complaints cite other sources of unhappiness, such as poverty or fate.

Conceit: A clever and fanciful metaphor, usually expressed through elaborate and extended comparison, that presents a striking parallel between two seemingly dissimilar things—for example, elaborately comparing a beautiful woman to an object like a garden or the sun. The conceit was a popular device throughout the Elizabethan Age and Baroque Age and was the principal technique of the seventeenth-century English metaphysical poets. This usage of the word conceit is unrelated to the best-known definition of conceit as an arrogant attitude or behavior.

Concrete: Concrete is the opposite of abstract, and refers to a thing that actually exists or a description that allows the reader to experience an object or concept with the senses.

Concrete Poetry: Poetry in which visual elements play a large part in the poetic effect. Punctuation marks, letters, or words are arranged on a page to form a visual design: a cross, for example, or a bumblebee.

Confessional Poetry: A form of poetry in which the poet reveals very personal, intimate, sometimes shocking information about himself or herself.

Connotation: The impression that a word gives beyond its defined meaning. Connotations may be universally understood or may be significant only to a certain group.

Consonance: Consonance occurs in poetry when words appearing at the ends of two or more verses have similar final consonant sounds but have final vowel sounds that differ, as with "stuff" and "off."

Convention: Any widely accepted literary device, style, or form.

Corrido: A Mexican ballad.

Couplet: Two lines of poetry with the same rhyme and meter, often expressing a complete and self-contained thought.

Criticism: The systematic study and evaluation of literary works, usually based on a specific method or set of principles. An important part of literary studies since ancient times, the practice of criticism has given rise to numerous theories, methods, and "schools," sometimes producing conflicting, even contradictory, interpretations of literature in general as well as of individual works. Even such basic issues as what constitutes a poem or a novel have been the subject of much criticism over the centuries.

D

Dactyl: See *Foot*

Dadaism: A protest movement in art and literature founded by Tristan Tzara in 1916. Followers of the movement expressed their outrage at the destruction brought about by World War I by revolting against numerous forms of social convention. The Dadaists presented works marked by calculated madness and flamboyant nonsense. They stressed total freedom of expression, commonly through primitive displays of emotion and illogical, often senseless, poetry. The movement ended shortly after the war, when it was replaced by surrealism.

Decadent: See *Decadents*

Decadents: The followers of a nineteenth-century literary movement that had its beginnings in French aestheticism. Decadent literature displays a fascination with perverse and morbid states; a search for novelty and sensation—the "new thrill"; a preoccupation with mysticism; and a belief in the senselessness of human existence. The movement is closely associated with the doctrine Art for Art's Sake. The term "decadence" is sometimes used to denote a decline in the quality of art or literature following a period of greatness.

Deconstruction: A method of literary criticism developed by Jacques Derrida and characterized by multiple conflicting interpretations of a given work. Deconstructionists consider the impact of the language of a work and suggest that the true meaning of the work is not necessarily the meaning that the author intended.

Deduction: The process of reaching a conclusion through reasoning from general premises to a specific premise.

Denotation: The definition of a word, apart from the impressions or feelings it creates in the reader.

Diction: The selection and arrangement of words in a literary work. Either or both may vary depending on the desired effect. There are four general types of diction: "formal," used in scholarly or lofty writing; "informal," used in relaxed but educated conversation; "colloquial," used in everyday speech; and "slang," containing newly coined words and other terms not accepted in formal usage.

Didactic: A term used to describe works of literature that aim to teach some moral, religious, political, or practical lesson. Although didactic elements are often found in artistically pleasing works, the term "didactic" usually refers to literature in which the message is more important than the form. The term may also be used to criticize a work that the critic finds "overly didactic," that is, heavy-handed in its delivery of a lesson.

Dimeter: See *Meter*

Dionysian: See *Apollonian and Dionysian*

Discordia concours: A Latin phrase meaning "discord in harmony." The term was coined by the eighteenth-century English writer Samuel Johnson to describe "a combination of dissimilar images or discovery of occult resemblances in things apparently unlike." Johnson created the expression by reversing a phrase by the Latin poet Horace.

Dissonance: A combination of harsh or jarring sounds, especially in poetry. Although such combinations may be accidental, poets sometimes intentionally make them to achieve particular effects. Dissonance is also sometimes used to refer to close but not identical rhymes. When this is the case, the word functions as a synonym for consonance.

Double Entendre: A corruption of a French phrase meaning "double meaning." The term is used to indicate a word or phrase that is deliberately ambiguous, especially when one of the meanings is risque or improper.

Draft: Any preliminary version of a written work. An author may write dozens of drafts which are revised to form the final work, or he or she may write only one, with few or no revisions.

Dramatic Monologue: See *Monologue*

Dramatic Poetry: Any lyric work that employs elements of drama such as dialogue, conflict, or characterization, but excluding works that are intended for stage presentation.

Dream Allegory: See *Dream Vision*

Dream Vision: A literary convention, chiefly of the Middle Ages. In a dream vision a story is presented as a literal dream of the narrator. This device was commonly used to teach moral and religious lessons.

E

Eclogue: In classical literature, a poem featuring rural themes and structured as a dialogue among shepherds. Eclogues often took specific poetic forms, such as elegies or love poems. Some were written as the soliloquy of a shepherd. In later centuries, "eclogue" came to refer to any poem that was in the pastoral tradition or that had a dialogue or monologue structure.

Edwardian: Describes cultural conventions identified with the period of the reign of Edward VII of England (1901–1910). Writers of the Edwardian Age typically displayed a strong reaction against the propriety and conservatism of the Victorian Age. Their work often exhibits distrust of authority in religion, politics, and art and expresses strong doubts about the soundness of conventional values.

Edwardian Age: See *Edwardian*

Electra Complex: A daughter's amorous obsession with her father.

Elegy: A lyric poem that laments the death of a person or the eventual death of all people. In a conventional elegy, set in a classical world, the poet and subject are spoken of as shepherds. In modern criticism, the word elegy is often used to refer to a poem that is melancholy or mournfully contemplative.

Elizabethan Age: A period of great economic growth, religious controversy, and nationalism closely associated with the reign of Elizabeth I of England (1558–1603). The Elizabethan Age is considered a part of the general renaissance—that is, the flowering of arts and literature—that took place in Europe during the fourteenth through sixteenth centuries. The era is considered the golden age of English literature. The most important dramas in English and a great deal of lyric poetry were produced during this period, and modern English criticism began around this time.

Empathy: A sense of shared experience, including emotional and physical feelings, with someone or something other than oneself. Empathy is often used to describe the response of a reader to a literary character.

English Sonnet: See *Sonnet*

Enjambment: The running over of the sense and structure of a line of verse or a couplet into the following verse or couplet.

Enlightenment, The: An eighteenth-century philosophical movement. It began in France but had a wide impact throughout Europe and America. Thinkers of the Enlightenment valued reason and believed that both the individual and society could achieve a state of perfection. Corresponding to this essentially humanist vision was a resistance to religious authority.

Epic: A long narrative poem about the adventures of a hero of great historic or legendary importance. The setting is vast and the action is often given cosmic significance through the intervention of supernatural forces such as gods, angels, or demons. Epics are typically written in a classical style of grand simplicity with elaborate metaphors and allusions that enhance the symbolic importance of a hero's adventures.

Epic Simile: See *Homeric Simile*

Epigram: A saying that makes the speaker's point quickly and concisely.

Epilogue: A concluding statement or section of a literary work. In dramas, particularly those of the seventeenth and eighteenth centuries, the epilogue is a closing speech, often in verse, delivered by an actor at the end of a play and spoken directly to the audience.

Epiphany: A sudden revelation of truth inspired by a seemingly trivial incident.

Epitaph: An inscription on a tomb or tombstone, or a verse written on the occasion of a person's death. Epitaphs may be serious or humorous.

Epithalamion: A song or poem written to honor and commemorate a marriage ceremony.

Epithalamium: See *Epithalamion*

Epithet: A word or phrase, often disparaging or abusive, that expresses a character trait of someone or something.

Erziehungsroman: See *Bildungsroman*

Essay: A prose composition with a focused subject of discussion. The term was coined by Michel de Montaigne to describe his 1580 collection of brief, informal reflections on himself and on various topics relating to human nature. An essay can also be a long, systematic discourse.

Existentialism: A predominantly twentieth-century philosophy concerned with the nature and perception of human existence. There are two major strains of existentialist thought: atheistic and Christian. Followers of atheistic existentialism believe that the individual is alone in a godless universe and that the basic human condition is one of suffering and loneliness. Nevertheless, because there are no fixed values, individuals can create their own characters—indeed, they can shape themselves—through the exercise of free will. The atheistic strain culminates in and is popularly associated with the works of Jean-Paul Sartre. The Christian existentialists, on the other hand, believe that only in God may people find freedom from life's anguish. The two strains hold certain beliefs in common: that existence cannot be fully understood or described through empirical effort; that anguish is a universal element of life; that individuals must bear responsibility for their actions; and that there is no common standard of behavior or perception for religious and ethical matters.

Expatriates: See *Expatriatism*

Expatriatism: The practice of leaving one's country to live for an extended period in another country.

Exposition: Writing intended to explain the nature of an idea, thing, or theme. Expository writing is often combined with description, narration, or argument. In dramatic writing, the exposition is the introductory material which presents the characters, setting, and tone of the play.

Expressionism: An indistinct literary term, originally used to describe an early twentieth-century school of German painting. The term applies to almost any mode of unconventional, highly subjective writing that distorts reality in some way.

Extended Monologue: See *Monologue*

F

Feet: See *Foot*

Feminine Rhyme: See *Rhyme*

Fiction: Any story that is the product of imagination rather than a documentation of fact. Characters and events in such narratives may be based in real life but their ultimate form and configuration is a creation of the author.

Figurative Language: A technique in writing in which the author temporarily interrupts the order, construction, or meaning of the writing for a particular effect. This interruption takes the form of one or more figures of speech such as hyperbole, irony, or simile. Figurative language is the opposite of literal language, in which every word is truthful, accurate, and free of exaggeration or embellishment.

Figures of Speech: Writing that differs from customary conventions for construction, meaning, order, or significance for the purpose of a special meaning or effect. There are two major types of figures of speech: rhetorical figures, which do not make changes in the meaning of the words; and tropes, which do.

***Fin de siecle*:** A French term meaning "end of the century." The term is used to denote the last decade of the nineteenth century, a transition period when writers and other artists abandoned old conventions and looked for new techniques and objectives.

First Person: See *Point of View*

Folk Ballad: See *Ballad*

Folklore: Traditions and myths preserved in a culture or group of people. Typically, these are passed on by word of mouth in various forms—such as legends, songs, and proverbs—or preserved in customs and ceremonies. This term was first used by W. J. Thoms in 1846.

Folktale: A story originating in oral tradition. Folktales fall into a variety of categories, including legends, ghost stories, fairy tales, fables, and anecdotes based on historical figures and events.

Foot: The smallest unit of rhythm in a line of poetry. In English-language poetry, a foot is typically one accented syllable combined with one or two unaccented syllables.

Form: The pattern or construction of a work which identifies its genre and distinguishes it from other genres.

Formalism: In literary criticism, the belief that literature should follow prescribed rules of construction, such as those that govern the sonnet form.

Fourteener Meter: See *Meter*

Free Verse: Poetry that lacks regular metrical and rhyme patterns but that tries to capture the cadences of everyday speech. The form allows a poet to exploit a variety of rhythmical effects within a single poem.

Futurism: A flamboyant literary and artistic movement that developed in France, Italy, and Russia from 1908 through the 1920s. Futurist theater and poetry abandoned traditional literary forms. In their place, followers of the movement attempted to achieve total freedom of expression through bizarre imagery and deformed or newly invented words. The Futurists were self-consciously modern artists who attempted to incorporate the appearances and sounds of modern life into their work.

G

Genre: A category of literary work. In critical theory, genre may refer to both the content of a given work—tragedy, comedy, pastoral—and to its form, such as poetry, novel, or drama.

Genteel Tradition: A term coined by critic George Santayana to describe the literary practice of certain late nineteenth-century American writers, especially New Englanders. Followers of the Genteel

Tradition emphasized conventionality in social, religious, moral, and literary standards.

Georgian Age: See *Georgian Poets*

Georgian Period: See *Georgian Poets*

Georgian Poets: A loose grouping of English poets during the years 1912–1922. The Georgians reacted against certain literary schools and practices, especially Victorian wordiness, turn-of-the-century aestheticism, and contemporary urban realism. In their place, the Georgians embraced the nineteenth-century poetic practices of William Wordsworth and the other Lake Poets.

Georgic: A poem about farming and the farmer's way of life, named from Virgil's *Georgics*.

Gilded Age: A period in American history during the 1870s characterized by political corruption and materialism. A number of important novels of social and political criticism were written during this time.

Gothic: See *Gothicism*

Gothicism: In literary criticism, works characterized by a taste for the medieval or morbidly attractive. A gothic novel prominently features elements of horror, the supernatural, gloom, and violence: clanking chains, terror, charnel houses, ghosts, medieval castles, and mysteriously slamming doors. The term "gothic novel" is also applied to novels that lack elements of the traditional Gothic setting but that create a similar atmosphere of terror or dread.

Graveyard School: A group of eighteenth-century English poets who wrote long, picturesque meditations on death. Their works were designed to cause the reader to ponder immortality.

Great Chain of Being: The belief that all things and creatures in nature are organized in a hierarchy from inanimate objects at the bottom to God at the top. This system of belief was popular in the seventeenth and eighteenth centuries.

Grotesque: In literary criticism, the subject matter of a work or a style of expression characterized by exaggeration, deformity, freakishness, and disorder. The grotesque often includes an element of comic absurdity.

H

Haiku: The shortest form of Japanese poetry, constructed in three lines of five, seven, and five syllables respectively. The message of a *haiku* poem usually centers on some aspect of spirituality and provokes an emotional response in the reader.

Half Rhyme: See *Consonance*

Harlem Renaissance: The Harlem Renaissance of the 1920s is generally considered the first significant movement of black writers and artists in the United States. During this period, new and established black writers published more fiction and poetry than ever before, the first influential black literary journals were established, and black authors and artists received their first widespread recognition and serious critical appraisal. Among the major writers associated with this period are Claude McKay, Jean Toomer, Countee Cullen, Langston Hughes, Arna Bontemps, Nella Larsen, and Zora Neale Hurston.

Hellenism: Imitation of ancient Greek thought or styles. Also, an approach to life that focuses on the growth and development of the intellect. "Hellenism" is sometimes used to refer to the belief that reason can be applied to examine all human experience.

Heptameter: See *Meter*

Hero/Heroine: The principal sympathetic character (male or female) in a literary work. Heroes and heroines typically exhibit admirable traits: idealism, courage, and integrity, for example.

Heroic Couplet: A rhyming couplet written in iambic pentameter (a verse with five iambic feet).

Heroic Line: The meter and length of a line of verse in epic or heroic poetry. This varies by language and time period.

Heroine: See *Hero/Heroine*

Hexameter: See *Meter*

Historical Criticism: The study of a work based on its impact on the world of the time period in which it was written.

Hokku: See *Haiku*

Holocaust: See *Holocaust Literature*

Holocaust Literature: Literature influenced by or written about the Holocaust of World War II. Such literature includes true stories of survival in concentration camps, escape, and life after the war, as well as fictional works and poetry.

Homeric Simile: An elaborate, detailed comparison written as a simile many lines in length.

Horatian Satire: See *Satire*

Humanism: A philosophy that places faith in the dignity of humankind and rejects the medieval perception of the individual as a weak, fallen creature. "Humanists" typically believe in the perfectibility of human nature and view reason and education as the means to that end.

Humors: Mentions of the humors refer to the ancient Greek theory that a person's health and personality were determined by the balance of four basic fluids in the body: blood, phlegm, yellow bile, and black bile. A dominance of any fluid would cause extremes in behavior. An excess of blood created a sanguine person who was joyful, aggressive, and passionate; a phlegmatic person was shy, fearful, and sluggish; too much yellow bile led to a choleric temperament characterized by impatience, anger, bitterness, and stubbornness; and excessive black bile created melancholy, a state of laziness, gluttony, and lack of motivation.

Humours: See *Humors*

Hyperbole: In literary criticism, deliberate exaggeration used to achieve an effect.

I

Iamb: See *Foot*

Idiom: A word construction or verbal expression closely associated with a given language.

Image: A concrete representation of an object or sensory experience. Typically, such a representation helps evoke the feelings associated with the object or experience itself. Images are either "literal" or "figurative." Literal images are especially concrete and involve little or no extension of the obvious meaning of the words used to express them. Figurative images do not follow the literal meaning of the words exactly. Images in literature are usually visual, but the term "image" can also refer to the representation of any sensory experience.

Imagery: The array of images in a literary work. Also, figurative language.

Imagism: An English and American poetry movement that flourished between 1908 and 1917. The Imagists used precise, clearly presented images in their works. They also used common, everyday speech and aimed for conciseness, concrete imagery, and the creation of new rhythms.

In medias res: A Latin term meaning "in the middle of things." It refers to the technique of beginning a story at its midpoint and then using various flashback devices to reveal previous action.

Induction: The process of reaching a conclusion by reasoning from specific premises to form a general premise. Also, an introductory portion of a work of literature, especially a play.

Intentional Fallacy: The belief that judgments of a literary work based solely on an author's stated or implied intentions are false and misleading. Critics who believe in the concept of the intentional fallacy typically argue that the work itself is sufficient matter for interpretation, even though they may concede that an author's statement of purpose can be useful.

Interior Monologue: A narrative technique in which characters' thoughts are revealed in a way that appears to be uncontrolled by the author. The interior monologue typically aims to reveal the inner self of a character. It portrays emotional experiences as they occur at both a conscious and unconscious level. Images are often used to represent sensations or emotions.

Internal Rhyme: Rhyme that occurs within a single line of verse.

Irish Literary Renaissance: A late nineteenth- and early twentieth-century movement in Irish literature. Members of the movement aimed to reduce the influence of British culture in Ireland and create an Irish national literature.

Irony: In literary criticism, the effect of language in which the intended meaning is the opposite of what is stated.

Italian Sonnet: See *Sonnet*

J

Jacobean Age: The period of the reign of James I of England (1603–1625). The early literature of this period reflected the worldview of the Elizabethan Age, but a darker, more cynical attitude steadily grew in the art and literature of the Jacobean Age. This was an important time for English drama and poetry.

Jargon: Language that is used or understood only by a select group of people. Jargon may refer to terminology used in a certain profession, such as computer jargon, or it may refer to any nonsensical language that is not understood by most people.

Journalism: Writing intended for publication in a newspaper or magazine, or for broadcast on a radio or television program featuring news, sports, entertainment, or other timely material.

K

Knickerbocker Group: A somewhat indistinct group of New York writers of the first half of the nineteenth century. Members of the group were linked only by location and a common theme: New York life.

Kunstlerroman: See *Bildungsroman*

L

Lais: See *Lay*

Lake Poets: See *Lake School*

Lake School: These poets all lived in the Lake District of England at the turn of the nineteenth century. As a group, they followed no single "school" of thought or literary practice, although their works were uniformly disparaged by the *Edinburgh Review.*

Lay: A song or simple narrative poem. The form originated in medieval France. Early French *lais* were often based on the Celtic legends and other tales sung by Breton minstrels—thus the name of the "Breton lay." In fourteenth-century England, the term "lay" was used to describe short narratives written in imitation of the Breton lays.

Leitmotiv: See *Motif*

Literal Language: An author uses literal language when he or she writes without exaggerating or embellishing the subject matter and without any tools of figurative language.

Literary Ballad: See *Ballad*

Literature: Literature is broadly defined as any written or spoken material, but the term most often refers to creative works.

Lost Generation: A term first used by Gertrude Stein to describe the post-World War I generation of American writers: men and women haunted by a sense of betrayal and emptiness brought about by the destructiveness of the war.

Lyric Poetry: A poem expressing the subjective feelings and personal emotions of the poet. Such poetry is melodic, since it was originally accompanied by a lyre in recitals. Most Western poetry in the twentieth century may be classified as lyrical.

M

Mannerism: Exaggerated, artificial adherence to a literary manner or style. Also, a popular style of the visual arts of late sixteenth-century Europe that was marked by elongation of the human form and by intentional spatial distortion. Literary works that are self-consciously high-toned and artistic are often said to be "mannered."

Masculine Rhyme: See *Rhyme*

Measure: The foot, verse, or time sequence used in a literary work, especially a poem. Measure is often used somewhat incorrectly as a synonym for meter.

Metaphor: A figure of speech that expresses an idea through the image of another object. Metaphors suggest the essence of the first object by identifying it with certain qualities of the second object.

Metaphysical Conceit: See *Conceit*

Metaphysical Poetry: The body of poetry produced by a group of seventeenth-century English writers called the "Metaphysical Poets." The group includes John Donne and Andrew Marvell. The Metaphysical Poets made use of everyday speech, intellectual analysis, and unique imagery. They aimed to portray the ordinary conflicts and contradictions of life. Their poems often took the form of an argument, and many of them emphasize physical and religious love as well as the fleeting nature of life. Elaborate conceits are typical in metaphysical poetry.

Metaphysical Poets: See *Metaphysical Poetry*

Meter: In literary criticism, the repetition of sound patterns that creates a rhythm in poetry. The patterns are based on the number of syllables and the presence and absence of accents. The unit of rhythm in a line is called a foot. Types of meter are classified according to the number of feet in a line. These are the standard English lines: Monometer, one foot; Dimeter, two feet; Trimeter, three feet; Tetrameter, four feet; Pentameter, five feet; Hexameter, six feet (also called the Alexandrine); Heptameter, seven feet (also called the "Fourteener" when the feet are iambic).

Modernism: Modern literary practices. Also, the principles of a literary school that lasted from roughly the beginning of the twentieth century until the end of World War II. Modernism is defined by its rejection of the literary conventions of the nineteenth century and by its opposition to conventional morality, taste, traditions, and economic values.

Monologue: A composition, written or oral, by a single individual. More specifically, a speech given by a single individual in a drama or other public entertainment. It has no set length, although it is usually several or more lines long.

Monometer: See *Meter*

Mood: The prevailing emotions of a work or of the author in his or her creation of the work. The mood of a work is not always what might be expected based on its subject matter.

Motif: A theme, character type, image, metaphor, or other verbal element that recurs throughout a single work of literature or occurs in a number of different works over a period of time.

Motiv: See *Motif*

Muckrakers: An early twentieth-century group of American writers. Typically, their works exposed the wrongdoings of big business and government in the United States.

Muses: Nine Greek mythological goddesses, the daughters of Zeus and Mnemosyne (Memory). Each muse patronized a specific area of the liberal arts and sciences. Calliope presided over epic poetry, Clio over history, Erato over love poetry, Euterpe over music or lyric poetry, Melpomene over tragedy, Polyhymnia over hymns to the gods, Terpsichore over dance, Thalia over comedy, and Urania over astronomy. Poets and writers traditionally made appeals to the Muses for inspiration in their work.

Myth: An anonymous tale emerging from the traditional beliefs of a culture or social unit. Myths use supernatural explanations for natural phenomena. They may also explain cosmic issues like creation and death. Collections of myths, known as mythologies, are common to all cultures and nations, but the best-known myths belong to the Norse, Roman, and Greek mythologies.

N

Narration: The telling of a series of events, real or invented. A narration may be either a simple narrative, in which the events are recounted chronologically, or a narrative with a plot, in which the account is given in a style reflecting the author's artistic concept of the story. Narration is sometimes used as a synonym for "storyline."

Narrative: A verse or prose accounting of an event or sequence of events, real or invented. The term is also used as an adjective in the sense "method of narration." For example, in literary criticism, the expression "narrative technique" usually refers to the way the author structures and presents his or her story.

Narrative Poetry: A nondramatic poem in which the author tells a story. Such poems may be of any length or level of complexity.

Narrator: The teller of a story. The narrator may be the author or a character in the story through whom the author speaks.

Naturalism: A literary movement of the late nineteenth and early twentieth centuries. The movement's major theorist, French novelist Emile Zola, envisioned a type of fiction that would examine human life with the objectivity of scientific inquiry. The Naturalists typically viewed human beings as either the products of "biological determinism," ruled by hereditary instincts and engaged in an endless struggle for survival, or as the products of "socioeconomic determinism," ruled by social and economic forces beyond their control. In their works, the Naturalists generally ignored the highest levels of society and focused on degradation: poverty, alcoholism, prostitution, insanity, and disease.

Negritude: A literary movement based on the concept of a shared cultural bond on the part of black Africans, wherever they may be in the world. It traces its origins to the former French colonies of Africa and the Caribbean. Negritude poets, novelists, and essayists generally stress four points in their writings: One, black alienation from traditional African culture can lead to feelings of inferiority. Two, European colonialism and Western education should be resisted. Three, black Africans should seek to affirm and define their own identity. Four, African culture can and should be reclaimed. Many Negritude writers also claim that blacks can make unique contributions to the world, based on a heightened appreciation of nature, rhythm, and human emotions—aspects of life they say are not so highly valued in the materialistic and rationalistic West.

Negro Renaissance: See *Harlem Renaissance*

Neoclassical Period: See *Neoclassicism*

Neoclassicism: In literary criticism, this term refers to the revival of the attitudes and styles of expression of classical literature. It is generally used to describe a period in European history beginning in the late seventeenth century and lasting until about 1800. In its purest form, Neoclassicism marked a return to order, proportion, restraint, logic, accuracy, and decorum. In England, where Neoclassicism perhaps was most popular, it reflected the influence of seventeenth-century French writers, especially dramatists. Neoclassical writers typically reacted against the intensity and enthusiasm of the Renaissance period. They wrote works that appealed to the intellect, using elevated language and classical literary forms such as satire and the ode. Neoclassical works were often governed by the classical goal of instruction.

Neoclassicists: See *Neoclassicism*

New Criticism: A movement in literary criticism, dating from the late 1920s, that stressed close textual analysis in the interpretation of works of literature. The New Critics saw little merit in historical and biographical analysis. Rather, they aimed to examine the text alone, free from the question of how external events—biographical or otherwise—may have helped shape it.

New Journalism: A type of writing in which the journalist presents factual information in a form usually used in fiction. New journalism emphasizes description, narration, and character development to bring readers closer to the human element of the story, and is often used in personality profiles and in-depth feature articles. It is not compatible with "straight" or "hard" newswriting, which is generally composed in a brief, fact-based style.

New Journalists: See *New Journalism*

New Negro Movement: See *Harlem Renaissance*

Noble Savage: The idea that primitive man is noble and good but becomes evil and corrupted as he becomes civilized. The concept of the noble savage originated in the Renaissance period but is more closely identified with such later writers as Jean-Jacques Rousseau and Aphra Behn.

O

Objective Correlative: An outward set of objects, a situation, or a chain of events corresponding to an inward experience and evoking this experience in the reader. The term frequently appears in modern criticism in discussions of authors' intended effects on the emotional responses of readers.

Objectivity: A quality in writing characterized by the absence of the author's opinion or feeling about the subject matter. Objectivity is an important factor in criticism.

Occasional Verse: Poetry written on the occasion of a significant historical or personal event. *Vers de societe* is sometimes called occasional verse although it is of a less serious nature.

Octave: A poem or stanza composed of eight lines. The term octave most often represents the first eight lines of a Petrarchan sonnet.

Ode: Name given to an extended lyric poem characterized by exalted emotion and dignified style. An ode usually concerns a single, serious theme. Most odes, but not all, are addressed to an object or individual. Odes are distinguished from other lyric poetic forms by their complex rhythmic and stanzaic patterns.

Oedipus Complex: A son's amorous obsession with his mother. The phrase is derived from the story of the ancient Theban hero Oedipus, who un-

knowingly killed his father and married his mother.

Omniscience: See *Point of View*

Onomatopoeia: The use of words whose sounds express or suggest their meaning. In its simplest sense, onomatopoeia may be represented by words that mimic the sounds they denote such as "hiss" or "meow." At a more subtle level, the pattern and rhythm of sounds and rhymes of a line or poem may be onomatopoeic.

Oral Tradition: See *Oral Transmission*

Oral Transmission: A process by which songs, ballads, folklore, and other material are transmitted by word of mouth. The tradition of oral transmission predates the written record systems of literate society. Oral transmission preserves material sometimes over generations, although often with variations. Memory plays a large part in the recitation and preservation of orally transmitted material.

Ottava Rima: An eight-line stanza of poetry composed in iambic pentameter (a five-foot line in which each foot consists of an unaccented syllable followed by an accented syllable), following the *abababcc* rhyme scheme.

Oxymoron: A phrase combining two contradictory terms. Oxymorons may be intentional or unintentional.

P

Pantheism: The idea that all things are both a manifestation or revelation of God and a part of God at the same time. Pantheism was a common attitude in the early societies of Egypt, India, and Greece—the term derives from the Greek *pan* meaning "all" and *theos* meaning "deity." It later became a significant part of the Christian faith.

Parable: A story intended to teach a moral lesson or answer an ethical question.

Paradox: A statement that appears illogical or contradictory at first, but may actually point to an underlying truth.

Parallelism: A method of comparison of two ideas in which each is developed in the same grammatical structure.

Parnassianism: A mid nineteenth-century movement in French literature. Followers of the movement stressed adherence to well-defined artistic forms as a reaction against the often chaotic expression of the artist's ego that dominated the work of the Romantics. The Parnassians also rejected the moral, ethical, and social themes exhibited in the works of French Romantics such as Victor Hugo. The aesthetic doctrines of the Parnassians strongly influenced the later symbolist and decadent movements.

Parody: In literary criticism, this term refers to an imitation of a serious literary work or the signature style of a particular author in a ridiculous manner. A typical parody adopts the style of the original and applies it to an inappropriate subject for humorous effect. Parody is a form of satire and could be considered the literary equivalent of a caricature or cartoon.

Pastoral: A term derived from the Latin word "pastor," meaning shepherd. A pastoral is a literary composition on a rural theme. The conventions of the pastoral were originated by the third-century Greek poet Theocritus, who wrote about the experiences, love affairs, and pastimes of Sicilian shepherds. In a pastoral, characters and language of a courtly nature are often placed in a simple setting. The term pastoral is also used to classify dramas, elegies, and lyrics that exhibit the use of country settings and shepherd characters.

Pathetic Fallacy: A term coined by English critic John Ruskin to identify writing that falsely endows nonhuman things with human intentions and feelings, such as "angry clouds" and "sad trees."

Pen Name: See *Pseudonym*

Pentameter: See *Meter*

Persona: A Latin term meaning "mask." *Personae* are the characters in a fictional work of literature. The *persona* generally functions as a mask through which the author tells a story in a voice other than his or her own. A *persona* is usually either a character in a story who acts as a narrator or an "implied author," a voice created by the author to act as the narrator for himself or herself.

Personae: See *Persona*

Personal Point of View: See *Point of View*

Personification: A figure of speech that gives human qualities to abstract ideas, animals, and inanimate objects.

Petrarchan Sonnet: See *Sonnet*

Phenomenology: A method of literary criticism based on the belief that things have no existence outside of human consciousness or awareness. Proponents of this theory believe that art is a process that takes place in the mind of the observer as he or she contemplates an object rather than a quality of the object itself.

Plagiarism: Claiming another person's written material as one's own. Plagiarism can take the form of direct, word-for-word copying or the theft of the substance or idea of the work.

Platonic Criticism: A form of criticism that stresses an artistic work's usefulness as an agent of social engineering rather than any quality or value of the work itself.

Platonism: The embracing of the doctrines of the philosopher Plato, popular among the poets of the Renaissance and the Romantic period. Platonism is more flexible than Aristotelian Criticism and places more emphasis on the supernatural and unknown aspects of life.

Plot: In literary criticism, this term refers to the pattern of events in a narrative or drama. In its simplest sense, the plot guides the author in composing the work and helps the reader follow the work. Typically, plots exhibit causality and unity and have a beginning, a middle, and an end. Sometimes, however, a plot may consist of a series of disconnected events, in which case it is known as an "episodic plot."

Poem: In its broadest sense, a composition utilizing rhyme, meter, concrete detail, and expressive language to create a literary experience with emotional and aesthetic appeal.

Poet: An author who writes poetry or verse. The term is also used to refer to an artist or writer who has an exceptional gift for expression, imagination, and energy in the making of art in any form.

Poete maudit: A term derived from Paul Verlaine's *Les poetes maudits* (*The Accursed Poets*), a collection of essays on the French symbolist writers Stephane Mallarme, Arthur Rimbaud, and Tristan Corbiere. In the sense intended by Verlaine, the poet is "accursed" for choosing to explore extremes of human experience outside of middle-class society.

Poetic Fallacy: See *Pathetic Fallacy*

Poetic Justice: An outcome in a literary work, not necessarily a poem, in which the good are rewarded and the evil are punished, especially in ways that particularly fit their virtues or crimes.

Poetic License: Distortions of fact and literary convention made by a writer—not always a poet—for the sake of the effect gained. Poetic license is closely related to the concept of "artistic freedom."

Poetics: This term has two closely related meanings. It denotes (1) an aesthetic theory in literary criticism about the essence of poetry or (2) rules prescribing the proper methods, content, style, or diction of poetry. The term poetics may also refer to theories about literature in general, not just poetry.

Poetry: In its broadest sense, writing that aims to present ideas and evoke an emotional experience in the reader through the use of meter, imagery, connotative and concrete words, and a carefully constructed structure based on rhythmic patterns. Poetry typically relies on words and expressions that have several layers of meaning. It also makes use of the effects of regular rhythm on the ear and may make a strong appeal to the senses through the use of imagery.

Point of View: The narrative perspective from which a literary work is presented to the reader. There are four traditional points of view. The "third person omniscient" gives the reader a "godlike" perspective, unrestricted by time or place, from which to see actions and look into the minds of characters. This allows the author to comment openly on characters and events in the work. The "third-person" point of view presents the events of the story from outside of any single character's perception, much like the omniscient point of view, but the reader must understand the action as it takes place and without any special insight into characters' minds or motivations. The "first person" or "personal" point of view relates events as they are perceived by a single character. The main character "tells" the story and may offer opinions about the action and characters which differ from those of the author. Much less common than omniscient, third person, and first person is the "second-person" point of view, wherein the author tells the story as if it is happening to the reader.

Polemic: A work in which the author takes a stand on a controversial subject, such as abortion or religion. Such works are often extremely argumentative or provocative.

Pornography: Writing intended to provoke feelings of lust in the reader. Such works are often condemned by critics and teachers, but those which can be shown to have literary value are viewed less harshly.

Post-Aesthetic Movement: An artistic response made by African Americans to the black aesthetic movement of the 1960s and early 1970s. Writers since that time have adopted a somewhat different tone in their work, with less emphasis placed on the disparity between black and white in the United States. In the words of post-aesthetic authors such as Toni Morrison, John Edgar Wideman, and Kristin Hunter, African Americans are portrayed as looking inward for answers to their own questions, rather than always looking to the outside world.

Postmodernism: Writing from the 1960s forward characterized by experimentation and continuing to apply some of the fundamentals of modernism, which included existentialism and alienation. Postmodernists have gone a step further in the rejection of tradition begun with the modernists by also rejecting traditional forms, preferring the antinovel over the novel and the antihero over the hero.

Pre-Raphaelites: A circle of writers and artists in mid nineteenth-century England. Valuing the pre-Renaissance artistic qualities of religious symbolism, lavish pictorialism, and natural sensuousness, the Pre-Raphaelites cultivated a sense of mystery and melancholy that influenced later writers associated with the Symbolist and Decadent movements.

Primitivism: The belief that primitive peoples were nobler and less flawed than civilized peoples because they had not been subjected to the corrupt influence of society.

Projective Verse: A form of free verse in which the poet's breathing pattern determines the lines of the poem. Poets who advocate projective verse are against all formal structures in writing, including meter and form.

Prologue: An introductory section of a literary work. It often contains information establishing the situation of the characters or presents information about the setting, time period, or action. In drama, the prologue is spoken by a chorus or by one of the principal characters.

Prose: A literary medium that attempts to mirror the language of everyday speech. It is distinguished from poetry by its use of unmetered, unrhymed language consisting of logically related sentences. Prose is usually grouped into paragraphs that form a cohesive whole such as an essay or a novel.

Prosopopoeia: See *Personification*

Protagonist: The central character of a story who serves as a focus for its themes and incidents and as the principal rationale for its development. The protagonist is sometimes referred to in discussions of modern literature as the hero or antihero.

Proverb: A brief, sage saying that expresses a truth about life in a striking manner.

Pseudonym: A name assumed by a writer, most often intended to prevent his or her identification as the author of a work. Two or more authors may work together under one pseudonym, or an author may use a different name for each genre he or she publishes in. Some publishing companies maintain "house pseudonyms," under which any number of authors may write installations in a series. Some authors also choose a pseudonym over their real names the way an actor may use a stage name.

Pun: A play on words that have similar sounds but different meanings.

Pure Poetry: poetry written without instructional intent or moral purpose that aims only to please a reader by its imagery or musical flow. The term pure poetry is used as the antonym of the term "didacticism."

Q

Quatrain: A four-line stanza of a poem or an entire poem consisting of four lines.

R

Realism: A nineteenth-century European literary movement that sought to portray familiar characters, situations, and settings in a realistic manner. This was done primarily by using an objective narrative point of view and through the buildup of accurate detail. The standard for success of any realistic work depends on how faithfully it transfers common experience into fictional forms. The realistic method may be altered or extended, as in stream of consciousness writing, to record highly subjective experience.

Refrain: A phrase repeated at intervals throughout a poem. A refrain may appear at the end of each stanza or at less regular intervals. It may be altered slightly at each appearance.

Renaissance: The period in European history that marked the end of the Middle Ages. It began in Italy in the late fourteenth century. In broad terms, it is usually seen as spanning the fourteenth, fifteenth, and sixteenth centuries, although it did not reach Great Britain, for example, until the 1480s or so. The Renaissance saw an awakening in almost every sphere of human activity, especially science, philosophy, and the arts. The period is best defined by the emergence of a general philosophy that emphasized the importance of the intellect, the individual, and world affairs. It contrasts strongly with the medieval worldview, characterized by the dominant concerns of faith, the social collective, and spiritual salvation.

Repartee: Conversation featuring snappy retorts and witticisms.

Restoration: See *Restoration Age*

Restoration Age: A period in English literature beginning with the crowning of Charles II in 1660 and running to about 1700. The era, which was characterized by a reaction against Puritanism, was the first great age of the comedy of manners. The finest literature of the era is typically witty and urbane, and often lewd.

Rhetoric: In literary criticism, this term denotes the art of ethical persuasion. In its strictest sense, rhetoric adheres to various principles developed since classical times for arranging facts and ideas in a clear, persuasive, appealing manner. The term is also used to refer to effective prose in general and theories of or methods for composing effective prose.

Rhetorical Question: A question intended to provoke thought, but not an expressed answer, in the reader. It is most commonly used in oratory and other persuasive genres.

Rhyme: When used as a noun in literary criticism, this term generally refers to a poem in which words sound identical or very similar and appear in parallel positions in two or more lines. Rhymes are classified into different types according to where they fall in a line or stanza or according to the degree of similarity they exhibit in their spellings and sounds. Some major types of rhyme are "masculine" rhyme, "feminine" rhyme, and "triple" rhyme. In a masculine rhyme, the rhyming sound falls in a single accented syllable, as with "heat" and "eat." Feminine rhyme is a rhyme of two syllables, one stressed and one unstressed, as with "merry" and "tarry." Triple rhyme matches the sound of the accented syllable and the two unaccented syllables that follow: "narrative" and "declarative."

Rhyme Royal: A stanza of seven lines composed in iambic pentameter and rhymed *ababbcc*. The name is said to be a tribute to King James I of Scotland, who made much use of the form in his poetry.

Rhyme Scheme: See *Rhyme*

Rhythm: A regular pattern of sound, time intervals, or events occurring in writing, most often and most discernably in poetry. Regular, reliable rhythm is known to be soothing to humans, while interrupted, unpredictable, or rapidly changing rhythm is disturbing. These effects are known to authors, who use them to produce a desired reaction in the reader.

Rococo: A style of European architecture that flourished in the eighteenth century, especially in

France. The most notable features of *rococo* are its extensive use of ornamentation and its themes of lightness, gaiety, and intimacy. In literary criticism, the term is often used disparagingly to refer to a decadent or overly ornamental style.

Romance:

Romantic Age: See *Romanticism*

Romanticism: This term has two widely accepted meanings. In historical criticism, it refers to a European intellectual and artistic movement of the late eighteenth and early nineteenth centuries that sought greater freedom of personal expression than that allowed by the strict rules of literary form and logic of the eighteenth-century Neoclassicists. The Romantics preferred emotional and imaginative expression to rational analysis. They considered the individual to be at the center of all experience and so placed him or her at the center of their art. The Romantics believed that the creative imagination reveals nobler truths—unique feelings and attitudes—than those that could be discovered by logic or by scientific examination. Both the natural world and the state of childhood were important sources for revelations of "eternal truths." "Romanticism" is also used as a general term to refer to a type of sensibility found in all periods of literary history and usually considered to be in opposition to the principles of classicism. In this sense, Romanticism signifies any work or philosophy in which the exotic or dreamlike figure strongly, or that is devoted to individualistic expression, self-analysis, or a pursuit of a higher realm of knowledge than can be discovered by human reason.

Romantics: See *Romanticism*

Russian Symbolism: A Russian poetic movement, derived from French symbolism, that flourished between 1894 and 1910. While some Russian Symbolists continued in the French tradition, stressing aestheticism and the importance of suggestion above didactic intent, others saw their craft as a form of mystical worship, and themselves as mediators between the supernatural and the mundane.

S

Satire: A work that uses ridicule, humor, and wit to criticize and provoke change in human nature and institutions. There are two major types of satire: "formal" or "direct" satire speaks directly to the reader or to a character in the work; "indirect" satire relies upon the ridiculous behavior of its characters to make its point. Formal satire is further divided into two manners: the "Horatian," which

ridicules gently, and the "Juvenalian," which derides its subjects harshly and bitterly.

Scansion: The analysis or "scanning" of a poem to determine its meter and often its rhyme scheme. The most common system of scansion uses accents (slanted lines drawn above syllables) to show stressed syllables, breves (curved lines drawn above syllables) to show unstressed syllables, and vertical lines to separate each foot.

Second Person: See *Point of View*

Semiotics: The study of how literary forms and conventions affect the meaning of language.

Sestet: Any six-line poem or stanza.

Setting: The time, place, and culture in which the action of a narrative takes place. The elements of setting may include geographic location, characters' physical and mental environments, prevailing cultural attitudes, or the historical time in which the action takes place.

Shakespearean Sonnet: See *Sonnet*

Signifying Monkey: A popular trickster figure in black folklore, with hundreds of tales about this character documented since the nineteenth century.

Simile: A comparison, usually using "like" or "as," of two essentially dissimilar things, as in "coffee as cold as ice" or "He sounded like a broken record."

Slang: A type of informal verbal communication that is generally unacceptable for formal writing. Slang words and phrases are often colorful exaggerations used to emphasize the speaker's point; they may also be shortened versions of an often-used word or phrase.

Slant Rhyme: See *Consonance*

Slave Narrative: Autobiographical accounts of American slave life as told by escaped slaves. These works first appeared during the abolition movement of the 1830s through the 1850s.

Social Realism: See *Socialist Realism*

Socialist Realism: The Socialist Realism school of literary theory was proposed by Maxim Gorky and established as a dogma by the first Soviet Congress of Writers. It demanded adherence to a communist worldview in works of literature. Its doctrines required an objective viewpoint comprehensible to the working classes and themes of social struggle featuring strong proletarian heroes.

Soliloquy: A monologue in a drama used to give the audience information and to develop the speaker's character. It is typically a projection of the speaker's innermost thoughts. Usually delivered while the speaker is alone on stage, a soliloquy is intended to present an illusion of unspoken reflection.

Sonnet: A fourteen-line poem, usually composed in iambic pentameter, employing one of several rhyme schemes. There are three major types of sonnets, upon which all other variations of the form are based: the "Petrarchan" or "Italian" sonnet, the "Shakespearean" or "English" sonnet, and the "Spenserian" sonnet. A Petrarchan sonnet consists of an octave rhymed *abbaabba* and a "sestet" rhymed either *cdecde, cdccdc,* or *cdedce.* The octave poses a question or problem, relates a narrative, or puts forth a proposition; the sestet presents a solution to the problem, comments upon the narrative, or applies the proposition put forth in the octave. The Shakespearean sonnet is divided into three quatrains and a couplet rhymed *abab cdcd efef gg.* The couplet provides an epigrammatic comment on the narrative or problem put forth in the quatrains. The Spenserian sonnet uses three quatrains and a couplet like the Shakespearean, but links their three rhyme schemes in this way: *abab bcbc cdcd ee.* The Spenserian sonnet develops its theme in two parts like the Petrarchan, its final six lines resolving a problem, analyzing a narrative, or applying a proposition put forth in its first eight lines.

Spenserian Sonnet: See *Sonnet*

Spenserian Stanza: A nine-line stanza having eight verses in iambic pentameter, its ninth verse in iambic hexameter, and the rhyme scheme *ababbcbcc.*

Spondee: In poetry meter, a foot consisting of two long or stressed syllables occurring together. This form is quite rare in English verse, and is usually composed of two monosyllabic words.

Sprung Rhythm: Versification using a specific number of accented syllables per line but disregarding the number of unaccented syllables that fall in each line, producing an irregular rhythm in the poem.

Stanza: A subdivision of a poem consisting of lines grouped together, often in recurring patterns of rhyme, line length, and meter. Stanzas may also serve as units of thought in a poem much like paragraphs in prose.

Stereotype: A stereotype was originally the name for a duplication made during the printing process; this led to its modern definition as a person or thing that is (or is assumed to be) the same as all others of its type.

Stream of Consciousness: A narrative technique for rendering the inward experience of a character. This technique is designed to give the impression of an ever-changing series of thoughts, emotions, images, and memories in the spontaneous and seemingly illogical order that they occur in life.

Structuralism: A twentieth-century movement in literary criticism that examines how literary texts arrive at their meanings, rather than the meanings themselves. There are two major types of structuralist analysis: one examines the way patterns of linguistic structures unify a specific text and emphasize certain elements of that text, and the other interprets the way literary forms and conventions affect the meaning of language itself.

Structure: The form taken by a piece of literature. The structure may be made obvious for ease of understanding, as in nonfiction works, or may obscured for artistic purposes, as in some poetry or seemingly "unstructured" prose.

Sturm und Drang: A German term meaning "storm and stress." It refers to a German literary movement of the 1770s and 1780s that reacted against the order and rationalism of the enlightenment, focusing instead on the intense experience of extraordinary individuals.

Style: A writer's distinctive manner of arranging words to suit his or her ideas and purpose in writing. The unique imprint of the author's personality upon his or her writing, style is the product of an author's way of arranging ideas and his or her use of diction, different sentence structures, rhythm, figures of speech, rhetorical principles, and other elements of composition.

Subject: The person, event, or theme at the center of a work of literature. A work may have one or more subjects of each type, with shorter works tending to have fewer and longer works tending to have more.

Subjectivity: Writing that expresses the author's personal feelings about his subject, and which may or may not include factual information about the subject.

Surrealism: A term introduced to criticism by Guillaume Apollinaire and later adopted by Andre Breton. It refers to a French literary and artistic movement founded in the 1920s. The Surrealists sought to express unconscious thoughts and feelings in their works. The best-known technique used for achieving this aim was automatic writing—transcriptions of spontaneous outpourings from the unconscious. The Surrealists proposed to unify the contrary levels of conscious and unconscious, dream and reality, objectivity and subjectivity into a new level of "super-realism."

Suspense: A literary device in which the author maintains the audience's attention through the buildup of events, the outcome of which will soon be revealed.

Syllogism: A method of presenting a logical argument. In its most basic form, the syllogism consists of a major premise, a minor premise, and a conclusion.

Symbol: Something that suggests or stands for something else without losing its original identity. In literature, symbols combine their literal meaning with the suggestion of an abstract concept. Literary symbols are of two types: those that carry complex associations of meaning no matter what their contexts, and those that derive their suggestive meaning from their functions in specific literary works.

Symbolism: This term has two widely accepted meanings. In historical criticism, it denotes an early modernist literary movement initiated in France during the nineteenth century that reacted against the prevailing standards of realism. Writers in this movement aimed to evoke, indirectly and symbolically, an order of being beyond the material world of the five senses. Poetic expression of personal emotion figured strongly in the movement, typically by means of a private set of symbols uniquely identifiable with the individual poet. The principal aim of the Symbolists was to express in words the highly complex feelings that grew out of everyday contact with the world. In a broader sense, the term "symbolism" refers to the use of one object to represent another.

Symbolist: See *Symbolism*

Symbolist Movement: See *Symbolism*

Sympathetic Fallacy: See *Affective Fallacy*

T

Tanka: A form of Japanese poetry similar to *haiku*. A *tanka* is five lines long, with the lines containing five, seven, five, seven, and seven syllables respectively.

Terza Rima: A three-line stanza form in poetry in which the rhymes are made on the last word of each line in the following manner: the first and third lines of the first stanza, then the second line of the first stanza and the first and third lines of the second stanza, and so on with the middle line of any

stanza rhyming with the first and third lines of the following stanza.

Tetrameter: See *Meter*

Textual Criticism: A branch of literary criticism that seeks to establish the authoritative text of a literary work. Textual critics typically compare all known manuscripts or printings of a single work in order to assess the meanings of differences and revisions. This procedure allows them to arrive at a definitive version that (supposedly) corresponds to the author's original intention.

Theme: The main point of a work of literature. The term is used interchangeably with thesis.

Thesis: A thesis is both an essay and the point argued in the essay. Thesis novels and thesis plays share the quality of containing a thesis which is supported through the action of the story.

Third Person: See *Point of View*

Tone: The author's attitude toward his or her audience may be deduced from the tone of the work. A formal tone may create distance or convey politeness, while an informal tone may encourage a friendly, intimate, or intrusive feeling in the reader. The author's attitude toward his or her subject matter may also be deduced from the tone of the words he or she uses in discussing it.

Tragedy: A drama in prose or poetry about a noble, courageous hero of excellent character who, because of some tragic character flaw or *hamartia*, brings ruin upon him- or herself. Tragedy treats its subjects in a dignified and serious manner, using poetic language to help evoke pity and fear and bring about catharsis, a purging of these emotions. The tragic form was practiced extensively by the ancient Greeks. In the Middle Ages, when classical works were virtually unknown, tragedy came to denote any works about the fall of persons from exalted to low conditions due to any reason: fate, vice, weakness, etc. According to the classical definition of tragedy, such works present the "pathetic"—that which evokes pity—rather than the tragic. The classical form of tragedy was revived in the sixteenth century; it flourished especially on the Elizabethan stage. In modern times, dramatists have attempted to adapt the form to the needs of modern society by drawing their heroes from the ranks of ordinary men and women and defining the nobility of these heroes in terms of spirit rather than exalted social standing.

Tragic Flaw: In a tragedy, the quality within the hero or heroine which leads to his or her downfall.

Transcendentalism: An American philosophical and religious movement, based in New England from around 1835 until the Civil War. Transcendentalism was a form of American romanticism that had its roots abroad in the works of Thomas Carlyle, Samuel Coleridge, and Johann Wolfgang von Goethe. The Transcendentalists stressed the importance of intuition and subjective experience in communication with God. They rejected religious dogma and texts in favor of mysticism and scientific naturalism. They pursued truths that lie beyond the "colorless" realms perceived by reason and the senses and were active social reformers in public education, women's rights, and the abolition of slavery.

Trickster: A character or figure common in Native American and African literature who uses his ingenuity to defeat enemies and escape difficult situations. Tricksters are most often animals, such as the spider, hare, or coyote, although they may take the form of humans as well.

Trimeter: See *Meter*

Triple Rhyme: See *Rhyme*

Trochee: See *Foot*

U

Understatement: See *Irony*

Unities: Strict rules of dramatic structure, formulated by Italian and French critics of the Renaissance and based loosely on the principles of drama discussed by Aristotle in his *Poetics*. Foremost among these rules were the three unities of action, time, and place that compelled a dramatist to: (1) construct a single plot with a beginning, middle, and end that details the causal relationships of action and character; (2) restrict the action to the events of a single day; and (3) limit the scene to a single place or city. The unities were observed faithfully by continental European writers until the Romantic Age, but they were never regularly observed in English drama. Modern dramatists are typically more concerned with a unity of impression or emotional effect than with any of the classical unities.

Urban Realism: A branch of realist writing that attempts to accurately reflect the often harsh facts of modern urban existence.

Utopia: A fictional perfect place, such as "paradise" or "heaven."

Utopian: See *Utopia*

Utopianism: See *Utopia*

V

Verisimilitude: Literally, the appearance of truth. In literary criticism, the term refers to aspects of a work of literature that seem true to the reader.

Vers de societe: See *Occasional Verse*

Vers libre: See *Free Verse*

Verse: A line of metered language, a line of a poem, or any work written in verse.

Versification: The writing of verse. Versification may also refer to the meter, rhyme, and other mechanical components of a poem.

Victorian: Refers broadly to the reign of Queen Victoria of England (1837–1901) and to anything with qualities typical of that era. For example, the qualities of smug narrowmindedness, bourgeois materialism, faith in social progress, and priggish morality are often considered Victorian. This stereotype is contradicted by such dramatic intellectual developments as the theories of Charles Darwin, Karl Marx, and Sigmund Freud (which stirred strong debates in England) and the critical attitudes of serious Victorian writers like Charles Dickens and George Eliot. In literature, the Victorian Period was the great age of the English novel, and the latter part of the era saw the rise of movements such as decadence and symbolism.

Victorian Age: See *Victorian*

Victorian Period: See *Victorian*

W

Weltanschauung: A German term referring to a person's worldview or philosophy.

Weltschmerz: A German term meaning "world pain." It describes a sense of anguish about the nature of existence, usually associated with a melancholy, pessimistic attitude.

Z

Zarzuela: A type of Spanish operetta.

Zeitgeist: A German term meaning "spirit of the time." It refers to the moral and intellectual trends of a given era.

Cumulative Author/Title Index

Cumulative Author/Title Index

Cumulative Nationality/Ethnicity Index

Subject/Theme Index